BLACKS IN BLACKFACE:

A Source Book on Early Black Musical Shows

by

HENRY T. SAMPSON

The Scarecrow Press, Inc.
Metuchen, N.J., & London
1980

All quotes from the Pittsburgh Courier and the
Baltimore Afro-American reprinted by permission of
the publishers: respectively, The New Pittsburgh
Courier Publishing Company, and the Afro-American
Company of Baltimore.

Library of Congress Cataloging in Publication Data

Sampson, Henry T   1934-
    Blacks in blackface.

    Includes index.
    1. Musical revue, comedy, etc.--United States.
2. Afro-American entertainers. I. Title.
ML1711.S25   782.81'08996073   80-15048
ISBN 0-8108-1318-1

This book is dedicated to the hundreds of black performers, composers, and producers whose accomplishments and contributions to the growth and development of the American musical theatre have been ignored, minimized, or forgotten.

ACKNOWLEDGMENTS

Information for this project was derived from a wide variety of sources. The theatre program collections at the UCLA Research Library, the Moorland-Spingarn Research Center at Howard University, and the Los Angeles Public Library were extensively used. The black newspapers identified in Appendix C were the primary source of information on blacks in show business before 1930.

The author is also grateful to the following individuals who provided supplementary information on their personal involvement: Lorenzo Tucker, Clarence Muse, George Wiltshire, Reginald Fenderson, Willie Covan, Robert Johnson, Alfred Chester, and Fayne Criner (wife of the late actor J. Lawrence Criner). The author also wishes to acknowledge the assistance of Charles Frazier and Thurman Edwards, who did much of the photographic work, and Stephanie Johnson, who did some of the editing and the typing of the first draft of the manuscript.

CONTENTS

LIST OF TABLES

PREFACE

I first became interested in the history of the black musical
theatre while researching an earlier book on black films and film
makers. * Many of the black film stars of the 1920's and 1930's
were actively involved in musical shows and several had begun their
careers in minstrel shows and, in general, were skilled in several
departments of the theatrical arts.

Many excellent books have been published on the American
musical theatre. They have ranged from encyclopedias and reviews
of the best Broadway shows to anthologies of musical shows. They
have treated all aspects of the musical theatre including musical
comedy, musical farce, revues, musical spectacles, musicals,
comic operas, and minstrel shows. They have presented detailed
information on songs, performers, composers, lyricists, producers,
directors, and so forth. Some have included black shows such as
Williams and Walker's "In Dahomey," Sissle and Blake's "Shuffle
Along," "Porgy and Bess," and a few others that had long runs in
white theatres. However, information on the hundreds of black
shows produced by blacks and performed in black theatres has not
been included in these earlier works. Since many of the songs,
dances, comedy routines, and music which eventually became an
integral part of the American musical theatre originated in pioneer
black musical shows, omission of this information has resulted in
a significant gap in the history of the growth and development of
this art form. It is the primary objective of this book to make a
first attempt to fill this gap.

The title of this book, <u>Blacks in Blackface</u>, refers to many
of the top black comedians who worked in blackface. This was a
tradition that originated in white minstrel shows in the mid-1800's

---

*<u>Blacks in Black and White</u>, Scarecrow Press, 1977.

and that persisted in black musical shows and vaudeville well into
the 1930's.   The comedian used blackface makeup and wore baggy
clothes and floppy shoes to achieve a comic effect and to maximize
the contrast between himself and the well-dressed "straight" characters in the show.   Most of the leading black comedians of the
period worked in blackface including Bert Williams, Flournoy E.
Miller, Irvin C. Miller, S. H. Dudley, Billy King, and Gallie
DeGaston.   Some examples of blackface comedy may be seen in the
films "Natural Born Gambler" (Bert Williams, 1916), Oscar Micheaux's
"Ten Minutes to Live" (Gallie DeGaston, 1932), "That's the Spirit"
(F. E. Miller, 1933), and "Yes Sir, Mr. Bones" (F. E. Miller and
white actors in blackface, 1951).   Although the vast majority of the
performers mentioned in this book did not perform in blackface,
many, especially those who had light complexions, were encouraged
to do so when they worked in white shows or performed in white
theatres.

        It was not my intention in this work to subject the black mu-
sical shows of yesteryear to a critical analysis using the rationale
of present day thinking.   Rather, I relied on black newspapers of
the period to provide the critical commentary from a black perspec-
tive.   These newspapers provided the most immediate reaction to a
new show and played a major influence in the financial success of
the show and the popularity of the leading performers.   A visit to a
city by such top shows as "The Smart Set" or "Black Patti's Troubadours" was front page news, and many papers provided biographical
information on the stars and sometimes printed the entire program
of the show.

        The first black newspaper to carry an entertainment page on
a continuing basis was the Indianapolis Freeman.   Starting in the
1890's, the Freeman's entertainment page included not only local attractions, but also news from shows appearing in other cities which
was usually mailed in by the proprietors or managers of these shows.
The Christmas issue of the Freeman carried an annual review of the
stage in which the top shows of the year were reviewed and the
prospects for the coming year were discussed.   By 1910, almost

all of the black weeklies in the large cities carried theatrical news,
but only the Freeman, the Defender (Chicago), the Whip (Chicago),
the Age (New York City) and the Amsterdam News (New York City)
carried a fulltime theatrical editor on the publication staff.   In the
years before the first World War, the top black theatrical writers
were Tony Langston (Chicago Defender), Lester A. Walton (the Age,
New York City), Dave Payton (Chicago Whip), Sylvester Russell
(Freeman), and Romeo Daugherty (Amsterdam News, New York
City).   Of this group, Walton and Russell were clearly the most
vocal regarding economic, political and racial issues as they related to the theatre.   They frequently used their columns to sharply
criticize black shows and performers who, in their view, did not
"measure up." They were also quick to react when they thought
that white reviews of black shows were tinted with racism or were
based on ignorance of the Negro race.   In the early 1920's, James
A. Jackson's column of theatrical news was carried by many of the
leading black weeklies.   Jackson also edited a full page of black
theatrical news which was carried between 1921 and 1925 in Billboard, a leading white trade publication.

    At this point, some comments on the contents of this book
are in order.   Chapter One presents an overview of the growth and
development of the black musical theatre from its origin in minstrels
through the golden years of the 1920's to its gradual decline in the
late 1930's.   The activities of some of the men who provided the
financial resources and built the theatres that provided much of the
foundation upon which the black musical theatre was built are
chronicled in Chapter Two.   Chapter Three discusses the leading
black show producers of the period whose creative talent and or-
ganizational skills provided the glue which held together all the
other essential elements which were necessary for successful musical productions.   The history of several famous black theatres is
discussed in Chapter Four.   It was in these theatres that many of
the black stars first gained popularity.   Chapters Five and Six
present information on black musical shows and biographical data
on many of the leading performers.   Some of the information in

both chapters is incomplete, but is included in order to provide a
starting point for other researchers in the field.   Appendix A con-
tains a typical T. O. B. A. contract of the mid-1920's.   An additional
list of shows not included in Chapter Five and a list of black newspapers (including those used as source material for this book) are
given in Appendixes B and C respectively.

Henry T. Sampson
March 1980

CHAPTER 1

EARLY BLACK MUSICAL SHOWS:
HISTORICAL OVERVIEW

The early black musical comedies in the first forty years of
the twentieth century had their roots in early minstrel shows of the
post-bellum period. Although Charles Hicks, a black man, organized the first all-black minstrel show in about 1865, virtually
all of the first minstrel shows were performed by whites in blackface, and were essentially grotesque imitations of black plantation
life in the South. Because of slavery, black entertainment did not
make much headway professionally until after the Civil War. However, as far back as 1859 there were a few blacks giving musical
concerts throughout the Eastern States including Blind Tom, Black
Swan, Thomas J. Brown, Frederick Everette Lewis, The Whitehouse
Sisters, Samuel Johnson, Joe White and others. The Hamilton
Brothers (Dave and Jake) had a concert group and toured the Midwest with great success. Before that, there were a few nomadic
minstrel and jubilee entertainers who somehow managed to eke out
a precarious living in the late eighteenth and early nineteenth cen-
turies, but very little is known about these performers. One of
the first black groups to gain popularity was the Lucca Family.
They began their travels sometime around 1853 and offered a program of folk concerts in halls, churches, and under tents in vacant
lots. The family disbanded in about 1879.

By the mid-1860's, black minstrel troupes were beginning to
organize, and their popularity grew rapidly. These early performers continued to blacken their faces in the tradition of the white
minstrels, and were an imitation of an imitation of plantation life
of Southern blacks. However, these black singers, composers, and
dancers brought an original vitality never before seen on the American stage. They brought a great deal that was new in dancing including the buck and wing, the stop-time, and the Virginia Essence
which constituted many of the fundamental steps in American jazz
dancing.

The early black minstrels were stereotyped depictions of the
life and pursuits of black people from the period of their arrival on
this continent to the time of and after their emancipation. Minstrel
performances were enacted in a manner apparently free of self-
consciousness; nevertheless, there was a subtle pathos underlying

1

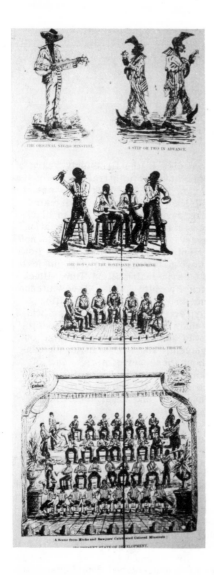

Graphic Depicting Development of
Black Minstrels, circa 1897

the entire structure, whose
appeal was irresistible.
This form of entertainment
was a developer of ability
because the artist was placed
on his own and was not aided
by scenery and stage effects
to get laughter.

A minstrel perform-
ance was usually conducted
with a group of at least
seventeen men, colorfully
costumed, their faces covered with burnt cork with
lips exaggerated with red or
white paint, seated in a half
circle.   At the center was
the interlocutor, the master
of ceremonies, who played
the straight role, set up
comedians, and who was the
butt of their jokes.   On either side of the interlocutor
were usually seven or eight
singers, dancers, mono-
loguists or other featured
performers and at the end of
each line were the "end
men," Mr. Bones and Tambo
(named for the instruments
they played: bones used
like Spanish castanets and
a tambourine), who were the
star comedians.   The band
was either located in the pit
or behind the performers.
The show always began with
the interlocutor's command,
"Gentlemen, be seated," and
followed by a noisy overture,
including cymbals, banjos
and drums, the performance
would begin with a scene of
assorted brilliance, color,
and apparent noise which,
however, would finally assume a tranquil and engaging
mobility abounding in humor,
side-splitting jokes, grotesque song and dance steps,
quaint dialogue and tidbits,

concluding with a "walk-around." This was called Minstrel First Part.

Aware that their audiences, mostly whites, were not ready to accept anything of a serious nature from them, these artists, most of them unlettered musically, put forth a series of selections of a sentimental nature, interspersed with dramatic recitations and sketches always offset with humor. This section was known as the Olio and was of a form more like later vaudeville and burlesque shows.

All through the period 1865 to 1900, minstrel shows, varying in caliber, abounded. Some of the great shows were "Lew Docke-stacler's," "Mahara's," "Callenders," "Georgia," "Billy Kersands," "The Eureka," and "Primrose and West," the latter consisting of forty white and thirty black performers. Many artists rose to fame from the ranks of these groups.

Sam (Dad) Lucas won a lasting fame in minstrel olios through a rendition of his version of "The Death of Uncle Tom" and Walker King, a silver-toned tenor, created a sensation throughout the world. Other black performers who won lasting fame as unique characters known as "end men" in minstrel shows were Billy Kersands, Ben Hunn, Tom McIntosh, Ernest Hogan, Harry Fiddler, Bob Kelly,

Big Four Minstrel Comedians, circa 1898

John Rucker, and Tom Fletcher, while Tom Brown was a famous
interlocutor.

Billy Kersands was considered to be the world's greatest and
most widely known black minstrel. He originated a famous dance
which he called the "Virginia Essence," and his big mouth made
him famous. He appeared before Queen Victoria in England where
she presented him with a stick pin in the shape of a horseshoe
which was later stolen in Savannah, Georgia.

The importance of the minstrel to the development of early
black theatre is best summed up by James Weldon Johnson in the
book Black Manhattan when he said:

> Minstrelsy was, on the whole, a caricature of Negro life,
> and it fixed a stage tradition which has not yet been en-
> tirely broken. It fixed the tradition of the Negro as only
> an irresponsible, happy-go-lucky, wide grinning, loud-
> laughing, shuffling, banjo-playing, singing, dancing sort
> of being. Nevertheless, the companies did provide stage
> training and theatrical experience for a large number of
> coloured men. They provided an essential training and
> theatrical experience which, at the time, could not have
> been acquired from any other source. Many of these
> men, as the vogue of minstrelsy waned, passed on into
> the second phase, or middle period, of the Negro on the
> theatrical stage in America; and it was mainly upon this
> training they had gained that this second phase rested.

The minstrel shows consisted entirely of male performers.
The first black women to gain success on the American stage were
the Hyer Sisters, who starred in several plays including "The
Underground Railroad" and "Out of Bondage." In the early 1870's
the Hyer Sisters--Madah and Emma, daughters of Sam B.
Hyers--started out from California with a company of violinists and
pianists. Their first tour carried them through the western United
States followed by engagements in the British provinces and Europe.
At the time, they were considered musical prodigies and their first
show was entitled "Out of Bondage," a sort of farce comedy, in
which the famous tenor Wallace King and a young Sam Lucas were
the bright stars.

Starting in about 1888, there were several successful shows
that did not follow the traditional minstrel format. Some of these
included blacks, but the featured parts were held by white men.
Perhaps the most popular show of this type was "South Before the
War" which was brought up from Louisville, Kentucky in 1891 by
two whites, Whallen and Martell. The show was made up of plantation scenes, songs, dances, and several specialties and played
for several seasons in the better burlesque houses. Billy McClain
headed the black end of this show and Snyder and Buckley the white
end.

Another all-black show of this period was "Darkest America"

Hampton and Johnson As They Appeared in John W. Vogel's "Darkest America," circa 1898

which was first presented by Nat Salsbury at Ambrose Park in South Brooklyn. Billy McClain was one of the stars and McClain later took the show over the regular theatrical circuits under the management of A. G. Fields. The November 11, 1896, edition of The Colored American, Washington, D.C., commented about the show:

> Al G. Fields' unique company, styled "Darkest America," has made a pronounced hit here this week, packing the Bijou Theatre nightly with the most brilliant audiences that the popular house has known this season. The organization comprises half a hundred of the best Afro-American talent in the country and the entertainment they give is full of clean, bright and wholesome fun and their singing, dancing and sketch work is strictly up-to-date. Their delineation of Negro life, carrying the race through all their historical phases from the plantation, into the reconstruction days and finally painting our people as they are today, cultured and accomplished in social graces, holds the mirror faithfully up to nature. "Darkest America" besides amusing, contributes a chapter to history. The scenic effects are noteworthy. The characters are in competent hands. Sam Lucas, the master of Afro-American comedians, leads the cast, ably seconded by his brilliant wife. Mr. Lucas, like wine, improves with age and his comedy scintillates with all the luster that won for him his exalted place in the mimic world. Despite the fact that Mr. Lucas is dubbed the dean of the Negro stage and that his name is associated with the early traditions of Afro-American theatricals, it would be a gross label to call him an old man. Mrs. Lucas is a

notions of modernity

splendid musician and renders difficult selections upon the
violin and cornet.   James Crosby comes in for a large
share of applause.   He is conscientious and has decided
talent.   His singing and dancing are among the best
"cards" of the show.   Billy Miller is a monologuist of no
mean ability.   Miss Florence Hines has established herself as the best male impersonator now before the public
and when she is billed her admirers join her in "hanging
the expense" and turn out to hear her form of songs.   The
enthusiastic feature is Prof. Henderson Smith's superb
military band.   It easily leads its class in the country and
reflects great credit upon the capacity of its painstaking
director.

     The St. Louis Post-Dispatch of May 1897, a white daily, of-
fers another view of this show:

     If you are a Southerner and acquainted with the "brother
     in black" you will find much entertainment in "Darkest
     America. "   If you come from the other side of the line
     and have formed your own ideas of Colored folks from
     the stage Negro and Darktown sketches, you will be in-
     structed and amused.   "Darkest America" is a big show,
     partly vaudeville and partly spectacular, and all the per-
     formers are Negroes.   There are all shades and sizes of
     Negroes in the company, and some of them are possessed
     of marked talent for dancing and making music.   The per-
     formance is a series of pictures of American Negro's life
     "from plantation to palace, " the program calls it.   It be-
     gan with scenes in slavery days and concludes with a
     swell function in Washington, where the Colored brother
     comes out strong in several ways.

     The first significant departure from the minstrel show format
occurred in about 1890 when Sam T. Jack, then a prominent burlesque theatre owner and manager, produced a sparkling musical
show from an idea originated by Sam Lucas.   "The Creole Show"
included 16 beautiful girls and an impressive supporting cast of
such skilled performers as Sam Lucas and his wife, Marie Lucas,
Fred Piper, Billy Jackson, and Irving Jones.   Although the show
contained none of the typical plantation settings found in the minstrel
show, it did follow the same general pattern.

     "The Creole Show" was an important first step in the devel-
opment of black musical comedy.   It was the first to feature a
beautiful female chorus and consisted of a minstrel first part, which
was different from the traditional minstrel shows in that the girl
was in the center of the line, and it had a female interlocutor, with
the men on the ends.   The show had an olio which preceded the
finale.

     "The Creole Show" opened in Boston in 1891 and later played
Sam Jack's Opera House during the season of the World's Fair.   It

later created a sensation in New York City at the old Standard
Theatre in Greeley Square.   The show played for five successful
seasons.

A description of "The Creole Show" is presented by the following article published in the Indianapolis Freeman, September 20,
1890:

> Sam T. Jack's Creole Burlesque Company recently opened
> at London Theatre, New York City.   The show commenced
> with a very pretty first part, attractive groupings of
> shapely femininity.   In "Tropical Revelries," Florence
> Brisco was the first conversationalist; Florence Hines,
> the greatest living female song and dance artist, second
> and Mrs. Sam Lucas third.   The olio sketches were very
> fine and called for numerous encores.   The burlesque,
> "The Beauty of the Nile, or Doomed by Fire," by Wil-
> liam R. Waits, is fine.   It is cast as follows: Nafra,
> Sadie D. Walfa; Choep, Florence Hines; Grip, Rurnell
> Hawkins; Zeno, Irving Jones; Isis, his Queen, Sarah
> LaRue; Amasis, King of Thebes, Florence Brisco; Ker-
> mack, Mammie Laning; Dinon, Eloise Pousett; Amon,
> Nina St. Jean; Zoilous, May Vorshall; Yeason, Miss
> Vaija; and Mr. and Mrs. Sam Lucas, musical sketch
> artists.

The Creole show, year after year, produced something
near forty different actors who later went on to become big
stars.   They included Bob Cole, Billy Johnson, Sam Lucas,
Charles Johnson, Charles Hunn, Frank Mallory, Edward Mallory,
Black Carl Danti, Walter Smart, George Williams, Sherman Coats,
Jim Grundy, Belle Davis, Dora Dean, Mattie Wilkes, Florence
Hines, Saddie Jones, Mazie Brooks, and a host of others.   In 1897,
the Creole show was still going strong.   The following description
of the show during this period is offered by the following article
published in the Indianapolis Freeman, January 1, 1897:

> Sam T. Jack's Creole played to packed houses at Brook-
> lyn, New York last week, and are presenting an elaborate
> bill.   The opening piece on the program is "H. M. S. Pina-
> fore."   Then follows specialties by Grundy and Mundy,
> grotesque dancers; Black Carl, the Creole Mahatma;
> George Wilson, blackface comedian; the Golden Gate Quar-
> tette with "Washday on the Levee"; and Hypolite, West
> Indian musical prodigy.   The show closes with a skit
> called "The Soiree."

A further departure from the old minstrel show form came
when a show entitled "Octoroons" was produced in 1895 by John
William Isham, who had been the advance man for "The Creole
Show."   The show featured 16 men and 17 women performers.   Although it still contained vestiges of the minstrel show, it was composed of three distinct parts.

The first part consisted of an opening chorus and a medley
of songs done by the various principals, generally assisted by the
girls of the chorus.   The middle part was a burlesque sketch in
which a number of specialties were strung on a very thin thread of
a story.   The show ended with a cakewalk jubilee, a military drill,
and a "chorus-march" finale.   The scenes of the show were laid in
New York City.

The original "Octoroons" company included the following per-
formers: Madam Flower and Fred Piper singing "Alice, Where Art
Thou?"; Billy Johnson, Bob Cole's first partner; Sweetie May; Ed
Barber, Frank and Ed Mallory; Tom Brown; Tom McIntosh;
Belle Davis; Hyer Sisters; Mattie Wilkes; Walter Smart; George
Williams; Aida Overton (later Aida Overton Walker, wife of
George Walker); Stella Wiley (later the wife of Bob Cole); Arthur
Maxwell; Mazie Brooks; Hattie McIntosh (then Mrs. Tom McIntosh
and later married to Billy King); and Grace Holliday.

Isham's next venture in 1896 was "Oriental America" which
consisted of the finest talent then available including Sidney Woodward, J. Rosamond Johnson, William C. Elkins, Maggie Scott, and
Inez Clough, who later won fame as a member of the Lafayette
Players Stock Company.   "Oriental America" was the first all-black
show to play on Broadway (at the old Palmer Theatre) and the first
to entirely break away from the slapstick and burlesque of the minstrel show.   Although it still was built on the minstrel show pattern, the afterpiece, instead of being made up of burlesque and
specialties, cakewalk, "hoe-down" and walk-around finish, was a
medley of opera selections.

The year 1897 marked a decided turning point in the history
of black theatricals in America.   It was about this time that Bob
Cole organized and headed the first black stock company in New
York City where black men and women could receive formal theatrical training.   Composed of 12 to 15 members, the group met at
Worth's Museum on Sixth Ave. and 30th Street.   At the time, the
26-year-old Bob Cole was both playwright and stage manager for
the group, and because of his fine creative talent and versatility,
he was able to lead the company to great popularity.

In the meantime, still unrecognized for their abilities, were
Bert Williams and George Walker playing the small-time vaudeville
(then called variety) circuits in and about Chicago.   In session at
West Baden, Indiana were the Show Managers of America.   A hur-
ried call was issued for acts to entertain these theatrical producers
who had come from all parts of the country.   Among the acts were
Williams and Walker, and they scored a veritable sensation.   In the
audience was Thomas Canary of Canary and Lederer, then unhappy
because his New York production "The Gold Bug" which had just
opened was unfavorably received by the press.   Without waiting to
see the rest of the program, Canary dashed backstage, signed up
Williams and Walker, and hustled them to New York to join the
tottering show.   The team repeated their West Baden act on Broadway and were the only hit of the show which closed after one week.

The first successful black road show to tour the East and South was "Black Patti's Troubadours" which was first produced in 1897 by Voelckel and Nolan, two whites from New York City who also managed the show.   The show was headed by Sissieretta Jones who was billed as "Black Patti. "   The show toured for many seasons between 1897 and 1920.

The year 1898 marked a major point in the development of black theatricals when Bob Cole produced "A Trip to Coontown. " This show was the first to make a complete break from the minstrel pattern, being written with a continuity, and having a cast of characters working out the story from beginning to end.   It was the first musical comedy featuring an all-black cast and was the first show to be written, produced, managed, and staged by blacks. Among the performers who worked with Cole was Billy Johnson, who later became Cole's first partner in vaudeville, and the first Johnson of Cole and Johnson; Sam Lucas; and Jesse Shipp, who later directed many of the subsequent Williams and Walker shows. The show was an immediate success and ran for three seasons between 1898 and 1900.

Table 1

BLACKS ENGAGED IN THE ENTERTAINMENT BUSINESS, 1910
(Compiled by U. S. Bureau of Census*)

Actors	1, 279
Showmen	100
Stage Carpenters	12
Stage Hands	321
Fortune Tellers and Hypnotists	50
Owners and Managers	93
Musicians	5, 804

The success of Bob Cole's show "A Trip to Coontown" in 1898 was the spark that fully ignited the development of black theatricals (see Table 1).   The next eleven years brought to fore the artistry of such great stars as Bert Williams and George Walker, Will Vodery, Sisserietta Jones, Ernest Hogan, Sam Lucas, Will Marion Cook, Aida Overton Walker, Jesse Shipp, S. H. Dudley, Alex Rogers, and J. Leubrie Hill.   This era also saw the unfolding of such great shows as the "Senegambian Carnival, " an operetta called "Clorindy" which was presented at the old Casino Roof Garden, "The Sons of Ham, " "In Dahomey, " "The Smart Set, " "Bandanna Land, " "Abyssinia, " "Shoofly Regiment, " "Rufus Rastus, " "The Red Moon, " and "The Oyster Man. "

---

*Published in Billboard, August 6, 1921.

After the deaths of Bob Cole, Ernest Hogan and George
Walker, black shows were usually absent from Broadway between
1911 and 1920. However, black theatricals continued to develop and
thrive. Stellar producer-performers such as S. H. Dudley, Salem
Tutt Whitney, J. Homer Tutt, J. Leubrie Hill, Billy King, Mabel
Whitman, Frank Montgomery, William Benbow and Irvin C.
Miller headed and produced road shows that played in black and white
theatres from New York City to Jacksonville, Florida and from New
Orleans to Chicago. The rapid construction of black theatres in the
South between 1916 and 1921 made it possible for these shows to
make several appearances in one city and reduced the traveling time
between cities that had theatres large enough to accommodate them.
In addition, several theatres like the Howard in Washington, D. C.
and the Grand in Chicago, as well as the Lafayette in New York
City, had resident stock companies which put on original shows on
a weekly basis.

The Negro Players, organized in the latter part of 1912, was
another of the early pioneer black stock companies. The company
included such talented performers as Alex Rogers, Henry S. Creamer, Andrew Bishop, Cassie Norwood, Alice Gorgas, Ruth Cherry,
Harrison Stewart and Charles Gilpin.

The first production of the Negro Players Company was "The
Old Man's Boy" which had its premier performance at the Casino
Theatre in Philadelphia in January 1913. The play was in three
acts with the first two consisting of singing, dancing, and dialogue.
The third act was constructed along dramatic lines and did not in-
clude any musical numbers. James Reese Europe conducted the
orchestra with production and music by Alex Rogers and Henry S.
Creamer. The company appeared under the direction of the Pioneer
Negro Amusement Company.

On the 17th of March 1913, the Negro Players opened at the
Lafayette Theatre in New York City in a tabloid musical comedy en-
titled "The Traitor" with Will Marion Cook assisting with the music.
At this time, Abbie Mitchell, Grace Lee Cook, Chris Smith, Billy
Harper, "Boots" Allen and William Shelton joined the company.

In an article appearing in the March 12, 1913, edition of the
New York Age, Will Marion Cook described the objectives of the
Negro Players as follows:

> The Negro Players, a company formed for the develop-
> ment of Negro music and drama, will begin at the Lafay-
> ette, a large theatre located in Harlem, on March 17, a
> series of productions. The founders of the organization
> aim to put into characterization a musical and dramatic
> form, real pictures of Negro life both city and plantation.
> The authors of the playlets will at first treat the lighter
> humorous characteristics of their people until Negro ac-
> tors shall have obtained a purer stage technique.
> The Negro's talent for music and dramatic expression

is now understood. The Negro Players hope to act in the development and perfection of this talent.

The Negro Players toured the South with the "Old Man's Boy" before disbanding in the latter part of 1913.

Concurrent with the organization of stock companies and the production of musical comedy shows in the East, similar developments were taking place in the South. In 1903 there were only a few honky-tonk theatres in the South where these shows were performed regularly. These included the Blue Room in Louisville, Kentucky, Tom Baxter's Place in Jacksonville, Florida, Tom Golden's Place in Savannah, Georgia, one each in Galveston and Houston, Texas, and The Hottentot in Pensacola, Florida.

However, by 1913 the South was the best playing field for black shows. At this time there were only a few first-class houses that played first class black shows. The advent of motion pictures closed most of the second-class houses to black shows making it very difficult to secure a profitable one-week stand in the Northern theatres, while the "one-nighters," except where there was a large black population, were not profitable. Thus, the financial prospects for most large black shows routed through the North were bleak.

However, with few exceptions, the first-class houses in every Southern city were available for black shows. In cities where there were not first-class white or black theatres, there were creditable black houses that would insure a reputable black company a profitable engagement.

It was a fact that in the segregated white theatres only the galleries and balconies were available for black patrons in the Southern cities. But this lack of seating capacity was offset by an increase in price for a one-night engagement. A good black show was always assured of a capacity black attendance while playing the South. Many white theatre managers, realizing this fact, frequently turned over the entire house to black patrons when playing a black show.

There were several serious drawbacks for black shows touring the South, however. In many cities hotel accommodations were not available so the performers had to find room and board in the private homes of the local black citizens. Also, black companies traveling in the South in their own private railroad cars suffered more inconvenience through race prejudice than they encountered in the North.

Playing all-white Southern towns such as Rogers, Arkansas or Aurora, Missouri was sometimes a trying experience for black performers. Members of a black company usually were not overly elated or over-jubilant when it was announced that they were booked to play an all-white town in the South or Southwest. The very existence of an all-white town usually meant the inhabitants were not above boasting: "We have no niggers here" or "We allow no niggers in this town" or posting signs such as "Nigger read and run, if you can't read, run anyway." Surprisingly, however, there were relatively few serious incidents between the local white citizens and traveling black performers.

The rapid increase in the construction of black theatres in the South coupled with the demand for talented performers who could stay at one house for several weeks resulted in the significant increase in house producers and house stock companies. When one group of performers met the approval of the patrons of a theatre and increased the attendance, the manager of that theatre, wishing to retain the drawing card, encouraged the performers to stay as long as they could change their program and please the patrons.

Robert Motts created the first successful stock company at his Pekin Theatre in Chicago, Illinois in 1906. After Motts blazed the trail, many other stock companies were organized that could play one theatre for an indefinite period and give satisfaction. They presented dramas, comedies, farce-comedies and musical comedies. These different shows were sometimes written and staged by a producer with the company or were chosen from several standard or stock plays that could be purchased.

The management of black theatres required the stock companies to change shows weekly, or semi-weekly. For example, during one engagement at the Lyric Theatre, Newport News, Virginia, Whitney and Tutt's Smart Set company changed programs nightly for more than twenty consecutive nights without repetition. No show they presented was shorter than 75 minutes and consisted mostly of musical comedies written by Salem Tutt Whitney with special music by T. L. Corwell and J. Homer Tutt and Henry Waterson. During this engagement they also produced three dramas, including "Uncle Tom's Cabin," two farce comedies and one musical show and one entire vaudeville bill. All of these shows had been played by the company at different towns.

At the time the Pekin Stock Company was disbanded following Bob Motts' death in 1911, there were several excellent stock companies working principally in the South where there was a large black population and where the black houses were in competition with white houses.

Probably the best of these was known as the Russell, Owens, Brooks Stock Company which originated at Tom Baxter's honky-tonk playhouse in Jacksonville, Florida. This company later split, leaving Bob Russell and Billy Owens at the head of one company and Marion Brooks and Speedy Smith leading another. The Russell and Owens company included the Brown Sisters, Madame LeRue, Lena Wiggins, Lillian Brown and others. Although they traveled throughout the South, their home base was Stile's Pekin Theatre in Savannah, Georgia.

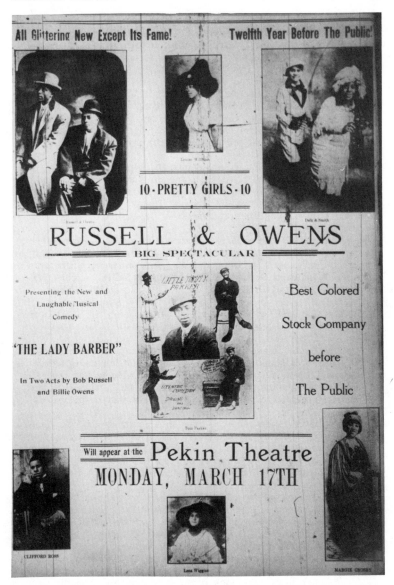

Ad for Russell and Owens Stock Company with Photos, circa 1913

Billy King first entered the field of stock while managing the
Central Theatre in Atlanta, Georgia. Billy's first company was
able to play at any one theatre indefinitely without losing prestige.
Lew Kenner's stock company was also a strong drawing card in the
South and especially at Frank Crowds' Globe Theatre in Jackson-
ville, Florida. Associated with Kenner were Hendricks and Lee,
Annie St. Clair, Rastus Mason, Billy Mills and others. Ed Lee's
Creole Bells company, Sidney Perrin's company and Tim Owsley's
company were also doing commendable work during this period.
Sidney Perrin was not only a noted producer, but he also wrote his
own plays and composed the music for the same.

A little later came the Stevens and Williams Company, Charley Williams and Gus Stevens with Joe Simms doing the comedy.
Next came the Billy Earthquake Company followed by John Rucker's
company, which started at the Temple Theatre in New Orleans with
Irvin C. Miller doing character parts.

During this same period, George Freeman of Birmingham,
Alabama started a company which included Clarence Muse, Lucille
Hegaman, and others. Then came the Benbow and Stringbeans Com-
pany which included Gallie DeGaston, Speedy Smith, Archie and Edna
Jones, Zed Bledsar, Emma Frederick, Bessie Smith, Eubie Barton,
Sadie Britton, Baby Benbow and others. Also starring about this
time were Gus and Trixie Butler, Julius McGarr, Billy McLaurin,
and Sandy Burns.

The development of talented stock comapnies was important
in the history of black theatricals. They provided their managers
good financial returns and they in turn were able to pay their performers good salaries. Typical salaries ranged from $5 a week
for chorus girls and from $20 to $35 weekly for the principals.

The experience received by a performer in a stock company
under a good director and producer was invaluable. It required that
the members of the company be versatile and self-reliant. It per-
fected talents and trained the performers to successfully enter almost any department of theatrical endeavor.

A major boost for black performers and shows was the organization of the first black theatrical circuits. The first was organized by S. H. Dudley in 1913; at the time he owned several
theatres in Washington, D. C. and Virginia. Dudley's headquarters
was located at 1818 Seventh Street N. W. in Washington. At one
time, twenty-one theatres were included in the Dudley circuit.

Another boost for black performers was the Theatre Owners
and Booking Association, T. O. B. A., which was organized in Chattanooga, Tennessee in 1920. The organization of the T. O. B. A. was
affected by a group of influential theatre owners in the South and
Midwest (see Table 2). Membership in the organization was offered
to any theatre owner by a purchase of three shares of capital stock
at par value of $100 per share. Members of the association

Table 2

THEATRE OWNERS WHO WERE ORIGINAL MEMBERS
OF T. O. B. A. IN 1920

H. J. Hury	Gay Theatre	Birmingham, Ala.
Milton Starr	Bijou Theatre	Nashville, Tenn.
E. B. Dudley	Vaudette Theatre	Detroit, Mich.
E. C. Foster	Brooklyn Theatre	Wilmington, N. C.
C. H. Turpin	Booker T. Washington	St. Louis, Mo.
N. C. Scales	Lafayette Theatre	Winston-Salem, N. C.
M. A. Eightman	Plaza Theatre	Little Rock, Ark.
A. Barrasou	Place Theatre	Memphis, Tenn.
Charles F. Gordon	Star Theatre	Shreveport, La.
J. J. Miller	Milo Theatre	Charleston, S. C.
T. S. Tinley	Lyceum Theatre	Cincinnati, Ohio
C. H. Douglass	Douglass Theatre	Macon, Ga.
Sam E. Reevin	Liberty Theatre	Chattanooga, Tenn.
William Warley	Lincoln Theatre	Louisville, Ky.
Bordeaux and Bennett	Lyric Theatre	New Orleans, La.
Clemmons Bros.	Lincoln Theatre	Beaumont, Texas
F. C. Holden	Liberty Theatre	Alexandria, La.
C. C. Schreiner	Pike Theatre	Mobile, Ala.
Chintz Moore	Park Theatre	Dallas, Texas
W. H. Leonard	Gayety	Waco, Texas
Lee and Moore	Lincoln Theatre	Galveston, Texas
C. H. Cattey	American Theatre	Houston, Texas
W. J. Stiles	Strand Theatre	Jacksonville, Fla.
K. W. Talbutt	New Royal Theatre	Columbia, S. C.
Bordeaux, Bennett and Gordon	Majestic Theatre	Montgomery, Ala.
W. J. Stiles	Pekin Theatre	Savannah, Ga.
O. J. Harris	Grand Central Theatre	Cleveland, Ohio
E. S. Stone	Washington Theatre	Indianapolis, Ind.
Lawrence Goldman	Lincoln Theatre	Kansas City, Mo.
Breaux and Whitlow	Alridge Theatre	Oklahoma City, Okla.
L. T. Brown	Dreamland Theatre	Muskogee, Okla.
L. T. Brown	Dreamland Theatre	Tulsa, Okla.

automatically became recipients of a free franchise for life for the
city in which they operated.   The original officers of the T. O. B. A.
were as follows: Milton Starr, Nashville, Tennessee, President;
J. J. Miller, Charleston, South Carolina, Secretary; and Sam E.
Reevin, Chattanooga, Tennessee, Treasurer and General Manager.
The Board of Directors included: T. S. Finely, Cincinnati, Ohio;
C. H. Douglass, Macon, Georgia; Clarence Bennett, New Orleans,
Louisiana; and H. J. Rury, Birmingham, Alabama.

        Eventually the circuit grew to include over 80 theatres and
could book black acts for a full season.   Although the T. O. B. A.
provided booking for hundreds of black performers (see Table 3),
many complained about unfair treatment by theatre managers.   Before taking a show out on the T. O. B. A. , the show manager had to
sign a contract (see APPENDIX A), the terms of which were clearly
in favor of the theatre manager.   In an article which appeared in
the August 18, 1928, edition of the Pittsburgh Courier, Clarence
Muse commented on the financial vulnerability of the show manager:

> At the beginning of the season, on or about Labor Day,
> six or seven week contracts will be issued to well-known
> producers and managers of shows.   The term of the con-
> tracts are carefully worded, unlike any other theatrical
> contract in the world.   But if the show fails to appear,
> they pay and pay dearly even more than the contract will
> earn, as I will explain in detail.   All of the contract is
> the party of the first part, meaning the manager of the
> theatre, and the party of the second part, meaning the
> show, is only mentioned with no protection at all.   For
> example, if it is a percentage date, and this is always
> the case, if the house does poor business, the contract
> will read, 50-50, must have 20 or more artists, names
> of artists in the show must appear and if they failed to
> arrive a liability clause in the contract demands the show
> has damaged the theatre manager in the sum of $1500.
> But if the manager sees fit not to play you, he is not
> compelled to even notify you only on a six-day notice, and
> on liability, even if you appear, and he doesn't care to
> play you.   There is seldom a show of this size that can
> earn $1500 for their share unless it falls on a holiday
> week.   And when the management can earn an average
> $1500 on percentage, he will buy the show-top salary
> $1200 take it or leave it or as low as $100 with an aver-
> age jump of $6 to $16 per capita.
>   Now, note that for this $1200 salary, with ridiculous
> road jumping, you must have at least 20 people, all ex-
> cellent artists with a reputation, at least eight chorus
> girls, and you must order and pay for at least $100
> worth of lithographs and share with all newspaper adver-
> tising that the theatre manager contracts for, and above
> all, $50 of the money must be paid to the T. O. B. A. as
> commission.   The tremendous balance is for the salaries
> of the capable artists.   And with the average jump given

Table 3

ROUTINGS ON THE T. O. B. A. CIRCUIT, OCTOBER 1926
(Baltimore Afro-American, October 31, 1926)

City, State	Theatre	Act
Chattanooga, Tenn.	Liberty	Marie and Clint, Charles Anderson, Dudley and Byrd, Snow and Snow
Nashville, Tenn.	Bijou	Susie Sutton Company
Memphis, Tenn.	Palace	Boisy De Legge Company
Hot Springs, Ark.	Vendome	Roscoe Montella Company
Shreveport, La.	Vendome	William and Brown, Dounvear and Dounvear, Hugh Turner
Dallas, Texas	Ella Moore	Dusty Murray Company
New Orleans, La.	Lyric	Thomas and Breeden, Green and Lane, Jones and Chatman, Fritz Jazz Lips, Jr. , Billy Arnet
Bessemer, Ala.	Frolic	Maggie Jones, Sledge and Sledge, Hampton and Hampton
Macon, Ga.	Douglass	Dudley and Byrd, Prince and Connie, Glasco and Glasco
St. Louis, Mo.	Booker T. Washington	Clifford Ross, Long and Jackson, Dooley and Robinson, Bessie Smith, Sam Gray Company
Kansas City, Mo.	Lincoln	William Benbow Company
Galveston, Texas	Liberty	Jackson and Rector Company
Houston, Texas	Best	Dusty Murray Company
Port Arthur, Texas	Lyric	Glasco and Glasco
Columbus, Ga.	Dunbar	Jack Johnson
Cleveland, Ohio	Globe	Whitney and Tutt
Chicago, Ill.	Grand	Shufflin' Sam from Alabam'

by the circuit, it will leave about $400 to pay off all the
artists, an average of $20 per capita.

Many show managers have been branded all over the
country by poor victims of the T. O. B. A. as thieves,
won't pay off, jumping board bills and all kinds of un-
pleasant expressions unbecoming a theatrical manager and
why?--Please keep in mind, the above average contract
mentioned and the terms therein.   There is a fund set
aside by this organization to take care of the initial cost
of production at the beginning of the season, but they immediately encourage reputable artists to take out shows as
we will advance you on your first date from $200 to $300
cash and your railroad tickets.   No, instead of taking this
money back, as all circuits do, a little at a time each
week, they demand and collect every cent on the first date.
This starts the pawn broker's department of the T. O. B. A.
and each and every week you are hustling for an advance
for the next date and only every third contract is on a
guarantee date, and many managers want advance money,
hence the sudden "bust-out. "   The pawn broker must be
paid and the starving artists are left unpaid.   The manager of the show is branded as bad.   The pawnbroker has
crushed his victim and the vandals of the T. O. B. A. are
smiling over their prey.

In another article which appeared in the December 21, 1929,
edition of the Pittsburgh Courier, William G. Nunn commented on
the decline of the quality of shows on the T. O. B. A. as follows:

We don't blame the producer, entirely.   A couple of years
ago, if memory fails to play us false, this same T. O. B. A.,
which is now hanging on the ropes, and has already taken
the "long count, " had some money to spare.   Did they give
one of our race producers a chance to improve their circuit?   Nay, Nay!   They gave the money to Mister (if you
please) Jack Goldberg, will-o'-the-wisp theatrical "promoter, " and one of the smartest men in the game when it
comes to looking out for Jack Goldberg.   Goldberg, if this
same memory of ours is still hitting on all fours, has
been connected with more different theatrical ventures than
any man around today.   It was he who reaped the harvest
from the original "7-11" company--a company which was
"made" through the efforts of no less a group of principals than the hardworking "Speedy" Smith, Mae Brown,
and Garland Howard, a delux dancing combination; "Chink, "
the best oriental impersonator of his day, and a chorus,
which, while not composed of high class beauties, stood
as one of the best-trained group of girls this writer has
ever seen.

This was the show which took the old Columbia Circuit
by storm for a year.   And Goldberg had been connected
with the Smith of "Blues Singer" fame and many others.
Goldberg, we repeat, was the man chosen by the T. O. B. A.

to give a NEGRO public an abundance of what the NEGRO
public likes. (His name tells his nationality.) And what
did Goldberg do? He started turning shows out at the rate
of one-a-week! In Goldberg's estimation, anything at all
was good enough for Negro patrons of Negro houses. But
the public failed to swallow Goldberg's "money bait."
They wanted class and artistry and something new in the
way of jokes. They desired a change from the old smut
line of nauseating jokes. They wanted a degree of intelligence. They didn't favor or relish the ideas of a leading
man coming to the front and splitting his verbs. They
didn't relish the ideas of girls appearing on the stage in
frayed, dirty costumes--and with run-over shoes. Why
these conditions prevailed, they did not know, but they did
know that they weren't to spend their money going to such
shows and their wishing they hadn't come.

From every angle--at the time Goldberg was given his
"chance"--condemnation of the action of this body was
heard. Why wasn't a Negro man of ability given this
chance? Any number of good men could have been found
who could have turned out shows which would have satisfied.

Most prominently mentioned of the entire bunch was
Irvin C. Miller, at that time overworked with the respon-
sibility of trying to manage about five different shows.
Miller's "Models," "All Girls' Revue," and "Red Hot
Mamma" were his outstanding hits, but still he was in a
position to get pretty girls, and he had apparently solved
the mystery of just what the Negro, going to a theatre,
is crazy about.

Miller already had a nucleus of shows with which to
start. He had corraled most of the available talent, and
would have been able to get other high-class entertainers
without a great deal of trouble. He appeared to be the
logical choice.

Since that time they have been slipping. Nothing of a
remedial nature has taken effect. And the result now is
that the circuit, the actors, and the managers of shows
are mere puppets, suffering from the balking of an over-
abused public.

We blame the T. O. B. A. There is no mixture of
sympathy in our condemnation. They had their chance
and they have flunked it. Our advise is for the theatrical
producers, who are supposed to be real members of the
T. O. B. A., but in reality are mere tools, to call a meeting of outstanding colored producers--if they can be obtained now--make them an offer and back this offer with
coin of the realm, if necessary.

In the years between 1912 and 1920, the leading show producers were J. Leubrie Hill, Salem Tutt Whitney, J. Homer Tutt,
Frank Montgomery, Billy King, Bob Russell, and Mabel Whitman,
and Irvin C. Miller. After taking over control of Gus Hill's "Smart

Set. " Whitney and Tutt produced over 13 new and original musical comedies during this period and helped develop such talent as Mamie Smith, then a famous blues singer, Adelaide Hall, Eddie Rector, Blanche Calloway, Harriet Calloway, Blanche Thompson, Margaret Simms, Alonzo Fenderson, Edna Barr, and Nat Cash. Dramatic stars who got their start with Whitney and Tutt include Charles Olden, Leigh Whipper, and Clarence Robinson.

This was a unique period in the history of black theatricals. It was a period when blacks produced, directed, wrote, and staged shows performed in black theatres, many of which were owned by blacks, before black audiences. In short, it was a period when blacks had a significant measure of control over every aspect of their productions. With the exception of relatively few black performers and shows who played the white vaudeville circuits (see Table 4), the vast majority of black performers and their songs and dances were seldom seen by white audiences.

Table 4

BLACK PERFORMERS ON WHITE THEATRICAL CIRCUITS, 1926
(Baltimore Afro-American, February 6, 1926)

KEITH ALBEE	WESTERN VAUDEVILLE
Plantation Review	Harris and Holly
Bryson and Jones	Tabor and Green
Gaines Brothers	
Dixie Four	PANTAGES
Jones and Peat	Chappelle and Stinnette
Harrington and Green	Sheftel's Revue
Joyner and Foster	
Bill Robinson	COLUMBIA *Burlesque*
Glen and Jenkins	Black and White Revue
Four Chocolate Dandies	Lucky Sambo
	Monkey Shines
ORPHEUM	Rarin' to Go
Covan and Ruffin	Seven-Eleven
	Sliding Billy Waston

It was "Shuffle Along" in 1921 that initiated the return of black shows to Broadway on a regular basis. The show was written, directed, produced and staged by Eubie Blake, Noble Sissle, Flournoy E. Miller and Aubrey Lyles. It was this show that first introduced a black chorus of partially garbed girls in the style of the white "Follies" or "Vanities" to the Broadway stage. At first, it was predicted that white audiences would not accept them, but their good looks and ability to dance with feverish precision and abandon made them instant hits. The Sepia torso-wielders were latent bundles of energy and their vivaciousness gave birth to the speed show which was to characterize black shows during the next twenty years.

Table 5

PARTIAL LIST OF BLACK ACTS PLAYING
CIRCUSES, CARNIVALS, AND FAIRS IN
THE UNITED STATES, 1900-1920

Pizarro's Tasmanian Troupe--Acrobats
Bessie Coleman--Aviatrix-Stunt Flyer
Maharajah--Mystic and Magician
Alphonso--Showman
Sidney Rink's Society Circus--Complete pony and trained mule show
Great Diamond Circus Side Show--C. E. Warren, Proprietor
Robert Mile's Anchor Concert Co. --Illusionists, magic, escapes, etc.
Billy Townsend's Athletic Show
Princess Wee Wee--Midget
Abnorma--Giantess
J. H. Dixon's Pit Show
Daye's Traveling Dance Orchestra
Watts Brothers--Acrobats
Ira Green--Acrobat
The Great Clemo--Contortionist and Acrobat
Edwards and Edwards--Wire Walkers and Balancers (man and woman)
Grey and Grey--Heavyweight Jugglers, Balancers (man and woman)
Billy English--Hoop Roller and Indian Club Juggler
DeWayman Niles--Contortionist
Boyd and Boyd--Contortionist and Acrobat (man and woman)
Wells and Wells--Horizontal bars, trapeze, rings, 21-foot high
    rigging (man and woman)
Gains Brothers--Acrobats, high wire, rings
Alie Johnson--"The Cat on the Wire"--Wire walking in comedy
    costume
Coy Herndon--Hoop Roller with elaborate equipment and costume
Lawrence Glover--Wire Walker
Dan Wiley--Trick- and Fancy-Skater
Clows Gentry--Ride down 100-foot incline and dive into a water tank
Amanzie Richardson--Wire Walker
Harry Wills--Heavyweight Fighter

After "Shuffle Along" came other great shows such as "Liza," "Dinah," "How Come," "Runnin' Wild," "Chocolate Dandies," and "Charleston Dandies." From these shows came many hit songs and popular dances such as the Blackbottom and the Charleston. These shows proved to a national audience that black performers could no longer be considered merely droll, harmony singing troupes, who did the cakewalk and the chicken wheel, and above all it proved that black shows were money makers.

It was this latter fact that induced whites to become interested in producing black shows, and this eventually led to the demise of the black producer. By the early 1930's almost all of the black musical comedy shows that played on Broadway were produced by whites, for example Lew Leslie and Jack Goldberg. Goldberg also organized the Majestic Theatrical Circuit in 1928 which booked blacks and produced shows for black theatres.

It was also about this time that black ownership and management of theatres in the large cities of the East significantly diminished. By the end of 1928, A. E. Lichman, white, had purchased black theatres in Washington, D. C. including Lincoln, Rosalia, and Jewell, and the Royal in Baltimore.

In 1929 Frank Schiffman, white, purchased four black theatres in Harlem: the Lincoln, Roosevelt, Douglass, and Odeon. Black control of theatres in the East virtually came to an end when John T. Gibson lost control of his Standard and Gibson (formerly the Dunbar) in Philadelphia.

By the mid-1930's, musical comedy shows and revues produced by, owned by and performed by blacks were well on the road to decline. By this time only Irvin C. Miller and a few others continued to produce shows on a regular basis. However, exceptional talent was not available to these men. Many of the headline performers were by this time appearing in nightclubs, a few were performing in white shows and others had gone to Hollywood to work in motion pictures.

It is ironical that once the pioneer black producers had proven through sheer grit that money could be made with black shows, Broadway accepted them and they were allowed to progress to the extent that they could be exploited. And by the end of the 1920's most of the profits from black shows went into the hands of white producers and owners.

In an article that appeared in the January 1, 1933, edition of the Baltimore Afro-American, Ralph Matthews commented on the state of black theatricals as follows:

> Many will contend that the Negro theatre has found its own level and that it has taken on a definite form that has buried the stigma of the past which once left it standing like a dingy jim crow car on the side line as the

palace coaches of the American theatre rumbled on their way.

My contention is that it has merely undergone a transition and that the basic principle upon which America has always accepted the Negro still remains. The old musical comedy scenes that showed him in overalls against a background depicting a Mississippi levee have given way to a nightclub panorama and Harlem has supplanted Dixie as the name synonymous with the Negro. The plunking banjo and the cotton field have been supplanted by the moaning saxophone and the rent party wail. The melancholy spirituals have been replaced by the equally melancholy, but less reverent, blues and the rhythm of the old plantation has vanished in the path of the weird and sensuous tempo of the jungle and the beat of the tom tom. The brass band in its flaming red coats has been replaced by the jazz orchestra with its dancing baton-wielders and skat singers. The big names among Negro performers are those who have appealed to the whimsicalities of the white race and conform to their ideas of what a Negro should be.

Those who have confined their activities to what we might term the Negro theatre exclusively have either vanished completely from the arena or are existing in mediocrity. The American black man honors only those whom the gods have chosen. The Negro theatre has not really progressed--it has merely been absorbed.

HIGHLIGHTS OF BLACK MUSICAL
SHOW PRODUCTION

1865   The first black minstrel company, the Georgia Minstrels, is organized by Charles Hicks.

1888   The Astor Place Company of Colored Tragedians opens at the old Cosmopolitan Theatre, Broadway and Forty-first Street, New York City, for a run, producing "Hamlet" and "Othello."

1891   Sam T. Jack produces "The Creole Show" which was the first black show to deviate significantly from the minstrel pattern.

Hyer Sisters' celebrated musical company play "Out of Bondage," "Blackville Twins," and "Colored Aristocracy" in the East.

1896   John W. Isham produces "Oriental America."

THE LARGEST AND BEST MINSTREL PARADE.

Graphic Depicting Rusco and Hollands' Minstrel Parade, circa 1898

1897   Bert Williams and George Walker star in their first big
        show, "Senegambaian Carnival" with a cast of 65.

        Williams and Walker, billed as the "Tobasco Senegambians,"
        score a hit at Koster and Bial's in New York City.

        Johnson and Dean, billed as the King and Queen of Colored
        Aristocracy, open on the Orpheum Circuit in San Francisco.

        Bob Cole and Billy Johnson open in vaudeville at Proctor's
        23rd Street Theatre in New York City.

        Lew Johnson's "Black Uncle Tom's Cabin" company tour
        California.

        Isham's "Oriental America" creates a sensation in Great
        Britain.

1898   Bob Cole writes and produces "A Trip to Coontown," the
        first black show to make a complete break from the minstrel
        pattern.

        "Clorindy, or the Origin of the Cake Walk" by Will Marion
        Cook and Paul Laurance Dunbar opens for a trial run on
        July 5 in Rice's "Summer Nights" at the Casino Roof Garden
        in New York City.

        W. C. Handy, the father of the Blues, gains a reputation as
        band master and cornet soloist with Mahara's Minstrels.

1899   Williams and Walker produce and perform in "4-11-44"
        (later changed to "The Policy Players").

Ernest Hogan, billed as the "unbleached American," leads the Afro-American Minstrel Show to Australia.

1900   Williams and Walker bring out "The Sons of Ham."

1902   Williams and Walker produce "In Dahomey" which opens at the New York Theatre in Times Square in New York City.

1903   "In Dahomey" runs for seven months at the Shaftesbury Theatre in London, England. On June 23, Williams and Walker present a command performance at Buckingham Palace.

1904   S. H. Dudley stars in "The Smart Set."

Robert Motts opens the famous Pekin Theatre in Chicago.

1905   Ernest Hogan stars in "Rufus Rastus."

1906   Williams and Walker produce and star in "Abyssinia" written by Jessie Shipp.

Bob Cole and J. Rosamond Johnson go on a European tour.

Bob Cole and J. Rosamond Johnson write and produce "The Shoofly Regiment."

1907   Williams and Walker produce and perform in their last show together, "Bandanna Land."

Miller and Lyles get their first professional engagement as playwrights at the Pekin Theatre in Chicago.

"The Oyster Man," starring Ernest Hogan, opens.

1908   Bob Cole and J. Rosamond Johnson produce "The Red Moon."

Lester A. Walton assumes duties as dramatic editor of New York Age, a black weekly in New York City.

An all-black show is presented for the first time before a white audience in the Bowery Section of New York when "A Trip to Africa" is presented by the Black Patti Musical Comedy Company.

Williams and Walker celebrate their 16th anniversary on the stage at a special performance at the Majestic Theatre in New York City on April 2.

Dunbar Theatre in Columbus, Ohio opens.

Robert Motts buys Columbia Theatre in Chicago.

Frogs Club, with Bert Williams, George Walker, Bob Cole, and Others

The Frogs, a famous theatrical club, is organized in New York City in July with Bert Williams as President.

Cole and Johnson's "The Red Moon" opens at the Majestic Theatre in Jersey City, New Jersey.

Black Pythians of the State of Louisiana opens new theatre for blacks in New Orleans.

1909   Ernest Hogan dies.

Bert Williams appears for the first time without his partner, George Walker, when "Bandanna Land" opens for the season at the Majestic Theatre in Brooklyn.

Bert Williams signs to do a single in vaudeville on the Keith-Procter Circuit.

Colored Vaudeville Benevolent Association is organized in New York City.

Bert Williams opens in his last all-black show when "Mr. Lode of Koal" is presented at the Casino Theatre in Toledo, Ohio.

1910   "Mr. Lode of Koal" closes on March 5.

J. Ed. Green, actor, playwright and director for the Pekin Theatre, dies in Chicago.

Cleff Club is organized in New York City with the famous orchestra director James Reese Europe as President and Founder.

Bert Williams opens in Ziegfeld's "Follies of 1910" at the Apollo Theatre in Atlantic City, New Jersey.

Cole and Johnson retire from the musical comedy field.

Flournoy E. Miller and Aubrey Lyles play vaudeville on the Keith Circuit.

Bob Cole retires from the stage because of illness.

S. A. Keys, F. Morris and L. Easley open the Hiawatha Theatre in Washington, D. C.

Magnolia Theatre in Cincinnati, Ohio opens for black patronage.

1911   George Walker of the famous Williams and Walker team dies. Bob Cole dies in New York.

J. Leubrie Hill's "My Friend from Dixie" opens at Columbia
Theatre in Brooklyn.

1912   Robert Motts, owner of Pekin Theatre in Chicago, dies.

S. H. Dudley buys his first theatre in Washington, D. C.

Irvin C. Miller produces his first musical comedy, "Mr.
Ragtime. "

Blacks open Lincoln Theatre in Jacksonville, Florida, W. T.
Clark, G. W. Walton, T. B. Pursley, proprietors.

1913   Florenz Ziegfeld, famous producer of the "Follies," pur-
chases the rights to use the finale to the first act and several song numbers from J. Leubrie Hill's "Darktown Follies."

The Frogs Club, a famous black entertainers' club, presents
"Frog Follies" in Baltimore featuring Bert Williams and S.
H. Dudley.

Charles Turpin opens Booker T. Washington Theatre in St.
Louis.

1914   Majestic Theatre, formerly Ford's Opera House, is leased
by blacks in Washington, D. C.

The Griffin Sisters, under the management of S. H. Dudley,
tour Europe.

Lottie Gee and Effie King (sister act) are one of the first
black acts to tour the Lowe Circuit.

The American Theatre is leased by S. H. Dudley and
Andrew Thomas and is added to the Dudley Circuit.

J. Leubrie Hill's "My Friend from Kentucky" opens on
Broadway June 1 at Hammerstein's Victoria Theatre.

The Daley Amusement Company, Inc. constructs $100,000
Daley Theatre in Baltimore at Pennsylvania Ave. and Green-
willow Street, William H. Daley, President.

Unique Theatre in Detroit opens, E. J. Johnson, owner.

The Old Fellows' Auditorium Theatre opens in Atlanta,
Georgia with opening addresses presented by Booker T.
Washington and Emmett J. Scott.   Theatre was located on
Auburn Ave. between Bell and Butler Streets.

1915   Bill "Bojangles" Robinson scores a hit at the Lafayette
Theatre in New York City.

Irvin C. Miller presents his first big show "Broadway Rastus" at the Apollo Theatre in Atlantic City, New Jersey.

Miller and Lyles stage "Darkydom."

Colored Vaudeville Benefit Association is organized in New York City with offices at 424 Lenox Avenue.

Anita Bush Stock Company opens at the Lafayette Theatre in New York City with a sketch entitled "Over the Footlights" with Anita Bush, Carlotta Freeman, Charles Gilpin, Andrew Bishop, and "Dooley" Wilson.

1916   Sam Lucas, the dean of black actors, dies in New York City.

The black-owned Colonial Theatre opens in Baltimore, Maryland.   White theatres in Baltimore open balconies to blacks.

After their phenomenal success as polite entertainers in the fashionable amusement resort of Palm Beach, Florida, Noble Sissle and Eubie Blake enter vaudeville as a team.

1917   Celebrated actor Tom Brown dies in Chicago.

1918   Billy King Stock Company starts several years' run at Grand Theatre in Chicago.

Influenza and pneumonia epidemic causes Health Department to close all black theatres in Baltimore from October 11 to November 1.

1919   Attucks Theatre built by blacks opens in Norfolk, Virginia.

1920   Quintard Miller produces his first big show, "Broadway Gossips."

First National Negro Theatre Coporation is organized in Baltimore.

1921   A dozen members of William Benbow's Company are disrobed and flogged in Mansfield, Louisiana by a mob of 500 whites. The trouble resulted from an argument between Mrs. Benbow and a white woman.

Theatre Owners and Booking Association, T. O. B. A. , is organized.

Harper and Blanks are the first black act to tour the Shubert Circuit of white theatres.

"Shuffle Along" opens a two-year run at the Daley's Sixty-third Street Theatre in New York City.

John T. Gibson buys Dunbar Theatre in Philadelphia.

John T. Gibson is selected by Milton Star, president of the
T. O. B. A., to be his Eastern representative.

"Put and Take" produced by Irvin C. Miller opens at town
hall in New York City.

Black Swan Record Company is organized by Harry H. Pace,
president of Pace Phonograph Corporation.   Pace had purchased the Remington Phonograph Company which was then
owned by the grandson of the inventor of the Remington rifle
and Remington typewriter.   Black Swan is the first black
owned record company in America.

E. B. Taylor and C. H. Jenkins organize the Dunbar Film
and Theatrical Corporation capitalized at $150,000.

New Dunbar Theatre, owned by the Savannah Motion Picture
Company, opens in Savannah, Georgia.   The first picture is
Oscar Micheaux's "Symbol of the Unconquered."

1922   The Douglass Theatre in Baltimore, owned by E. C. Brown,
opens with a performance by the Lafayette Players Stock
Company.

Dunbar Theatre in Philadelphia adds vaudeville to drama and
picture program.

"Strut Miss Lizzie," produced by Henry Creamer and Turner
Layton, opens on Broadway.

Irvin C. Miller's "Liza" plays at Daley's Sixty-third Street
Theatre in New York City.

1923   "Plantation Days" opens in London, England.

Bessie Smith and Company broadcast over WSB radio in
Atlanta, Georgia.

A performance of "Shuffle Along" at the Pitt Theatre in
Pittsburgh is broadcast over radio station KDKA.

Ethel Ridley introduces the Blackbottom dance on Broadway
in Irvin C. Miller's "Dinah."   Miss Ridley was taught the
dance by Perry Bradford.

1924   Musicians Protective Union is organized by blacks in Norfolk,
Virginia.

Ella B. Moore Theatre owned by Chintz and Ella Moore
opens in Dallas, Texas.

"Dixie to Broadway" cast including Florence Mills broadcast over radio station WGN in Chicago.

Director of Dressing Room Club presents Florence Mills with a diamond medal in recognition of her outstanding success.

The Charleston dance created by blacks is introduced to New York, America, and the world in the Miller and Lyles show "Runnin' Wild."

1925   Tony Langston quits as drama editor of Chicago Defender.

James A. Jackson's page is dropped from Billboard. W. T. Donaldson, publisher, states that the page was discontinued because of the lack of black advertising in the publication.

I. H. Herk, white, president of Mutual Burlesque Circuit, orders that no black acts or companies be engaged for the Mutual houses.

U. S. Interstate Commerce Commission requires southern railroad companies not to distinguish between private railroad cars owned by blacks and those owned by whites. Ruling resulted when a southern railroad refused to move the Chappelle show because Chappelle was black.

Sissle and Blake play the Metropol Club in London, England.

Brown and Stevens Bank in Philadelphia fails.

1926   Florence Mills stars in "Blackbirds" produced by Lew Leslie.

Clarence Muse produces and performs in "Charleston Dandies."

Bessie Coleman, famous airplane stunt flyer, dies in a plane crash in Jacksonville, Florida.

Jack Goldberg granted exclusive franchise to produce black shows on the Columbia Circuit.

A. E. Lichman, white, buys Howard Theatre in Washington, D. C.

Pythian Theatre, built by Knights of Pythian (black), opens in Columbus, Ohio.

1927   Florence Mills dies in New York City.

Lincoln Theatre in Los Angeles, California opens.

Regal Theatre in Chicago opens.

Columbia Burlesque Circuit drops shows featuring mixed casts.

John T. Gibson changes the name of his Dunbar Theatre to the Gibson Theatre.

Jack Goldberg organizes enterprises to produce all-black musical comedy shows.

Arthur Rockwald's "Struttin' Sam from Alabam'" is closed after three-day run at the Majestic Theatre in Los Angeles because of boycott of show by blacks who protested the "Jim Crow" policy of the theatre.

William Benbow's "Get Happy" company tours Cuba.

1928   Jules Hertig, white, who opened the first vaudeville house in Harlem, dies.

Whitman Sisters Company is booked for a year run on the Publix Circuit.

The Official Theatrical World, a national directory and guide of black performers in the theatre, is published.   The publication staff is headed by Irvin C. Miller.

Walker Theatre, located on the ground floor of the Madame C. J. Walker building in Indianapolis, Indiana, opens.

Moss and Fry sail for London to begin a five-month tour of Europe.

Fair Theatre in Washington, D. C. hires "spotters" (blacks hired to pick out other blacks passing for whites) to bar blacks from a performance of "Porgy."

"Blackbirds" opens in London, England.

1929   Irvin C. Miller is elected president of Florence Mills Theatrical Society.

Shelton Brooks appears in black film "Gayety," a vitaphone short with Hamtree Harrington and Ida Anderson.

William Benbow's "Miami Follies" company tours Costa Rica.

John T. Gibson leases his Gibson Theatre to whites.

"Blackbirds" is hit of season at the Moulin Rouge in Paris, France.

Mrs. Maria C. Downs sells Lincoln Theatre in New York City to Frank Schiffman.

1930   Irvin C. Miller appears in black film "Dark-Town Scandals Revue" produced by Oscar Micheaux. Cast includes Sara Martin, Maude Mills, Club Alabam Stompers, Dixie Jubilee Singers, Harlem Strutters.

Charles C. Gilpin dies.

Sidney Kirkpatrick and Henry Creamer die in New York City.

Drs. P. W. and B. J. Burnett open Savoy Theatre in Rocky Mount, North Carolina.

Shelton Brooks and "Bird" Allen broadcast twice weekly over CBS and are billed as "Egg and Shell."

S. H. Dudley sells his Mid-City Theatre in Washington, D. C. to a white corporation.

Fascists try to break up "Shades Over Harlem" during a performance at a theatre in Germany claiming that black shows were ruining German culture.

Alex Rogers, song writer of Williams and Walker company, dies in New York City.

1932   Aubrey Lyles dies in New York City at age 49.

Fats Waller has daily radio show on WLW in Cincinnati, Ohio.

1933   Madam Sissieretta Jones, "Black Patti," dies in Rhode Island.

1934   Salem Tutt Whitney dies.

Jessie A. Shipp, pioneer showman, dies in Jamaica at age 65.

The "Tree of Hope" which stood in front of Lafayette Theatre at Seventh Avenue and 132nd Street in New York City is cut down.

1935   Andrew Tribble dies.

Whitman Sisters' Musical Comedy disbands after about 25 years in show business.

Charleton Moss stages pageant depicting the history of the black man in America at the Wadleigh Annex Theatre in New York City.

Federal Theatre Project is established by the U. S. Government Works Progress Administration.

1936   Evon Robinson, wife of J. Leubrie Hill, dies in New York
        City.

1937   John T. Gibson, pioneer black theatre owner and producer,
        dies.

        Negro Actor's Guild is organized in New York City with Bill
        Robinson as honorary president, Fredi Washington as execu-
        tive director, Murial Rahn as recording secretary, W. C.
        Handy as treasurer, Cab Calloway as chairman of the execu-
        tive board, Leigh Whipper as second vice president, J.
        Rosemond Johnson as chairman of bylaw committee, Rev.
        Adam Clayton Powell, Jr., as chaplain, and Simon Fenstein
        as general counsel.

CHAPTER 2

BLACK POWER IN THE 1920's

In the years just before and after the First World War, several black men played an important role in the development of black theatricals through the financing and ownership of theatres, amusement companies and publishing and record companies. Through sheer determination, and the willingness to invest huge sums of capital in the construction of theatres, these individuals provided the means for hundreds of black performers to exhibit and develop their talents, and most importantly, to earn a living. Above all, it meant that during this brief period blacks had considerable control over virtually all aspects of their theatrical enterprises. Although many blacks were involved in the financial end of black show business, a few individuals stood out. These include E. C. Brown, John T. Gibson, Sherman H. Dudley and Harry Pace.

BROWN AND STEVENS

E. C. Brown and A. F. Stevens organized the Douglass Amusement Company in 1919. The objective of the corporation was to raise capital for the construction of a theatre on the southwest corner of Broad and Lombard Streets in downtown Philadelphia. The corporation was capitalized at $100,000 and Grant Williams, then a successful publicity man, was the manager with E. C. Brown serving as president and A. F. Stevens the treasurer.

E. C. Brown was educated in Philadelphia. His mother died when he was nine years old and his father left him at the age of eighteen. In school, Brown was an exceptionally bright student. After graduating from the public schools, he was employed by a mercantile agency as mail clerk which he filled for three years. This position, however, simply inspired him for more responsible work. During this period he took a course at the Spencerian Business College in stenography and typewriting. After completing the course, William T. Bell, then vice president of the National Railroad Company, engaged him as his stenographer. In this position the young Brown came in touch with the leading steel and railroad magnates. After the company merged with a larger concern, E. C. Brown and other employees lost their positions. After spending some time diligently seeking work as a stenographer and finding

Dunbar Theatre at Broad and Lombard Streets in Philadelphia, circa 1921

that his color and not his competency was against him, he, with that indomitable courage and ability to think and act judiciously under such circumstances, went South still determined to forge a career in business.

Arriving in Newport News, Virginia, with only a few dollars in his pockets, he worked hard and eventually succeeded in interesting a successful businessman to go into partnership with him. So the real estate firm of Brown and Brown was started and soon had signs on vacant buildings all over the city.

In 1909, E. C. Brown began a banking business in Newport News by organizing the Crown Savings Bank, which eventually became a success. In May 1909, he secured a charter for a corporation known as the Brown Savings and Banking Company, which had a flourishing business in Norfolk, Virginia. In the same building, Brown had a real estate department, which did a large business. During the same period Brown served as director of the Southern Aid Society of Richmond, Virginia and as the treasurer of the Colored Bankers' Association.

In about 1915, E. C. Brown moved to Philadelphia and established a bank with A. F. Stevens as his partner.

In 1919, Brown and Stevens purchased the Quality Amusement

from Robert Levey, and thereby also gained control of the Lafayette
Players Stock Company and the Lafayette Theatre in New York City.
Their next venture was the construction of the Dunbar Theatre in
Philadelphia and they made plans to expand the Quality Amusement
Company's theatrical attractions to include four companies of Lafay-
ette Players, a Comic Opera Company, a grand opera company,
musical comedy companies, and a vaudeville company. By the end
of the year, the corporation either owned or controlled the follow-
ing theatres: Dunbar Theatre, Philadelphia; Lafayette Theatre, New
York City; Howard Theatre, Washington, D. C.; Avenue Theatre,
Chicago; the Putnam Theatre, Brooklyn, New York; and the Pershing
Theatre in Pittsburgh, Pennsylvania.

In 1919, the prospects for the Quality Amusement Company
never looked brighter. E. C. Brown secured the services of Alex
Rogers to produce several musical productions which were to be
presented in theatres owned or controlled by the corporation. Later,
C. Luckeyth Roberts was engaged as musical director to work in
collaboration with Alex Rogers.

The first productions put out by Rogers and Roberts were
"This and That" and "Baby Blues." Soon after, the Quality Amuse-
ment Corporation presented a revival of J. Leubrie Hill's "My
Friend from Kentucky" at the Lafayette Theatre in New York with
Andrew Tribble portraying the role of Mandy Lee, the part original-
ly played by J. Leubrie Hill.

The addition of the Lincoln Theatre in Norfolk, Virginia
brought the number of theatres under the corporation's control to
seven, and E. C. Brown announced that "by the end of the year,
nearly every large city in the country will have a first class theatre catering to race people which they can be proud of and feel at
home." Later in 1920, Brown announced ground breaking for the
construction of the Douglass, a $500,000 theatre in Baltimore which
was to be the newest link in his theatre chain.

In 1921, however, the fortunes of the corporation took a
downward turn. In April of that year, Quality Amusement Corporation withdrew from the Avenue Theatre in Chicago citing "bad business and the public's complaints, in general, against treatment accorded at the Avenue."

A few weeks later, E. C. Brown sold the Dunbar Theatre to
John T. Gibson and in 1922 the Brown and Stevens Bank in Philadelphia was sold at auction to John M. Dotterer of Wayne, Pennsylvania for $190,000.

The Douglass Theatre in Baltimore was the last piece of
property to be sold by Brown and Stevens. Having opened in February 1922, the theatre was sold for $125,000 at public auction to
two whites from New York City, J. Elmer and Samuel Porter.

JOHN T. GIBSON

John T. Gibson stood only five feet, three inches tall and
weighed only 110 pounds, but he was the giant of black theatricals
in the 1920's. Gibson--as theatre owner, directing manager, and
producer--made a permanent contribution to the development of the
black entertainment in the East. Through grit, nerve, daring and
intelligence, Gibson forged a theatrical empire in Philadelphia which
eventually made him a wealthy man. Known as the "Little Giant,"
Gibson's Standard Theatre which stood on South Street was considered one of the class houses on the vaudeville circuit.

John T. Gibson was born in Baltimore, Maryland on February 4, 1878. After finishing the public school in Baltimore, he attended Morgan College Preparatory School for two years.

After going to Philadelphia in the 1890's, Gibson peddled
meat, upholstered chairs, and did other odd jobs. But always lurk-
ing within him was the urge for wealth and power. Although slight
in stature, the young Gibson was headstrong and slightly arrogant.

Gibson's initial venture into the theatrical business began in
1910, when Samuel Reading, a Philadelphia businessman, took the
ambitious Gibson in as a partner in a moving picture and vaudeville
house, known as the North Pole. At the time the house was doing
poorly and Reading hoped that Gibson could turn it around. The
North Pole was the first movie house constructed on South Street
which, at the time, was the State Street, Lenox Avenue, Beal
Street, and Central Avenue of Philadelphia.

The partnership was not agreeable and a little more than a
year later it was dissolved. Gibson, realizing the great possibilities
of the business, bought out his partner's interest for $800. Thus
began the rise to fame and fortune for the shrewd and ambitious
John Trusty Gibson.

At first, the North Pole was a success in a small way, but
Gibson's heart and mind were set on bigger and better things. After a short time, he closed the house and moved into the Standard,
a larger and a more modern playhouse on South Street. This
proved to be a brilliant move. The post-World War I prosperity
brought wealth to Gibson. The Standard Theatre became a veritable
gold mine. Every week the receipts were well above $12,000.

Many stars of the 1920's and 1930's gained their first experience at the North Pole and Standard Theatre. These included
Ethel Waters, the Whitman Sisters, Buck and Bubbles, Butterbeans
and Susie, Bessie Smith, George Wiltshire, and the Nicholas Brothers. The comedy team of Fairchild and Lovejoy (Alec), Sandy
Burns and Bilo, Johnny Woods the ventriloquist, were a few who
kept the first row audiences (usually white) in stitches with their
Jewish, German, and Italian dialogue.

Although the Standard was enormously successful, Gibson
was ambitious and he cast a designing eye about for more profitable
business ventures.   The banking firm of Brown and Stevens held and
operated the modern Dunbar Theatre, and this was Gibson's next
venture.   The Dunbar, despite the best efforts of Brown and Stevens,
failed to pay and Gibson bought it for $120,000.

However, to his surprise Gibson found he had a "white ele-
phant" on his hands.   One problem was that blacks who patronized
his Standard Theatre would not attend his Broad Street house.   Gibson responded by bringing the topflight stars of the time to the Dunbar including the celebrated Lafayette Players, musical comedies
like "How Come" and "Liza," the leading orchestras and road shows.
Still Gibson had no better success than his predecessors and much
of the profits from the Strand were used to carry the Dunbar.

Often Gibson was heard to remark "Colored people should
own property on Broad Street."   He liked to stand in front of the
Dunbar and say "John T. Gibson has a theatre on Broad Street."
He literally patted the building like one caressing an infant.

Gibson was also civic minded, realizing the importance of
being a part of black organizations.   Consequently, he sought membership in many of the leading civic clubs.   He also donated $5,000
to Morgan College in Baltimore.   Following this, Gibson was elected
a trustee of the College and in June 1928, he received the honorary
degree of Doctor of Laws from Morgan.

Gibson also loved the "good life."   He purchased a beautiful
estate at Meadowbrook which he named "Elmira" after his wife
whose first name was Ella.   The gorgeous countryside manor was
tastefully furnished by one of the then leading Philadelphia interior
decorators.   It became the showplace of the East and the envy of
Gibson's white neighbors.   His next venture was real estate: he
acquired an apartment house, near downtown, a row of houses in an
exclusive section of West Philadelphia, and several tenements in
South Philadelphia.

Then came the crash of 1929.   Gibson found his back up
against the wall and like a house of cards his empire came tumbling
down.   Real estate holdings were wiped out, the country estate was
swept away, the Dunbar was sold, and finally the Standard went too.
The early 1930's found Gibson just a step ahead of poverty.   The
only thing he managed to salvage from his huge fortune was a house
in West Philadelphia which had been shielded by joint ownership with
his wife.   It was there that Gibson died on June 12, 1937.

SHERMAN H. DUDLEY

Sherman H. Dudley, famous comedian of the original "Smart
Set" company earned a permanent place in the history of black theatricals by organizing the first black theatre circuit in 1913.   He

Sherman H. Dudley, circa 1908

was born in Dallas, Texas and for a brief period in his youth Dudley tried horse racing. During his association with racing, he met a man who, appreciating his wit, persuaded him to join a medicine show which gave performances on the street corner of Austin, Texas. He sang a song entitled "Dese Bones Shall Rise Again" with such effect and spirit that many of the spectators thought he was a minister of the faith. This was in 1875.

Subsequent to this, Dudley was in great demand for variety shows and at music halls. About this time, Dudley and Andrews organized the Ideal Minstrels which ran for four weeks of barnstorming before becoming stranded. Dudley then proceeded to organize the Dudley Georgia Minstrels, which interested a number of wealthy people of Galveston, Texas to put up the capital to finance the company. The Galveston News (July 30, 1897) had the following to say about Dudley's company:

> ' Despite the bad weather large houses greeted Dudley's
> Georgia Minstrels at their matinee and night performances
> yesterday and the merit of the show was equal to the size
> of the audience. The Dudley Georgians are all typical
> Negroes and give a sure enough Negro minstrel show.
> The stage setting in the first part is one of the prettiest
> ever seen here, and in fact, grander than any put on a
> Galveston stage by other shows of like nature. The set-
> ting represents a room in a palace in Morocco and is
> richly painted, being adorned with large arches, heavy
> pedestals and rich draperies. The men, all richly cos-
> tumed, are seated in four rows, one above the other.
> Down the center is built a stairway. The jokes were new
> and funny, the songs catchy and the dancing graceful.
> The opening overture was well put on and heartily encored.
> Helen Brown sang a sweet melody in a rich manner and
> did some good dancing.

After touring with this company for two seasons, Dudley joined P. T. Wright's Nashville Students, and afterwards went into vaudeville with the famous comedian, Tom McIntosh, heading "Hot Old Time in Dixie." Later, with Sam T. Croker, Jr. he joined the Clorinda Company and toured the Eastern and Middle Atlantic States. It was during this time that Dudley met and married the actress, Bertie Ormes.

For a while, Dudley and his wife worked in vaudeville with Dudley singing that one-time popular song, "Good Morning, Carrie." In 1902, he held the position of stage manager and amusement director with Richards and Pringle's Famous Georgia Minstrels company no. 1. With this show he produced and staged the afterpiece "The Darktown Ping Pong Club" in which he was also the featured comedian.

Dudley was a good musician as well as a great minstrel end man. With the McCabe and Young Minstrels he acquired the nick-

name of "Happy"; when one of the end men would call out "Is everybody happy?" Dudley would pick an opportune moment to yell "Happy" and the audience would roll over with laughter.

He became famous in 1904 when he led a mule on the stage
as part of his act while a member of the Smart Set company's production of the "Black Politician." The show at that time was under
the ownership of Gus Hill, white, of New York who was one of the
founders of the Columbia Circuit. Hill at that time had fourteen
shows. He had moved a mule from a play called "McFadden Flats"
to three or four other revues and it did not fit any place. So his
last resort was Dudley, who was playing in Cleveland, Ohio. Dudley received the mule and wondered what he was going to do with
the animal. There was a race horse scene in which he gave an
extemporaneous monologue, but nobody had seen a race horse on the
stage. Dudley reasoned that there was nothing to do but try the
scheme; if it flopped, it just flopped, that's all. He marched out
on the stage leading the mule and the house went wild. It was a
decided hit, and Dudley soon became the riot of the comedic world.
In 1907, Dudley joined Dave Marion, another white producer, and
continued the mule act. Between 1904 and 1917, Dudley had four
mules. One was killed accidentally while being removed from a
railroad car and the others died from old age. With his mule and
his rendition of the song "Come After Breakfast," Dudley made the
original Smart Set company famous.

S. H. Dudley first publicly disclosed his idea for a black
theatre circuit in the following letter which was published in the
January 20, 1912 edition of the Indianapolis Freeman:

> Dear Sir: I am adopting this method of putting up square-
> ly to any prominent Negroes throughout the country who
> may be interested in theatricals, the following question,
> which I trust will be answered through your valuable col-
> umns. The things I wish to know are as follows:
> How many colored men with money are willing to in-
> vest in theatres? The day is now ripe, the time has
> come; there is more profit in show business than any
> other business you can invest your money in, if properly
> managed.
> Why should you lose this opportunity? Give me ten
> theatres in ten cities and I will keep the doors open 365
> days per year and guarantee a success. I mean by this,
> if I am provided with real theatres, planned and operated
> by colored men, and not backed by white men. These
> houses must be theatres. They are easy to get at this
> time. If you are in doubt, write me and I will tell you
> why. You don't have to build them. In nearly every city
> there are theatres for lease. This is due to the passing
> of the "pistol drama" for Whites, which has seen its last
> days, thereby leaving a vast amount of theatrical property
> practically valueless for immediate usages. Ingenuity,
> experience and business foresight must be exercised in

securing possession of this property without paying enough
rent to buy the houses.   Therefore I insist if you are interested, write me and I will give you, in detail, my
modus operandi.   The following cities are available and
the ones I most desire as a starter: East-Philadelphia,
Pa.; New York City; Baltimore, Md.; Washington, D. C.;
Richmond, Va.; and probably Newport News, Va. and
Norfolk, Va.; West-Chicago, Ill.; Louisville, Ky.; St.
Louis, Mo.; Cincinnati, Ohio; Indianapolis, Ind.; and
probably Columbus, Ohio.

The most money in theatres has been made in recent
years in the "burlesque wheel. "   This is due to the fact
that it is a wheel within a wheel.   This is what I want to
accomplish in the establishment of a chain of Negro theatres controlled and operated exclusively by business men
of the race.

I am offering to all persons interested my time, professional experience and money (which is not as much as
that of Rockefeller and Morgan).

I thank the editor of the Freeman for the use of this
valuable space and trust that through its columns I may
be able to establish the proposition outlined in this letter.

Signed, S. H. Dudley

In March 1912, after starring in a performance of "Dr.
Beans from Boston" at the Apollo Theatre in Atlantic City, Dudley
announced that he was retiring from the stage to devote more time
to implementing his idea of establishing a chain of black theatres
(see page 49).   Interviewed by a reporter from the Freeman, Dudley explained his retirement as follows:

> ... I must devote most of my time to my enterprises to
> make them a success.   I know it is a hard task and a
> great undertaking.   Still I mean to make it a success and
> with the aid of good, competent surroundings and the loy-
> alty of the vaudeville performers, I cannot see anything
> but success.   It is only a matter of time, as the white
> theatres don't care to play us.   Some one has got to make
> a start to find something for those hundreds and hundreds
> of Colored performers to do.   I am going to find work for
> them.   The time is right and all we need is a few more
> theatres like the Howard in Washington and the Grand in
> Chicago.   I wish I could get about ten houses in ten lead-
> ing cities, and we would have what we have never had.
> There are Negroes capable of playing from low comedy to
> Shakespeare's heaviest plays.   This would give them a
> chance.   At present my enterprise is in its infancy, but
> it will grow.   It takes time.   I want the management of
> all good acts in the business.   I can and will get them
> money and work.   I want all managers of real vaudeville
> to cooperate with me.   No honky-tonk halls, but high class

(cont'd on page 48)

Table 6

THEATRES OWNED AND OPERATED BY BLACKS, 1910-1930

Location	Theatre & Type*	Original Owner/Manager
Alabama		
Decater	Mykes--E	Sykes
Mobile	Dixie Park--E	?
Florance	Bessie--P	Mrs. Reasle Foster
Sheffield	Fields--E	Elija Fields
Opelika	Dreamland--V	?
Arkansas		
Helena	Placa--P	Mrs. Eliza Miller
Hot Springs	Vendome--P, V	?
Texarkana	?--?	Jason S. Douglass
Delaware		
Wilmington	National--E	Johns Hopkins
District of Columbia		
Washington	Hiawatha--P	Murray A. Ryan
Washington	Dunbar--P	G. Rufus Byars
Washington	Dudley--V	S. H. Dudley
Washington	Foraker--V	Murray
Washington	Mid-City--V	S. H. Dudley
Washington	Rine Mouse--V	M. Martin
Washington	Florida--P	Mr. Colfax
Washington	Maceo--V	?
Florida		
Bartow	Picture--?	?
Daytona	?--E	?
Jacksonville	Austin--V	Buddy Austin
Jacksonville	Globe--V, P ⎫	W. S. Sumter, Dr. J.
Pensacola	Lincoln--P ⎬	Seth Hills, Frank Crowd
Pensacola	El Dorido--V	?
Pensacola	Electric--V	M. Jacoby
St. Augustine	?--E	?

*V = Vaudeville or Road Show
 E = Equipped for shows, but at the time showing pictures only
 P = Pictures only
 D = Dramas

Location	Theatre & Type	Original Owner/Manager
Georgia		
Athens	Morton--V	William G. Garter and Jas. P. Davis
Athens	Pastime--V	?
Atlanta	Paradise--V	Elijah Davis
Atlanta	Auditorium--V	S. L. Lockett (K of P)
Atlanta	Arcade--?	?
Atlanta	Famous--V	J. B. Kelly
Atlanta	Palm Garden--V	W. G. Gray
Augusta	Lenox--V	J. A. Moffett
Brunswick	Pekin--V	?
Brunswick	Palace Photo Play Theatre--P	J. S. Buggs
Columbia	Ocmulgee-V	W. M. Rainey
Decater	Luna Park--V	?
Macon	Old Douglass--V	C. H. Douglass
Macon	Woverline--V	Willie Braswell
Macon	New Douglass	C. H. Douglass
Savannah	Pekin--V	W. J. Stiles
Savannah	Dunbar--P	Savannah Motion Picture Corporation (Walter Scott, President)
Savannah	Star--P	Savannah Motion Picture Corporation
Savannah	Globe--P	Savannah Motion Picture Corporation
Valdosta	?--P	?
Waycross	Star--V	H. A. Hunter
Illinois		
Chicago	Pekin--D, V	Robert (Bob) Motts
Chicago	Rose Bird--P	W. C. Gates and Son
Chicago	Star--P	Teenan Jones
Chicago	Western--P	S. L. Owens
Chicago	Dunbar--V	Dr. Richerson
Chicago	Columbia--V	Robert (Bob) Motts
East St. Louis	Olympic--P	King and Davis
Indiana		
Indianapolis	Washington--V	F. S. B. Stone
Indianapolis	Indiana--E	Dr. O. Puryear
Indianapolis	Airdome--V	R. S. Geyer
Indianapolis	Columbia--V	Hill Bros.
Indianapolis	Two Johns--V	John A. Hubert and John H. Victor
Kentucky		
Lexington	Pekin--V	Gray and Combs
Louisville	Taft--V	Luther Edwards
Louisville	Thirteenth Street--V, P	Edward D. Lee
Louisville	Pekin--V	Edward D. Lee

Location	Theatre & Type	Original Owner/Manager
Kentucky (cont.)		
Louisville	New Odd Fellows Theatre--V	Edward D. Lee
Paducah	Hiawatha--P	Dr. S. George
Louisiana		
Baton Rouge	Bernard--V	?
Homer	?--?	?
New Orleans	L. K. Mitchell--P	Luther K. Mitchell
New Orleans	Temple--?	E. S. Cheeberg
New Orleans	Bordeaux--P	Bordeaux and Camp
New Orleans	Pythian Temple	K. of P. Lodge
Scotland	?--P	?
Maryland		
Baltimore	Dunbar--P	Brown and Stevens/ Josiah Diggs
Baltimore	Renard--P	?
Michigan		
Detroit	Vaudett--V	E. B. Dudley
Detroit	Shook--V	Ben Shook
Detroit	Unique--P	J. W. Hamilton
Mississippi		
Greenwood	Bijou--V	B. F. Seals
Jackson	American--V	W. J. Latham
Mound Bayou	Casino--P	Fred Miller
Missouri		
St. Joseph	Dudley--P	Charles T. Phelps
St. Louis	Booker T. Washington--V	C. H. Turpin
St. Louis	Vendome--?	Mrs. Noah Warrington
St. Louis	Barrett's Theatorium--V	Richard D. Barrett
Nebraska		
Omaha	Cameraphone--V	?
New York		
New Rochelle	North Avenue	Sydney B. Chase
New York City	Renaissance--P	William Roach (W. C. Roach Company)
North Carolina		
Charlotte	Dixie--V	?
Concord	Alpine--V	?
Durham	Rex--V	Frederick K. Watkins, Arthur E. Benjamin
Durham	Wonderland--P	Frederick K. Watkins
New Bern	?--P	?
Rocky Mount	Sandy--V, P	Drs. P. W. and E. J. Burnett
Winston Salem	Lafayette--V	W. S. Scales
Ohio		
Cincinnati	Pekin--P	Oscar Hawkins
Cincinnati	Gaither--V	Edward Gaither

Location	Theatre & Type	Original Owner/Manager
Ohio (cont.)		
Cincinnati	Lincoln Theatre--?	?
Columbus	Empress--E	J. A. Jackson and Ruby Williams
Columbus	Dunbar--V	J. A. Jackson
Dayton	Dunbar--?	?
Hamilton	Vendome--V	?
Oklahoma		
Ardmore	?--?	Tobe Crisp
Guthrie	Lyric--V	A. L. Sneed
Muskogee	Dreamland--V	Mrs. L. T. Williams
Oklahoma City	Aldridge--?	Mrs. Zelia Beaux and Whitlow
Okmulgee	Dreamland--V	Mrs. L. T. Williams
Tulsa	Dreamland--V	Mrs. L. T. Williams
Tulsa	Pekin--V	?
Pennsylvania		
Philadelphia	Dunbar--V, D	Brown and Stevens / Grant Williams (later purchased by John T. Gibson)
Philadelphia	Auditorium--V	Sam Reading
Philadelphia	Standard--V	John T. Gibson
Pittsburgh	Lincoln--V	Harry Tennenbaum
Pittsburgh	Star--V	Charles P. Stinson
South Carolina		
Bennettsville	Lincoln--E	King and Covington
Camden	?--P	?
Charleston	Lincoln--V	J. C. Cannon/C. P. McClane
Charleston	Milo--V	?
Florence	Princess--V	V. C. Brown
Florence	Elite--V	?
Rock Hill	Broadway--P	W. S. Alston
Tennessee		
Columbia	Livingstone--V, P	Livingstone Mays
Jackson	Pekin--V	William Blakely
Knoxville	Lincoln--V	?
Memphis	Gem--V	?
Memphis	Pekin--V	?
Memphis	Savoy--V	F. A. Barrasso
Nashville	Lincoln--P	?
Nashville	Star--P	?
Texas		
Beaumont	Verdun--?	A. N. Adams
Beaumont	Lee's Tent--V	Edward Lee
Bonham	Star--P	Charles Jordan
Dallas	Park--V	Chintz Moore
Dallas	Ella B. Moore--P	E. B. Moore
Dennison	Dreamland--P	P. Woods

Location	Theatre & Type	Original Owner/Manager
Texas (cont.)		
Fort Worth	Washington--P	?
Galveston	Lincoln--V	?
Galveston	Ruby--V	?
Greenville	Pastime--V	?
Houston	Lincoln--P	Olen Pullum DeWalt
Houston	American--V	C. A. Caffey
Houston	Palace--V	?
Houston	Peoples--V	Frank McKensie
Paris	Alhambra--V	?
Rusk	Queen--P	Ed Conley
Sherman	Andrews--E	?
Temple	Rink--?	J. J. Dawson
Virginia		
Alexandria	S. H. Dudley--V, P	S. H. Dudley, Brown and Stevens
Hampton	Hampton--?	Hampton Theatre, Inc. (C. Tiffany Tolliver, pres., T. Green, vice-pres., Dr. B. Downing, sec., A. F. Brooks, treas., Major W. B. F. Crowell, auditor)
Hampton	Strand--?	Hampton Theatre, Inc.
Norfolk	Attucks--V, D	Twin City Amusement Corporation/Robert Cross/Rufus Byars
Norfolk	Pekin--P, V	C. W. Moseley
Norfolk	Globe--V	?
Norfolk	Clark--V	F. E. Alexander
Petersburg	Loraine--P	William Wilkins
Petersburg	S. H. Dudley--V	S. H. Dudley
Petersburg	Rialto	Jas. M. Wilkerson, president of stock company
Petersburg	Idle Hour--V	S. H. Dudley
Staunton	Sunnyside--V	Mrs. R. I. Paunell
Wisconsin		
??	Rose--V	W. McKinney, J. D. Brachelor
West Virginia		
Charleston	Majestic--?	?

houses. We have a few, and what we managers need and must do is to consolidate, and we will in time. Stop worrying about who and what can I get next week for my show. I am going to spend all of my entire time and energy to make it a success. I want the help of the per-formers and managers. Then success will be guaranteed.

Between 1911 and 1913, Dudley purchased several theatres in Washington, D. C. including the Mid-City, S. H. Dudley, Fairyland, Foraker and the Blue Mouse. His first purchase outside the city of Washington was in Newport News, Virginia. He made Leigh Whipper the manager. At this time, Whipper, who later became a respected actor of stage and screen, was doing monologue on the vaudeville circuit with a partner. Soon, Dudley convinced other theatre managers to join the circuit: the Dixie, Richmond, Virginia; the Globe, Norfolk, Virginia; S. H. Dudley, Newport News, Virginia. The above eight houses were the original members of the Dudley circuit. All were booked by Dudley with Lew Henry as general manager. By 1916 the Dudley Circuit consisted of over 28 theatres covering the South, East and Midwest. This circuit made it possible for the first time that a black act could get contracts for eight months out of one office.

The onset of the great depression caused Dudley to sell his theatres and by the end of 1929, his theatrical empire came to an end when he sold his Mid-City Theatre to a white corporation.

Acts Playing the S. H. Dudley Circuit in November 1914
(Chicago Defender, November 30, 1914)

S. H. Dudley Theatre, Lew Henry, Manager, Washington, D. C.	Martin and Motely Stock Company
Howard Theatre, Andrew J. Thomas, Manager, Washington, D. C.	J. Leubrie Hill's Darktown Follies Company
Foraker Theatre, George Tucker, Manager, Washington, D. C.	Dick and Struffin
Fairyland Theatre, Mr. Ross, Manager, Washington, D. C.	Drake and Walker Trio
Chelsea Theatre, D. Gentry, Manager, Washington, D. C.	Special pictures
Green's Opera House, Zel Bledseaux, Manager, Richmond, Virginia	Nit and Tuck
Hippodrome Theatre, W. J. Goulter, Manager, Roanoke, Virginia	Davis and Green, Brown and Pinkey
Boston Theatre, C. C. Andrews, Manager, Lynchburg, Virginia	Whitman Sisters
Ford's Theatre, R. F. Johnson, Manager, New Bern, North Carolina	Bonnie and Samoura Clark

Dixie Theatre, J. H. Williams, Manager, Danville, Virginia	Ricks and Talbert
Columbia Theatre, W. A. Don-levy, Manager, Philadelphia, Pennsylvania	Massengale and Crosby
New Standard Theatre, J. T. Gibson, Manager, Philadelphia, Pennsylvania	Wiggins and Wiggins, Arthur Allen, Butler and Johnson, Jones Ross, and Pellelon Trio
Vaudette Theatre, E. L. Dudley, Manager, Detroit, Michigan	Kelly and Davis
Crown Winter Garden Theatre, Billy Smith, Manager, Columbus, Ohio	Three Cuban Nightingales
Lincoln Theatre, Marion Brooks, Manager, Cincinnati, Ohio	Watts Brothers
Ruby Theatre, Wilholt and Col-lier, Managers, Louisville, Kentucky	Reed's Georgia Troubadours
Crown Garden Theatre, Tim Owsley, Manager, Indianapolis, Indiana	Burton and Hock
Church Park Theatre, S. T. Beer, Manager, Memphis, Tennessee	Clark Company Company, Jones and Jones, Denslow and Denslow
Dixie Theatre, Danville, Virginia	Anita Wilkins, Hugh Turner

PACE AND HANDY

The scope of black ownership in the entertainment business included music publishing companies and at least one record company. In 1908, Harry H. Pace, then a twenty-four-year-old professor of Greek and Latin at Lincoln University, Jefferson City, Missouri, and W. C. Handy (the father of the Blues), who was teaching music in Memphis, collaborated on songs and later organized the Pace and Handy Music Company, Inc.

In 1909, W. C. Handy orchestrated the "Memphis Blues" which he copyrighted and published in 1912. In 1913, Pace and Handy published "Jogo Blues" and "The Girl You Never Have Met" under the firm's name. Pace then left for Atlanta to become secretary-treasurer of the Standard Life Insurance Company. A year later Handy wrote the words and music of the famous "St. Louis Blues." It was on Beale Street in an office over the Solvent

W. C. Handy As Bandmaster with Mahara's Minstrels, circa 1904

Savings Bank that Handy continued to write and publish not only
Blues, but marches, hymns, spirituals, and popular songs. The
business of Pace and Handy grew rapidly and eventually it became
necessary to move from Beale Street to Broadway in New York City.
Pace came back to the firm at about the same time. Bert Williams' recording of "O Death, Where Is Thy Sting?" and Eddie
Green's song "A Good Woman Is Hard to Find" established the
firm's name throughout the world, and it became known as the
"House of the Blues"; millions of phonograph records were sold by
artists performing the firm's songs.

    Later, Harry Pace, sensing the growth of the recording in-
dustry, and being a good businessman, severed connections with the
publishing firm and organized the Pace Phonograph Company in 1921,
which manufactured records under the label of Black Swan.   Black
Swan Records was the first record label to be manufactured by a
black company, and the original officers and directors of the company were: Harry H. Pace, president and treasurer; D. L. Haynes,
secretary; Dr. W. E. B. Dubois; John F. Nail; Levi C. Brown; T.
K. Gibson; Emmett J. Scott and William Lewis.   The company's
business offices were originally located at 257 West 138th Street in
New York City, but were later moved to 2289 Seventh Avenue.   The
recording studios and pressing plant were located in Long Island,
New York.

    It is quite likely that Harry Pace decided to name his record
label after the famous black concert singer, M. Magalene Tartt,
who toured the South under the billing The Black Swan.   The young
Pace probably first heard the talented soprano during his stay in
Memphis, Tennessee between the years of 1908 and 1914.   It was
during this period that The Black Swan reached the height of her
popularity.   Although Mme. Tartt had a truly remarkable voice,
she never gained the national and international fame of her two
famous contemporaries, Anna Patti Brown and Sissieretta Jones
(Black Patti).

    An advertisement which appeared in the June 2, 1923, edi-
tion of the Chicago Defender described the company in the following
manner:

> Only bonafide Racial company making talking machine
> records.   All stockholders are colored, all artists are
> colored, all employees are colored.   Only company using
> Racial Artists in recording high class song records.   This
> company made the only Grand Opera records ever made
> by Negroes.   All others confine this end of their work to
> blues, rags, comedy numbers, etc.   Pioneer company in
> this field.   List of Artists includes many of the most
> prominent concert artists as well as vaudeville stars.
>   Offices of the company are located on 2289 7th Avenue,
> New York City.

In 1923, the following artists were recording for Black Swan: Ethel

Label of First Black-Owned Phonograph Record Company, circa **1921**

Waters, Trixie Smith, Josie Miles, Lucille Hegamin, Florence Cole Talbert, Antoinette Garnes, Charles Winter Wood, Kemper Harreld (violinist, and later professor of music at Morehouse College, Atlanta, Georgia), Revella Hughes, F. H. Henderson, Sammy Swift's Jazz Band, the Jazz Masters, Etta Mooney, Henderson's Dance Orchestra, Four Harmony Kings, Hattie King Reavis, Marion Harrison, William H. Farrell, Inez Wallace, Marianna Johnson, Earl B. Westfield, Manhattan Harmony Four, Fred Smith's City Orchestra, Harry A. Delmore, Lena Wilson, Carroll Clark, Creamer (Henry) and Layton (Turner), J. Arthur Gaines, Alberta Hunter, Julia Moody, and Maud DeForrest.

The brightest young star of Black Swan records was Ethel Waters, and the demand for her public appearances was so great that Harry Pace sponsored a tour for Miss Waters and a small band, and they were billed as "The Black Swan Troubadours." The group played all the large black theatres in the East and Midwest with Miss Waters singing all of her hit recordings. The tour not only enhanced the popularity of Miss Waters, but also boosted record sales for Harry Pace.

With Ethel Waters' recording of "Down Home Blues" and
others, Harry Pace started a stampede in the recording industry.
All the large white companies added "race catalogues" as they were
called then.   Hundreds of black artists became recording artists
overnight.   Black bands couldn't supply the demand for the blues.
For a time, the Pace company made huge profits but eventually his
competition proved too stiff.   Paramount, Columbia and other large
companies flooded the market with recordings at prices so low that
Pace could not compete and the company had to fold.   But Harry
Pace had set a trend in the recording industry that resulted in a
great demand for black singers and musicians.

After the failure of his record company, Pace turned his remarkable talents to the insurance business.   In 1925 he was the
founder and first president of the Northeastern Life Insurance Company of Newark, New Jersey.   In 1928 Pace was elected president
of the National Negro Insurance Association which was composed of
thirty insurance companies operating throughout the United States
and having over 300 million dollars of insurance in force.

The Handy Brothers Music Company, Inc., became the suc-
cessor to the Pace and Handy Company, with Charles E. Handy,
president, and W. C. Handy, secretary-treasurer and employing a
staff of arrangers, copyists, bookkeepers, pianists, stenographers,
pluggers, salesmen, and everything that was involved with a music
publishing firm.   Later, a prominent London firm contracted for
foreign rights for Continental Europe and the whole British Empire.
A firm in Rio de Janeiro contracted for South American rights, and
another in Sydney, Australia represented the firm in that country
and the Far East.

The Handy Brothers Music Company was a member of the
Music Publishers' Protective Association and the American Society
of Composers, Authors and Publishers, and received royalties
quarterly from the use of the music on radio, in theatres, cabarets,
dance halls, hotels, and all other places where the music was performed.

Thirty Songs Written by Black Composers,
Published by Pace and Handy Music Co., Inc.
(Advertisement in Chicago Defender, Oct. 16, 1920)

Title	Composer
Think of Me, Little Daddy	Alberta Whitman
That Thing Called Love	Perry Bradford
Long Gone	Charles Smith
Oh, You Darktown Regimental Band	Maceo Pinkard
Remember and Be Careful Every-day	Dave Payton, Brown and Lemonier
I'm Dying with the Worried Blues	Dave Payton
I Never Had the Blues Till I Left Old Dixieland	Spencer Williams

Pee Gee Blues	H. Q. Clark
A Good Man is Hard to Find	Eddie Green
Sweet Child	Ewing and Stovall
I Wonder If Your Loving Heart Still Pines for Me?	W. Benton Overstreet
Lonesome Road Blues	Will Nash
Nighti Night	W. Max Davis
Florida Blues	W. King Phillips
Why Did You Make a Plaything of Me?	J. Berni Barbour
Deep Sea Blues	Q. Roscoe Snoden
Campmeeting Blues	W. T. Carroll
Preparedness Blues	Chas. Hillman
The Insect Ball	Jim Burris
Louisiana Dip	Bobby Lee
Sliding Fever	Alexander Valintine
I'm Going Back to My Used-to-Be	Jimmie Cox
I'm Looking All Around for a Vampire	Creamer and Layton
The Tom Cat Blues	Butler and Pankey
No Matter What You Do	William Grant Still
Blind Man's Blues	McLaurin and Green
Manvolyne Waltz	Fred M. Bryan
Young Black Joe	Simms and Warfield
Thinking of Thee	Harry H. Pace
Saint Louis Blues	W. C. Handy

CLARENCE WILLIAMS

Clarence Williams, internationally known music composer, pianist, radio and recording artist was also a pioneer black music publisher. Williams was born in 1904 in Plaquemine, Louisiana, a small town on the outskirts of New Orleans, where he spent his early life. He attended grammar school, but quit at an early age in order to secure a job to help his parents, who were poor. He worked as a waterboy on a railroad gang, of which his father was the foreman. He also worked as a bootblack, bus boy, errand boy, and a tailor's apprentice.

He learned to play the piano at an early age and his first job in the music business was as a piano player in a wine room in New Orleans. Whenever a patron would request any number except the two he knew, "Some of These Days" and "Lonely Joe," he always excused himself by saying he did not have the music with him. Later he would buy the music of the requested number and have a girl play it over and over until he learned to play it by ear.

Each time the girl played a song for him, it would cost him $1.00, so he decided it would be cheaper to take piano lessons at 25 cents per lesson. He started out, but at the end of his eighth lesson he was satisfied that he was equipped with enough of the fundamental knowledge of piano playing to make any selection easy for him.

Ad for Clarence Williams Music Publishing Co., circa 1924

Williams wrote his first songs in 1910: "You Missed a Good Woman When You Picked All Over Me" and "Brownskin Who for You?" He had difficulty in trying to get them published so he saved every penny he could and published them himself and sold them on street corners, peddled them from door to door, and went around to cabarets and dance halls and played and sang them, which created a demand for the songs.

A few years later, he formed a partnership with A. J. Piron and opened a store upstairs over a cabaret and began writing more songs. He also opened a music store in Chicago and later went to New York because of the opportunities there for recording his music.

Williams was one of the first blacks to demonstrate music in the five and ten cent stores from New Orleans to Texas and from there to New York. Later, he organized the first swing trio on radio which consisted of Clarence Todd, himself and his wife, Eva Taylor. He also wrote the book and music and produced the show "Bottomland" in 1927 which starred his wife.

Some of the songs Williams authored and published included "Baby, Won't You Please Come Home?" 1917; "Royal Garden Blues" 1918 (with Spencer Williams); "Sugar Blues" (later the theme song of Clyde McCoy and his Sugar Blues Orchestra); "You're Some Pretty Doll" 1919; "Who Made You Cry, Sugar Baby?" (with Spencer Williams); "If You Want Me, Please Don't Dog Me 'Round" (featured in the Ziegfeld Follies of 1919); "Sister Kate" 1923; "Everybody Loves My Baby" 1924; "Rhapsody in Love"; "De Da Da"; and "I'm Falling for You."

The Williams' catalogue contained over 2,000 songs, spirituals, and instrumentals, and the firm had representatives in every European country, Asia, South America, and Australia. Williams died in 1967.

CHAPTER 3

PIONEER BLACK SHOW PRODUCERS

MINSTREL MEN

After the end of the Civil War, blacks began to take to the stage in increasing numbers, performing in minstrel companies and advertising themselves as the genuine article. Although these early minstrel performers adopted many of the racial stereotype portrayals of plantation life portrayed by white minstrel shows which originated in America several decades earlier, this form of entertainment was used by many black performers as a springboard to branch out into other forms of higher class entertainment. Although the profits of most of the black minstrel shows went into the hands of white owners, there were several blacks who owned and managed some of the most successful companies that toured America and abroad.

Black minstrel companies began to emerge as early as the mid-1850's, but it was Charles Hicks who organized the first successful black-owned aggregation. Starting out as a manager of Brooks and Clayton's Georgia Minstrels, the first black minstrel company, Hicks, then known as Barney Hicks, organized his first troupe in 1866 and started out from Cincinnati, Ohio, and traveled through Indiana, Illinois, Ohio, Pennsylvania, and New York. His original company was composed of about eight men: five musicians, one middle man, and two end men. The names of these men are not recorded, but it is claimed that the first show was responsible for the well-known words, "Why did the chicken cross the road?" Hicks' company was very successful and in 1870 went to Germany carrying several well-known artists including Jimmy Jackson, Jake Hamilton, Dick Slayter, Abe Cox, Abe Bishop, Lem Williams, Prof. Lyons, Tom Corniss and others. They stayed four or five years before returning to the United States. Shortly afterwards, Charles Callender purchased the company from Hicks, and put it out as the Original Georgia Minstrels which was one of the best shows of this type during this period.

After Charles Hicks, Lew Johnson was the next black man to own a minstrel company. He put together his first group in Chicago in 1867, but it was not very successful and soon went to the wall. Johnson's next venture was a traveling brass band which played in halls, theatres and opera houses in the Midwest. His first success-

Mallory Brothers--Featured Performers with Williams and Walker
Shows, circa 1899

ful minstrel company was organized in 1871 and consisted of about
fifteen performers including Will Terrell, Frank Essex, Sonnie
Black, Ben Nash, Ed Rector, Charlie Swerer, Spencer Drake (the
only black drum major in the business at the time), Eugene Ewing,
Joe Woodson, Bob Bodie and Sam Butler's Orchestra, and Alf
White.   Henry Bridgewater was their advance agent.   Perhaps Johnson's best company was organized in St. Louis about 1878 and was
billed as Lew Johnson's Plantation Minstrels.   They played all the
principal cities of the Northwest and carried such stellar artists as
the Mallory Brothers, Sam Lucas, McCabe and Young, King Billy
Speed and others.

Another popular minstrel company owned by blacks in the
early 1900's was McCabe and Young's Minstrels.   After the original
co-owner, D. W. McCabe, died in Wyoming in 1907, the show was
taken over by his younger brother, William McCabe.   William
McCabe was born in Kansas City, Missouri, January 6, 1873.   He
gained his early stage experience by performing several seasons
with his brother's show, part of the time being billed as the "Boy
Wonder. "   After a time, the young McCabe traveled with W. S.
Cleveland's Minstrels and eventually rejoined his brother, Dan, who
was at this time managing the "Black Trilby" company.

In 1900, William McCabe branched out for himself, organizing the Georgia Troubadours.   For over ten seasons this was one of

the most popular shows touring the Western states, primarily the Dakotas, Iowa, Michigan, and Minnesota.   By the season of 1910, McCabe's show consisted of ten performers headed by "Clever" Bill Young and including Cassie Binder, Edna McCabe (Mrs. McCabe), Ada Smith, Edith Gordan, Hattie Lewis, Tom Warren, and Jack Winbush, with Fred W. Burns as musical director.   The afterpiece performed by the company during this season was "A Trip to the Jungles."

Perhaps the best of the minstrel companies owned and managed entirely by blacks was the Rabbit's Foot Company organized in 1900 by Pat Chappelle.   Before organizing this company, Chappelle had had many years of experience as a performer and as a theatre owner.   After several years of touring the leading vaudeville houses of the East and West, Chappelle returned to Jacksonville, Florida, his hometown, where he bought a hotel and billiard parlor on Bay Street.   He later remodeled this building into a concert hall where many famous black performers of the day appeared.   In the season of 1899-1900, Chappelle organized his first company, the Famous Imperial Minstrels, which toured the Southern states.   Later, after associating himself with a man named Donaldson, he opened the Mascotte Theatre-Saloon in Tampa, Florida.   The shows presented soon became the talk of the town and the theatre was crowded night-

Ad for Pat Chappelle's Rabbit's Foot Company, circa 1900

ly. The success made at this house prompted Chappelle and Donaldson to open the Buckingham Theatre in Ft. Brooks, Florida.

The Rabbit's Foot Company show was written for Chappelle by Frank Dumont, and the company consisted of about fifty performers. The business staff consisted of Pat Chappelle, owner and general manager; L. W. Chappelle, assistant general manager; J. E. Chappelle, talent agent; D. Ireland Thomas, secretary; George L. Moxley, stage manager; George Jones, band master; T. C. Williams, advance agent. The performers included Happy Howe, leading comedian; Amos Gillard, William Thomas, Lewis Williams, J. M. Gayles, Frank Hopkins, E. N. Collins, Oscar Hicks, Freddie Goodman, Willie Goodwin, Prince Okasuma, Inman and Davis, Bose Reese, the Reevers, William Nicholas and wife, J. D. Rainey, Jose Miller, Laura Logan, Ada Harris, Mattie Harris, Kemp and Hicks, W. C. Pinkney, David Johnson and Johns Hopkins. The company carried their own brass band and orchestra and traveled in their own private railroad car.

In the season of 1905, Chappelle added a new feature to his company in the style of a professional baseball team which played the local club of each city where the company played. During the ballgame, the Rabbit's Foot concert band usually performed a program of classical music.

After Pat Chappelle's death in Tampa, Florida in November 1911, the show he had originated passed out of black ownership and was sold outright to Fred S. Walcott who was then the owner of F. S. Walcott Carnival shows. The Rabbit's Foot company was put back on the road in November 1912 with 45 persons, including 25 stage performers. The personnel of the company included: F. S. Walcott, owner and manager; Ed (Dad) Howard, stage manager; George Williams, band leader. On the stage were: John Mesns, T. H. Durman, Joe Douker, Billie Freeman, Carter Lockheart, Mose Watkins (extremes), Frank Tansel and Original Happy Howe (semi-circle), Ed (Dad) Howard (interlocutor), Frank Dukes, Lillian Lockheart, Joseph M. Means, Lillian Dukes, Robert Reeves, Frank Means, Frank Reed, Carrie Collum, and Nettie Howard. The last act put on by the company this season was "A Judge for a Day." The Rabbit's Foot show continued to tour the Southern United States until well into the 1940's.

JOHN W. ISHAM

In 1893, the Indianapolis Freeman stated that John W. Isham "Has done more for the advancement of the colored race in all America than any other man since the day of its emancipation." Isham was born in 1866 in Utica, New York, where he acquired his first taste for show business. Being of very fair complexion, Isham frequently passed for white and thereby was able to secure responsible positions with various show companies which allowed him to acquire valuable experience in the management and advertis-

ing end of the business.   In the season 1883-1884, he worked in the
advertising department with Ryan and Robinson's Circus.   In 1885-
1886, Isham was engaged by the Sell's Brothers shows and from
1886 to 1888, he held a responsible position with the Barnum and
Bailey shows.

His first real break came when he was engaged by Sam T.
Jack as advance man for the Creole Company.   It was during this
period that he conceived the idea of organizing his own company
under the title of John W. Isham's Octoroons.   This company of
talented artists not only presented a series of high class musical
entertainment, but performed equally well in grand opera and comic
opera, intermingled with specialties.   For eight seasons this was
one of the most successful shows on the road.   By 1897 the popularity of the company had become so great that Isham put out two
additional companies of Octoroons.

The original Octoroon cast included Madame Flowers, Fred
Piper, Jesse Shipp, Billy Johnson, Mamie Emerson, Bell Davis,
Bob Kelly, Tom Brown, Frank Mallory, Edward Mallory, Tom
McIntosh, Hattie McIntosh, Shorty May, Ed. Furber, and George
Hammond.   An article published in the Indianapolis Freeman on
July 3, 1897, provides a description of the Octoroon show during
this period:

> Isham's Octoroons, no. 2 is a well equipped company of
> Colored artists; the performance is thoroughly enjoyable,
> many of the company being superior to the average white
> performer.   "The Blackville Derby," an amusing travesty
> upon the race track, serves to introduce a number of
> comedians, chief among the funmakers being Tom McIntosh,
> who is genuinely funny.   "Thirty Minutes Around the Op-
> era," a melange of operatic selections, in which the lead-
> ing characters are taken by Miss Bertha Lee, an excellent
> soprano, and Harry M. Jackson, a pleasing tenor, is prov-
> ing surprisingly good.   In the Olio, Mr. and Mrs. Tom
> McIntosh are easily the leaders.   Both have an intelligent
> idea of low comedy, and their act is full of new and orig-
> inal humor.   Harry Fidler, an excellent character mimic,
> is amusing, and Sam Lucas is giving a clever monologue.
> Others who appear on the bill are Billy Jackson, comedi-
> an, the "Twentieth Century Swells," Bethel and Jones in a
> character sketch, and the Spanish Serenaders.

In 1897, Isham decided to put out a larger and better show
entitled "Oriental America."   In the original cast were Tom Brown,
Harry Fidler, Ruby Shelton, J. Rosamond Johnson, Billy Eldridge,
Strout Pane, Ed. Winn, Jesse Shipp, Jim Burris, Sidney Woodward,
William Elkins, Mattie Wilkes, Inez Clough, The Meridith Sisters,
Lottie Carrie, Pearl and Maggie Scott, Jennie Eldridge, and others.
This was the first show of this type to open on Broadway at Pal-
mer's Theatre.   The show was not a huge success but was consid-
ered one of the best singing shows of the time.   The following

JOHN W. ISHAM'S FAMOUS OCTOROONS.

John W. Isham's Famous Octoroon Company, circa 1898

article in the November 9, 1896, edition of the Morning Times, Washington, D. C., provides a description of the show:

> Scarcely ever has an audience left the theatre more thoroughly pleased and delighted over a performance than the one which filed out of the Academy of Music last week. The attraction was Isham's Oriental America, presented by a company of sweet singers and talented performers, the cream of the colored race. The show is regarded, among

The Brittons Comedy Team As They Appeared with Isham's Octo-roons, circa 1902

the leading aggregation of similar character, as one of the strongest on the road.   It is a company full of strong soloists, well supported by a powerful and well-balanced chorus, and the selections rendered were pleasing in the extreme.   From the rise of the curtains on the opening chorus, the audience, which filled the house to the doors, were first surprised, then pleased, then delighted, and reached the climax of enthusiasm in rounds of applause when the last curtain fell on the magnificent rendition of the bridal chorus sextette from "Lucia di Lammermoor" in which all the stars appeared.

Mr. Isham has certainly eclipsed all his former efforts

in this line.   The program, although a collection of most
difficult selections for soloists and ensemble voices, is
rendered in an artistic and finished manner.   The several
scenes in each act have been given the benefit of very attractive and elaborate scenic and electric embellishment
and especially is this so in the last act, wherein are presented prominent scenes using appropriate costumes from
well-known standard operas of the several schools, to
which fully forty minutes were devoted.

Miss Mattie Wilkes, the leading soprano of the company, has undoubted talent of high degree, and handles well
her birdlike voice, whose upper register is strong and
clear and pleasing in the extreme.   Her rendition of the
"Last Rose of Summer" in the third act was a gem, and
called for round upon round of applause to which she responded with a pretty ballad.

The comedian of the company, Billy Eldridge, is the
next great feature of the show.   He provided a laughter
without effort, and his talent as an originator of comic
business far above the ordinary, and his dancing has seldom been equalled here.   He made a decided hit in his
specialties with Jennie Eldridge.   Miss Margaret Scott's
selections of vocal gems were well received.   The famous
Colored tenor, Sidney Woodward, fully justified all that
has been written about him.   He has good presence and is
in every way in voice and manner an ideal tenor.   His
rendition of the Aria from "Rigoletto" was enthusiastically
received.   Those who appeared in the quartet from the
same opera with him and scored a success were Misses
Margaret Scott and Jube Johnson.

J. Rosamond Johnson gave his armorer's song from
DeKoven's "Robin Hood" in costume and earned a recall.
Jesse Shipp and Edward Winn were clever as descriptive
vocalists.

Among the many features of the great show were a
Japanese dance, cleverly rendered by Fanny Rutledge,
Pearl Meredith, Alice Mackey and Carrie Meredith, who
sang and danced equally well and were prominent in all
the ensemble scenes of the performance.   A quartet of
cycling girls in bloomers and twentieth century maids,
the maids of the Oriental Huzzars, led by Miss Belle
Davis, as well as the hunting scene and opening chorus
form the "Bells of Cornville." All these and many more
were attractive numbers of the performance.   Miss Belle
Davis gave a pleasing imitation of May Irwin in "I Want
You, Ma Honey" and other popular songs, and Billy Eldridge brought down the house with "Hot Tamale Alley"
which he sang as it has never been presented here before.
A flower ballet by a bevy of pretty girls, assisted by
Naby Ray, was an attractive number in the second act.

By 1900, John Isham found that his shows could not compete
with the productions of Bob Cole and Williams and Walker, so he

retired from show business management.   John Isham's brother,
Will, who had joined him in the season of 1887 as actor and manager of the Octoroon company, decided to make one last effort to
put out a successful show.   In the season 1900-1901, the Octoroon
company took the road playing a production entitled "King Rastus"
which had the old minstrel man Billy Kersands in the starring role.
The show was a complete failure.   One critic who saw the show in
Memphis, Tennessee, commented as follows (March 30, 1901 edition of the Indianapolis Freeman):

> Isham's Octoroons in the operatic comedy "King Rastus"
> made their appearance at the Auditorium in Memphis,
> Tennessee March 19 and 20.   As a whole the show was
> one that the citizens of this place care not to see repeated.
> It is a slander on the Negro of America; for example, here
> are some of their sayings: "Who raised you, a Colored
> woman?"; "If a Negro left those things here, give them
> back to him."; "Say, gal, give me them White folks mon-
> ey."; "That's the reason White folks don't let niggers hold
> office, because they want to rule the earth.".   And worse
> than all was when they say "Every nation has a flag but a
> coon."   Every flag was displayed with honor, then a rag
> with a chicken and watermelon on it was displayed, and
> on it was this inscription: "Our rag," signifying that the
> Negro would spill his last drop of blood to get into some-
> body's chicken coop and watermelon patch.   The costumes
> and dancing were very vulgar.   The White people enjoyed
> this flag business and niggers in the White folks yard, but
> for me, we say shame, shame!

After "King Rastus" closed the Octoroons continued to play
for several more seasons with decreasing popularity.   These shows
took on a more conventional musical comedy form and the operatic
selections so prominent in earlier shows were dropped.   Isham's
Octoroons and Oriental America, however, were important links in
the development of black theatricals in America.

BOB COLE AND J. ROSAMOND JOHNSON

Early black show producers spearheaded the transition of
black theatricals from the minstrel show to musical comedy and
serious dramatic plays.   Robert "Bob" Cole is credited with having
produced the first black-cast musical comedy which made a complete break from the minstrel show format.   Bob Cole's contribution to the development of the early black theatricals cannot be un-
derstated.   James Weldon Johnson, in his book Black Manhattan,
referred to Cole as "the greatest single force in the middle period
of the development of the Negro in American Theatre."

Robert Cole was born in Athens, Georgia in July, 1868.
His father was prominent in politics in the South during the carpet-
bag period.   Cole received his education in the public schools of

COLE AND JOHNSON.

J. Rosamond Johnson [standing] and Bob Cole--One of America's
Pioneer Producing, Composing, and Vaudeville Teams, circa 1903

Atlanta, Georgia and at Atlanta University. Cole left college, however, and secured a job as a bellboy in a hotel in Jacksonville,
Florida. Later he left the South and went to New York where he
did hotel work, but it was not long before he drifted to Chicago
where he divided his work between hotels and clubs.

About this time, the young Cole began to attract attention as
a guitar player, singer and song writer. His first work as an actor
came when he formed a vaudeville team with Lew Henry. The young
team, however, was not successful and soon broke up. Cole then
did a single turn consisting of a monologue and songs written by him.
His first songs were "Parthenia Takes a Likin' to a Coon" and his
next number was "In Shin Bone Alley." Both songs were published
in Chicago by Bill Rossiter.

Cole's reputation as a song writer and actor slowly grew and
his next venture as a team member was with Pete Staples with
whom he formed a comedy musical act which met with only fair success. Cole's first work with a large company was with Sam T.
Jack's Creole Show where he was one of several comedians. He
also was stage manager of the show, and at the age of twenty-three
was probably one of the youngest stage managers in the business.
In the Creole Company was a clever soubrette, Stella Wiley, with
whom Bob Cole formed a team known as Cole and Wiley. They
played some good vaudeville time in the East, and were later married, but the marriage only lasted a few years.

Cole then joined the All Star Stock Company at Worth's Museum, at Sixth Avenue and 30th Street in New York City. This was
probably the first stock company in America organized by blacks.
The members of this historic company were: Billy and Willie Farrell, Tom Brown, Fred Porter, Mamie Flowers, Billy Johnson, Ben
Hunn, Jerry Mills, Mattie Wilkes, Aline Cassell, Hen Wise, Will
Proctor and Stella Wiley.

Bob Cole next became associated with the Black Patti Troubadours as writer and producer. He was assisted by Billy Johnson,
and his ability as a writer, producer and actor attracted wide attention. Cole wrote the hour-long farce "Jolly Coon-ey Island" and the
dramatic critics were very complementary of his tramp character
and his work in the production was directly responsible for the replacing of vaudeville at Proctor's 58th Street house with large shows.
At the time the Black Patti company was composed of Aida Overton
(later Aida Overton Walker), Maggie Davis, Stella Wiley, the DeWolf
Sisters, Lena Wise, Mme. Reed, Lloyd G. Gibbs, Groggins and
Davis, Rastus and Grant, Hen Wise, Anthony D. Byrd, Charles L.
Moore, Billy Johnson, Bob Cole, Black Patti and a chorus of fourteen. All did not go well for Cole, however. He and the manager
of the company, Rudolph Voelckel, were unable to agree on salary
after Cole had made such a big hit. Cole later left the company,
but not before he and Voelckel had become involved in litigation over
the music which Cole wrote and refused to give up.

Cole's Famous Tramp Character "Willie Wayside" First Introduced
with Black Patti's Troubadours, circa 1900

Ad for First Black Musical Comedy, circa 1900 (third season)

The trouble between Cole and Voelckel initiated a series of other controversies between white managers and black performers with such people as Voelckel and Nolen on one side and Cole and Jesse A. Shipp, Tom Brown, Bob Kelly, Billy Johnson, and Lloyd Gibbs as leaders on the other.

The misunderstanding between managers and players led directly to Cole organizing his first company, "A Trip to Coontown." The company, under black management, stormed the country with eighteen players consisting of Bob Cole, Billy Johnson as stars; Vincent Bradley, the Freeman Sisters, Jennie Scheper, George Brown, William (Black) Carl, Tom Brown, Jesse A. Shipp, Walter Dixon, Lloyd G. Gibbs, Sam Corker, Jr. and Sam King. The "A Trip to Coontown" company had to play the worst houses in every city its first year, but played some of the better houses its second season. The show opened on September 27, 1897, at South Amboy, New Jersey and was first seen in New York at Miner's

Eighth Avenue Theatre.   By the end of the following year the black
company was playing at the Grand Opera House and Casino Roof.
It was during this period that Bob Cole's portrayal of the tramp
character "Willie Wayside" brought him fame.

Billy Johnson, Bob Cole's first partner, was born in Charleston, South Carolina, and he attended the public schools and high
school in Augusta, Georgia.   His first important professional engagement was with Charles Hicks of the famous Hicks and Sawyer Minstrels in the season of 1887-1888, making his debut in New York
City August 27, 1887.   During the next few years, he worked his
way from a song-and-dance man to specialty artist.   After traveling
six seasons with this company, he next joined Isham's Original
Octoroons for the season of 1895-1896 where he created the role
of the bookmaker in "Darkville Derby."   The following season he
joined Black Patti's Troubadours where he met Bob Cole for the
first time.

After the closing of the "A Trip to Coontown" company, Cole
and Billy Johnson* dissolved partnership and the famous song-
writing team of Cole and Johnson, with J. Rosamond Johnson as the
new member, was formed.

J. Rosamond Johnson was born in Jacksonville, Florida on
August 11, 1873.   His mother, a talented musician, was the assistant principal of Stanton Public School and his first teacher.   At the
age of four, young Rosamond was an accomplished pianist.   Completing his public school education in Jacksonville, he entered the
New England Conservatory of Music in Boston for a long period of
diversified study which was later supplemented by a private course
in composition in London, England under Samuel Coleridge Taylor.

In 1905, the talented team of Cole and Johnson was the most
popular song-writing team in America.   They were the composers
of "Under the Bamboo Tree," "The Maiden with the Dreamy Eyes,"
"Congo Love Song," and many other hits.   They also wrote for
Klaw and Erlanger and for many white Broadway stars.   They wrote
the music for "Humpty Dumpty" which appeared on Broadway in 1906
and for "Nancy Brown" in which the white star May Irvin starred for
several seasons all over the United States.   Because of their immense popularity, the team was induced to go into vaudeville.   They
sang their own songs which were so artistically done that they were
soon known in vaudeville as headliners.

In the summer of 1906, after returning from a successful
engagement at the Palace Theatre, London, England, Cole and Johnson made preparations to produce "A Shoofly Regiment" which opened
under their management in Washington, D. C. during the Fall of 1906.
At the time, Williams and Walker Company and Ernest Hogan were
two leading black attractions on the road and Cole and Johnson had

---

*See Chapter 6 for more biographical information on Billy Johnson.

difficulty getting suitable booking.   They were given one-night stands
throughout the South, although carrying about sixty people and much
scenery.   The had considerable financial difficulties and expended
several thousand dollars of their own money to keep the show intact.
At the start of the theatrical season of 1907-8, "A Shoofly Regiment"
played a short engagement at the Bijou Theatre on Broadway, and
this is where Stair and Havlin became interested in the production.

Prospects looked bright for Cole and Johnson at the beginning
of the season of 1908-9 when they put out "The Red Moon" which
was produced with some success for two seasons.   At the closure
of the season of 1909-10, Cole and Johnson announced their retirement from the musical comedy field, giving as their reason that
large productions could not make money any longer by playing popular priced theatres owing to the booking furnished by Stair and
Havlin.

America's Foremost Colored Comedians

COLE & JOHNSON

In their Successful and Artistic Musical Comedy,

'The Red Moon'

Everything New but the Title.

50 The Greatest Colored Cast
and Chorus in the World **50**

INCLUDING

FANNIE WISE, MOLLIE DILL, ELIZABETH WILLIAMS, LE-
ONA MARSHALL, REBECCA ALLEN, MAYME BUTLER, SAM
LUCAS, WESLEY JENKINS, ARTHUR TALBOT, HENRY
GANT, BENNY JONES, EDGAR CONNOR, FRANK FOW-
LER BROWN and

Aida Overton Walker

All New Songs and Costumes.

Ad for Cole and Johnson's Last Production, "The Red Moon,"
circa 1909

The team returned to vaudeville at $750 per week and in the Fall of 1910 made their reappearance as vaudevillians at Keith's Fifth Avenue Theatre. It was on the last night of their engagement at the Fifth Avenue Theatre that Cole suffered a nervous breakdown and the next day was taken to Bellevue Hospital in New York City. He was next sent to Manhattan Hospital, on Ward Island, where he remained until the first of July 1911 when he was taken to a private sanitarium in Amityville, much improved. On Saturday, July 29 of the same year, Cole left Amityville accompanied by his mother, for the Catskills, and was there only four days before he drowned in a lake. Many at the time believed he took his own life since he was known to be an excellent swimmer.

Lester A. Walton payed a tribute to Bob Cole in the August 8, 1911, edition of the New York Age. The article concluded as follows:

> He was a man whose mind was rich with imagination and pregnant with ideas; an omnivorous reader and lover of debate; a man who did not fear to express his convictions; a Negro who believed in his race and in the equality of mankind; a dutiful son and devoted brother; one who was liked and admired and respected for his ability and force of character; a man who died by his own genius, firey overwork of brain and unquenchable ambition.

In his autobiography, Along This Way, James Weldon Johnson observed that "Bob Cole was one of the most talented and versatile Negroes ever connected with the stage. He could write a play, stage it, and play a part. Although he was not a trained musician, he was the originator of a long list of catchy songs." Among the songs Cole composed were "Louisiana Lizzie," "I Must Have Been a'Dreaming," "No One Can Fill Her Place," "Katydid," "The Cricket and the Frog," and "The Maiden with the Dreamy Eyes." He and his partner, J. Rosamond Johnson, wrote "Under the Bamboo Tree," "Big Indian Chief," "Bleeding Moon," and "Oh, Didn't He Ramble."

After the death of Bob Cole in 1911, J. Rosamond Johnson formed an act with Charlie Hart, previously of Avery and Hart. The team went abroad and later Johnson was given charge of the large chorus at one of the leading theatres in London. In February, Johnson returned to America and appeared in vaudeville for a short time with the noted actor Tom Brown, later doing a single turn. In 1912, Rosamond Johnson became musical director of Oscar Hammerstein's Grand Opera House in London, and on July 3, 1913, he married Nora Ethel Floyd of Jacksonville, Florida in a brilliant London wedding.

In 1914, Johnson was appointed Director of the Music School for Colored People, then located on 131st Street and Fifth Avenue in New York. Within several months, he had increased the enrollment of the school to 2,016.

Johnson also served with distinction as second lieutenant in the Fifteenth Regiment in World War I. Later in his career he wrote several authoritative books on American music.

During the 1920's, Johnson appeared in several black shows including "Harlem Rounders" in 1925. In the same year, he put out his own Syncopation company and made a successful tour of the Midwest and East. In addition to Johnson the company included such fine artists as "Peggy" Holland, Edward H. Hanson, Lee Langston, Leon Abbey and Miss E. Bennett. The act consisted of singing, dancing and selections on the banjo and violin. After viewing a performance, a theatrical critic for the Minnesota Messenger commented that "We have often wondered, why blackface entertainers? After witnessing J. Rosamond Johnson and his Negro company, we wonder again why Theatre Managers and bookers ever sign up Negro imitators when the race itself has the very best of entertaining ability?"

J. Rosamond Johnson was in his sixties when he performed in the stage production of "Porgy and Bess" in 1935. Prior to this he had appeared in the hit shows "Fast and Furious" in 1931 and "Mamba's Daughters" with Ethel Waters, and one of his last appearances was in "Cabin in the Sky" in 1941. In 1939, he played a small role in the black film "Keep Punching" which featured Henry Armstrong. Johnson died in New York City on November 11, 1954.

J. ED. GREEN

When Robert Motts decided to build a theatre for blacks on the south side of Chicago in about 1904, he selected J. Ed. Green to organize a stock company and to stage and manage the company's productions. The productions at the Pekin gave the little house fame and standing throughout the country. Much of the Pekin's success was due directly to the hard work and talents of J. Ed. Green.

Mr. Green was born in New Albany, Indiana on November 24, 1872, where he attended the public schools and completed his high school education. As a boy he showed marked ability as a dramatic reader and vocalist. He made his debut as a performer at the Masonic Temple Theatre, Louisville, Kentucky, with Madame Selika, singing a very difficult baritone solo, "Bandit's Life." For several seasons thereafter, he confined his efforts to entertaining at clubs and church concerts and his work met with such approval that he decided to branch out into vaudeville, so during the season 1892 he organized the famous Diamond Quartet composed of himself and three of his fellow townsmen, Ed. Hood, I. M. Smith and La Force. The group went to Cincinnati where they joined Botwick's Specialty Company and toured the principal cities of Canada.

During the season of 1894-1895, Green and his quartet were engaged by Whallen and Martell for "South Before the War." Green directed the chorus for this organization and played the role of "Young Eph." In the summer of 1896, Green wrote and staged at

Havelin's Theatre, Chicago, the big production entitled "Fred
Douglass' Reception" which was performed by the Black American
Troubadours Company.

Next, the youthful actor and budding playwright joined the
Oliver Scott Company and was successful as stage manager and
interlocutor, so much so that the management of the Georgia Minstrels secured him as interlocutor and later made him stage manager.   This was in the season 1897-1898.

The following season, Mr. Green produced the King and
Bush Minstrels and later joined the Black Patti Troubadours, serv-
ing in the capacity of stage manager and being featured as the
"Bronze Chesterfield" which later became his nickname.

In collaboration with Bob H. Kelly, Green wrote and produced the "Queen of the Jungle" featuring Mme. Flowers and Allie
Gillam.   Next he was seen in the "Smart Set" company where he
created the character of "Kane" in which role he scored the hit of
his career as a character actor.   During this period he wrote two
songs, "The Girl That I Would Wed," and "Letters We All Love to
Read."   He also wrote two plays, "The Hoosier Detective" and
"Jack's Return from Africa."

It was with the first season with the "Rufus Rastus" company
with its star Ernest Hogan that Green staged the production and
played the role of "Beasley," the head waiter.   The staging of
"Rufus Rastus," especially the minstrel first part in the first act,
was generally praised by the critics.   At the end of the season's
success of "Rufus Rastus," Green went to Chicago to stage a white
burlesque show and was later engaged by Robert T. Motts as amusement director for the Pekin Theatre.   His first task was to change
the house to a popular family theatre which was no small undertaking.   However, through his efforts the Pekin Theatre soon became
one of the theatrical successes of America and an inspiration to all
black performers.   It was Green who most influenced the early development of the young playwrights, Miller and Lyles.

With the advent of the small vaudeville theatres in Chicago,
which caused the manager of the Pekin Theatre to change its policy
to a ten-cent vaudeville house, J. Ed. Green and Marion A. Brooks
organized the Chester Amusement Company, operating three theatres
in Chicago and booking several others.   It was the eventual failure
of this venture which contributed to his physical breakdown.   Green
died February 13, 1910, in Chicago at the home of Mrs. A. W.
Baker, 3213 Wabash Ave.

A list of productions by J. Ed. Green at the Pekin and
Columbia Theatres includes "Haddon Chambers," "Captain Swift,"
"The African Princes," "My Nephew's Wife," "Mayor of Dixie,"
"Queen of the Jungles," "My Friend from Georgia," "Count of No-
Account," "In Zululand," "The Man from Bam," "The Grafter,"
"Doctor Dope," "The Husband," "The Bachelor," "The Hoosier,"

"Isle of Night," "Peanutville," "Panama," "Young Mrs. Winthrop,"
"Uncle Eph's Dream," and "Darktown Circus."

Songs authored by Green include "Cupid, Will You Always
Wear a Smile?," "Tears," "Two Tender Dreamy Eyes," and "All
for Your Love."

WILLIAMS AND WALKER

Two years before Bob Cole produced "A Trip to Coontown,"
Bert Williams and George Walker, America's greatest comedy team,
came East from the West Coast. They brought with them their famous Cakewalk dance and their song "Has Anybody Seen Dora Dean?"
Newspaper accounts of the period describe George Walker as unfor-
gettable and as being the personification of his song "Bon Bon Buddy," with spats, a high silk hat, gloves, monocle and malacca cane,
tailored suits, and colored shirts. Walker had a magnificent phy-
sique except for the spindle legs and flat feet that one never sus-
pected as he stepped through his peerless cakewalk.

Bert Williams, however, was really lighter in complexion
than his partner, Walker, and blackened up several shades darker
than George. In his style of comedy and dancing, or in his delivery
of a song, Bert Williams was inimitable. No American comedian has
ever reached his heights. His facial expression and pantomime surpassed the greatest clowns. The great Chaplin could hold an audience no better. In the slow, talking delivery of his songs, he was
without parallel. Each song was a mood and one never missed a
nuance of feeling.

Williams was born in New Providence, Nassau, Bahama

Famous Comedy Team George Walker [left] and Bert Williams,
circa 1900

Islands in 1876 and at the age of two was brought to New York City
by his parents.   His father was a papier-mâché maker.   From New
York City the family moved to Riverside, California, where Williams graduated from high school.   He later went to San Francisco
intending to study to be a civil engineer, but instead he joined a
minstrel company known as "The Mastodon Minstrels," which played
the lumber and mining camps of California.

George Walker was born in Lawrence, Kansas in 1873.   His
first acting job came when he was hired to appear in a medicine
show which took him to San Francisco.

In an article published after Walker's death and which ap-
peared in the January 14, 1911, edition of the Indianapolis Freeman,
Bert Williams gave the following account of how he first met George
Walker and their early years together.

> We came together almost by accident.   I was in San
> Francisco with Martin and Selig's Mastodon Minstrels,
> composed of five whites, one Mexican, and four Colored
> minstrels.   The Mexican drove the four-horse team and
> played trombone.   That was over 18 years ago.
> A man was wanted for the end opposite me.   George
> Walker was in town.   He could dance, and I was learning
> dance steps from him.   He was picked up by Dr. Wait in
> Lawrence, Kansas as a good subject for sticking pins in
> and having men stand on his chest for which he received
> 50 cents a night.   This brought him into a medicine show
> that one day landed him in San Francisco.   I asked him
> where I could find a certain fellow that I wished to get for
> the opposite end to me.   We could not find him, and then
> I turned to George and said: "What's the use lookin' any
> longer?   You're the right man anyhow."   And he surely
> proved to be.
> We were with that minstrel troupe for five months,
> getting a salary off and on.   When we got it, his salary
> was $8 per week and cakes.   I received $1 more for act-
> ing as stage manager.   I think we had three paydays that
> season.   Once we were stranded in Bakersfield, California.
> Tired and tried, we returned to San Francisco, where for
> two years we were at Halahan Homan's Midway, after
> which Gustave Walters, who formed the Orpheum Circuit,
> sent us to Los Angeles, where another act had made a
> failure.   Clifford and Stuth, getting $300 a week, were
> the headliners.   Our eyes popped out of our heads when
> Billy Clifford showed us $300 in gold.   We were supposed
> to stay three weeks as trial, we stayed four at $60 a
> week and went from there to Denver.
> At Denver, a medicine man engaged us to go to Cripple
> Creek.   He got scared when he saw the miners and jumped
> his own show, but as we were already into his debt for
> $80 we did not care.   With that money we went to Chicago,
> reaching there with an outfit of music and in rags.   Walter

J. Plummer gave us a start in Chicago.   Montgomery and
Stone had been booked for a theatre in Pittsburgh.   They
refused to fill the engagement and we took their place.
That helped us to more work.
    At West Baden we met Tom Canary who engaged us for
"The Passing Show," after which we went to New York and
joined the ill-fated "Gold Bug" company, which lasted only
one week on Broadway.   In 1896 we got one week with the
Sandow Show in which were Ed Captian and Wood & Sheppard among others.
    We were in with Peter F. Daily in "A Good Day" at
the Hollis Street Theatre, Boston, came back to the Casino
in New York, but were transferred to Will A. McConnell
at Koster & Bial's.   I have never heard of a vaudeville
run at one house to equal that of our Koster & Bial record.   Yvette Guilbert, La Belle Otero and the Barrion
Sisters were there at different times during the run.

When Williams and Walker reached New York in 1895, "coon"
songs were all the rage and a number of white stars including Lew
Docksteader and George Primrose were making reputations as blackface comedians.   Williams and Walker were billed as "Williams and
Walker, the Two Real Coons."   By this time, Williams did the
comedy and George Walker was the straight man.

    It was during their Koster & Bial's run that Williams and
Walker popularized the "Cake Walk," a dance that had originated on
the slave plantations of the South.   An article which appeared in the
March 3, 1897 edition of the Indianapolis Freeman gives the following graphic description of their Koster & Bial act:

        The first half is made up of conventional singing, dancing,
        and joking, but it ends with a "cake walk."   That is about
        the best feature of the bill.   There are but two couples,
        and as the cake is now in evidence the walkers promptly
        get down to business.   One pair hold the floor at a time,
        and the men's manners are in strong contrast.   One chap
        is clownish, though his grotesque paces are elaborate,
        practiced, and exactly timed, while the other is all airi-
        ness.   It is a revolution to most observers to see so much
        of jauntiness in one human being.   The elder Turkeydrop
        could not hold a candle to such incandescent deportment.
        The airy man's attire is gorgeous.   Pointed shoes, tight
        trousers, red and white striped shirt front, and shining
        silk hat are not out of harmony with mock diamonds that
        are as big as marbles, and there is a smile that for size
        and convincingness is unequaled.   Away up stage he and
        his partner meet and curtsey, she with utmost grace, he
        with exaggerated courtliness.   Then down they trip, his
        elbow squared, his hat held upright by the brim, and with
        a mincing gait that would be ridiculous were it not abso-
        lute in its harmony with the general scheme of airiness.
        With every step his body sways from side to side and the

outstretched elbows see-saw but the woman clings to his
arm, and this grandest of entities is prolonged till the
footlights are reached.   Then a turn at right angles brings
another elaborate curtsey before the two pass along parallel to the footlights.   Here he faces the audience, and no
lack of grace comes from his unusual position in walking.
The smile is thus in view throughout the promenade, and,
if one could doubt that this chap is a dandy of dandies, it
should be dispelled.   Its expansiveness is only limited by
the Negro's face, and it is genuine in large degree, else
the sparkling eyes belie it.   The other chap's rig is rusty,
and his joints work jerkily, but he had his own ideas about
high stepping, and carries them out in a walk that starts
like his companion's but that ends at the other side of the
stage.   Then the first fellow takes both women, one on
each arm, and, leaving the other man grimacing vengeful-
ly, starts on a second tour of grace.   Even then he walks
across the front of the stage with that huge smile wide
open, and goes off, leaving the impression that he'd had
a pretty good time himself.

Shortly after they closed at Koster & Bial's, Williams and
Walker went to England in 1897 where they played an engagement
at the Empire Music Hall in London under the billing of "Tobasco
Senegambians. " After their return from Europe they played a six-
week engagement at Koster & Bial's and then went on tour with the
Hyde's Comedians.   This was the last appearance of them as a
team in a white production.

In 1899, Bob Cole's "A Trip to Coontown" was launched and,
in order to compete with this show, Williams and Walker signed
with Lederer and McConnell and made their first appearance as
musical comedy stars in a "Senegambian Carnival. " Paul L. Dunbar wrote the book and lyrics and Will Marion Cook the music.
The original cast was composed of the following: Williams and
Walker, Joe Hodges, Charles Davis, Lord Bonnie, William Elkins,
Charles L. Moore, Henry Williams, Mamie Emerson, Lottie
Launchmere, Mazie Brooks, Lottie Thompson, and Black Carl,
magician.   In the chorus were Ada Overton, Grace Halliday and
others.   Harry T. Burleigh led the orchestra and George Walker
introduced his big hit song, "The Hottest Coon in Dixie. "

Their next show in 1900 was produced with the backing of
Hurtig and Seamon and was called "The Policy Players. "   The show
first came out as "4-11-44" and centered around a dream in which
Williams wins by playing the numbers 4-11-44.   This show had only
a limited success.

It was during this time that Williams and Walker married
actresses in their company.   George Walker married Aida Overton
on June 22, 1899.   Aida Overton had joined the company as a
young soubrette.   A year later, Bert Williams married Lottie
Thompson who had joined the cast of "The Senegambian Carnival" in 1898.

Ad for Williams and Walker's First Big Show, "The Policy Players,"
circa 1900

Getting better and better each season, the Williams and
Walker shows were booked into better and larger theatres.   In 1902,
they produced "In Dahomey" which was written by Jesse Shipp, then
an accomplished actor and playwright.   This show was a great success and played the New York Theatre in Times Square, and in
1903 it was taken to London where it ran for several months at the
Shaftesbury Theatre.   While there, the company received a Royal
Command for a performance at Buckingham Palace on June 23 in
honor of the birthday of the Prince of Wales.   As they had done before in America, Williams and Walker made the Cakewalk a social
fad in England and France.   George Walker commented on their
visit to the Royal Palace in England as follows:

> We were treated royally.   That is the only word for it.
> We had champagne from the Royal cellar and strawberries
> and cream from the Royal garden.   The Queen was per-
> fectly lovely, and the King was as jolly as he could be
> and the little princes and princesses were as nice as they
> could be, just like little fairies.

One of the most profitable seasons experienced by Williams and

Walker was in 1904-5, shortly after their return from England when
"In Dahomey" was presented in theatres across the country going as
far west as San Francisco.

Breaking with Hurtig and Seamon, the team joined forces
with Melville B. Raymond who put them out in their most pretentious of all early black productions, "Abyssinia, " in 1906. Jesse
Shipp wrote the play for them, and "Abyssinia" had an African background which involved the Lion of Judah, an ancestor of King Solomon. The show had elaborate scenery and a large cast including
live camels. After an out of town tryout at the Convention Hall in
Washington, D. C. , the show opened at the Majestic Theatre in New
York, then located on Columbus Circle at the corner of 58th Street.
The show was an immediate success and received great notices in
the newspapers.

Differences with Raymond led them to sign contracts to appear under the management of F. Ray Comstock, then representing
the Shuberts, and for the next two seasons, 1907-9, they successfully starred in their next production, "Bandana Land. " With the
book by Jesse Shipp, the plot concerned an old black couple living
in the South and how a black corporation was formed and bought
their land and called it "Bandana Land. " This show was also a hit
and in it Williams sang a song "Late Hours" and introduced for the
first time his famous pantomime poker game which became his
trademark. (Williams' "Poker Game" may be seen in the film
short "Natural Born Gambler" made in 1916.) From then on, it
made no difference what he said or sang, the audience would never
let Bert Williams leave the stage until he did the poker game and
did his dance to the time of his themesong "Nobody. "

In his book 100 Years of Negro Entertainment, Tom Fletcher
claims that Bert Williams first got the idea for his famous poker
game pantomime while visiting a friend at a hospital in Lincoln,
Nebraska. While there, Williams happened to observe a mentally
ill patient playing an imaginary poker game. The patient was all
alone in his room talking to himself and acting as though he were
in a poker game involving several other people. Williams watched
the man deal several rounds before Jesse Shipp, who was with Williams, turned to him and said "Bert, there you are. "

Much of Williams and Walker's success with "Bandana Land"
was attributed to Will Marion Cook's ensemble numbers which tended
to give the production a classical tone and helped significantly in
making it a Broadway production. During the last four weeks of
"Bandana Land's" stay on Broadway, Cook, with the assistance of
Alex Rogers, gave the public an example of dramatic singing of a
kind never before seen in a black musical comedy. The number,
the "Conjure Man, " was sung as the finish of the first set in which
all the members of the company participated.

George W. Walker was last seen in "Bandanna Land" during
the season of 1908-9. While playing at the Great Northern Theatre

in Chicago, it was noticed that he was not himself, and his physician advised that he take a much needed rest.   When the show appeared in Louisville, Bert Williams was compelled to appear alone and Aida Overton Walker sang her husband's numbers dressed in male attire. After spending months visiting health resorts in Michigan and receiving the care of his mother and relatives at his home in Lawrence, Kansas, he returned to New York and entered one of the institutions at Central Islip, where he died in 1911.

In the January 12, 1911, edition of the New York Age, Lester A. Walton paid the following tribute to George Walker:

> George W. Walker was a talented artist, a fact which cannot be overlooked.   His character of the "dandy darky" which brought out hundreds of imitators, that famous stage smile and his fame as a fashion plate of the sartorial art cannot be readily blotted from our minds.   Yet, the man was a dominating force in the theatrical world more because of the service he rendered the colored members of the profession, more because of the opportunities he created than for the types he has originated.
>
> There are several colored performers today who possibly could fill Mr. Walker's shoes as a straight man with some degree of success, but there is not one who could don the uniform of the commander-in-chief of the colored theatrical forces and bring about conditions providing positions for colored workers, composers, and performers--positions paying large salaries.
>
> It was George Walker's chief aim to elevate the colored theatrical profession, and the race as well.   It was his desire to give us elaborate productions as the white shows and play the best theatres.   For years he struggled valiantly to realize his ambition, having to put his seemingly inopportune and foolhardy ideas (from a white man's standpoint) against those of managers who did not believe that the time was ripe for the presentation of first-class colored shows.   And much of his ill health can be attributed to the mental and physical energy he expended in his tireless endeavor to make progress for his profession, his race and his country.
>
> An instance is cited to show what an aggressive fighter George Walker was.   Some years ago he and his partner had a conference with Abraham Erlanger of Klaw and Erlanger.   Mr. Erlanger is known as the theatrical czar of the country.   On this occasion the comedians asked to be given first-class booking.   The theatrical magnates expressed the opinion that the day was far distant before a colored aggregation would be given the opportunity to entertain a Broadway audience; that the time was not propitious.
>
> George Walker disagreed with Mr. Erlanger, which greatly vexed the latter.   The comedians left the office of Klaw and Erlanger after a stormy scene, with the head of

the syndicate in bad humor.   The comedian vowed that he
would prove that the claims of Mr. Erlanger were untrue,
and set to work to accomplish that end.   He had great
satisfaction in seeing the big promoter in a box at the
Majestic Theatre one evening during the long run of the
Williams and Walker Company in "Bandana Land."   The
show was playing to a Broadway audience and doing an
enormous business.

Bert Williams opened the 1910 season in vaudeville doing a
single at the Victoria Theatre in New York City.   During this period, he introduced several new songs including "The Barber Shop
Chorale," "Some Folks Call it Chantecleer, But It's Plain Chicken
to Me," and "I'll Lend You Anything but My Wife, and I'll Make
You a Present of Her."   He always finished his act with his themesong "Nobody."

In September 1910, Williams played a high-class playhouse
in Chicago--the Colonial--for the first time in his career as a member of Ziegfeld's "Follies of 1910."   Although there were large numbers of white comedians, singers and dancers in the show, the
critics were unanimous in acknowledging that Williams was the hit
of the show.

Constance Skinner in the Chicago Evening American, in his
review of the show, wrote in part:

> The principal congratulatory item, however, is Mr. Bert
> Williams.   Bert Williams is not one of the "Follies," he
> is the wisdom and wit before F. Ziegfeld ever committed
> a folly.

The 1911 season of the "Follies" opened with Bert Williams
over the objections of many of the white performers in the company.
However, because of his tremendous success of the previous season,
Williams was given an opportunity to display his talents to a larger
extent than in the "Follies of 1910."   The big hit of the "Follies of
1911" was a sketch performed by Williams and Leon Errol.   Errol
recalled the sketch as follows:

> In the Grand Central scene, Williams was the porter,
> carrying Errol's luggage.   Errol was a British tourist.
> Their destination is the upper level and their trip is
> hazardous because the whole place is torn up and filled
> with temporary passages, where exposed girders and un-
> finished iron work abound.
>   Williams, as the husky "red cap," has tied a rope to
> the neat little tourist, the other end of which encircles
> his own waist.   They are proceeding cautiously along like
> mountain climbers in the Swiss Alps, when Errol becomes
> impressed with the structural work and stops in the center
> of the stage to discuss it.   Williams has seen "plenty" of
> it and can not enthuse with him, nor does he give expres-

sion verbally nor facially to anything except the fear that
his passenger may fall off. Errol's nervous little move-
ments and wide gestures with his arms finally do the trick.
He falls off, but Williams pulls him back with a labored
hand over hand pull.   Just as he has succeeded in pulling
the struggling man up to the foothold, instead of Errol
grasping the girder, he asks: "Porter, have you got a
match?"

Williams, exhibiting a single track mind, immediately
lets go of the rope to feel in his pockets for a match.
Realizing that the Britisher is falling below into space
again, he quickly pulls and hauls again until he succeeds
in landing him back to the spot where he had asked so
thoughtlessly for the match.   He is gasping for breath,
but as he catches hold of the girder he manages to say,
"Never mind the match, Porter, I broke my pipe."

There were gales of laughter at this and then Williams
cautions him and they stand there and do about fifteen
minutes of very funny dialogue.   It was one of those
scenes which Mr. Errol mentions as being built by the
two men from nothing.   They worked many topics of the
day into the dialogue.   Errol, as a stranger, asked Williams many questions about the terminal, about his work
and his home life:

"You have a wife and family I suppose?"
"Oh yes, sir; I'se married an' I'se got three chil'un."
"Is that so.   Ah that's very commendable."
"Yes, sir, so it is."
"What are the names of your children?"
"Well, I names 'em out de Bible.   Dar's Hannah
and den dar's Samuel and de las' one name 'Iwilla.'"
"Iwilla?   I don't remember that name in the Bible."
"Sure 'tis.   Don't you 'member where it say,
'IWILLA rise'?"

Mr. Errol is impressed with his guide's fine family
instinct and promises him five cents.   Then he gives him
five cents.   Williams looks at the nickle scornfully and
mutters and grumbles.   Errol slips again.

He falls off.   Down, down, down, the coils of rope
feed and jerk as if he will never reach the bottom.   Williams stares straight out from his elevated foothold and
into the eyes of the screaming audience.   He braces himself as best he can.   There is a tug at the rope to show
that Errol has fallen several stories into the excavation
pit.

Williams mutters "five cents" in a scornful tone and
then determinedly undoes the knot of rope at his waist and
it whizzes down.   His passenger has descended farther.
He picks up the suit case which he has been carrying for
him and hurls it down after him.   There is a terrific explosion.   They are still blasting rock.   Williams looks off
into space and then says: "Thar he goes, way up, up...."
As if the blast of dynamite has thrown Errol high into the

air. He keeps watching high in the air, "Ah, there he
goes, now he's near the Metropolitan tower. Ef he kin
only grab that little gold ball on the top--uh-uh, he muffed
it. "
    When the curtain fell on these scenes there was no way
of managing to have the show go on. The audience felt
that in spite of the wonderful comedy value, they must
have more of Williams. Accordingly, his specialty, a
group of songs, always followed directly. One number,
which Williams wrote, to the lyrics of Bert Clark is
"Dat's Harmony. "

> "Mister Shubert's serenade is grand.
> I cert'nly love to hear a big brass band
> Play Sousa's marches by the score
> An' I likes good opera, what is more.
> Dat pleasing melody in F
> Is sho' some music--well I guess,
> But folks makes a mistake you see
> When dey say dat's all to harmony.

> Chorus

> 'Cause when your wife says 'Come to your dinner,
>   John'--
> Dat's harmony!
> When you jes gits a whiff of what she's bringin' on
> Dat's HARMONY!
> Wid all due credit to a big brass band
> De sweetes' music in de land
> Is when you hear de sizzle from de fryin' pan
> Man, dat's HARMONY!"

Again the critics were unanimous in their praise of his work.
A few examples follow:

> [New York Times:] Then came Bert Williams and Leon
> Errol in a scene at the Grand Central Station, Bert Wil-
> liams, solus, followed with some new songs. Mr. Wil-
> liams' collection of melodies this season is equal to any
> he has had, and he seems to have improved his hereto-
> fore almost perfect work.

> [New York World:] It remained, however, for that dusky
> vaudeville genius, Bert Williams, to make the big hit of
> the night. He had already been funny in "Everywife" but
> he was sidesplitting when he appeared as a "red cap" to
> pilot an English tourist to the train over the almost inac-
> cessible fastnesses of New York Central Station. This
> dialogue, in which the tourist fell off a girder into the
> depths below, the audience nearly went into convulsions.
> Mr. Williams, as usual, had some new songs. "Woods-
> man Spare That Tree" was enough to win his audience,
> but his second song: "That's Harmony, " and his panto-

mime of a fatal poker hand brought him twice the amount
of applause that any performer received during the evening.

[New York Morning Telegraph:] The big comedy hit of the
night arrived late with Bert Williams garbed as a railroad
station porter, appearing on top of a steel girder, tugging
after him a passenger bound for a New York Central train.
This travesty on conditions at the Grand Central Station
was a gorgeously humorous conceit, and Williams made it
excruciatingly funny. He was ably assisted by Leon Errol
in the sad plight of a passenger. Williams then rendered
two songs in his inimitable style, and capped the climax
of a glorious night for himself by telling the story of a
poker game in pantomime. Williams began to shine. Mr.
Williams is cast as Nobody, a sort of explanatory prologue
to each scene. Whether serious, grotesque, or just simply
funny, this dark-skinned man demonstrated again that he is
one of the most finished actors on the American stage.

The "Follies of 1912" opened on Broadway in October 1912,
and again Bert Williams was the big star. In the first two seasons,
Williams had scenes only with white men, but was not permitted to
appear on the stage whenever any of the females were around for
fear of "inciting a riot" among the white audiences. When he finished his work he retired to his dressing room, and left the theatre
in his street attire long before the show was completed. However,
in the 1912 edition of the "Follies," he had dialogue with women and
at the finale of both the first and second acts he appeared with all
the principals. One of his hit songs of the show that season was
"Borrow from Me."

During the next eight years Williams continued to star in the
"Follies" which was considered to be one of America's greatest
musical attractions of the period. His last Ziegfeld show was the
"Follies of 1919" which included Eddie Cantor, Eddie Dowling, Ben
Ali Haggin, and Mary May.

During his long career Bert Williams recorded songs which
sold thousands of records for Columbia. The titles include "The
Moon Shines On," "Oh Death Where is Thy Sting?," "Everybody
Wants a Key to My Cellar," "Bring Back Those Wonderful Days,"
"Unlucky Blues," "Brother Low Down," "It's Getting So You Can't
Trust Nobody," "It's Nobody's Business But My Own," "Elder Eat-
mor's Sermon on Throwing Stones," and "Ten Little Bottles."

Bert Williams had been in failing health for over a year before his collapse during the first performance of "Under the Bamboo
Tree" at the Garrick Theatre in Detroit, Michigan. He died of
pneumonia at his home, 2309 Seventh Avenue, New York City, at
12:03 a.m. on Sunday, March 5, 1922. He was 46 years old and
was survived by his wife. They had no children.

The Williams and Walker shows used some of the finest
talent available at the time.   In addition to Jesse Shipp who wrote
the book and directed, there was Alex Rogers, the lyricist, and the
author of the words to many of the most popular of Williams and
Walker's songs, among them: "Why Adam Sinned," "I May Be
Crazy, But I Ain't No Fool," "The Jonah Man," "Bon Bon Buddy,"
"The Chocolate Drop," and "Nobody." The talented performers in
the company included Rosalie Tyler, Abbie Mitchell, Anna Cook,
Inez Clough, Lottie Gee, Lloyd Bibbs, The Original Golden Gate
Quartet, Lewin Saulsburg, George (Bass) Foster, George Pickett,
Adolf Henderson, Clarence Tisdale, J. Leubrie Hill and Anita Bush.

In his time, no performer in the history of the American
stage enjoyed the popularity and esteem of all people and classes of
theatregoers to the extent as did Bert Williams. His name in lights
in front of any theatre meant "capacity" attendance, no matter what
the vehicle.   Booker T. Washington once said: "Bert Williams has
done more to make white people appreciate the Negro Race than any
man, living or dead, past or present." W. C. Fields said of Williams, "The funniest man I ever saw and the saddest man I ever
knew."

In an article which appeared in the December 1917 issue of
American Magazine, Bert Williams provides a rare insight into his
philosophy concerning his approach to comedy, his work in the theatre, and his personal views on racism in America.   The article is
presented here in its entirety:

> One of the funniest sights in the world is a man whose hat
> has been knocked in or ruined by being blown away--
> provided, of course, it be the other fellow's hat! All the
> jokes in the world are based on a few elemental ideas,
> and this is one of them.   The sight of other people in
> trouble is nearly always funny.   This is human nature.
> If you observe your own conduct whenever you see a friend
> falling down in the street, you will find that nine times out
> of ten your first impulse is to laugh and your second im-
> pulse is to run and help him get up.   To be polite you will
> dust off his clothes and ask him if he has hurt himself.
> But when it is all over you cannot resist telling him how
> funny he looked when he was falling.   The man with the
> real sense of humor is the man who can put himself in
> the spectator's place and laugh at his own misfortune.
>   That is what I am called upon to do every day.   Nearly
> all of my successful songs have been based on the idea that
> I am getting the worst of it.   I am the "Jonah Man," the
> man who, even if it rained soup, would be found with a
> fork in his hand and no spoon in sight, the man whose
> fighting relatives come to visit him and whose head is al-
> ways dented by the furniture they throw at each other.
> There are endless variations of this idea, fortunately; but
> if you sift them, you will find the same principle of human

nature at the bottom of them all.   The song the "Slippery
Ellam Tree" at first sight seems to be different.   It
starts as a parody, if you remember, on George P.
Morris' "Woodman Spare That Tree."   But the tree revolves itself into a peg on which I hang my troubles.   It
is the tree I climb when I am running away from my wife,
my refuge whenever there is action, a hiding place from
my wife's relations, my creditors, the police, and the dog
next door.

Troubles are funny only when you pin them to one particular individual.   And that individual, the fellow who is
the goat, must be the man who is singing the song or telling the story.   Then the audience can picture in their
mind's eye and see him in the thick of his misfortunates,
fielding flatirons with his head, carrying large bulldogs on
the seat of his pants, and picking the bare bones of the
chicken while a wife's relatives eat the breast and so forth.

It was not until I was able to see myself as another person that my sense of humor developed.   For I do not believe there is any such thing as innate humor, it has to be
developed by hard work and study, just as every other human quality.   I have studied it all my life, unconsciously
during my floundering years, and consciously as soon as I
began to get next to myself.   It is a study that I shall
never get to the end of, and a work that never stops, except when I am asleep.   There are no union hours to it
and no let-up.   It is only by being constantly on the look-
out for fresh material, funny incidents, funny speeches,
funny traits in human nature that a comedian can hope to
keep step with the public.

Most of the successful songs I have had were written
by Alexander Rogers.   He was the author of the words of
"Nobody," "Jonah Man," "I May Be Crazy But I Ain't No
Fool," and many others.   The tunes to several of these I
wrote myself, or perhaps it would be more correct to say
that I assembled them.   For the tunes to popular songs
are mostly made up of standard parts, like a motor car.
The copyright law allows anybody to take no more than
four bars of any existing melody.   As a machinist assem-
bles a motor car then, I assembled the tunes to "Nobody,"
"Crazy," "Believe Me," and one or two others.   It would
be wrong for me to say that I composed these tunes, because as a composer I am a one finger artist.   I did study
harmony and through bass, but that is as far as I went.

Before I got through with "Nobody," I could have
wished that both the author of the words and the assembler
of the tune had been strangled or drowned or talked to
death.   For seven whole years I had to sing it.   Month
after month I tried to drop it and sing something new, but
I could get nothing to replace it, and the audiences seemed
to want nothing else.   Every comedian at sometime in his
life learns to curse the particular stunt of his that was
most popular.   "Nobody" was a particularly hard song to

replace.   Song writers say that I am a particularly hard
man to write a song for.   Whenever they have a song a
man can use, they seem to want a portion of his life before they will sell it to him.   They want war prices for
their songs, but I have not observed any war salaries being paid to artists.   The way some of them deal with me
is to calculate what my income ought to be for the next
ten years, and then ask ten percent of that.

Not that I grudge paying for a song; in fact, one is
only too glad to pay for a really good song.   My ambition
is not that of Mr. Lauder.   I don't want people to say of
me when I am dead, "how much did he have?" but rather--
if they say anything--"how much did he enjoy?"

At one time it seemed to me that almost everybody in
the United States was writing a song just like "Nobody. "
It never occurred to any of them that to be just like "Nobody" a song would need to have the same human appeal
as "Nobody" mixed in with it humor, the human appeal of
the friendless man.   Most of these imitations were called
"Somebody, " and that was the only single solitary idea
they had, just a feeble paraphrase of "Nobody, " with the
refrain switched around to "Somebody. "   The majority of
writers apparently think that one idea spread over three
or four verses and the refrain is enough to carry a song.
A really good song must be fairly packed with ideas.
There should be at least two every stanza and two more
in the refrain.   Take, for example, a number of songs I
am singing or rather talking, in the Follies now, by Ring
Lardner; "Home, Sweet Home--That's Where the Real
War Is. "   Every line carries an amusing picture, and
each verse is built so that it leads to a fresh laugh in the
refrain.

In picking a song I always consider the words.   The
tune will take care of itself.   I should feel sorry for a
song that depended on its tune if I had to sing it!   When
I was a lad I thought I had a voice, but I learned differ-
ently in later years.   I did not take proper care of it,
and now I have to talk all of my numbers.   And even what
little voice I have left has to be nursed and petted like a
prize car.   I study carefully acoustics of each theatre I
appear in.   There is always one particular spot on the
stage from which the voice carries better more clearly
and easy than from any other.   I make it my business to
find that spot before the first performance, and once I
find it I stick to it like a postage stamp.   People have
sometimes observed that I practice unusual economy of
motion and do not move about much as other singers do.
It is to spare my voice and not my legs that I stand still
while delivering a song.   If my voice were stronger I
could be as active as anybody, because it is much easier
to put a song over if you can move about.

I hope nothing I have said will be mistaken to mean
that I think I have found a recipe for making people laugh,

or anything of that sort.   The man who could find the
recipe would be bigger than Klaw and Erlanger and the
Shuberts put together.   Humor is the one thing in the
world that is impossible to argue about, because it is a
matter of taste.   If I could turn myself into a human
boomerang; if I could jump from the stage, fly out over
the audience, turn a couple of somersaults in the air,
snatch the toupee from the head of a bald man in the
front row of the balcony, and light back on the stage in
the spot I jumped from, I could have the world at my
feet--for a while.   But even then I would always have to
be finding something new.   Look at Fred Stone; he can do
anything the human body can be trained to do, but he is
always learning something new, and always just about six
months ahead of his imitators.

People sometimes ask me if I would not give anything
to be white.   I answer, in the words of the song, most
emphatically, "No. "   How do I know what I might be if I
were a white man?   I might be a sand-hog, burrowing
away and losing my health for eight dollars a day.   I
might be a street car conductor at twelve or fifteen dollars a week.   There is many a white man less fortunate
and less well equipped than I am.   In fact, I have never
been able to discover that there was anything disgraceful
in being a colored man.   But I have often found it incon-
venient--in America.

I had not the slightest idea of going on the stage at
first, nor any very definite ambition except to get an education.   I went through high school in Southern California
and was going to Leland Stanford University.   A bunch of
us, three white boys and myself, thought it would be nice
and easy to make spending money by touring through the
small towns on the coast in a bus and giving entertain-
ments.   That bus tour was the beginning of several dis-
astrous years.   We got back to San Francisco without a
stitch of clothing, literally without a stitch, as the few
rags I wore to spare the hostility of the police had to be
burned for reasons that everybody will understand who has
read of the experiences of soldiers in trenches.   It was
then that I first ran up against the humiliations and per-
secutions that have to be faced by every person of colored
blood, no matter what his brain, education, or the integ-
rity of his conduct.   How many times have hotel keepers
said to me, "I know you, Williams, and I like you, and I
would like nothing better than to have you stay here, but
you see we have Southern gentlemen in the house and they
would object. "

Frankly I can't understand what it is all about.   I
breath like other people, eat like them--if you put me at
a dinner table, you can be reasonably sure that I won't
use the ice cream fork for my salad; I think like other
people.   I guess the whole trouble must be that I don't
look like them.   They say it is a matter of race prejudice.

But if it were prejudice a baby would have it, and you
will never find it in a baby. It has to be inculcated on
people. For one thing, I have noticed that this "Race
prejudice" is not to be found in people who are sure enough
of their position to be able to defy it. For example, the
kindest, most courteous, most democratic man I ever met
was the King of England, the late King Edward VII. I
shall never forget how frightened I was before the first
time I sang for him. I kept thinking of his position, his
dignity, his titles; King of Great Britain and Ireland, Emperor of India, and half a page more of them, and my
knees knocked together and the sweat stood out on my
forehead. And I found the easiest, most responsive,
most appreciative audience any artist could wish. I am
lucky in that he liked my stories, and he used to send
for me to come to the palace once or twice a week to
tell some story over that he had taken a liking to, and
found he couldn't tell correctly.

He was not the only man in England in whom I found
courtesy and kindness.

Each time I come back to America this thing they call
race prejudice follows me everywhere I go. When Mr.
Ziegfeld first proposed to engage me for the Follies there
was a tremendous storm in a teacup. Everybody threatened
to leave, they proposed to get up a boycott if he persisted;
they said all sorts of things against my personal character.
But Mr. Ziegfeld stuck to his guns and was quite undis-
turbed by everything that was said. Which is one reason
why I am with him now although I could make twice the
salary in vaudeville. There never has been any contract
between us, just a gentleman's agreement. I always get
on perfectly with everybody in the company by being polite
and friendly but keeping my distance. Meanwhile, I am
lucky enough to have real friends, people who are sure
enough of themselves not to need to care what their brainless and envious rivals will say if they happen to be seen
walking along the street with me. And I have acquired
enough philosophy to protect me against things which would
cause me humiliation and grief if I had not learned independence. It was not people in the company, I since discovered, but outsiders who were making use of that line
of talk for petty personal purposes.

Meanwhile, I have no grievance whatsoever against the
world or the people in it. I'm having a grand time. I
am what I am, not because of what I am, but in spite of
it.

J. LEUBRIE HILL

Between 1911 and 1916 John Leubrie Hill established himself
as a first rate show producer and one of the most important figures
in American show business. Hill was born in Memphis, Tennessee

J. Leubrie Hill, circa 1912

in 1873. He was the son of John W. and Rachel Hill. Before
first going East, Hill gained a reputation throughout the South as an
entertainer. He was above average as a singer, a piano player and
his services were very much in demand. In 1896, Hill was associated with Alex Rogers who was also born in Tennessee. Later in
the same year, after filling a successful engagement at the Centennial Exposition, held in Nashville, Hill went to Cincinnati where he
worked as an entertainer until the following year when he went East
and formed a partnership with Shepard N. Edmonds. The team
secured a position at Sontagh and were one of the pioneer black
teams in vaudeville.

In 1902 Hill became a member of the Williams and Walker
Company with which organization he remained during the seasons of
1902-3, 1903-4, and 1904-5. He made the trip to England with the
company in 1903 appearing with this famous aggregation before the
King of England at Buckingham Palace on June 23, 1903. He wrote
the song "My Dahomian Queen" which was sung very successfully by
George Walker.

During the season of 1905-6, Hill was prominent in the cast
of Ernest Hogan's "Rufus Rastus" company and the following season
he remained in New York entertaining and writing songs. In 1907
he again joined the Williams and Walker Company and was one of
the comedy leads in the corporation scene of "Bandana Land" as
Sandy Turner. After playing two seasons in "Bandana Land," Hill
went out with Bert Williams' Company in "Mr. Lode of Koal," playing one of the leading roles. At the close of the season he formed
his first stock company appearing principally in Philadelphia and
Washington, D. C.

His first musical comedy was "My Friend from Dixie" which
was put on the road after playing several weeks in Newark at the
Columbia Theatre. As a result of this show, Hill gained immediate
recognition for his music and for his "mammy" character and rapidly rose to the highest rank as a show producer. He later called
his show the "Darktown Follies" to make it plain that the production
was black, but Hill was not a good businessman and hard luck
seemed to always overcome his best efforts.

Later, poor health forced Hill to retire from the stage for a
while. During the season of 1913-14 Hill recovered his health
enough to come back, and with a revision of his old play which he
renamed "My Friend from Kentucky" he captured the nation as a
composer. Opening at the Lafayette Theatre, the production made
an instantaneous hit. The musical numbers "At the Ball, That's
All," "Night Time is the Right Time," and "Rock Me in the Cradle
of Love" were among the musical gems of the show. The show
played at the Lafayette Theatre for six weeks with great success
and all the subsequent engagements except the last, in February
1915, were largely patronized by Harlemites who had become warm
admirers of "Darktown Follies." Flo Ziegfeld, seeing the piece,
bought the rights for several songs which subsequently were incor-

porated into the famous "Follies." Hill's last work, which was
written with Alex Rogers, was too much of a physical strain on
Hill who was ill at the time. Hill died in New York on August 30,
1916.

On the staff of Hill's "Darktown Follies" Company was Will
H. Vodery who wrote the music, Alex Rogers who did the lyrics
and assisted with the book; Hill did the producing, staging and performed in the show, usually taking the part of a female character.
His wife, Evon Robinson, was one of the stars of the company and
other members included Babe Townsend, Arthur Ray, Alonzo Fenderson, Edna Morton, Julius Glenn, Eddie Rector, and Eddie Stafford.

BILLY KING

Billy King, talented performer and prominent black show
producer, was born in Whistler, Alabama in 1875 on a large farm,
where at the age of ten he was considered one of the best plough
hands. But this rural labor did not satisfy little Billy who dreamed
of being a show performer. So one day, he ran away from home,
hopping a freight for he knew not where. Drifting about the country,
Billy eventually fell in with some actors. A little later, he organized his own minstrel company which was billed as "King and Bush,
Wide Mouth Minstrels." They toured the south in the early 1890's.
After the closing of his company, Billy joined Richard and Pringle,
Rosco and Holland's Georgia Minstrel Company. At the time, Billy
Kersands was the star. After a season with this company, King be-
came stage manager and producer of the company. Billy Kersands,
Clarence Powell, James Crosby, and King were known as the "Big
Four" comedians.

After King quit the Georgia Minstrels, he made his home in
Chicago, Illinois where he opened an office for booking and producing shows and vaudeville acts. The season of 1911 found Billy King
teamed with James Mobley in a successful vaudeville act. Their
humor, although somewhat low key and unobtrusive, always seemed
to please the audience wherever they played. The next season King
formed his first stock company in Atlanta, Georgia. Billy wrote
and produced all of the company's plays and engaged a very talented
group of artists including Billy Higgins, then just making a name
for himself as a comedian, W. Henri Bowman, then a well-known
singer, Madame Eva LaRue, dramatic soprano, Bessie Brown,
male impersonator, Charles Huggins, baritone soloist, Butler and
Butler, a unique singing and dancing act, J. P. Reed, a bass soloist. "The Two Bills from Alaska" was the big hit of the 1912 season.

In 1913, Billy King went to the Lyric Theatre in Kansas
City, Missouri, and organized another successful stock company
which included such veteran performers as Hattie McIntosh, Mrs.
Cordelia McClain, Georgia Kelly, Ursel Burnette, Aida Overton,
Mabel Wiggins, W. Henri Bowman, Billy Henderson, Hugh Kelly,

Billy King, circa 1914

Jack "Ginger" Wiggins, the sensational dancer, and Billy Higgins.
King's company played 21 weeks at the Lyric before going to the
Star Theatre in Savannah, Georgia in 1914.   He stayed there for a
full season producing a new show every week.   The next year, 1915,
King moved his company to the Grand Theatre in Chicago where he
produced shows for the next eight seasons.   King's company put on
a new show each week and King was responsible for bringing in
many new innovations into musical comedy including girls clowning
at the end of chorus lines.   The latter routine was used by Josephine Baker to gain her first real notice in the chorus of Sissle
and Blake's "Chocolate Dandies."   King also wrote several popular
songs, several of which were introduced by his protegee, Gertrude
Saunders.

Some of the performers who first made their mark on the
stage with King include Marshall "Garbage" Rogers, Gertrude
Saunders, Ernest Whitman, Howard Kelly, Dink Stewart, Jerry
Mills, Andrew Tribble, Mildred Smallwood, and Jack Wiggins.

WHITNEY AND TUTT

The most prolific producing, acting, writing team of this
period was that of the brothers, Salem Tutt Whitney and J. Homer
Tutt.   Between 1910 and 1925 they produced, wrote and directed
over 25 tabloids, two dramas, sixteen musical comedies, at least
150 vaudeville sketches, 300 poems and 50 songs.

Whitney and Tutt along with J. Leubrie Hill and Billy King
practically forged the link of continuity in black theatricals between
Bob Cole and Williams and Walker to Irvin C. Miller.   Between
1910 and 1914 they were the only bigtime black producers in the
field.   Their sway really extended to "Shuffle Along" in 1921 which
was produced by Miller and Lyles, Sissle and Blake.

The elder brother, Salem Tutt Whitney, was born in Logansport, Indiana and started his theatrical career with the Puggsley
Brothers' Tennessee Warblers in the seasons 1895-1898.   This company included the following artists: Mr. and Mrs. James, musical
and sketch; Salem Tutt Whitney, vocalist and comedian; C. H.
Puggsley, tenor; James Moore, monologist; Little Carcia and Irma
Puggsley, vocalists and impersonation; W. Baynard, trick and descriptive pianist; L. E. Puggsley, operatic tenor soloist; Emma A.
Baynard, prima donna soprano; Mme. Bessie Gee, comedienne and
vocalist; and Puggsley Brothers, proprietors.

As a youngster Salem Tutt Whitney started out singing baritone, but while he was on the road his voice changed to a deep bass.
In 1899, he led his own company, The Oriental Troubadours, on a
road tour of the South.   They played one week stands and introduced
a complete change of program nightly.   At this time the personnel
of the company included: Charles H. Puggsley, tenor; W. A.
Baynard, piano specialist; Salem Tutt Whitney, banjo, comedian,

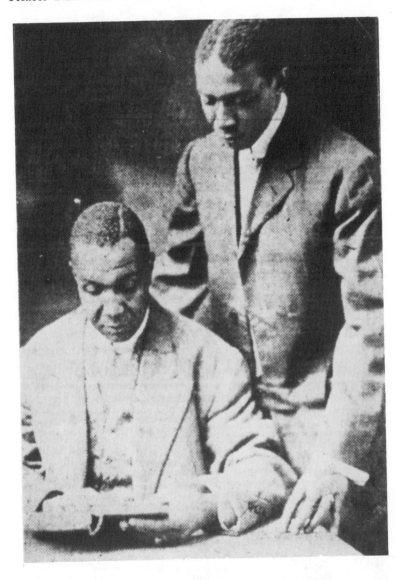

Salem Tutt Whitney [left] and J. Homer Tutt, circa 1917

Ad, circa 1909

and stage manager; J. C. Lewis, character artist; Walter Emery, eccentric dancer and acrobat; Emma A. Baynard, prima donna; Lillian C. Brown, Boston Nightingale; The Taylor Sisters, Nettie and Jennie, instrumentalists.

In 1901 he opened his first musical comedy, "The Ex-President of Liberia," under the management of Ed. Dale, then the owner of the Dale Hotel at Cape May, New Jersey. Whitney not only wrote the show, but staged it, wrote the music, arranged the numbers, and designed the costumes. It was during this period he called on his brother, J. Homer Tutt, as understudy and who was later to help make the name Whitney and Tutt famous.

In 1905, Whitney joined the "Smart Set" Company then headed by S. H. Dudley. After serving a short time in the chorus, he was given a leading straight role as John Gain in "George Washington Bullion" and he later also assumed the duties of stage manager. While with Gus Hill's "Smart Set" Company, Salem Tutt Whitney composed several songs and playlets. His songs included "The Man that Rules the Town," "My Spanish Maid," "I Ain't Built That Way," "Love You Best of All," "Lula, Be My Lady Lee," "O, My Miss Mandy." His playlets included "Prince Bungaboo," "Blackville Strollers," "Two Jolly Tramps," "The Recruit," "Derby Day," and "Hodge and Hodge."

In 1907, Homer and Salem joined Black Patti's Troubadours. In 1909, they organized the second company of the original "Smart Set" Company under the management of Gus Hill, and in 1916 Whitney and Tutt gained control of the company and renamed it Whitney and Tutt's "Smart Set" Company.

J. Homer Tutt was also born in Logansport, Indiana. At the age of five he was a cow-dogger, a shepherd for a herd of cows, at 25 cents a head. Tutt graduated from Manual Training High School in Indianapolis, Indiana. In high school he was a champion sprinter and broad jumper. J. Homer Tutt made his debut as a featured player by creating the role of the one-legged soldier, "Silas Jackson," in "The Black Politician" in 1905. He performed for two seasons with the "Smart Set" Company

The AMERICAN Theater

Always a New Show

THE SMART SET
40 People. Nearly All Girls.
In the New Musical Comedy

HIS EXCELLENCY
THE PRESIDENT
— with —
Salem Tutt Whitney and the
Bronze Beauty Chorus—
Scene & Costume Girls New Costumes

11th & Pa. Avenue, N. W.

Thomas and Dudley, Props.

A New Theater for the People for Ladies and Gentlemen

GRAND OPENING

MONDAY, AUGUST 24

with the Celebrated SMART SET

Ad for "His Excellency the President," One of Whitney and Tutt's
Most Successful Productions, circa 1913

before joining the Black Patti Troubadours, playing leading straight
parts. He also composed several songs for the star, Sissieretta
Jones, including "Good Night, Marie."

Whitney and Tutt wrote the following two-hour musical comedies: "Sunny Africa," "Mayor of Newton," "How Newton Pre-
pared," "Jump Steady," "Prince of Bungaboo," "His Excellency the
President," "Blackville Strollers," "George Washington Bullion
Abroad," "Bamboula," "Up and Down," "Oh Joy," "North Ain't
South," "Deep Harlem," "My People," "Darkest Americans"; one
of the best shows was "Children of the Sun." The book was written by Whitney and Tutt assisted by George Wells Parker, Omaha,
Nebraska, then a celebrated archaeologist, historian, and author.
The music was written by James Vaughn who had earlier served in
a similar capacity with the Williams and Walker shows.

In the field of tabloids, they were also active. A tabloid
ran for approximately one and one-half hours and was sandwiched
between feature motion pictures. They wrote "Betwixt and Between,"
"Who Struck John?," "Messin' Around," "Keep Fit," "Blues Singer,"
"When Malinda Sings," "Nonsense," "Rainbow Chasers," "Circus
Days," "Two Jolly Tramps," "Hide and Seek," and "Needmore Hotel."

J. Homer Tutt was also a composer as well as an author and lyricist and some of the songs to which he wrote both words and music were: "There's Nothing About You Gives Me a Thrill," "The Dream Is Over," "I'm Tired of Doin' the Lovin'," "I Craves to Be Loved," "I've Still Got My Song," "Silas Green from New Orleans," "The Expression on Your Face Makes Me Hesitate," "Lucinda Be My Lady Love," "Honey, Won't You Come to Me" (made popular by Black Patti), "Goodnight, Marie," "Dat's Sufficiency," "Oh My Mis' Mandy," "Smile on Sue," "Wedding of the Flower and the Bee," "Tell Me Rose," "Manny's Golden Rule," "Dat's Fair Enough," "I'm Free," "Too Late," "When You're Away from Home," and "It's Hard, but It's Fair." Perhaps Tutt's best work was done as a collaborator with such then nationally famous composers as C. Luckyth Roberts, James Vaughn, Edgar Powell, Donald Heywood, Joe Jordan, Russell Smith and Henry Watterson.

The first and only of Tutt and Whitney's shows to play on Broadway was "Oh Joy" which had a four-week run in 1922 at the Bamboo Isle Theatre, then on Broadway and Fifty-Seventh Streets. Some of the principals were Ethel Waters, Ethel Williams, Amon Davis, Emmett Anthony, Andrew Tribble, J. Francis Mores, Julia Moody, Emma Jackson, Margaret Simms, Jim Vaughn and Alonzo Fenderson. Blanche Thompson, the famous prima donna of the "Smart Set" Company, was discovered by Salem Tutt Whitney at the Sharp Street M. E. Church in Baltimore where she was a leading soprano.

Although Salem Tutt Whitney and J. Homer Tutt were brothers, they had different names. It appears that when Whitney first started out with the Puggsley Brothers, Louis, the manager of the company, could not remember Salem or Tutt, so he told him he would add Whitney to his last name which he could easily remember, as it was the name of a very famous white concert basso, Myron W. Whitney.

Salem Tutt Whitney was the creator of perhaps the longest running tent show ever to play in the United States, "Silas Green from New Orleans." It ran continuously in the South from 1904 to the early 1940's. Although the members of the cast changed and many novelties were added during the years, the basic plot of the show remained the same. The original script was written by Salem Tutt Whitney.

J. Homer Tutt, in an article which appeared in the August 15, 1936, edition of the Baltimore <u>Afro-American</u>, recalled the story of how the Silas Green show was born:

> Back in 1902 Salem Tutt Whitney was traveling through the South with S. H. Dudley's "Jolly Ethiopians" and later joined the "Smart Set" which was a winter season show, traveling in the North. To keep busy during the summer months, he formed Whitney and Bernards' Troubadours and traveled under canvas through the South.

About that time, Eph Williams, one of the race's greatest pioneer showmen, who had a twenty-car dog and pony circus, ran into difficulty and lost all of his paraphernalia except his dogs and ponies.

Whitney took the ponies and with the troubadours formed the street parade when his show opened in a town. This show was called "Silas Green from New Orleans."

While playing Hampton, Virginia in 1905, a big storm wiped the whole show out, and Whitney and Tutt sat down on a stump and watched their tent being wrecked and their trunks of costumes buried in the mud and decided that nothing could be done about it.

They made a deal with Eph Williams that if he could salvage the show out of the mud they would give him the book and lyrics and the title to the show, and if he ever made any money he could pay them for it.

A few days later, after the storm abated, Eph, with his ponies, pulled the show over to Phoebus, Virginia and with the help of his wrecking crew, put on a show. From that day until this "Silas Green from New Orleans" has been an institution throughout the Southland. Every big actor of Harlem has at some time or other played with "Silas Green." Two generations of Dudleys have been affiliated with the show and Eph Williams passed the show on to his heirs, who in turn sold it to Charles Collier, white, for a large consideration, and Collier has in turn grown independently rich through its management.

"And until this day," lamented Tutt, "neither my brother nor I have received one nickel for the show."

When Eph Williams died he was worth about $30,000 in cash and owned considerable land in Florida and had other holdings. But, old Eph never forgot his obligation to us. Every summer for years, he would write to spend our vacations with him, and when our winter tour ended we would go down and visit him on the show. For the first few days everything was fine. About the fourth day Eph would tell his audience, "I've got some big stars from up North visiting us and I know you would like to see them do a little number," and before we knew it, old Eph would have us working every show without paying us a cent.

When Eph Williams died in December 1921, he left his daughter a considerable sum of money and half interest in the Silas Green Show. Charles Collier, white, had purchased the other half shortly before Williams' death. A few years later, the famous Silas Green from New Orleans show passed entirely from black control when Mr. Collier assumed full ownership of the show. Salem Tutt Whitney died on February 12, 1934.

WHITMAN SISTERS

The Whitman Sisters company was one of the most respected

The Whitman Sisters' "Romping Thru Company," circa 1926

and successful groups to play the black theatrical circuits in the
1920's and 1930's.   The company was headed by Mabel Whitman,
then popularly known as "Sister Mae" who was the manager, director and producer.

Mabel Whitman was born in Lawrence, Kansas; while still a
young girl, she and her sisters, Essie and Alberta, took a prominent part in church and concert work, their father, Albany A. Whitman, being a minister of the gospel.   George Walker, also a native
of Lawrence, first saw the Sisters during a visit to Lawrence on
his return from his first trip to San Francisco.   He tried to sponsor the sisters for a trip to New York for the purpose of starting
them on their professional career, but was met with parental objections.   Mabel and her sisters received their grammar school education in the public schools of Lawrence and later went to Boston,
Massachusetts where they attended the New England Conservatory of
Music for five years under the tutelage of George M. Davis.   They
also studied at Morris Brown College in Atlanta, Georgia after the
family moved to that city.

Their first professional engagement was as a "filler" for an
open spot on the bill at the Orpheum Theatre in Kansas City which
at the time was under the management of a Mr. Lehman.   They had
come to Kansas City at the end of a short evangelical tour with
their father.

Later, Essie and Mabel were given a short singing and dancing skit by William Accoe of New York and were billed as the
"Daznette Sisters."   They were an instantaneous hit, and soon after
Lehman obtained permission from their parents to sign them at a
good salary; later, they traveled, chaperoned, over the Orpheum,
and Kohl and Castle circuits, appearing on the same bills with
such acts as Joseph Hart, Carrie DeMan, Carter DeHaven, Baby
Lund, the Four Cohans, Grant Jones and Grant, Gracie Emmett,
and Jenie Dandy.   This was in 1899-1900.

The Whitman Sisters Novelty Company opened their winter
season of 1900 at the Augusta Grand Opera House, Augusta, Georgia

and from there they went to Savannah Theatre, Burbridge's Opera
House in Jacksonville, Florida and all of the leading Southern houses.
They also had the honor of being the first black females to play the
Greenwald Circuit. During this period, they were under the man-
agement of their mother and carried a company of twelve. A Bir-
mingham daily had this to say about their act:

> These three bright, pretty, mulatto girls are the daughters
> of the pastor of the A. M. E. Church of Atlanta, Georgia.
> They have wonderful voices, that of Essie being the lowest
> contralto on record. The sisters play banjos and sing coon
> songs with a smack of the original flavor. Their costum-
> ing is elegant; their manner graceful and their appearance
> striking in elegance as they are unusually handsome.

When the season of 1904 opened, the Sisters were billed as
the Whitman Sisters New Orleans Troubadours and were under the
management of Mabel, the older sister. By this time, their act had
developed into a high class vaudeville nature consisting of a comedy
first part arranged especially to show the original comedy of Willie
Robinson, the "Little Georgia Blossom." The singing of Tony Jackson and Baby Alice Whitman usually brought down the house.

In 1906, they went to New York City, and through the efforts
of Will Marion Cook, then a famous composer, were placed on the
program of a private musicale held at the Waldorf Astoria in the
honor of a Judge Gray. Their next New York engagement was at
the Palm Gardens in May of the same year. After that they played
the entire Keith and Proctor Circuit, all of the Percy G. Williams
houses, and the Poli and Fox circuit as well as the leading theatres
in and around New York. Following that, they were signed over the
Pantages time by Al Sutherland, shortly before the death of their
mother in Atlanta. In 1914 Mabel and Essie and the Picks, Sammy
and Aaron, played independently, being featured on the Family United
circuit, spending about twenty weeks in and around Boston. Mabel's
likeness appeared in the Boston papers along with such white stars
as Fanny Brice, Weber and Fields, Joan Sawyer and Irene LaTour,
Frank Sylvester and others.

By the season of 1910, the Whitman Sisters had established
themselves as one of the most popular acts on the road. The roster
of the company at this time included: Essie, Mabel and Alberta
Whitman; Baby Alice Whitman; Thomas Hawkins, the Toy Comedian;
Willie and Lulu; "Too Sweet" Paul Carter; Cliff Rhodes, contortionist; Billy Mills; Raymond Clark; Walter Smith; Kite Fisher; Billy
Earthquake; Slim Henderson, stage manager; Albert Carroll, director of music; Mabel Whitman, amusement director and manager of
the company.

During the season of 1911-1913, the Whitman Sisters split up
with Alberta and Essie forming a small vaudeville group and playing
the Eastern theatres, and Mabel doing a single in Southern houses.

By the season of 1914, the Sisters including "baby" Alice were back together again playing with their small company which included the "Picks," Aaron and Sambo.

"Pops" Whitman was the son of Alice Whitman and began his career in show business at the age of three. As a child prodigy, he played many of the leading vaudeville houses in the country with his mother and aunts. When the sisters disbanded in the 1940's after the death of Mabel Whitman, "Pops" teamed with Louis Williams and they toured the country with some of the top bands of the period. "Pops" died in Chicago in 1946 at the age of 26.

The Whitman Sisters show in the 1920's and 1930's played a profitable circuit of rural communities in the South and Southwest, punctuated by engagements in the metropolitan centers of the Midwest and East. For the performers of the troupe it was a severe but thorough school in which to learn show business. Playing on a continuous performance basis, the show had to appease patrons who stayed in the theatre for several consecutive performances and who were audible in their disapproval if each repeat show was not sufficiently different from the one before. This called for considerable ingenuity on the part of the whole company. The real test in the judgment of the audience was the amount of unrehearsed high jinks the actors could produce.

In an article which appeared in the Baltimore Afro-American in December 1931, Mabel Whitman was asked if they liked to work white houses or colored, and this was her reply:

> "I think beyond question that a colored audience is our favorite, for there we get full appreciation without grudge, for what we do and there is no such thing as a nasty little feeling that we are breaking in where we are not really wanted.
> "As a matter of fact," she continued, "you never have a real light colored star on the white stage. When we get too light, as we are (humorously), they won't really welcome you, but still it is a pleasure to know that you are able to qualify as a first class entertainer for that kind of audience; but, as for us, give us a colored audience any old day in the week."

In another article which appeared in the January 19, 1929 edition of the Baltimore Afro-American, Mabel Whitman offers an insight on problems faced by show managers. She was interviewed during an engagement at Gibson's Standard Theatre in Philadelphia regarding her opinion on "What's the matter with show business?" The following is part of her reply:

The trouble with this game is a set of unscrupulous owners

Opposite: Bert (Alberta) and Alice Whitman [right], circa 1922

and managers who seemingly have syndicated themselves together to stifle the progress along the lines of art and entertainment.   They feel that any kind of show is good enough for a colored audience and their only desire is to have a comedian and a few half-naked girls on hand to keep the doors open.

They insult the intelligence and prey on Negro patrons. They sense that the people must have some place to go for amusement; instead of giving them the best talent possible, they palm off the worst as long as they can.

When the crowd gets fed up on that sort of diet, they try to work a good show and try to get it for the same money they pay an amateur company which was made up overnight.   This is what a certain owner told me--and I'll name him when and if necessary--"I have been losing money all year and I have to get out of the red on your engagement here.   Therefore I won't pay you what you want.   You have a family company.   You don't need money because you all work and live together.   Come in at my price or stay out. "

Well I stayed out.   I am staying out and I never in life will pay for a man who tells me I have to foot the losses he has suffered from bum shows.

Let me give you some figures in this particular case. Years ago, when I had a smaller show, he refused to pay me a guarantee of $1400.   I went in on a percentage and took away $2700 for my end of the receipts.   The last time we played his house my cut for the week was $3750. Then, when he tried to get me this fall, he offered me a guarantee of $1600 instead of the usual percentage and explained himself by saying that I, Mae Whitman, had to made up for the bad weeks other people had given him.

He offered me $1600 for a company of 30 people.   He offered me $1600 and it would cost me $490 in railroad fare, exclusive of baggage transportation, to get there (Excuse me if I am not as calm as usual.).

What encouragement does a producer get out of that sort of stuff?   How can you improve and develop your shows and people if there is no more money available for a good show than for a misfit outfit?

This is what an owner did here in Philadelphia.   He went to the individual members of a show in his house and asked them what their salary was, offering as an excuse that he was about to produce a show and wanted to use them in it.   At the end of the week he paid off the performers himself and paid the producer a musician's salary.

What does "Mabel Whitman" mean to men of that type? Does my name stand for anything with them?   For no more than "Mabel Jack Rabbit"?

With them it is an insolent "What are you going to do about it?   Take it or leave it. "

If these birds pay you a living wage they want you to guarantee that it will not rain or snow during the week you

are booked with them.   Something must be done and done
quickly.
     But there is another picture, a bright and cheerful one.
All owners are not in that category.   In this game there
are men who appreciate your work and your worth.   They
will either pay what you ask or not book your show at all
until they feel they can do so.   And they will pay you the
same money or percentage for return engagements.   They
try to give their patrons leading entertainment and you always work harder for such managers.   Believe me,
twenty years experience by Mae Whitman means something to them.   In the West, in Pittsburgh, Newark, New
York, Atlantic City, and here in Philadelphia are owners
who will always give us enough times to make out a season.   They don't do it out of sympathy, they don't do it
out of charity.
     True, they are our friends, but they realize that we
own more scenery and more costumes than any similar
organization, thus reducing the house overhead.   They
know we are money-makers.   They apprecaite these things.
That's why, in the course of a season, we play from two
to eight weeks with Mr. Gibson and other high-class theatrical men.   Indeed, I spend so much time in Philadelphia
that it is a second home for me.
     And now do you know what is the matter with show
business?

FRANK MONTGOMERY

     Frank Montgomery is another black producer whose contribu-
tions to the American theatre cannot be overlooked.   With his wife,
Florence McClain, he produced several hit shows during the early
1920's including the "Hello" series and "Broadway Rounders."   In
the season of 1911, Montgomery put out the first company under his
ownership, The Dixie Flyers Company, presenting the play "Ethiopiaville."   This company was composed of Frank Montgomery, Russell
Smith, Eddie Stafford, James Brown, Elwood Wooding, Sallie Jones,
Maude Hudson, Bessie Stafford, Mayme Brown, Bonnie Clark,
Florence McClain and Senora McClain.

     Montgomery was also an instructor of dance, producer of
numbers, and author of many burlesque hits.   He assisted in the
staging of three companies of "Barney Google."   He also put in a
song of his own and most of the dance numbers for Cain and Davenport's "Dancing Around," a white show.   Later, he contributed to
other white shows including Lew Talbot's "Wine, Women and Song"
and Lew Berstein's "Bathing Beauties" and Max Field's "Fashion
Review."   Montgomery also supervised the revision of dance numbers for Eddie Hunter's "How Come?"   Some of Montgomery's hit
shows were: "Hello, 1919"; "Hello, 1921"; "From Speedville to
Broadway," 1916; "On the Way to Boston," 1916; "In the Old Home
Town," 1916; "The Two Detectives," 1917; and "Why Spoil It?,"
1922.

EDDIE HUNTER

Eddie Hunter, composer, performer, and producer, was born and reared on the east side of New York City, then one of the roughest parts of the city. He learned rhythm from his banjo playing father and his white mother urged him to always fight for what he wanted.

Hunter first started producing minstrels at old McFarland's Hall, then located on East 98th Street and Third Avenue. Having been forced to quit school at an early age, he was handicapped by a lack of formal education, but this did not deter him in his writing of sketches and playlets. At night after his job as a switchboard operator in a large apartment house, he labored long into the night perfecting his sketches. By a chance of fate, he caught the eye of the famous Enrico Caruso, who took an interest in him and arranged to have him tutored by show producers. After that, Eddie wrote many shows including "How Come?," produced on Broadway, and "Good Gracious," produced in London.

The book for "How Come?," the sensation of 1923, was born in a lodge room where Eddie was being initiated into the Masons. Eddie was working on his show and had it partially completed, but wanted a strong opening. The actual happenings in the lodge room that night, where the brothers were discussing finances, proved so ludicrous to the comedian that he wrote them into a skit and it became one of the funniest bits in the show. Later, he did the bit in his vaudeville act.

IRVIN C. MILLER

The Miller Brothers, Irvin C. and Flournoy E. and Quintard, made a lasting contribution to black theatricals. Sometimes in collaboration, but mostly working independently, the brothers produced many great shows between 1920 and 1940, several of which were performed on Broadway. They all were born in Columbia, Tennessee and their father at one time was the editor of the Nashville Globe, a black weekly newspaper. Irvin C., the oldest, was born in 1884. He attended the public schools of Columbia before attending Fisk University in Nashville, where he excelled in football and basketball, although acting was always his first love.

After finishing Fisk, he decided to make acting his career and secured his first engagement at the old Pekin Theatre in Chicago, which was the home of the famous Pekin Stock Company. His first performance there was in a play entitled "Colored Aristocrats," written by Aubrey Lyles and Irvin's brother Flournoy.

After Bob Motts died, Miller left the Pekin Theatre and Chicago to join John Rucker's company in New Orleans. Miller played straight roles and wrote plays for the company. His first play was entitled "Happy Sam from Bam" which was first performed

Irvin C. Miller and His Tango Girls with Mr. Ragtime Co., circa
1915. [First row, left to right, sitting]: Esther Bigeou, Irvin C.
Miller, Lottie Turner, Trixie Butler, and Lulu Whidby. [Standing]:
Mamie Ashford, Magnolia Cox, and Frances Wood.

by Rucker's company at the Temple Theatre, New Orleans in December 1912. At this time, Rucker's company included Irvin C.
Miller, Wallace and Nina Stovall, the Valeria Sisters, Lillian and
Maye, J. C. Boone, J. Francis Mores, formerly of the Peking
Stock Company, La Belle Glean, Esther Bigeou, Tillie Johnson,
Beatrice F. Moore, Isfael James, George Allen, and Henry Pashal
who wrote the music for "Happy Sam from Bam" and directed the
chorus. Miller and J. Francis Mores staged the musical numbers
and the song hits of the play were "Goodbye Rose," "Dearest Mem-
ories," "You're My Baby," "The Undertaker Man," "Gee Whiz,"
"It's Tough to be Poor," "Last Man," and "Molasses and Candy."

In the season of 1913, Miller formed a team with Esther
Bigeou, whom he later married, and went out on the vaudeville circuit playing the principal cities of the Midwest. Their act this season opened with a song, "Uncle Joe," followed by Miss Bigeou singing "My Persian Rose" followed by Miller doing an "old man" song
and dance. Miss Bigeou then sang "Robert E. Lee" and the closing
number which usually brought down the house was their rendition of
the "Texas Tommy" dance.

Miller and Bigeou played vaudeville until the beginning of the
1914 season when they joined Kid Brown's company in Chicago.
Shortly afterwards, Miller wrote his next musical play called "Mr.

Ragtime" which was a farce comedy in which Miller and Brown had
the leading straight and comedy roles, respectively.

Next, Miller wrote and staged acts in the burlesque wheel,
finally landing in Philadelphia in 1915. With him he brought the
book of "Broadway Rastus." He took it to John T. Gibson and convinced him to finance the show. It turned out to be Miller's first
hit show. It packed theatres and brought instant fame to the young
producer. This was in 1915. "Broadway Rastus" first opened for
a run of several weeks in Atlantic City, New Jersey, at the Apollo
Theatre and included such talented performers as Leigh Whipper,
Lottie Grady, Billy Ewing and Henry Jines. W. C. Handy, soon
to become recognized throughout the world as a composer, assisted
in writing the music for the show.

Miller's next big venture was "Put and Take" in 1920. This
show opened at Town Hall in New York City, but did not prove the
success he had expected, so he abandoned the producing business for
a while, selecting a partner and going into vaudeville as Miller and
Anthony. While they were filling engagements, Miller was working
on the book for "Liza." After the book was completed, Miller organized a company and the show opened in 1922. Although the show
was a financial success, it did not achieve the fame of "Shuffle
Along" which was playing in New York during the same period. But
"Liza" enjoyed a long run and is credited as the first black musical
comedy owned and produced on Broadway entirely by black capital.

In 1923 Irvin C. Miller wrote and produced "Dinah" which
was the show that introduced the Blackbottom dance to New York.
The Blackbottom achieved a nationwide popularity second only to
the Charleston, another dance created by blacks. In 1923 over
1,000 pupils practiced the Blackbottom daily in New Wayburn's
school of stage dancing. Among them were such white society leaders as Marjorie Oelrichs and Mrs. Frederick Church and Consuelo
Vanderbilt, as well as such stage stars as Ann Pennington and
Marilyn Miller to say nothing of the many dancing teachers from
all over the country.

Miller may be best remembered for his annual production of
"Brownskin Models." The idea for the show came to Miller one
day when he was standing in front of a Broadway theatre where the
blazing lights announced that Flo Ziegfeld was "Glorifying the American Girl." As he viewed the pictures displayed in the lobby, his
attention was attracted to a beautiful, well shaped black lady walking
down the street. The idea popped into his head, "Why not glorify
the brown skin girl?" This he was determined to do and "Brownskin Models" came into being.

When "Models" was first introduced to the show world it
toured the country with great success, playing the big theatre chains
for forty weeks. From then on, up until the start of World War II,
it was an annual event. When the war curtailed the use of buses
for show traveling, "Models" toured the USO circuit of Army camps.

After the war, Miller continued to produce condensed versions of
the show until his retirement in the early 1950's.   Later, Miller
married Blanche Thompson, one of the featured performers of the
show.   Irvin Miller died in 1967.

MILLER AND LYLES

One of the most popular producing-performing teams of the
1920's was Flournoy E. Miller and Aubrey Lyles.   Starting out as
playwrights with the Pekin Stock Company in the early 1900's, the
team became a hit on the vaudeville stage and later contributed
their producing, writing and performing talents to some of the most
successful black musical comedies of the 1920's.

Like his older brother, Irvin, Flournoy E. Miller was born
in Tennessee in 1889.   He and Aubrey Lyles, who was born in
Jackson, Tennessee in 1882, were childhood friends.   They attended
Fisk University in Nashville where they produced and performed in
their first amateur shows for the school.

Miller and Lyles left Fisk before completing their scholastic
work and went to Chicago where they were engaged by Bob Motts as
playwrights for the Pekin Stock Company during the years 1905-1909.
Their most popular works were "The Mayor of Dixie," "The Husband," and "The Man from Bam."   They also made their professional acting debut playing small parts in the productions.

In 1908, after a brief vaudeville tour, Miller and Lyles decided to write a new play entitled "The Colored Aristocrats."
Flournoy Miller persuaded his brother, Irvin, to put up the money
to back the new production.   It was in this play which opened at the
Pekin Theatre in August 1909 that Irvin, Flournoy and Aubrey Lyles
made their debut as starring performers.   It was also in this play
that F. E. Miller first introduced the characters Steve Jenkins
(Miller) and Sam Peck (Lyles) that would become famous a decade
later in their Broadway hit production of "Shuffle Along."

In April 1908, Marion A. Brooks and Flournoy Miller took a
dozen or more players from Chicago to Montgomery, Alabama for
the purpose of establishing a stock company at the newly opened
Bijou Theatre.   The stock company was called the Bijou Stock Company and the Bijou Theatre was one of the first black theatres in
the South.

The first productions were "Queen of the Jungle" and
"Ephraham Johnson from Norfolk."   The latter show was a frolic
of music and comedy in three acts.   It was written by Miller and
Brooks and staged under the personal direction of the latter.

Although their initial productions appeared to achieve moderate success, the stock company eventually failed.   The company returned to Chicago and the Bijou subsequently closed in May 1908.

Flournoy E. Miller and Aubrey Lyles [right] As They Appeared in
Vaudeville, circa 1920

        In 1909, Miller and Lyles went out in vaudeville as comedi-
ans in Chicago and after playing the small time were booked on the
larger circuits.   They went East for the first time to New York in
August 1910, and opened at a theatre in Yonkers, which was then
known as a try-out house for the United Booking Office.   They were
a big success and later were booked for thirty weeks.   In February
1911, the team first played New York City at Hammerstein's Victoria Theatre.   Their act was unique in that, unlike other comedians of
the period, Miller and Lyles did not sing nor dance.   It consisted of
ten minutes of patter which bristled with wit and humor followed by
an original acrobatic boxing exhibition.   This routine was successful
so they later incorporated it into several of their successful shows
of the 1920's.   In 1913, the team returned to Chicago where they
produced a tabloid musical comedy entitled "The Cabaret."

        The first major black musical comedy which starred Miller
and Lyles was "Darkydom," produced in 1915.   The piece opened at
the Howard Theatre, Washington, D. C., and later played the Lafayette in New York City.   Lester Walton was producer and Will Marion Cook and James Reese Europe wrote the music.   The show was
staged by Jesse A. Shipp and the lyrics were written by Henry
Creamer and the book was by Henry Troy.   Besides Miller and

Lyles, the show featured other well-known performers such as Allie
Gilliam, Fannie Wise, the dancer Ida Forsyne, and a great singing
choir.

For the next six years, Miller and Lyles continued to play
the Keith circuit; however, they continued to write and produce
plays.   They produced "Who's Stealing?" in Chicago in 1918.   In
1921 they teamed with Noble Sissle and Eubie Blake to produce the
sensational musical comedy "Shuffle Along" which had a long run
on Broadway.   "Shuffle Along" was the hit of the 1921 season and
is credited as being responsible for bringing black musicals back
to Broadway in the fashion of Williams and Walker.   The show
opened in New York City at the Sixty-third Street Theatre and all
New York flocked to see fast and exhilarating dancing and to hear
such song hits as "I'm Just Wild About Harry," "Gypsy Blues,"
"Love Will Find a Way," "I'm Cravin' for That Kind of Love" and
"Shuffle Along."

In 1922, Miller and Lyles wrote a three-act drama entitled
"The Flat Below."   The plot dealt with the hardships of a poor fam-
ily in Harlem.   Members of the cast included Clarence and Ophelia
Muse, Jack Carter, Lena Wilson and Estelle Cole.   The play opened
May 8 at the Lafayette Theatre where it had a successful run.

Next, Flournoy E. Miller directed his writing talents to
drama and the result was a three-act play entitled "Going White"
which starred Gus Smith, Edna Thomas, Dora Deane, and Barrington Carter.   The play had a short run at the Lafayette Theatre and
had a racial theme dealing with a mulatto family who leave their
home in the South.   This move was necessary because the son had
defended his sister from an attack by a white man and in doing so,
killed him.   He escapes and his mother and sister follow him to a
northern city.   The daughter, in order to get work, passes for a
white actress.   After two years, she is a star and her mother is
posing as her maid.   She is eventually discovered to be black by
her manager, but since he has invested a large amount of money in
the show, he does not reveal her true racial identity to the public.
She is finally, however, forced out of show business and two years
later the brother and sister complete a course in dentistry in Chicago.   Their happiness is complete when a former neighbor in the
South visits them and tells them that the man the brother was supposed to have killed did not die from the blow he struck, and that
he was not wanted by the police.

After "Shuffle Along" closed on the road in 1924, Miller and
Lyles came out with another musical comedy "Runnin' Wild" which
opened on upper Broadway on October 29, 1924.   The show made
theatrical history by first introducing one of America's most popular
dances to Broadway, America and the World--the Charleston.   The
musical score for the show was written by James P. Johnson.

In 1925, Miller and Lyles produced two musical comedy
tabloids, "Backbiters" and "Honey," neither one of which achieved

much success.   In 1927 they put out "Rang Tang" which included
such talent as Evelyn Preer, Inez Davis, Jerry Mills and May
Barnes.   In 1928 they tried their luck with "Keep Shufflin'," but
the show was not a big success and shortly afterwards the team
broke up.

Lyles went to Africa where he stayed for a year.   Upon his
return, he tried making it alone and produced a show entitled "Runnin' De Town" which was not successful.   During this period, Miller wrote and appeared in Lew Leslie's "Blackbirds of 1930."   At
the intervention of Flournoy's brother, Irvin C. Miller, the pair
were brought together again and soon after made two talking shorts
for RKO Pictures and had a fifteen-minute spot for the summer on
the Columbia Circuit.

In 1931 they produced their last show together, "Sugar Hill."
A year later, Aubrey Lyles died in New York City, having left an
everlasting impression on the world of show business.

Lyles, the little man of the team, contrived to involve himself in situations which demanded bravado and the exercise of discretion.   In his character, he was brave until the time came to
flee, and generous in the distribution of his bits of heavy wisdom.
He was ridiculously funny.   Perhaps the best known stunt developed
by the team was their boxing act.   In this bit, the larger Miller
was challenged by the midget Lyles into a pugilistic travesty which
became a classic on the American stage.

It was in "Shuffle Along" that Lyles' boastful, big-talking
character earned lasting fame.   He and Miller were cast as the
chief officials of a Utopia called Jim Town, in which there was
nothing but singing, dancing, pretty girls.   Miller was the mayor
of that city, and Lyles, the mite, was the loud-mouthed Chief of
Police, exercising not only his authority, but sometimes spreading
out into the affairs of the mayor.

At the time, many felt that the then famous radio team of
Amos and Andy had copied its manner and material from Miller and
Lyles.   The latter sought to collect damages insisting that Amos
was a copy of Miller and Andy was a copy of Lyles and that Miller
and Lyles' gags had been stolen.   They met with no success in their
suit and later contracted to provide the Columbia Broadcasting System with a similar act on radio which failed to achieve the popularity of the alleged imitators.

After Aubrey Lyles died, Miller teamed with Mantan Moreland and they traveled on the road with their own units and doing
vaudeville.   They both came to Hollywood in 1936 and appeared in
the first all-black Western, "Harlem on the Prairie."   They were
featured in many other black-cast pictures between 1940 and 1950.

CHAPTER 4

FAMOUS BLACK THEATRES

The growth and the development of black theatricals in the
first quarter of the twentieth century was directly related to the
erection of black theatres which served as a training ground for
black performers and the principal source of entertainment for
blacks.   Although many black performers eventually became successful and played on the "big time" white circuits, almost all of
them got their start in black theatres playing before predominantly
black audiences.

Many of the black theatres in the early years were owned
and operated by blacks and many had resident stock companies
which put new shows on a weekly basis and offered guaranteed
booking for the road shows.   Along with the black churches, the
black theatres were one of the few institutions in the early days
controlled by blacks where blacks could develop their talents and
exhibit them relatively free from the influences of the dominant
white society.

The first legitimate black theatre in the United States was
founded and established by Robert Motts in Chicago, Illinois.
Motts, who owned a buffet restaurant on the south side of Chicago,
first thought about opening a theatre in about 1904.   After consul-
tation with his many friends, Fred Cary assisted him in remodel-
ing his buffet and getting the house in readiness to open as a music hall and vaudeville theatre on June 18, 1904.   The Pekin, located on 27th and State Streets, was not a large theatre even by
the standards of the time, but it was artistically designed and
adorned with gold and red embellishments in the interior.

The opening bill presented Hen Wise and Katie Milton and
their two pickaninnies, Eugene King and Leo Bailey.   Hen Wise
was then given charge of what can be termed a miscellaneous stock
company, staging musical numbers and lively vaudeville, alternate-
ly.   Motts advertised his theatre in all the leading black newspapers as "The only theatre in America playing colored artists
exclusively. "

Following Hen Wise, Charles S. Sager was engaged as stage
manager.   Soon afterwards, a fire ruined the interior of the Pekin.

115

Repairs implemented by Motts included enlarging the stage and add-
ing a balcony so that the New Pekin opened in the spring of 1905 as
a regular theatre and, as Bob Cole said, "This was the beginning
of the colored theatres." Motts next made William Foster his acting manager, and J. Ed. Green the producer with Jerry Mills as
Green's assistant. Other members of the staff included Joseph (Joe)
Jordan, director of music; R. J. Moxley, scenic artist; Judge W. H.
Moore, press agent; and Thomas F. Motts, treasurer.

Initially the performances at the Pekin were mostly of a musical nature, with serious as well as comedy effects. Because of
this, the theatre, over several years, maintained a large number of
reputed musical directors. These included Will Marion Cook, one-
time musical director of the Williams and Walker shows; Tim Bryman, one-time director of S. H. Dudley's "Smart Set" company; Joe
Jordan, the first Pekin director; and H. Lawrence Freeman, who at
one time directed the "Rufus Rastus" company which starred Ernest
Hogan.

The first musical comedy produced at the Pekin was in 1906
and was under the direction of J. Ed. Green. It was entitled "The
Man from Bam" with a book by Flournoy E. Miller and Aubrey
Lyles and the music by Joe Jordan. The principal comedian in the
cast was Sam Henderson. Andrew Tribble was also a feature, and
the play enjoyed a three-week run. Other plays which followed were
"The Mayor from Dixie," "Two African Princes," "My Friend from
Georgia," which was revised by J. Ed. Green. For the first
time a black people's theatre manned on both sides of the footlights by men and women of the race, presenting a product of
black playwrights and composers had been organized in America.

A new show opened at the Pekin every two weeks. This
meant that since the shows were all original as to book and music
(the latter generally consisting of twenty new musical numbers), they
had to be not only conceived and composed, but orchestrated, rehearsed and staged with the ongoing show (giving ten performances
weekly) still playing. Sometimes one composer wrote all of the music for an entire show.

"The Husband" was produced at the Pekin on April 22, 1907.
This comedy was written by Miller and Lyles with music by Joe
Jordan and T. Brymn. The cast included Harrison Stewart, Lottie
Grady, Jerry Mills, Matt Marshall, May White, Jennie Ringgold,
Pearl Brown, Nettie Lewis, George White, J. F. Mores, Beulah
White, Charles Gilpin, Adolph Henderson, George Day, Madeline
Cooper, Oma Crosby, Pauline Freeman, John Turner and Elora
Johnson.

The next production at the Pekin was "The Queen of the Jungles," a comedy by Bob A. Kelley. This play had the same cast
as "The Husband," but also included Lawrence Chenault, Charles
Young, Cecil Watts, Viola Stewart, Effie King, Charles Foster and

Leon Brooks. "Captain Rufus,"
a military comedy, was next
produced. The book was by J.
Ed. Green and Alfred Anderson
with the music by H. Lawrence
Freeman and additional music
by Joe Jordan, and Brymn.

Owing to the success of "Captain Rufus" and "The Husband"
and through the influence of Ernest Hogan, Bob Motts sent these
two plays to New York City with
J. Ed. Green in charge. Miller
and Lyles went along and were
in the cast of both plays which
opened at Hurtig and Seamon's
Music Hall Theatre, August 12,
1907, for two weeks.

Bob Motts also gave several
professional matinees with much
success: two for Williams and
Walker and one each for Black
Patti and Cole and Johnson. He
also made his theatre available
for church and charitable bene-
fits. Other plays produced at
the Pekin were "The Idler,"
"Captain Swift," "The Man Upstairs," "Montana," "The Pet
Dog" and "Sambo."

The Pekin was responsible
for the early development of
many singers and actors who
went on to win national fame
and renown. Among these were
Lottie Grady, Austin Wilkins,
Abbie Mitchell, Charlotta Freeman, Leona Marshall, Effie King,
Ada Banks, Elvira Johnson, Charles H. Gilpin, Charles (Bass)
Foster, Lawrence Chenault, J. Francis Mores, Walter Crumbly,
J. Wesley Johnson, Harrison Stewart, Matt Marshall, Dooley Wil-
son, Louis Mitchell, Kinky Cooper, Horse Crawford, Flournoy E.
Miller, Aubrey Lyles, Irvin C. Miller, and Quintard Miller.

One of the first orchestras of black musicians to give a
serious delineation of theatrical musical accomplishments was performed at the Pekin. Among the noted musicians of this period
were William Tyler, master violinist and nephew of the great comedian Bert Williams, William (Pop) Riley, Samuel Barnes, William Bailey, and one of the most versatile of all orchestra pianists,
Edward Harding.

Newspaper ad, circa 1906

H. Lawrence Freeman--Orchestra Conductor for Pekin Stock Company, circa 1906

After William Foster left the Pekin, Motts engaged William H. Smith to fill in from time to time as acting manager. Shortly after this, J. Ed. Green also left and Motts changed the policy of the house to mixed vaudeville.

Motts' last venture in musical comedy came when he hired Sam Croker, formerly business manager for Cole and Johnson, as his acting manager. Through Mr. Croker, Motts also secured Jesse A. Shipp, already a famous playwright and producer, to produce musical comedies. "Dr. Herb's Prescription, Or It Happened in a Dream" and the "Lime Kiln Club" were two of the best plays produced by Shipp. The latter was the last appearance of the Pekin Stock Company on its own stage. Among the members of the company were Jesse A. Shipp, Tom Brown, Alice Gilliam, Charles

Gilpin, Clarence Tisdale, Lloyd Gibbs, William C. Elkins, Jerry
Mills, Shelton Brooks, Billy Johnson, Hattie McIntosh, and others.
Jesse Shipp had wanted to produce big musical comedies that would
enjoy a long run, but Mr. Motts wanted new plays every week, a
venture that was too difficult to attain and eventually led to the closing of the company.

After the stock company closed, the house returned to vaudeville and Motts remodeled the outside of the theatre.   A new brick
wall replaced the wooden building on the 27th Street side and a ce-
ment front was added on the State Street side.   Shortly before this
work was completed, Motts was taken ill and never returned to the
theatre.   Bob Motts died in July 1911.

Before his death, Bob Motts signed his theatre to his younger
half-sister.   In November 1912 the Pekin reopened under the management of Aft C. Harris, a Chicago performer.   The opening attraction was Sidney I. Perrin in "The Kissing Trust" which scored
a big success.   In August 1913 the Pekin Theatre was sold to
George Holt, white, who was the proprietor of the Brunswick Hotel
in Chicago.   The property was sold for $35,000.

Robert Motts deserves a special place in the history of
American theatricals for having given birth to the Pekin Theatre
and its famous stock company.   At the time of his death, nearly
every large city in the United States had a black theatre patterned
after the idea he originated.

Meanwhile, in New York City, when Harlem was first beginning to grow into what was eventually to become a major black
population center, the old Lincoln Theatre was established in 1908
at the corner of 135th Street and Lenox Avenue, with Jack Dempsey
(not the fighter), manager, and an individual known as Frenchy as
the proprietor.   The old Lincoln was originally known as the Nickel-
ette, presumably because a nickel was the admission price.   Soon
the price was raised, a makeshift stage was built for vaudeville,
and the name was changed to the Lincoln.   The theatre consisted of
an elongated one-story building, dingy and gloomy in the interior,
with its floor lower than the level of the sidewalk.

It was in this environment that Eddie Hunter, at that time
of the well-known team of Hunter and Tom Chappelle, conceived and
evolved outstanding shows that eventually made his work famous as
a travesty of humor and fun.   Hunter and Chappelle had organized
a company of fine performers and were presenting fifteen-minute
original sketches which proved to be a great drawing card.   One of
the most famous of the Hunter and Chappelle company's presentations was the sketch entitled "Subway Sal," which was characterized
by Andrew Tribble in blackface.

These sketches, which were the creations of Eddie Hunter,
followed one another in weekly succession and formed the basis
upon which his subsequent international fame evolved.   After leaving

the old Lincoln, Hunter and Chappelle organized a new company, based on the more meritorious elements of the original and added Charlotta Freeman as prima donna and H. Lawrence Freeman as manager.   The company was booked in the Loew Theatres of New York City, New Jersey, Long Island, Staten Island, and Westchester.

After discontinuing this company, Chappelle and his wife Juanita Stinette became feature vaudeville artists.   Hunter went on to produce and perform in shows such as "How Come" and many others.

Among the large number of performers who passed through the dingy portals of the old Lincoln Theatre to world recognition were Chris Smith, composer-pianist, Tom Fletcher, star comedian, Bobbie and May Kemp, headline vaudeville stars, and Clarence Muse, noted film and dramatic actor.

The new Lincoln Theatre, erected on the site of the old Lincoln by Maria C. Downs, was the place of origin of the Anita Bush Stock Company which was organized and managed by a talented and enterprising black woman whose name it had.   The company was the first legitimate dramatic repertoire ensemble to operate in a recognized theatre in greater New York City.

The Anita Bush Stock Company opened at the new Lincoln Theatre in 1914, and created a veritable sensation through the superior quality of the plays presented as well as the unexpected excellence of the cast of performers.   The individual members of the company each had previous training and stage experience and, as a consequence, their performances were marked with a profes-sional stamp.

Anita Bush, who played the ingenue roles, was a prominent member of the Williams and Walker Company from the time of its inception until the final curtain of "Mr. Lode of Koal."   Not only was she an excellent singer, as proved by her subsequent years of high class vaudeville, but she was also one of Aida Overton Walker's special dancers of former years.   She was also a pioneer black screen actress having appeared in several black silent films including "The Crimson Skull" and "The Bull Dogger."

Charlotta Freeman, who portrayed the emotionally dramatic characterizations, was an outstanding performer as well as the prima donna of Ernest Hogan's "Rufus Rastus" company, the Pekin Stock Company, John Larkin's company, and H. Lawrence Free-man's Negro Grand Opera Company.

Another distinguished member of the company was Charles H. Gilpin, later to become famous in the title role of the stage production "Emperor Jones" and in "All God's Chillun Got Wings" and other international productions of stage and radio.   Gilpin also enacted the role of the lieutenant in "Captain Rufus," the music of which was composed by Joe Jordan and H. Lawrence Freeman.

Andrew Bishop, a native of New York, had made his stage debut in Alex Roger's play "The Old Man's Boy" under the stage direction of Jesse Shipp in 1912. Bishop subsequently became the leading juvenile of the celebrated Lafayette Players Stock Company and later appeared in a number of all-black films in the 1920's and 1930's.

Dooley Wilson, another original member of the Anita Bush company, was a pioneer vaudeville performer, an outstanding singer, entertainer, and floor manager of some of the most popular of Harlem's emporiums. He later played the role of the inspector in Dr. Rudolph Fisher's "The Conjure Man Dies" at the Lafayette Theatre in 1935, and became nationally known for his performance in the movie "Casablanca."

Some of the initial presentations of the Anita Bush company included "The Girl at the Fort" and "Almost Two O'Clock." The company presented several other productions during a period of six months after which time the owner of the theatre, Mrs. Downs, decided to organize the New Lincoln Stock Company, whereas the Bush company moved to the Lafayette Theatre.

After establishing the Lincoln, Mrs. Downs did not enjoy a corner on the Harlem amusement market very long. Soon the Crescent Theatre was opened in 1910 farther down on 135th Street toward Fifth Avenue. It was under the management of Flugelman and Johnson and later Martinson and Nibur, two liquor dealers in Harlem, took it over and the theatre soon became the Mecca of the more affluent class of people who wished to see higher grades of entertainment along with the motion pictures.

The Lincoln and the Crescent did a land office business. More and more black families were crossing the residential dividing line in Harlem, which was then Seventh Avenue, and Martinson and Nibur decided to gamble on the erection of a theatre at 132nd Street and Seventh Avenue called the Lafayette. When the Lafayette was completed, it was uncertain whether its clientele would be white or black. The word soon spread among the blacks that the new theatre would draw the color line and the owners soon saw the effect of this rumor in the decrease in business at their liquor store and decrease in attendance at the Crescent Theatre. They decided to invest heavily in advertising to assure their black customers and their prospective audiences at the Lafayette that they were looking for black trade.

About the time that Martinson and Nibur made public that they contemplated erecting the Lafayette, the Johnson Amusement Company, a black concern, was organized to build a theatre on 138th Street between Fifth and Lenox Avenues. The work of excavation on both theatres was started about the same time, but only the Lafayette was ever completed. Although Thomas Johnson, President of the Johnson Amusement Company, assured all stockholders that their money was safe, the firm went bankrupt several months after starting the project.

The Lafayette Theatre was known in Harlem as the "House Beautiful" and was the home base of the Lafayette Players Stock Company which is still considered one of the best dramatic stock companies ever developed in America.

Lester A. Walton, while managing the Lafayette Theatre in 1914, transplanted the Anita Bush Stock Company from the New Lincoln Theatre to the Lafayette Theatre.

When the Anita Bush company moved, Mrs. Downs formed an organization of her own, recruiting performers from the ranks of vaudeville headliners who had had little, if any, dramatic experience and training. As a consequence, the enterprise failed. Among the performers involved in the unsuccessful venture was the team of Muse and Muse--Clarence Muse who later starred with The Lafayette Players and his talented wife, Ophelia Muse; Walker Thompson, the straight man of a then famous vaudeville team; Charlie and May Olden, dancing stars of J. Leubrie Hill's musical comedy company; and Evelyn Ellis, who had no previous stage experience.

During the short period of inception and dissolution of the Downs company, the Anita Bush company carried on at the Lafayette until the theatre was forced to close temporarily as a result of mismanagement.

Out of the remnants of the defunct Lincoln and Bush Players, Charles H. Gilpin initiated the Lafayette Players Stock Company which was to carry on continuously at the Lafayette for the next seven years. About the same time, Robert Levy, white, had reopened the Lafayette, and he engaged some of the most famous Broadway play directors to train and develop these players. Current plays on Broadway, featuring white casts, were performed by the Lafayette Players using scenery that had been used in the original productions. Some of these initial successes were "The Deep Purple," "Kick In," "Within the Law," "The Count of Monte Cristo," "Five Fathers," "Faust" (dramatized version), "Third Degree," "The Wolf," "The Chocolate Soldier," and "Dr. Jekyll and Mr. Hyde" in which Clarence Muse played the title role in whiteface.

A new play opened every Monday afternoon. There was a daily matinee, and during the period of the current production the play for the following week was being rehearsed, beginning on Tuesday morning and continuing each morning thereafter. This mode of operation was a regular routine followed by the players for seven full years without a break.

After a time, two additional companies of the Lafayette Players were organized and operated with one at the Howard Theatre, Washington, D. C. and the other at the Dunbar Theatre in Philadelphia. Later, a fourth company was organized and operated at the Avenue Theatre in Chicago. Later Brown and Stevens, black Philadelphia bankers, bought the Quality Amusement Company from Robert Levy. This purchase included the Lafayette Theatre and the Lafayette Players. They placed Lester Walton in charge as manager.

Some of the great dramatic stars of yesteryear who made their marks with the Lafayette Players included Cleo Desmond, Anita Bush, Inez Clough, Abbie Mitchell, Charlotta Freeman, Mattie Wilkes, Marie Young, Iris Hall, Ruth Carr, Laura Bowman, Ida Anderson, Evelyn Ellis, Lillian Gillian, Hilda Oftley, Susie Sutton, May Kemp, Ruth Cherry, Lillian Woods, Ophelia Muse, May Olden, Theresa Blueford, Evelyn Preer, Rosalie Tyler, Isabel Jackson, Elizabeth Williams, Charles Gilpin, Clarence Muse, Sidney Kirkpatrick, Andrew Bishop, J. Francis Mores, Walker Thompson, Lawrence Chenault, Thomas Mosely, A. B. Comathiere, Dooley Wilson, Bob Slater, Luke Scott, Lionel Monagas, Jim Burroughs, Charles Olden, Will Cook, Arthur Ray, Walter Robinson, Barrington Carter, Charles Moore, Tom Brown, J. Lawrence Criner, Arthur Simmons, Hayes Pryor, Creighton Thompson, Opal Cooper, Edward Thompson, and Nathanial Guy.

It was 1921 before the first theatre in New York City, owned and managed by blacks, was constructed. The Renaissance, located at Seventh Avenue and 133rd Street was built by the Sares Realty Company, headed by William Roach.

Following closely upon the advent of the erection of black theatres in Chicago and New York, the first vaudeville house opened in Philadelphia in 1910. This theatre, the North Pole, was owned and managed by John T. Gibson. The North Pole occupied a bleak, barren barnlike building with dressing rooms located in a loftlike attic.

Later, Gibson moved from the North Pole into the Standard Theatre, which had all the earmarks of a legitimate playhouse. It was there that the Whitman Sisters were given the first opportunity to develop from the raw recruits of early days to the stellar artists that they eventually became. These beautiful and talented young women were capable of performing either individually or in a group formation acts and exhibitions ranging from complete shows or revues, which embraced the charming ingenue and the lady of quality to the dainty and piquant soubrette and comedienne of the early 1890's. Alberta, Mabel, and Alice were dominating personalities of this talented group.

The Griffin Sisters of "Easy Rider" fame were also products of the Standard. Also during the early 1920's the Standard had its own stock comapny headed by Sandy Burns. The Burns company put on original productions on a weekly basis and provided early training for such stellar artists as George Wiltshire, Quintard Miller, and Marcus Slayter.

After Brown and Stevens acquired the Lafayette Theatre in New York City, they decided to erect and control a similar playhouse in their own home town of Philadelphia. The Dunbar Theatre was the result of this enterprise. Located on the southwest corner of Broad and Lombard Streets, it was a structure with an exterior of brown stucco effect enhanced by embellishments of Arabic design. Situated upon a spacious thoroughfare, just two blocks

from the Academy of Music, then the home of the Metropolitan
Opera Company, the Philadelphia Symphony Orchestra, this new
theatre occupied a most conspicuous and ideal location.

The opening performance featured the celebrated Lafayette
Players Stock Company.   John T. Gibson subsequently purchased
the Dunbar and later changed its name to the Gibson Theatre.   By
this purchase, Gibson became the owner of all of the black theatres
in Philadelphia.   However, they passed out of his hands, ending
what was the greatest era of black theatredom and marked the down-
fall of black ownership, to any large degree, in the cities of the
East.

The eventual failure of Gibson was the beginning of white in-
roads into the black theatre world which later advanced rapidly in
Washington, Baltimore, New York City, and Philadelphia so that by
1930 the black operator as a controlling factor in the large cities
of the East was reduced to almost nothing.

The year 1910 was one of the most memorable in the history
of black theatres as many big cities harkened to the demand for exclusive theatres for blacks.   In the wake of the Lafayette in Harlem
and the North Pole in Philadelphia came the Howard Theatre in
Washington, D. C.   The Howard was the first abode of Washington's
cultured black society.   Andrew Thomas, its manager, was a prominent member of the younger set.   With him was Rufus Byras as
his assistant manager and Thomas' brother Sylvester was the leader
of the house orchestra.

The Howard Theatre opened on a Monday evening in August
1910.   The opening was an auspicious one with the leading black
citizens of Washington on hand.   In the pit the orchestra was under
the direction of Will Vodery who was billed on the program as
"Professor Will Vodery."   The ushers were selected from students
attending Howard University.   Those appearing were Abbie Mitchell,
the Five Largards, the Pekin Trio, E. E. Larner, Hatch and Company, Clermonto and Miner, Mr. and Mrs. Tom Lancaster, Johnson
and Johnson, and the Seymour Sisters.

The opening bill had historic significance because it was the
first time in the history of Washington that white acts appeared before a black audience.   They were well received, but the big hit of
the evening was the singing of Abbie Mitchell.

The first legitimate road show to play the Howard was the
John Larkins Musical Comedy Company of which H. Lawrence Freeman was the musical director.   The great road shows of those days
did not carry a full orchestra as each theatre maintained a standard
group of its own--usually members of the local symphony orchestra,
or other musical units.   The Larkins company carried one first
violinist and one tap-drummer only.   Consequently, it was impera-
tive that a new orchestra had to be rehearsed in a different city
every Monday morning where the show appeared.   It was at the

Howard that Allie Ross, a violinist who later gained international fame, made his initial debut.

During the first five years of operation, the Howard featured musical shows featuring Frank Montgomery, J. Leubrie Hill, Salem Tutt Whitney, Irvin C. Miller, and S. H. Dudley companies alternating between Washington, New York, Philadelphia, and Norfolk and Savannah. Vaudeville acts and Sunday concerts were also very popular.

The Globe Theatre, Jacksonville, Florida, was the Southern anchor of the tour for black road shows and vaudeville artists. The Globe originally opened as the Bijou and was founded by Frank Crowd. It first opened on July 16, 1908 with a seating capacity of 218. Motion and Illustrated pictures was the order; eventually a stage was installed and light vaudeville was added, which significantly increased the popularity of the house. The owner and manager, Frank Crowd, left nothing undone to please the public insofar as the quality of the shows presented. At this time, the Bijou was the first and only playhouse in Jacksonville where motion pictures could be seen by blacks in refined surroundings.

It was not long, however, before two whites, Joel and Glickstein, opened the Air Dome next door to the Bijou. The Air Dome had a seating capacity of 700, a six-piece orchestra under the direction of Eugene Framen Mikell, a large stage, appropriate scenery and a strong company. The crowds then flocked to the Air Dome and Frank Crowd wondered what he would do.

The doors of the Bijou were closed for five months and on January 17, 1910, the theatre opened again with a new name, the Globe. The theatre had been completely remodeled. The first and second floors were torn out and a balcony arranged in true theatre fashion. Other improvements included inclined floors, two private boxes, seating six persons each, a stage large enough to accommodate the largest traveling minstrels (first part), scenery by Anthony J. Solomon of Boston and the Imperial Curtain Company of New York. The third floor over the stage was taken out, forming a tower, and dropping curtains were added. Wiring, switchboard, dimmer, and electrical effects were installed by the Interior Conduit and Insulation Company of New York. A tungsten lighting system was used exclusively. Interior decorations were by Maloleu. Six hundred comfortable theatre chairs occupied the orchestra and dress circle sections, and the balcony was enlarged to 400 seats, making a total capacity of 1000 seats, including 100 emergency folding chairs for the aisles.

To finance this massive project, Frank Crowd organized the Globe Amusement Corporation with an incorporated capital of $25,000. The original directors of the Corporation were W. S. Sumter, president; Frank Crowd, vice-president and general manager; Dr. J. Seth Hills, secretary and treasurer.

Thereafter, the house played to standing room only for the
two shows presented every night of the week. The company at the
Globe included the following talented artists: Bob and Alice Russell,
Billy Owens, Speedy Smith, Cora (Fisher) Glenn, William Glenn,
Pauline Crampton, Mattie Garrett, Georgia Davis, L'Don Bradford,
Evelyn White, Barbara Santana, Butler May and Maggie Dixon.
Eugene Mikell directed the house orchestra. The opening produc-
tion of the house was "Booker T. Cruising on the High Seas."

In 1918, the black population on the South side of Chicago
was growing rapidly and ever since the close of the Pekin a few
years earlier, the Grand and the Avenue Theatres were vying for
the patronage of black theatre goers. The Grand Theatre, situated
at State and Thirty-first Streets, always catered to blacks, but the
Avenue Theatre, established in 1914 and located at Indiana Avenue
and Thirty-first Street at first was lukewarm to black patrons and
frequently the management chose to segregate them in jim crow
balconies.

However, as more blacks moved into the district where the
Avenue Theatre was situated, and whites moved out in large numbers, the theatre management, seeing the handwriting on the wall,
actively competed with the Grand for black patronage. Breaking
with previous policy, black acts were brought in for weekly runs
where previously the black vaudevillians were "persona non grata."
The Avenue Theatre was a moderately large house with a seating
capacity of 1200. Prior to 1918, no blacks were engaged in an official capacity in the front, not even as cashier. By the early
1920's this policy had changed.

In the early 1920's the Avenue was the western spur of the
operations of the Lafayette Players and incidentally caused the formation of a fourth company of Players. The sojourn of the various
companies of the Lafayette Players at the Avenue was usually prolonged from three to six months and the appreciative audiences began to accept each of the successive groups as their own. Some of
the memorable performances during this period were rendered by
Evelyn Preer, Sidney Kirkpatrick, Ivy Hubbard, and Rosalie Tyler.
Chicagoans also had the pleasure of welcoming the return of some
of their old favorites of the early Pekin Theatre days such as
Abbie Mitchell, Charlotta Freeman, Lawrence Chenault, J. Francis
Mores and others.

The Grand Theatre was a vaudeville house and in the early
1920's did a capacity business. A large measure of the theatre's
success was due to the Billy King Stock Company which presented
new and original musical comedies and tabloids every week between
1915 and 1923. The featured performers with this celebrated company included Gertrude Saunders, Marshall Rogers, Andrew Tribble,
Lottie Gee, and Dink Stewart.

During this period, the only theatre in Chicago under black
management was the Star Theatre, owned by Jessie Binga, and

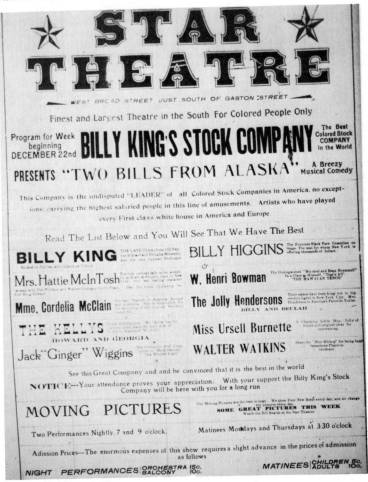

Ad for Billy King's Stock Company at Star Theatre, Savannah, Georgia, circa 1914

leased to Teenan Jones. It was a motion picture house, situated at State and Thirty-ninth Streets. The theatre was never very successful and offered no real competition to the Avenue and Grand.

Perhaps the most famous of all of Chicago's black theatres was the Regal, where just about all of the leading black performers played during the forty years after it first opened in 1928. Situated on South Parkway near 47th Street, the Regal was in the heart of the fashionable section of Chicago's south side. Dave Payton was the first musical director of the theatre which had a house orchestra

of 22 musicians that was augmented by the Right Quintet imported
from New York City where they had supported many Broadway
shows.   The 3000-seat theatre opened with Fess Williams and his
Joy Boys with Sammy Williams at the organ.   The Regal was torn
down in the early 1970's to make way for a parking structure.

One of the stops on the circuit for all of the road shows in
the early 1920's was the Attucks Theatre in Norfolk, Virginia.
With the completion of the Attucks Theatre in 1919, the black people of Norfolk and vicinity were given a theatre with, at the time,
all the latest up-to-date conveniences and equipment.   Silent movies,
spoken drama, vaudeville, musical comedies and minstrels constituted the attraction of the theatre.   In 1920, the Attucks was part
of a circuit of theatres which featured productions booked by the
Quality Amusement Company, then owned by blacks.   The circuit
included the Lafayette in New York, the Putnam in Brooklyn, the
Dunbar in Philadelphia, the Howard in Washington, D. C. , the Douglass in Baltimore, the Lincoln in Norfolk, Virginia, the Avenue in
Chicago, the Pershing in Pittsburgh.   Among the featured attractions playing this circuit were the Lafayette Players, "Darktown
Follies" company, Frank Montgomery, "Hello" annual, Quintard
Miller's and Irvin C. Miller's productions, Billy King's creations
and Brown and Gulfport as leading vaudeville acts.

In the years before World War I, Atlanta, Georgia could
also boast of having one of the finest theatres of any city its size.
The New Auditorium Theatre located in a magnificent building occupying a whole block of Auburn Avenue between Bell and Butler
Streets was without question the finest playhouse in the South.   It
was owned and managed by blacks.   The theatre had a seating
capacity of 538 on the main floor and 75 in the gallery.   It was
opened Monday, May 4th by the Southern Amusement Company and
was a favorite playhouse for many of the black road shows and
vaudeville acts.

The magnificent Lincoln Theatre in Los Angeles was opened
October 7, 1927.   Located in the then heart of the black business
district at 23rd Street and Central Avenue, the theatre was erected
at a cost of $500,000.   The building was a massive reinforced con-
crete structure of simple Moorish design.   With a main auditorium
and balcony, it had a seating capacity of 2100 and had a pipe organ
costing $35,000.   The auditorium with its indirect lighting system,
was marked by lavish ornamentation.   The mohair upholstered seats
were provided for the patrons both upstairs and down.

The opening performance at the Lincoln was the "Chocolate
Scandals, " a fast stepping attraction imported from the East and
featuring Sam Russell, Sarah Martin, Ali Brothers and the Mosby
Dixieland Blue Blowers, a Los Angeles organization, Albertine
Pickens, formerly a movie star with the black-owned Lincoln Motion
Picture Company, and Doc Straine as the principal comedian.

Adolph Ramish, white millionaire, was the owner, Sam

Opening of Lincoln Theatre in Los Angeles, circa 1927

Kramer, white, was the director, and Curtis Carpenter, black, was the house manager. The staff included a well-trained force of beautiful girls, the "Pantalette" usherettes. In the late 1920's the Lincoln was the scene of some of the last performances of the Lafayette Players Stock Company.

The most fashionable theatre on the T. O. B. A. circuit in the Southwest was the Ella B. Moore Theatre in Dallas, Texas, which was opened in October 1924. The theatre was the property of Chintz and Ella B. Moore, husband and wife, who also owned the Park Theatre in Dallas. The theatre, which opened with a performance of the Lafayette Players Stock Company, was modern in every particular. It had a ground floor which could accommodate 600 persons, a balcony that seated 500, loge seats for 100 and four boxes. It also had an office, an automatic entrance gate operated from the office, a reception room, and an office for the use of traveling managers. The structure was topped with a roof garden and there were seven dressing rooms and an orchestra room. There was also a shower bath for the artists backstage.

CHAPTER 5

BLACK MUSICAL COMEDY SHOWS, 1900-1940

To some degree, all of the modern day American musical comedies have been influenced by black musical shows performed in the first quarter of this century. Many of the dances first introduced in these shows (e.g., the Lindy Hop, Blackbottom, Charleston, and Truckin') were the precursors of dances performed on the stage today. Many of the hit songs written for these shows, such as "I'm Just Wild About Harry," "Ain't Misbehaving," "Honeysuckle Rose," and many others, are still popular favorites. The fast-stepping, high-kicking ladies of the modern chorus lines are a direct off-shoot of the beautiful bronze beauty chorus girls that flashed across the stage in such hit shows as "Shuffle Along," "Liza," "Runnin' Wild," and "Blackbirds." In general, the "Speed Show" idea was born during this period. Many white and black comedians "went to school" on Bert Williams, Ernest Hogan, Miller and Lyles and others.

The early black musical shows were a transition phase in the development of the black theatrical tradition in America. They offered black performers their first opportunity to break away from the minstrel pattern with its burlesque and stereotype characterization of the race. They offered talented blacks their first opportunity to demonstrate on a national basis that they could produce, compose, stage, manage and finance their productions. These shows also gave black women their first opportunity to share the footlights on an equal basis with male performers.

It was not easy for the black producer to break away from the "coon show" pattern that had its roots in the minstrel shows which were popular before 1900. Many of these shows were severely criticized by white critics for being insufficiently "Negroid." The following examples illustrate that point:

> [From a review of "Bandanna Land" in the <u>Dramatic Mirror</u> (1908):] What the management's objective object in permitting most of the men and nearly all of the women to wear straight hair, however, is difficult to understand. The types would be very much closer to natural if it were not for this point. But it really does not matter, and the singing of the straight-haired chorus is just as vigorous as it would be with the kinks.

[From a review of Cole and Johnson's "Red Moon," which appeared in the New York Sun:] Although the company is made up entirely of colored performers there were times when one fairly ached for the sight of a man or woman who was really black and wasn't ashamed of it.

[In commenting on a performance of the Black Patti Company in 1910, a Dallas critic commented:] Have you ever watched an audience that was three parts animated, joyous, eager, squirming colored folks and one part languid, rather uncomfortable and mostly disturbed members of the Caucasian race at a show that was solely, altogether nigger? Don't look disgusted, they're pretty good stuff, these coon shows--and it's a revelation to watch the people in the balconies, an education in plain human nature, to observe the pit.

And don't think for a minute that the colored aggregation is lacking in talent. There is as much downright funniness to the square inch in such musical comedy, as can be discovered in ordinary productions. A nigger that is willing to come right out and be pure nigger, to avail himself of the delicious peculiarities of his race, can be quite the funniest thing going, and the one who pompously apes the mannerisms of his brother in white can be just a tiny bit funnier and the combination is positively hilarious.

Then, too, there's music in the soul of every true son of Ham and a big bunch of darkies can always manage to coax a lot of tunefulness out of any melodious music with the throaty gurgle and the sort of vocal somersault that comes between, that can be approached by no human and there's a plaintive note that is purely African and wholly delightful.

And then the dancing! From pickaninny days the buckwing has been his own private possession, and the Negro comedian is in his element when his feet are describing eccentric circles and fantastic evolutions to the rhythmic evolutions of his companions. For humor undenied the Negro comedian is pretty apt to satisfy the fun loving hunter of amusement.

Nine years later, Jack Lait commented as follows on a performance of "Put and Take" at Town Hall in New York City:

There is, throughout, too much effort to be "dressed up" and dignified. Only at the very end does it become the novelty that it should be if it wants to survive at all and have any excuse for invading Times Square.

Colored performers cannot vie with white ones, and Colored producers cannot play within an apple's throw of Ziegfeld and try to compete with him. On 39th Street another attraction failed the night before ("The Mask of Hamlet") because the Italians wanted to out-Americanize

Americans. And here Colored folks seemed to have set
out to show the Whites they are just as white as anybody.
They may be as good, but they're different--and, in their
entertainment, at any rate, they should remain different--
distinct--indigenous.

A quarter hacked away in dress suits when it would
have been a success in plantation jumpers, etc. The
girls' wardrobe runs to tawdry gowns and frocks when
they should have been fancifully dressed as picks, Zulus,
cannibals, or cotton pickers. There wasn't enough true
Colored stuff in the show--until the finale.

In order to achieve financial success the large black companies, consisting of from 40 to 50 people, had to play the large white
and black houses. To be successful, therefore, the black show producer had to retain enough of the "plantation" element in his shows
to appeal to whites and to convince managers of white houses to book
the show while at the same time not make the show so demeaning
that it would not appeal to blacks. One of the early black producers
who was successful at walking this "thin line" was J. Leubrie Hill.
His shows were generally well received by both whites and blacks.
In a review of Hill's, "My Friend from Dixie," in 1912, a white
critic writing in the Louisville Courier Journal observed that:

As Thomas Nelson Page has pointed out, there are about
as many forms of Negro dialect used in the United States
south of Mason Dixon's Line, and the fact that J. Leubrie
Hill, in "My Friend from Dixie," the current attraction at
the Walnut, employs the rich, haunting and at times crooning intonations of the Virginia darky adds materially to the
pleasure afforded by the excellent comedy work.

When he speaks--or to be exact, when she speaks,
since Hill appears in the role of a female Virginia darky--
one is inclined to the belief that he could give an excellent
reading of some of Page's stories, especially "Marse
Chan" and "Mah Lady."

Wisely eschewing the lure of paint and powder and
frizzed hair, upon which so many companies of Negro performers are apt to go to pieces, "My Friend from Dixie"
introduces the familiar to all who have lived in small
Southern towns or in the country. Very black and very
bad pickaninnies, with tightly braided hair, farm hands,
crap shooting boys and "likely looking cullud gals" wearing bandannas and gorgeously colored calicoes, give life
and spirit to the piece.

It appears when whites went to see a black show for the first
time and were surprised to see other than one with kinky hair and
raucous behavior many were probably surprised to learn that there is
no certain "type" of black and that blacks could perform in a cultured and refined manner. So it appears that the early black shows
are not only interesting from an historical point of view, but also
from a psychological point of view as well.

A few white critics of this period were able to judge black
shows on merit only.   For example, an article which appeared in
the Brooklyn Eagle contained the following comments about "Bandanna Land":

> With all due respect to that clever comedienne Margie
> Cahill and to that wonderful whirlwind Elsie Janis, the
> best performance in Brooklyn this week is that of Williams
> and Walker in "Bandanna Land" and the Majestic Theatre.
> These clever artists play at a popular price house because
> they are Negroes.   But art knows no color line and it is
> single justice to say that our stage has no white comedian
> so good as Bert Williams, or any singing soubrette with
> the grace and distinction of style which adds a touch of
> Gallic eloquence to the work of Aida Overton Walker.
> George Walker, the co-star with Williams, is the same
> entertaining dandy darky that he always has been since
> the "team" became known in vaudeville, a most amusing
> poseur and graceful dancer.   But he is essentially an
> entertainer of a type very common on our musical stage,
> while his two chief associates are artists of such fine
> creative talent and such finish and distinction of style that
> their work is entitled to be judged upon its merits without
> regard to prices of admission or any color line.   On their
> merits those actors stand in the very forefront of the
> American stage in their respective lines--if not all alone
> in the forefront.
>   For the rest of "Bandanna Land" is a play dealing with
> the humors of Southern Negroes of the present day as they
> are seen by the humorists of their own race.   For the
> most part, white managers have kept their hands off this
> time and allowed the authors, J. A. Shipp and Alex Rog-
> ers, the composer of the music, Will Marion Cook, and
> the three chief actors to work out and build up a play
> which should be to the likes of their race in the South,
> something like what "the Old Homestead" is to the life of
> New England.   It is not an ambitious effort and not at all
> the sort of play that will go ringing down the ages.   But
> it is genuine and honest and--what matters most for the
> audience--it is so funny that you laugh yourself tired over
> it.   All the authors are actors and in such a play the
> actor always gets a chance for everything he can do.
>   The piece is naturally full of songs and dances for the
> principals and those are the things which arouse the white
> spectators to something like a fury of applause.   The
> touches which portray the life and character of the ordin-
> ary Negro arouse quick and hilarious laughter among the
> colored audience, pretty good evidence that the authors and
> actors have told the truth.   There are half a dozen other
> good actors and singers in the company, including that
> wonderfully sympathetic soprano, Abbie Mitchell Cook.
> There is a large well-trained chorus.   Mr. Cook has
> written some excellently tuneful and characteristic Negro

melodies and the whole performance moves with spirit, precision and finish.   Anyone who loves laughter but stays away from "Bandanna Land" in fear that it is an ordinary rough and tumble "darky show" will make an unfortunate mistake.

　　Black theatrical writers of the period were very sensitive to negative criticism of black shows in the white press.   One of the most vocal was Lester Walton, then the dramatic editor of the New York Age.   In the December 24, 1908, edition of the Age, Walton states that:

> White critics are, as a rule, as ignorant of how the Negro really lives in everyday life as the white performer who depicts such inconsistencies.   And what is more amusing at times is that they seek to show the Negro performer just how he should do his work on the stage in order that it might prove acceptable to the public from a Negro standpoint.

In the same article, Walton concludes as follows:

> As there is a dark and a bright side to every question, so is there relative to the subject herein discussed.   The bright side is the good work the colored shows in particular are doing to offset all mistakes which white actors who are playing Negro characters make.   Our colored musical comedies are setting such pace that minstrelsy has been entirely revolutionized in recent years, and much of what is vulgarly termed "niggerism" has been eliminated, while it is a fact that many whites are influenced by the white man's characterization of the Negro and Negro life, the colored shows are informing hundreds daily with the great progress the race is making and the current way we talk, dress, sing and carry ourselves generally.   Thus, we have two forces working against each other on the stage; the one seeking to convey the truth to the public, the other, while not wishing to misrepresent and distort, doing so because of ignorance and an improper insight into Negro life.   Which will the public ultimately accept? Will it wake up to the true conditions affecting the Negro or will it close its eyes and blindly follow ignorance and sometimes prejudice?   The writer feels confident that the colored shows will wield more influence in making acceptable stage types depicting Negro life than any other influence, and on the other hand, it behooves the white man on the stage to stop fooling himself and others and seek to portray the true Negro of today, for while fooling himself he is also doing the white race an injustice.

　　While one may disagree with Walton on the relative influences of racism and ignorance on the reaction of white critics to black shows, there is no doubt that early black musical comedy shows had a major influence on the acceptance of positive black characterizations on the American stage.

Some vestiges of the minstrel shows prevailed in the black musical shows of the 1920's and 1930's. The black face comedian still prevailed. Even today, traces may be found in black shows, although in a more subtle form. It is interesting to compare the comment of Lester Walton made in 1908 with the following comment made by Lance Morrow in an essay which appeared in Time Magazine of March 27, 1978:

> Blacks know something about whites too. But whites in the U. S. still do not know all that much about blacks; most whites possess no automatic focus mechanism to tell them what is nonsense and what is not. Whites receiving a brutalized, stupid or stereotyped image of blacks through TV are liable to tell themselves, "Why, yes, that's the way blacks are."

The information about the black shows presented in the remainder of this chapter was derived from black weekly newspapers and original theatre programs. In many cases, the information is incomplete. The text has been edited but most of the original description has been retained in order to preserve the flavor of the period.

SHOW SYNOPSES

Scene from "Abyssinia," circa 1906

ABYSSINIA (1906)
Producers: Bert A. Williams, George Walker
Book, Lyrics: Jesse A. Shipp, Alex Rogers
Music: Will Marion Cook, Bert A. Williams

Cast of Characters:

From the U. S. A.

Jasmine Jenkins, always with the money	Bert A. Williams
Rastus Johnson, U. S. A. --"the money"	George W. Walker
Elder Fowler, pastor of the largest colored Baptist church in Wilson County, Kansas	Chas. H. Moore
Miss Primly, a dear friend of Ras' family	Lottie Williams
Aunt Callie Parker, Ras' aunt and leading sister in Fowler's flock	Hattie McIntosh
Wong Foo, a Chinese cook	George Catlin
Serena, Miss Primly's niece	Maggie Davis
Lucinda ⎫ Friends of Ras' and Nettie ⎬ members of Daphne ⎭ Fowler's choir	⎧ Lavinia Rogers ⎨ Ada Guigesse ⎩ Aline Cassel

From Abyssinia

King Menelik II, king of kings of Abyssinia	R. Henri Strange
The Affa Negus Tegulet, King Menelik's chief justice	J. A. Shipp
Shambal Bollasso, Tegulet's nephew, a captain in King Menelik's army	Alex Rogers
Zamish, Tegulet's trusted servant	J. E. Lightfoot
Omreeka ⎫ Shambal Bollasso's Semra ⎭ escort	⎧ Chas. L. Moore ⎩ Wm. Foster
Hadji, a messenger	Wm. C. Elkins
Lion	Clemo Harris
Camel	Messrs. Payne and Lillard
Tai Tu, queen of Abyssinia	Annie Ross
Varinoe ⎫ Market Allamo ⎭ girls	⎧ Hattie Hopkins ⎩ Katie Jones
Miriam, also a market girl	Aida Overton Walker

Flower girls, sweets sellers, Tej girls, ribbon girls, wood carriers, water carriers, citizen types, etc. by the Misses Clarke, Christian, DePas, DeMoss, E. Brady, B. Brady, Tapley, Payne, Martin, Hawkins, Meredith, Day, Ellis, Vaughan, Puggsley, Allen, Barnes, Bolden, Mitchell Adams, M. Brown, L. Brown and Ringgold.

Soldiers, servants, priests, donkey boys, citizens, etc. by Messrs. Tapley, Payne, F. Williams, Henderson, Gibbs, Rex, Chenault, R. Young, Thomas, C. Young, C. Williams, Gilpin, Chappelle, Jas. Nelson, Hall, Guillaume, Saulsbury, Lillard, Randall, Roberts and Johnson.

Story: (No information)

Bert Williams [sitting] and George Walker in a Scene from
"Abyssinia," circa 1906

Synopsis:
Scene 1--Borema Springs, the last camping place before reaching
    Addis Ababa, the capital of Abyssinia. Time, Tuesday after-
    noon.
Scene 2--Market place outside the walls of Addis Ababa.   Time,
    Wednesday.
Scene 3--King Menelik's audience chamber. Time, Thursday,
    5 a. m.   (Note: All affairs of state and official business in
    Abyssinia transacted at this hour.)
Scene 4--King Menelik's throne room.   Time, Thursday evening.
    The queen's birthday.
Note: Meaning of Abyssinian words used in the play: Janhoi--King,
    emperor. Affa negus--Chief justice. Shambal--Captain, leader
    of 1000 men. Ras--a prince. De jas--A general. Bijirondi--
    Baggage man. Tej--The national drink (intoxicant). Es-shi--
    All right, we all agree, etc. Salam allah--May the peace of
    God be upon you.

Musical Numbers: Director of Music, Jas. Vaughan. The over-
    ture to "Abyssinia" is a blending of native African and Ameri-
    can Negro melodies, and although foreign to the thematic ma-
    terial of the play, is nevertheless intended to suggest its char-
    acter.

Scene 1

"Ode to the Sun"	Entire Chorus
"Jolly Jungle Boys"	Charles Young and Male Chorus
"Ode to Menelik"	Male Chorus
"The Lion and the Monk" (Die Trying)	Aida Overton Walker and nine Abyssinian Maids
"Where My Forefathers Died"	Hattie McIntosh and Chorus

Scene 2

Opening--"Holiday in the Market"	Entire Chorus
"Rastus Johnson, U. S. A. "	George W. Walker and Chorus
"Answers That You Don't Expect to Get"	Lottie Williams
(Assisted by Alex Rogers and Bert A. Williams)	
"I'll Keep a Warm Spot in My Heart for You"	Aida Overton Walker
"It's Hard to Find a King Like Me"	George W. Walker and Chorus
Finale--"The Capture of Yaraboo"	Williams and Walker and Chorus

Scene 3

"Here It Comes Again"	Bert A. Williams

Scene 4

"Menelik's Tribute to Queen Tai Tu"	Arranged and led by Aida Overton Walker
The Dance of the Falasha Maids	Williams and Walker
The Dance of the Amhara Maids	

(Assisted by the Drum Majors, Randall, Roberts and Johnson and the Dixie Ballet)

ACES AND QUEENS (1925), 2 Acts 14 Scenes
Producer: Foster and Marino
Book, Lyrics and Music: Porter Granger and Freddie Johnson
Stage Director: Freddie Johnson
Musical Director: Fred Tunstall
Stage Manager: Harold Douglas
Assistant Stage Manager: Bill Andrews

Cast of Characters:

John Whitby	Rudolph Gray.
June Whitby	Grace Smith
Mary Whitby	Henrietta Lovelass
Turkey Bosom (Porter at Whitby's Hotel)	E. E. Pugh
Rufus Perkins (another Porter)	Joe Byrd
Sam Houston, a Big Town Slicker	Billy Andrews
George Brown, a Detective	James Fuller
Jack Stafford, June's Sweetheart	Thaddeus Drayton
Jacquellin Thompson, the Town Vamp	Lelia Wilson
Cafe Proprietor	Rufus Greenlee
Dancing Nan	Grace Smith

Dancing Daisies--Lottie Ames, Nina Hunter, Margaret Fall, Florence
    Lester, Grace Michacis, Madeline Hawkins, Gertrude Robinson,
    Jewel Thomas, Vivian Harris, Mamie Ellis, Alice Coleman,
    Corine Coleman

Plot: The story is about an oil well stock swindle and the courtship of June and Jack.

Musical Numbers:
Opening Ensemble, "Happy"   Entire Chorus
"Stop"   Grace Smith and Chorus
"Dandy Dan"   Rufus Greenlee
"Anybody's Men Has Been My   Lelia Wilson
    Man"
"June"   Grace Smith and Thaddeus
                                         Drayton
Dance Specialty   Clifton
"Will You Love Me While   Mildred Brown and Billy
    You're Gone"   Andrews
"Aunt Jemima (I'm Going   Lelia Wilson and Plantation
    Home)"   Folk
"Black Bottom" (dance)   Rufus Greenlee
"Coal Oil"   Billy Andrews and Town People
"Not So Long Ago"   Mildred Brown
"Strolling"   Rufus Greenlee and Girls
"Dreary, Dreary, Rainy Days"   Henrietta Lovelass and Chorus
"Midnight Cabaret"   Dancing Waiters: James Gaines,
                                         James Harrison, Herbert
                                         Walker, Joe Scott, Willie
                                         Coles, Aaron Elwood.

"Don't Forget Bandanna Days"   Grace Smith and Chorus
"Havin' a Wonderful Time"   Lelia Wilson and Chorus
Specialty   Greenlee and Drayton
"Take Me Back to Dixie Blues"   Trio: Lelia Wilson, Henrietta
                                         Lovelass, Mabel Brown
Dance Specialty   Herbert Walker
"Runnin'"   E. E. Pugh and Joe Byrd
"Dancing"   Grace Smith and Chorus
"Keep a Diggin'"   Entire Chorus

AN AFRICAN PRINCE (1920)
Presented by the Quality Amusement Company, E. C. Brown,
    President

Cast of Characters:
Agustus Keene Shaver   Charles Olden
Erastus Underholt   J. Francis Mores
Others--Edward Thompson, Lionel Monagas, Will A. Cook, A. B.
    DeComathiere, Edward Saunders, Alice Gorgas, Susie Sutton,
    Edna Scottron, Ethel Pope, Katie Shipley.

Story: The story deals with a man who has made a fortune raising

hogs in Kansas. His two daughters persuade him to come to New
York where they expect to get into the best set of society. Father,
however, has other plans; he plans to use his money to buy the
nomination for some high office in the government of the African
Republic that is about to be established.

The father becomes disgusted with his son who is a playboy,
and threatens to disown him if he doesn't shape up. Being stubborn,
the son fails to heed his father's advice and one day, in a drunken
stupor, brings home with him a stranger whom he has met in a bar.
The next morning, in fear of being kicked out of his home, the son
decides to introduce the stranger as the "African Prince" who has
arrived to help in the selection of the governing body of the new republic. From this point on, the comedy begins and at the end the
father decides it is better for him to return to Kansas and raise
hogs than to go to Africa.

Musical Numbers (20 were presented):
"Any Time, Any Day, Anywhere"   Edna Scott
"Lonesome at the Cabin"   J. Francis Mores

AFRICANA (1922), 2 Acts 12 Scenes
Producer: George Taylor (comedian)

Cast of Characters: Soley Grant, Frank Keath, Billy English,
    Charles Barry, Lillian Barry, Sadie Long, Lizzie Maylor,
    Chick McIntosh

Story: The story tells of the efforts of a Princess of Ethiopia to
locate her brother who has gone off to America. A reward of
$10,000 inspires a couple of crooked individuals to secure this
large sum and the situations which follow are the basis for a funny
series of conditions.

Musical Numbers: (No information)

AFRICANA (1927)
Producer: Earl Dancer
Music, Lyrics: Donald Heywood
Dances and Ensembles: Louis Douglass
Orchestra Direction: Allie Ross

Synopsis:
Orchestral Overture--"Africana   Southland Syncopators
    Medley"

Part I, Scene 1

Entre--"Black Cargo"   Taskiana Four and Africana
                                            Girls

Sons of Aunt Hagar   Mordecia and Burnham
Dance--"Bugle Blues"   Ed Pugh
"Weary Feet," introducing "I'm   Ethel Waters
    Coming Virginia!"

Tap Drill by Aunt Hagar's Chil-   Miss Waters and the Girls
   dren

Scene 2

Specialty--"A Step a Second"   Taylor and Johnson (the 2 Black
                                     Dots)

Scene 3

At the Railroad Station   Messrs. Glenn and Jenkins

Scene 4

The Original Black Bottom   Miss Waters and the Girls
   Dance
Tap Black Bottom Dance   Taylor and Johnson (the 2 Black
                                     Dots)

Scene 5

"Jedgement Day." Scene--The Courtroom in Catch Air, Miss.
   Time--Any Monday Morning
Cast of Characters:
Defense Attorney   James Mordecia
Prosecutor   Paul Bass
Officer Allblack   Ed Pugh
His Honor the Judge   Columbus Jackson
One Lung   Paul Floyd
Sadie Go About   Margaret Beckett
A Suspicious Character   Paul Meers

Scene 6

"Here Comes My Show Boat"
Song   Ethel Waters
Dance of the Tambourines   Africana Girls
A Little Minstrel and Spiritual   Africana Eight
   Harmony
Finale--"The Cake Walk Strut"   Snow Fisher

Part II, Scene 7:   The Mississippi

Song--"Time Ain't Very Long"   Africana Octette
Song--"Smile"   Miss Waters

Scene 8

"Shine 'Em Up!"   Snow Fisher, Robichaux, John-
                                   son, Taylor and Johnson

Scene 9

Porter and Ex-Porter   Messrs. Glenn and Jenkins

Scene 10:   A Romantic Interlude

Song--"Clorinda"   Paul Bass and Edna Barr
The Boy--Margaret Beckett   The Girl--Theresa Mason
Clorinda Girls and Boys   The Taskiana Four

Scene 11

Some Songs You Have Home on   Miss Waters
   Your Records

Scene 12

Harlem Transplanted to Paris
Scene--"Chez Florence," a colored Parisian Cafe
Master of Ceremonies   Paul Bass
Specialty   African Jazzers Directed by
                                   Allie Ross
"Banana Maidens à la Josephine   Margaret Beckett and the Ten
   Baker"   Little Bananas

The Broom Dance	Messrs. Glenn and Jenkins
The Count and Countess	Ethel Waters and Donald Heywood
Song--"Africana Stomp"	Miss Waters, Mr. Heywood and the Girls
Grand Finale	The Entire Company

Ladies of the Ensemble--Margaret Beckett, Theresa Mason, Bertye Byrd, Margaret Burns, Laronia Bradley, Eva Bradley, Adelaide Jones, Jenny Salmons, Lucille Smith, Rose Young, Ethel Moses, Lucia Moses, Dolly McCormick, Aslean Lynch.

AFRICANA (1934), 2 Acts 25 Scenes
Producer: Donald Heywood

Cast of Characters:

King's Son	Walter Richardson
King	Jack Carr
Princess	Heshla Jamanya
Missionary's Daughter	Gertrude Branch

Others--Ismay Andrews, Olivette Miller, Ethel Williams, Leo Bailey, Don Michaels, Joe Byrd, Four Virginians, Abriam Cosse (African Dancer)

Story: The son of the King of the Belgian Congo is sent away to Europe to college, where he acquires an education, and then wants to go back home and educate his people.

His plans to persuade them to throw off witchcarft and adjust to modern ideas fail to click when he sets foot on his native soil. Instead, his former pals and playmates laugh at him.

The best known villager, the witch doctor, openly declares she is angry and that she will make him the town's laughing stock. The son, however, is warmly received by his father, the King, and is given the royal crown during a happy home-coming feast. But now the villagers turn openly against him when they learn that he has fallen in love with the daughter of a missionary who had come to town while he was away.

Love-crazed and asserting his superiority, the prince continues his love affair until the angry father threatens to disown him and have the girl driven from the community.

Musical Numbers: (No information)

ALABAMA BOUND (1921)
Producer: Irvin C. Miller
Book: Irvin C. Miller

Cast of Characters: Emmett Anthony, Irvin C. Miller, Ida Brown, Anita Wilkins, Mildred Smallwood, Lena Leggett, Ernest Whitman, William E. Fountain, Ferdo Robinson

Story: (Review from Norfolk Journal and Guide, March 12, 1921):

"You will agree with us when you follow Broadway Rastus (Irvin C.
Miller) and Gang (Emmett Anthony) down the road a piece until they
come to the grave yard scene or 'Land of Silence' when wit and
humor runs riot among the tombstones.   Then on down the road
further as they stumble upon a baker shop 'In Old Virginia' in the
moment of their extreme hunger when a loaf of bread has more
charm than the prettiest 'brown' in Virginia or the contents of a
fat pocket book on the whirl and excitement of a congested thoroughfare.   Say man, have you been as hungry as that?   Gee, but this
is a scream.   Then you wouldn't miss seeing these hungry fellows
at the carnival where they secure jobs in the band and take on new
life after several days of 'three hots per day.'   They are also impressed with the chorus of girls."

Musical Numbers:

"The Dog"	Emmett Anthony
"Come Back to Me Daddy"	Ida Brown
"Baby Blues"	Ida Brown
"When Honey Sings an Old Time Song"	Anita Wilkins
"Good Night My Dear"	William Fountain, Ida Brown
"Love's Funny Proposition"	?
"Ballet Girl"	?
"Gingham Girl"	Ida Brown
"Beautiful Girl"	?
"Yodle Song"	?
"Musical Rass"	Emmett Anthony
"Alabama Bound Blues"	Emmett Anthony and Ferdo Robinson
"Dreamy Eyes Girl"	William Fountain
"Day By Day"	Ida Brown and Chorus
"Answer"	Irvin C. Miller, Mildred Small-wood and Chorus
"Sundown"	John Churchill and Girls
"Love is a Fable"	Anita Wilkins and William Fountain
"McGory Girl"	Ernest Whitman
"Home Again"	Alma and Company

ALABAMA CHOCOLATE DROPS (1909)
Producer: William Benbow

Program:

First Part

Bones	Will Bell, Dave Perclus
Tambos	Lewis Hines, Kid Jones
Opening Overture	Prof. Smith's Orchestra

Musical Numbers:

"Carrie"	Lewis Hines
"Black Salome"	Balor Young
"Come Right In"	Dave Perdue
"Yankee Doodle Town"	Company

Finale, First Part:
Olio

"If Good Eating Gwine to Kill Me, I'm Ready to Die"	William Benbow
"Good Evening, Caroline"	Young and Hines
"Beautiful Eyes"	Laura Blackburn
"The Baseball Fans"	Bell and Perdue

Closing Afterpiece: Camp Meeting on Fog Island

Parson Dunn	Will Bell
Aunt Dinah Lee	Dave Perdue
Tough Lizie	Jessie Burney
Bad Pete	Lewis Hines
Policeman Dogan	Will Strozer
Miss Jennie Flip	Belor Young
Willie the Dude	James Mills

Finale by William Benbow, "Who Throwed that Brick"

Good Night

ANNIE OAKLEY (1924)
Producer: Quintard Miller, Marcus Slayter

Cast of Characters: Quintard Miller, Marcus Slayter, Amon Davis, Eddie Lemons, Carrie Yates, Rosa Henderson, Bill Cousby
Story: Two brothers (Amon Davis and Eddie Lemons) have blind trusting faith in two erring wives. These better halves are attracted, like moths, by the "bright lights" and hooch, set out to see the world, taking a path that leads them down, down, down to peril and destruction.
Musical Selections: (No information)

BABY BLUES (1919)
Presented by the Quality Amusement Co., E. C. Brown, President
Book, Lyrics: Alex Rogers
Music: C. Luckeyth Roberts

Cast of Characters:

Baby Blues	Ida Brown
Wash Wadson	"Dink" Stewart
Granny Wadson	Alex Rogers
Sid Green	Jim Burris
Dilsey Dorsey	Estelle Cash
Mrs. Darrling	Lavinia Rogers

Others--Al F. Watts, Perry Solston, Lottie Harris, Elida Welsh, Theresa West, Jesse Paschell.

Story: Granny Wadson's grandson, Wash (Washington Wadson), on coming into manhood, sells some lots which his father had bought many years before. He gets $11,000 for the land. Wash has always been a trifling, good-for-nothing uneducated fellow and wild, but, like most grandmothers, Granny loves him and has always rather indulged him.

There is a girl going to school and stopping at Granny's house. Wash is madly in love with this girl, whose name is Lulu Darrling--called by her friends "Baby Lou" because she sings the "Baby Blues" better than any of the others, and, too, because her mother had always called her "Baby."

Some time before the play opens, Lou had promised Wash that if he got the money he was expecting, she would marry him. Although this promise was made in a somewhat playful manner, when she finds out that he is really going to get the money, she figures that after all it shouldn't be such a bad bargain. She is afraid to tell her mother, as Wash is homely and rather rough, and her mother, Mrs. Darrling (Mamma Darrling) has great hopes that Lou might marry one Webb Grayson. Grayson is neat, nice-looking, etc., but is really a "bad-egg."

Mrs. Darrling visits Granny's home in the first scene of the first act and first learns that her daughter, Lou, is going to marry Wash, and afterwards she sees Wash and the trouble starts to brew. However, "Mamma Darrling" is somewhat pacified when she learns about the money Wash is about to get the following day. As soon as Webb finds out for certain that Wash is to be married to Lou, he (Webb) starts to make trouble.

In the second scene of the first act, Wash gets the money at the bank and he insists on having the entire $11,000 paid to him in $1 bills, claiming that big bills are dangerous, hard to handle, etc. He also insists that he be allowed to carry all his money around with him and he has built for himself a contraption of his own invention, a sort of combination safe-dress suitcase. He and Lou are to be married within three weeks and in the third scene the people are seen on their way to Garson's Grove, which place Wash has hired for the wedding because Lou has insisted on believing in an old saying that "To marry in June in the open air brings happy days--it brings a charm that keeps away the blues. Unhappy is the bride that rain falls on." In the fourth scene of the first act comes the wedding.

In the first scene of the second act, Wash and Lou are in Indianapolis where a ball is being given in their honor. Something happens. The next scene is in a small park in Indianapolis that same night and something else happens. Then comes the scene where there is a surprise turn of events. In the third and final scene of the second act, the climax occurs. (Eighteen musical numbers)

Musical Numbers:
"Baby Blues"
"Rock-a-By-Baby Blues"
"The Rain Song"
"The Wedding"
"Jewel of the Nile"   Lena Stanford
"Daddy Moon"   Charlie Woody

BAMBOULA (1921)
Producer: Whitney and Tutt

Book: Whitney and Tutt
Music and Lyrics: Edgar Powell, James Vaughn

Cast of Characters:
Jasper Jazz   Salem Tutt Whitney
Raspberry Razz   J. Homer Tutt
Professor Loveling   Alonzo Fenderson
Henpecked Husband   Alexander White
Sally Swift   Emma Jackson

Story: Professor Loveling, a musical fanatic, hears the first four
measures of "Bamboula," an ancient African melody.   Not knowing
the origin of the melody, he conceives the idea of tracing the origin
in order to prove that the African, as well as other peoples, have
contributed to the music of the world.   In this attempt to carry out
his plan, he elicits the aid of Jasper Jazz and Raspberry Razz who
have already gained a great reputation as travelers.   The trip that
follows leads them to the African continent where a great deal of
action takes place.

Musical Numbers: (No information)

BANDANNA LAND (1908), 3 Acts
Producer: Williams and Walker
Book: Jessie A. Shipp
Music: James Vaughn
Lyrics: Alex Rogers

Cast of Characters: Bert Williams, George Walker, Aida Overton
    Walker, Abbie Mitchell Cook, Henry Troy, Alex Rogers (Amos
    Simmons), Jessie A. Shipp (Mose Blackstone), J. Leubrie Hill,
    Ada Gulguesse, G. Henry Tapley, Lloyd G. Gibbs, L. H. Sauls-
    bury, J. P. Reed, Arthur Payne, George Catlin, James E.
    Lightfoot, M. Allen, R. Henri Strange, Charles H. Moore,
    Matt Housley, Lavina Rogers, Hattie McIntosh, Bertha Clark,
    Maggie Davis, Ida Day, Bessie Brady, Marguerite Ward, Katie
    Jones, Ada Vaughn.

Story: The plot involves Skunton Bowser (Bert Williams), a simple-
minded fellow who falls heir to a considerable sum of money.   Just
about the same time a group of Blacks organize the T. S. C. R. O.
Company for the purpose of real estate investment.   Bowser's money is used to finance this organization through the ingenuity of his
friend and guardian, Bud Jenkins (George Walker).

Musical Numbers:
"Bon Bon Buddy"   George Walker
"It's Hard to Love Somebody   Aida Overton Walker
    When Somebody Don't Love
    You"
"Red Red Rose"   Abbie Mitchell (Cook)
"Just the Same"   Henry Troy

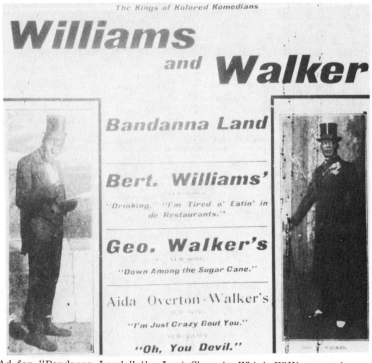

Ad for "Bandanna Land," the Last Show in Which Williams and Walker Performed As a Team, circa 1909

"I Ain't Gwine to be No Rain"   Alex Rogers
"Late Hours"   Bert Williams
"You to You is You"   Bert Williams
"I'd Rather Have Nothin' All of
    the Time Than Something
    for a Little While"   Bert Williams

THE BLACK POLITICIAN (1907)
    (The Smart Set Company)
Producer: Sherman H. Dudley
Book: S. H. Dudley, S. B. Cassion
Music, Lyrics: James Reese Europe, R. C. McPherson (Cecil
    Mack)

Cast of Characters:
Walter Tiese, Manager of the   James Burris
    Overland Burlesquers
Remus Boreland, Candidate for   Tom Logan
    Mayor

Ephriam Grindle, also a Candidate	Irvin Allen
Silas Jackson, a Relic of the Civil War	John Smith
Cephas Knott, a Vigilant Sheriff	Will Carrington
Dolphis Grindle, son of Ephriam	Will Ramsey
Palora Boreland, daughter of Remus	Jennie Pearl
Flossie Conn, Leading Lady of the Burlesquers	Rose Lee
Samantha Grindle, Ephriam's wife	Alberta Ormes
Jimmie Blackburn, a thoroughbred race horse	Teddy
Penuts, a four-footed friend of Doo's	by Himself
Hezekiah Doo, the Black Politician	S. H. Dudley

Jockeys--Lucille Collins, L. Brown, Josie Luzzo.
Spanish Maids--Ella Jones, Dora Naever, Florence Green, Rebecca
      Ropper.
Society Ladies--Jennie B. Hillman, Luventa Williams, Pauline
      Brown, May York, Irene Tucker, Henrietta Robinson, Harriet
      Lucas.
Politicians and Race Track Officials--Matt Johnson, George
      McClain, William Ramsey, Frank Montgomery, R. Williams,
      Fred Jennings, T. J. Sadler.

Story: The plot concerns a contest between two candidates for
mayor of the town of Marco. Ephriam Grindle, one of the candidates, hires Hezekiah Doo to manage his campaign. After taking
over Grindle's campaign, Doo finds himself the victim of two
scheming jokers, Walter Tiese and Flossie Conn, rejects of a
stranded burlesque troupe. They are trying to use poor Hezekiah
to gain control of the campaign funds. After many funny circumstances, Hezekiah makes good by winning a horse race. In the
end, Grindle wins the race and Hezekiah Doo wins the hand of
Polora Boreland, the daughter of the rival candidate.

Synopsis of Scenes:
Act 1
Scene 1. Exterior of Grindle's Home at Marco, Georgia
Scene 2. Street Leading to Depot at Marco, Georgia
Act 2
County Fair Race Track
Act 3
Lawn adjacent to Assembly Room, City Hall, Marco, Georgia

Musical Numbers:
Act 1

Potpourri of Vocal Gems	Company
"When I Rule the Town"	Irvin Allen

"Spooney Sam"	James Burris
"The Darktown Band"	Matt Johnson
"Help Yourself"	Jennie Pearl
"Don't Take Him Away"	Ensemble

Act 2

"Races, Races"	Company
"Likin' Ain't Like Livin' "	Rosa Lee Tyler and Chorus
"Down Manilla Bay"	Ella Jones, Florence Green and Chorus
"Hezekiah Doo"	Jennie Pearl, S. H. Dudley
"The Smart Set Carbineers"	Robert Williams and Chorus

Act 3

"Society"	Company
"Lolita"	Rosa Lee Tyler
"I Don't Like School"	Female Chorus
"Crow"	S. H. Dudley and Scholars
Grand Medley Finale	Entire Company

Executive Staff for Smart Set Company:

Gus Hill	Owner
J. E. Comeford	Manager
Al Holstein	Business Manager
Tom Logan	Stage Manager
James Reese Europe	Musical Director

BLACKBIRDS OF 1928
Producer: Lew Leslie
Lyrics: Dorothy Fields
Music: Jimmy McHugh

Principal Cast of Characters: Bill Robinson, Mantan Moreland,
   Aida Ward, Adelaide Hall, Tim Moore, Cecil Mack Choir.

Synopsis:

Prologue: Way Down South
Scene and Place: Dixie

"The Call of the South"	Cecil Mack Blackbird Choir
"Shuffle Your Feet" (Song)	Ruth Johnson and Marjorie Hubbard
"Dixie" (Song)	Aida Ward and Entire Company

Review--Part I

| Aunt Jemima Stroll | Crawford Jackson, Blue McAllister, Lloyd Mitchell |

Scene in Jungleland:

| "Diga, Diga, Do"* (Song) | Adelaide Hall and her Blackbird Chorus |

Bear Cat Jones' Last Fight
Scene at Mrs. Jasmine Wilson's Lawn

| Bill Green (A Fight Promoter) | George W. Cooper |

---

*Song later popularized by Lena Horne in the black musical film,
"Stormy Weather" in 1943.

Jack Sterling (Time Keeper)	Lloyd Mitchell
Eberneezer Doozenbury (A Bully)	Tim Moore
Sam Skinner (His Buddie)	Mantan Moreland
Bear Cat Jones (Champion)	Blue McAllister
Big Boy (Bear Cat's Second)	Harry (Shorty) Lucas
Mrs. Jasmine Wilson	Eloise Uggams

I Can't Give You Anything But Love

Song	Aida Ward and Chester Jones
Trio (Song)	Adelaide Hall, Aida Ward and Chester Jones

What a Night

Slippery Jim	Lloyd Mitchell
The Sheriff	George W. Cooper
Billy the Dope	Mantan Moreland
The Woman	Elizabeth Welsh

Bandanna Babies

Song	Adelaide Hall, Ruth Johnson, Crawford Jackson and the Blackbird Chorus

Playing According to Hoyle
Scene: A Gin Mill Somewhere in Harlem

Spike Jones	Blue McAllister
Jim Jackson	Tim Moore
Billy Henry	Mantan Moreland
Smithie	George W. Cooper
Bar Tender	Lloyd Mitchell
Policeman	Phillip Patterson

Three Bad Men from Harlem
Blue McAllister, Mantan Moreland and Lloyd Mitchell

Porgy
Song--Aida Ward and Billie Cortez; also Cecil Mack Blackbird Choir, including: Joseph Attles, George W. Cooper, Phillip Patterson, Willard McLean, James Strange, Clement Hall, Elizabeth Welsh, Mabelle Staples, Eloise Uggams, Burkie Jackson, Margaret Rhodes and Rosie White.
(With Apologies to the Theatre Guild and Dorothy and DuBois Heyward)

Finale--Part I	Entire Company

Review--Part II

Magnolia's Wedding Day
Bridesmaids: Ruth Johnson, Thelma Salmonds, Irma Miles, Dorothy Irving, Marjorie Hubbard, Asalyn Lynch, Bernice Smith, Dorothy Dobson, Julia Noisette, Lydia Bourke, Alice Hoffman, Blanche Howell, Margaret Cherot and Dorothy Williams.

Aunts: Louise Uggams, Billie Cortez, Elizabeth Welsh and Mable Staples.

Uncles: Phillip Patterson, Willard McLean, James Strange, Clement Hall and Joseph Attles.

Preacher	Tim Moore
Intruder	Aida Ward
Bride	Blue McAllister
Groom	Mantan Moreland

Earl Tucker Giving His Conception of the Low Down Dance
Picking a Plot

Undertaker	George W. Cooper
Ross Jones	Tim Moore
Do Little Jackson	Mantan Moreland
Grave Digger	James Strange
A Departed Brother	Willard McLean
Little Bits	Harry (Shorty) Lucas
Another Departed Brother	Phillip Patterson
A Friend of the Departed	Mamie Savoy

Doin' the New Low Down

Song	Bill Robinson and the Blackbird Chorus

Getting Married in Harlem
Scene: Reverend Green's Apartment on 135th Street

Maid	Rosa White
Ross	Tim Moore
Pandora	Elizabeth Welsh
Do Little	Mantan Moreland
Lizzie	Billie Cortez
Atta Boy	Blue McAllister
Minnie	Eloise Uggams
Sister Low Down	Baby Banks
Big Boy	Harry (Shorty) Lucas
Reverend Green	George W. Cooper

I Must Have That Man

Song	Adelaide Hall

Wilton Crawley accompanied by his Low Down Clarinet
Here Comes My Blackbird

Song	Adelaide Hall, assisted by Blue McAllister, Crawford Jackson and the Blackbird Chorus
A Memory of 1927	Impersonated by Aida Ward
Finale--PartII	Entire Company

Orchestral Arrangements: Will Vodery, Ken MacComber and Arthur
    Goodman
Credits: Costumes and gowns designed by Kiviette and executed by
    Mahieu.   Haberdasher--Nat Lewis.   Shoes--I. Miller and Sons.
    Scenery by the Premier Scenic Studios.   Lighting by Display
    Stage Lighting Company.   Pianos used, by Steinway.
Executive Staff for Mr. Leslie:

Manager	Harry Rankin
Stage Manager	Fred Sutton
Press Representatives	Ben F. Holzman and Nat N. Dorfman
Master Carpenter	Charley Googins
Master Electrician	Tom Nolan
Master Properties	Edward Cartier
Wardrobe Mistress	Minnie Jones
Wardrobe Mistress	Fanny Powell

BLACKBIRDS OF 1929
Producer: Lew Leslie
Lyrics: Dorothy Fields
Music: Jimmy McHugh

Principal Cast of Characters: Sandy Burns, Beebee Joyner, Har-
    riet Calloway, Clarence Foster, John Worthy, Eddie Thompson,
    Hilda Perleno, Rollin Smith, Henry "Gang" Jines, Cecil Mack
    Choir, Derby Wilson, Maggie Jones, Myrtle Watkins, Lloyd
    Mitchell

Synopsis: ˴
                    Prologue: Way Down South
        Scene and Place: Dixie
"The Call of the South"   Cecil Mack's Blackbird Choir
"Shuffle Your Feet"   Myrtle Watkins and Mamie Savoy
"Dixie" (Song)   Hilda Perleno and Entire Com-
                                      pany
                         Review--Part I
Aunt Jemima Stroll   John Worthy, Ed Thompson,
                                      Aarons Palmer and Derby
                                      Wilson

        Scene in Jungleland
"Diga, Diga Do" (Song)   Harriet Calloway and Blackbird
                                      Chorus

        We Must Have "It"
        (A Colored Version Based on Eleanor Glyn's Novel)
Ham   Sandy Burns
Sudds   Henry "Gang" Jines
Sam   Clarence Foster
Miss Mandy   Mamie Savoy
Miss Wilson   Alice Gorgas
Miss Moore   Myrtle Watkins
(Written and Staged by Salem Tutt Whitney)
        I Can't Give You Anything But Love
Song   Hilda Perleno and Roy White
Trio (Song)   Hilda Perleno, Roy White and
                                      Harriet Calloway
Quartette   Ray Yeates, Ernest Boyd,
                                      Jimmy Lucas and Wm.
                                      Edmondson
Intruders   Henry "Gang" Jines and
                                      Charlotte Lewis

        What a Night
Slippery Jim   Lloyd Mitchell
The Sheriff   Roy White
Billy the Cope   Aarons Palmer
Woman   Hilda Perleno
        Bandanna Babies
Song   Harriet Calloway, Myrtle Wat-
                                      kins, John Worthy, Ed
                                      Thompson, Derby Wilson
                                      and Blackbird Chorus

Playing According to Hoyle
Scene: A Gin Mill Somewhere in Harlem
Bill Henry   Henry "Gang" Jines
Jim Jackson   Sandy Burns
Smithie   Clarence Foster
Spike Jones   Ed Thompson
Bartender   Lloyd Mitchell
Policeman   Roy White
     Sherman Robinson in An Impersonation of Johnny Hudgins
          The Man Who Talks Too Much
Prologue   Hilda Perleno
     Porgy--Travesty
Cecil Mack's Blackbird Choir--Maggie Jones, Ester Hayes, Alice
     Gorgas, Louise Howard, Jewel Jennifer, Ruth Boston, May
     Haygood, Bertha Wright, Ernest Boyd, James Robinson, Ray
     Yeates, Jimmy Lucas, Roy White, Raymond Giles, William
     Edmondson, and Bamboo McCarver.
Finale--Part I   Entire Company
                    Review--Part II
     Magnolia's Wedding Day
Bridesmaids: Mamie Savoy, Myrtle Watkins, Marion Jones, Pearl
     Howell, Margaret Jackson, Natalie Caldwell, Charlotte Lewis,
     Adelaide Jones, Odis Sitgraves, Billie Yarbo, Ernestine
     McClain, Josephine McClain, Edith Smith, Catherine Brown,
     Juinata Boyd and Susie Baker.
Aunts: Ester Hayes, Alice Gorgas, Maggie Jones, Ruth Boston,
     Jewel Jennifer and May Haygood.
Uncles: Ernest Boyd, James Robinson, Ray Yeates, Jimmy Lucas,
     Roy White, Raymond Giles, William Edmondson, and Barrington
     Guy.
Preacher   Henry "Gang" Jines
Intruder   Harriet Calloway
Bride   Ed Thompson
Groom   Sandy Burns
Impression of Snakey Hips Dance   Freddie Taylor
          Picking a Plot
Undertaker   Clarence Foster
Boss Jones   Sandy Burns
Do Little Jackson   Henry "Gang" Jines
A Departed Brother   Ray Yeates
Another Departed Brother   Roy White
Little Bits   Charlotte Lewis
A Friend of the Departed   Alice Gorgas
          Doin' the New Low Down
Song   Aarons Palmer and Blackbird
                                             Chorus
Bill Robinson Duo   John Worthy and Ed Thompson
(All Steps Created and Staged by Bill Robinson)
          Just Pals
Beebee Joiner and Clarence Foster
          I Must Have That Man
Song   Harriet Calloway

Mr. Leslie Presents Rollin Smith in a Spiritual Specialty and
    an Operative Version of "I Can't Give You Anything But Love"
Scene: Musical Studio; Place: New York
Inspiration   Hilda Perleno
The Composer   Rollin Smith
Metropolitan Chorus   Cecil Mack's Blackbird Choir
Metropolitan Orchestra   Plantation Orchestra
(Conceived, Written and Staged by Mr. Leslie. Musical Arrange-
    ment by Russell Wooding)
    Bad Men from Harlem
John Worthy, Ed Thompson, Aarons Palmer, Lloyd Mitchell, Derby
    Wilson, and Bamboo McCarver
    Here Comes My Blackbird
Song   Harriet Calloway, assisted by
                                             John Worthy, Ed Thompson
                                             and the Blackbird Chorus

A Memory of 1927   Impersonated by Harriet Callo-
                                             way

Finale--Part II   Entire Company

Orchestral Arrangements: Will Vodery, Ken MacComber, and
    Arthur Goodman

BLACKBIRDS OF 1933
Producer: Lew Leslie
Sketches: Nat N. Dorfman, Mann Hollister, Lew Leslie
Lyrics, Music: Alberta Nichols, Joseph Young, Ned Washington,
    Victor Young
Costume Design: Charles LeMaire
Settings: Mabel A. Buell

Cast of Characters: Lionel Monagas, Edith Wilson, John Mason,
    Eddie Hunter, Speedy Smith, Kathryn Perry, Toni Ellis,
    Martha Jones, Musa Williams, Mary Mathews, Phil M. Scott,
    Inez Gray, Josephine Grier, Judy Sunshine, Cynthia Richardson,
    Viola Paradees, Alberta Cash. Chorus: Inez Persaud, Evelyn
    Shepard, Toni Ellis, Baby Simmons, Gertrude Williams,
    Louise Patterson, Deanie Gorden, Emma Smith, Thelma Wil-
    liams, Murial Cook, Maudine Simmons, Clarice Cook, Ronett A.
    Hutchens, Lillian Roberts, Dorothy Saunders, Kathryn Evans.
    Cecil Mack Choir, Duncan Sisters (Inez and Laura), Eloise Ug-
    gams, Jessie Zachary, Annabell Ross, Charlotte Junins, Edyth
    Sewell, Musa Williams, David Bethe, Clarence Lenton, James
    Armstrong, David Collins, W. E. Allen, James Skelton, Alonzo
    Bogan, Frank Jackson, Earl L. Sydnor.

Synopsis:
Prologue--This part shows how the performers desert their homes,
    house rent parties, and street corners to rush for parts in the
    new Blackbirds revue.
Second Scene--All the performers are congregated backstage where
    Lionel Monagas, the stage director, puts them through their paces.

Skit--Takeoff on "Emperor Jones"	John Mason and others
Song--"A Hundred Years from Today"	Kathryn Perry
Song--"Your Mother's Son-in-Law"	Edith Wilson, John Mason, Toni Ellis, Martha Jones
Skit--"Design for Harlem" (a takeoff on "Design for Living"	Edith Wilson, John Mason, Eddie Hunter, Speedy Smith
Skit--"No Dinner for Eight"	Edith Wilson, John Mason, Eddie Hunter, Musa Williams, Toni Ellis, Lionel Monagas, Mary Mathews, Phil Scott

Scene from Gilbert and Sullivan's "Mikado"
Finale--"What--No Dixie?"

A BLACKVILLE CORPORATION (1915)
   (Adapted from Messers Shipp, Rogers and Cook's BANDANNA LAND)
   Producer: J. Leubrie Hill

Cast of Characters:

Sandy Turner	J. Leubrie Hill
Jasper Jenkins	Alex Rogers
Matilda Jenkins	Mme. Fairfax
Bankus Blackville	Dink Stewart
Rastus Brown	James Burris
Rube Jenkins	Anthony Byrd
Mandy Jenkins	Evon Robinson
Diana Jenkins	Sarah Byrd Green
Sister Sparks	Ethel Williams
Sue Jenkins	Mattie Harris
Cynthia Jenkins	Kate Barnett
Elder Sparks	Emmett Anthony
Country Green	Charles Olden
Brother Jackson	Toots Davis
Brother Morgan	Will Mandeleff
Brother Wilson	Joe Hatch
Brother Black	Willis Gross
Brother Brown	Eddie Rector
Brother Green	Harry Stafford
Brother Watson	Hamilton White
Mose Lewis	Fred Cox
Lawyer Tom Collins	Al Stewart

Song Hit: "The Harlem Prince" sung at the end of the last act by
   Evon Robinson and company, uniquely staged by J. Leubrie
   Hill.

BLACKVILLE STROLLERS (1908), One Act
Producer: Black Patti Troubadours
Book, Lyrics, Music: Salem Tutt Whitney and J. Homer Tutt

Cast of Characters:

Sureta Walkback, Mgr. of Black-ville Strollers	J. Homer Tutt
Count-de-Ties, a dusty Knight of the Road	W. A. Cook
Percy Harold, who can't see it	Charles Bougla
Allah Board, conductor	Gus Hall
Rueben Fern, a rustic traveller	George Day
Kitty, Silas' daughter	Sara Venable
Mandy Martina, leading lady of the Strollers	Sarah Green
Sara Heartburn, understudy	Marie Bell
Sal Solome, looking for a position	Jeanette Murphy
Aunt Jemimah, going to town	Anthony Byrd
Flossie	Beatrice Hodge
Glossie	Ruby Taylor
Cynthe	Ada Alexander
Pliney	Daisy Brown
Margy	Vera Davenport
Pansy	Theresa Burroughs
Blossom	Loretta Wooden
Crissy	Irene Gaines
Head Porter	Slim Henderson
Head Waiter	Henry Wooden
Station Agent	James Goodman
Silas Green	Salem Tutt Whitney

Musical Numbers: (No information)

THE BOARD OF EDUCATION (1918)
Producer: Billy King

Principal Cast of Characters: Billy King, Howard Kelly, Gertrude
    Saunders

Story: The story deals with the passing off as members of the
Board two "hustlers" who are covering the world on foot and who
use this means of getting a lot of free sleeps and eats to say nothing of a wardrobe from time to time. The two are played by
Howard Kelly and Billy King. Their schemes work out all right,
until a detective who has trailed the pair from a distant city lands
in their midst and from there on until the final curtain when the
pinch comes off there is enough excitement to please everybody.

Musical Numbers:

"Wait Till the Cows Come Home"	Gertrude Saunders
"Sleep, Kentucky Home"	Girl Quartette

"Worked on Me for the Very   Billy King
    Last Time"
"Land of Cotton" (closing num-   Entire Cast
    ber)

BOMBOLLA (1929)
Producer: Irving Cooper
Book, Staging: D. Frank Marcus
Lyrics, Music: D. Frank Marcus, Bernard Martin

Cast of Characters (In the Order of Their First Appearance):

Ed ⎫   ⎧ Robert Ecton
Jeb ⎪ The Harmonizers   ⎪ Oliver Foster
Ned ⎬   ⎨ Charles Lawrence
Fred ⎭   ⎩ Claude Lawson
Rhodendra Frost   Mercedes Gilbert
'Lije Frost   Monte Hawley
Sheila Nesbit   Hilda Perleno
Sampson Frost   Percy Winters
Ludlow Bassom   George Randol
Anna Frost   Isabell Washington
Deputy Sheriff   Ray Giles
Sambo   John Mason
Dusty   "Dusty" Fletcher
Stage Doorman   Ray Giles
First Pedestrian   Cora Merano
Second Pedestrian   Ruth Krygar
J. Quentin Creech, the Star   Billy Andrews
Myrtle Wyms, the Soubrette   Billie Cortez
Tom Gin, "The Chief Comedian"   Brevard Burnett
"The Song Bird"   Revella Hughes
Anna's Maid   Cora Merano
The Preacher   Ray Giles
Cecil Mack's Southland Singers
The Swanee Four--Messrs. Ecton, Foster, Lawrence and Lawson
Bombolla Dusky Damsels--Alice Bowen, Fannie Cotton, Violet
    Fisher, Estella Finley, Clara Howard, Pearl Howell, Mabel
    Hopkins, Ruth Krygar, Carmen Lopez, Adelaide Marshall,
    Josephine McClain, Ernestine McClain, Jenny Salmons, Ollie
    Schoonmaker, Edna Scarez, Georgina Spelvina, Marion Tyler,
    Catherine Upshur.
The Bombolla Steppers--Chas. Banks, Johnnie Bragg, Ernest
    Creanshaw, Frank Davis, Kenneth Harris, Dominick Mendez,
    Arthur Oliver.

Story: The story concerns a rather uneventempered girl from the
South whose ambition towards stage success lures her North to
Harlem where her name is to blossom forth in lights. This is
brought to pass when she is given the starring role in a revue
called "Bombolla."

Synopsis of Episodes:

Part I--Act 2
Brevard Burnett's One-Man Crap Game
Mason & Fletcher's Strange "Inter-Feud"
(With Due Apologies to the Theatre Guild)

The Hot Dog Man	John Mason
The Soft Shell Crab Man	"Dusty" Fletcher
First Customer	Ruth Krygar
Second Customer	Billie Cortez
Cop	Chas. Lawrence

Cecil Mack's Southland Singers, Swanee Four, Members of the
    Ensemble

Two in One

(a) Clothes Make the Woman

The Wife	Hilda Perleno
The Friend	Georgina Spelvina
The Husband	Monte Hawley

(b) "Suicide"

Sambo	John Mason
"Dusty"	"Dusty" Fletcher
The Woman in the Case	Billie Cortez

The Wall Between

The Husband	"Dusty" Fletcher
The Wife	Hilda Perleno
The House Man	Brevard Burnett
First Poker Player	John Mason
Second Poker Player	Ray Giles
Third Poker Player	Charles Lawrence
Additional Specialties By	
The Boy with the Shifty Shoes	"Derby" Himself

Percy Winters and Cora Merano
Johnnie Bragg
Timoney Gladstone
Swanee Four
Cecil Mack's Southland Singers
The Bombolla Steppers

Synopsis of Scenes:
Act I, Scene 1
Front Yard of the Frost Home on the Outskirts of Savannah, Later
    Afternoon September.
Scene 2
Stage Entrance of the Jackson Theatre, New York.   Four Weeks
    Later.
Scene 3
The Stage of the Jackson Theatre During Rehearsal.   Immediately
    Following.
Act 2, Part I
The Stage of the Jackson Theatre on the Opening Night of "Bom-
    bolla."   (It will be obvious that the listing of the necessary
    scenic changes is not feasible.)
Part II
Scene 1--Anna's Dressing Room.   Immediately Following.

Scene 2--The Wedding Procession.   The Following Night.
Scene 3--The Stage of the Jackson Theatre.   Immediately
    Following.

Musical Numbers:
                        Act I, Scene 1
"Evenin"   Cecil Mack's Southland Singers
                                  and Swanee Four
"Ace of Spades"   Miss Perleno, Mr. Winters and
                                  Ensemble
"Dixie Vagabond"   Mr. Randol and Ensemble
"Rub-a-Dub Your Rabbit's Foot" Miss Washington
(Dance by Johnnie Bragg and Ensemble)
                        Scene 2
"The Way to Do Bombolla"   Miss Cortez, Mr. Winters and
                                  Ensemble
"Somebody Like Me"   Miss Washington, Mr. Randol
Finale   Ensemble
                        Act 2, Part I
"Tailor Made Babies"   Miss Cortez, Mr. Bragg and
                                  Ensemble
"African Whoopie"   Miss Washington and her Wild
                                  Animals
"Tampico Tune"   Misses Perleno and Hughes,
                                  Mr. Andrews, "Derby" and
                                  Girls
"Song of Harlem"   Miss Washington and Swanee
                                  Four
"Shoutin' Sinners"   Misses Cortez, Perleno,
                                  Messrs. Burnett, Fletcher,
                                  Southland Singers and
                                  Swanee Four
"Anna"   Miss Washington, Mr. Andrews
                                  and Ensemble
Specialty   "Derby"
                        Part II, Scene 1
Reprise   Mr. Randol and Quartette
                        Scene 2
Wedding Procession   Ensemble
                        Scene 3
"Hot Patootie Wedding Night"   Miss Washington and Company
Finale   Entire Company

BON BON BUDDY, JR. (1922), 2 Acts 12 Scenes
Producer: Irvin C. Miller
Book: Irvin C. Miller
Music: Maceo Pinkard
Stage Directors: Irvin C. Miller, B. Eugene Field

Cast of Characters:
Liza Norris   Gertrude Saunders
Sheriff   William DuMont

Bon Bon Buddy, Jr.   George Wright
Alice Dole   Lydia Brown
Jim Norris   William Simms
Jason Davis   Adrian Joyce
Uncle Pete   Parker Ramsey
Uncle Plummer   Quintard Miller
Uncle Epheas   Theopolis Miller
Agneria   Alice Brown
Rastus   Irvin C. Miller
Rasmus   Emmett Anthony
Aunti Jemima   Elizabeth Terrell
Sam Johnson   Doe Doe Green
Bad Man   D. Eugene Field
Oscar Wilber   Fred Falls
Mary Baines (Soubrette)
Show Girls--Hilda Farnum, Bee Freeman, Alice Lynch, Doris
     Magnotle, Budois DeGaston, Louise Hardaway
Dancing Girls--Viola Branch, Billie Kelly, Aurora Davis, Elna
     Adams, Louise Erne, Angelyn Hammond, Eunice Porter, May
     Green, Viola Garvie, Elcie Anderson, Marion Davis, Clara
     Townsend
Dandies--Reuben Brown, Lloyd Mitchell, Henry Jackson, Jarvis
     Chisolm, Sinclair Dotson

Story: (No information)

Synopsis of Scenes:
Act 1
Scene 1   Stage Lafayette Theatre
Scene 2   Main Street, Bowling Green Kentucky
Scene 3   Jim Norris' Home, Bowling Green
Scene 4   Specialty, H. Brown
Scene 5   Sam Johnson's Barber Shop
Scene 6   Main Street, Bowling Green, Kentucky
Scene 7   Fire! Fire! Fire!
Act 2
Scene 1   Town Store
Scene 2   Main Street
Scene 3   U. B. D. Graveyard
Scene 4   Specialty, Gertrude Saunders
Scene 5   Douglass Park

Musical Numbers:
Act 1, Scene 1
Opening Chorus--Introducing--"Struttin' Town, " "Creole Girls from
     the Follies, " "Bandana Girls, " "Dixie Girls, " by Struttin' Girls
     and Dandies
"Give Me Plenty"   Gertrude Saunders
"I'm the Sheriff"   William DuMont and Chorus
"Bound Me in My Mammy's   Lydia Brown and Chorus
     Arms"
Scene 2
"The Dog"   Emmett Anthony

Scene 3

"Forget All Your Troubles (and   William Simms and Chorus
    Smile)"
"Liza"   Wright, Saunders and Chorus

Scene 4

"The Day Bert Williams Said   Lydia Brown and Girls
    Goodby"

Scene 5

"Just Another Barber Shop   "The Gang" (Emmett Anthony)
    Choral"
"My Old Man"   Emmett Anthony

Scene 6

"Who's Tendin' to the Fire-   Irvin C. Miller
    man's Fire"

Act 2, Scene 1

"Raggedy Blues"   Alice Brown and Chorus
"For a Girl Like You"   Lydia Brown and Girls

Scene 2

"Bon Bon Buddy, Jr."   G. Wright and Dandies

Scene 3

"Love Me (While Loving Is   Gertrude Saunders
    Good"

Scene 4

"Ticklin' Tune"   Alice Brown and Chorus

Scene 5

"Dance"   Mae Barnes
"Walk You Baby Doll"   Company

BORN HAPPY (1943)
Producer: Sid Grauman
Special Songs: Lew Pollock and Charles Newman
Orchestrations: Lou Katzman and Charles Koff
Dance Director: Addison Cary

Principal Cast of Characters: Emmett "Babe" Wallace, Bill Robin-
    son, John Mason, Delta Rhythm Boys

Synopsis and Musical Numbers:

Act I

Overture
Scene 1--Maternity Hospital
Scene 2--Maternity Ward
    Distracted Husband   Babe Wallace
    Dr. Flash   Johnny Virgel
    Song--"Born Happy" (Writ-   Claudia Oliver and Born Happy
        ten by Lew Pollock and   Chorus
        Charles Newman)
"Smoke Gets in Your Eyes"   Holmes and Jean
"The Chee Chee Girl"   Rose Murphy
Eccentric Dancers   Pot, Pan and Skillet
John Mason, Assisted by Johnny Vigal
(Scene--Harlem After Dark)

Bill Robinson and His Born Happy Chorus
(Song--"I Can't Do Without Love"--Written by Deke Moffett)
Song Stylist   Velma Middleton
Decca Recording Artists   Delta Rhythm Boys
The Originals   Whitey's Jitterbugs
First Act Finale   Born Happy Chorus
Song--"You Can Hear a Pin   Judy Carol and Jimmy Ander-
    Drop" (Written by Lew Pol-   son
    lock and Charles Newman)

Act II

Scene--Outside Church in Deep South
    Reverend "Spiker" Bruce   John Mason
    Deacon Jones   Johnny Virgel
    Sister Full Blossom   Velma Middleton
    (Assisted by Ensemble)
Singing Comedienne   Mabel Scott
"Delightful, Delicious, Delovely"   Three Peppers
"Is There a Latin in the House?"   Judy Carol and Claudia Oliver
    (Written by Lew Pollock and   and Born Happy Chorus
    Charles Newman)
"Mr. Born Happy Himself"   Bill Robinson
Finale   Entire Company

BOTTOM LAND (1927)
Producer: Clarence Williams
Book, Lyrics, Music: Clarence Williams
Settings: Beaumont Studios
Staging: Clarence Williams, Aaron Gates
Orchestra Director: Clarence Williams

Cast of Characters:
Mary, Mandy Lee   Eva Taylor
At the Piano   Clarence Williams
Mammy Lee   Sara Martin
Pappy Lee   James A. Lilliard
Jimmy   Louis Cole
Tough Lilly   Katherine Henderson
Joshua   Slim Henderson
The Dumb Waiter   John Mason
Henry Henpeck   Charles Doyle
Shiftless Sam   "Naggie" Johnson
Skinny   Raymond Campbell
Rastus   Edward Farrow
Sally   Olive Otis
Mammy Chloe   Willie Porter
Kid Slick   Emanuel Weston
Policeman Doolittle   Edwin Tondel
Specialty   Craddock and Shadney
Chorus: Dot Campbell, Alice Carter, Bertha Wright, Billie Yar-
    brough, Dolly Langhorn, Portier Hands, Edith Dunbar, Mildred
    Prictchard, Walter Miller

Story: (No information)

Synopsis of Scenes:
Act 1
Scene 1   Bottom Land
Scene 2   A country road in Bottom Land
Scene 3   A barbecue restaurant in Bottom Land
Act 2
Scene 1   A street in New York City
Scene 2   A cabaret in Harlem
Act 3
Bottom Land

BROADWAY RASTUS (1915)
Producer: Irvin C. Miller
Book: Irvin C. Miller
Lyrics: Leigh Whipper
Music: Domer C. Brown assisted by Bob Ticketts and W. C.
    Handy (composer of "St. Louis Blues")

Cast of Characters:

John Miller, a baker	James Hicks
Sadie Williams, a student	Juanita Hicks
Rastus King, Crazy about Money	Irvin C. Miller
Mose Smith, his pal	Henry Jines
Mabel Durant, a somnambulist	Carrie Purnell
Madame Durant, her mother	Mae Boyd
Keen Johnson, a detective	Westley Hill
Happy Ben, a town character	Charles Gibbs
Ethel Norris, a popular girl	Esther Bigeou
Mae West, her friend	Eloise Johnson
Archie Love, a popular young man	Billy Ewing
Dandy Dan, a sport	James Calloway
Wallace Page, a fair promoter	Frank Brown
Dave Wallace, a booster	Russell
Bill Mays, Manager of the Birth of an Onion	Leigh Whipper
La EsMarelda, a fortune teller	Billie Young

Story: (No information)

Synopsis of Scenes:
Scene 1.   Interior of Elite Cafe No. 3
Scene 2.   Exterior "The Corner" (31st Street and State Street)
Scene 3.   Interior of the Blue Ribbon Hotel

Musical Numbers:

"Bye and Bye"	Billy Ewing
"Whip-o-Will"	Billy Ewing
"Every Woman's Got a Man but Me"	Billie Young

"Some Day"   Esther Bigeou
"You Go Your Way and I'll Go   Esther Bigeou
    Mine"
"I Was Mad for You"
"You'd Too"
"Every Shut Eye, Ain't Asleep"
"Every Goodby Ain't Gone"

BROADWAY RASTUS (1925 edition)
Producer: Irvin C. Miller
Book: Irvin C. Miller
Music: Maceo Pinkard
Stage Director: Irvin C. Miller
Music Director: Clarence Marks

Principal Cast of Characters: Irvin C. Miller, Blanche Thompson,
    Flo Brown, Cecil Rivers, Aurora Greeley, John Henderson,
    Gallic DeGaston

Story: (No information)

Musical Numbers:
                         Act 1, Scene 1
Opening Chorus--"Levee Moon,"   Ensemble
    "Plantation Follies,"
    "Levee Nights"
"Going South"   Flo Brown, Cecil Rivers &
                                      Chorus
"Black Bottom Dance"   Lilly Yuen and Chorus
                         Scene 2
"Orange Grove"   Cecil Rivers and Chorus
                         Scene 3
"Savannah"   Aurora Greeley, Flo Brown,
                                      and Chorus
"Runnin' Wild Blues"   Ensemble
                         Act 2
Opening Chorus--"Hello"   Liza Girls
"Planning"   John Henderson
"Too Tired"   Aurora Greeley and Chorus
"Old-Fashioned Rose"   John Henderson
Specialty   Gallie DeGaston and Yuen
Specialty   Rivers and Brown
"Dandy"   Aurora Greeley and Chorus
"Dance, Let's Waltz"   Irvin Miller and Blanche
                                      Thompson
Dance Eccentric   Lloyd Mitchell
Closing Chorus   Entire Company

THE BROADWAY ROUNDERS (1921), 2 Acts 16 Scenes
Producer: Frank Montgomery

Principal Cast of Characters: Frank Montgomery, Florence
     McClain, Leon Diggs, Alice Gorgas, "Bamboo" McCarver,
     Margaret Scott, Wells and Wells, Ardell Townsend, Chinese
     Walker, Brown and Brown, Edward Gray

Story: (No information)

Musical Selections:
"All by Myself"   Florence McClain
"Feeling Mighty Gay"   ?
"Sadie from Hackensack"   ?
"Mable"   ?
"Jack Johnson Blues"   ?

BROWN BUDDIES (1930)
Producer: Padrae, Inc.
Book: Carl Rickman
Music: Joe Jordan, Millard Thomas
Additional Musical Numbers: Shelton Brooks, Ned Reed, Porter
     Grainger, J. C. Johnson, J. Rosamond Johnson
Staging: Ralph Rose

Cast of Characters (In order of first speaking):
Spider Bruce   John Mason
Mathews   Thomas Moseley
Hamfat   "Little Ferdie" Lewis
Mammy Johnson   Ada Brown
Jessie Watkins   Alma Smith
George Brown   Andrew Tribble
Ukulele Kid   Putney Dandridge
Bill Jones   Walter Brogsdale
Pete Jackson   Maurice Ellis
Deacon Siccomore   Shelton Brooks
Mabel   Ethel Jackson
A Woman   Nancy Sharpe
Sam Wilson   Bill Robinson
Betty Lou Johnson   Adelaide Hall
A Policeman   Sam Jones
A Trumpeter   Hank Smith
Lieutenant Pugh   Wm. E. Fountaine
Houstin Charlie   Joseph Willis
Captain Andrews   James A. Lillard
Medical Officer   Carroll Tate
Orderly   Pete Thompson
A Guard   Edgar Brown
Privates Red and Struggy   Red and Struggy
Y. M. C. A. Man   Thomas Wye
A Corporal   Archie Toms
Soliders, Sailors, Dixie Dancing Girls and Male Chorus

Story: The story is about a company of soldiers who left the mud
flats of East St. Louis during the early stages of America's partici-

pation in World War I, to do their bit for Uncle Sam in the muddy trenches of France.   They are followed by a troupe of black YMCA entertainers from the old home town and a pretty romance is developed between the star of the "Y" unit, Adelaide Hall, and the top sergeant, Bill Robinson.

Synopsis of Scenes:
Act I
Scene 1--A street in the mud flats of East St. Louis.   Late summer 1917.
Scene 2--Outside the barracks.   One month later.
Scene 3--Aboard a transport.   Early spring 1918.
Act II
Scene 1--Y. M. C. A. entertainment hut.   Somewhere in France.
Scene 2--A road to the front.
Scene 3--A forest trail.
Scene 4--A street in East St. Louis.   July 1, 1920.
Scene 5--The home of Captain Andrews in East St. Louis; July 1920.
Musical Numbers (Charles L. Cooke, Conductor):
Act I
Overture	Brown Buddies
"Gettin' Off"	Ukulele Kid and Jessie
"Happy"	Sam and Betty Lou
"Brown Buddies"	Sam and Boys
"When a Black Man's Blue"	Mammy and Boys
Specialty	Sam
"Sugar Cane"	Ukulele Kid and Jessie
"My Blue Melody"	Betty Lou
Finale--"Carry On"	Captain and Entire Company

Act II
Opening Chorus	
"Dance Away Your Sins"	Mammy and Ensemble
"I Lost Everything Losing You"	Lieutenant Pugh
"Sweetie Mine"	Dixie Dancing Girls
Specialty	Red and Struggy
"Give Me a Man Like That"	Betty Lou
Specialty	Ukulele Kid and Boys
"Betty Lou"	Mammy
"In Missouria"	Ukulele Kid and Boys
"Taps"	Sam and Girls
Finale	Entire Company

BROWN SKIN MODELS OF 1925
Producer: Irvin C. Miller

Principal Cast of Characters: Irvin C. Miller, Lily Yuen, Margaret Bolden, H. L. Pryor, Eva Metcalf, Bee Freeman, George Crawford

Synopsis:
Prologue Song--"Painting a Picture of You"	Cecil Rivers

Bits of Posing	Edna Barr, Bee Freeman, Hazel McPherson
Monologue	Irvin C. Miller
Comedy Skit: "Relief Bureau"	George Crawford and Girls
"Argentine"	Chorus
"Mary Ann"	Eva Metcalf
Bedroom Comedy Skit	Entire Company

BROWN SUGAR (1927)
Producer: Amy Ashwood Garvey (wife of Marcus Garvey)
Book: Marcus Garvey, Sam Manning

Principal Cast of Characters: Sam Manning, Mercay Marquez

Story: "Brown Sugar" is a beautiful brown girl who is admired by
a mechanic and a rich Prince from India. The conflicts between
these two furnish the largest part of the production and take the
audience to far-off India furnishing ample opportunity for dramatic
scenes as well as comical ones.

Musical Selections: (No information)

BURNS AND RUSSELL CO. (1922)
    (Title of Presentation not known)
Producer: Sandy Burns and Sam Russell

Principal Cast of Characters: Sandy Burns, Marcus Slater, George
    Wiltshire, Alexander Peel, Fred Hart, Edna Burns, Inez Wilt-
    shire, Anita Spencer, Tiny Gray, Mary Heever, Lillian Carroll

Story: Burns plays the role of a one-legged veteran of the Spanish
American War and Russell plays the role of his wife. The plot has
to do with the recruiting of soldiers to go to war.

Musical Numbers: (No information)

BURNS AND RUSSELL CO. (1922)
    (Title of Presentation not known)
Producer: Sandy Burns and Sam Russell

Cast of Characters:

Neighborhood Gossip	Edna Burns
Policemen	Fred Hart and George Wiltshire

Others: Sandy Burns, Sam Russell, Inez Wiltshire, Alexander Peel,
    Coony Conners, Helen Pope, Anita Spencer, Tiny Gray, Mary
    Heever, Lillian Carroll

Story: The story deals with the efforts of police to break up booze-
selling and coke-peddling that is being carried on in a small neighborhood.

Musical Numbers: (No information)

CABARET PRINCE (1930)
Producers: Quintard Miller, Marcus Slayter

Cast of Characters:

Manager of the Blue Bird Night Club	Lloyd Curtis
Cora Blake	Edith Spencer
Mary Doyle	Lottie Gee
Billy Dexter	Marcus Slayter
Sally, an entertainer	Aurora Greeley
Steve Randolph	Amon Davis
Boddidly	Gallie DeGaston
Larry	Leroy Broomfield
Daisy	Irine Pondexter
Rastus Jones	Quintard Miller

Story: (No information)

Synopsis: A Spectacular Musical Comedy Drama of Night Life in New York City
Scene 1--Private party room of the Blue Bird Night Club
Scene 2--In front of a fashionable restaurant
Scene 3--Blue Bird Night Club
Scene 4--A street in New York
Scene 5--A gambling room at the Blue Bird

Musical Numbers:

Opening, "Cabaret Nights"	Miller and Slayter Girls
"Get Out and Get Under"	Miss Spencer and Girls
"To Be With You"	Mr. Broomfield, Miss Greeley and Chorus
Specialty	Mr. Slayter
"Anytime"	Miss Hawkins and Chorus
Specialty	Miss Gee
"Deep Henderson"	Miller and Slayter Girls
Specialty	Miss Greeley and Mr. Broomfield
Finale	Entire Company

CABIN IN THE SKY (1941)
Producer: Albert Lewis in Association with Vintin Freedley
Book: Lynn Root
Lyrics: John Latouche
Orchestra Director: Max Meth

Cast of Characters (In the order of speaking):

Georgia Brown	Katherine Dunham
Dr. Jones	Louis Sharp
Brother Green	J. Rosamond Johnson
Lily	Georgie Burke
Petunia Jackson	Ethel Waters
Lucifer, Jr.	Rex Ingram
"Little Joe" Jackson	Dooley Wilson

Imps $\left\{\begin{array}{l} \text{Archie Savage} \\ \text{Jieno Moxzer} \\ \text{Rajah Chardieno} \\ \text{Alexander McDonald} \end{array}\right.$

The Lawd's General	Todd Duncan
Fleetfoot	Milton Williams
John Henry	J. Louis Johnson
Dude	Al Moore
First Henchman	Earl Sydnor
Second Henchman	Earl Edwards
Third Henchman	Maurice Ellis
Messenger Boy	Wilson Bradley
Domino Johnson	Dick Campbell

Katherine Dunham Dancers--Calude Brown, Talley Beattey, Rita Christiana, Lucille Ellis, Lawrence Kennard, Roberta McLaurin, Alexander McDonald, Jieno Moxzer Harris, Rajah Ohardieno, Evelyn Pilcher, Carmencita Romero, Edith Ross, Archie Savage, Lavinia Williams, Thomas Woosley, J. Emanuel Vanderhans, Candido Vicenti.

J. Rosamond Johnson Singers--Wilson Bradley, Rebecca Champion, Helen Dowdy, Clarence Jacobs, Ella MacLashley, Fradye Marshall, Arthur McLean, Louis Sharp, Eulabel Riley, Thomas Anderson, Laura Vaughns

Synopsis:
Act 1
Scene 1.   Exterior of the Jacksons' home, somewhere in the South. Night.
Scene 2.   Little Joe's Bedroom.
Scene 3.   The Jacksons' Backyard.   One month later.
Scene 4.   The Head Man's Office in Hades.   Three months later.
Scene 5.   The Jackson's Front Porch.
Act 2
Scene 1.   The Jacksons' Backyard.   One month later.
Scene 2.   Exterior of John Henry's Cafe.   One month later.
Scene 3.   John Henry's Cafe.
Scene 4.   At the Pearly Gates.

Musical Numbers:
Act 1
"The General's Song"	Lawd's General and Saints
"Pay Heed"	Lawd's General
"Taking a Chance on Love"	Petunia
"Cabin in the Sky"	Petunia and Little Joe
(a) "Holy Unto the Lord"	Petunia, Little Joe, Parson Green and Churchmembers
(b) "Dem Bones"	Petunia, Helen and Churchmembers
"Do What You Wanna Do"	Lucifer, Jr. and Imps
Reprise: "Taking a Chance on Love"	Petunia and Little Joe

Act 2
"Fugue"	Lawd's General and Saints

"My Old Virginia Home on the Nile"	Petunia and Little Joe
(Vision) Egyptian Ballet	The Dunham Dancers
"It's Not So Good to Be Bad"	Lawd's General
"Love Me Tomorrow"	Georgia Brown and Little Joe
"Love Turned the Light Out"	Petunia
(a) Lazy Steps	The Dunham Dancers
(b) Boogy Woogy	The Dunham Dancers
"Honey in the Honeycomb"	Georgia Brown and Boys
"Savannah"	Petunia (dance with Archie Savage)

Finale.

Orchestration by Dominico Savino, Charles Cooke, Fudd Livingston, Nathan VanCleve. Vocal Arrangements by Hugh Martin.

CALLENDER'S FAMOUS GEORGIA MINSTRELS (1875)
Proprietor: Charles Callender
Stage Manager: R. G. Little

Synopsis:

Part First

Overture	Callender's Georgia Minstrels
Blow Me Horn	J. Grace
Never Miss the Water Till the Well Runs Dry	E. P. Smith
Oh, Git Way	P. Devonear
Old Home Ain't What It Used to Be	A. A. Lucas
Carve Dat Possum	Sam Lucas
Bring Back the Old Folks	Wallace King
John's Gone Down on the Island	W. (Billy) Kersands
Beneath the Maple on the Hill	R. Little

Concluding with the Comic Plantation Sketch Characters by the Company

Part Second

Ballad, Wallace King
Ladder of Fame

Mr. Hallup	P. Devonear
Call Boy	Al Smith
John Trampon	Sam Lucas

Master Willie Lyle
Prima Donna, in his Burlesque Sketches
Ham Town Students
Devonear, Grace, Little, and Lucas
Kersands in his Specialties
Dat Ticket's Too Big

Manager	E. P. P. Smith
Big Ticket	Sam Lucas
Mose	J. Grace
Dairy Maid	W. Lyle
Dummy	P. Little
Lize	W. (Billy) Kersands
Rag Picker	Al Smith

Whole to Conclude with 6 O'Clock in Georgia
By Company

CANARY COTTAGE (1920)
Producer: Panama Amusement Co.
Lyrics: Oliver Morosco
Music: Earl Carrol, Shelton Brooks

Cast of Characters:

Jerry Summerfield	Shelton Brooks (in blackface)
Sam Asbestos	Olie Powers (in blackface)
"Jag"	Billy Moss
Pauline Hugg	Evelyn Preer
Betty Fay	Alberta Hunter
Widow	Marguerite Lee
Mrs. Hugg	Berlena Blanks
Mile Finnegan (boy)	Charles Shelton

Others: Jestina McKinney, Hattie Cash, E. C. Caldwell

Story: The story is concerned with the love affairs of Jerry Sum-
merfield. These cover an affair with a wealthy matron whose husband divides his time between the bottle and any stray "chickens"
which might strut his way; an engagement with the pretty daughter
of the widow of a rich handkerchief manufacturer; and the wooing
and final marrying of the housekeeper of the cottage. It is through
the situations of Jerry's attempts to keep the subjects of his fickle
affection from wising-up on him and among themselves that a world
of screaming comedy is created.

Musical Numbers:

"It Ruined Marc Anthony"	Hunter, Preer, Lee
"Wake Up with the Blues"	Alberta Hunter

THE CANNIBAL KING (1901)
Producer: Bob Cole
Book: Paul Lawrence Dunbar, J. Rosamond Johnson
Lyrics: Bob Cole, J. Rosamond Johnson
Music: Will Marion Cook

Principal Cast of Characters: Bob Cole, Ernest Hogan, Ben Wise,
    Coley Grant, J. Rosamond Johnson, Theo. Pankey, Lewis Salis-
    bury, Reginold Burleigh, "Kid" Frazier, Abbie Mitchell Cook,
    Aida Overton Walker, Kati Milton, Mamie Grant, Muriel Ringold,
    Cecil Watts, Anna Cook, Mollie Dill, Odena Warren, Willie
    Dancy, Midget Price, Gertie Peterson, George Archer, John
    Boyer, The Alabama Comedy Four.

Story: "The plot of the comedy hinges upon the ludicrous attempts
of a colored headwaiter at a fashionable Florida hotel, who suddenly
becomes wealthy, to elevate the members of his race and make
them eligible to society."--Indianapolis Freeman, November 9, 1901

Musical Numbers: (No information)

Ad for "Captain Jasper," Black Patti's Musical Comedy Company,
circa 1912

CAPTAIN JASPER (1907)
    (Black Patti Troubadours)

Principal Cast of Characters: Sissieretta Jones (Black Patti),
    "Happy" Julius Glenn, Sarah Green, Will A. Cook, A. F.
    Watts, Charles Bougia, George W. Tarant, Jennette Murphy,
    Marie Hendricks, Johnny Livingston, Grace Stewart, Jesse
    Hart, Mamie and Edith Rose, Blanche Howell, Fanny Hudson,
    Roy White, Dore Green, Eddie Borden, Tracey Jordan, John
    Grant, John Phillips, Jesse Triplett, James Reed, Louis Wen,
    Archie Johnson, Clayton Cook, Ernest Green.

Story: Captain Jasper, Colonel Warsaw and his daughter on the eve
of their departure for the Philippine Islands for a pleasure trip discover the theft of very valuable government papers concerning secret

plans of an attack on the Philippine stronghold, and documents given
in trust to the Colonel by his friend, Sergeant Jackson, which are
intended to be given to his daughter, Cheteka, when she becomes of
age.   These latter papers concern a valuable grant of land in the
United States, which one day would make Cheteka very wealthy.

Before departure for the Philippines, Colonel Warsaw is informed that a certain Major Drummond, who was commissioned to
the Islands several months prior to the discovery of the theft, had
committed the crime.   Captain Jasper is commanded to search for
Drummond and to recover at all risks the secret plans and the valuable documents given to the Colonel by Sergeant Jackson.   Mrs.
Jackson (formerly Cheteka Castro, a native of the Philippine Islands), whose relations with her husband have become estranged,
and having a longing for her native land, decides to return and take
her daughter Cheteka with her.   There she meets Major Drummond
who acquaints her with the contents of the valuable missing documents left in trust to Colonel Warsaw.   Through much persuasion,
false promises, etc., he finally induces Cheteka to sign a power of
attorney, authorizing him to dispose of her property rights given to
her by her father.   Just as he is negotiating to dispose of same,
he is detected by one U. R. Swift and his friend Captain Jaster
Charcoal (posing as the real Captain Jasper) who afterwards com-
plicates things for Drummond.   Upon the arrival of Drummond to
the United States, he attempts to escape from the real Captain Jasper and is killed.   The stolen papers are eventually returned to
their real owners.

Musical Numbers: "Sun-Blessed Are You," "The Nightingale," "The
    Belle of New York," "Sugar Babe"

CAPTAIN RUFUS (1907)
    (Pekin Stock Company, Chicago)
Producer: J. Ed. Green
Book: J. Ed. Green, Alfred Anderson
Music: H. Lawrence Freeman
Dances: Bill Johnson
Staging: J. Ed. Green

Cast of Characters:
Captain Rufus   Harrison Stewart
Colonel   J. Ed. Green
Sergeant   Dan Wromley
Major Drummond   Jerry Mills
Lt. Stokes   Charles H. Gilpin
Colonel's Daughter   Jennie Ringgold
Filipino Girl   Lottie Grady
West Point Cadet   Lawrence Chenault
Russell Wallace, War Corres-   Russell White
    pondent
Rufus' Manager   Matt Marshall

Story: (No information)

Musical Numbers: "Morning is Dawning," "I've Got Good Common Sense," "The Tale of the Monkey and the Snake," "Song of the Witches," "The Lilly"

CAPTAIN RUFUS (1914)
Producer: Pekin Stock Company (Jerry Mills)
Book: Talford Anderson
Stage Director: Jerry Mills

Cast of Characters:

"Captain Rufus"	Sidney Kirkpatrick
Leon Carlos	Charles Liverpool
Cheteka Castro	Lizzie Wallace
Lucy	Bessie Tribble
War Correspondent	Mayme Carter
Col. Warsaw	Charles Moore
Lt. Stokes	Leon Crosby

Others--Andrew Tribble, Jack Smith, George Hall, Lem Crosby, Sergeant W. Jones, D. Acklen, The Pekin Orchestra under the direction of Beecher Todd

Story: The story is laid in the Philippines and is about "Captain Rufus," a bogus captain.

Musical Numbers:

"Amazon Land"	Lizzie Wallace
"My Mandiline"	Leon Crosby
"You Ain't Nothin' Yet"	Andrew Tribble
"Tail of the Monkey and the Snake"	Mayme Carter
"Chief of the Aggregation"	Jack Smith
"The Sword and the Flag"	Sidney Kirkpatrick
"Just for a Night	Bessie Tribble and Company
"Back to the U.S.A."	Entire Company

CATCHING THE BURGLAR (1918)
Producer: Billy King

Principal Cast of Characters: Billy King, Bessie Brown, Leon Brooks, James Thomas, Blaine Brown

Story: The story tells of the acts of a burglar who makes many visits to the home of a wealthy family. Billy King is hired as a detective to ferret out that mysterious intruder and his efforts along the line are what make up the play. He finally winds up his connection with the case by pinching the man of the house and allowing the real culprit to escape.

Musical Numbers:

"My Place of Business"	Billy King

"I Wish You Good Luck"   Bessie Brown
"Before the World Began"   Leon Brooks
"I Miss the Mississippi Miss"   James Thomas
"Our Own Broadway"   Blaine Brown and Company

CHANGE YOUR LUCK (1930), 2 Acts
Producer: Cleon Trockmorton
Book: Garland Howard
Music and Lyrics: J. C. Johnson
Dances: Lawrence Deas and Speedy Smith
Singing Numbers: Stanley Bennett

Cast of Characters:
Big Bill   Alec Lovejoy
Hot Stuff Jackson   Garland Howard
Cateye   Jimmy Thomas
Malindy   Alberta Perkins
Profit Jones   Sam Cross
Skybo Snowball   Speedy Smith
Bandana Babe Peppers   Cora La Redd
Romeo Green   Sterling Grant
Josephine Peppers   Neeka Shaw
Mary Jane   Alberta Hunter
Diamond Joe   Chick McKinney
Ebenezer Smart   Hamtree Harrington
Mathilda   Mabel Gant
Evergreen Peppers   Leigh Whipper
Passionate Sadie   Millie Holmes
Rat Row Sadie   Emma Maitland
Tack Annie   Aurelia Wheeldin
                        ⎛ Dottie   Dorothy Embry
Sisters of Mercy   ⎨ Mary   Mary Mason
                        ⎝ Lil   Lillian Cowan
Hot Popper Henry   Henry Davis
Hot Popper Jimmy   James Davis
Hot Popper Van   Van Jackson
Ansy   Bertha Roe
Percolatin Gertie   Gertie Chambers
Short Dog, the Hoofer   Yank Bronson
Charleston Sam, the Hoofer   Sammy Van
Shake a Hip, Bellboy   Louie Simms
Shake a Leg, a Bellboy   Buster Bowie
Captain Jones   J. Lewis Johnson
The Four Flash Devils   S. W. Warren, Chas. Gill,
                                   Billy Cole, C. P. Wade
Stanley Bennett and His Syncopators--Dancing Girls, Levee Maids,
    Rat Row Rowdies, Roustabouts, Stevedores, High Yellows
    and Seal Skin Browns, Church Folks and Citizens of
    Sundown.
Members of the Uplift League--Pauline Jackson, Fred McCoy,
    Charlie Downz, Mae Haywood, Alice Cannon, DeWitt Davis,

Harry Watkins, Millie Holmes, Luther Henderson, J. W. Mobley, Angeline Lawson, J. Louis Johnson, James McPeters, Sally Goldman, Frederick Wheeldin, Sylvia Collins, Emma Thomas, Ida Dewey, Chester Jones, Ida Rowley and Cy Williams.

Story: (No information)

Synopsis:

Act I

Scene 1--The Levee, Sundown, Mississippi.
Scene 2--Street in Sundown.
Scene 3--Sunflower Lane.
Scene 4--Interior of Evergreen Pepper's Funeral Parlor.
Scene 5--Same as Scene 2.
Scene 6--Lobby of Sundown Hotel.

Act II

Scene 1--Rat Row, Across the River.
Scene 2--Street in Rat Row.
Scene 3--Lawn Fete at Evergreen Pepper's Home.

Musical Numbers:

Act I

Opening Chorus	Ensemble
"Sweet Little Baby o'Mine"	Josephine, Hot Stuff, Simms & Bowie, and Ensemble
"Can't Be Bothered Now"	Bandana Babe, Four Hot Peppers and Sisters of Mercy
"Ain't Puttin' Out Nothin'"	Bill and Malindy
"Religion in My Feet"	Sundown Trio, Four Flash Devils, Sam Van and Ensemble
"You Should Know"	Josephine, Romeo and Ensemble
"Waisting Away"	Mary Jane and Diamond Joe
"Walk Together, Children"	Profit Jones and Uplift League
"Honesty"	Romeo, Josephine, Sundown Trio and Dance Sextet
"Mr. Mammy Man"	Josephine, Hot Stuff and Girls
Dance Specialty	Louise Simms and Buster Bowie
"My Regular Man"	Bandana Babe, Sammy Van and Ensemble
"I'm Honest"	Romeo and Sundown Trio
Reprise	Entire Company

Act II

"We're Here"	Malindy and Ensemble
"Low Down Dance"	Diamond Joe, Sam Van and Girls
"Open That Door"	Snowball and Passionate Sadie
"Change Your Luck"	Smart and Mary Jane
"Percolatin'"	Bandana Babe and Girls
Dance Specialty	Gertie Chambers
"Travellin'"	Profit Jones, Mary Jane and Ensemble

"St. Louis Blues"   Four Hot Poppers
"What Have I Done?"   Josephine and Romeo
Dance   Romeo, Hot Stuff and Josephine
"Rhythm Feet"   Louis Simms and Buster Bowie
Finale   Entire Company

CHICAGO FOLLIES (1916)
Producer: Tim Moore*

Principal Cast of Characters: Tim Moore (comedian), Gertrude
    Moore (Mrs. Moore, leading lady), Kid Brown (straight),
    Brownie Campbell (boy), Ethel Watts (soubrette), Eddie Staf-
    ford (characters), Eva Smith, Jessie Cowan and Florance Seals
    (choristers)

Brief Synopsis:
Opening--Chorus with Brown and Campbell, song and dance
Moore (Tim) and Moore (Gertrude)--Comedy
Miss Stafford and Chorus
Brown, Campbell and Moore--Comedy
Watts, Cowan, Moore (Gertie)--"My Old Kentucky Home"
Closing--Burlesque

CHIEF OUTLANCHETTE (1918)
Producer: Billy King
Book: Billy King

Cast of Characters:
Villain   Jerry Mills
Indian Chief   Jim Reed
Hero   Leon Brooks
Wild Bill   Howard Kelly
Heroine   Bessie Brown
Handy Man   Billy King

Story: The story is about a hero who is a half-cast and is in love
with the pretty Mildred Lindsay.   He, however, is faced with an attempt at double-crossing by the villain who is aided by his gang.
It finally comes to a place where the girl is called upon to either
accede to the demands of the outlaw or stand and see the whip ap-
plied to her lover.   Just as the climax comes, there is a great
rescue; the villain is killed, the hero and the girl are thrown into
each other's arms, and the comedian does his stuff and everyone
begins living happy forever.

Musical Numbers: (No information)

---

*Gained national recognition in his role as the King Fish in the
"Amos and Andy" TV show in the early 1950's.

THE CHILDREN OF THE SUN (1919)
Producers: Salem Tutt Whitney, J. Homer Tutt
Book: Salem Tutt Whitney, J. Homer Tutt

Principal Cast of Characters: Salem Tutt Whitney, J. Homer Tutt,
    Edward Tolliver, Carrie King, Virginia Wheeler

Story: Dean Kelly Miller of Howard University, Washington, D. C.,
embarks on a voyage of archaeological research, when he discovers
valuable records which he claims establishes the antiquity of the
Negro race.   These records, having been translated, are read at a
Race Conference at Howard University.
        The records speak of Ethiopia as the mother of nations, and
her offspring as "Children of the Sun"; also of fabulous wealth, and
how King Solomon obtained his wealth from his mines.   The legend
concludes with the prophesy that whoever locates the original site of
the "Children of the Sun" will discover a mountain of gold.
        A Japanese student attending Howard tells of his people being
sun worshippers, which causes an expedition to immediately proceed
to Japan.
        Abe and Gabe Washington, by reason of their experience
from the previous expedition, are elected to head the second expedition, and after traveling through Japan, Persia, India, and Egypt in
a fruitless search, at last arrive at the site of ancient Ethiopia, and
learn the true story of the "Children of the Sun. "

Musical Numbers:
"Women All Go for Mine"   J. Homer Tutt, assisted by May
                                        Olden, Virginia Wheeler,
                                        Julia Moody, Allice Smith,
                                        Bertha Roe, Grace Howell.
"Travelin' "
"We're Travelin' "
"Dear Old Dixie Home"
"Come and Dance with Me"
"Something About You I Like"

CHINA TOWN (1920), 2 Acts
Producer: Billy King, Darktown Follies Co.
Orchestra Director: Marie Lucas

Principal Cast: Billy King, Dink Stewart, Leon Diggs, Lottie Har-
    ris, Jesse Paschall, Will Cook, Lillian Gardner, Helen Baxter,
    May Crowder, Evon Robinson, Percy Colston

Musical Numbers:
"Old Home Jim"   Jesse Paschall
"Sweet Sixteen"   Leon Diggs
"Ruling Power"   Dink Stewart
"Kentucky Home"   Will Cook
"Acalon"   A. Thiggs
"High Jinks"   Lillian Gardner and Chorus

"Don't Take My Blues Away"	Helen Baxter
"My Dream of the U.S.A."	Leon Diggs
"Margie"	Lottie Harris
"Some Day"	May Crowder
"China Town"	May Crowder
"Japanese Sandman"	Evon Robinson
"Gay White Way"	Evon Robinson
"After You're Gone"	Dink Stewart
"Rose"	Percy Colston

Story: (No information)

CHOCOLATE BROWN (1921)
Producer: Irvin C. Miller
Special Music and Lyrics: Spencer Williams

Cast of Characters: Andrew Tribble, Mildred Smallwood, PeeWee
    Williams, William Fountain, Lillian Gardner, Mae Crowder,
    Mary Bradford, William Thiefl, Percy Colston, Archie Cross,
    The Broadway Four

Story (Review by Dave Payton, Chicago Whip, May 28, 1921): "A
scant propaganda theme runs through the play just enough to be interesting and is based on Negro society, turning its back on the
southern brother, who chooses to migrate north, and the lesson
brought out is of moral value, teaching to help them and educate
them and not to turn them loose here in ignorance to become jail-
birds and public charges."

Musical Numbers: (No information)

THE CHOCOLATE DANDIES* (1924-1925), 2 Acts 12 Scenes
Producer: B. C. Whitney
Book: Noble Sissle and Lew Payton
Music, Lyrics: Noble Sissle, Eubie Blake
Stage Director: Julian Mitchell

Cast of Characters:

At the Piano	Eubie Blake
Mandy Green, The Deacon's Wife	Amanda Randolph
Sammy, Mandy Green's Baby	Pauline Godfrey
Black Joe, Jr.	Addison Carey
That Comely Chorus Girl	Josephine Baker

---

*Essentially the same show was performed on the road in 1924
under the title "In Bamville" prior to its opening in New York
at the Colonial Theatre, April 1, 1924. See page 234 for
synopsis.

Struttin' Drum Major and His Bamville Band	J. Mardo Brown
Bill Splivins, Plantation Owner	W. H. Hann
Mr. Hez Brown, President of Bamville Fair	William Grundy
Mrs. Hez Brown, the Wife	Inez Clough
Angeline Brown, the Daughter	Lottie Gee
Jessie Johnson	Elizabeth Welsh
Manda, Bill Splivin's Niece	Valaida Snow
Uncle Eph	Fred Jennings
Dobby Hicks	Noble Sissle
Dan Jackson	Ivan H. Browning
Shorty	Ferdie Robinson
Johnnie Wise	Russell Smith
Mose Washington	Lew Payton
Joe Dolks	Johnny Hudgins
Silas Green	Lee J. Randall
Bookmaker	George Jones, Jr.
Snappy	Charlie Davis
Sandy Scarecrow's Jockey	Curtis Carpenter
Jump Steady	John Alexander, Chic Fisher
In the Bank:	
Bank Policeman	Ferdie Robinson
The Porter	Fred Jennings
Secretary	Valaida Snow
Cashier	Richard Cooper
Bookkeeper	Percy Colston
Draft Clerk	Claude Lawson
Auditor	Addison Carey
Four Harmony Kings (Quartette)	
At the Wedding:	
Mischief	Mildred Smallwood
A Deserted Female	Josephine Baker
Her Bunco Attorney	Lloyd Keyes

Road Show Cast: J. Mardo Brown, Addison Carey, Hattie King, Reavis, Catherine Perry, Andrew A. Copeland, E. Campbell Cauldwell, Lew Payton, "Onions" Jeffrey, Buris Brown, Howard Elmore

Story: (No information)

Musical Numbers: "Mammy's Little Chocolate Cullud Chile," "Have a Good Time Everybody," "That Charleston Dance," "The Slave of Love," "I'll Find My Love in D-I-X-I-E," "There's No Place as Grand as Bandana Land," "The Sons of Old Black Joe," "Jassamine Lane," "Dumb Luck," "Breakin' 'Em Down," "Jockey's Life for Mine," "Dixie Moon," "Down in the Land of Dancing Pickaninnies," "Thinking of Me," "All the Wrongs You've Done to Me," "Manda," "Run on the Bank," "Chocolate Dandies"

Added After New York Opening: "You Ought to Know," "Jazztime
    Baby"
Dropped from the Show Before New York Opening: "There's a
    Million Little Cupids in the Sky"
The show was unique because it featured a simulated horse race on
    the stage using real horses.

CHOCOLATE TOWN (1923)
Producer: Raymond Day
Stage Director: Coy Herndon

Principal Cast of Characters: Coy Herndon, Leon Diggs, Billy
    Arnette, Jazz Warren, Bessie Brown, "Pork Chops" Gibson,
    Cecelia Coleman, Elaine Horn, Louise Washington, Josephine
    Jones, Ernest Montaguas' 18-piece Jazz Band, W. Kelly's Or-
    chestra, Flapper Chorus

Story: (No information)

Musical Numbers:

Act 1

"Hot Lips"	Cecelia Coleman
"Old Lang Syne"	Charles Trice Trio
"Jennie's Jubilee"	"Rastus" Brown
"Bell in the Light House"	Frank Gibson
"May Be Your Man"	Louise Washington
"Long Gone"	Billy Arnete
"Beautiful Moonshine"	Jazz Warren
"Tomorrow"	Leon Diggs and Company

Act 2

"Kicky Koo"	?
"Society"	?
Comedy Sketch: "The Oklahoma Wild Cat Oil Co."	
"The Frolics and Pastimes of 1865"	Entire Company

THE COLORED ARISTOCRATS (1909)
Producers: Irvin C. Miller, Flournoy E. Miller, Aubrey Lyles
Book: Flournoy E. Miller, Aubrey Lyles
Music: Sidney Perrin

Cast of Characters:

Steve Jenkins	Flournoy E. Miller
Sam Peck	Aubrey Lyles
Harry Fast	Irvin C. Miller
Dodson Moseby	Cliff Green
Matilda Moseby	Cassie Burch
Frank Cole	Arthur Malone
Rose Little John	Carmen Lawson
Laberta Birdsong	Vivian Forrest

Mrs. Bootnose	Alice Christy
Mrs. Fainty	Eva Simpson
Mrs. Hatchethead	Georgia Hutchinson
Mrs. Solate	Edith Grodon
Mrs. Meddlesome	Julia Turner
Mrs. Nuffsed	Sourthey DeJole
Policeman 13-13-13	Clyde Brooks
Jim, the Lime Man	Alfonso Walker
Happy Harry	Thomas Pierson

Story: (No information)

Musical Numbers: "Why Moses Never Saw the Promised Land,"
    "Caroline," "Fare Thee Well," "Dreamy Day," "Chocolate
    Mandy," "Meet Me by the Candy Pole," "For the Last Time,
    Call Me Sweetheart," "Pleading Eyes"

COME ALONG MANDY (1924)
Producer: Salem Tutt Whitney, J. Homer Tutt
Book, Lyrics: Whitney and Tutt
Music: Donald Heywood

Principal Cast of Characters: Salem Tutt Whitney, J. Homer Tutt

Story: It all starts in Hopeville, Georgia at what should have been
a peaceful party for Mandy. However, because of Zack and Sudds
it is more like a battle ground because of a dispute over the bound-
ary line between plantations. Lovey Joe tries to act as peacemaker
but only adds to the confusion. Al LaBabor, a thief, poses as a
lawyer when he finds Zack and Sudds so busy fighting, and makes
away with the deeds to their property. The theft is discovered and
the chase leads throughout many exciting scenes with Zack and Sudds,
Joe, Lucinda, and Krispy all acting as detectives. Mandy is invited
to come along and the thief is finally cornered at a reception in New
York. Zack and Sudds shake hands and all ends happily.

Musical Numbers: (No information)

THE CON MAN (1918)
Producer: Billy King

Principal Cast of Characters: Billy King, Howard Kelly, James
    Reed, Bessie Whitman, Ernest Whitman

Story: The story tells of a widow who had a lot of cash left her,
and she wants to get a pet on which to spend her affections. Howard Kelly, playing the part of a coarse hustler, disguises Billy King
as a mongrel dog and takes him around to the widow's house telling
her about how cleverly the dog has been trained. The fact that the
rich widow puts the dog through a lot of stunts provides the major
portion of the comedy of the show. Also, before the widow has

even seen the pair, Kelly has used his pal for everything from a
scarecrow to a marble statue in his efforts to surround some easy
money.

Musical Numbers:
"Rolling Stones"   James Reed
"Real Kind Mamma"   Bessie Whitman
"You're Just Like a Mother to   Ernest Whitman
    Me"
"Cotton Bales"   Billy King

DARKEST AMERICANS (1918), 2 Acts
Producers: Salem Tutt Whitney, J. Homer Tutt
Book, Lyrics: Whitney and Tutt
Musical Director: C. Luckeyth Roberts

Principal Cast of Characters: Salem Tutt Whitney, J. Homer Tutt,
    Emma Jackson, Virginia Wheeler, Al F. Watts, Alonzo Fender-
    son, Julian Keith, William Fountain, Nat Cash, Boots Marshall,
    George Lynch, Lena Stanford Roberts, Carrie King, Estelle
    Cash, Edna Gibbs, Helen Jackson, Ora Dunlop, Tillie Cottman,
    Teresa West, Bertha Yokum, Katie Thompson, Viola Mander,
    Estelle Irvin, Mattie Lewis, Rosina Alexander, Bertha Cottman,
    Ellen Mander, Alica Jason.

Musical Numbers: "Jolly Jazz Joy Ride, " "Blue Fever, " "That
    Creole Flower Garden of Mine, " "The Sambos Will Get You If
    You Don't Watch Out"

DARKEST AMERICANS (1919), 2 Acts
Producers: Salem Tutt Whitney, J. Homer Tutt
Music: C. Luckeyth Roberts

Principal Cast of Characters:
Abraham Dubois Washington   Salem Tutt Whitney
Gabriel Douglass   J. Homer Tutt
Professor, Howard University   Alonzo Fenderson
Dean Kelly Miller, Howard   Alfred E. Watts
    University
R. Vernon, Journalist   Wilber White
President of U. S. A.   Ed Tolliver
Vice-President of U. S. A.   Nat Cash
Red Cap   Sammie Lewin
Others--Lena Sanford Roberts, Estelle Cash, Edna Gibbs, Emma
    Jackson, Virginia Wheeler
Story: Dean Kelly Miller of Howard University, Washington, D. C. ,
goes on an archaeological research trip in the interest of his uni-
versity. Abe and Gabe enter Howard University under false pre-
tense. Dean Kelly Miller is lost and Abe and Gabe are commissioned by the university to search for him. This search carries
them to all parts of the globe and they are the participants in many

exciting and ludicrous adventures.   The Dean is found and returns
home where everything ends happily.

Musical Numbers: (No information)

DARKTOWN AFFAIRS (1929)
Producer: Jake Strouse
Book, Lyrics, Music: Garland Howard, Mae Brown, Speedy Smith,
    Jesse Shipp
Music Director: Stanley Bennett

Cast of Characters:

Hot Stuff Jackson, The Dixie Dude probation officer	Garland Howard
Sally Ann Peppers, Evergreen Pepper's angel child	Miss Mae Brown
Jack Snowball, proprietor of Sundown Hotel	Speedy Smith
Milindy, cook at Sundown Hotel and owner of Hoggery across in Rat Row	Hattie Noles
Diamond Joe, the gigolo	Robert Davis
Liza, just a gal	Kitty Brown
Pinky, a tot	Ada Banks
Sweet Singing Eddie	Joe Loomis
Officer Green	Andrew Copeland
Sarah Go About	Zudora DeGaston
Detective Smart	Leo Broadner
Prophet Jones	Andrew Fairchild
Pansy Sunshine	Angie Mitchell
Just Two Hot Papas	Moxie and Al
Bellboys	Teddy and Eddie
Black Bill, bad man	Coley Grant
Duksy Chinberry	Frank Carter
Miscellaneous Frank ⎫ Members of ⎧	Sam Lee
Keystone Atterbury ⎬ literary club ⎨	Aril Doe
Juniper Wheatley ⎭ ⎩	Jim Glover

Show Girls, Maids, Dancers, Expressmen, Toughs, Roustabouts,
    Village Choir, Rat Row Rowdies, etc.

Story: (No information)

Synopsis:

Act I
Scene 1--Interior of Evergreen Pepper's funeral parlor and living
    room, Sundown, La.
Scene 2--Low Down Street
Scene 3--Sundown Hotel

Act II
Scene 1--Rat Row, across the river
Scene 2--The Stroll
Scene 3--Interior of Evergreen Pepper's funeral parlor.   The Social
    Function Jamboree

Musical Numbers:

Act I

Overture
Opening Chorus   Company
"Home Brew"   Ensemble
"How About Me?"   Hot Stuff, Sally Ann, Pansy,
                                     Dock and Chorus
"Your Sins Will Find You Out"   Liza and Diamond Joe
"Loving Friends"   Hot Stuff and Ensemble
"Page Mr. Jackson"   Sally Ann and Teddy the Bellboy
Hot Foot Dance   Teddy
Social Function Stomp   Milindy
Chicken Bone   Snowball
"Liza"   Sweet Singing Eddie and Liter-
                                     ary Club
"Sally Ann"   Sally Ann, Hot Stuff and En-
                                     semble

Act II

"Milindy"   Company
"Kicking the Mule"   Sarah Goabout, Gals, Red
                                     Lincoln
"Foolishness"   Smart and Pinky
"Walk Together"   Ensemble
"Function Bound"   Al and Moxie
"Going to Miss Me"   Snowball and Sarah Goabout
"Under the Moon"   Sweet Singing Eddie
Dance Porto Rico   Hot Stuff and Sally Ann
"Milindy Blues"   Milindy
"Wedding Day"   Liza
Sally Ann Revival   Company
Finale

DARKTOWN CIRCUS DAY (1903)
Black Patti Troubadours
Book: Bob Cole

Cast of Characters:
Josiah Johnson, the Poo-Bah of   John Green
   Darktown
Marish Johnson, his wife, with   Anthony D. Byrd
   an eye on Josiah
Primus ⎱ (their sons with a   Will A. Cook
Reuben ⎰ love for the circus)   Charles Bougla
Little Willie, their youngest,   James Crosby
   with lengthy aspirations
Momselle Hoplightly, the queen   Ida Forcen [Forsyne]
   of the arena
Professor Blackenback, with a   J. Ed. Green
   circus on his hands
Handy Andy, with troubles of   Bobby Kemp
   his own
Policeman 7-11, a guardian of   Leslie Triplett
   the peace

Bill Barber, a circus pealer   Mac Allen
    with the dope
Henri Tenori, from the opera   James Worles
Percy Hamfat, an actor   J. P. Reed
Bells of Darktown--Bessie Gillam, Nettie Lewis, Jeanetta Murphy,
    Olivette Williams, Sarah Green, Emma Thompson, Lizzie Tay-
    lor, Maude Turner, Henrietta Percaud, Mable Turner, Ella
    Carr
Candy Butchers, Peanut Vendors, Animal Attendants, Actors,
    Actresses, Freaks, Monkeys, Bears, Elephants and Others

Synopsis:
                            Part I
Time--Present
Scene 1.   Exterior of Darktown Circus
Scene 2.   Interior of Darktown Circus
Scene 3.   Interior of Theatre
Musical Numbers:
"When the Circus Comes to   Chorus
    Town"
"Strolling Around the Circus   Entire Company
    Tent"
"Castle on the Nile"   James Crosby and Company
"What Became of the Monk"   Messrs. Kemp, Byrd, Crosby
                                          and Triplett
"Mandy"   Ida Forcen and Chorus
"Ain't Going to Stay Here Any   John Green and Chorus
    Longer"
"Under the Bamboo Tree"   Nettie Lewis and Bobby Kemp
Finale--Buck Dancing Contest
    (Intermission)
                            Part II
Emma Thompson   Comedienne
Around the Camp Fires in the
    Philippines
James Crosby, Bon Mots of 1903
    Sisseretta Jones   The Black Patti
Bobby Kemp's Wang Doodle Four   Black Wire Equilibris
    Mac Allen
William Nicholas   Mimic
Selections for Grand and Comic Opera in Costume--Sisseretta Jones
    (Black Patti); Sarah Green, Contralto; James E. Worles, Tenor;
    J. Ed. Green, Baritone; James P. Reed, Bass; and a chorus
    selected from the best Negro voices in the country
Conspirator's Chorus (Mme.   Company
    Angot)
"Miserere" (Trovatore)   Black Patti, J. E. Worles and
                                          Chorus
"In Lovers Lane"   James P. Reed
"Behold the Queen" (Ensemble)   Chorus
"Waltz Song" (Belle of New   Black Patti and Company
    York)
"Quintette" (Martha)   Black Patti, Sarah Green, James

Worles, J. Ed. Green and A.
D. Byrd
Orchestra Selections--Anton Gloeckner, Musical Director
March--In Dahomey, Johns
Overture--Ceitic, St. Clair
Revelie--Falling Star, Richmond
Waltzes--Hearts Courageous, Blanke
Characteristic--Nasturium, Jones
March--Ching a Ling a Loo, Hoffman

Chorus Line of J. Leubrie Hill's "Darktown Follies" Company,
circa 1913

DARKTOWN FOLLIES (1916 edition)
Producer: J. Leubrie Hill
Book: Alex Rogers
Lyrics, Music, Staging: J. Leubrie Hill

Cast of Characters:
Dora Dean	J. Leubrie Hill
Jim Thomas	Opal Cooper
Andrew J. Dean	Dink Stewart
Pop Potter	J. W. Mobley
Elder Crawford	DeKovan Thompson
Professor Payne	Alonzo Fenderson
Cicero W. Jones	Alex Rogers
Toussaint L'Ouverture Brown	Jim Burris
Buddy Boyd	Charles Woody

Six Trip Around the World Girls: Bessie Breece, Evon Robinson,
    Nellie Newton, Marjorie Shipp, Philis Phavor, Hilda Oftley,
    Clara Charrington, Sadie Tapin, Irene Inlington, Emma Ceruti,
    Ruth Richardson, Elida Webb

Uncle Joe	J. W. Mobley
Stenographer	Julia Rector
Murray Jib	J. W. Mobley
Jake	Opal Cooper
Nellie Newton, a Chorus Girl	Irma Baptiste
Jerk	Babe Townsend
Court Officer	Hamilton White
Court Clerk	Samuel Billig
Judge	Alex Rogers
Hoola	Bessie Simms

Zola   Josephine Larro
Boola   Lackaye Grant
Sing Ki   Arthur T. Ray
Yippi Ki-Yink   Gerti Townsend
Isha, Temporary Ruler of   Opal Cooper
    Somali Land
High Yaller Man   Elliot Scott

Story: (No information)

Synopsis of Scenes:
Act 1
Scene 1.   Living room of Andrew Jackson Dean's home, Tuscaloosa,
    Alabama, about 10 o'clock at night (ten hours are supposed to
    elapse between scenes 1 and 2)
Scene 2.   Outside of the railroad station, Tuskegee, Alabama (no
    time elapses between scenes 1 and 2)
Scene 3.   Lawn in front of Tuskegee's (Institute) main building (five
    minutes has elapsed between scenes 2 and 3)
Scene 4.   Corridor leading to Dean's Office (no time has elapsed
    between scenes 3 and 4)
Scene 5.   Interior of Dean's Office
Act 2
(Two days are supposed to have elapsed between Acts 1 and 2)
Scene 1.   Exterior of Pekin Theatre, Chicago, Illinois (no time
    elapses between scenes 1 and 2)
Scene 2.   Stage of Pekin Theatre (several hours are supposed to
    have elapsed between scenes 2 and 3)
Scene 3.   Interior of court room (fifteen days are supposed to have
    elapsed between scenes 3 and 4)
Scene 4.   Honolulu (about three weeks are supposed to have elapsed
    between scenes 4 and 5)
Scene 5.   China (about one month is supposed to have elapsed be-
    tween scenes 5 and 6)
Scene 6.   Outskirts of Somaliland (five days are supposed to have
    elapsed between scenes 6 and 7)
Scene 7.   Interior of Palace--Somaliland
Act 3
(One month is supposed to have elapsed between Acts 2 and 3)
Scene 1.   Exterior of cabaret building (no time elapses between
    scenes 1 and 2)
Scene 2.   Interior of cafe and cabaret

Musical Numbers:
Opening Chorus, "Musical   Company
    Pleasure"
"Trombone Man"   Ruth Ruffin and Chorus
Trombone Solo   J. W. Mobley
"Lou My Lou"   Tim Thomas
"Goodby Forever"   Ensemble, J. Leubrie Hill and
                                      Chorus
"Here, There and Everywhere"   Alex Rogers, Jim Burris,
                                      Charles Woody

"Tuskegee"	Ensemble, Company
"Keep a Little Love Light Burning"	Irma Baptiste
"Summer Nights"	Tuskegee Sextette
"Darktown Follies Dance"	Senior Girls, High School Cadet Boys
"When the Right Boy Comes Along"	Bessie Breece
"Do Re Mi Ragtime"	Dancing Darktown Follies Girls and Boys
"Ragtime"	Dink Stewart and Chorus

Act 4

"Sure Cure for the Blues"	Nina
"Hoola-Boola Love Song"	Opal Cooper, Hunt, Irma Baptiste and Chorus
Dance	Bessie Simms
"Chink, Chink Babe"	Arthur T. Ray, Gerti Townsend and Chorus
"It's a Long Way from Here to Dixie"	Six Trip Around the World Girls (see cast)
"Milo"	Creighton Thompson and Invisible Male Chorus
Dance-Ragtime Soldier Boys	Darktown Follies Boys
"Syncopation"	Bessie Breece and Entire Company

Act 5

Dance-Darktown Follies Buck and Wing	Eddie Rector and Ruth Ruffin
"Cabaret Shows"	Dora Dean and Company
Two Different Styles of Dancing	Lackaye Grant, Bessie Simms and Ruth Ruffin
Grand Finale-"Goodby Ragtime"	Opal Cooper and Entire Company

Executive Staff of "Darktown Follies": Press Representative, David Galwey; Business Manager, Leon Williams; Stage Manager, Babe Townsend; Assistant Stage Manager, Hamilton White; Musical Director, Clarence G. Wilson; Stage Carpenter, J. W. Ellis; Property Master, J. F. Murphy; Electrician, Al Gorda; Wardrobe Mistress, Mme. Florrie; Costumes by Mathiev.

DARKTOWN SCANDALS (1927)
Producer: Eddie Hunter
Book: Eddie Hunter

Principal Cast of Characters: Eddie Hunter (Rastus Lime), Sidney Easton, Billy Mitchell, Maggie Johnson, Martha Copeland (singer, dancer), Julia Moody, Raymond Campbell, Edward Farrow.

Story: The plot concerns the organizing of a Steamship Company in a Southern town. The salesman of the company winds up running a gin mill. He is arrested and imprisoned for his activities, but he manages to escape.

DARKYDOM (1915)
Producer: Lester A. Walton
Book: Henry Troy
Lyrics: Henry S. Creamer
Music: Will Marion Cook, James Reese Europe

Cast of Characters:

Mose Montgomery, a Barber	Cliff Green
Bransford Johnson, a Son of Rest	Will A. Cook
Aloysius Washington, a Son of Rest	Allie Gilliam
Mrs. Ethel Green, a Manicurist	Fannie Wise
Henry Shaw, a Valet	Henry Troy
Jefferson Dibb, a Nut	DeKoven Thompson
Mrs. Hazel Black, Air Insurance Agent	Hilda Oftley
Ah Sing, a Chinaman	Frank Walker
Mrs. Top Note, a Teacher of Music	Abbie Mitchell
Steven Jenkins ⎫ Two Crosstie Sam Peck ⎭ Inspectors	Flournoy E. Miller Aubrey L. Lyles

Story: (No information)

Musical Numbers:

"Cairo"	Fannie Wise
"Lady's Lips"	Abbie Mitchell
"Mammy"	Opel Cooper
"The Ghost Ship"	Creighton Thompson
"Scay-A-Da-Hootch," dance	Ida Forsyne
"Magnolia Time"	Nettie Anderson
"Dreamy Town"	Lillian Grade (song written by one Clarence Williams)
"Rat-A-Tat"	Helen Baxter

THE DEVIL (1922)
Producer: Quintard Miller

Principal Cast of Characters:

The Devil	Purcelle Cuff
Young Man	Quintard Miller
Poverty	Henrietta Lovelass
Young Man's Friend	"Monkey" Johnson
Marion Ablaunche	Soubrette
Purity	Helen Chapelle
One Lung, a Chinaman	Eugene Shields
Others: Ruby Jones, Catherine Peace, Estelle Cash	

Story: The plot of the story involves the attempt of the Devil to lure a young man into the path of ruin and destruction. However,

a friend of the young man, who was not tempted by the devil, res-
cues the young man by "shooting up" the Chinese "dive" where he
(the young man) has been lured.

Musical Numbers: (No information)

DINAH* (1923), 2 Acts, 10 Scenes, 18 Musical Numbers
Producer: Irvin C. Miller
Book: Irvin C. Miller
Lyrics and Music: Tim Brymn

Cast of Characters:

Policeman	Lemuel Jackson
Uncle Joe Davis	Will A. Cook
Lucinda	Florence Brown
Mandy	May Barnes
Diral Davis	Margaret Simms
Walter Davis	Cecil Rivers
Sambo Johnson	Sterling Grant
Uncle Amos	Archie Cross
Corine	Ethel Ridley
Sam Sykes	Doe Doe Green
Sambo Smith	Irvin C. Miller
Slow Kid	Billy Mills
Dinah Lee	Gertrude Saunders
Just Different	Harry Smith
Harry Jenkins	Alonzo Fenderson

Dinah Dancing Girls--Aurora Greely, Blanche Thompson, Millie
    Cook, Helen Fenderson, Glaydes Scott, Alberta Baker, Sylvia
    Collins, Alberta Boyd
Honey Girls--Angeline Hammond, Helen Reed, Eva Carriera, Bessie
    Williams, Coressa Madison, Roberta Lowery, Helen Jackson,
    Daisy James
Dandy Sambos--Lloyd Mitchell, Charles Lawrence, Percy Wintters,
    Aberdeen All, Willis Cross, Albert Flasher

Story: The story has to do with a young man stealing the inheritance of his niece whose guardian, his father, was to invest in stock
in a dance hall that the town is building. It turns out that the money he stole was not his niece's, but had been found in a haunted
house and was supposed to be returned to the bank.

Musical Numbers: (No information)

DIXIE GOES HIGH HAT (1938)
Producer: Flournoy E. Miller

---

*In this show the famous Blackbottom dance was first danced in
New York by Ethel Ridley.

Cast of Characters:

Steve Jenkins	Flournoy E. Miller
Ceason Jones	Mantan Moreland
Ma Jenkins	Mae Turner
Georgie	Marguerite Robinson
Sally Jenkins	Dorothy Dandridge
Harry Hopkins	Otis Rene
Marmadulie Sylvane	Rudolph Toombs
Elder Loore	Spencer Williams
Half Dollar Bill	Leonard Christmas
Cindy	Juneda Carter
Jackson	Marcus Slayter
Mose	Quintard Miller
Socrates	Jessie Cryner
Solomon	Leonard Dixon
Owl	George Cooper

Story: Miller and Mantan escape on a plane from the all colored village of "Jim Town" to Africa.

Musical Numbers: (No information)

DIXIE TO BROADWAY (1924)
Producer: Lew Leslie
Book: Walter DeLeon, Tom Howard, Lew Leslie, Sidney Lazarus
Lyrics: Grant Clarke, Roy Turk
Music: George W. Meyer, Arthur Johnston

Principal Cast of Characters: Florence Mills, Shelton Brooks, Hamtree Harrington, Will Vodery, Plantation Orchestra, Cora Green, Johnny Nit, Willie Covan, U. S. Thompson

Synopsis:

Act I

Scene 1--Prologue--Evolution of the Colored Race
Scene 2--
"Put Your Old Bandanna On"

Danny Small, Maud Russell, the Plantation Chocolate Drops and the Plantation Steppers

Scene 3--
"Dixie Dreams"   Florence Mills and Company
Scene 4--
"A Few Steps in Front of the   The Plantation Steppers
    Curtain"
Scene 5--"Treasure Castle" by Tom Howard
Sam   Hamtree Harrington
Slim   Shelton Brooks
Charlie   Danny Small
Svengali   William DeMott
Scene 6--
"He Only Comes to See Me   Cora Green
    Once in a While"

Scene 7--
"Jungle Nights in Dixieland"   Florence Mills and the Planta-
                                       tion Chocolate Drops
Scene 8--
"Prisoners Up-To-Date"   Johnny Nit, Byron Jones, Lew
                                       Keene
Scene 9--"The Right of Way" by Walter DeLeon and Lew Leslie
The Cop   Walter Crumbley
The Victim   Hamtree Harrington
Mr. and Mrs.   Shelton Brooks and Maud Russell
Miss High Hat   Cora Green
(Oldsmobile used in this scene from Boston Oldsmobile Company)
Scene 10--"Mandy, Make Up Your Mind"
The Groom   Florence Mills
The Bride   Alma Smith
Bridesmaids   Billy Cain, E. Moses, Gwendo-
                                       lyn Graham, Anita Rivera,
                                       Jerry Clarke, Marian Tyler
4 Maids of Honor   Maud Russell, Lillian Brown,
                                       Eva Metcalf, Aida Ward
4 Best Men   Danny Small, Juan Harrison,
                                       Ralph Love, Charles Foster
Scene 11--
"Hanging Around"   Hamtree Harrington and Cora
                                       Green
Scene 12--
"Jazz Time Came from the   Florence Mills, Alma Smith,
   South"   Billy Cain
Scene 13--
"Jazz Time Came from the   Entire Company
   South"

                          Act II
Scene 14--
"If My Dream Came True"   Juan Harrison
Scene 15--"If My Dream Came True"--First Episode
"Georgia Cohans"   Willie Covan, Byron Jones,
                                       Charlie Walker

     --Second Episode
"Eva Tanquays"   Alma Smith, Billy Cain, E.
                                       Moses, Gwendolyn Graham,
                                       Anita Rivera

     --Third Episode
"Gallagher & Shean"   U. S. Thompson, Lew Keene,
                                       Danny Small, Ralph Love,
                                       Brown and William DeMott

     --Fourth Episode
"Belasco's Kiki"   Marian Tyler, Theresa West,
                                       E. Meadows, Jerry Clarke,
                                       Anita Rivera, Aida Ward,
                                       Eva Metcalf, Natalie Cald-
                                       well

     --Fifth Episode
"George Walker"   Snow Fisher, Johnny Nit, Dick
                                       Whalen

--Sixth Episode
"Bert Williams"   Shelton Brooks, Sam Vander-
                                        hurst, Charles Foster

Scene 16--Shelton Brooks
Scene 17--"Darkest Russia" (with apologies to the eminent Balieff
    and Morris Gest)
"Katinkas"   Danny Small and the Plantation
                                        Chocolate Drops

"Wooden Soldiers"   Florence Mills and Plantation
                                        Steppers

Scene 18--
"The Sailor and the Chink"   Winfred and Brown
Scene 19--
"Dixie Wildflowers"   Cora Green and the Plantation
                                        Chocolate Drops

Scene 20--
"I'm a Little Blackbird Looking   Florence Mills
    for a Blue Bird"
Scene 21--"A Nice Husband" by Sidney F. Lazarus
The Maid   Maud Russell
Georgette   Cora Green
Freddy   Hamtree Harrington
Jimmy   Shelton Brooks
Scene 22-
"Dance Specialty"   U. S. Thompson and Willie
                                        Covan

Scene 23-
"Trottin' to the Land of Cotton   Cora Green, Danny Small and
    Melodies"   Entire Company
Scene 24--Finale   Entire Company

DR. BEANS FROM BOSTON (1912), 3 Acts
Producer: S. H. Dudley
Music: Will H. Vodery
Lyrics: Henry S. Creamer

Cast of Characters:
Mr. Waterbury Lee, Proprietor   Arthur Talbot
    of Bay Shores Hotel
Miss Susie Lee, his Daughter   Daisy Martin
Bill Simmons, a Hustler   James Burris
Larry Smith, a Druggist   Henry Troy
Jimmy Quickste, a Messenger   Roley Gibson
Alex, a waiter   William Ramsey
Dr. Beans from Boston   Frank DeLyons
Madam Sahara Heartburne,   Ella Revans
    Primadonna
Queen Sophenia, a Fortune   Robert Williams
    Teller
Jessie Jenkins, a Telephone   Robert Williams
    Agent
A Cash Girl   Hattie Burris
A Drug Clerk   Jessie Harris

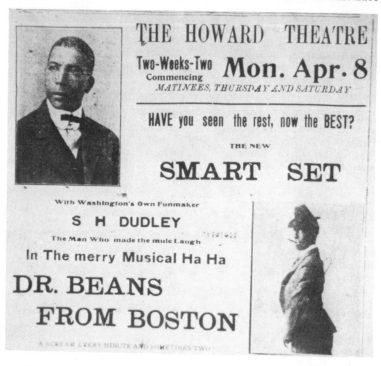

Ad for "Dr. Beans from Boston," Starring S. H. Dudley, circa 1912

Patric, Butt's Friend   S. H. Dudley's Mule
Gymnasium Butts, Ex-Minstrel   S. H. Dudley
Bathing Girls--Hattie Smith, Marie Hendrick, Erline Brown, Carrie
    Sutton
Babies--Tillie Cottman, Rosana Alexander, Ida Bindford, Maggie
    Sewell
Auto Girls--Jennie Hillman, Jessie Harris, Belle Morgan, Dora
    Weaver
Matrons--Hattie Burris, Lizzie Carrington, Beatrice Owens, Belle
    Walcott
Boys--William Ramsey, Robert Williams, Harry Watson, Billy
    Moore, James Reed, Frank DeLyons, Arthur Wilson, J. Harris

Story: The plot of "Dr. Beans from Boston" deals with the adventures of Gymnasium Butts, who passes himself off as the real Dr.
Beans, and gets possession of a drug store.   His confederate is
Bill Simmons, whose suggestions are usually accepted and carried
out.   The principal asset of the drug store is a love potion, which
the comedian finds after a diligent search, and then gives, in large
quantities, to Susie Lee, for whom his heart palpitates.   It is while
Gymnasium Butts is "going big" with Susie Lee that the real Dr.

Beans from Boston comes on the scene while a big dance is going
on at Buckroe Beach. When confronted by the real thing, the im-
poster grabs a club and tries to make a home run with Dr. Beans'
head, evidently so shaking up the latter's mental faculties that he
forgets just what and who he is. So that there was a happy ending
for Gymnasium Butts.

Synopsis:

Act 1

Scene 1.   Exterior of the Bay Shore Hotel
Scene 2.   The Beach Drug Store

Act 2

The Summer Garden at the Bay Shore Hotel
Time: In June
Place: Buckroe Beach, Virginia
(Note: Buckroe Beach was an actual summer resort for black peo-
    ple in the early 1900's, and during each season was crowded
    with visitors from all over the country, and was considered one
    of the prettiest spots in Virginia.)

Musical Numbers:

Act 1

Opening Chorus	Ensemble
"Sunshine"	Daisy Martin and Chorus
"Messenger Boy"	Roley Gibson and Male Quartette
"Virginia"	James Burris and Chorus
"Bathing"	Ella Bevans and Girls
"Rain"--Finale	Entire Company

Act 2

"Idle Dream"--Opening	Chorus
"Dearest Memories"	Henry Troy and Chorus
"Let's Make Love"	Daisy Martin and Chorus
"Dr. Beans from Boston"	S. H. Dudley and Chorus
Old Virginia Dance	S. H. Dudley, Daisy Martin, and Chorus

Act 3

"Drinking"--Opening	Chorus
"Eternity"	Henry Troy
"What Did I Say That For?"	S. H. Dudley
Grand Finale	Entire Chorus

DUMB LUCK (1922), 2 Acts 12 Scenes
Producer: Moss and Frye

Principal Cast of Characters: Moss and Frye, Revella Hughes,
    Justa (toe dancer), Alberta Hunter, Boots Marshall, Dick Wells,
    Ruby Mason, Will Elkins, Male Glee Club, Joe Bright (as
    county sheriff), Lawrence Criner, India Allen (in blackface),
    Cleo Desmond (as the mother)

Synopsis: The story deals with Tom Wilson (Moss), and Jerry
Walsh (Frye) who leave Honeysuckle, South Carolina to sell some

home products and their triumphant return, which they had antici-
pated might be followed by a jail sentence, but instead was the occasion of much hilarity.   The scenes take place in Honeysuckle, New
Orleans, and Argentina.

Musical Numbers: "My Old Kentucky Home Sweet Home," "Little
    Red Shawl," "Melody of Love," "Strolling," "Argentina Says
    Farewell"

THE EDDIE HUNTER CO. (TABLOID) (1922), 1 Act, 2 Scenes
    (Title Not Known)
Producer: Eddie Hunter
Book: Eddie Hunter
Music: William Fountain

Principal Cast of Characters:
Forger   Eddie Hunter
Aristocratic Hostess   Evon Robinson
Warden   William Fountain
Guard   James (Jim) Burris
Others--Alec Lovejoy, Madeline Belt, Nina Hunter, Erstelle Aiken,
    May LaVere, Sonia Somers, Al Curtis, Lawrence Dewson, Dick
    Conway

Story: The story is about the arrest and escape of a forger.   The
arrest occurs during a social affair at the home of an aristocratic
hostess.

THE EMPEROR OF DIXIE (1908), 2 Acts
Producer: No Information

Cast of Characters:
Bill Skeemar, Lina's Sweetheart   Walter Crumbley
Plain Sam, Just Barely Living,   E. I. Henderson
    That's All
Amos Johnson, a Wealthy Old   S. H. Lane
    Farmer
Betty Johnson, his Wife who   Odessa Crosby
    Craves Notoriety
Mandy, her Cousin, a Village   Carlene Jefferson
    Flirt
Sally Thompson, Mrs. John-   Corinne Brown
    son's Sister
Eph Thompson, her Mischievous   Sidney Perrin
    Son
Professor Quickstep, a Poet,   Arthur Rhoads
    Vocalist and Dancing Master
Captain Hardy, the Hearty Cap-   Jack Johnson
    tain on a Furlough
Phoebie, the Captain's Sweet-   Mena Caldwell
    heart

Vardefoots, of the Village   T. White
Prince Black, in Search of an   F. L. Mitchell
    Heiress
Skagga, a Village Weary who   Billy Bradley
    Does Chores
Areta   Ada Fisher
Tulip   Leona Miller
Lucy   Daisy Miller
Mme. Belle   Myrtle Freeman

Story: (No information)

Musical Numbers:

Act 1

Opening Chorus   Entire Company
"When De Dinner Horn Blows"   Perrin, Rhoads, White, Crumb-
                                        ley, Butler
"I've a Never Dying Love All   Corrine Brown
    For You"
"The Emperor of Dixie"   Walter Crumbley
"When the Trees Shed Their   J. Johnson and Miss Caldwell
    Leaves in the Fall"
"Give Me My Three Nickels"   E. L. Henderson
"When the Band Played Old   Walter Crumbley and Chorus
    Yankee Doodle Dandy"

Act 2

Opening Chorus, "Drink and Be   Entire Company
    Merry"
"The Tallaho Song"   Entire Company
"Salam"   F. L. Mitchell and Chorus
"All Hail the Prince"   Entire Company
"Much Obliged to You"   E. L. Henderson
"Emperor of Dixie," Grand   Entire Company
    Finale

EPHRAHAM JOHNSON FROM NORFOLK (1908), 3 Acts
    (Bijou Stock Co.)
Producer: No Information
Book: Flournoy E. Miller, Marion Brooks
Staging: Marion A. Brooks

Cast of Characters:
Ephraham L. Johnson, from   James Moore
    Norfolk
Bill Smart, Looking for Money   Flournoy E. Miller
Harry Blue, Eph's Friend from   Marion A. Brooks
    Home
Johnny Fast, a Wise Boy who   Master Dozzel
    Strayed from Home
Harry Wilkes, a Social Leader   Henderson Bowen
Dick Stopen, Some Detective   Irvin Jones
Mrs. Flanders, the Widow   Ivy Hubbard

Fanny Lenox, News Reporter   Carmen Lawson
Barth Lewis, Very Stylish   Blanch Arlington

Story: (No information)

Musical Numbers:

Act 1

Opening Chorus--"Society"   Entire Company
"Hard to Love Somebody When   Blanch Arlington
    Somebody Don't Love You"
"Here Today but When Tomor-   Flournoy E. Miller and Chorus
    row Comes, I'll Be Gone"
"Napinee"   Tom Overton and Boys
"On One Summer Night"   Dixie Mattison and Boys

Act 2

Opening Chorus--"Since You   C. W. Atkins
    Called Me Dear"
"I'd Like to Know Your Ad-   Camden Lawson and Flournoy
    dress"   E. Miller
"Darktown Grenadiers"   Henderson Bowen and Chorus

Act 3

Opening Chorus--"What Will   Henderson Bowen and Chorus
    Your Answer Be?"
"I Want You"   Ivy Hubbard and James Moore
"Nuf Sed"   James Moore and Ivy Hubbard

EXPLOITS IN AFRICA (1919)
Producer: Billy King

Principal Cast of Characters: Billy King, Billy Higgins, Marguerite
    Scott, Ernest R. Whitman, Theresa Brooks, Gertrude Saunders

Story: (No information)

Musical Numbers:
"Bleeding Moon"   Marguerite Scott
    (assisted by Ernest Whitman)
"You Can't Get Lovin' When   Theresa Brooks
    There Ain't No Lovin' "
"Itsy Bitsy Doll"   Gertrude Saunders

FAST AND FURIOUS (1931)
Producer: Forbes Randolph
Music, Lyrics: Gordon and Revel
Additional Music: J. Rosamond Johnson, Porter Grainger, Joe
    Jordan, Allie Wrubel
Sketches: Forbes Randolph, John Wells, Zora Neal Hurston, Tim
    Moore, Clinton (Dusty) Fletcher, Jackie Mabley
Orchestra Director: Joe Jordan

Synopsis:
Introduction
To establish the atmosphere of this production the stage is set to
represent a street in Waycross, Georgia, as soon as the doors of
the theatre are opened.   Early comers may witness the inhabitants
of Waycross engaged at "woofing."   "Woofing" is the term employed
by the Negroes of the South to describe their animated, self-
laudatory conversation.

   During this introduction two songs never before heard in the
North will be introduced.   They are "John Henry" and "East Coast
Blues"; they originated in the colored work camps of the South. --
Forbes Randolph
Overture
Singing by Fast and Furious Quartet and Rosamond Johnson Quartet
Parody of "The Band Wagon"
   "Fast and Furious"

Sung by	Grace Smith
Danced by	4 Dancing Boys and Chorus

(Music and lyrics by Gordon and Revel)
   "The Last Word" by Tim Moore

The Husband	Tim Moore
The Wife	Baby Goins

   "In the Cigar Store" by Clinton (Dusty) Fletcher

Proprietor	Clinton (Dusty) Fletcher
First Customer	Grace Smith
Second Customer	Juano Hernandez
Third Customer	Russell Lee

   "Walking On Air"

Sung by	Orlando Roberson
Danced by	Chickieta Martin, Wilhelmina Wade and Chorus

(Music and lyrics by Gordon and Revel)
Baby Goins
Theatre Pantomime
With apologies to Mazie Gay, "Cochrane's Revue," London, 1929.
   "Frowns"

Sung by	Lois Deppe

(Music and lyrics by Gordon and Revel)
   "The Three Dames Ziegfeld Failed to Glorify"

Sung by	Lee (Boots) Marshall, Melva Boden, and Gene Donnell

(Music and lyrics by Porter Grainger)
   "Rumbatism"

Sung by	Lily (Pontop) Yuen and Jackie Mabley
Danced by	Miss Yuen and Chorus

(Music and lyrics by Gordon and Revel)
   "So Lonesome"

Sung by	Orlando Roberson

(Music and lyrics by Joe Jordan and Rosamond Johnson)
   "The Court Room" by Zora Neale Hurston

Judge	Tim Moore

Clerk of Court	Maurice Ellis
Prosecuting Attorney	Clarence Todd
Lawyer	Lloyd Mitchell
Officer Simpson	Melva Boden
John Barnes	Juano Hernandez
Cliff Mullins	Russell Lee
Mrs. Mullins	Jackie Mabley
Jessie Smith	Emma Maitland
A Lawyer	Lloyd Mitchell
Eva	Etta Moten

"The Silent Bootlegger" by Clinton (Dusty) Fletcher

The Bootlegger	Clinton (Dusty) Fletcher
First Customer	Grace Smith
Second Customer	Baby Goins
Detective	Clarence Todd

"Gymnasium"

Sung by	Neeka Shaw
Dances by	Neeka Shaw, Jackie Mabley, and Chorus
Boxing by	Aurelia Wheeldin and Emma Maitland

(Music and lyrics by Gordon and Revel)

Edna Guy

Madrassi Nautch (East Indian street dance)
(Through the courtesy of Miss Ruth St. Denis)

Gracie Smith

"Raid on Jake's" by Tim Moore

Jake	Tim Moore
Dizzy	Melva Boden
A Guest	Etta Moten
Another Guest	Earl Shanks
Two Detectives {	Juano Hernandez Joe Willis
Other Guests	Maurice Ellis, Billy Wallace, Lloyd Mitchell, and Aurelia Wheeldin

Frank Walker

"Shadows on the Wall"

Sung by	Etta Moten
Shadows	Clarence Todd, Joe Willis, Earl Shanks, Lloyd Mitchell, and Marion Hairston

(Music and lyrics by Gordon and Revel)

"Scene on 135th Street" by Jackie Mabley

Mrs. Smith	Jackie Mabley
Mr. Smith	Melva Boden
Detective	Maurice Ellis
Policeman	Joe Willis

"Boomerang"

Sung by	Midgie Lane
Danced by	Helmsley Winfield, Midgie Lane, and Chorus

(Music and lyrics by Rosamond Johnson and Joe Jordan)

Rhumba Band
Dance by   Senorita Ofelia Diaz
Song by   Fast and Furious Quartet
  "Jacob's Ladder"
Elder Simmons   Lois Deppe
Cigarette Girl   Neeka Shaw
Rhythm Girl   Marion Hairston
Cabaret Dancer   Midgie Lane
Singing Waiters   Messrs. Todd, Willis, Mitchell,
                                          Shanks
Number King   Gilbert Holland
Danny   Helmsley Winfield
Sisters and Brothers of the   Forbes Randolph's Choir
  Church
Guests at the Cabaret
(Conceived and written by Rosamond Johnson and Allie Wrubel)
Act II
  "Football Game" by Zora Neal Hurston
Capt. of Howard's Team   Tim Moore
Capt. of Lincoln's Team   Clinton (Dusty) Fletcher
Referee   Lois Deppe
Cheerleaders   Jackie Mabley and Zora
                                          Hurston
Lincoln's Wrestler   Gilbert Holland
Howard's Wrestler   Juano Hernandez
Teams, Bands, Chorus, and Choir.
  "Happy Ending"
Sung by   Ruby Elzy
(Music and lyrics by Gordon and Revel)
  "Hot Feet"
Sung by   Neeka Shaw
Danced by   Al Richard, Midgie Lane, and
                                          Chorus
(Music and lyrics by Gordon and Revel)
  "Pansies" by Lottie Meaney
Young Man   Helmsley Winfield
Business Man   Russell Lee
Gardner   Lee (Boots) Marshall
  "The Flowers"
Orchid   Melva Boden
Violet   Jean Donnell
Forget-me-not   Alexander Moody
Lily   Larri Loerear
Daffydill   Penman Lovingood
Dancing Pansies   Thos. Smith, Edw. Jones,
                                          Frank Walker, and Maurice
                                          Young
(Music and lyrics by Porter Grainger)
  "Poker Game" by Zora Neal Hurston
Nunky   Clinton (Dusty) Fletcher
Tush Hog   Tim Moore
Too Sweet   Clarence Todd
Sack Daddy   Russell Lee

Black Baby   Maurice Ellis
Peckerwood   Juano Hernandez
Mrs. Dilson   Jackie Mabley
   "Hell"
Tushog   Tim Moore
Nunky   Clinton (Dusty) Fletcher
First Assistant to the Devil   Frederic A. Wheeldin
Second Assistant to the Devil   Carl H. Taylor
The Devil   Grace Smith
The Angel   Edna Guy
Too Sweet   Clarence Todd
Sack Daddy   Russell Lee
Peckerwood   Juano Hernandez
Black Baby   Maurice Ellis
Imps, Angels, and Sojourners in Hell
   "Road to Heaven"
The Devil   Grace Smith
Singing by   Messrs. Shanks, Willis, Todd,
                                             and Mitchell

   "Heaven"
The Lord   Lois Deppe
Angel Gabriel   Maurice Ellis
Angel Michael   Russell Lee
The Devil   Grace Smith
Singing by   Messrs. Shanks, Willis, Todd,
                                             and Mitchell
                      Al Richard
   "Macbeth" by John Wells and Wm. Shakespeare
The Doctor   Melva Boden
A Gentlewoman   Etta Moten
Lady Macbeth   Jackie Mabley
A Servant   Earl Shanks
Seyton   Juano Hernandez
Macbeth   Tim Moore
A Messenger   Joe Willis
Young Siward   Maurice Ellis
MacDuff   Clinton (Dusty) Fletcher
King of Scotland   Russell Lee
Prompter   Clarence Todd
   "Modernistic"
Sung by   Lily (Pontop) Yuen
Danced by   Miss Yuen and Chorus
(Music and lyrics by Porter Grainger)
                 Fast and Furious Quartet
   "Asaka-Saba (Dance of the Moods)"
Danced by   Helmsley Winfield
(Music by Porter Grainger)
                 Clinton (Dusty) Fletcher
         Rhumba Band and Four Dancing Boys
   "Snowball Blues"
Forbes Randolph's Choir and Dancing Girls
Forbes Randolph's Choir--
   Girls: Ruby Greene, Sibol Cain, Ruby Elzy, Gladys Freeland,

Marion Hairston, Rosina Lefroy, Emma Maitland, Julia Mitchell,
Aurelia Wheeldin, Billy Wallace.
Boys: Cecil Burrows, Jean Donnell, Maurice Ellis, Element D.
Hall, Larri Loerear, Penman Lovingood, Alexander O. Moody,
Carl H. Taylor, Frederic A. Wheeldin.
Dancing Girls--Doris Alexander, Juanita Boisseau, Bertie Boyd,
Thelma Brunder, Mary Goodwin, Marion Green, Virginia
Groves, Chickita Martin, Inez Persaud, Carolyne Rich, Edna
Richardson, Evelyn Sheppard, Katherine Upshur, Wilhelmina
Wade, Pearl White, Grace Hall, Cleopatria Ward.
Dancing Boys--Edward Jones, Thomas Smith, Frank Walker,
Maurice Young.

FASTSTEPPERS (1930)
Producer: Mabel Whitman

Principal Cast of Characters: Whitman Sisters (Alberta, Alice,
Essie), Willie "Toosweet," "Show Boy" and "Cut-Out," "Pops"
Whitman, Joey Jones, Leona Curry, Frank McClennon, "Five
Oke Boys," Elfreda Orman, Margaret Watkins, Annie Mae Price

Musical Numbers:

"Why Can't You Love Me That Way?"	Alberta and Alice Whitman
"I Don't Want Your Kisses"	Alberta and Alice Whitman
"When My Dreams Come True"	Lena Curry
"Honeysuckle Rose"	Alice Whitman and Chorus
"He's So Unusual"	Margaret Watkins
"At the End of the Road"	Annie Mae Price
"Am I Blue"	Annie Mae Price

FOLLOW ME (1923 edition), 2 Acts, 16 Scenes, 24 Songs
Producer: I. M. Weingarden

Principal Cast of Characters: Valaida Snow (introducer), Billy Hig-
gins, Ernest Whitman, Clifford Ross, Julian Costello, Julia
Moody, Coleman Troy, Edna Taylor, Sallie Gates, Sylvia
Mitchell, William Gunn, Edward Cadwell, Follow Me Four,
Cornell and Baytie
Pony Ballet--Sallie Gates, Toy Tytas, Irene Cornell, Mazella
Lewis, Doris Saunders, Billie Jackson, Adelle Townsend, Eva
Jones
Regular Chorus--Lena Leggett, Ora Johnson, Jessie Taylor, Maris
Wade, Elvira Johnson, Alice Framptson, Louise Warner, Doris
Hudson, Erskine Wrighton, Chester Jones, Walter Badie, Cole-
man Tytus, Ernest Smith, Edward Taylor, Edward Caldwell

Story: (No information)

Musical Numbers: (No information)

FUNNY MONEY (1930)
Producer: Tim Owsley (also at this time was the producer of Silas
    Green from New Orleans Show)
Special Music: F. B. Woods and George Gillins
Lyrics: Tim F. Owsley
Special Dancing Chorus: Bobby Gillins, Katie Bryant

Cast of Characters:

Mr. Meddla	Kike Gresham
Lila Bean	Manzie Campbell
Nancy Green	Marion Gresham
Silas Green	Fred Wiggins
A Street Angel	Princess White Durah
Hubbard	Frank Keith
Wife	Mildred Scott
Man	Mose Penny
Woman	Evelyn White
Lawyer	Sean Johnson
Officer	Freddie Durras
Uncle Ruco	Frank Smedelay
Miss Watsey	Katie Bryant
Miss Ritsen	Bertle Davis

Townspeople: Bobby Gillins, Bernice Carter, Henrietta Pinkney,
    Bethel Monroe, Hazel Walker, Katie Buckhalter, Cleo Wong,
    Rosibell Hunter
Special Added Attractions: Tim Green and Reberta (comedy and
    songs), Allie Johnson (wire artist)

Synopsis:
Act 1
Scene 1.   Front Yard of the Green Home
Scene 2.   Nearby Street
Scene 3.   Public Craceyard
Scene 4.   Nearby Street
Scene 5.   City Park
Scene 6.   Nearby Street
Act 2
Scene 7.   Living Room of the Green Home

Musical Numbers: "The Same Old Silas," "All the Time in Dixie,"
    "A Little Kiss," "Whoopee," "In Love With You," "Absence,"
    "Dance of the Ghost," "Steppin'," "For Sale," "My Soul," "It's
    All Over Now"
Special:

"Blue"	Princess White Durrah
"Can't Help It" ·	Evelyn White

GEORGE WASHINGTON BULLION ABROAD (1915), 3 Acts
Producer, Book, Lyrics: Salem Tutt Whitney, J. Homer Tutt
Music: Salem Tutt Whitney, J. Homer Tutt, James Vaughn

Cast of Characters:

George Washington Bullion	Salem Tutt Whitney

Sam Cain, Bullion's Friend	J. Homer Tutt
Chameleon Norman, Detective (creating five characters)	Luke Scott
Grafton Smooth, a Slick Article	Will Dixon
Captain Raymond, Captain of Vessel	Frank Jackson
Jack Snow	Sam Gardner
Jed Simpkins	George McClain
Willie Little	Sam Grey
Ephram Howe	George Boutte
Poor Little Henpecko	O. D. Carter
First Mate	Will Brown
Second Mate	Edward Marshall
Amanda Henpecko	Julian Costello
Geraldine Shantz, the New Schoolteacher	Blanche Thompson
Mrs. Dewar	Ethel Marshall
Moana Sweet, Bullion's Ward	Hattie Akers
Louis Dillingham, Smooth's Confederate	Ethelyn Proctor
Martha Bullion, Bullion's Sister	Irene Tasker
Clover Leaf, Schoolgirl	Emma Jackson
Susie Young	Josie Graham
Emany Poorly	Mattie Lewis
Militant Parkfurst	Mamie Palmer
Oriental Dancing Girls:	
Salome	Ora Dunlap
Salina	Helen Jackson
Lysia	Helen Brown
Niphrara	Bernidene Small
Ziska	Virginia Wheeler
Zora	Carrie King
Maoma	Esther Small
Cleo	Marie Hearde
Zabastic	Tom Hall
Happy Sam	Will Norwood
Peter Joy	Theodore Peyton

Plantation Hands; Deck Hands, Sailors; Guards; School Girls; Waiting Maids; and Society Belles.

Story: (No information)

Synopsis:

Act 1
Scene 1.   Bullion's Tobacco Plantation
Scene 2.   Main Street, Bowling Green, Kentucky
Scene 3.   Boat Landing

Act 2
Scene 1.   Deck of Ship
Scene 2.   On a Raft
Scene 3.   The Rajah's Garden

Act 3
Same as Act 1, Scene 1.

Musical Numbers:

Act 1

"Dinner Bells," opening chorus	Company
"Golden Days," conversation song and dance	Carter and Boutte assisted by Hattie Akers, Maude Palmer and Chorus
"Love Me Anywhere"	Louise Proctor, Will Dixon and Others
"Shine On Southern Moon"	Blanche Thompson, and School Girls
"Don't Do That to Me Dear"	Salem Tutt Whitney, and Hattie Akers
"Dog Gon I'm Young Again," song and chorus	Old Folks
"Italy and My Rose," solo	Luke Scott
"Levee Pastimes"	Boutte and Carter, Mamie Palmer and Josie Graham
"Goodby My Old Kentucky Home"	Ensemble and Company, (Soloists: Blanche Thompson, Carrie King)

Act 2

"We're Sailing Along," opening chorus	Chorus
"Moonlight Pace," modern dance	J. Homer Tutt, Blanche Thompson, and Chorus
"The Deep Blue Sea," solo and chorus	Frank Jackson
"Help Cometh from Above," octette	Principals
"Allah Oh! Alla!," ensemble	Entire Company
"Body Guards of the Prince," song and drill	Eight Guards
"Maryauna," song and chorus	Blanche Thompson and Chorus
"Dance of Death"	Ethel and Luke Scott
"No Matter How Good You Treat the World You Never Get Out Alive"	Salem Tutt Whitney
"Going Back to Dixieland"	Ensemble and Company (Soloists: Emma Jackson, Ora Dunlap, Helen Jackson, Virginia Wheeler)

Act 3

"Strutting Sam"	J. Homer Tutt and Chorus
"Gin, Gin, Gin," a toast	Salem Tutt Whitney
"When You Hear the Old Kentucky Blues," Grand Finale	Ethel Marshall and Chorus

Executive Staff:

J. Martin Free	Business Manager
Salem Tutt Whitney	Amusement Director
George Boutte	Assistant Stage Manager
Bus Williams	Traps
J. C. McCormack	Advance Agent

J. Homer Tutt	Stage Manager
James Vaughn	Music Director
Jennie Hillman	Wardrobe Mistress

GET SET (1923)
Producer: Harlem Producing Co.
Music and Lyrics: Donald Heywood and Porter Grainger
Book: Joe Bright
Additional Music: Bob Ricketts, William Benton Overstreet
Dances: Boots Marshall, John Dancy

Cast of Characters:

Fred Douglass, Soldier of Fortune	Lawrence Chenault
Officer L. C. All	Henry Rector
Grafton Smooth, a Schemer	Walter Richardson
Bud Feret, a Secret Service Man	Bennie Clark
Mrs. Douglass, Trying to Get into Society	Hilda Thompson
Clementina, a Flapper	Jennie Plate
Dolly Jess, Town's Fashionplate	Ruby Mason
Mandy Snow, a Lady of Color	Mable Johnson
Dot, the Pride of the Town	Rose Brown
Madam LaRue, a Society Leader	Ida Anderson
Dolly Springtime, a Village Belle	Toosie Delks
Senorita Lopez, a Butterfly from Old Madrid	Ella Deas
Pansy Blossom, from Boston	Louise Dunbar
Madam Jack, of the Opera	Mattie Harris
Marie Antoinette, from Paris	Edna Scotron
Messenger Boy, All His Life	Lloyd Gibbs
Isthmus and Peninsula, Two Unbleached Americans	Joe Bright and Joe Russell

Musical Numbers:

Act 1

Opening--Delegates	The Company
"Tee-dle-oo"	Rose Brown and Dancing Girls
"Two Eyes in Dixie"	Bennie Clark and Chorus
Dancing Specialty	Henry Rector
"Trying"	Walter Richardson and Chorus
"They Won't"	Joe Bright and Ponies
"Hoo Che Ans"	Ella Deas and Senoritas
"Jigi Hoo"	Joe Bright and Rose Brown
"Melody of Love"	Walter Richardson and Ruby Mason
"Old Kentucky Blues"	Joe Russell and Dancing Girls
Finale First Act	Ruby Mason and Entire Company

Act 2

"Pay Day"	Ensemble

"Strolling"	Ladies and Gentlemen of the Company
"Get Set"	Ethel Williams
"Shake It"	Toosie Delk and Dancing Girls
"Lindy Lee"	Jessie Lawson and Dandies
"Georgia"	Joe Russell
"Jimmie and Charlie"	Ruby Mason, Boys and Girls
The Treat of the Evening, the Famous Black Swan Record Star	Ethel Waters
A Few Musical Moments with	Donald Heywood and Walter Richardson
Grand Finale--"Let's Forget Bandana Days"	Entire Company

Where It Happened:
Act 1.   Lawn and Garden of Mr. Douglass, Louisville, Kentucky
Act 2, Scene 1.   Lobby, Dunbar Hotel
Act 2, Scene 2.   State Street, Chicago, Illinois
Act 2, Scene 3.   Ball Room, Star Casino, Chicago, Illinois

GINGERSNAPS (1929)
Producers: J. Homer Tutt, Salem Tutt Whitney
Book, Lyrics: J. Homer Tutt, Donald Heywood, George Morris
Music: Donald Heywood
Dance Arranger: George Stamper

Principal Cast of Characters: J. Homer Tutt, Vivian Baber, Barrington Guy, Roscoe "Red" Simmons, George Stamper.

Synopsis:
First Carton
Snap I--Birth of Dixie (A plantation set on the stage of the Harlem Theatre)

The Singer	Roscoe "Red" Simmons
--A Fowl Deed	
Boots	Boots Swan
John	John Lee
The Sheriff	Homer Tutt
Lindy	Vivian Baber
Snap II--Crazy Walk. A new dance creation.	
	Bobby DeLeon and Snapperettes
Snap III--The Same Old Clown	
The Clown	Barrington Guy
Snap IV--Sweet Lips	
	Ethel Moses, Roscoe "Red" Simmons, Bobby DeLeon and Selma Smith

Snap V--"Hot Shots" and "Snapperettes"
Let's Make Hey, Hey (While the Sun in Shinin')
Dance specialty by "The Five Hot Shots"

Snap VI--In Agan and Out Agan
Mr. Inagan   Boots Swan
Mr. Outagan   John Lee
The Warden   J. Homer Tutt
Snap VII--Sambo's in the Movies (Location--Hollywood)
The Director   Roscoe "Red" Simmons
The Cameraman   James Monday
Aunt Jemima   Bertha Wright
Armour's Chef   Walter Meadows
The Gold Dust Twins   Bobby DeLeon and Selma Smith
    --Travesty on "Hallelujia"
Daniel Haynes   Homer Tutt
Nina Mae McKinney   Vivian Baber
Victoria Spivey   Maud DeForest
The Preacher   Barrington Guy
The Southland Choir: Anthony Gaytzera, Larry Seymour, Walter
    Hilliard, Joseph Loomis, Walter Meadows, J. Grace Walton,
    Bertha Wright, Thelma Rhoten, Mary Mason, Margaret Watson
                        Second Carton
Snap I--My Jungle Home
Tar Zan   Barrington Guy
Boola   Vivian Baber
The Jungle Maids and Tom-Tom Beaters
Snap II--Hot Stuff
Boots Swan   Himself
John Lee   Ditto
Snap III--Change My Luck
The Janitor   J. Homer Tutt
The Scrubwoman   Maud DeForest
Snap IV--Spread Your Knees
                                        Vivian Baber and Snapperettes
Snap V--Big Boy, I Gotta Belong to You
                                        Bobby DeLeon and Selma Smith
Snap VI--See the Point
The Stranger   George Stamper
The Croupier   James Monday
The Proprietor   J. Homer Tutt
Snap VII--Some Stepping
                                        5 "Hot Shots"
                                        "Low" Stepping, Frank (Pim-
                                            ples) Davis   .

Snap VIII--He Always Gets His Man!
    A Drama of the Canadian Wilds
    Time--The Present
    Locale--A.   Somewhere in the Saskatchewan
            B.   Interior of Cabin
    Cast (in order of appearance):
George Stamper as Jean Baptiste   a trapper
J. Homer Tutt as Marcel Corot   a sled driver
Larry Seymour as Gitchie   a halfbreed
Boots Swan as Rastus   a cook
Barrington Guy as "Strangler"   a fugitive from justice
    Crane

Roscoe "Red" Simmons as   of the Canadian Royal North-
    Benchley   western Mounted Police
Snap IX--Let's Make "Hey, Hey"
Specialty   Bobby DeLeon
Snap X--I'll Do Anything for Love (A Lenox Avenue Incident)
Boots Swan and Johnny Lee
Barrington Guy and Vivian
    Baber
Maude DeForest and Roscoe
    "Red" Simmons
Snap XI--Finale: You're Something to Write Home About
(Meaning "You," our Dear   Bobby deLeon and Selma Smith
    Audience   with the Entire Company
A Bevy of "Snapperettes"--Mabel Garey, Ethel Moses, Marion
    Fleming, Estello DePolanco, Marie Robinson, Gladys Bronson,
    Frankie Scott, Elvire Sanches, Marie Aken, Enid Morgan,
    Margaret Jackson, Ruth Curtiss.

GREAT DAY (1929)
Producer: Vincent Youmans
Book: John Wells, W. Cary Duncan
Lyrics: William Rose and Edward Elison
Dances: John Boyle
Choral Singing Direction: Will Marion Cook and Russell Wooding

Cast of Characters:
Pooch Starling   Herbert Corthell
Emmy Lou Randolph   Gladys Baxter
Lasses Snow   F. E. Miller
Skeetes Johnson   A. L. Lyles
Chick Carter   Don Lanning
Heliotrope Snow   Cora Green
Maurice Arnot   Alberto Carillo
Francine LaRue   Allys Dwyer
Jackson Rolfe   Alan Goode
Dubose   Jackson Sheppard
Croupier   Lynn Eldridge
Harry   Len Saxon
Tom   Don Cortez
George   Jack Martin
Phillip   George D'Andria
Ida Lee   Alice Douglas
Mary Ellen   Mildred Newman
Grace Fullerton   Mable Ellis
Marion Wittier   Lillian LaMont
Genevieve   Ann White
Lazy Bones   J. DeWitt Spencer
Elijah   Lois Deppe
Hattie   Billie Wallace
Waitress   Kitty Coleman
Piano Player   Harold Arlen
Panzy   Frances Stevens
The Intoxicated Gentleman   Andrew Hicks

The Gold Digger   Blanche Underwood
Ladies and gentlemen of the Southern Smart Set, Race Track Char-
    acters, Mardi Gras Revelers, Gambling House Frequenters,
    Plantation Hands, Waitresses, Hostesses, Pickaninnies, etc.

Story: The story concerns the efforts of Chick Carter to make good
on a sugar plantation backed by money supplied by Emmy Lou, the
girl he loves and who worships him, and who takes a job in a New
Orleans gambling casino to raise the cash.   He allows himself to
become entangled with a French siren, however, and Emmy Lou
goes down the trade of life until she is a figure in a low cabaret.
The climax is reached when, just as Chick announces his engagement to the French girl, Francine. Emmy Lou arrives on the scene
to break news that the levee has given away and the plantation faces
ruin.   This is sufficient to cause Francine, who had been aided and
abetted in her scheme by the casino owner, Maurice Arnot, to de-
part in a hurry for the city.

Synopsis:
Act I
Scene 1.   A Square in the French Quarter, New Orleans.   Mardi
    Gras Time, 1912.
Scene 2.   A Street in New Orleans.
Scene 3.   The Gambling Casino.   Three Months Later.
Scene 4.   By the Roadside.
Act II
Scene 1.   The "Hot Ace" Dance Hall.   Six Months Later.
Scene 2.   ".Telephone Booths."
Scene 3.   The Levee.
Scene 4.   The Road from the Levee.
Scene 5.   The House on Chick Carter's Plantation.   The Same
    Night.

Musical Numbers:
Act I
"Mardi Gras"   Ensemble
"Happy Because I'm in Love"   Chick, Emmy Lou and
                                          Ensemble

Finaletto.
(Reprise) "Happy Because I'm   The Ballet
    in Love"
"Sweet Emmy Lou"   Ensemble
"More Than You Know"   Emmy Lou
"Sweet Sunshine"   Plantation Workers
"Without a Song"   Elijah and Plantation Workers
Act II
"Doo, Dah, Dey"   The Piano Player and Ensemble
(Reprise) "More Than You Know"   Emmy Lou
"Two Black Dots"   Graham and Johnson
"Mean Man"   Heliotrope
"Great Day"   Elijah and Plantation Workers
(Reprise) "Without a Song"   Elijah
(Reprise) "Great Day"
Finale Ultima.

THE GREEN PASTURES (1935)
  (New York City Production)
Producer: Laurence Rivers
Book, Lyrics: Suggested by Roark Bradford's Southern Sketches,
  "Ol' Man Adam an' His Chillun"

Cast of Characters (In the order of their appearance):

Mr. Deshee	Charles H. Moore
Myrtle	Alicia Escamilla
First Boy	Jazzlips Richardson, Jr.
Second Boy	Howard Washington
Third Boy	Reginald Blythwood
Vangie	Fredia Langshaw
A Cook	Frances Smith
Custard Maker	Homer Tutt
First Mammy Angel	Anna Mae Fritz
A Stout Angel	Josephine Byrd
A Slender Angel	Edna Thrower
Archangel	J. A. Shipp
Gabriel	Samuel Davis
The Lord	Richard B. Harrison
Choir Leader	McKinley Reeves
Adam	Daniel L. Haynes
Eve	Geraldine Gooding
Cain	Lou Vernon
Cain's Girl	Benveneta Washington
Zeba	Edna M. Harris
Cain the Sixth	James Fuller
Boy Gambler	Louis Kelsey
First Gambler	Collington Hayes
Second Gambler	Ivan Sharp
Voice in Shanty	Josephine Byrd
Noah	Tutt Whitney
Noah's Wife	Susie Sutton
Shem	Milton J. Williams
First Woman	Dinks Thomas
Second Woman	Anna Mae Fritz
Third Woman	Geneva Blythwood
Fourth Woman	Benveneta Washington
First Man	Emory Richardson
Flatfoot	Freddie Archibald
Ham	J. Homer Tutt
Japheth	Stanleigh Morrell
First Cleaner	Josephine Bryd
Second Cleaner	Florence Fields
Abraham	J. A. Shipp
Isaac	Charles H. Moore
Jacob	Edgar Burks
Moses	Alonzo Fenderson
Zipporah	Mercedes Gilbert
Aaron	McKinley Reeves
A Candidate Magician	Reginald Fenderson
Pharaoh	George Randol

The General	Lou Vernon
The Admiral	Charles Winter Wood
First Wizard	Emory Richardson
Head Magician	Arthur Porter
Joshua	Stanleigh Morrell
First Scout	Ivan Sharp
Master of Ceremonies	Collington Hayes
King of Babylon	Emory Richardson
Prophet	Ivan Sharp
High Priest	J. Homer Tutt

The King's Favorites { Leona Winkler, Mabel Ridley, Constance Van Dyke, Mary Ella Hart, Inez Persand

Officer	Emory Richardson
Hezdrel	Daniel L. Haynes
Another Officer	Stanleigh Morrell

The Children--Philistine Bumgardner, Margery Bumgardner, Fredia
    Longshaw, Wilbur Cohen, Jr., Verdon Perdue, Ruby Davis,
    Willmay Davis, Margerette Thrower, Viola Lewis.
Angels and Townspeople--Amy Escamilla, Elsie Byrd, Benveneta
    Washington, Thula Oritz, Ruth Carl, Geneva Blythwood.
Babylonian Band--Carl Shorter, Earl Bowie, Thomas Russell,
    Richard Henderson.
The Choir--Evelyn Burwell, Assistant Director
    Sopranos: Bertha Wright, Geraldine Gooding, Marie Warren,
    Mattie Harris, Gertrude DeVerney, Massie Patterson,
    Marguerite Avery, Juanita Hall.
    Altos: Ruthena Matson, Leona Avery, Mrs. Willie Mays, Viola
    Mickens, Charlotte Junius.
    Tenors: John Warner, Joe Loomis, Walter Hilliard, Harold
    Foster, Adolph Henderson, William McFarland, McKinley
    Reeves, Arthur Porter.
    Baritones: Oliver E. Foster, Gerome Addison, Walter Whit-
    field, D. K. Williams, Benjamin John Ragsdale.
    Bassos: Cecil McNair, Tom Lee, Walter Meadows, Frank
    Horace.

Story (from Program of Mansfield Theatre presentation, April 13,
1931): "'The Green Pastures' is an attempt to present certain aspects of a living religion in the terms of its believers. The religion is that of thousands of Negroes in the deep South. With terrific spiritual hunger and the greatest humility these untutored black
Christians--many of whom cannot even read the book which is the
treasure house of their faith--have adapted the contents of the Bible
to the consistencies of their everyday lives.

"Unburdened by the differences of more educated theologians
they accept the Old Testament as a chronicle of wonders which happened to people like themselves in vague but actual places and of
rules of conduct, true acceptance of which will lead them to a tangi-
ble, three-dimensional Heaven. In this Heaven, if one has been
born in a district where fish frys are popular, the angels do have

magnificent fish frys through an eternity somewhat resembling a
series of earthly holidays.   The Lord Jehovah will be the promised
comforter, a just but compassionate patriarch, the summation of all
the virtues His follower has observed in the human beings about him.
The Lord may look like the reverend Mr. DuBois as our Sunday
School teacher speculates in the play, or he may resemble another
believer's own grandfather.   In any event, His face will have an
earthly familiarity to the one who has come for his reward.
        "The author is indebted to Mr. Roark Bradford, whose re-
telling of several of the Old Testament stories in 'Ol' Man Adam
an' His Chillun' first stimulated his interest in this point of view.
        "One need not blame a hazy memory of the Bible for the
failure to recall the characters of Hezdrel, Zeba and others in the
play.   They are the author's apocrypha, but he believes persons
much like them have figured in the meditations of some of the old
Negro preachers, whose simple faith he has tried to translate into
a play. "

Synopsis:

Part I

Scene 1--The Sunday School.
Scene 2--A Fish Fry.
Scene 3--A Garden.
Scene 4--Outside the Garden.
Scene 5--A Roadside.
Scene 6--A Private Office.
Scene 7--Another Roadside.
Scene 8--A House.
Scene 9--A Hillside.
Scene 10--A Mountain Top.

Part II

Scene 1--The Private Office.
Scene 2--The Mouth of a Cave.
Scene 3--A Throne Room.
Scene 4--The Foot of a Mountain.
Scene 5--A Cabaret.
Scene 6--The Private Office.
Scene 7--Outside a Temple.
Scene 8--Another Fish Fry.

Musical Numbers:

Act I

"Oh, Rise and Shine"
"When the Saints Come Marchin' In"
"Cert'n'y Lord"
"My God Is So High"
"Hallelujah!"
"In Bright Mansions Above"
"Don't You Let Nobody Turn You Roun' "
"Run, Sinner, Run"
"You Better Min' "
"Dere's No Hidin-Place Down Dere"
"Some o' Dese Days"

"I Want to Be Ready"
"De Ole Ark's a-Moverin"
"My Soul is a Witness"
Entr-Acte--City Called Heaven

Act II

"My Lord's a-Writin' All de Time"
"Go Down, Moses" (Bass solo by Cecil T. McNair)
"Oh, Mary, Don't You Weep"
"Lord, I Don't Feel Noways Tired"
"Joshua Fit de Battle of Jericho"
"I Can't Stay Away"
"Hail de King of Babylon!"
"Death's Gointer Lay His Cold, Icy Hands on Me"

HAM'S DAUGHTER (1932)
Producer: Dennis Donoghue

Cast of Characters:

Dad Jones	Thurston Lewis
Eliza	Dr. Mary Jane Watkins
Mother Jones	Trixie Smith
Ned Daniels	Lorenzo Tucker
Rastus	Robert Johnson
Slick Harris	Alvin Childress
Detective Jim Bronson	Marty Crossman
Smitty	Speedy Smith
Emma	Millie Holmes
Kitty	Ponchita Aublaunche
Lola	Gwendolyn Clarke
Sam Wheeler	Thomas Lee
Police Officer	Allen Cohen
Prison Keeper	Thomas Lee
The Rev. Mr. Washington	Victor Archer
Brother Amos	Lawrence Lomax
Sister Freeman	M. Holmes
Margaret	Queenie Estwick
Sister Mary	Dorothy Harris

Story: A Southern lassie (Dr. Mary Jane Watkins) is lured by the
city slicker (Alvin Childress) from her psalm-singing Southern home
and a devoted lover (Lorenzo Tucker) and faithful Man Friday (Robert Johnson) to a wicked Northern city where she is disillusioned
and deserted, but ultimately saved by the clever detective (Marty
Crossman).   She is re-established in the good graces of her family
and married to her Southern beau.

Musical Numbers: (No information)

HARLEM ROUNDERS (1925), 2 Acts
Producer: Frank Montgomery*
Musical Director: J. Rosamond Johnson
Stage Manager: Eddie Williams

Principal Cast of Characters: Billy Higgins, Florence McClain,
    Billy Gulfport, Abbie Mitchell, Kitty Brown
The Bunch of Beauties with "Harlem Rounders"--Alma Henderson,
    Linda Nicholson, Dorothy Hooper, Dorothy Wilson, Pearl Dar-
    riel, Thelma Ragsdale, Aurella Fisher, Marie Warren, Daisy
    Azarro, Maxine Harrison, Alice Robinson, Nova Rodriguez.
The Dancing Boys--Eddie Dent, Charles Newby, Jimmie Sadler,
    Leon Walker, Arthur Richardson, Ellwood Ford.
Note: J. Rosamond Johnson composed "Under the Bamboo Tree,"
    "Phoebe Brown," "Lazy Moon," and the following shows:
    "Shoofly Regiment," "The Red Moon," "Come Over Here,"
    and others.

Synopsis:
                          Scene--Dixie
"Trucking Cotton"   Billy Higgins, Billy Gulfport,
                                      Ed Peat and Men
"Honey Bunch"   Kitty Brown and Will Brown
"Alabam"   Florence McClain and Chorus
Comedy Scene   Billy Higgins, Florence
                                      McClain, Ed Peat
"Too Tired"   Kitty Brown and Girls
                          Olio
Specialty   Ed Peat
"Effervescing Lady"   ⎫
"The Mysterious Bowl"   ⎬   Eloise Bennett and Girls
                             ⎭
                          Olio
Specialty--"Follow the Swallow"   Eddie and George
                       Scene in Italy
Italian Number, "Rose of   Abbie Mitchell
    Montmartre"
"Does My Sweetie Do What I   Florence McClain
    Want To?"
Hotel Chateau, Comedy Safe   Lion, Billy Higgins, Billy
    Robbery Scene   Gulfport
                          Olio
Selections   The Southern Four
                      Scene in Mexico
Indian Jazz   Florence McClain and Indian
                                      Squaw
Specialty   Kitty Brown
Phoebe Brown   Eloise Bennett and Mexican
                                      Girls

---

*Frank Montgomery wrote, staged, and produced "Hello, 1919,"
"Dancing Around," "The Broadway Rounders," "The Toy Shop,"
and staged the dancing numbers in "How Come" and others.

Specialty	Billy Gulfport
"Step On It, Johnny"	Will Brown and Entire Company
Intermission	

Act 2
Apache Scene

Apache Dance	Eloise Bennett and William Thrill
Specialty	Billy Higgins

Charleston Scene

"Charleston Town"	Florence McClain and Charleston Rose Buds
Bomb Hit	Billy Higgins, Will Brown, Billy Gulfport, Ed Peat, Eddie and George

Old Broadway Scene

Specialty	Dewey Weinglass, Jessie Crowford, George Phillips
Holdup Scene	Billy Higgins, Florence McClain, Billy Gulfport, Billy Brown, Eddie and George, Kitty Brown, Ed Peat

Monte Carlo Scene

J. Rosamond Johnson and his Troubadour Band--A. Jackson, sax, oboe, clarinet; H. Sapario, banjo; E. Bullock, sax, clarinet; A. Walker, drums; A. Thompson, sax, clarinet; I. Myers, piano; T. J. Frazer, trombone, euphonium; R. Ysaguerro, tuba.

Olio
Russian Scene

Specialty	Gulfport and Brown
"Song of Songs"	Abbie Mitchell and Chorus
Russian Dancers	Dewey Weinglass and Dancing Demons, and Chorus
Burlesque	Billy Higgins, Gulfport and Brown, Ed Peat
Finale	Entire Company

THE HEART BREAKERS (1918)
Producer: Billy King

Principal Cast of Characters: Billy King, Howard Kelly, Georgia Kelly, James Thomas, Bessie Brown, Gertrude Saunders

Story: The story tells of the efforts of a young lady to keep company with a young man who her parents do not like and the latter have engaged Bill to keep a weather eye out toward the girl's protection. His efforts in this connection is the main comedy theme.

Musical Numbers:	
"Flirtation"	Beaus and Belles
"Hid Away"	Billy King
"Cotton Picking Time"	Bessie Brown
"Little Lump of Sugar"	Gertrude Saunders
"Going to Carolina"	Billy King and Company

HELLO DIXIELAND (1920)
Producer: Billy King

Principal Cast of Characters: Billy King, Arthur Bruce, Lelia
    Mitchell, Berlina Blanks, Clarence Beasley, Charles Williams

Musical Numbers:
"Mandy"   Arthur Bruce
"Yama"   Lelia Mitchell
"Don't Take My Blues Away"   Berlena Blanks
"Rose"   Ollie Hickman
"Come Back, Mandy"   Clarence Beasley
"Hey, Hey"   Charles Williams and Company

HELLO 1919 (1919), 2 Acts 11 Scenes
Producer: Frank Montgomery

Cast of Characters: Frank Montgomery, Early West, Tiny Ray,
    Clarence Robinson, Raymond Miller, Ardelle Townsend, Dyke
    Thomas, Alice Ramsey, Willie Ingram, Millie Holmes, Marie
    Rich, May Bird, Nona Burk

Musical Numbers:
"Hello Everybody"   Early West, Tiny Ray, Clarence
                                   Robinson, Raymond Miller
"Ballyhoo Baby"   Ardelle Townsend
"Impossible"   Dyke Thomas
"High Brown Baby's Ball"   Alice Ramsey and Chorus
"Distinguished Ball"   Broadway Octet (Tiny Ray, Earl
                                   West, Willie Bird, Willie
                                   Ingram, Millie Holmes,
                                   Marie Rich, May Bird,
                                   Nona Burk
"Yo Son"   May Bird and Chinese Girls
"Sand Dunes"   ?
"Great Big Baby Boy"   ?
Synopsis:

Act 1

"A minstrel scene with Mr. Butler and Mr. Thomas doing
the comedy sitting on miniature boxes on each side of a semi-circle.
At the center of the semi-circle a gentleman was being interrupted
by someone sitting in the audience with whom he took issue.   After
much nonsense, the gentleman in the audience was invited on the
stage to do what he could do and it proved to be none other than
Frank Montgomery (the star comedian) who makes a nice prologue
speech, accompanied by a sweet musical strain and then the show
began. "

Act 2

"The second act takes place in the Capitol, Palm Beach, the
Boardwalk and a hotel lobby in the Island of Yap (last scene). "
Review by Dave Payton, Chicago Whip, July 4, 1920.

HEY HEY (1926)
Producer: Mrs. Amy Ashwood Garvey (wife of Marcus Garvey)

Principal Cast of Characters: Sam Manning, George McClennon,
    Alberta Bryne, Evelyn Ray, Clarence Beasley

Story: The story is centered about the desires of Sam and George
to find their lovemates by traveling to Africa to match ribs from
which their women were made. Having been thrown out of their
homes by their wives, they are more determined than ever to find
their soul-mates. In Africa they do match the ribs, but the women
who possess them are their original wives who had preceded them
to Africa.

Musical Numbers: (No information)

HIS EXCELLENCY, THE PRESIDENT (1915)
Producer, Book Lyrics, Music: Salem Tutt Whitney and J. Homer
    Tutt

Cast of Characters:

His Excellency, O Saymore	William (Babe) Townsend
Dud White	Salem Tutt Whitney
Monsieur LaFritz	Greenberg Holmes
Mandy Simpkins	Helen Harper
Senator Comeback	Frank Jackson
Enuff Dessert	Will Dixon
Mrs. James Brown Douglass	Ethel Marshall
Lady Winterbottom	Pauline Parker
Letter Dance	Emma Jackson and Babe Brown

Story: (No information)

Musical Numbers: (No information)

HIS HONOR THE BARBER (1909), 3 Acts 7 Scenes
Producers: Barton and Wiswell
Book: Edwin Hanford
Music, Lyrics: James Bryman, James Burris, Chris Smith

Cast of Characters:

Raspberry Snow	Sherman H. Dudley
Babe Johnson	Andrew Tribble
Mose Lewis	James Burris
Capt. Percival Dardelin	Lawrence Chenault
Caroline Brown	Aline Cassals
Lady White	Jennie Pearl
Ella Wheller Wilson	Mrs. S. H. Dudley
"Patrick"	The Mule

Story: The story deals with Raspberry Snow whose main ambition

Ad for "His Honor the Barber," Featuring S. H. Dudley, circa 1909

in life is to shave the President of the United States.   The closest
he gets to realizing his desire is in a dream in the second act.

Musical Numbers:
"Leave 'Fore Supper Time"	S. H. Dudley
"Corn Shucking Time"	Irving Allen
"Merry Widow Brown"	Aline Cassals
"The Isles of Love"	Jennie Pearl
"Rainbow Sue"	?
"Consolation Lane"	?
"Crybaby Moon"	?

HOT CHOCOLATES (1929)
Producer: Connie Immerman
Staging: Leonard Harper
Comedy Sketches: Eddie Green
Lyrics: Andy Razaf
Music: Thomas "Fats" Waller, Harry Brook

Principal Cast of Characters: Baby Cox, Edith Wilson, "Jazzlips"
    Richardson, Jimmie Baskette, Six Crackerjacks, Billy Higgins,
    Eddie Green, Cabell (Cab) Calloway, Margaret Simms, Wooding's
    Jubilee Singers, LeRoy Smith and His Orchestra, the Sixteen
    Hot Chocolate Drops, the Eight Bon Bon Buddies.
The Hot Chocolate Drops--The Misses Billie Bow, Dolly McCormack,
    Virginia Wheeler, Anise Boyar, Jean Roundtree, Juanita
    Boisseau, Marion Davis, Dorothy Young, Bernice Aiken,
    LaRoma Bradley, Rita Walker, Hazel Cole, Dorothy Irving,
    Frances Sheppard, Lucille Smith and Thelma Salmons.
The Bon Bon Buddies--The Messrs. George Norton, James Love,
    Lewellyn Crawford, Lloyd Mitchell, Freddie Heron, Bobby
    Johnson, Julius Howard and John Perry.

Synopsis:
Prologue (at Connie's Inn)

Porter	"Jazzlips" Richardson
Head Waiter	J. E. Lightfoot
Doorman	Clarence Todd
First Waiter	Jesse Wilson
Second Waiter	J. W. Loguen
Attendant	Thomas R. Hall
Master of Ceremonies	Jimmie Baskette
Guests, Orchestra and Entertainers	
Waltz Divine	Paul and Thelma Meeres
The Club Revue: Pickaninny Land	Florence Parham, the Six Crackerjacks, the Hot Chocolate Drops and Bon Bon Buddies

Act I, Scene 1

"Song of the Cotton Fields"	Russell Wooding's Jubilee Singers

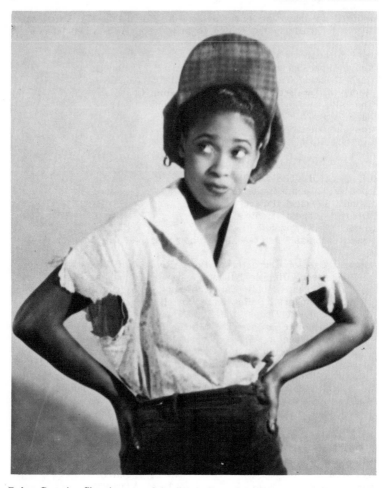

Baby Cox As She Appeared in "Hot Chocolates," circa 1934

"Sweet Savannah Sue"	Margaret Simms, Paul Bass, the Hot Chocolate Drops, Bon Bon Buddies and Jubilee Singers

Scene 2

The Unloaded Gun	Eddie Green, Billy Maxey and Jimmie Baskette

Scene 3

"Say It with Your Feet"	Baby Cox, the Hot Chocolate Drops and Bon Bon Buddies

Scene 4

"Ain't Misbehavin'"	Margaret Simms, Cabell Callo-

way and Russell Wooding's
Jubilee Singers

Scene 5

Rowland Holder

Scene 6

Big Business:
Kid Licorice   "Jazzlips" Richardson
Manager   Eddie Green
Promoter   Billy Higgins
A Reporter   Billy Maxey
Gamblers   Jessie Wilson, Dick Campbell,
                                       J. E. Lightfoot
Referee   Thomas R. Hall
Moving Picture Magnate   A. A. Haston

Scene 7

"Goddess of Rain"   Jimmie Baskette; dance by
                                       Louise Cook with Ensemble

Scene 8

"Dixie Cinderella"   Baby Cox and Billy Maxey

Scene 9

Negro Spiritual   Russell Wooding's Jubilee Sing-
                                       ers (Ina Duncan, Elice Todd,
                                       Mary Pervall, Natalie Long,
                                       Anita Reed, Louise Wil-
                                       liams, Gladys Jordan, Dick
                                       Campbell, A. A. Haston,
                                       Thomas R. Hall, J. W.
                                       Loguen, Jessie Wilson,
                                       Clarence Todd, J. E.
                                       Lightfoot, Toussaint Duers.

Scene 10

Harlem Street Scene   Billy Maxey, Cabell Calloway
                                       with Bernice Aiken, LaRoma
                                       Bradley, Frances Hubbard

Scene 11

"Black and Blue"   Edith Wilson and Cabell Callo-
                                       way

Scene 12

"That Rhythm Man"   Paul Meeres and the Entire
                                       Company
Finale Specialty   Louise Cook, Paul and Thelma
                                       Meeres

Entre'Acte: Trumpet Solo by Louis Armstrong

Act II, Scene 1

The Wedding of the Rabbit and the Bear
Hostess   Edith Wilson
Bunnies   Paul and Thelma Meeres
Bear   Baby Cox
Rabbit   Florence Parham
Fox   Cabell Calloway
Monkeys   Mary Prevall, Louise Williams,
                                       Natalie Long
Pussy-Cat   Margaret Simms

Frogs	Midnight Steppers
Sister Twister	Louise Cook
Jackass	Billy Maxey
Zebras	Bon Bon Buddies
Birds	Jubilee Singers

Scene 2

Somewhere in Harlem	Edith Wilson, Eddie Green, Billy Higgins, Jimmie Baskette and Louise Williams

Scene 3

"Can't We Get Together?"	Baby Cox and Florence Parkham

Scene 4

"Redskinland"	Jimmie Baskette

(Specialty dance by Paul and Thelma Meeres)

Scene 5

"Jazzlips" Richardson

Scene 6

Traffic in Harlem:

The Chaufferettes	Hot Chocolate Drops
Motorcycle Cops	Bon Bon Buddies
The Sergeant	Billy Maxey
Lieutenant	"Jazzlips" Richardson
Captain	Billy Higgins
Specialty	The Six Crackerjacks
An Entertainer	Margaret Simms
Cabaret Girls	Hot Chocolate Drops
"Snake Hips' Dance"	Margaret Simms and Girls

Scene 7

In a Telegraph Office

Clerk	Jimmie Baskette
Hallow	Eddie Green

Scene 8

"Off-Time"	Margaret Simms and the Bon Bon Buddies and Entire Company

THE HOT MIKADO (1939)
(Based on the Gilbert and Sullivan Classic)
Producer: Michael Todd
Book: Hassard Short
Topical Lyrics: Dave Greggory and William Tracy
Musical Adaptations and Orchestra Arrangements: Charles L. Cooke
Dances: Truly McGee

Cast of Characters (In order of appearance):
The action of the play might have taken place in Japan.

Nanki-Poo (Son of The Mikado, in love with Yum-Yum)	Bob Parrish
Pish-Tush (a Noble Lord)	James A. Lillard
Ko-Ko (The Lord High Executioner)	Eddie Green

Pooh-Bah (The Lord High Everything Else) .... Maurice Ellis

Yum-Yum .... Gwendolyn Reyde

Pitti-Sing   3 Sisters, Wards { Frances Brock

Peep-Bo   of Ko-Ko .... Roseeta LeNoire

Messenger Boy .... Freddie Robinson

Katisha (Prospective Bride-to-be of Nanki-Poo) .... Rose Brown

The Mikado .... Bill Robinson

Red Cap .... Vincent Shields

Singing Girls--Alyce Ajaye, Fay Banks, Ethel Brown, Alice Carter, Maggie Carter, May Daniels, Vivian Eley, Marie Fraser, Marion Hairston, Ethel Harper, Pearl Harrison, Bruce Howard, Julie Hunter, Irene Johnson, Massie Patterson, Idelle Pemberton, Edna Rickes, Ann Simmons, Theresa Stone, Geneva Washington, Waldine Williams, Mary Young, Ethylnn Edmonson, Josephine Hall.

Singing Boys--Charles Banks, Lemuel Bullock, William Barber, Russell Carrington, Archie Cross, Travers Crawford, John Diggs, Leslie Grey, Otho Gains, Marshall Haley, John Jackson, Harry Lewis, Elmaurice Miller, Walter Mosby, Maynard Sandridge, Vincent Shields, Larry Seymour, Harold Slappy, Clyde Turner, George Turner, Anthon Taylor, Ben Wailles, Roy White, Moke Wilson.

Dancing Girls--Ronetta Batson, Valerie Black, Mitzi Coleman, Elaine Dash, Elizabeth Dozier, Claudie Haward, Sylvia Lee, Jackie Lewis, Cleo Law, Pearl McCormack, Ruby Richards, Mary Robinson.

Jitterbug Girls--Gladys Crowder, Geneva Davis, Belle Hill, Connie Hill, May Miller, Mildred Pollard.

Jitterbug Boys--Eddie Davis, Leon James, Walter Johnson, Lee Lyons, Albert Minne, Russell Williams.

"Tap-a-Teers"--Louis Brown, Jules Adger, Ernest Frazier, Fred Heron, Chick Lee, Eddie Morton.

Guards--Sam Brown, Vincent Anderson, Willie Dinkins, Gershon Meyers, John Williams, Luther Williams.

Quartette--Travers Crawford, Otho Gains, Harry Lewis, Elmaurice Miller.

Story: (No information)

Musical Numbers:

(Note: The entire score of this production is that of Sir Arthur Sullivan's "The Mikado" set to modernized tempos. There is no interpolated music of any kind.)

Act I

"If You Want to Know Who We Are" .... Ensemble

"A Wandering Minstrel" .... Nanki-Poo, Male Chorus and the "Tap-a-teers"

"Our Great Mikado" .... Pish-Tush, Male Chorus and the "Tap-a-teers"

"Young Man Despair" .... Pooh-Bah, Pish-Tush and

"Behold the Lord High Execu-   Nanki-Poo
   tioner"   Ko-Ko and Male Chorus
"I've Got a Little List"   Ko-Ko and Male Chorus
"Comes a Train of Little Ladies" Girls' Chorus
"Three Little Maids"   Yum-Yum, Pitti-Sing, Peep-Bo,
                                    The "Tap-a-teers" and
                                    Dancing Girls and Jitterbugs
"So Pardon Us"   Yum-Yum, Pitti-Sing, Peep-Bo,
                                    Pooh-Bah, Pish-Tush and
                                    Girls' Chorus
"Were You Not to Ko-Ko   Yum-Yum and Nanki-Poo
   Plighted" (Duet)
Finale of Act I   Nanki-Poo, Ko-Ko, Pish-Tush,
                                    Pooh-Bah, Yum-Yum, Pitti-
                                    Sing, Peep-Bo, Katisha,
                                    and Entire Ensemble

Act II

"Braid the Raven Hair"   Ensemble
"The Moon and I"   Yum-Yum and the Harmoneers
"Here's a How-de-do"   Yum-Yum, Nanki-Poo and Ko-Ko
The Mikado   Mikado and Katisha, and Entire
                                    Ensemble
(a) "I'm the Emperor of Japan"   Mikado and Katisha
(b) "My Object All Sublime"   Mikado
"Flowers That Bloom in the   Pitti-Sing, Yum-Yum, Nanki-
   Spring"   Poo, Pooh-Bah, and Ko-Ko
(a) Dance   The "Tap-a-teers," Dancing
                                    Girls and Jitterbugs
(b) Dance   Mikado and Dancers
"I, Living I"   Katisha
"Titwillow"   Ko-Ko
Finale of Act II   Entire Company

HOT RHYTHM (1930)
Producer: Will Morrissey
Sketches: Ballard MacDonald, Will Morrissey, Edward Hurley,
    Johnny Lee Long, Dewey "Pigmeat" Markham
Music, Lyrics: Donald Heywood, Porter Grainger

Principal Cast of Characters (In the order of their appearance):
    Johnny Hudgins, Eddie Rector, Arthur Bryson, Johnny Lee
    Long, Edith Wilson, Mae Barnes, George Wiltshire, Amon
    Davis, Jarahal, Dewey "Pigmeat" Markham, Doris Rheubottom,
    Laura Duncan, Revella Hughes, Ina Duncan, Inez Seeley, Hazel
    Van Vlerah, Sam Paige, Slaps Wallace, Lois Simms, Buster
    Bowie, Al Vigal, Hilda Perleno, Willie Taylor, Billy Sheppard,
    Hendricks Mattingly, King Washington, Joseph Brown, St. Clair
    Dodson, Natalie Long, Mal Dumas, Freddie Waithe, Llewelyn
    Ransom, Larri N. Lorear, Madaline Belt, Tousaint Duers,
    Roland Smith.
Ladies of the Ensemble--Isabelle Peterson, Lenora Gadson, Evelyn

Ortez, Erlise Thopson, Doris Alexander, Juanita Boyd, Dorothy
Seeton, Hazel Miles, Julia Noissette, Regina James, Helen
Robinson, Eda Bell, Alberta Puggsley, Dolores Watson, Mabel
Gary, Elverta Brown, Blanch Farrow, Madge Fox, Ethel Carr
and Dorothy Saunders.
Singers--St. Claire Dodson, Natalie Long, Mel Dumar, Larrie
Lawlor, Freddie, Lou Rasom.
Musical Director: Maurice Coffin
Master of Ceremonies: Eddie Rector

Synopsis:
Act I
Scene 1--Tree of Hope.   Believe it or not Ripley will vouch for the
actors' wishing tree in Harlem.   Songs by Al Vigal and Mel
Dumar and ensemble.
Scene 2--Nora Green.   Miss Seeley, Messrs. Simms, Bowie, Dod-
son, Taylor.
Scene 3--A Harlem Rent Party; Long, Markham, Wiltshire,
Misses Wilson, Van Vlerah, Rheubottom.   "Mama's Gotta Get
Her Rent"--sung by Miss Wilson.
Scene 4--Miss Mae Barnes.   Who Boop-Boop-a-Dooped a Lotta
Boops Long Before Helen Kane Ever Heard of Boop.   "Say the
Word That Will Make You Mine."
Scene 5--A Harlem Spelling Bee.   (He graduated from High School
at eight--in the evening.)   Miss Rheubottom, Mr. Wiltshire and
a no-good brat.
Scene 6--Loving You the Way I Do.   Revella Hughes, Al Vigal,
Mae Barnes, Arthur Bryson and ensemble.
Scene 7--Rector Rhythm.   100° Fahrenheit.   Miss Belt, Mr. Rec-
tor and ensemble.
Scene 8--The Penalty of Love.   Miss Seeley, Messrs. Davis,
Taylor, Wiltshire, Dumar, Sheppard, Long and Markham.
Sung by Mr. Duers and ensemble.   Condemned man, Mr.
Sheppard.   Mr. Hudgins Broadcasts.
Scene 9--"Since You Went Away."   Sung by Miss Perleno and Mr.
Vigal.   Danced by Simms & Bowie.
Scene 10--A Certain Lady on Trial.   Miss Barnes, Messrs. Long,
Markham, Davis, Wiltshire, Dodson, Rector.
Scene 11--Ravella Hughes Trio.   With Ina and Laura Duncan.   In
Sepia Melodies (A Ravella Hughes Arrangement).
Scene 12--Floradora Sextette (A La Harlem).   Ensemble Post-
Graduates.   Also that Hudgins Guy.
Scene 13--"Jarahal."   A Gangster Incident.
Scene 14--The Cave.   A hot spot in hot Harlem.   1--Rector Girls.
"Alabamy," sung by Miss Belt.   3--A Harlem Skate.   J.
McGarver.   4--Tumbling Around.   Baby Goins.   5--The Tor-
nado.   Mr. Bryson.   6--Finale--Sepia Vanities.   Beautifying
Harlem.
Act II
Scene 1--(a) "Up in the Sky," sung by Miss Seeley and Mr. Vigal.
(b) "Afro-Fresh Air, Inc.," Mr. Long and Markham.
Scene 2--"In the Air."
Scene 3--Anywhere in Africa.   "Tropical Moon," sung by Miss

Hughes and ensemble.   Dramatic Interlude--Mr. Sheppard.
Scene 4--Sam Paige and Slaps.   Perhaps.
Scene 5--Hungry for Love.   Sung by Miss Perleno.   Cupid's Hospi-
    tal.   Nurses, Revella Hughes with Laura and Ina Duncan.   Dr.
    Smith, Mr. Wiltshire.
Scene 6--Episodes.   Of a Broadway Producer.   Misses Wilson,
    Van Vlerah, Messrs. Wiltshire, Vigal, Markham, Rector.
Scene 7--Hot Rhythm.   Sung by Mae Barnes and Girls.
Scene 8--Miss Wilson Struts her Stuff.   Eddie Rector and Madaline
    Belt.
Scene 9--Othello--Put on the Spot.   Mae Barnes, Mr. Long, Mark-
    ham, Davis.   Another Strange Interlude (Musical).   Mr. Hudgins
    on the Old Sole Hour.
Scene 10--Steppin' on It.   Eddie Rector and Madaline Belt.   Arthur
    Bryson Shakes a Foot.
Scene 11--Finale.   Entire Company.

HOTTEST COON IN DIXIE (1906)
Producer: I. E. Gideon
Book, Lyrics: Ferdos and Carter
Music: George Byrant

Cast of Characters:

Jeff Jackson, Hottest Coon in Dixie	A. A. Copeland
Lilly Snow White, Jeff's means of support	H. M. Prince
Mamie Brown, just from college	Josephine Lazzo
Parson Brown, typically Southern	Thomas Deaker
Nancy Brown, Parson's wife	L. E. Gideon
Sue Simpkins, very kittish	Emma Prince
Will Daily, club man	Sidney H. Carter
Jube Jones, race horse tout	J. A. English
Rastus Brown, just for fun	Clarence Dotson
Miss Eager	Amos Scruggs
Mose Jenkins, the law	Earle Burton
Isaac Murphy, jockey	Will Burton

Story: (No information)

Musical Numbers:

"My Old Kentucky Home"	Edythe Drake and Chorus
"Allus de Same in Dixie"	Josephine Lazzo and Chorus
"All Wise Chickens Follow Me"	Andrew Copeland
"Love Me and the World is Mine"	Irving Richardson
"I Like Your Way"	Sidney Carter and Chorus
"I Don't Know Where I'm Going, But I'm On My Way"	H. M. Prince
"Sweet Mamie"	Andrew Copeland and Chorus

Olio

Queen Dora	Manipulation in flames
Clarence Dotson	Song and dance

Marvelous Petitts   Magic
Dixie Comedy Four   Musical selections
The Great English   Hoop manipulator

HOW COME (1923)
Producer: Eddie Hunter

Principal Cast of Characters (1923): Eddie Hunter, Amon Davis,
    George Cooper, Alberta Hunter, Johnny Nit, Rastus Wilson,
    Leroy Broomfield, Nina Hunter, Alice Brown, Andrew Tribble
    (Deacon Long Track), Nat Cash, Alfred "Slick" Chester.
Principal Cast of Characters (1925): Eddie Hunter, Barrington
    Carter, Caroline Williams, Nina Hunter, Madlyn Odlum, Leroy
    Broomfield, Billy Higgins, Doe Doe Green, Nona Marshall,
    George Lynch, George W. Cooper, Emma Jackson, Norman
    Astwood, Alberta Perkins, Amy Spencer, Jessica Zack, Mabel
    Gant, Adrian Joyce, Duck Victor.

Synopsis: The main theme of the musical comedy has to do with the
formation of a business and making away with the funds by the
crooked secretary urged on by a scheming companion. Hunter in
blackface portrays the secretary and George Cooper has the part of
companion. Other sketches support the main theme including one
dealing with a bootblack parlor which is really a "front" for a boot-
legging joint.

Musical Numbers: (No information)

HOW NEWTOWN PREPARED (1916), 2 Acts
Producer, Book, Staging, Lyrics: Salem Tutt Whitney, J. Homer
    Tutt
Music: Salem Tutt Whitney, J. Homer Tutt, Taylor L. Corwell
    and Clarence G. Wilson

Cast of Characters:
George Washington Bullion   Salem Tutt Whitney
Sam Cain, Bullion's Friend   J. Homer Tutt
Pedro Gomez, Mexican Spy   Al Watts
Eagle Eye, Indian Chief   Dave Liston
Said Pasha, Turkish Prince   Julian Costello
Major Bragg, Civil War Relic   Sam Gardner
Elder Toots, Newtown Pastor   Tommy Hall
Captain Marmon   Alonzo Fenderson
Eph Snow, New Oracle   Sam Gray
Veterans of the U. S. A.
    Private Arsenal   Lee Marshall
    Corporal Remington   Nathan Cash
    Sergeant Duposal   Charles Hicks
    Lieutenant Krupp   O. D. Carter
    Major Bragg   Charles M. Lawrence
    Colonel Hullabaloo   Albert Crane

Martha Bullion   Helen Clinton
Moana Sweet, Bullion's Ward   Mattie Lewis
Louise Dillingham, Society Lady   Carrie King
Samantha Haskfort, Suffragette   Julian Costello
Peggie Flipp, News Dispenser   Emma Jackson
Pargaret Simpson   Helen Jackson
Mandy Lee   Estelle Cash
Lucinda Thompson   Sweetie May
Senora Flores, Secret Service   Blanche Thompson
    Agent
Soldiers, Farmhands, Turks, Sailors, Citizens, etc.: Edna Gibbs,
    Juanita Hicks, Josie Graham, Ora Dunlop, Virginia Wheeler

Story: The town of Newtown is celebrating a reunion of the Grand
Old Veterans of the U. S. A. The young people are for preparedness
but the veterans and old heads believe in the efficiency of a volun-
teer army or peace at any price.
        Bullion is at the head of the older element of the town and
they visit his plantation to be instructed by him just what stand to
take. While there, news reaches them of the battle of Carrizal and
the gallant fight made by the Tenth (black) Cavalry. After a dramatic recital of the conflict, they are unanimously for preparedness.
        A spy in the employ of the Mexican government makes his
appearance and tries to discourage their preparations and urges them
to fight on the side of Mexico. Failing in this, he manages to get
the entire regiment under Bullion, who has been made Colonel,
aboard a boat controlled by his secret agents. When the fact becomes known, the boat is far from its original destination. Soon
after, the boat encounters a gale and is blown to pieces. Those on
board are rescued by a foreign warship. When this vessel lands,
the Bullion party finds itself in one of the Turkish possessions where
they are forced to take sides with the Turks in their war against the
Allies. After many vicissitudes, the company is rescued by the
troops of an American man-of-war and all ends happily.

Musical Numbers:

Act 1

Opening Chorus	Company
Grand Old Veterans in the U. S. A.	Sam Gardner and Veterans
Study in Black and White	J. Homer Tutt and Carrie King
Girls Quartette	Carrie King, Emma Jackson, Helen Jackson, Mattie Lewis
Old Veterans Jubilee	O. D. Carter, Sam Gray, Lee Marshall, Sam Gardner
"The Wedding of the Flower and the Bee"	J. Homer Tutt, Estelle Cash
"All I Want is Plenty of Loving"	Billie Young and Chorus
"My Sweet Hawaiian Home"	Blanche Thompson and Male Quartette
"Sweet Melody Blues"	Sweetie May and Chorus
Buck Dancing	O. D. Carter and Lee Marshall
"Little Boy, Little Girl"	Ora Dunlop, Virginia Wheeler,

	Juanita Hicks, Helen Jackson, Sam Gray, Alonzo Fenderson, J. Hicks, Nat Cash
Finale Farewell	Blanche Thompson, Salem Tutt Whitney, J. Homer Tutt and Entire Ensemble

Act 2

"The Tar's Farewell"	Soldiers and Nurses
"The Zoo"	Blanche Thompson, J. Homer Tutt and Entire Chorus
"Help Cometh from Above"	Blanche Thompson, Salem Tutt Whitney, J. Homer Tutt, Mattie Lewis, Sam Gardner, Dave Liston
"Ode to Allah"	Chorus
"Turkish Drill"	Turkish Soldiers
"Turkey"	J. Homer Tutt, Blanche Thompson and Company
"The Pasha's Dream"	Julian Costello
"If I Could Make the Sun Stand Still"	Salem Tutt Whitney
"Dixie Land is Calling Me"	Entire Company

Executive Staff:

T. L. Corwell	Manager
H. D. Collins	Business Manager
Clarence G. Wilson	Musical Director
J. Homer Tutt	Stage Manager
Ora Dunlop	Wardrobe Mistress
William Walton	Stage Carpenter
Elmer Jenkins	Property Man

HUMMIN' SAM (1933)
Producer: No Data

Cast of Characters:

Hummin' Sam	Gertrude "Baby" Cox
Uncle Ned	Speedy Smith
Totem	Alonza Bozen
Hot Cakes	Bunny Allen
First Jockey, Second Jockey	The Two Chesterfields
Yellow George	Lionel Monagas
Edward Holton	Lorenzo Tucker
Mr. Conners	John Lee
Mike	Sandy
Madge Carter	Madeline Belt
Caesar, Cicero	Jones and Allen
Mr. Carter	Al Wells
Mae Carter	Flo Brown
Freddie Marlowe	Cecil Rivers
Nina May	Edith Wilson

Clara   Hannah Syvester
Drum Major   J. Merdo Brown
Miss Jitters   Louise Cook

Musical Numbers: (No information)

THE HUSBAND (1909 edition)
    (Pekin Stock Company, Chicago)
Producer: J. Ed. Green
Book, Lyrics: Flournoy E. Miller, Aubrey Lyles
Music: Joe Jordan
Staging: J. Ed. Green

Cast of Characters:
The Husband   Harrison Stewart
His Wife   Lottie Grady
Friend of the Wife   Jennie Ringgold
The Cook   Ada Smith
Hanna   Elvira Johnson
Mr. Durant   Jerry Mills
Butler   C. B. Winfrey
Dishrag   Charles H. Gilpin
The Maid   Nettie Lewis

Story: (No information)

Musical Numbers:
"Lulu"   Nettie Lewis
"Oh, You Kid"   Nettie Lewis
"Good Evening, Caroline"   Elvira Johnson
"You Dear"   J. F. Mores
"Dissipation"   Harrison Stewart
"Happiness"   Florence Brown
"Take Your Time"   Harrison Stewart
"Iv'e Got Good Common Sense"   Harrison Stewart
"Friend of the Family"   Matt Marshall
"Mine, All Mine"   Jennie Ringgold
"Susanna" (Bob Cole and Rosa-   Nettie Lewis
    mond Johnson)
"Running Wild" (James Brymn)   Elvira Johnson

IN BAMVILLE (1924)
Producer: Noble Sissle, Eubie Blake
Book: Noble Sissle, Lew Payton
Music, Lyrics: Noble Sissle, Eubie Blake
Staging: Julian Mitchell

Cast of Characters:
At the Piano   Eubie Blake
Mandy Green, the Deacon's   Amanda Randolph
    Wife

Sammy, Mandy Green's Baby   Gwendolyn Fenster
Black Joe, Jr.   Addison Carey
That Comedy Chorus Girl   Josephine Baker
Struttin' Drum Major and His   J. Mardo Brown
     Bamville Band
Bill Splivena, Plantation Owner   W. A. Hann
Mr. Hez Brown, President of   William Grundy
     Bamville Fair
Mrs. Hez Brown, the Wife   Inez Clough
Angeline Brown, the daughter   Lottie Gee
Jessie Johnson   Elizabeth Welsh
Manda, Bill Spliven's Niece   Valaida Snow
Uncle Eph, Trainer of Rarin'   Fred Jennings
     To-Go
Dobby Hicks, Race-Horse Tout   Noble Sissle
Dan Jackson, Owner of Rarin'   Ivan H. Browning
     To-Go
Shorty, Dumb Luck's Jockey   Ferd Robinson
Johnnie Wise, Village Rube   Russell Smith
Mose Washington, Owner of   Lew Payton
     Dumb Luck
Joe Dolks, Owner of Jump   Johnny Hudgins
     Steady
Silas Green, the Deacon   Lee J. Randall
Bookmaker   George Jones, Jr.
Snappy (Rarin' To-Go's Jockey)   Charlie Davis
Sandy Scarecrow's Jockey   Curtis Carpenter

In the Bank

Bank Policeman   Ferd Robinson
The Porter   Fred Jennings
Secretary   Valada Snow
Cashier   Richard Cooper
Bookkeeper   Percy Colston
Draft Clerk   Claude Lawson
Auditor   Addison Carey
Four Harmony Kings (Quartette): Ivan H. Browning, W. H.
     Berry, George Jones, Jr., W. A. Hann.

At the Wedding

Mischief   Mildred Smallwood
A Deserted Female   Josephine Baker
Her Bunco Attorney   Lloyd Keyes
Town Flappers, Bank Clerks, Barbers, Citizens, Clerks, etc.
Bamville Opera House Band--Joe Smith, Director; J. M. Brown,
     Drum Major; E. C. Caldwell, J. W. Mobley, Ferdie Robinson,
     George Dosher, Horace Langhorne, L. J. Randall, R. Cooper,
     Willard Sinkford.
Jazzy Jassmines--Carmen Marshall, Aimee Bates, Edith Simms,
     Rose Young, Anita Alexander, Cecilia Butler.
Bandanaland Girls--Bertha Wright, Ruby Barbee, Mae Cobb, Hilda
     Perleno, Ruth Walker, Marie Fraine, Mae Fortune, Mildred
     Hudgins, Marion Gee, Lolita Hall, Evelyn Harris, Viola Jack-
     son, Jimmie Jordan, Thelma McLaughlin, Josie Miles, Helen
     Mitchell, Mabel Nichols, Catherine Parker, Jennie Salmon,

Bobbie Smith, Mary Scott, Clara Titus, Essie Worth, Mildred
Smallwood.

Bamville Vamps--June Johnson, Doris Mignotte, Francie Williams,
Jaculine Williams, Margaret Tyson, Rose Russell.

Syncopated Sunflowers--John Alexander, Chic Fisher, Howard Elmore, Richard Wheaton, Willie Sheppard, Lloyd Keyes, Earl
Crompton, Bournis Brown, Benjamin Mifflin, Carl Tomlinson.

Story: (No information)

Synopsis:

Act I
Last Day of the Bamville, Mississippi Fair
Scene 1--South and Main Streets, Bamville.
Scene 2--Stables at the Fair Grounds.
Scene 3--Betting Ring at the Fair Grounds.
Scene 4--Paddock.
Scene 5--Bamville Race Trace (in the stretch).

Act II
Evening of the Same Day
Scene 1--Lawn Party, Bill Spliven's Plantation Home.
Scene 2--Street in Bamville Next Morning.
Scene 3--Bamville County Bank the Following Day.
Scene 4--Sissle and Blake's Studio.
Scene 5--Wedding of Dan and Angeline on the Stage at the Bamville
Opera House.

Musical Numbers:

Act I

"Have a Good Time, Everybody"	Opening Chorus
"That Charleston Dance"	Elizabeth Welsh
"Fate Is the Slave of Love"	Miss Gee and Mr. Browning
"I'll Find My Love in D-I-X-I-E"	Noble Sissle and His Dixie Darlings
"Bandanaland"	Lee Randall, Russell Smith, and Bandanaland Girls
The Sons of Old Black Joe	By Syncopated Sunflowers
Old Black Joe	W. A. Hann
"Jassamine Lane"	Miss Gee, and Mr. Browning and Jassamine Chorus
"Jump Steady--Dumb Luck"	Johnny Hudgins, Lew Payton
"Breakin' 'Em Down"	Valaida Snow and Chorus
(Introducing Joe Smith--Jazz Cornetist)	
"Jockey's Life of Mine"	Charlie Davis and Jockeys

Act II

"Dixie Moon"	George Jones, Jr. and Chorus
"Manda"	Valaida Snow and Syncopated Sunflowers
"All the Wrong You've Done Me"	Lew Payton and Johnnie Hudgins
"Thinking of Me"	Miss Gee and Mr. Browning
"Land of Dancing Pickaninnies"	Charlie Davis and Bamville Picks

Selections   Four Harmony Kings
"Take Down Dis Letter"   Lew Payton
In Their Studio--A Few Minutes   Sissle and Blake
    with Chocolate Dandies
(By Sissle and Blake and their Struttin' Co.)
Vocal and Orchestra Arrangements by Lorenzo Calduel.

IN DAHOMEY (1903)
Producers: Bert A. Williams and George Walker
Book, Staging: Jesse A. Shipp
Lyrics: Paul Lawrence Dunbar, Alex Rogers
Music: Will Marion Cook

Cast of Characters, Prologue:
    Time--Three months before beginning of Play.
    Place--Dahomey
Je-Je, a caboceer   Chas. Moore
Menuki, Messenger of the King   Wm. Elkins
Mose Lightfoot, Agent of Daho-   Wm. Barker
    mey Colonization Society
Soldiers, Natives, etc.

Cast of Characters, Acts I and II:
Shylock Homestead, called "Shy"   Bert A. Williams
    by his friends
Rareback Pinkerton, "Shy's" per-   George W. Walker
    sonal friend and adviser
Hamilton Lightfoot, president of   Pete Hampton
    a colonization society
Dr. Straight (in name only),   Fred Douglas
    street fakir
Mose Lightfoot, brother of   Wm. Barker
    Hamilton, thinks Dahomey a
    land of great promise
George Reeder, proprietor of an   Alex Rogers
    intelligence office
Henry Stampfield, letter carrier,   Walter Richardson
    with an argument against
    immigration
Me Sing, a Chinese cook   George Catlin
Hustling Charley, promoter of   J. A. Shipp
    Get-the-Coin Syndicates
Leather, a bootblack   Richard Conners
Officer Still   J. Leubrie Hill
White Wash Man   Green Tapley
Messenger Rush, but not often   Theodore Pankey
Pansy, Daughter of Cecilia   Abbie Mitchell
    Lightfoot, in love with
    Leather
Cecilia Lightfoot, Hamilton's   Mrs. Hattie McIntosh
    wife
Mrs. Stringer, dealer in for-   Mrs. Lottie Williams

George Walker [left] As Rareback Pinkerton and Bert Williams As
Shylock Homestead with Aida Overton Walker in "In Dahomey" at the
Shaftesbury Theatre, London, circa 1903

saken patterns and editor of
fashion notes in "Beanville
Agitator"

Rosetta Lightfoot, a troublesome   Aida Overton Walker
   young thing

Colonists, Natives, etc.

Story: A group of unscrupulous business men in Boston proposed
to colonize some land in Africa as a haven for oppressed Negroes,
sending "Rareback Pinkerton" down to Florida to persuade a wealthy
but senile Negro to finance the scheme.   "Shylock Homstead, " a
happy simpleton who beat a drum in a Salvation Army Band, went
to Florida with the crooks, unknowingly being used as a dupe by
Rareback in the presentation of the scheme.   When businessmen
learned that Shylock was the heir to the great Florida fortune,
Rareback dazzled him by offers of friendship, just so that he would
be appointed trustee to the estate.   In possession of Shylock's money, Rareback blossomed in glorious clothes and became the leader
of Florida and Dahomey society, while Shylock remained the bump-
kin with a blind faith in his friend's goodness.   Finally after Rareback made such a preposterous demand for money that Shylock found
the strength to refuse, the simpleton signed over the remainder of
his inheritance to the Dahomey colony.

Synopsis:

Prologue--Scene: Garden of the Caboceer (Governor of a Province)

Act I.   Public Square, Boston

Act II.   Scene 1--Exterior of Lightfoot's House, Gatorville, Florida
         Scene 2--Road, one-and-a-half miles from Gatorville
         Scene 3--Interior of Lightfoot's Home

Special: At Finale of last Act will be presented a Grand Spectacu-
    lar Cake Walk

Musical Numbers:

Prologue

Dahomian Queen	Anna Cook, Morris Smith and Company
"Caboceers Choral"	Company

Act I

Overture	
Opening Chorus: "Swing Along, " "Mellie Green"	Henry Troy and Chorus
"My Castle on the River Nile" (interpolated)	George Walker and Chorus
"Broadway in Dahomey" (inter- polated)	Williams, Walker and Company
Entire Act	

Act II

"Actor Lady"	Aida Overton Walker
"Brown Skin Baby Mine"	Abbie Mitchell, Richard Con- nors and Chorus
"Leaders of Coloured Aristoc- racy"	Hattie McIntosh and Company

"Society" (Soprano solo by Ella   Pete Hampton, Hattie McIntosh,
    Anderson)   Lloyd Gibbs, Richard Con-
                                             nors and Company
"The Jonah Man" (interpolated)   Bert Williams
"A Rich Coon's Babe" (inter-   Aida Overton Walker
    polated)
"The Czar"   George Walker assisted by Aida
                                             Overton Walker and Com-
                                             pany
"Emancipation Day"   Williams, Walker and Company
Emancipation Day March and Cake Walk Finale
(The statue in this scene is done by Mr. Walter Richardson.)
The Orchestra under the direction of the composer, assisted by
    Mr. James Vaughan.
Lyrics of "Broadway in Dahomey," "Jonah Man," "Rich Coon's
    Babe," "The Czar" by Alex Rogers.   "Dahomian Queen" written
    by F. B. Williams and J. Leubrie Hill.

IN ETHIOPIAVILLE (1913)
Producer: Frank Montgomery
Book, Lyrics, Music: Frank Montgomery

Cast of Characters:
Shylock Holmestead   Frank Montgomery
Dandy Jones Pinkerton   Ed Lea Coleman
Joseph Green   Charlie Ross
Georgiana Green   Florence McClain
Semantha Green   Emma Morton
George Augusta Stokes, a   Charles Nickerson
    Policeman
Eliza Jones, Nurse   Lila Moore
Lucinder Jones, the Lady   Belle Smedley
    from Boston
Little Willie Jones, the Village   Sollie Jones
    Pest
Saddie Green, His Little   Edna Coleman
    Sweetheart
"Nick Carter," the King of   Harry McDonald
    Detectives
Village Boys and Girls: Sadie Thompson, Blanche Thompson, Will
    Duncan, Mary Thompson, Elwood Woodring, Mamie Garrett,
    Belle Thompson, George Smith, Bessie Bullard, Beah Moore.

Story: The plot had to do with a jewel case which was stolen from
old man Green. The robbery occurred after Green and his family
had decided to move to Boston. The case must be recovered and
detectives are sent for to ferret out the deed. In the meanwhile,
two down and out minstrel men appear on the scene; learning of
the theft and the reward, they decide to impersonate the real detectives to take advantage of the situation. The play ends with
Shylock Holmestead stumbling onto the lost case in a card game,
thus proving to be a real detective in spite of his objections to
the role which he had decalred would only land him in jail.

Musical Numbers:

"Bless Your Everloving Little Heart"	Billy Ewing
"Musical Moon"	Billy Ewing and Chorus
"On the Mississippi"	
"Dixie"	
"Syncopated Boogie Boo"	
"Oh, Ho, In the Morning"	
"Peace Wid the World"	Frank Montgomery
"Old Boston Town"	
"Crazy About Some Boy"	
"Our Old Man"	
"I Wonder Why They Call Me Snowball"	
"When Will I Plant the Tree"	

IN THE JUNGLES (1911)
    (Black Patti Troubadours)
Book: Will A. Cook, Al F. Watts
Music: Will Marion Cook, Alex Rogers
Staging: Jerry Mills

Principal Cast of Characters: Sissieretta Jones (Black Patti), Will
    A. Cook, Julius Glenn, Al F. Watts, Tillie Seguin, Charles
    Bongia, Jeanette Murphy, William Greer, Fanny Morton, Mabel
    DeHeard, Rose Rayne, Johnny Livingstone, Zittella Mason,
    Mayme Smith, Mary Evans, Ada Douglass, Nellie Peterson.

Story: The story deals with a Baptist Missionary Society that is
interested in rescuing a young lady who has been lost in the jungles but who is later discovered to be safe having been made a
Queen by the natives. She is later returned to her native land
through the efforts of a confidence man, a detective and his valet.

Musical Numbers:

"My Jewel of the Nile"	Black Patti
"Home Sweet Home"	Black Patti
"Never Let the Same Bee Sing You Twice"	Julius Glenn
"Plant a Watermelon by My Grave"	Julius Glenn
"Roll a Little Pill for Me"	Will A. Cook
"Baby Rose"	Black Patti
"Love is King"	Black Patti, Charles Bongia
"Ragtime Love"	Marie Greer
"Let the Juice Ooze Through"	Julius Glenn
"O, Say Wouldn't That Be a Dream"	Julius Glenn
"My Dreamland"	Julius Glenn

JAZZBO REGIMENT (1929)
Producer: No Data

Principal Cast of Characters: Sam Grismond, Andrew Tribble (as
    Ophelia Snow), Clinton "Dusty" Fletcher, John Mason, Gertrude
    Saunders, Chappelle and Stinnette, Columbus Jackson, Pearl
    McCormack, Joe Jordan

Story: The tale of the adventures of two hillbillies from Kentucky
who join a marine regiment and are sent off to a mythical isle somewhere, an isle where many adventures await them. They become
heroes in a variety of amusing ways.

Musical Numbers: (No information)

JUMP FOR JOY (1941)
Synopsis:
Overture

Act I

Scene 1--Sun-Tanned Tenth of the Nation. Lyrics by Paul Webster,
    Music by Hal Borne and Otis Rene. Entire Company.
Scene 2--Prologue. Duke Ellington.
Scene 3--It's Only Propaganda. Paul White and Wonderful Smith.
Scene 4--The Brown Skin Gal in the Calico Gown. Lyrics by Paul
    Webster, Music by Duke Ellington.

The Boy	Herb Jeffries
The Girl	Judy Carol
Calico Girls	Artie Brandon, Lucille Battle, Avanelle Harris, Doris Ake, Myrtle Fortune, Suzette Johnson
Dance by	The Hi-Hatters

Scene 5--Bli-Blip. Lyrics by Sid Kuller, Music by Duke Ellington.

Girl	Marie Bryant
Boy	Paul White

Scene 6--Resigned to Living, by Hal Fimberg.

Gertrude	Suzette Johnson
Noel	Al Guster
First Caller	Herb Jeffries
Second Caller	William Lewis
Man	Wonderful Smith

Scene 7--Pot, Pan and Skillet.
"Bugle Break, "--"Subtle Slough"   Music by Duke Ellington
Scene 8--Chocolate Shake. Lyrics by Paul Webster, Music by
    Duke Ellington.

Bartender	Paul White
Boy	Al Guster
Girl	Ivy Anderson
Cigarette Girl	Marie Bryant

Scene 9--Wonderful Smith. Monologue by Wonderful Smith.
Scene 10--"I Got It Bad and That Ain't Good. " Lyrics by Paul
    Webster, Music by Duke Ellington.

Singer	Ivy Anderson

Scene 11--Two Left Feet. Lyrics by Paul Webster, Music by Hal
    Borne.

Herb Jeffries and Judy Carol As They Appeared in Duke Ellington's
"Jump for Joy," circa 1941

Schoolboy	Paul White
Cindy	Marie Bryant
First Sister	Avanelle Harris
Second Sister	Lucille Battle
Fairy Godmother	Evelyn Burrwell
Prince Charming	Lawrence Harris

Jitterbugs--Hit-Hatters, Artie Brandon, Myrtle Fortune, Millie
    Munroe.
Scene 12--Joe Turner.
Scene 13--The Life of Our Time, by Hal Fimberg.

Carlyle	Wonderful Smith
Ephedrine	Louise Franklin
Sharpie	Pan
Streetwalker	Alice Key
Kit Carson	Pot
Johnny	Skillet

Scene 14--Al Guster. "Stomp Caprice" by Mercer Ellington.
Scene 15--Whether or Not. Pan and Skillet.
Scene 16--Uncle Tom's Cabin is a Drive-In Now. Lyrics by Paul
    Webster, Music by Hal Borne.

Uncle Tom	Roy Glenn
Aunt Jemima	Evelyn Burrwell
Hostess	Ivy Anderson
Waitress	Marie Bryant

Hit-Hatters, Ensemble
Overture

Act II

Scene 1--"Jump for Joy." Lyrics by Sid Kuller and Paul Webster,
    Music by Duke Ellington Choir and Ensemble.
Scene 2--If Life Were All Peaches and Cream. Lyrics by Paul
    Webster, Music by Hal Borne.

First Couple	Judy Carol and Herb Jeffries
Second Couple	Marie Bryant and Paul White

Scene 3--"Nothin'." Lyrics by Sid Kuller and Ray Golden, Music
    by Hal Borne.

Singer	Ivy Anderson

Scene 4--You're in the Army Now, by Sid Kuller.

Doctor	Roy Glenn
First Draftee	Paul White
Second Draftee	Pan
Third Draftee	Skillet
Fourth Draftee	Pot

Scene 5--Concerto for Klinkers. Music by Duke Ellington.
Scene 6--Shh! He's on the Beat. Lyrics by Sid Kuller and Hal
    Fimberg, Music by Duke Ellington.

Proprietor	Roy Glenn
Waitress	Marie Bryant
Bartender	Wonderful Smith
First Couple	Hyacinth Cotten and Bene Greene
Second Couple	Alice Key and Paul White
Third Couple	Clarence Landry and Udell Johnson

Fourth Couple	Avanelle Harris and Pot
Cop	Pan
Police Captain	Joe Turner

Scene 7--Vignettes, by Sid Kuller.

The Duke	Duke Ellington
First Couple	Judy Carol and Herb Jeffries
Second Couple	Marie Bryant and Udell Johnson

Scene 8--The Tune of the Hickory Stick. Lyrics by Paul Webster, Music by Hal Borne.

Singer	Judy Carol
Dancer	Al Guster

Scene 9--Willie Lewis.
Scene 10--Sidewalk Incident.

Panhandler	Wonderful Smith
Passerby	Paul White

Scene 11--Made to Order, by Sid Kuller.

First Tailor	Pan
Second Tailor	Skillet
Customer	Pot

Scene 12--Sharp Easter. Lyrics by Sid Kuller, Music by Duke Ellington.
Scene 13--Finale. Entire Cast.

Duke Ellington's Orchestra:

Lawrence Brown--Trombone	Ben Webster--Tenor Saxophone
Juan Tizol--Valve Trombone	Otto Hardwick--Alto Saxophone
Jimmy Blanton--Bass Viol	Harry Carney--Baritone Saxo-
Sonny Greer--Drums	phone
Freddie Guy--Guitar	Rex Stewart--Trumpet
Johnny Hodges--Alto Saxophone	Ray Nance--Trumpet
Barney Bigard--Tenor Saxophone	Wallace Jones--Trumpet
	Joe Nanton--Trombone

Girls of the Ensemble: Artie Brandon, Lucille Battle, Avanelle Harris, Ethelyn Stevenson, Myrtle Fortune, Alice Key, Doris Ake, Hyacinth Cotten, Millie Munroe, Louise Franklin, Patsy Hunter.
Choir: Maudie Bilbrew, Eddievies Flenoury, Evelyn Burrwell, Elizabeth Green, Edward Short, Bene Greene, Lawrence Harris, Roy Glenn.
The Hit-Hatters: Clarence Landry, Vernod Bradley, Udell Johnson.

JUMP STEADY (1922), 2 Acts 11 Scenes
Producers: Salem Tutt Whitney and J. Homer Tutt

Principal Cast of Characters: Salem Tutt Whitney, J. Homer Tutt, Margaret Lee, Henrietta Lovelass, Percy Colston, Margaret Simms, Nat Cash, Helen Fenderson, Bessie Simms, Elvita Davis, Elizabeth Campbell, Edith Simms, Joyce Robinson, Hazel Springer, Helen Warren, Viola Mandero, May Oliver, Ethel Pope, George Randol, Jennie Dancy, Bernice Winston, Chester Jones, George Phillips, Henry Thompson, Dick Conway, John Dancy, Leroy Bloomfield, Amon Davis

Story: Amon Davis is the victim of schemers Hamford (J. Homer
Tutt) and Samford (Salem Tutt Whitney) who swindle him out of a
large sum of money.

Musical Numbers:
"Dear Old Southland"   Margaret Lee
"Syncopated Blues"   Margaret Lee
"Ja Da Blues"   Julia Moody
"Breaking a Leg Dance," a song and dance during which Lottie
     Harris, Nelly Brown, Julia Moody, and Margaret Simms sang
     and danced up and down the aisles.

K OF P (1923)
Producer: Collington Hayes

Cast of Characters: Collington Hayes, Helen Hayes, Bessie White,
     Newell Morse, Olivette West, Malachia Smith

Story: The story is about two men who pretend to be attending
lodge meetings as a subterfuge to get away from their wives.

Musical Numbers: "Tomorrow," "Ghost of Mr. Jazz," "Asleep in
     the Deep," "Got My Habits On," "Royal Garden Blues," "Da Da
     Strain"

KEEP IT UP (1922)
Producer: I. M. Weingarden

Principal Cast of Characters: Billy Higgins, Ernest Whitman,
     Clifford Ross, Alice Gorgas, Susie Sutton, Lena Leggett,
     Henrietta Leggett, Edna Hicks, Ollie Burgoyne, Bob Brawlet,
     Al Curtis, Iola Young

Story: The show included the following two sketches: First Act
Sketch: "Circus at the Cut Out Inn"--Billy Higgins portrays the
role of a hotel porter. Second Act Sketch: "The Greedy Man"--
Billy Higgins portrays a judge.
     Another highlight of the show was Clifford Ross' impersona-
tion of Bert Williams in a song entitled, "At the Poker Club."

Musical Numbers: (No information)

KEEP SHUFFLIN' (1928)
Producers: Flournoy E. Miller and Aubrey Lyles
Book: Miller and Lyles
Lyrics: Henry Creamer and Andy Razaf
Music: Jimmy Johnson and "Fats" Waller
Orchestration: Will Vodery
Musical Director: Jimmy Johnson
Dances and Ensembles: Clarence Robinson

Cast of Characters:

Boss	Paul Floyd
Brother Jones	John Gregg
Mose	John Virgel
Grit	Greta Anderson
Walter	Clarence Robinson
Scrappy	Byron Jones
Evelyn	Evelyn Keyes
Honey	Honey Brown
Alice	Jean Starr
Mrs. Jenkins	Margaret Lee
Steve Jenkins	Flournoy E. Miller
Sam Peck	Aubrey Lyles
Maude	Maude Russell
Yarbo	Billie Yarbo
Hazel	Hazel Sheppard
Marie	Marie Dove
Bill	Gilbert Holland
Joseph	Herman Listerino

In Orchestra

At the Piano   Jimmy Johnson
(Piano courtesy Baldwin Company)
Behind the Bugle   Jabbo Smith

Ladies of the Ensemble--Hazel Sheppard, Gussie Williams, Ethel
    Moses, Marion L. Tyler, Vivienne G. Brooks, Lila Brogdan,
    Evelyn Irving, Gladyce Bronson, Gertrude Gaines, Violet
    Speedy, Marie Dove, Shirley Abbey, Jean Kane, Peggy Bur-
    nett, Billie Rickmon, Madeline Odlum, Clarice Egbert, Ruth
    Cherry, Ruth Lambert, Greta Anderson, Thelma Green, Edythe
    Parker.

Jubilee Singers and Dancers--Charles Lawrence, Herman Listerino,
    Lloyd Mitchell, Howard Browne, Joseph A. Willis, Chris Gor-
    don, Edwin Alexander, Sandy Brown and Kenneth Harris.

"Alabama Day" Paraders, Citizens of Jimtown, etc.
The entire production owned and operated by "Still Shufflin', Inc. "

Story: (No information)

Synopsis:

Act I
Scene 1--Exterior of Industrial School, Jimtown.
Scene 2--Street in Jimtown.
Scene 3--Front Yard of Steve Jenkins' Home.

Act II
Scene 1--Town Hall.
Scene 2--Main Street, Jimtown.
Scene 3--Interior of Steve Jenkins' Home.
Scene 4--Outskirts of Jimtown.
Scene 5--Back in Front Yard of Steve Jenkins' Home.

Musical Numbers:

Act I
Opening Chorus (by Creamer and Vodery)   Ensemble

"Teasing Mama" (by Creamer and Johnson)	John Virgel, Greta Anderson, and Company
"Choc'late Bar" (by Razaf and Waller)	Evelyn Keyes and Byron Jones
"Labor Day Parade" (by Razaf and Todd)	Clarence Robinson and Company
"Give Me the Sunshine" (by Creamer, Johnson and Conrad)	Jean Starr, John Virgel, Clarence Robinson
"Leg It" (by Creamer, Todd and Conrad)	Maude Russell and Company
Exhortation Theme from Hamekraw Negro Rhapsody (by Creamer and Johnson)	John Virgel and Jubilee Glee Club
"Sippi" (by Creamer, Johnson and Conrad)	Maude Russell
"How Jazz Was Born" (by Razaf and Waller)	Jean Starr and Company
Finale	Entire Company

Act II

"Keep Shufflin'" (by Razaf and Waller)	John Virgel and Company
"Everybody's Happy in Jimtown" (by Razaf and Waller)	Male Octette
"Give Me the Sunshine"--Reprise (by Creamer, Johnson and Conrad)	Miller and Lyles
"Dusky Love" (by Creamer and Vodery)	Maude Russell, Clarence Robinson and Company
"Charlie, My Back Door Man" (by Creamer and Todd)	Jean Starr and Strut Men
"On the Levee" (by Creamer and Johnson)	Maude Russell and Girls
Finale--"Skiddle de Scow" (by Johnson and Bradford)	

LIZA (1922)
Producer: Irvin C. Miller
Book: Irvin C. Miller
Lyrics and Music: Maceo Pinkard
Special Lyrics: Nat Vincent
Staging: Walter Brosics

Cast of Characters (In order of appearance):

Squire Norris	Alonzo Fenderson
Liza Norris	Margaret Simms
Nora	Gertrude Saunders
Uncle Pete	William Simms

Opposite: Ad for Irvin C. Miller's "Liza," circa 1924.

Parson Jordan	Packer Ramsey
Judge Plummer	Quintard Miller
Ras Johnson	R. Eddie Greenlee
Dandy	Thaddius Drayton
The Sheriff	Will A. Cook
Ice Cream Charlie	Irvin C. Miller
Bodiddily	Emmett Anthony
Tom Liggett	Billy Mills
Sam Sykes	Doe Doe Green
Mammy	Elizabeth Terrill
Mandy	Maude Russell
Harry Davis	Snippy Mason
Bill Jones	Donald Fields

Brown-Skin Vamps: Misses Bee Freeman, Doris Mignotte, Agnes
    Anthony, Thelma Greene, Zudora DeGaston, Gladys Robinson,
    Louise Dunbar and Elizabeth Welch.
Jimtown Flappers: Misses Blanche Thompson, Helen Dunmore,
    Lena Dukes, Edith Simms, Marion Jones, Ethel Taylor, May
    Green and Mary Fortune.
Dancing Honey Girls: Misses Aurora Davis, Viola Branch, Clara
    Townsend, Millie Cooke, Angeline Hammond, Cornell Vigai,
    Gladys Scott, Helen Fenderson.
Struttin' Dandies: Messrs. Ruben Brown, St. Clair Dotson, Charles
    Lawrence, Lloyd Mitchell, Franklyn O'Cause, Cornelius Burton,
    John Gaelard, and Paul Sullivan.

Story: Review: Patterson James, Chicago Whip, 1924: "Comedy
of this kind is not suited to Negro players, but they insist on doing
it. Instead of working out their own ideas giving them the flavor of
their own racy uniqueness, they rehash white men's concepts of
Negro character. In doing that they lose all semblance of reality
and naturalness and become tiresome."

Synopsis:
Act I
Scene 1--In Front of Squire Norris's Home.
Scene 2--Town Jail.
Scene 3--Sam Sykes' Barber Shop.
Scene 4--A Street in Jimtown.
Scene 5--"On the Levee."
Act II
Scene 1--Jimtown Square.
Scene 2--A Street in Jimtown.
Scene 3--Jimtown Graveyard.
Scene 4--Street in Jimtown.
Scene 5--Corridor of Jimtown Ball Room.
Scene 6--The Ball Room.
Time: Summer Time. Place: Jimtown, South Carolina.

Musical Numbers (Orchestra under direction of Lieut. Tim Brymn):
Act I, Scene 1
Opening Chorus--"Tag Dag"	Ensemble
Song--"Pleasure"	Gertrude Saunders and Chorus

Song--"I'm the Sheriff"	Will Cook and Boys
Song--"Liza"	Thaddius Drayton, Margaret Simms, Gertrude Saunders, and Chorus

Scene 2

Specialty--(Memories)	Agnes Anthony, Viola Branch, May Green, Gladys Taylor, Ethel Taylor and Angeline Hammond

Scene 3

Song--"Just a Barber Shop Cord"	The Gang

Scene 4

Song--"That Brown-Skin Flapper"	Gertrude Saunders and Flappers

Scene 5

Ensemble--"On the Moonlit Swanee"	Town Folks
Dance--"Essence"	Greenlee and Drayton and Boys
Dance--"Forget Your Troubles"	Boys and Girls
Song--"My Old Man"	Elizabeth Welch, Emmett Anthony and Quintette
Song--"Runnin' Wild Blues"	Misses Saunders, Simms, and Messrs. Greenlee and Drayton and Entire Company

Act II, Scene 1

Song--"The Charleston Dance"	Maude Russell and Girls
Song--"Dandy"	Margaret Simms and Dandies
Song--"My Creole Girl"	R. Eddie Greenlee and Girls

Scene 2

Duet--"Planning"	Margaret Simms and Thaddius Drayton

Scene 3

The Ghost Dance	Dotson and Mitchell

Scene 4

Song--"Love Me"	Gertrude Saunders

Scene 5

Dance	Four Steppers
Jimtown Speedster	Eddie Fields
Specialty	Emmett Anthony
Specialty	Greenlee and Drayton
Song--"Don't Be Blue"	Gertrude Saunders
Finale	Entire Company

LUCKY SAM FROM ALABAM' (1914)
    (Black Patti Troubadours)

Cast of Characters:

Miss Inez Jones, Principal of the Colored Schools	Sissieretta Jones (Black Patti)
Sam Toles	Harrison Stewart
"Ray," a good-natured tramp	Will A. Cook
A Lassie	Viola Stewart
Pansy Wilson	Tillie Seguin

Others--Jeanette Murphy, George Howard, John Grant, Ethel
  Williams

Story: The story hinges about the fortunes of Sam Toles, a re-
markably keen-witted man, who, by his ambition and luck, rises
from the humble status of a white-washer to the ownership of a
prosperous bootblack parlor, and finally is selected as the teacher
of the public school of the little town in which he lives.

Musical Numbers:
"Goodby"   Sissieretta Jones
"No One"
"Hostess of Social Functions"   Sissieretta Jones and ensemble
"Mornful Rag"
"Going No Place in Particular"   Harrison Stewart
"Pleading Eyes"   Ethel Williams and Chorus
"Watch Your Steps"   Tillie Seguin

LUCKY SAMBO (1925)
Producer: Hertig and Seamon
Music, Book, Lyrics: Porter Grainger, Freddie Johnson
Stage Manager: Jessie A. Shipp
Dances: Leonard Harper

Cast of Characters:
John Whitby   Westley Hill
Mrs. Whitby   Gertie Moore
June   Monette Moore
"Doc" August   Arthur Porter
Rastus Johnson   Joe Byrd
Sambo Jenkins   Tim Moore
Jacks Stafford   Freddie Johnson
Farch   Lena Wilson
Edith Simpson   "Happy" Williams
John Law   Billy Ewing
Jim Nightengale   Clarence Robinson
Hitt Keys   Porter Grainger
Red Cap   Johnny Hudgins
Oil Promoter   Ernest Whitman
Others--Three Dixie Songbirds (Hilda Perleno (soprano), Amanda
      Randolph (second soprano), Berlena Blanks (contralto))

Story: The story is of the discovery of an oil well in the backyard
of rural houses, the oil diggers, the watered stock turned into money, landing in jail, and the modern floor show at the cabaret.

Musical Numbers:
"If You Can't Bring It"   Julia Moody
"Dancing in the Moonlight"   Hilda Perleno, Ernest Whitman
"The Big Parade"   Ernest Whitman

MAGNOLIA (1926)
Producers: Alex Rogers, Luckeyth Roberts
Book, Lyrics: Alex Rogers
Music: Luckeyth Roberts
Dances: Charley Davis

Cast of Characters:

Henry Upton, Bellboy	Dink Stewart
Peggy Switch	Hilda Rogers
Harvey	Paul Bass
Jody	Percy Colston
Mr. Workem	Lionel Monagas
Jasper Downson	Barrington Carter
Johnny Page	George Randol
Chelf	Claude Lawson
Dusty Snow	Alberta Perkins
Sherman	Eddie Hunter
Jerry	Estelle Floyd
Widow Love	Lena Sanford Roberts
Geraldine	Mabel Grant
Magnolia	Catherine Parker

Musical Numbers: (No information)

THE MAN FROM BALTIMORE (1934)
Producer: Joe Hurtig
Book: John Raines
Music: Wen Talbert
Lyrics: Alonzo Govern
Ensembles and Dances: Lew Crawford, John Dancey
Staged by Joe Hurtig

Cast of Characters:
Act 1

Ben Gibs, a Sailor	Alfred "Slick" Chester
Matilda Jensarp, Rufus' Best Girl	Baby Joyce
George Ormas, A Detective	Percy Verwayen
Policeman	Archie Cross
Samuel Austin, Promoter of Blazassus Scheme	Lionel Monagas
Sisters of the Flock	Hattie King, Dora Thompson, Mabel Howard, Massie Patterson, Bertha Powell, Viola Anderson
Aunt Jemima, Brother Smith's Wife	Trixie Smith
Belk Cowan, Angeline Gaillard's Chum	Pearl Gaines
Sunny Sam, Rufus' Side Pardner	Dinah Scott
Angeline Gaillard, Graduate of Tuskegee	Hilda Perleno

Rufus Rastus, Oyster Peddler   Billy Higgins
Useless, Rufus' Dog   Joe Brown

Act 2

Courier   Fred Brown
King of Bahaha   Alfred "Slick" Chester
Palm Girls   Virginia Wright, Hazel Cheek
Native Men   Billy Anderson, Jerry Pierce,
                                     Robert Lee
King's Guards   John Lee, Lovel Wilis
Princess Ito, King's Favorite   Mabel Howard
   Daughter
General Debility   Henry Davis
General Delivery   Sylvan Greenridge
Seeress   Pearl Gaines
Minister Pleni Potentiary (from   Archie Cross
   USA)
Royal Cook   Trixie Smith
Dogolo, Sacred Dog   Joe Brown
Secretary of the Navy   Willie Alant

Wen Talbert's Choir--Hattie King, Dora Thompson, Mabel Howard,
   Massie Patterson, Bertha Powell, Viola Anderson, James
   Skelton, William Winters, Sylvan Greenridge, Harris Davis,
   Archie Cross, Roger Alford
Sixteen Oysterettes--Gwen Graves, Virginia Wright, Fredrica
   Phoenix, Ollie DeSilva, Beulah, Hilda Bendischer, Ruth Dash,
   Lillian Crawford, Marjorie Jackson, Marion Saltan, Juanita
   Boyd, Margaret Nelson, Virginia Groves, Mimi Whiley, Hazel
   Cheek, Grace Michael
Eight Baltimoreans--Roberta Lowery, Judy Sunshine, Beatrice
   McGill, L. Bruce, E. Brown, L. Humphrey, R. Ford, Dorothy
   Jackson
White Wing Brigade--Fred Brown, Billy Anderson, Jerry Pierce,
   Robert Lee, H. Lee, Lovey Willis, Willy Avant
Specialties--Ofelia and Pimento, Three Rhapsodians, Lee and Lee,
   Cora LaRedd, Baby Joyce, Three Ebony Steppers

Story: The story is of a poor man becoming a King on a mythical
island. A city slicker sells a group of suckers tickets for a cruise
to Blazassus, island of plenty, where no one works. The boat, en
route to the island of Blazassus, is shipwrecked and the passengers
and crew are cast upon the island of Bahaha, where Rufus Rastus
becomes King after he promises to marry the princess. However,
the villain is exposed as Samuel Austin and everything ends happily.

Musical Numbers: (No information)

THE MAN FROM 'BAM (1906)
   (Pekin Stock Company, Chicago)
Book: Flournoy E. Miller, Aubrey Lyles
Music: Joe Jordan, Will H. Vodery
Staging: Charles S. Sager

Cast of Characters:
Elder Cashingberry   Charles Sager
Jube Johnson, the man from   L. D. Henderson
  'Bam
Hester Johnson, Jube's wife   Andrew Tribble
Henry Johnson   Joe Weatherly
Captain D. Young   R. T. Thomas
Pete Jones   Henry Reed
Others--Cook Sisters, Josephine Smith, Dolores Thomas, Irwin
    Allen, George Henry, Ethel Jones, Lizzie Wallace, Ora Gris-
    wald, Nina Smith

Story: Good fortune smiles on Jube Johnson of Mobile, Alabama
and former employee of the Illinois Central Railway when he picks
a winner at the race track. With his money he decides to throw a
party for some of his friends in Darkville, a suburb of Chicago.
He does not, however, tell his wife Sarah and when she finds out
she follows Jube to the party and denounces him with no apparent
effect. Later, Jube bets on another horse, Bullfinch, and convinces his friends to do the same. But Jube's wife plays another
horse in the same race called "Jonah Man" because, as she says,
the horse Jube picks will surely drop dead at the post. Poor Jube
loses all of his money as well as his many friends. Sarah, making
a lot of money on Jonah Man's victory, soon becomes a rich woman
while her husband is reduced to poverty. He begs her to take him
back. Sarah relents after much persuasion and many promises from
Jube to do better and all ends serene and happy for "The Man from
'Bam. "

Musical Numbers: "The Man from 'Bam," "Feather Your Nest,"
"I'd Like to Steal You," "I'm Just from 'Bam," "Strolling," "The
Alabama Cadets"

THE MAN FROM 'BAM (1920), 3 Acts
Producer: Chicago Producing Company (Dave Payton, President
    and Treasurer; Joseph Jordan, Vice-President and Manager;
    Jerry Mills, Stage Director)
Music: Joe Jordan

Cast of Characters:
Lazy Dancing   Medill Thompson
Sarah Peabody   Alberta Perkins
Hanna   Mabel Gant
Matron-singer   Margaret Lee
Mandy Lee   Berlena Banks
Young Lady-singer   Maud Russell
Jack Fairfax   Louis Taylor
Bob Skinner (male lead)   Jerry Mills

Musical Numbers: (No information)

MANDY GREEN FROM NEW ORLEANS (1928)
Producer: Majestic Theatrical Circuit (Jack Goldberg)

Principal Cast of Characters: "Babe" Brown, Johnny Stevens, John
    LaRue, Harry "Shrimp" Brock, Johnny Woods, Coleman Titus,
    Johnny Stevens (juvenile), Marguerite Watkins, Billie Jackson,
    Elvira Johnson, Paulestine Stone, Lauretta O'Brien, Margaret
    Ross, Willie B. Young, Lulumay Jackson, Ella Bolden, Susie
    Stevens, Helen Taylor, Maurice Mitchell, Francis Watson

Story: The story starts with the marital problems of Sam Green
(in blackface), hen-pecked husband who does the housework while
his wife, Mandy, spends her time charming the neighbors. Sam is
uncomplaining, in fact he defends his "missus" in her domination of
him. He, indeed, cannot force himself to harm her after she, believing him to be dead, promises to give her insurance money to
her lover. The story winds up in Mexico.

Musical Numbers: (No information)

THE MAYOR OF JIMTOWN (1923)
Producer: Miller and Slater

Principal Cast of Characters: Emmett Anthony, Blanche Thompson,
    Marcus Slayter, Quintard Miller
Story: The plot deals with two partners who operate a grocery
store and who are running for Mayor of Jimtown against each other.

Musical Numbers: (No information)

THE MAYOR OF NEWTOWN (1909)
Producer: Salem Tutt Whitney
Book, Lyrics, Music: Salem Tutt Whitney, J. Homer Tutt

Cast of Characters:

Lem Lee, His Excellency the Mayor	Salem Tutt Whitney
Ned Jenkins, Lem's Protege	J. Homer Tutt
Pedro Manuel, Mexican Half-breed	Russell Smith
Ephraim Snow, Shoemaker and Politician	Al Stauder
Major Jinks, Civil War Veteran	Will Dixon
Eagle Eye, Indian Chief	Frank Jenkins
Jeremiah Blackstone, Shyster Lawyer	George Warden
Zook Swift, Town Constable	Sam Grey
Elder Toots, Preacher	John C. Wright
Loco Pete, Bad Man	Blaine Waters
Lieutenant Fear, of Newtown Guards	Charles Olden

Marie Bellfonte, Coquette	Blanche Thompson
Evelyn Stockholm, Schoolteacher	Lena Roberts
Pocohontas, Indian Princess	Ethel Marshall
Sumantha Mandrake, Suffragette Leader	Hattie Akers
Alice Darling, Book Canvasser	Babe Brown
Phoebe Brown	Ora Dunlop
Dolly Dimple	Nina Marshall
Sally Slymley	Grace Kneff
Helyn Summers	Emma Jackson
Pattie Broenson	Alice Russell
Freezie Winters	Margaret Langford
Mianie Thanks	Stella Moore

Musical Numbers: (No information)

MAYOR OF NEWTOWN (1912)
Producers: Salem Tutt Whitney, J. Homer Tutt
Book, Lyrics: Tutt and Whitney
Music: T. L. Corwell, Tutt, Henry Watterion

Cast of Characters:

Lem Lee, the Mayor	Salem Tutt Whitney
A Man with Modern Ideas	J. Homer Tutt
Pedro Manuel	Ed. Tolliver
Mayor Jinks	Leigh Whipper
Eph Snow	Alfred Strauder
Eagle Eye, Indian Chief	Frank Jackson
Village Belle	Ethel Marshall
Pocahontas	Maybelle Brown
A Suffragette	Babe Brown
School Teacher	Nettie Taylor

Others--W. Blaine, Fred Redant, John Wilson, Nina Marshall,
    Goldie Chappelle, Hattie Akers, Julia Gideon, Cleo Mitchall,
    Belle May, Alice Russell, Virginia Wheeler, Grace Kneff

Story: (No information)

Musical Numbers:

"I'm the Mayor of Newtown"	Salem Tutt Whitney
"Here I Is and Here I Stay"	Salem Tutt Whitney
"Hot Tamale Sam"	J. Homer Tutt
"Good Night, Marie"	Ethel Marshall
"Neat Ned Nuff Sed"	J. Homer Tutt
"Tell Me Rose"	Blanche Thompson
"I Could Learn to Love a Boy Like You"	Blanche Thompson
"You, Babe, Only You"	Salem Tutt Whitney, Nettie Taylor

MERRY WIDOWER (1908)
    (Pekin Stock Company-Chicago)

Producer: Robert Motts
Director: J. Ed. Green
Book, Lyrics: Victor H. Smalley

Cast of Characters:
Popoven Chickenian, Ambassador	Charles H. Gilpin
Notty Head, his Wife	Mae White
Prince Dan-Low, the Merry Widower	Jerry Mills
Dish, Messenger of the Embassy	Harrison Stewart
Phonia	Lottie Grady
Tipp-Mah, Head Waiter of Mack's Inn	Walter Crumbly
Maid at Mack's Inn	Josephine Devance
CoCo	Willie Ingalls
CoLa	Ada Fisher
O Mee	Madeline Cooper
O Mii	Effie King

Musical Numbers: (No information)

MESSIN' AROUND (1929)
Producer: Louis Isquith
Lyrics: Perry Bradford
Music: Jimmy Johnson

Principal Cast of Characters: Paul Floyd, Cora LaRedd, Freda
   Jackson, Billy McLaurin, James (Slim) Thompson.
"Messin' Around" Choir--Charlee Downz, Inez Glover, Oliver Ball,
   Pearl Johnson, Gladys Wells, Lena Shadney, Audrey Thomas,
   Monette Moore, Arthur Porter, James Thomas, Sam Cross,
   Louis Craddock, Joseph Willis, James Shank, Bamboo
   McCarver, Fred A. Wheeldin, James K. Love.
Our Gang Kids (Dancing Waiters)--William Tyds, Quentin Gregory,
   Charles Johnson, James Dyer and "Pimples."
Maids--Pearl McCarver, Anna Brown, Joyce Richardson, Rachel
   Beech, Enid Morgan, Vincent Boyce, Bebe Lynn, Vernet
   Christie.
Chorus--Freda Jackson, Queenie Price, Catherine Upshur, Pearl
   McCarver, Bebe Lynn, Pearl McLaurin, Emily Malloy, Enid
   Morgan, Edith Randolph, Vincent Boyce, Anna Brown, Vernet
   Christie, Joyce Richardson, Gladys Webster, Rachel Beech,
   Evelyn Dickerson.

Synopsis:
Prologue
"On to Harlem"   Paul Floyd
Part I
Scene 1--Harlem Street Scene
Place: Lenox Avenue and 135th Street, New York City
"Harlem Town" (song)   "Messin' Around" Choir
I'm the Law   Paul Floyd

Makin' Time	Maids
Papers	Our Gang Kids
Blues	Monette Moore
Reprise--"Harlem Town" (song)	Entire Company
On Parade	Paul Floyd, Freda Jackson, Monette Moore, Arthur Porter, Cora LaRedd
"Skiddle-De-Scow" (song)	Cora LaRedd, Our Gang Kids, James Dwyer and Company
"Get Away from My Window" (song)	Audrey Thomas, Billy McLaurin, James (Slim) Thompson
"Your Love Is All I Crave" (song)	Hilda Perleno, Sterling Grant and Chorus
Predictions	Walter Brogsdale, Paul Floyd, Freda Jackson, Queenie Price, Our Gang Kids and Entire Company
"Shout On" (song)	Walter Brogsdale, Arthur Porter, Paul Floyd and "Messin' Around" Choir

Scene 2

Specialty	William McKelvey

Scene 3--Telling Fortunes, Place: A Gypsy Camp Fire

Fortune Teller	Olive Ball
He	Sterling Grant
She	Hilda Perleno
A Fortune Seeker	Billy McLaurin
His Friend	James (Slim) Thompson

Scene 4

"I Don't Love Nobody" (song)	Audrey Thomas, Sam Cross, Evelyn Dickerson, Rachel Beech, Queenie Price, Pearl McLaurin, Bebe Lynn, William Tyds, Quentin Gregory, James Dyer, William McKelvey and "Pimples."

Scene 5--Dynamite

Crook	Paul Floyd
Guardian	James (Slim) Thompson
Dummy	Billy McLaurin

Scene 6--Mississippi

"Roustabouts" (song)	Arthur Porter, Joseph Willis, Bamboo McCarver, James Thomas, Sam Cross, "Pimples," Queenie Price, William McKelvey, "Messin' Around" Choir and Chorus
Mississippi Moan	Walter Brogsdale and Entire Company
"Mississippi" (song)	Walter Brogsdale and Entire Company

Part II
Scene 1--At the Carnival
Place: Outside the Entrance of Main Tent.
Barker   Paul Floyd
"Circus Days" (song)   Chorus
Tapso, the Dancing Skater   Bamboo McCarver
Applicant   Billy McLaurin
Second Applicant   James (Slim) Thompson
Rolo   James K. Love
Jolo   James Skank
Scene 2--Battle for World's Female Championship
World's Female Junior Light-   Emma Maitland
  weight Champion
World's Female Bantamweight   Aurelia Wheeldin
  Champion
(Note: Miss Maitland and Miss Wheeldin are the only two licensed
  female boxers in America.)
Miss Maitland's Second   Billy McLaurin
Miss Wheeldin's Second   James (Slim) Thompson
Referee   Fred A. Wheeldin
Spectators   Entire Company
Scene 3--Paying Off
(Same as Scene 1)
La Ballerina   Susie Wroten
Carnival Barker   Paul Floyd
First Second   Billy McLaurin
Second Second   James (Slim) Thompson
Scene 4
Spirituals   Three Harmony Sisters, Olive,
                                      Pearl and Gladys
Scene 5--Harlem's Midnight Frolic
Master of Ceremonies   Sterling Grant
Tapcopation   Cora LaRedd and Dancing
                                      Waiters
"Sorry" (song)   Hilda Perleno and Sterling
                                      Grant
Russian Specialty   Frank Davis
Hopping the Buck   William McKelvey
"Put Your Mind Right On It"   Monette Moore, Joseph Willis,
  (song)   Guests, "Messin' Around"
                                      Choir, Dancing Waiters,
                                      Cora LaRedd and Chorus
Yamekraw (Piano Symphony)   Jimmy Johnson
First Guest   Billy McLaurin
Second Guest   James (Slim) Thompson
Whirlwind   Ebony Trio (Aubrey Thomas,
                                      James Thomas, and Sam
                                      Cross)
"Messin' Around" (song)   Monette Moore
Finale   Entire "Messin' Around"
                                      Company

MISS BANDANA (1927)
Producer: Clarence Muse
Orchestra Director: Russell Smith

Principal Cast of Characters: Clarence Muse, Salem Tutt Whitney,
    R. M. Cooper, George Backer, L. Randall, J. Mabley, Onion
    Jeffries, Walter Crumbley, Mable C. Ridley, Ike Paul, Alice
    Gorgas, Geraldine Goodway, Ollie Burgoyne, John Henderson,
    Cecil Graham, Gordon Wilson, Hope Black, Three Brownies.

Story: The opening scene is laid on a Mississippi levee, where
romance starts between a stage-struck country girl and her youthful admirer. The story follows her adventures in the Mississippi
valley and in New York City.

Musical Numbers: (No information)

MISS CALICO (1926)
Producer: Earl Dancer
Lyrics: Earl Dancer
Music: Donald Heywood
Stanging: Earl Dancer

Principal Cast of Characters: Ethel Waters, Alec Lovejoy, Marshall
    Rogers, Lionel Monagas.
Chorus Beauties Include--Alberta Boyd, Juanita Boyd, Theresa
    Mason, Gladys Jones, Hazel Miles, Lillian Stokes, Oletha
    White, Margaret Beckett, Maude Collins and Marion Davis.

Synopsis:
                             Act I
Overture   Featuring Thornton Brown,
                                      Cornetist
Opening: America's Black   Taskiana 4, with Cocoa-Brown
    Cargo   Skinned Maids, George
                                       Stanton, Alec Lovejoy
"I'm Coming, Virginia"   Miss Ethel Waters
Specialty   Jimmie and Eddie White
I'm Satisfied   Alec Lovejoy
Black Bottom   Miss Waters and Calico Girls
A Revival Meeting: Written by
    Gene Hooten and Staged by
    Earl Dancer
    Spiritual Singers   Taskiana 4
    Sister Few Clothes   Ida Hooten
    Elder Full Bosum   Marshall Rodgers
    Sister Get Happy   Ethel Waters
    Presiding Elder Low Down   Gene Hooten
Specialty   Lew Keene
A Few Moments with   Ethel Waters
Down Home Stomp   Margaret Beckett, White Bros.
                                       and Chorus

Finale.

Act II

A Few Moments with the Calico Syncopators and Louisa V. Jones	Thornton Brown, Director
The Dance of the Old Black Crow	Lew Keene and Girls
"Sweet Mamma, Lulu Belle" (written by Earl Dancer, with apologies to Mr. Belasco)	Miss Waters and Lionel Monagas
Shadows on the Wall	George Stanton and Cocoa-Brown Skinned Models
Specialty	Taskiana 4
Bamborina	Margaret Beckett and Bamboo Girls
A Court Scene--from Catch Air, Mississippi	
Chink	Lew Keene
Police Man--All Black	Gene Hooten
Prosecuting Attorney	Lionel Monagas
Attorney for Defense	Jimmie White
Judge--Nothing but Years	Alec Lovejoy
Sophie Go Bout	Margaret Beckett
A Darktown Divorce Seeker	Ethel Waters
Tack Annie	Ida Hooten
Razor Jim	Marshall Rodgers
(written by Earl Dancer)	
The Drill of Aunt Hagar's Children	Calico Girls and White Bros.
Specialty--Some Songs That You Have Heard in Your Homes (Pearl Wright at the Piano)	Miss Waters
Finale	Entire Company

MISS NOBODY FROM STARLAND (1920), 21 Musical Numbers
Producer: No Data

Principal Cast of Characters: Shelton Brooks and others

Story: The scene is laid onboard the Aquitania. All passengers
on board have become thoroughly acquainted with each other and as
the day draws near for the landing on home soil, a stowaway is
discovered in the person of Niva, an Egyptian princess. The captain is about to send her to the authorities but she is saved by
Preston Haliday, the son of Henry Haliday, the hair restorer maker.
The young Haliday had fallen in love with a conniving widow who is
in reality an actress who is smuggling some jewelry into the country. She persuaded Haliday to back a show for her which her brother has written. In the second act, the show is in the making and
the audience is led into the backstage secrets and is shown how
numbers are staged and produced and how the scenes are built and
developed.

Musical Numbers: (No information)

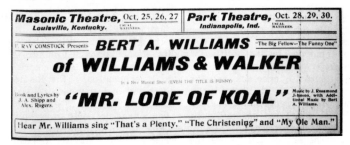

Ad for "Mr. Lode of Koal," Bert Williams' Last Black Show,
circa 1909

MR. LODE OF KOAL (1909)
    (Broadway Production, Majestic Theatre, November 1909)
Producer: Bert Williams
Book, Lyrics: Jesse A. Shipp, Alex Rogers
Music: J. Rosamond Johnson
Additional Music: Bert Williams

Cast of Characters:

Chester A. Lode	Bert Williams
Buggsy	Alex Rogers
Gimlet	Tom Brown
Gluter, Gimlet's silent partner	Siren Nevarro
Buttram	J. Leubrie Hill
"Cap"	Henry Troy
Singlink, Court messenger	Charles McKenzie
"Sarg"	J. E. Lightfoot
Woozy, Commander-in-Chief of the Army	Hattie McIntosh
Weedhead	Charles H. Moore
First Lieutenant	Sterling Rex
Second Lieutenant	J. M. Thomas
Third Lieutenant	Clarence Redd
Blootach	Matt Housley
Whirling, Court Jester	Siren Nevarro
Mysteria	Lottie Grady
A Sailor	Ada Banks
Kinklets	Georgia Gomez
What	Bessie Brady
Ho	Anita Bush
Rubuena	Lavinta Rogers
Diano	Maggie Davis
Ovec	Jessie Ellis
Discretta	Ida Day
Giddina	Katie Jones

Citizens, Guards, etc.--Messrs. Hawks, Payne, Holland, Cooper,
    Gibbs, Foster, Saulsbury, Tapley, Hillard, Tolliver, Chappell.
Flower Girls, Dancers, etc.--Misses M. Brown, Inez Clough, F.
    Brown, Lewis, Yorke, Vaughn, King, DeVance, Gulguesse,
    Payne.

Story: The opening scene of the play is laid in the courtyard of the King, Big Smoak, ruler of the mythical island of Koal. Poor Chester arrives just in time to take the place of the King who has been kidnapped by the political bandits of the island. Chester is introduced to the populace as the new ruler, while his sponsors subject him to ingenious and tyrannical persecution. The luscious, sleep-compelling fruit growing on the island and served exclusively to the King is eaten by Chester, who at once begins to enjoy one of the most satisfying and delightful dreams that he could have wished for, had he the magic of Aladdin's lamp at his command.

The second act shows the "Dream Scene" with the feasting and dancing. The picturesque "Dance of the Veiled Mugs," "In Far Mandelay," "The Lament," and the "Harbor of Lost Dreams," are among the musical numbers which are produced in this act.

In the last act, Chester awakens, Big Smoak returns, and poor Chester is condemned to be one of the King's servants.

Additional Musical Numbers: "My Ole Man," "Christening of the Baby," "That's a Plenty," "Chink Chink Chinyman," "Blue Law," "Mum's the Word," "Bygone Days in Dixie," "Believe Me"

MR. RAGTIME (1914)
Producers: Irvin C. Miller, Kid Brown
Book, Lyrics: Irvin C. Miller
Music: Will Dorsey

Cast of Characters:

Mme. Winfrey, Proprietor of Hotel	Ethel James
Daisy Lewis, Waitress	Eva Harris
Dora Jones, Hair Dresser	Tillie Cross
Mabel Webster, Entertainer	Orena James
Louise Day, Manicurist	Carrie Caisons
Thomas Green, Porter	Kid Brown
Sarah Green, His Wife	Eleanor Johnson
Alleen Dean	?
James Wilberforce, from New York	Irvin C. Miller

Visitors, Maids, Guests, and Others.
Scene: Interior of Dumas Hotel; Time: Present; Place: New Orleans

Story: (No information)

Musical Numbers:

Opening Chorus--"Ragtime Chimes"	Company
"All Aboard for Dixie Land"	Ethel James and Chorus
"Croony Melody"	Esther Bigeou and Irvin C. Miller
"Every Road"	Orena James and Chorus
"I'm Going to Exit"	Kid Brown

"Hello Little Miss U. S. A. "	?
"Bleeding Heart"	Ethel James
"Flippity Flop"	Kid Brown and Chorus
"When You Sang the Rosary to Me"	Miss Bigeou
"Hesitation Waltz"	?
"Carmina"	James Sisters
"Long Lost Blues"	Miss Johnson and Company
"Finale"	Entire Company

MOONSHINE (1922 edition), 2 Acts 11 Scenes
Producer: Billy King

Cast of Characters:

Mrs. Sallie Booker (the wife)	Margarette Scott
Winnie Booker (the daughter)	Ethel Jackson
Billy Booker (the father)	Billy King
Silas Jenkins (the bootlegger)	Marshall Rogers
Vamp	Genevieve Stern

The Incomparable Steppers: Dink Thomas, Marrie Warren, Ida Bennett, Marion Moore, Sallie Gates, Christine Russell and her Radio Girls, Baby Cox

Story: The first act has to do with the operation of a bootlegger who "carries it on the hip. " Billy, as Billy Booker, is the fellow's principal customer, with Marshall Rogers, as Mose of the wet ideas, pursuing him into his home in his efforts to keep Bill "lit up. " This latter furnishes the grounds for the occurrences throughout.
        In the second act, the reading of the will of a deceased uncle forms the foundation for the proceedings of the entire act.

Musical Numbers:
Scene 1
Opening--"Darktown Medley"	Entire Company and Jasper Johnson's Syncopated Band
"The Dancing Fool"	Willie Thrill and Girls
"The Jazzbo Strut"	Doc Straine and Girls

Scene 3, A Street
Billy King, William Gunn, Genevieve Stern, Ike Young, Willie Thrill

Scene 4, A Picnic in the Moonshine
"Hello Everybody"	Entire Company
"The Old Time Ball"	Bessie Brown and Girls
"Moonshine Blues"	Happy Chorus

Act 2, Scene 1
"We're on the Jury"	The Jurors
"Take Him Away"	Entire Company

Scene 2
Specialty	Sensational Jack Wiggins, the Unique Entertainer

Scene 3
"Madagascar"   May Bell Brown and Girls
Scene 4
"Magnetic Maids"--Trombone   Marie Lucas
    Solo
"Old Black Joe"   Anna Belle Cook
Violin Solo   Gertrude Rustill
"Just Vamping That's All"   Bessie Brown and Magnetic
                                          Maids
"Jazz Me"   Bessie Brown
Scene 5
Specialty   Hightowers and Jones
Scene 6, A Quiet Evening in
Billy Booker's Home
"Step On It"   Jennie Straine and Girls
"Voo Doo"   Billy King
"Classics"   Margarette Scott
"Moonshine"   Scott, Gunn and Girls
?   Baby Cox and Girls
"Good Night"   Entire Company

MUTT AND JEFF (1922), 2 Acts 14 Scenes
Owner: Joseph Conoly and Gus Hill
Stage Producer: Richard F. Carroll
Book: Bud Fishey and Richard F. Carroll
Music, Lyrics: T. A. Hammel, Frank Montgomery, Leroy Brown,
    Phil Worde, Joseph Conoly, Richard Carroll
Musical Director: Frank Montgomery
Orchestration: Robert W. Ricketts
Orchestra Director: Phil Worde

Cast of Characters:
Chiquita, Daughter of Mexican   Marguerite Lee
    Rebel President
Carmencita, her Aunt   Lillian Russell
Jack Manley, a Sporty Young   Henry Sapara
    American
Plunger Wiggles, Horse Owner   Joe Russell
    and Man About Town
Racetrack Gatekeeper   Ben Williams
Mutt, the Long of It   Leroy Brown (Stringbeans)
Jeff, the Short of It   Tausha H. Hammond
Doper, the Dip   Ed Fraction
Jacquille Manly, Posing as a   Florence McClain
    Widow
A Blind Man   E. C. Caldwell
Ophelia   Bee Freeman
Desdemonia Newmonia   Dempale Braxton
A Dude   Charles Hawkins
Captain Jinks of the Good Ship   Frank Montgomery
    "Hot Tamale"
Others--Marie Rich, Kitty Rover, Dorothy Sweeting, Helen Hodges,

Beulah Bevere, Daisy Pizarro, Catherine Huckleby, Bebie
Daniels, Mable Jones, Elsie Fisher, Gladys Hunt, Gertrude
Russell, J. F. Lafayette.

Story: (No information)

Musical Numbers:
Act 1

Opening Chorus--"Hello, Belmont Park"	Frank Montgomery and Chorus
Entrance--Wiggles, Chiquita, Jack and Carmen	
"Wild About Rose"	T. A. Hammond
"No One Like You"	Sapara and M. Lee
"Pretty Melody"	Quintette (Lee, F. McClain, Russell, Sapara, J. Russell)
"Echoes of Jazzland"	Russell and Russell
"Two Handsome Men"	Brown and Hammond (Mutt and Jeff)
"Chiquita"	Sapara and Spanish Girls
"My Cavalier"	M. Lee
"The Shimmy Wedding"	Ensemble
"The Jockey Jamboree"	Conoly and Carroll
"Widow Kiddo"	J. Russell and F. McClain
"The Sport of Kings"--Finale	Entire Company

Act 2

"Carolina Sue"--Opening Ensemble	Entire Company
"The Cabaret Entertainers"	Sapara and Lee
"Poor Little Me"	T. Hammond
"The Tale of the Mermaid"	M. Lee and Mermaids
Specialty	Montgomery and McClain
"Jefferson Jazz Band"	J. Russell, L. Russell, Jingling Joy Jiggers
"How Long"	Montgomery and High Steppers and Ensemble
Good Night Number	Ensemble

MY FRIEND FROM KENTUCKY (1909)
Producers: Salem Tutt Whitney, J. Homer Tutt
Book, Lyrics: Whitney and Tutt
Music: Taylor L. Corwell, Salem Tutt Whitney, J. Homer Tutt

Principal Cast of Characters: Salem Tutt Whitney (Abraham Lincoln
    Brown), J. Homer Tutt, Sam Gardner, Frank Jackson, Sank
    Simms, James Woodson, Linsey Lewis, Daisy Martin, Nettie
    Taylor, Mabel Dehearbe, Nina Marshall, Mamie Gardner,
    Blanche Simms, Georgie Davis, H. S. Wooton, James Weaver,
    Al Stauder, James Woodson

Story: Abraham Lincoln Brown arrives in an auto (wheelbarrow)

and meets his host and a party of friends waiting to welcome "The
Man that Rules the Town of Bowling Green." He is welcomed by
so many good looking girls that he declares, after being introduced
to the charming Daisy Martin, that he was never going back to
Bowling Green no more. The funny situations arise when he is
initiated in the Lodge, when he becomes a soldier and when he goes
on the field of honor as a result of an insult.

Musical Numbers:

"Come Out, Dear Louise"	Nettie Taylor and Sextette
"The Man that Rules the Town"	Salem Tutt Whitney
"Strutting Sam"	J. Homer Tutt and Chorus
"Hymn by the Royal Roosters"	Company
"Way Back in Dixie Land"	Ethel Marshall and Ensemble
"My Spanish Maid"	Babe Brown and Spanish Maids
"Smile On, Sue"	Daisy Martin, J. Homer Tutt
"Pride of Company B"	Whitney and Gardner
"Reminiscing of Dixie"	Company
"Where I Long To Be"	Frank Jackson and Chorus
"Dat's Sufficiency"	Tutt and Whitney and Daisy Martin
"For Honor"	Company

MY FRIEND FROM KENTUCKY (1913)
Producer: J. Leubrie Hill
Book: J. Leubrie Hill

Cast of Characters:

Jasper Green, Rich Colored Plantation Owner of Leesburg, Virginia	Sam Gaines
Juliette Lee	Edna Morton
Susie Lee	Adel Johnson
Emmaline	Daisy Brown
Clemantine	Anna Packey
Jimmy Moon, Country Lad, Very Shy	Tiny Ray
Jim Jackson Lee, Jasper's Son-in-Law	Julius Glenn
Mandy Lee, Jasper's Eldest Daughter	J. Leubrie Hill
Bill Simmons, a Representative of the Colored Man's Business League, with Big Ideas	Will Brown
Madame Langtree, a Jolly Grandwidow of Washington, D. C.	Jennie Schepar
Miss Lucinda Langtree, her Youngest Daughter	Evon Robinson
Miss Lillian Langtree, Oldest Daughter	Alice Ramsey
Katie Krew, Society Reporter	Effie Hollman

of Washington, D. C. and
"Busy Bee"

Carrie Nation Brown, President of and Treasurer of the Colored Women's Suffragettes, Also a Friend of the Langtrees	Ethel Williams
Hannal Belmont Jackson, Vice-President and Secretary of the Colored Women's Suffragettes, Also a Friend of the Langtrees	Kattie Wayn
Chauffeur	Johnnie Peters
Mose Lewis, a Prominent Lawyer of Leesburg, Virginia	Eugene L. Perkins
Dr. Moore	Theo. L. Pankey
Officer Jones	Billy Moore
Spikie, the Newsboy	Grace Johnson
Shine, the Bootblack	Ray Webster
Cab Driver	Will Thomas
Red Cap Sam	Eddie Stafford
Lady Ensom	Pauline Parker
Head Waiter Thompson	Arthur V. Carr

Country Lads and Lassies--William Kelly, Eddie Rector, Eddie
Stafford, George Hatch, Arthur Ames, Ed Cossens, Daisy
Brown, Lillian Hunter, Jennie Ray, Edna Morton, Evelyn
Moore, Erma Batist, Hilaria Friend

Old Men's Quartette--Hamilton White, William Smith, Eddie Scott,
William Thomas

Newsboys Quintette--Grace Johnson, Tiny Ray, Eddie Rector,
Arthur Ames, William Kelley, Eddie Cozzens

Belles and Beaus and Special Guests at Lucinda Langtree's Tea
Party--Pauline Parker, Ethel Holleman and others

Story: The story tells of the enticing from his southern home of
Jim Lee, a wealthy plantation owner, by a smooth young man, Bill
Simmons, who has gained some experience by a stay in the north.
Jim Lee is elected president of the Colored Men's Business League
over Jasper Green. Simmons, the man from Kentucky, convinces
Jim Jackson Lee if he changes his name to Booker T, he can be
elected president of the Colored Men's Business League at Washington. He is persuaded to mortgage his wife's house for $3000
and go to Washington. Jim's father-in-law has arranged for a vacation in Washington, D. C. and has arranged to bring a whole flock
of his neighbors with him. Jim's wife, who learns after the latter's
departure that he has planned a mortgage on the holdings, decides
to join the party along with her children, her object being to find
her recreant spouse. The latter is presented into society by the
smooth young man who introduces Jim as a single man. A marriage is arranged between Jim and Lucinda Langtree, youngest
daughter of a popular society matron. There is a lawyer and a
physician carried along in the story who lend class to the play,
and it is about the above mentioned that the show is built.

Musical Numbers:

Act 1

Opening--"No Place Like Dixie-land"	Ensemble
*"Night Time Is the Right Time"	Country Lads and Lassies
"Dear Old Dixie"	Sam Gaines and Chorus
"Waiting All Day Long"	Anna Pankey and Chorus
"Happy Time"	Old Men's Quartette
"Goodby, Dixieland"	J. Leubrie Hill, Anna Pankey, Eugene L. Perkins and Chorus

Act 2, Scene 1

Opening Chorus--"Waiting at the Depot"	Ensemble
"Lou, My Lou"	Grace Johnson and Quintette
Buck Dance	
"Has Anybody Seen Jim Jackson?"	J. Leubrie Hill

Act 2, Scene 2

Opening Chorus--"Gay Manhattan Rag"	Company
Ragtime Dance	Dixie Sextette
"You"	Theo. L. Pankey
"My Friend from Kentucky"	Will Brown, Julius Glenn and Chorus
*"Rock Me in the Cradle of Love"	Alice Ramsey and Chorus
"That's the Kind of Man I Want"	Evon Robinson and Chorus
"Goodtime While I Can"	Jennie Schepar
"Take Me Away to Jail"	Big Chorus

Act 3, Scene 1

Few Minutes with Jim Jackson Lee	Julius Glenn

Act 3, Scene 2

"What's the Matter with Jasper Green?"	
"The Man of the Hour"	Will Brown and Chorus
Three Styles of Dancing	Johnny Peters and his Dancing Girls--Ethel Williams, Daisy Brown, Edna Morton
*"At the Ball, That's All"-- Grand Finale	Entire Company

Costumes by Orange, N.Y.; Shoes by Cammeyers, N.Y.; Tights and Stockings by Sigmund and Weyl; Men's Hats by Young Bros.; Wigs by Hepnew

Staff for Lafayette Producing Company: Benjamin Nibur, General Manager; Joseph Loew, Manager; Clarence W. Logan, Business Manager; Jas. J. Vaughn, Musical Director; Babe Townsend, Stage Manager; Tiny Ray, Assistant Stage Manager; William

---

*Rights to these numbers were purchased by Flo Ziegfeld and subsequently incorporated into the famous "Follies."

Emerson, Stage Carpenter; Fred Tollamn, Property Man; Lou
Brown, Drummer; Joseph Brown, Master of Transportation;
Mabel Brown, Wardrobe Mistress.

MY RICH UNCLE (1918)
Producer: Billy King

Principal Cast of Characters: Billy King Company

Story: A rich uncle of a beautiful young girl wants to marry off in
high society. A smooth city chap (Howard Kelly) comes along and
with his fine appearance and smooth manners tips over the beans.
Billy King, who is in on the deal with the smooth gent, goes into
various disguises and finally allows himself to be dressed up in
baby clothes and to be deposited at the home of the girl. What
happens next is a world of fun and the climax of the show.

Musical Numbers: (No information)

NEGRO NUANCES (1924)
Producer: Will Marion Cook
Book: Abbie Mitchell, Miller and Lyle
Orchestra Director: James P. Johnson
Music, Lyrics: Will Cook

Principal Cast of Characters: Abbie Mitchell, Lucille Handy
    (daughter of W. C. Handy, composer of St. Louis Blues),
    Louis Douglass, F. E. Miller, A. Lyles.

Story: The play traces the musical history of blacks starting in
Africa, moving with the slave ships, the lamentations of pre-civil
war days to the reconstruction period as typified by the early minstrels of Jim Bland's day.

Musical Numbers: (No information)

THE NEW AMERICAN (1920)
Producer: Billy King

Principal Cast of Characters: Billy King, Marshall Rogers, Julia
    Rector, Bruce and Bruce, Ollie Herman, Edna Hickman, Prof.
    Dillard (a magician)

Story (Review, Dave Payton, Chicago Whip, December 18, 1920):
"The plot, if such may be called, which lacked continuity and introduced a new feature in the field of comic entertainment inasmuch as
it introduced a serious subject, and handled it masterfully, that is
of vital concern to all America--the status of the Negro--The New
American. "

Musical Numbers: (No information)

NORTH AIN'T SOUTH (1923)
Producers: Salem Tutt Whitney, J. Homer Tutt
Book: Tutt and Whitney, Jesse Shipp
Music: Donald Heywood
Dance Director: Frank Montgomery

Cast of Characters: Salem Tutt Whitney, J. Homer Tutt, Jesse
    A. Shipp, George McClennon, Edna Gibbs, Mae Kemp, Hilda
    Bendischer, Marion Harrison.

Story: The story is about a group of black singers and dancers in
Plainsville, Georgia whose collective ambition is to go North and go
on the stage.   One day, a New York producer stops overnight in the
town and is invited to see a show put on by the local performers.
The show includes several scenes from Shakespeare's "Othello" (the
burlesque scenes from "Othello" were performed by Salem Tutt
Whitney and Maud DeForrest).   The New York producer (Jesse
Shipp) is impressed, especially with one of the beautiful young female singers in the group.   He promises her work if she will ac-
company him to New York City.   The entire company follows her
to New York, but they have trouble landing jobs so they eventually
return home with the declaration that "North Ain't South."

Musical Numbers: "What Kind of a Woman Does a Man Expect?,"
    "Po' Little Lamb," "Pickaninny All Dressed Up," "On Parade,"
    "Shake a Leg," "Keep-A-Stepping Along"

OCTOROONS (1900)
Producer: John W. Isham

Principal Cast of Characters: Pete Hampton, Smart and Williams,
    William English, Billy Miller, Joe Britton, Marion Henry,
    Sally Lee, Ada Mickey

Program:
Opening--Musical Skit, 7-11-77   written by Bob Cole
Olio--
    Billy Miller   Comic monologue and songs
    The Brittons   Comedy sketch and dancing
    Belle Davis   Songs
    Smart and Williams   Comedy sketch, "The Booking
                                           Agency" (assisted by Marion
                                           Henry and Belle Davis)
    William English   Novelty
Finale--Thirty Minutes Around
    the Opera

OH, JOY! (1922)
Producer: Louis T. Rogers
Book, Lyrics, Music: Salem Tutt Whitney, J. Homer Tutt

Principal Cast of Characters: Salem Tutt Whitney, Homer J. Tutt,
    Ethel Waters, Andrew Tribble (Ophelia Johnson), Julian
    Costello, Amon Davis, Emmett Anthony, Paul Morefield,
    Alonzo Fenderson, Frances Mores, Rosco Wickham, George
    Phillips, Dick Conroy, J. J. Jasper, Wilton Dyer, Budde
    William, Nat Cash, Walter Richardson, Marguerite Lee,
    Margaret Simms, Ethel Williams, Lottie Harris, Bessie Sims,
    Nellie Brown, Helen Fenderson, Elvita Davis, Elizabeth
    Campbell, Daisy Martin, Helen Springer, Violet Williams,
    Ollie McNaley, Ethel Pope, Madeline Alsoton, Edith Sims,
    Helen Warren, Viola Mander, Jewel Thomas, Joyce Robinson,
    Jane McCarthy, Peck Fortune, Anita Robinson, Sally Evans,
    Leroy Broomfield, Chester Jones, Al Lawrence.

Story: (No information)

Musical Numbers:
"Valley of the Nile"   Julian Costello
"Georgia Rose"   ?
"What's the Use?"   ?

AN OIL WELL SCANDAL (1924)
Producer: Freddie Johnson

Cast of Characters: Bill McLaurin and E. H. Pugh (Turkey
    Bosom and Mose), Clarence Robinson, Mattie Harris, Ruth
    Cherry, Tillie Marshall, Daisy Pizarro, Howard Douglass,
    James Fulton, Thomas Morris

Story: The oil scandal is brought about by a slick city guy going
to a little country town and disposing of several thousand dollars of
worthless oil well stock to the unsuspecting populace of that town
through the aid of Mose and Turkey Bosom, who were accused and
put in jail. The real culprit was eventually captured and Mose and
Turkey Bosom are released much to the joy of the populace.

Musical Numbers: (No information)

THE OLD MAN'S BOY (1913)
Producers: Alex Rogers and Henry Creamer (Negro Players Stock
    Company)

Cast--Synopsis:
                        Prologue
Sitting Room in Hiram Wilson's House
Cast in Order of Appearance:
Hiram Wilson, Jr., the Old   Andrew Bishop
    Man's Boy
Martha, the Mother   Lavinia Rogers
Hiram Wilson, the Old Man   Alex Rogers
Others--Alice Gorgas, Billy Harper, Charles Gilpin, Jessie Ellis

(the singing nightingale), George LeCook (buck and wing dancer),
Ruth Cherry, C. W. Tyrant, Charles Woody (pride of the levee)

Act 1

Rehearsal of the Negro Players Company at Lafayette Theatre.
Three weeks are supposed to have elapsed between the Prologue
and the first act.

Stage Manager	Henry Creamer
Hiram Wilson, Jr., Newest Member of the Company	Andrew Bishop
Hiram, Jr.'s Wife, Principal Dancer	Ruth Cherry
Comedian of the Company	Billy Harper
Phrenological Vocal Director	Charles Gilpin
The Prima Dona	Alice Gorgas
Assistant Stage Manager	Cassie Norwood
The New Soubrette	Grayce LeCook
The Orchestra Director	Marie Lucas (wife of Charles Lucas)
That Scrapping Drummer	Cricket Smith
LaBelle, a Dancer	Jessie Ellis
Gwen, a Dancer	Gwendolyn Walton

Act 2

Continuation of Act 1 Dress Rehearsal.

King Jung-a-boo	Billy Harper
Prime Minister	Henry S. Creamer
Tuff-Tuff, the Court Jester	Andrew Bishop

Act 3

Same as Prologue: Hiram Wilson's House

Hiram Wilson, Sr.	Alex Rogers
Hiram Sr.'s Lifelong Friend, Tom Bolden	Charles Gilpin
Martha, the Wife	Lavinia Rogers
Hiram Wilson, Jr.	Andrew Bishop
Pearl, Hiram Jr.'s Wife	Ruth Cherry
Hiram Wilson, III, the Baby	by Himself
Grace, a Visiting Friend	Alice Gorgas
May and Emma, Hiram, Jr.'s Sisters	Jessie Ellis and Grayce LeCook

Other members of the company--Goldie Cisco, Mayme Furber,
Lula Lawson, Edna Smith, Lucille Sterette, Hortense Sterette,
Carrie Boyd, Howard Durry, Edward Brown, John Reeves,
Tracy Jordan, William Crawford, John Powell, Ray Amos,
Robert Murry, Charles Woody, John Peterson

Musical Numbers:

Act 1

"June Time"--Opening Chorus	Company
"Dixie Land March Song"	Ellis and Chorus
"All Day Long"	Edward Brown, Goldie Cisco and Chorus
"Hello, Mr. Moon"	Alice Gorgas and Chorus
"Oh, You Devil Rag"--Dance	Ruth Cherry, Cassie Norwood and Company

"You'll Want My Love"	Grayce LeCook and Howard Durry
Trombone Solo	Marie Lucas
The Blues--Trombone and Cornet	C. Smith and Marie Lucas
"Brazilian Dreams"	Jessie Ellis and Company
"I Lost My Way"	Billy Harper
"International Rag"	Grayce LeCook and Company

Act 2

Swanee River Dance	Ruth Cherry and Company
Specialty Song	Alice Gorgas
"You've Got to Bag It"	Jessie Ellis, Cassie Norwood and Chorus
Panama Dance	Ruth Cherry, Howard Durry
"Hanging Around and Gone, Gone, Gone"	Grayce LeCook
"Uncle Remus at the Races"	Charles S. Gilpin
"King Love 'Em All" and "The Castle on the Isle of Koal"	Billy Harper and Company

Act 3

"Sweet Thoughts of Home"	Alice Gorgas

OVER THE TOP (1919)
Producer: Billy King

Principal Cast of Characters: Billy King, Billy Higgins, Gertrude
    Saunders, Ernest Whitman, Rosa Lee Tyler, Ida Forsyne,
    Theresa Brooks, Ollie Burgoyne, Berlena Blanks, Ruth Cherry,
    Sadie McCarver, Jim Reed, Clarence Stevens, Maio Gerwood,
    Marcus Slayter, Mazie King, Ernie Ford, Rebecca Thomas,
    Zuleaker Daniels, Lena Turner, Belle West, Ella Gadson,
    Mary Bradford, Ethel Jackson, Ethel Bolton, Mammie Morales,
    Edna Hicks, Dolly Smith, Geneve Stearn, Laura B. Hall, J. W.
    Coleman, H. Crawford, Leonard Burton, R. Fractor.

Story: The story deals with the return of Captain Austin from
overseas and his subsequent mission to the Peace Conference held
near Paris, where he is denied admittance and is compelled to return to the United States without accomplishing his mission.   In the
last act several speeches are made dealing with the mistreatment
of black Americans.

Musical Numbers: (No information)

THE OYSTER MAN (1907)
Producer: Ernest Hogan
Music: Will H. Vodery

Cast of Characters:

Baltimore Oyster Vendor	Ernest Hogan
Sunny Sam	John Rucker

Society Leader, Graduate of   Carita Day
    Tuskegee
Oyster Man's Girl   Muriel Ringgold

Musical Numbers: (No information)

PANAMA (1908)
    (Pekin Stock Company, Chicago)
Producer: J. Ed. Green
Book: Marion A. Brooks, Charles A. Hunter
Staging: J. Ed. Green
Music: James T. Brymn, H. Lawrence Freeman

Principal Cast of Characters: Harrison Stewart, Abbie Mitchell,
    Pekin Chorus assisted by "Pekin Ponies"

Story: The plot of the story deals with the troubles of inhabitants
of a humble Kentucky town who were induced by a smooth promoter
to invest in a mythical piece of property in Panama. The acts of
the piece take place in Brandyville, Kentucky and then shift to the
canal region of Panama.

Musical Numbers: "Julius Caesar Johnson," "Awful," "What I
    Know I Knows," "Put It Right in My Hand," "Happy Sam Chow,"
    "Things Ain't Just Right," "The Summertime," "I'd Like to Run
    Away with You."

PEPPER POT REVUE (1927)
    (New York Production)
Producer: Leonard Harper

Principal Cast of Characters: Bill Robinson, Small and Mays (two
    mahogany princes), Madeline Belt, Marie Preval, Byrd and
    Billy Higgins

Synopsis:

Opening--"Under the Dixie Moon"	Small and May and Chorus
"Emaline"	Bill Robinson, Marie Preval
Sketch, "Find and Dod"	Byrd and Billy Higgins
"Jes the Same," "Sundown"	Small (ukulele), Mays (banjo)
Dance Number (up and down	Bill Robinson
stairs)	

PLANTATION REVUE (1922)
Producer: Lew Leslie
Orchestra Director: Will H. Vodery

Opposite: Ad for Ernest Hogan's Last Show, "The Oyster Man,"
circa 1907

Synopsis:

Opening--Introduction	Shelton Brooks
"The Bugle Call"	Jonnie Dunn (on the Cornet)
"Old Black Joe"	Plantation Quartet with U. S. Thompson and Lew Keene
"Southern Hobby"	Plantation Quartet with U. S. Thompson
"Robert E. Lee"	Edith Wilson and Six Dixie Vamps
"Southland"	Chappelle and Stinnette
"Mandy"	Florence Mills and Six Dixie Vamps
Specialty	U. S. Thompson and Edith Wilson
Finale--"Minstrels on Parade"	Entire Company

THE POLICY PLAYERS (1900)
    (Original Title, "A Lucky Coon")
Producers: Bert Williams, George Walker

Principal Cast of Characters: Bert Williams, George Walker,
    Mattie Wilkes, Reese Bros., Fred Douglass, George Catlin,
    Mallory Bros., Mazie Brooks, Lottie Thompson, Aida Overton,
    Edward Harris

Story: The first act shows Dusty Cheapman (Bert Williams), a lot-
tery fiend from Thompson Street, who eventually wins a lot of money, and desires to enter high society and is introduced to Happy
Hotstuff (George Walker) who engineers the scheme very successfully.
    The second act shows a very elaborate scene at the house of
the Astrobilts on the Hudson River. Mr. Readymoney, butler of
the Astrobilt family, is anxious to become one of the Black 400
and Happy Hotstuff agrees to furnish the means by which the coveted
distinction is acquired for the sum of four hundred dollars. Hotstuff induces the butler to allow an affair to take place at the resi-
dence of his employers on the Hudson by promising to have his personal friend, the Ex-President of Haiti (Bert Williams) stop by on
his tour around the world and grace the grand gathering of the
Colored 400 with his presence. The Ex-President of Haiti arrives
at the affair amid much band playing and gaiety when many funny
incidents occur.

Musical Numbers:

"The Broadway Coon"	Aida Overton
"The Medicine Man"	
"The Man in the Moon Might Tell"	
"Honolulu Bells"	

PORGY AND BESS (1935)
    (Founded on the play "Porgy" by DuBose and Dorothy Heyward)

Presented by: Theatre Guild
Music: George Gershwin
Libretto: DuBose Heyward
Lyrics: DuBose Heyward, Ira Gershwin
Director: Rouben Mamoulian

Cast of Characters (In the order of appearance):

Mingo	Ford L. Buck
Clara	Abbie Mitchell
Sportin' Life	John W. Bubbles
Jake	Edward Matthews
Maria	Georgette Harvey
Annie	Olive Ball
Lily	Helen Dowdy
Serena	Ruby Elzy
Robbins	Henry Davis
Jim	Jack Carr
Peter	Gus Simons
Porgy	Todd Duncan
Crown	Warren Coleman
Bess	Anne Brown
Detective	Alexander Campbell
Two Policemen	Harold Woolf, Burton McEvilly
Undertaker	John Garth
Frazier	J. Rosamond Johnson
Mr. Archdale	George Lessey
Nelson	Ray Yeates
Strawberry Woman	Helen Dowdy
Crab Man	Ray Yeates
Coroner	George Carleton

Residents of Catfish Row, fishermen, children, stevedores, etc.:
The Eva Jessye Choir--Catherine Jackson Ayres, Lillian Cowan,
Sara Daigeau, Darlean Duval, Kate Hall, Altonell Hines, Louisa
Howard, Harriet Jackson, Rosalie King, Assota Marshall, Wil-
nette Mayers, Sadie McGill, Massie Patterson, Annabelle Ross,
Louise Twyman, Helen R. White, Musa Williams, Reginald
Beane, Caesar Bennett, G. Harry Bolden, Edward Broadnax,
Carroll Clark, Joseph Crawford, John Diggs, Leonard Franklin,
John Garth, Joseph James, Clarence Jacobs, Allen Lewis,
Jimmie Lightfoot, Lycurgus Lockman, Henry May, Junius
McDaniel, Arthur McLean, William O'Neil, Robert Raines,
Andrew Taylor, Leon Threadgill, Jimmie Waters, Robert Wil-
liams, Ray Yeates.
Choral Conductor--Eva Jessye
Children--Naida King, Regina Williams, Enid Wilkins, Allen
Tinney, William Tinney, Herbert Young.
The Charleston Orphan's Band--Sam Anderson, Eric Bell, Le
Verria Bilton, Benjamine Browne, Claude Christian, Shedrack
Dobson, David Ellis, Clarence Smith, John Strachan, George
Tait, Allen Tinney, William Tinney, Charles Williams, Herbert
Young.

Synopsis and Program Notes (Calvin Theatre, New York City, October 10, 1935): Place: Charleston, S. C.; Time: The recent past.

Act I

Scene 1--Catfish Row. A summer evening.

Clara sings a lullaby to her baby. Robbins enters crap-
game while his wife begs him not to play. Porgy enters and also
joins crap-game. He is accused of being "soft on Crown's Bess."
Crown and Bess enter. The crap-game culminates in a fight between Crown and Robbins in which Robbins is killed. Crown escapes, while Bess seeks sanctuary in Porgy's room.

Scene 2--Serena's Room. The following night.

The "saucer burial" of Robbins who has died penniless.
Friends contribute to the funeral expenses. A detective enters and,
to secure a witness to the Robbins murder, arrests Peter. Serena
is told that unless the body of her husband is buried on the following day it will be given to the medical students. The undertaker
enters and agrees to bury the body on the following morning.

Act II

Scene 1--Catfish Row. A month later.

Porgy and Bess are at their window. Sporting Life, the
dope-peddler, enters. Lawyer Frazier enters and sells Bess a
divorce from Crown. Sporting Life offers Bess dope and is
threatened by Porgy. The Negro community leaves for the picnic.
Bess goes, leaving Porgy alone in Catfish Row.

Scene 2--A Palmetto Jungle. Evening of the same day.

The picnic party pauses for a final celebration on the way
back to the excursion steamer. Bess is detained by Crown, who
has been in hiding on the island. He forces her to remain with
him for the night.

Scene 3--Catfish Row. Before dawn. A week later.

Bess has returned to Catfish Row and her voice raving in
delirium can be heard from Porgy's room. Serena leads a prayer
for Bess' recovery. Street vendors enter, crying their wares.
Bess joins Porgy on the doorstep. They confess their love for each
other and Porgy promises to protect her from Crown. A bell sounds
the hurricane alarm, and Clara, whose husband, Jake, is out with
the fishing fleet, falls in a faint. The storm descends upon Catfish
Row.

Scene 4--Serena's Room. Dawn of the following day.

The storm is raging while the frightened Negroes sing and
pray. A knock is heard at the door which they believe to be the
summons of death. Crown enters. He ridicules Porgy. From the
window Bess sees that Jake's boat has been wrecked. Clara gives
her baby to Bess to keep until she returns and rushes out. Crown
laughs at the frightened Negroes, defies the storm and leaves to
help Clara. He warns Bess that he will return for her.

Act III

Scene 1--Catfish Row. The next night.

In one of the rooms a group of women are mourning for
the dead of the storm. Sporting Life enters and intimates to Maria
that Crown is still alive. In Porgy's room Bess can be heard singing to the baby. Crown enters and approaches Porgy's door. He
is seized by Porgy and in the ensuing fight is killed.

Scene 2--Catfish Row. Early morning.

The detective and coroner enter determined to discover

Crown's murderer.   They interrogate the residents of the court but
are unsuccessful.   The coroner insists that Porgy go with him to
identify the body of Crown at the inquest.   Filled with superstitious
terror at the thought of looking on his victim's face, Porgy refuses
and is dragged away.   Bess is approached by Sporting Life who
tries to persuade her to go to New York with him.   She refuses.
Sporting Life leaves a small packet containing "happy dust" upon
her doorstep and departs.   In despair of losing Porgy she opens
her door and picks up the "happy dust."

Musical Numbers:

Act I, Scene 1

Lullaby, "Summer Time"	Clara
"A Woman Is a Sometime Thing"	Jake and Ensemble
Entrance of Porgy: "They Pass By Singing"	Porgy
Crap Game Fugue	

Scene 2

"Gone, Gone, Gone!"	Ensemble
"Overflow"	Ensemble
Arioso, "My Man's Gone Now"	Serena and Ensemble
Train Song, "Leavin' Fo' De Promis' Lan' "	Bess and Ensemble

Act II, Scene 1

Rowing Song, "It Takes a Long Pull to Get There"	Jake and Fishermen
"I Got Plenty o' Nuttin' "	Porgy
Divorce Scene, "Woman to Lady"	Porgy, Bess, Frazier and Ensemble
Duet, "Bess, You Is My Woman Now"	Porgy and Bess
Picnic Song, "Oh, I Can't Sit Down"	Orphan Band and Ensemble

Scene 2

"It Ain't Necessarily So"	Sportin' Life and Ensemble
Duet, "What You Want with Bess?"	Crown and Bess

Scene 3

"Time and Time Again"	Serena and Ensemble
Street Cries, Strawberry Woman, Crab Man.	
Duet, "I Loves You, Porgy"	Porgy and Bess

Scene 4

"Oh, de Lawd Shake de Heaven"	Ensemble
"A Red Headed Woman"	Crown and Ensemble
"Oh, Doctor Jesus"	Principals and Ensemble

Act III, Scene 1

"Clara, Don't You Be Down-hearted"	Ensemble

Scene 2

"There's a Boat That's Leavin' Soon for New York"	Sportin' Life and Bess

<u>Scene 3</u>

Occupational Humoresque
Trio, "Where's My Bess"   Porgy, Serena and Lily
"I'm On My Way"   Porgy and Ensemble
Scenery built and painted by New York Studios. Costumes by
    Theatre Guild Workroom under supervision of Jean Tate. Nets
    by the R. J. Ederer Net & Twine Co. Steinway piano used in
    this production.

A PRINCE OF DIXIE (1911)
Book: George Taylor

Cast of Characters:
Will Daley   Frank Montgomery
Mamie Brown   Bessie Brady
Mose Jenkins   James Brown
Rastus Brown   Pearl Churchill
Messenger   Elwood Woodring
Parson Brown   Eddie Stafford
Aunt Mirandy   Mamie Jones
Lilly Snow Jackson   Lena Mitchell
Jube Jones   Mayme Brown
Sue Simpkins   Maude Hudson
Jeff Jackson   George Tucker
Teacher   Lizzie Hart

Story: (No information)

Musical Numbers:
"All Wise Chickens Follow Me"   George Taylor
"I Ain't Going to Walk Back
    Home"
"I Am the Man with All the
    Dough"

RAISIN' CAIN (1923), 2 Acts 8 Scenes
Producer: Nat Nazarro
Book, Music: Frank Montgomery
Music Director: Jules Laster

Cast of Characters:
Nomo, a Chief   Emory Hutchins
Leila, Chief's Daughter   Jean Starr
Neila, Chief's Daughter   Corressa Madison
Bilo, a Lost Soldier   Sam Russell
Mrs. Brown, Mother of Bilo   Josephine Gray
Shaky, a Buddy of Bilo   George McClennon
Flash Jones   Demos Jones
Speed Green   Tony Green
Slick, a Bad Man   Emory Hutchins
Weary, a Prophetess   Josephine Gray

Leila's Chum   Percy Wiggins
Cliff   Cliff
Others--Carrie (Sublette), Amy Roden, Jean Kane, Irene Lauder,
    Ruth Green, Edith Dunbar, Pearl Darrell, Mozelle Tibbs,
    Gladys Robinson, Florence Hill, Margaret Bolden, D. Mitchell,
    George Staten, William Spencer, Alexander Peel, James Taylor,
    James Andrews, Ernie Henry, Roscoe Simmons, Howard El-
    more, Charles Lanchaster

Synopsis:

Act 1

In Africa
Scene 1.   In Senegambia
Scene 2.   On a Jungle Trail
Scene 3.   Interior of Chief Nomo's Hut

Act 2

New York City; Time: Present (1923)
Scene 1.   Music Store, Upper Seventh Avenue, Harlem
Scene 2.   Lafayette Theatre Block
Scene 3.   Restaurant of Bilo and Shaky
Scene 4.   Hotel Conservatory
Scene 5.   Ballroom

Musical Numbers:

Act 1

"Tropical Chant"--Opening Chorus	Ensemble
"When My Man Comes Home"	?
"Mammy's Black Baby"	Josephine Gray
"Jungle Jump"	Percy Wiggins and Chorus
"Happenings"	Demos Jones
"Senegambian Moon"	Jones and Chorus
"Sentimental Oriental Blue"	Jones and Chorus
"Come Out"	Green and Chorus
"Let's Go"	Leita Neila, Green, Jones and Entire Company

Act 2

"Harmony"	Ensemble
Specialty	A few moments with Buck and Bubbles, world famous entertainers
"Laughing Clarinet"	George McClennon
"Barber Shop Harmony"	Buck, McClennon, Russell, Jones
Dance	Bubbles
"Call a Cop"	Corressa Madison and Chorus
"Voice from the Congo"	Josephine Gray
"Hot Chops"	Ensemble
"Fattening Frogs for Snakes"	Corressa and Chorus
"Raisin' Cain"	Jones, Green and Ensemble
"Oh, Foot"	Sam Russell, George McClennon
Specialty	Jean Starr (Fred Tunball at piano)

Passing Review:
    "Strut, Miss Lizzie"
    "Plantation"
    "Shuffle Along"
    "Liza"
    "How Come"
    "Williams and Walker"   Buck and Bubbles
Grant Finale   Entire Company

RANG TANG (1927)
Producers: Flournoy E. Miller, Aubrey Lyles
Book: Kaj Gynt
Lyrics: Jo Trent
Music: Ford Dabney
Staging: Flournoy E. Miller

Principal Cast of Characters: Flournoy E. Miller, Aubrey E.
    Lyles, Edward Thompson, Evelyn Preer, Crawford Jackson.

Story: The plot of the tale is about two barbers who are run out of
"Jimtown," steal an airplane and land in Africa. Their adventures there form the comedy situations for the play.

Synopsis:
<u>Act I, Scene 1: Public Square, Jimtown</u>
Daybreak
    Mrs. Jenkins   Lillian Westmoreland
    Laborers, Washwomen, Cottonpickers
Barber Shop Business
    Customer   James Strange
    Villagers   B. Jackson, A. Allen, E.
                          Thompson
"Everybody Shout"--sung by villagers and Jimtown Quartette (S.
    Mason, J. Willis, C. Todd, A. Allen)
Dance Specialty--Crawford Jackson
"Sammy and Topsy"--Sung by Inez Draw and May Barnes
    Magnolia   Zaidee Jackson
    Mrs. Jenkins   Lillian Westmoreland
"Brown"--Sung by Zaidee Jackson and Jimtown Dandies
Dance Specialty--Crawford Jackson
"Pay Me"--Sung by Jimtown Business Men
    Steve Jenkins, a Barber   F. E. Miller
    Sam Peck, Another Barber   A. Lyles
    Sheriff   Edward Thompson
"Sambo's Banjo"   Zaidee Jackson and Banjo
                          Ensemble
<u>Scene 2: Loafer's Lane, Jimtown</u>
Missing   Mrs. Jenkins, Alice and Vil-
                          lagers
"Some Day"--Sung by Miss Josephine Hall and Jimtown Trio (J.
    Willis, Miss Revells, Miss Simmons)
Spirituals   Jimtown Glee Club

(Special arrangement by Daniel L. Haynes and Clarence Todd)

<u>Scene 3: Adrift</u>

The Aviators   Miller and Lyles

<u>Scene 4: The Shores of Africa</u>

"Come to Africa"--Sung by Josephine Hall and Native Girls

<u>Scene 5: A Jungle Trail</u>

Steve and Sam   Miller and Lyles

<u>Scene 6: The Bamboo Forest</u>

"Zulu Fifth Avenue"--Sung by Evelyn Preer and Zulu Steppers

Dance Specialties--Barnes and Mack, Crawford Jackson

Jungle Love

    Jungle Rose   Evelyn Preer

    King of Madagascar   Daniel Haynes

"Jungle Rose"--Sung by Daniel L. Haynes

Monkey Business

    Steve and Sam   Miller and Lyles

    Jungle Rose   Evelyn Preer

    Simian   L. Ransom

"Monkey Land"--Sung by Miller and Lyles

    Apes, Monkey Band, Missing Links, Baboon Quartet,
    Chimpanzees, Monkeys

<u>Act II, Scene 1:</u>

A Dream

    Jungle Rose   Evelyn Preer

    (Handmaidens and Birds)

    Tribal King   Edward Thompson

    His Handmaiden   Gertrude Williams

Nymph Dance by Marie Mahood

    The Queen of Sheba   Josephine Hall

    A Courier   Frankye Maxwell

    (Lantern Bearers, Handmaidens and Couriers)

"Sweet Evening Breeze"   Josephine Hall

A Jungle Family

    Chief Bobo   Joe Willis

    The Six Little Wives   Margie Hubbard, Marie Mahood,
                                     Evelyne Keyes, Thelma
                                     McLaughlin, Hazel Miles
                                     and Frances Hood

The Jungle School

    The Teachers   Miller and Lyles

    The Natives   L. Ransom and C. Gordon

    Native Children

Moon Dance--By Natives

<u>Scene 2: The Desert</u>

"Summer Nights"   Josephine Hall

    Dance by Barnes, Mack, and Byron Jones

The Prospectors   Miller and Lyles

    The Queen of Africa   Lillian Westmoreland

The Mirage

The Jungle Rose Dancing Girls

<u>Scene 3: The Native Village</u>

The Captive

"Tramps of the Desert"--Sung by George Battles and Natives

The Prisoner	F. E. Miller
The King	A. Lyles
Chief	George Battles
Jungle Rose	Evelyn Preer
King of Madagascar	Daniel Haynes
"Voodoo"	
Voodoo Chief	Gilbert Holland

<u>Scene 4:   A Jungle Trail</u>

The Settlement	
Chief	George Battles
Steve and Sam	Miller and Lyles
Fisticuffs	Miller and Lyles

<u>Scene 5:   Exterior of a Harlem Cabaret</u>

"Harlem" (Song)	Evelyn Preer, Harlem Sextet
	and Harlemites
Dance Specialty--Barnes and Mack	
The Richest Man in the World	Miller and Lyles
Doorman	L. Ransom
Officer	Jerry Mills

<u>Scene 6:   Interior of a Harlem Cabaret</u>

A Couple of Live Ones	Miller and Lyles
Head Waiter	Joe Willis
Cigarette Girl	Marie Mahood
Manager	Edward Thompson
A Beauty	Le 'Etta Revells

Dance Specialty by Byron Jones
A New Dance
"Rang Tang"--Sung and Danced by Evelyn Preer and Entire Company
Male Chorus--Daniel L. Haynes, Ambrose Allen, Howard Brown,
    C. H. Gordon, Gilbert Holland, Burkie Jackson, Snippy Mason,
    Llewellyn Ransom, James Strange, Joseph Willis, Clarence Todd,
    Edwin Alexander, George Battles and Edward Thompson.
Ladies of the Ensemble--Le 'Etta Revells, Pauline Jackson, Susie
    Baker, Gladyce Bronson, Doris Colbert, La Valla Cook, Inez
    Draw, Teddy Garnette, Alice Hoffman, Margie Hubbard,
    Frances Hubbard, Evelyn Keyes, Marie Mahood, Frankye Max-
    well, Thelma McLaughlin, Hazel Miles, Thula Ortez, Thelma
    Rhoton, Gladys Schell, Helen Smith, Norma Smith, Gomez
    Boyer, Mildred Coleman, Leonore Gadsden, Isabel Peterson,
    Ethelyn Boyd, Irma Miles, Marie Simmons, Anna Humphrey,
    Gertrude Williams.

THE RED MOON (1908), 3 Acts
Producer: Bob Cole, J. Rosamond Johnson
Book, Lyrics: Bob Cole
Music: J. Rosamond Johnson
Additional Lyrics: Charles Hunter
Additional Music, Music Director: James Reese Europe

Cast of Characters:

Plunck Brown	Bob Cole
Slim	J. Rosamond Johnson

Minnehaha	Abbie Mitchell
John Low Dog, Indian Chief	Arthur Talbot
Indian Bruce	Theo. Pankey
Bill Gibson	Henry Gant
Wench	Andrew Tribble
Amanda Gibson	Mollie Dill
Lucretia Martin	Elizabeth Williams
Bill Webster	Sam Lucas

Others--Wesley Jenkins, Benny Jones, Fanny Wise, Edgar Connors,
  Daisy Brown, Leona Marshall
Chorus--Mayme Butler, Lulu Coleman, Bessie Tribble, Bessie
  Simms, Blanche Deas, Tillie Smith
The Ada Girls--Marie Young, Pauline Hackney, Tootsie Delk,
  Marie Lucas, Mattie Harris, Millie Deas
The Dancing Picks--Daisy Brown, Leona Marshall, Marion Potter,
  Lottie Gee, Pearl Taylor, Bessie Brown
College Boys--Frank DeLyons, Frank Brown, W. E. Phelps,
  Herbert Sutton, Robert Young, Will Waters
The Policemen--W. H. Tunstill, William Waters, Samuel Gray

Cast of Characters, 1909 Season:

Red Feather	Theo. Pankey
Lilly White	Andrew Tribble
Bill Webster	Sam Lucas
Bill Gibson	Henry Gant
Bill Armour	Wesley Jenkins
Bill Simmons	Benny Jones
Lureretia Martin	Elizabeth Williams
Amanda Gibson	Mollie Dill
Waneta	Marie Young
Eagle Eye	Frank Brown
Sally Simmons	Leona Marshall
Sue Simmons	Daisy Brown

Story: The story of the play has to do with a romantic episode
opening in and around a Government School for Indians and Blacks
at "Sunshine Land." The first act opens with an exterior view of
the school and grounds. It develops that Minnehaha, the half-breed
daughter of an Indian Chief who fifteen years before had deserted
her when she was an infant and returned to the land of his people
in the "Land of the Setting Sun," suddenly returns and claims his
daughter over the protest of the black mother and her friends. The
Chief, with the help of "Red Father," an Indian student at the
school who is in love with Minnehaha, finally prevail in their mission and the maiden is forcibly taken back to her father's tribe.

      In the second act the curtain goes up on a very elaborate
mountainous setting where Minnehaha has been taken by her father.
After many funny situations the girl is rescued by Plunck, a show-
manager (Bob Cole) and Slim, a ragtime piano player (J. Rosamond
Johnson). These two are masquerading as a doctor and lawyer.

      In act three, Minnehaha, having been restored to her home
and friends, is married to Plunck as a reward for his bravery.

Musical Numbers (1908):
"Checkers"   Herbert Sutton
"Ada"
"Bleeding Moon"   J. Rosamond Johnson
"Big Red Shawl"   J. Rosamond Johnson
"On the Road to Monterey"   Edgar Connors assisted by
                                          Daisy Brown, Leona
                                          Marshall
"I've Lost My Teddy Bear"
"Cupid Is an Indian Pickininny"   Abbie Mitchell
"I Ain't Had No Lovin' in a   Andrew Tribble
    Long, Long Time"

Musical Numbers (1909):
"Wildfire"   Aida Overton Walker
"Phoebe Brown"   Aida Overton Walker
"As Long as the World Rolls   Abbie Mitchell
    On"
"Coola-Woo-la"   J. Rosamond Johnson
"Sambo"   Edgar Connors

RHAPSODY IN BLACK (1931)
Producer: Lew Leslie
Lyrics and Music: George Gershwin, Dorothy Fields, Jimmy
    McHugh, Mann Holiner, Alberta Nicholi, Ken Macomber, J.
    Rosamond Johnson, Cecil Mack, W. C. Handy
Vocal Arrangements for Spirituals and Folksongs: Cecil Mack

Principal Cast of Characters: Ethel Waters, Valaida Snow, Berry
    Brothers, Earl (Snakehips) Tucker, Eddie Rector, Blue McAl-
    lister, Al Moore, Cecil Mack Choir, Pike Davis' Continental
    Orchestra

Synopsis:
                            Prologue
       "Harlem Interlude" by Nat. N. Dorfman
Liza explains to George Washington Aaron Burr Brown that all the
world is a rhapsody and that the ghetto of New York City known as
Harlem is a rhapsody in black.
Liza   Ethel Waters
George Washington Aaron Burr   Robert Raines
    Brown
Cecil Mack Choir--Eloise Uggams, Avis Andrews, Louise Howard,
    Mayme Richardson, Seleta Pettiford, Geneva Washington, Olive
    Ball, Maude Simmons, Ernest Boyd, Frank Jackson, Robert
    Raines, Ernest Allen, Harold Thompson, James Skelton.
Patrons, Hangers-on, Visitors, etc.
(The Scene is a Gin Mill in Harlem)
                            Part I
Rhapsody in Black   Valaida and Pike Davis' Con-
                                          tinental Orchestra
(A musical transition of the Negro from Africa to Harlem--by Ken
    Macomber and Pat Carroll)

"Gettin' Up Mornin' "   Ernest Boyd and Cecil Mack
                                          Choir
"Heard Nobody Pray"   Eloise Uggams and Cecil Mack
                                          Choir
Wash Tub Rub-sody   Ethel Waters
(Pearl Wright, Accompanist)
(By Mann Holiner and Alberta
   Nichols)
"'Till the Real Thing Comes   Valaida and Pike Davis' Con-
   Along"   tinental Orchestra
Reprise   Berry Brothers
(By Mann Holiner and Alberta
   Nichols)
"Exhortation"   Ernest Allen and Cecil Mack
                                          Choir
"Chloe"   Geneva Washington and Cecil
                                          Mack Choir
Harlem Rhumbola   Valaida, Al Moore and Pike
(By Dorothy Fields and   Davis' Continental Orches-
Jimmy McHugh)   tra
Dance Hall Hostess   Ethel Waters
(Pearl Wright, Accompanist)
(By Mann Holiner and Alberta
   Nichols)
George Gershwin's "Rhapsody   Valaida, Pike Davis' Continental
   in Blue" (Vocal arrangement   Orchestra, Cecil Mack
   by Rosamond Johnson)   Choir and Ananias Berry.
                                          Joseph Steel at the piano.

Part II

"St. James Infirmary"   Valaida, Cecil Mack Choir and
   (Choral arrangement by   Pike Davis' Continental
   Russell Wooding) (Special   Orchestra
   music and lyrics for choir
   by Valaida)
"What's Keeping My Prince   Ethel Waters
   Charming?"
(Assisted by Blue McAllister)
(Pearl Wright, Accompanist)
(By Mann Holliner and Alberta
   Nichols)
Rhythm in Rhapsody   Earl (Snakeyhips) Tucker and
                                          Bessie Dudley
"Eli Eli"   Avis Andrews, Eloise Uggams
                                          and Cecil Mack Choir
"The Two Guitars"   Valaida and Cecil Mack Choir
Rhapsody in Taps   Eddie Rector
"You Can't Stop Me from Loving   Ethel Waters
   You"
(Assisted by Blue McAllister)
(Pearl Wright, Accompanist)
(By Mann Holiner and Alberta
   Nichols)

Dream of the Chocolate Soldier   Valaida, Eddie Rector and Pike
    (Victor Herbert, Special Ar-   Davis' Continental Orches-
    rangement by Ken Macomber)   tra
Finale   Entire Company

RICHARDS, PRINGLE-RUSCO AND HOLLANDS BIG MINSTREL
FESTIVAL (1899)

Program:
First Part

Opening Chorus: "Lady Africa"   Company
J. Ed. Green, master of cere-
    monies, introducing Bobby
    Kemp and John Rucker,
    star endmen
"Kill It Babe"   Dick Thomas
"Tired of Dodging Dat Stall-   Bobby Kemp
    ment Man"
"Ain't I Your Honey Boy No   John Rucker
    More"
"I Am Living Easy"   Harry Fiddler
"When a Coon Sits in the   Billy Kersands
    President's Chair"
Selections by the St. Paul
    Cathedral Choristers

Olio

Christian, the Wonder Skater,
    assisted by Dick Thomas,
    Clever Comedian
Florence Hines, Male Imper-   "I Can't See My Money Go
    sonator   That Way"
Encore by Miss Hines   "I'm a Millionaire's Son"
McCarver, Reed and McCarver,
    the original Georgia Cracker
    Jacks, dancing and acrobatics
Allie Brow, King of the slack
    wire
John Rucker, the original "Ala-   monologue and song, "Luck-
    bama Blossom"   iest Coon in Town"
Leach and Dodd   selections on novel musical
                                            instruments
Marsh Craig, the human enigma
Four Broadway Girls   Songs
The Kersands, Billy and Louise   Comedy sketch, "Deacon and
                                            the Widow"
Afterpiece

"Darktown is Out Tonight"
Music under the direction of Prof. James Lacy

ROCKWELL'S SUNNY SOUTH COMPANY (1908)

Program:

First Act

Plantation Songs	Company
Opening Medley: "On the Bank of the Ohio River"	Company
Coons Prancing--To Two-Step Rather than Waltz	
"Let Me Be Your Lemon Coon"	Young Rastus
"Big Chief Battle Axe"	Daisy Fox
"My Old Kentucky Home"	Robert Edmonds' Sunny South Ladies Quartette (Louise Turner, Lilly Green, Daisy Fox, Blanche Fuller)
"Who Me, I'm Not the Man"	Clifford Brooks
"Be My Little Teddy Bear"	Blanche Fuller
"Good Old Georgia"	Robert Fuller
"What the Rose Said to Me"	Lillian Weathers
"I Was Born in Virginia	Nellie Thornton
Our Whirlwind Buck and Wing Dancers	Entire Company--watch Mammy!

Second Act

Miss Blanche Fuller, the Sunny South Nightingale
The Turners (James and Louise), the Encyclopedia of Comedy
Bob Purcell and Nellie Thornton, comedians, singers and novelty Buck and Wing dancers
Daisy Fox, the Little Magnet
Green and Weather, Novelty trick and fancy unicyclists
Sunny South Male Quartette
Albert Harris, Robert Edmonds in a budget of old time melodies: introducing our colored Bells and Swells in songs and dances

Third Act

Farce: "Fun in Camp"
Cast of Characters:

Jake, a new recruit	J. W. Turner
Capt. Big Head, who thinks he knows it all	Cliff Brooks
Sergeant Nocount	Robert Purcell
Ambolinas Snow	Louise Turner
Privates and Visitors: Introducing the whole Sunny South Company	

Business Staff of Sunny South Company:

J. C. Rockwell	Proprietor and Manager
J. C. Comer	Business Manager
J. W. Turner	Stage Director
Ed. Fox	Leader of the Band
W. Washington	Leader of Orchestra

ROSIE'S WEDDING DAY (1924)
Producer: Tim Moore, Chicago Follies Company

Principal Cast of Characters: Tim Moore, Willie Singleton, Pete
    Gentry, Fred Moore, Fred Durval, Edna Brown, Early Smith,
    Rachel King, Eva Simmons

Story: The plot involves the attempt to two young lovers to elope
and the bitter opposition of the parents.   The father locks the girl
in a room and leaves the key in charge of Jake, the hired hand.
        Tim Moore plays the part of Jake and his original antics and
spontaneous witticisms which culminate in his telling of a fable to
Rosie's father and mother of a similar Rosie who likewise tried to
elope fifty years before.   By fitting the action to the moment of the
present young couple, Moore furnished the comedy that kept the audience in an uproar of merriment.

Musical Numbers:
"Log Cabin Blues"   Willie Singleton
"Loving Song"   Pete Gentry

RUFUS RASTUS (1906)
Producer: J. Ed. Green
Book: William D. Hall
Lyrics: Frank Williams
Music: Tom Lominer, Joe Jordan, Ernest Hogan
Ensemble Music: H. Lawrence Freeman

Cast of Characters:

John Drake, second waiter at the Ponce de Leon Hotel	J. F. Mores
Dr. Fo-Jo, dealer in lucky charms	J. Leubrie Hill
Sophronia, housekeeper at Ponce de Leon Hotel	Anna Cook Pankey
Hugo, the porter, successful and satisfied	Harry Fiddler
Noah Beasley, head waiter at the Ponce de Leon Hotel	J. Ed. Green
Angelica Newcomb, looking for a job for her friend	A. D. Byrd
Bill B. Dam	Will Wilkins
Rev. Nightingale, Slipback New-comb, a man of many call-ings	R. A. Kelly
Federica, their educated daughter	Alice Mackey
Snowflack, their youngest off-spring	Muriel Ringgold
Enoch, the bell boy ⎫ Cousin Monk ⎬ Catasterphe ⎭	Theo. Pankey

Opposite: Ad for "Rufus Rastus," circa 1906

Lazarus Tuttle, stage manager   Henry Troy
   and theatrical promoter
Selina Giltedge, prima donna   Carita Day
   of Coontown 400
Mandy Jones, leading soprano   Mamie Emerson
   of Ragtime Opera Company
Rufus Rastus, unfortunate   Ernest Hogan
Samson Strong, with hallucina-   Harry Gilliam
   tions
Officer   Matt Housley
Belmoral, Hugo's sweetheart   Pauline Hackney
Floor Manager   Bill Moore
Hotel Help, Jubilee Singers, Minstrels, Terpsichorean Artists,
   Masqueraders
Choristers:
Scrub Women--Pearl Lavan, Sarah Green, Amy Leslie
Nurse Girls--Pearl Brown, Jeanette Foster, Madge Warren,
   B. Gillespie
Chambermaids--Nellie Dansy, Georgia Mickey, Maude Jones,
   M. Sullivan
Laundresses--Pauline Hackney, Pinky Cooper, M. Thomas, Anita
   Wilkins
Bell Boys--Jennie Thompson, Maude Turner, Mabel Turner
Yardmen--Billy Moore, Matt Housley, George Lynnier, William
   Spicer
Waiters--Will Wilkins, Angelo Housley, R. C. Baker, J. F.
   Mores
Footmen--William Pierce, J. L. Grant, Beverly Housley
Chefs--James Worles, Edward Gray, Walter Robertson, John Hill
Newsboys--Pearl Brown, Maude Turner, Amy Leslie, Jennie
   Thompson, Sarah Green, Jeanette Foster, Mabel Turner,
   Madge Warren

Story: The plot involves Rufus Rastus, an unfortunate man, who
owes twenty-two dollars, but who at last, through the gift of a
brainless tramp, accidentally finds himself in possession of the sum
of twenty-two thousand dollars hidden in a box of Quaker Oats.

Musical Numbers:
"Consolation"   Henry Troy
"Maude"   Alice Mackey
"Hornet and the Bee"   Carita Day
"My Mobile Mandy"   Mamie Emerson
"Old Kentucky Home"   Sallie Green
"The Isle of Repose"   Anna Cook Pankey

RUN LITTLE CHILLUN' (1933)
   (Original New York Production which opened at Lyric Theatre)
Producer, Book, Music: Hall Johnson

Cast of Characters (New York Production):
Ella   Edna Thomas

Children:
    Organist   Esther Hall
    Bessie Hicks   Marietta Canty
    Jeems Jackson   Jimmie Waters
Other Children--Henri Wood,
    Bennie Tattnall, Nell Tay-
    lor, Edna Comodore
The Rev. Sister Luella Strong   Olive Ball
Sister Mattie Fullilove   Mattie Shaw
Sister Flossie Lou Little   Bertha Fowell
Brother Bartholomew Little   Ray Yeats
Bro. Esan Redd, Church Dea-   Walter Price
    con, Board of Hope Baptist
    Church
Sister Mahalie Ockletree   Rosalie King
Sister Judy Ann Hicks   Pauline Rivers
Sister Lulu Jane Hunt   Lula Hunt
Sister Susie Mae Hunt   Carolyn Hughes
Brother George Jenkins   Edward Broadnax
Brother Jeremiah Johnson   Milton Lacey
Brother Goliath Simmons   Service Bell
The Rev. Jones, Pastor of   Harry Bolden
    Hope Baptist Church
Jim (Rev. Jones' Son)   Alston Burleigh
Sulamai   Fredi Washington
Brother Lu-te, Chief Singer of   James Boxwill
    New Day Pilgrims
Brother Jo-be, Herald of Joy   Gus Simons
Sister Mata, Priestess   Ethel Purnello
Reba (Daughter of Kenda)   Waldine Williams
Mother Kenda (Daughter of   Ollie Burgoyne
    Tongola)
Brother Moses, Young Priest   Jack Carr
Elder Tongola, Prophet of the   Harold Sneed
    New Day Pilgrims
Belle, of Toomer's Bottom   Bessie Guy
Mame, of Toomer's Bottom   Mabel Diggs
Mag, Sulamai's Mother   Cecil Scott
Sue Scott, of Toomer's Bottom   Lula King
The Rev. Ebenezer Allen,   Andrew Taylor
    Local Preacher

RUN LITTLE CHILLUN' (1938)
    (Los Angeles Production)
Producers: Clarence Muse, Hall Johnson
Sponsored by Federal Music and Theatre Project

Cast of Characters:
Jim   Alfred Grant
Sulamai   Florence O'Brien
Elder Tongola   Arthur Ray
Young Minister   Roy Glenn

Old Minister   Jess Lee Brooks
The Rev. Sister Strong   Olive Ball
Others--Ruby Elzy, Gertrude Saunders, Myrtle Anderson, Eva
    Grant, Valena Miller, Cleo Desmond (former Lafayette player),
    Onest Conley, Bessie Gray, Thaddeus Jones, Elizabeth Sprat-
    ley, Guernsey Morrow, Henry Thomas, Arnestly Williams,
    Mabel Massengill, Larry Harrison, Clarence Hargraves, Ana
    Swanson, Myrtle Dunham, Earl Mitchell

Story: The story deals with the troubles of the pastor of Hope
Baptist Church into whose evangelistic domain has drifted a band of
pilgrims who worship under the moon and expose their bodies and
writhe and wiggle in the name of religion and they are drawing members of the Hope Baptist Church into their meetings.
        Jim, the son of Pastor Jones, who has carried on an open
love affair with Sulamai, a pretty girl from Toomer's Bottom, in
spite of a God fearing wife at home, follows his paramour to the
meetings, deserting his own church.
        Sulamai is also courted by Brother Moses, handsome bronze
priest of the pilgrims, but she ignored his protestations of love until Jim turns her down when she tells him she is to become a
mother.
        Brother Moses predicts a dire tragedy will befall Sulamai,
but she follows Jim to the Hope Baptist Church revival where Jim's
good wife and father have been praying for his redemption.   Jim is
re-converted but the worshippers turn on Sulamai when she too
comes seeking Jesus.   Jim's religion weakens and he goes after
her, but it is too late--the warning of Brother Moses comes true
in the form of a bolt of lightning that kills the soul-wrecked Sulamai,
ending the eternal triangle.   The play ends with Jim holding the
limp body of his sweetheart in his arms as the incantations of the
revivalists soar to heaven.

Musical Numbers: (No information)

RUNNIN' DE TOWN (1930)
Producer: No Data
Lyrics and Music: J. C. Johnson
Book: Leigh Whipper

Cast of Characters:
Sister Rebecca   Ollie Perkins
Sister Matilda   Marie Young
Missie   Susan Brown
Brother Dixon   Sam Cross
Josephine Dixon   Muriel Rahn
Fred Briggs   Leigh Whipper
Bob Jenkins   Paul Ford
Sister Drucilla   Angeline Lawson
Yaller   Yank Brunson
Foots   James McPheetus
Happy   Henry Davis

Rastus Brown   Fred Wheeldin
Chief of Police   Aubrey Lyles
Stanley Bennett's Jimtown Choir, Jimtown Flash Devils and Jimtown
     Steppers
Time--The Present (1930)
Place--Jimtown Dixie

Story: The plot involves two rival lodges and the efforts of the
hen-pecked chief of police to settle matters for all concerned.

Musical Numbers: (No information)

RUNNIN' WILD (1923)
Producers: Flournoy E. Miller, Aubrey Lyles
Book: Flournoy E. Miller, Aubrey Lyles
Music, Lyrics: James P. Johnson, Cecil Mack
Dances: Lydia Webb

Cast of Characters (In order of their appearance):

Uncle Mose	C. Wesley Hill
Uncle Amos	Arthur D. Porter
Tom Sharper	Lionel Monagas
Ethel Hill	Revella Hughes
Jack Penn	George Stephens
Detective Wise	Paul C. Floyd
Mrs. Silas Green	Mattie Wilkes
Mandy Little	Ina Duncan
Adelaide	Adelaide Hall
Steve Jenkins	F. E. Miller
Sam Peck	A. L. Lyles
Willie Live	Eddie Gray
Chief Red Cup	Tommy Woods
Head Waiter	Billy Andrews
Ruth Little	Elizabeth Welch
Silas Green	J. Wesley Jeffrey
Boat Captain	James H. Woodson
Sam Slocum	George Stamper
Lucy Lanky	Katherine Yarborough
Angelina Brown	Georgette Harvey

Story: (No information)

Synopsis:
                                   Act I
Scene 1--Market Place, Jimtown.
Scene 2--Railroad Station.
Scene 3--Four Corners, St. Paul, Minnesota
Scene 4--Rondo Street, St. Paul, Minnesota
Scene 5--Cabaret, St. Paul, Minnesota
                                   Act II
Scene 1--Levee, Jimtown.
Scene 2--Street, Jimtown.

Scene 3--A Deserted Barn, Jimtown.
Scene 4--Street, Jimtown.
Scene 5--Country Club, Jimtown.

Musical Numbers:

"Open Your Heart"	George Stephens
"Log Cabin Days"	Georgette Harvey and Male Quartet
"Old Fashion Love"	Ina Duncan, A. Porter, Adelaide Hall
"Love Bug"	Adelaide Hall
"Ginger Brown"	Adelaide Hall, Bob Lee (a struttin' fool) and Chorus
*Charleston (dance)	Elizabeth Welch and Chorus
"Juba Dance"	Elizabeth Welch and Chorus
"Keep Movin'"	Clarence Robinson
"Sun Kist Rose"	?
"Showtime"	?
"Heart Breaking Joe"	?
"Banjoland"	?
"Pay Day on Levee"	?
"Slow An' Easy Goin' Man"	?
"The Sheik of Alabam'"	?
"A Brown-Skin Vamp"	?

ST. LOUIS WOMAN (1946)
Producer: Edward Gross
Book: Arna Bontemps and Countee Cullen
Lyrics: Johnny Mercer
Music: Harold Arlen

Cast of Characters (In the order in which they speak):

Badfoot	Robert Pope
Little Augie	Harold Nicholas
Barney	Fayard Nicholas
Lila	June Hawkins
Slim	Louis Sharp
Butterfly	Pearl Bailey
Della Green	Ruby Hill
Biglow Brown	Rex Ingram
Ragsdale	Elwood Smith
Pembroke	Merritt Smith
Jasper	Charles Welch
The Hostess	Maude Russell
Drum Major	J. Mardo Brown
Mississippi	Milton J. Williams

Opposite: George Stamper, Dancer, As He Appeared in Miller and
Lyles' "Runnin' Wild," circa 1923

*Charleston dance was first introduced to Broadway in this show.

Dandy Dave	Frank Green
Leah	Juanita Hall
Jackie	Joseph Eady
Celestine	Yvonne Coleman
Piggie	Herbert Coleman
Joshua	Lorenzo Fuller
Mr. Hopkins	Milton Wood
Preacher	Creighton Thompson
Waiter	Carrington Lewis

Choral Group--Olive Ball, Rhoda Boggs, Miriam Burton, Rosalie King, Maude Russell, Zelda Shelton, Lori Wilson, J. Mardo Brown, John Diggs, Leon Edwards, Lorenzo Fuller, Theodore Hines, Jerry Laws, Arthur Lawson, Merritt Smith, Charles Welch.

Dancers--Rita Garrett, Dorothea Greene, Gwendolyn Hale, Betty Nichols, Marguerite Roan, Royce Wallace, Enid Williams, Theodore Allen, Smalls Boykins, Norman DeJoie, Frank Green, Lonny Reed, Arthur Smith, George Thomas.

Story: (No information)

Synopsis:
The action takes place in St. Louis, 1898.

Act I

Scene 1--A stable, early afternoon of a day in August.
Scene 2--Biglow's bar, late afternoon, the same day.
Scene 3--Outside Barney's room, at twilight.
Scene 4--A ballroom, evening of the same day.

Act II

Scene 1--Augie's and Della's home, late afternoon, the following week.
Scene 2--The alley.
Scene 3--Funeral Parlor.

Act III

Scene 1--Augie's and Della's home, early evening.
Scene 2--The alley.
Scene 3--The bar.
Scene 4--The stable.
Scene 5--Street corner close to the race track.

Musical Numbers (Orchestration by Ted Royal, Allan Small, Menotti Salta, and Walter Paul. Choral Arrangements by Leon Leonardi.):

Act I

Overture	Orchestra
"Li'l Augie Is a Natural Man"	Badfoot
"Any Place I Hang My Hat Is Home"	Della
"I Feel My Luck Comin' Down"	Augie
"True Love"	Lila
"Legalize My Name"	Butterfly
"Cake Walk Your Lady"	
Drum Major	J. Mardo Brown

Quartet	Rhoda Boggs, Rosalie King, Robert Pope, Milton J. Williams
Competing Couples	Betty Nichols, Smalls Boykins; Rita Garrett, Theodore Allen; Dorothea Green, Milton Wood; Royce Wallace, Lonny Reed; Gwendolyn Hale, Norman JeJoie; Enid Williams, George Thomas; Pearl Bailey, Fayard Nicholas; Ruby Hill, Harold Nicholas.

Act II

"Come Rain or Come Shine"	Della and Augie
"Chinquapin Bush"	Children
"We Shall Meet to Part, No Never"	Piggie
"Lullaby"	Della
"Sleep Peaceful"	Lila
Funeral Scene	
"Leavin' Time"	Choral Group

Act III

Reprise: "Come Rain or Come Shine"	Della
"A Woman's Prerogative"	Butterfly
"Ridin' on the Moon"	Augie and Ensemble
"Least That's My Opinion"	Badfoot
"Racin' Form"	Leah
"Come On, Li'l Augie"	Ensemble
Finale	Entire Company

SEPTEMBER MORN (1920), 3 Acts
Producer: Arthur Gillespie
Orchestra and Choral Direction: Shelton Brooks

Cast of Characters:

Professor Plastic	Shelton Brooks
Will Bunkum	Ollie Powers
"Suance"	Alberta Hunter
The Mother	Margaret Lee

Story: The story is derived from a famous painting of that name (September Morn). Argentina, a famous Parisian dancer, is about to make her debut in New York City and her press agent devises a scheme to make her famous by suggesting to the public that she is the subject of the painting. He has the real picture stolen and takes it to Professor Plastic's studio to have it retouched and to have Argentina's head placed in the original painting. The theft is discovered and traced to Plastic's studio only to find that it had been sent to the artist's home. Counter complications are developed in which many laughs and excruciating situations are expounded.

Musical Numbers: (No information)

7-11 (1923)
Producer: Barrington Carter
Book: Barrington Carter, Garland Howard, Sam Cook
Music: Speedy Smith

Cast of Characters:

Jack Storal	Speedy Smith
Hotstuff Jackson	Garland Howard
Elder Berry	Dink Thomas
Diamond Joe	Bill Grundy

Others--Sam Cook, Evon Robinson, Mae Brown, Barrington Carter,
    Elnora Wilson, Eugene Williams, Eddie Gray, Addison Cary,
    Charles Mason, Josephine Cary, Roscoe Wickham, Iris Hall
Chorus--Lillian Williams, Katie Woolford, Bessie Simms, Lillian
    Page, Marie Rich, Salmona Sisters, Jennie Day, Jacqueline
    Ghans, Mary Scott, Alice Whitfield, May Cooper, Zedora
    DeGaston, Hattie Thomas, Marlon Watson, Lottie Ames, Lydia
    Clark, Eugene Williams, Willis Cross, Arthur Ames, Addison
    Cary, Roscoe Wickham, Henry Rector

Musical Numbers: (No information)

SHADES OF HADES (1923), 2 Acts 7 Scenes
Producer: J. Samuel Stanfield
Book: Tim Owsley
Music, Lyrics: Dave Payton
Stage Director: Julia Rector

Cast of Characters:

"Sam Green," Pullman Porter	Tim Owsley
John Drinkmore	B. B. Joyner
Green's Wife (a lawyer)	Laura Bowman
Satan	Sidney Kirkpatrick

Others--Sylvia Mitchell, Walter Richardson, Richard Gregg, Charles
    Moore, Ollie Smith, Hester Kenton, Mary Bradford, Earl
    Simms, Charles Grundy, Ora Johnson, Isadora Mitchell

Story: Hannah, wishing to cure her husband, Sam, of his intensely
jealous actions, strikes upon a plan, which, when carried out,
causes him to lose his memory.   His memory is restored, however, when the same incident which caused his loss is re-enacted.
The action of the play shows Sam what he was going through during
the absence of his memory.

Musical Numbers:

"Caroline"	T. B. Thomas
"The Nashville Blues"	Hester Kenton
"Holiday in Hades Today"	?

Opposite: Act for Cole and Johnson's "Shoo Fly Regiment,"
circa 1907

COLE

AND

JOHNSON

IN THEIR LATEST CREATION

"The Shoo-Fly Regiment"

With the Best Singing Ensemble ever Collected
Together by a Colored Organization
"Under the direction of Prof. Harry Williams"

In the Perfection of its

PRESENTATION

It Climaxes all Previous Efforts of

COLORED ENTERTAINMENTS

The Brightest and Catchiest Music ever Written by
COLE & JOHNSON,
America's Greatest Song Writers.
Far Different from Anything ever Offered to the
Public by the Negro on the Stage, Creating a
New Thought in the Field of
Dramatic Possibilities.

THE FIRST REAL

AMERICAN NEGRO PLAY

With Original Music.

SHOO FLY REGIMENT (1907)
Producers: Bob Cole, J. Rosamond Johnson
Music: J. Rosamond Johnson
Lyrics: James Weldon Johnson

Cast of Characters:

Brother Doolittle, on the Board of Education	Sam Lucas
Doolittle's Partner	Wesley Jenkins
Uncle July Jackson	Henry Gant
Aunt Phoebie, Jackson's Wife	Elizabeth Williams
Mailman	J. J. Porter
Farmer Randolph	Arthur Ray
Napoleon Bonaparte Lampkins	Arthur Ray
Ophelia	Andrew Tribble
Martha	Anna Cook Pankey
Rose	Fannie Wise
Lieutenant Dixon	Theodore Pankey

Others--Bob Cole, J. Rosamond Johnson, Nettie Glenn, Arthur
    Talbot

Story: "The plot develops a clever story of Negro industrial education in the South and the recruiting of a Negro regiment which is
later sent to the Philippines.   The most elaborate and picturesque
portion of the production is seen in the act in which the beautiful
singing act is introduced.   Cole plays the part of an eccentric character creation and is a genuine comedian who extracts continuous
fun from everything he does on the stage.   Johnson furnishes an
equally pleasing portion of the entertainment with his clever songs
and piano playing. " (Review from New York Age, June 6, 1907)

Musical Numbers:

"Who Do You Love?"	Andrew Tribble, Matt Marshall
"If Adam Hadn't Seen the Apple Tree"	Bob Cole
"Bode of Education"	Sam Lucas and Allen
"Little Gal"	J. Rosamond Johnson and Chorus
"The Ghost of Deacon Brown"	Bob Cole and Chorus

SHUFFLE ALONG (1921)
Producer: Nikko Producing Company (John Scholl, Al Mayer,
    Flournoy E. Miller, Aubrey Lyles, Noble Sissle, Eubie Blake)
Book: Flournoy E. Miller, Aubrey Lyles
Music, Lyrics: Noble Sissle, Eubie Blake
Stage Director: Walter Brooks
Dances: Lawrence Deas, Charles Davis
Musical Arrangements: William Vodery
Orchestra Direction: Eubie Blake

Principal Cast of Characters:

Jim Williams, Proprietor of Jim Town Hotel	Paul Ford

Fight Scene from "Shuffle Along." Foreground: Flournoy E. Miller [in Blackface; left], and Aubrey Lyles, circa 1921

Jessie Williams, his Daughter	Lottie Gee
Ruth Little, her Chum	Gertrude Saunders*
Harry Walton, Candidate for Mayor	Roger Matthews
Board of Aldermen	Richard Cooper
	Arthur Porter
	Arthur Woodson
	Snippy Mason
Mrs. Sam Peck, Suffragette	Mattie Wilks
Tom Sharper, Political Boss	Noble Sissle
Steve Jenkins, Candidate for Mayor	Flournoy E. Miller
Sam Peck, Another Candidate for Mayor	Aubrey Lyles
Jack Penrose, Detective	Lawrence Deas
Rufus Loose, War Relic	C. Wesley Hill
Soakum Flat, Mayor's Body-guard	A. E. Baldwin
Strutt, Jim Town Swell	Billy Williams
Uncle Tom	Charles Davis
Old Black Joe	Bob Williams
Secretary to Mayor	Ina Duncan

Jazz Jasmines--Misses Goldie Cisco, Mildred Brown, Theresa West, Jennie Day, Adelaide Hall, Lillian Williams, Beatrice Williams, Evelyn Irving

Happy Honeysuckles--Misses Ruth Seward, Lucia Johnson, Marguerite Weaver, Bee Freeman, Marion Gee, Mamie Lewis, Marie Roberts

Syncopating Sunflowers--A. E. Baldwin, Charles Davis, Bernard

*Later played by Florence Mills after Gertrude Saunders left the show.

Johnson, Robert Lee, Snippy Mason, Miles Williams, Arthur
Woodson and Bob Williams

Majestic Magnolias--Misses Edna Battles, Ina Duncan, Lula Wilson,
Hazel Burke and Paula Sullivan

Story: (Note: Miller and Lyles based the plot and the characters
of this show on two earlier works, "Mayor of Dixie" written for the
Pekin Stock Company in 1905, and a later play entitled "Who's Stealing?" in 1918. The comedy fight was based on a routine first introduced in their famous vaudeville act.)

The story involves a mayoralty race in the small town of
Jim Town. The candidates are Steve Jenkins, Sam Peck and Harry
Walton. Jenkins and Peck also are the co-owners of a grocery
store. They are both taking funds from the business to finance
their respective campaigns. They complicate matters further by
hiring the same detective to check up on each other.

Jenkins wins the election, assisted by an unscrupulous campaign
manager, Tim Sharper. After he takes office, Jenkins appoints Sam
Peck as Chief of Police of Jim Town. Peck's main duty is to
"Salaam the Mayor." However, Peck interprets "Salaam" to mean
"slam" and a comedy fight between the two results.

In the end, the reform candidate, Harry Walton, takes over
and runs Jenkins and Peck out of town.

Synopsis:

Time--Election Day

Place--Jim Town in Dixieland

Act 1

Scene 1.   Exterior of Jim Town Hotel
Scene 2.   Possum Lane
Scene 3.   Jenkins' and Peck's Grocery Store
Scene 4.   Public Square

Act 2

Scene 1.   Calico Corners
Scene 2.   Possum Lane
Scene 3.   The Mayor's Office
Scene 4.   Saunders Lane
Scene 5.   Ballroom of Jim Town's Hotel

Musical Numbers:

Act 1

Opening Chorus	Entire Company on Election Day
"Simply Full of Jazz"	Gertrude Saunders and Synco-pated Steppers
"Love Will Find a Way"	Lottie Gee and Roger Matthews
"Bandana Days"	Arthur Porter and Company
"Sing Me to Sleep, Dear Mammy"	Roger Matthews and Board of Aldermen
"Honeysuckle Time"	Noble Sissle
"Gypsy Blues"	Lottie Gee, Gertrude Saunders, Roger Matthews
Grand Finale	Entire Company

Act 2

"Shuffle Along"	Jim Town Pedestrians and Traffic Cop

"Wild About Harry"   Lottie and Jim Town Sunflowers
"Jimtown's Fisticuffs"   Flournoy E. Miller, Aubrey
                                    Lyles
"Syncopation Stenos"   Mayor's Staff
Selections   Board of Aldermen
"If You Haven't Been Vamped   Flournoy E. Miller, Aubrey
    by a Brown Skin, You   Lyles, and Jim Town
    Haven't Been Vamped at   Vamps
    All"
"Uncle Tom and Old Black Joe"   Charles Davis and Bob Williams
"Everything Reminds Me of   Lottie Gee and Roger Matthews
    You"
"Oriental Blues"   Noble Sissle and Oriental
                                    Chorus
"I Am Craving for That Kind of Gertrude Saunders
    Love"
A Few Minutes With   Noble Sissle and Eubie Blake
"Baltimore Buzz"   Noble Sissle and Jim Town
                                    Jazz Steppers
"African Dip"   Flournoy E. Miller and Aubrey
                                    Lyles
Finale   Entire Company

SHUFFLE ALONG (1930 edition)
Producers: Flournoy E. Miller, Aubrey Lyles
Book: Flournoy E. Miller
Music: James P. Johnson, Thomas "Fats" Waller
Lyrics: Andy Razaf
Staging: Irvin C. Miller

Cast of Characters:
Green Ford, Foreman   James Lillard
Laborers   Richard Cooper, Walter Thomas,
                                    Edward Brown, George Ed-
                                    wards, Frank Lewis, Wil-
                                    lian Anderson
Mose   Johnie Virgel
Virginia Four   Sam H. Gray, Edward Ray,
                                    Frank Jackson, Ray Miles
Bess   Margaret Simms
Billy   Allen Virgel
Valaida   Valaida Snow
Ruth   Hilda Perleno
Punk Willis   Mr. Miller
Mrs. Willis   Billie Young
Sam Peck   Mr. Lyles
Jimmy Strutt   Derby Wilson
Tommee Taps   Howard Elmore
Tom   Herman Listerino
Sambo   Herman Jenkins
Andy   Herman Edwards
Ragtown Belles--Marion Davis, Beulah Smith, Mildred Lind, Baby
    Fisher, Marion Aiken, Mabel Hopkins, Ethyl Taylor, Mary

King, Gladys Scott, Myte Descano, Kay Saunders, Marie Bailey, Gladys Osorio, Lela Easterly, Catherin Jarvis, Estela Finley.

Story: (No information)

Synopsis:
Time--Present
Place--Ragtown, Virginia

Act I
Scene 1--Construction of Ragtown School.
Scene 2--Main Street of Ragtown.
Scene 3--Exterior of Punk Willis' Home.
Scene 4--Willow Tree.
Scene 5--Main Street
Scene 6--Banjo Land.

Act II
Scene 1--Equal Got League.
Scene 2--Main Street, Ragtown.
Scene 3--Interior of Punk Willis' Home.
Scene 4--Valaida Snow.
Scene 5--Ragtown Cemetery.
Scene 6--Exterior of Punk Willis' Home.

Musical Numbers:

Act I

Opening Chorus: "Work, Work, Work"	Show Boat Male Chorus and Ragtown Belles
"Teasing Baby"	Hilda Perleno and Johnie Virgel
"Chocolate Bar"	Margaret Simms and Allen Virgel
"Labor Day Parade"	
"Porter's Love Song"	Valaida Snow and Allen Virgel
"Sippi"	Hilda Perleno
"Brothers"	Johnie Virgel and Show Boat Male Chorus
"Willow Tree"	Valaida Snow and Male Chorus
Dance--Taps and Wings	Three Brown Spots
"Banjo Land"	Ensemble

Act II

"Shufflin'"	Johnie Virgel and Jimtown Belles
"Rhythm Man"	Valaida Snow, Girls and Boys
"Loving Honey"	Hilda Perleno and Ragtown Belles
"Taps"	Derby Wilson
Dance	Miller's Dancing Girls
"Spirituals"	Virginia Four
"Poor Little Me"	Valaida Snow
"Go Harlem"	Ensemble

SIMPLE MOLLIE (1908), 1 Act
Producer: Robert Motts, Pekin Stock Company
Lyrics, Music: Henri Wise

Cast of Characters:
Lucy Johnson	Lottie Grady
Jim Slick	Tim Owsley
Wild Bill	Lew Lammar
The Preacher	Augusta Stevens
Mollie-O	Katie Milton
Jake Blossome	Henri Wise

Synopsis:
Scene 1.   Picnic in Love Hollow
Scene 2.   Main St. in Duckville
Scene 3.   Parlor of Johnson's Home

Story: (No information)

Musical Numbers:
"Sweet Mollie-O"	Company
"Summer Time"	Miss Boyd and Company
"Poor Little Maid"	Katie Milton
"Taffy Finally"	Lottie Grady and Company

SINGING THE BLUES (1931), 3 Acts 7 Scenes
Producers: Alex A. Aaron, Vinton Freedley
Book: John McGowan
Staged by: Bertram Harrison
Dances: Sammy Lee
Settings: Donald Oenslager
Costumes: Kivette
Music, Lyrics: Jimmy McHugh, Dorothy Fields

Cast of Characters:
"Potato-Eyes" Johnson	Ashley Cooper
"Knuckles" Lincoln	Mantan Moreland
Jim Williams	Frank Wilson
"Bad Alley" Joe	John Sims
Dooley	James Young
Colored Policeman	Joe Byrd
Rocky	Johnny Reid
Eddie	Shirley Jordan
Mazie	Billie Cain
Jay	S. W. Warren
Dave Crocker	Jack Carter
Edith	Estelle Bernier
Sam Mason	Ralph Theodore
"Whitye" Henderson	Mildred Mitchell
Tod	Dick Campbell
Sid	Percy Wade
Susan Blake	Isabell Washington
Elise Joyce	Fredi Washington
Jack Wilson	Percy Verwayen
"Sizzles" Brown	Maude Russell
Officer Frank	James Young

The Lindy Hoppers   Jordan & Jordan, Shorty &
                                       Esalene, Jenkins & Jenkins
Four Flash Devils
Wen Talbert's Choir
Eubie Blake and His Orchestra
Members of the Magnolia Club Chorus--Billie Cain, Estelle
    Bernier, Aurelia Hallback, Hazel Coles, Frances Sheppard,
    Dolores Watson, Jennie Salmons, Lucia Moses, Dora White,
    Leah Roode, Julia Moses, Reta Walker, Marie Saunders,
    Terrasa Jentry, Iram Miles.

Story: A card game is raided in Johnson's Poolroom in Chicago.
In the excitement the hero, Jim Williams, shoots a policeman and
makes a getaway with his pal to New York. The two chaps meet up
with a couple of girls who steer them to Crocker's Place, a Harlem
speakeasy where the hero meets and falls in love with the top girl
entertainer. She returns his affections, moves him to her room,
and after finding out that he is being hunted for the shooting in
Chicago, manages his escape.

Synopsis:
                            Act I
Scene 1--Johnson's Poolroom, Chicago.
Scene 2--A Chicago Street.
Scene 3--Crocker's Place, Harlem, New York City.
Scene 4--Susan's Room.
Scene 5--The Magnolia Club.
                            Act II
Scene 1--A Dressing Room at the Magnolia Club.
Scene 2--Stage of the Magnolia Club.
Scene 3--Same as Scene 1, Act II.
Scene 4--The Harlem Police Station.
Scene 5--Crocker's Office.

Musical Numbers: (No information)

SONNY BOY SAM (1929)
Producer: No Data

Principal Cast of Characters: Sam Robinson (Sonny Boy Sam),
    Zablo Jenkins, Hunter and Warfield, C. D. Davis, James
    "Kid" Austin, O'Brien and McKenny, Paul Foster, Blake Mor-
    ril, Gertie Davis

Story: The plot revolves around a rugged black boy and his pal
from the cotton fields of the South with an ambition to gain fame
and fortune in any manner possible.

Musical Numbers: "Sonny Boy," "Tomorrow," "Sweet Sue," "There
    Must Be a Silver Lining"

SONS OF HAM (1900)
Producers: Bert Williams, George Walker
Book: Jesse A. Shipp, Bert Williams, George Walker
Lyrics: Alex Rogers
Music: Will Cook

Principal Cast of Characters: Bert Williams, George Walker, Aida
   Overton Walker, Lottie Thompson (Williams), Hattie McIntosh,
   Jesse A. Shipp.

Story: Williams and Walker play two itinerant derelicts who find
themselves in Denver, Colorado.   While there they are mistaken
for a pair of twin brothers who are expected to return from boarding school and claim a large family fortune.   Ham, the father of
the twins, has not seen his sons for many years, and he readily
accepts the two bums as his own children.   Bert and George are
enjoying their new found fortune when it is learned that the real
twins had learned to be acrobats and gun-jugglers at boarding
school.   The two imposters are put on the spot as they try to
prove that they are acrobats and thereby avoid exposure as phonies.
Finally, the real sons arrive in Denver to claim their inheritance
and run the imposters out of town.
      In this piece, Aida Overton Walker and Lottie Thompson
(later Mrs. Bert Williams) acted and sang as Denver citizens,
Jesse Shipp played the father, Ham, and the Reese Brothers,
vaudeville acrobats, played the real twin brothers.

Musical Numbers:
"The Phrenologist Coon"	George Walker
"My Castle on the Nile"	George Walker
"Zulu Babe"	Bert Williams and George Walker
"The Leader of the Ball"	George Walker
"Beyond the Gates of Paradise"	Lloyd Gibbs

SONS OF REST (1927)
Producer: Sidney Easton and Joe Simms
Music, Lyrics: Sidney Easton, Robert Warfield

Cast of Characters:
Spiritualist	Angeline Lawson
Old Man	Coley Grant
Indian Chief	"Billy" Moore
Old Man's Daughter	Harriet Williams
Government Agent	Paul C. Floyd
Sheriff	Addison Carey
Juvenile Part	Louise Williams, Arthur Noble

Others--Sidney Easton, Joe Simms, Josephine Noble, Taft Rice
   (dance specialty), Robert Warfield (dance specialty), Charles
   Taylor, Henry Lawson, Sam Davis (at piano), Chorus: Mildred
   Lee, Viola Gray, Joyce Browne, Agnes Talbot, Ethel Smiley,

Virginia Roundtree, Bobbie Andrews, Dolores Andrews, Lena Williams

Story: The town is troubled by a spiritualist who has been cheated out of her land and a government agent is sent to clear up the trouble. In straightening out the land tangle, the comic situations and some novel skits are offered.

Musical Numbers: (No information)

STEP ALONG (1924)
Producers: Quintard Miller, Marcus Slayter

Principal Cast of Characters: Quintard Miller, Marcus Slayter (in blackface), Amon Davis (in blackface), Burch Williams, Eddie Lemons, Homer Hubbard, Belle Johnson, Irene Parker, Bessie Wrightson, Mildred Brown, Myrtle Bryson, Viola Williams, Edith Randolph, Gladys Mitchell, Carrie Yates

Story: Amon Davis who plays a smart fellow who knows everything but is stumped by such questions as, "When I get on a train, where am I going?," and "When the wind blows, who is pushing it?," does manage to reply to the query "How much is a whole lot?" with "A whole lot more." However, he is startled to know that money originated in Noah's Ark when the total sum on hand was $3.01. His expression is ludicrous as it is explained to him that the frog had a green back, the lamb, four quarters, the duck, a bill, and the pole cat one scent.

Musical Numbers: (No information)

STEP CHILDREN (1923)
Producers: Boatner and Clark

Principal Cast of Characters: Boatner and Clark, Clem Mills, Eulalia Smith, Mary Hicks, Vergie Williams, Mary Green, Katie Smith

Story: The plot of the story has to do with the attempt of a stepmother to defraud the two stepchildren out of their inheritance and keep it for her own two children.

Musical Numbers: (No information)

STRUTT YOUR STUFF (1920)
Producer: Aaron Gates
Book, Lyrics: "Babe" Townsend
Music, Stage Direction: Dave Payton

Principal Cast of Characters: Billy Brown, Billy Gulfport,

Gertrude Saunders, Margaret Ward Thomas, Ida Forsyne,
India Allen, Mary Bradford, Charles Shelton, E. E. Caldwell,
LaMont Harris, Leonard Scott, Harvey Dagget, Buddy Jones
Chorus--Margaret Trimble, Wilse Simmons, Helen Wright, Irene
Summers, Myrtle Roberts, Louise Holmes, Viastie Ferguson,
Amanda Gibson, Irene Clemmons, Mary Jones

Story: (No information)

Musical Numbers:

"Hold Me"	Ida Forsyne
"The Wedding Blues"	Margaret Ward Thomas
"Honey Child"	Saunders, Brown
"Darktime Dancing School"	?
"Dancing is the Work of the Evil One"	Leonard Scott
"I Want to Shimmy"	Mary Bradford
"Louisiana Blues"	Billy Gulfport
"Summer Time"	Charles Shelton

STRUTTIN' HANNA FROM SAVANNAH (1927)
Producers: Will Mastin, Virgie Richards
Book: Eddie Hunter

Cast of Characters:

Creola	Virgie Richards
Mandy	Chick MacIntosh
Sam Green	Charlie Smith
Bill Simmons (the Villain)	Will Mastin
The Child	Daisy Randolph
Rastus	Rastus Airship
Mandy's Dad	C. C. Parker

Others--Wallace Lewis, Sam Davis, James Greenlee, Mae Larkin
(contortionist), Cecil Smith (banjoist), Richard Tilman, Henry
Red Davis, Sarah Venerable, Ruth Johnson
Chorus--Ethel Hart, Katherine Burt, Mae Selby, Maybelle Winbush,
El Vera Sanchez, Irene Lauda, Melba Graves, Thelma Bytops

Story: The plot has to do with a group of people in New Orleans
who are playing the numbers and everybody is trying to win on 4-
11-44. Smith, the henpecked husband, has a hard time getting
along with his wife and when he takes her six bits to play the numbers, he tries to stay out of her sight by hiding behind a well.
Later he is seen in Harlem and is doing well until his wife has
him arrested for the theft of the deeds to their property. Just
when the law is taking him away, he calls for his wife; the scene
then shifts back to the well behind which Smith has fallen asleep.
It was all a dream.

STRUTTIN' SAM FROM ALABAM' (1927)
Producer: Arthur Hockwald
Book, Lyrics, Music: Charles Alpin

Cast of Characters (Arranged in the order in which they first speak):

Kukula, A Samoan Princess	Frieta Shaw
Officer Blue	Tom Cross
Blossom	Mildred Washington
Charles Towne	Malcolm Patten
Sam Brown	Tom Harris
Chinatown Phil	Buddy Brown
Tong Fuey	Edward Tolliver
Mandy	Boston Webb
Cleopatra	Amy Loften
Molano	Margaret Jackson
Deacon Jones	Duke Johnson

Chinese Girls, Alabama Strutters, Samoan Girls and Boys, etc., etc.

Specialty--Helena Justa and Boys, Charles Hart, John Jackson, Ali Bros.

Story: (No information)

Synopsis:
Time: Present
Places: San Francisco, Alabama and Samoa.
Scene 1--Dupont Street, San Francisco.
Scene 2--A Plantation in Old Albama.
Scene 3--The King's Royal Garden on the Isle of Samoa.
Scene 4--Same as Scene 1.
Scene 5--The Dark Town Strutters' Club.

Musical Numbers:

Part I

"Clever People, These Chinese"	The Creole Chorus
"The Ragtime Struttin' China Girl"	Mildred Washington and Chorus
"Chin Chin Chinaman"	Edward Tolliver and Chorus
"I'd Rather Be a Street Sweeper"	Tom Harris and Street Sweepers
"Dancing on the Old Plantation"	Mixed Chorus
Specialties	Margaret Jackson, Ali Bros., Tommy Gates, Charles Weaver
"Struttin' Sam is Coming Back to Dixie"	Boston Webb and Mixed Chorus
"The Girl I Left in Zanzibar" (Danse Oriental)	Mal Patton, Helena Justa and Girls
"Don't Think Because My Name is Cleopatra"	Amy Loften
"The Samoan Dancing Girl"	Tom Harris and Chorus
Finale	

Part II

A Few Moments with Helena Justa and Boys	
"I'm a Samoan Maid"	Freita Shaw and Mixed Chorus
"I'm the King"	Tom Harris and Chorus
"Guide Me Mystic Moon to Dixieland"	Freita Shaw Chorus and Quartette

"On Our Carolina Honeymoon"   Mal Patten and Mildred Washington

"My Queen of Poppyland"   Buddy Brown and Mixed Chorus
Specialty   Helena Justa and her Four
                               Dancing Boys, direct from
                               Europe

Introducing Margaret Jackson
   (The Black Galli Curci)
The Evolution of the Dance   Freita Shaw and Entire Company
   Master Ceremony--Quadrill   Duke Johnson
   Cake Walkers   John Jackson, Billy Drew,
                               Gladys Johnson, Aberdeen
                               Ali, Ruth Edmondson
   Posma La   Tommy Gates
   Texas Tommy   Mildred Washington, Buddy
                               Brown
   Shimmy   Marbelle DeLandro
   Charleston   Charles Weaver

SUGAR HILL (1931)
Producer: Flournoy E. Miller
Book: Flournoy E. Miller

Cast of Characters:
Gyp Penrose   Broadway (Henry) Jones
Lucinda   Juanita Stinnette
Jasper   Chappy Chappelle
Iceman   Flournoy E. Miller
Janitor   Aubrey Lyles
The Other Woman   Etta

Story (Review: Houston Informer, January 9, 1932): "A sketch of
life in Harlem's aristocratic section. Horseplay, Comedy, a few
plaintive songs, including "Fate Misunderstood Me" and a great deal
of shuffling make up what proves at best a poor attempt to bring
Negro laughter and gaiety to Broadway."

THEY'RE OFF (1919)
Producer: Billy King

Principal Cast of Characters: Billy King, Edna Hicks, Berlena
   Blanks, R. L. Tyler, "Four Happy Girls" (Hall, Blanks,
   Daniels, Johnson), C. Barbour, Ernest Whitman, Edna Hicks,
   Gertrude Saunders, Ida Forsyne, Theresa Burroughs Brooks,
   Ollie Burgoyne, Clarence Green

Story: The opening is in the lobby of a big hotel where the sporting guests are waiting for the boat that will take them to the racetrack at Saratoga. Next, there is the opening chorus followed by a
song called "Dusting" in which the shapely maids of the hotel do
their stuff. "Yama Blues" is the first specialty sung by Edna Hicks
and "You Can't Shake Your Shimmie Here" is sung by Berlena

Blanks assisted by a chorus. "Room 16" is sung by R. L. Slayter.
In scene two, there are specialties done by "Four Happy Girls"
made up of Misses Hall, Blanks, Daniels and Johnson.   There is a
quartet and a novelty.

    The second act is at the track at Saratoga Springs and is
opened with a march by the entire company.   Next, "Derby Day in
Dixie" is sung by Clarence Green.   Then there is a specialty by
Ida Forsyne, a dancer, assisted by the Jolly Girls.   Theresa Burroughs sings a specialty, "Up in My Aeroplane," and a real plane
is used in which she "flies" over the audience.   Ernest Whitman
sings a song followed by Billy King who sings "Jungle Jazz."   Gertrude Saunders sings "Hot Dog Ball."   Next, Ollie Burgoyne does a
classic dance called "Brazil."

Musical Numbers:
"You Can't Shake Your Shimmie   Berlena Blanks
    Here"
"Kiss Me"   Laura B. Hall
"Kiss Waltz"   Rosa Tyler
"Up In My Aeroplane"   Theresa Brooks
"Hot Dog"   Gertrude Saunders

THIS WAY OUT (1922)
Producer: Quintard Miller

Cast of Characters:
Husband   Quintard Miller
Wife   Henrietta Lovelass
Spinster   Henrietta Lovelass
Home-Wrecker   Purcell Cuff
Professor   Eugene Shields

Story: The tale is of a faithless wife who is persuaded by her
paramour to desert her husband and baby and run away with him,
but is prevented by the return of her husband who missed his train.

Musical Numbers: (No information)

THE THREE TWINS (1916)
Producer: Quality Amusement Co., Robert Levey
Lyrics: C. A. Hauerback
Music: Karl Hoschna
Dances: "Babe" Townsend
Staging: A. C. Winn

Cast of Characters:
Ned Maryland, in Love with   J. Francis Mores
    Isabel
General Stanhope, a Martyr   Tom Brown
    to Dyspepsia
Tom Stanhope, his Father's Son   Walker Thompson

Kate Armitage, Tom's Sweetheart	Abbie Mitchell
Isabel Howard, the General's Ward	Gertie Townsend
Mrs. Dick Winters, a Cheerful Weeper	Laura Bowman
Molly Summer, Always Happy	Susie Sutton
Harry Winter, Molly's Expected Bridegroom	E. R. Brown
Matthew, a Keeper	G. G. Gibbs
Dr. Siegrrid Hartman, Bug Nut	Babe Townsend
Bessie Winters	Adel Townsend
Billy Winters, Dick's Child	Mildred Smallwood
Dick Winters, Somewhat Nervous	George E. Brown

Guests, Tennis boys, Tennis girls, Bathing girls, Yama Yama girls, Nurses, Keepers, Visitors, etc.

Synopsis:
Act 1.   The General's Home Town, on the Hudson
Act 2.   Reception Room of Dr. Hartman's Sanitarium

Musical Numbers: (No information)

TOO MANY IN THE HOUSE (1909)
    (Allen's Troubadours)

Cast of Characters:

Bluffey Ann, Proprietor of restaurant	Daisy Reynolds
Old Sloppy Sal, the cook	Josephine Plummer
Copper Goodhill, the policeman	Richard Carr
Hank, the black-eyed pea man	G. W. Allen
Jim Hobbs, his partner	Jolly Ed Stewart
Customers of the restaurant:	
Winkle Lou	Sarah Terry
Butter Bean Lizie	Annie Lee
High Life Sam	Jim Brown
Cat Fish Mame	Mme. L. Price
Molly High Grass	Stella Carr

Program:
Opening Scene--"Trouble Over Black-Eyed Peas in Dryade Street Restaurant"
Specialties--

"Picture Single Life"	Brown and Carr
"I Wish I Was in Heaven Sitting Down"	Allen and Lazell
"If I Had a Thousand Lives to Live"	Lazell, Carr, Reynolds, Terry and Company
"I Love My Wife, But Oh, You Kid"	Allen, Lazell, Stewart
"The Family Clock"	Lazell, Reynolds, Carr, Lee, and Terry

"Merry Widow Chorus"	G. W. Allen
"Trans-May-ni-fi-can-ham- dam-uality"	Mme. Lazell Price
"Oh, You Loving Gal"	Daisy Reynolds
"Good Evening, Caroline"	Company
"Too Many Men in the House"	Company

TOWN TOP-PIKS (1920)
Producer: Aaron Gates

Principal Cast of Characters: Billy Gulfport and Brown, Gertrude
    Saunders, Edith Wilson, Ruth Allison, Ollie Burgoyne, Leonard
    Scott, Aaron Gates, James Thomas, Ida Forsyne, Anna Free-
    man, Mary Bradford

Story: (No information)

Musical Numbers:

"Land of Creole Girls"	Leonard Scott (written by Spencer Williams)
"Shimmy Kate"	Mary Bradford
"I'll Get Even"	Gertrude Saunders and Will Brown
"Rose of Washington Square"	Gertrude Saunders
"Sweet Daddy"	Gertrude Saunders
"Dixie Jazz"	Anna Freeman
"Babylon"	Anna Freeman
"Mississippi Blues"	Billy Gulfport

TRIP AROUND THE WORLD (1921)
Producer: Billy King

Principal Cast of Characters: Billy King (Kid Bumpsky), Marshall
    Rogers, Dink Thomas, James Thomas, Jason Stevens, Arthur
    Bruce, Madam Bruce, Fred Vaughn, Leonard, Mrs. Bryant,
    Lelia Mitchell, Allegrete Anderson, Maude Russell, Ollie Hick-
    man, "Gator" and the "Bull."

Story: The action features artistically and picturesquely the costumes and pastimes of Cuba, France, Spain, Italy, China, Japan,
Turkey, and Africa.   It ends with the then famous "Bull Fight"
scene with Billy King in a hair-raising struggle between King and
the Bull.   King finally stabs the animal and then does his victorious
strutt.

Musical Numbers: (No information)

A TRIP TO AFRICA (1908 edition), 2 Acts
    (Black Patti Musical Comedy Company)
Producer: John Larkins

Cast of Characters:
King Jasper   "Jolly" John Larkins
Jim Grafter   Tom Logan
A Bear   George Reese
Mail Carrier   Herbert Sutton
Miss Sapollo   Clarice Wright
Waiter   John Grant
Detective   James Marshall
Others--Muriel Ringgold, W. J. Jenkins, Elizabeth Wallace, Julia
    James, Black Patti, Anne Bordenane, Alice Alix, Etta Grass,
    Essie Williams, Ada Mickey, Fannie Edwards, Hazel Carring-
    ton, Marjorie Shipp.

Musical Numbers:
                            Act 1
"Royal Coon"   "Jolly" John Larkins
"Dolly Brown"   "Jolly" John Larkins
"The Man in Grey"   Herbert Sutton
                            Act 2
Opening Chorus, "Pekaboo"   Entire Company
"Kentucky Home"   Herbert Sutton
"Hoodoo Man"   W. J. Jenkins
"Dolly Brown"   "Jolly" John Larkins

A TRIP TO AFRICA (1910 edition)
    (Black Patti Musical Comedy Company)
Producer: John Larkins

Cast of Characters:
"Razz Jim"   John Larkins
King Rastus   John Larkins
Secret Service Agent   W. A. Cook
Dr. Foolemall   H. Morgan
Sam Williams   Charles Bougia
Hank Williams   George Taylor
A Kleptomaniac   Louis Hunter
Chief Zamboo   Guss Hall
Thomas Cot   J. A. Grant
Cat Maria   J. C. Boome
Janitor   William Wilken
Chief Chef   George Hayes
Chorus--Zennie Hunter, Jenette Murphy, Ada Alexander, Emma
    Price, Ruby Taylor, Estella Carter, Mamie Compson, Levita
    Cash, Nellie Watkins, Rose Hawkins, Fannie Allen, Ella Dunn.

Musical Numbers:
"Suwanee River"   Sissieretta Jones (Black Patti)
"Mother's Chile"   John Larkins

Ad for Black Patti's Troubadours in "A Trip to Africa," circa 1908

"All Hail the King"	John Larkins
"A King Like Me"	John Larkins
"A Trip to Africa"	John Larkins
"The Jungle Drill"	John Larkins
"O You Loving Man"	John Larkins

A TRIP TO COONTOWN (1899)
Producer: Bob Cole
Book, Lyrics: Bob Cole, Billy Johnson

Cast of Characters:

Willie Wayside, a tramp	Bob Cole
Jim Flimflammer, the bunco artist	Billy Johnson
Old Man	Sam Lucas
Detective	Tom Brown

Others--Walter Dison, Thomas Craig, Barrington Carter, Molly
Dill, Pauline Freeman, Clara Freeman, Jennie Hillman,
Wiletta Duncan, Pear LaVan, Myrtle Cousins, A. Martin,
Alice Mackay, Edna Alexander.

Story: (No information)

Musical Numbers (1899 season):

| "I Must O' Been a Dreaming" | Bob Cole |
| "Picking on a Chicken Bone" | Bob Cole |

Musical Numbers (1901 season):

"If That's Society, Excuse Me"	
"Pickin' on a Chicken Bone"	
"I Can Stand for Your Color, but Your Hair Won't Do"	Sam Lucas

Office Staff:

Edward Lark	Manager
Ed. H. Lester	Assistant Manager
Sam Lucas	Stage Manager
George Brown	Master of Transportation
Willis Accooe	Musical Director
Jennie Hillman	Wardrobe Mistress

UP AND DOWN (1922)
Producers: Salem Tutt Whitney, J. Homer Tutt
Book, Lyrics: Tutt and Whitney
Music: Tutt and Whitney

Cast of Characters:

Miss Green	Blanche Calloway
Miss Pink	Jennie Dancey
Miss White	Alberta Jones
Miss Sunshine	Margaret Simms

Ad for Whitney and Tutt's "Up and Down," circa 1921

Miss Purple	Virginia Wheeler
Miss Red	Elizabeth Campbell
Miss Lavender	Helen Jackson
Miss Crimson	Nellie Brown
Miss Summer	Marion Bradford
Miss Black	Viola Mander
Miss Tempest	Elvira Davis
Miss Yellow	Edith Simms
Miss Winter	Bobby Reno
Miss Maytime	Helen Warren
Miss Fall	Hazel Springer
Miss Autumn	Joyce Robinson
Dr. Sunnyside	J. Francis Mores
Prof. Boosowisk	Alonzo Fenderson
Jed Thompson	Henry Thompson
Bill Splivins	John Dancey
Sergeant Oderly	Nat Cash
Jimmie Beets	Wilson Dyer
Lee Lung Chang	George Phillips
Archie Felton	?
Elbert Singer	Chester Jones
Wilton Frayne	George Phillips
Silas Perkins	Amon Davis
Sam Hamford	J. Homer Tutt
Ham Sanford	Salem Tutt Whitney

Story: The plot revolves around Ham Sanford and Sam Hamford, two get-rich-quick schemers who are chased all over the country by Silas Perkins for the money he has lost through promoting their schemes.

Musical Numbers:
"We Want to Booze"	Alonzo Fenderson
"Backbiting Me"	Amon Davis
"When You're Crazy Over Daddy"	Marion Bradford and Chorus
"Male Vamps"	J. Homer Tutt and Chorus
"Rock Me, Daddy"	Jennie Dancey

WATERMELON (1926)
Produced for the Majestic Theatrical Circuit (Jack Goldberg)

Principal Cast of Characters: Garland Howard, Speedy Smith, Mae Brown

Story: Two fakirs, too up-to-date for the little town on the banks of the Mississippi from which they had left, return later with a great idea of making watermelons grow on trees overnight. The fellows get the townfolk to finance their scheme and with the money they proceed to go on a pleasure tour of the world on which they visit the various capitals of Europe. What happens to them there is what forms the comedy of the piece.

Musical Numbers: (No information)

WHERE THE TRAIL ENDS IN MEXICO (1921)
Producer: Hambone Jones

Principal Cast of Characters: S. Gray, Virginia Liston, Bob Davis,
   Rosa Knight, Dolly Brown, Henrietta Leggett (younger sister of
   Josephine and Lena Leggett), Annie Bell Cook

Story: The play involves S. H. Gray as the U. S. Army Officer
who, prior to his departure from France, becomes engaged to be
married to Miss Davis, a pretty American girl, who was later kidnapped and taken across the border into Mexico by Mexicans.   Going
in search for his lover immediately upon his return from the front,
Sam comes into contact with much treachery at the hands of jealous
natives of the Southern Republic, but finally succeeds in rescuing
the girl with assistance of his colleague, Lockett, as the soldier
private.

Musical Numbers:
"Loromba"   Virginia Liston
"Papa Loving Joe"   Virginia Liston
"From My Kentucky Home"   Misses Rosa Knight, Dolly
                                       Brown and Quartette
"Old Man Shouts What a Time"   S. H. Gray, Giles, Davis and
                                       Clarke
"In the Mexican Blues"   Virginia Liston and Chorus
"Chili Beans"   Henrietta Leggett

WHITMAN SISTERS' REVUE (1923)
Producers: Whitman Sisters

Principal Cast of Characters: Mabel, Alice and Alberta Whitman,
   Little Maxie, Jr., Walter Johnson, Elsie Feribee, Pearl Chap-
   man, Sammy Jenkins, Dorothy Washington, Katie Douglass, Lou
   Gilbert, Ernest Michael, Miles Washington, Gallie DeGaston

Musical Numbers:
"Sweet Indiana Home"   Mabel Whitman
"Tomorrow"   Alice Whitman
"Remember Your Mother"   Gallie DeGaston
   (recitation)
"Nobody"   Gallie DeGaston

WHO'S STEALIN' (1918)
Producers: Flournoy E. Miller, Aubrey Lyles
Book: Miller and Lyles

Cast of Characters:
Department Store Owner   Flournoy E. Miller
Department Store Owner   Aubrey Lyles
Owners' Wives   Bessie Miller and Mrs. Andrew
                                       Tribble

Mrs. Fairfax (widow)	Cossie Slaughter
Adelaide (widow's daughter)	Myrtle Porter Lyles
Dr. Rockwell	A. J. Twigg
Crooked Detective	Roger Jones
"Onions," Grocery Man	Andrew Tribble

Others--Charley Bruce, Clara Lewis, Mary Carpenter, Minnie
    Kinsey, Cornell Richardson, Adorallia Alix, Leon Diggs, Daisy
    Collins

Story: Miller and Lyles play the principal male characters, owners
of a department store in Baxton, Iowa. They are supposed to be
married, according to the story, to the prettiest women in the town
and there is a rivalry between them (the wives) as to which will dress
in the more fashionable manner, as well as a desire on the part of
both to outdo all the women in town. In order to allow their wives
to make good along those lines, the two store owners start a system of "knocking down" the cash receipts. As a result, there isn't
much in the way of profits, so they each, unknown to the other,
send to Chicago for a private detective to come and catch the other
stealing. The letters fall into the hands of a crook who shows up
and impersonates the "bull" to both of them, and who, when he
finds out that they have both been crooked, gets busy himself and
starts a system of thieving that forces them to again call for help.
This time the letters are not miscarried and a detective called
"Big 7" appears on the scene. What follows is the climax of the
show.

Musical Numbers:

"Hand in Hand"	Leon Diggs and Chorus
"Just Like a Gypsy"	Leon Diggs and Chorus
"Four Eyes Told Me So"	Daisy Collins
Oriental Dance	Julia Rector
Specialty	Woods Sisters

WIFT WAFT WARBLERS (1921)
Producers: Davis and Stafford

Principal Cast of Characters: Amon Davis (in blackface), Eddie
    Stafford (in blackface), Elveta Davis, Ethel Watts, Alfonzo
    Robinson, Alex Jackson, Harold Douglass, Willie Carter,
    Josephine Leggett, Warbler's Quartet, Julia Pay, Lester
    Miller

Story: The story tells of the elopement of the daughter of a
wealthy family with a straightforward young man. The father had
framed a match between the girl and a ne'er-do-well, not realizing
the true character of the man. The pursuit of the elopers lays the
groundwork for the ensuing scenes which carry the audience to a
merry climax.

Musical Numbers:

"Jail House Now"	Amon Davis and Eddie Stafford

"My Home Town"	Alex Johnson
"Once in a While"	Harry Jackson
"Strutting Your Stuff"	Julia Ray
"Old Fashioned Garden"	Ethel Watts and Girls
"Kaffir Babe"	Harry Jackson
"Home Again Blues"	Lester Miller
"Down in China Town"	Ethel Watts

THE WRONG MR. PRESIDENT (1914)
Producers: Salem Tutt Whitney, J. Homer Tutt
Book, Lyrics: Whitney and Tutt
Music: Russell Smith, Trevor Corwell
Musical Director: Clarence G. Wilson

Cast of Characters:

Bud White, His Excellency	Salem Tutt Whitney
Dan Jenkins, Secretary to His Excellency	J. Homer Tutt
Monsieur LaFitz, Agent of Rebel Faction	Greensbury Holmes
Ellias Simpson, Proprietor of Ginger Springs Hotel	Alfred Strauder
Senator Conback, U. S. Minister to Haiti	Frank Jackson
Willie Jump, Bell Boy	O. D. Carter
Oh Saymore, Real President of Haiti	William "Babe" Townsend
Enuff Desert, Secretary to the Real President	Will Dixon
Menee Lick, Ambassador of Abyssinia	James Woodson
Moore Menas, Secretary of Legation	Matt Johnson
Sylam Bughouse, Resident of Ginger Springs	George Boutts
Carmencia Gomez, Agent of Rebel Faction	Blanche Thompson
Mr. James Brown	Douglas Barrymore
Dashing Widow	Ethel Marshall
Lady Winterbottom, A Society Belle	Pauline Parker
Mandy Simpkins, Wife of Ellias	Helen Clinton
Lydia Harkfurst, Old Maid Suffragette	Hattie Ackers
Letter Dance, Hotel Maid	Emma Jackson

Society Belles--Helen Jackson, Carrie King, Geneva Harley,
    Pauline Parker, Marie Hurley
Tango Dancers--William Williams, Goldie Cisco, Emma Jackson,
    Virginia Wheeler
Politicians--Cornelius Robinson, Walter Moore, Wilson Lee
Foreign Celebrities--Matt Johnson, James Wooden, Harry Atkins

Story: The scene is laid at "Ginger Springs," a popular health resort in Georgia, and the story deals with the adventures of two lively tourists of color, who have more philosophy, humor and appetite
than cash.   They are "gentlemen of leisure in reduced circumstances"
and "blow into town" just in advance of an exiled President and Secretary of the Republic of Haiti, who are traveling incognito while
awaiting the outcome of one of the periodic revolutions in their native land.   The landlord and his ambitious and fashionable young
wife, expecting the arrival of the two Haitian officials, mistake Bud
White and Dan Jenkins for them, and attribute their trampy appearance to their previously announced desire to keep their identity concealed.   The soldiers of fortune, in search of a square meal and
some easy money, readily assume the roles forced upon them and
throughout the large portion of the two long acts the "messes" they
get into as the bogus President and Secretary of the Haitian Republic furnish the vehicle for fun.

Musical Numbers: (Note: "Just a Pickaninny All Dressed Up" and
    "Tutt's Tudalo" were written for the exclusive use of the Smart
    Set Company by Lewis T. Thomas.)

Act 1

"Tourists Are We"--Opening Chorus	The Company
"What You Need is Ginger Springs"	Al Strauder and Chorus
"Good Advice," comedy duo	Salem Tutt Whitney and J. Homer Tutt
"Come Out," song and dance	Boutte and Carter, assisted by Lilliam Williams and Goldie Cisco
"Ye Old Quadrille," square dance	Matt Johnson and Company
"The Love You Can't Forget," novelty	Frank Jackson and Octette
"Romance Espanola"	Blanche Thompson and Chorus
"Just A Pickaninny All Dressed Up"	Whitney and Tutt
"When Your Country Calls to Arms," drill	Greensbury Holmes and Chorus
"The Intruder," finale	Ensemble

Act 2

"Hesitation Waltz"	Company
"All I Ask Is to Forget You"	Blanche Thompson
"Have Patience, Don't Worry," comedy duo	Whitney and Tutt
"Smart Set Tango"	Company
"We Welcome Thee"	Company
"Hawaiian Tango" ⎰demonstration⎱	Whitney and Tutt, Blanche
"Twilight Dreams" ⎱of latest⎰ dances	Thompson, Hattie Akers
"For Honor," dramatic ensemble	Company
"Tutt's Tudalo," finale	Danced by the Entire Company

CHAPTER 6

BLACKS IN BLACKFACE:

One of the most curious and interesting phenomena associated
with the early American stage was the immense popularity and lon-
gevity of the blackface artist.   Many white and black performers
used burnt cork make-up and during the early 1900's approximately
three times as many whites appeared over the large vaudeville circuits doing blackface acts as did black artists.   This was a period
when many black performers complained bitterly that white theatre
managers would turn down a black act to give a white act that did
blackface an engagement.   Two of the most popular whites using
burnt cork were McIntyre and Heath.   They played black parts long
before Williams and Walker first formed a team and left California.
Later, Al Jolson and Eddie Cantor used blackface as a ticket to
fame and fortune.   Correll and Gosden of "Amos and Andy" fame
used Negro dialect and stereotyped black characterizations to put
together one of the most popular shows on early radio at a time
when black comedians were barred from this entertainment medium.

In the early 1900's when all-black companies were becoming
popular, many blacks chose to blacken-up and imitate white performers doing stereotyped blackface comedy.   Although this was an
accepted and widespread practice, many black artists had serious
reservations as explained by George Walker:

> All that was expected of a colored performer was singing
> and dancing and a little story telling, but as for acting,
> no one credited a black person with the ability to act.
>   Blackfaced white comedians used to make themselves
> look as ridiculous as they could when portraying a "darky"
> character.   In their make-up they always had tremendous-
> ly big red lips, and their costumes were frightfully exag-
> gerated.   The one fatal result of this to the colored per-
> formers was that they imitated the white performers in
> their make-up as "darkies."   Nothing seemed more absurd
> than to see a colored man making himself ridiculous in
> order to portray himself.

Although Walker recognized the serious negative implications
of blacks doing low comedy in blackface, he and Williams exploited
the popularity of the blackface artist and did much to prolong this

form of entertainment. They billed themselves as the "Two Real
Coons" which Walker rationalized as follows:

> There were many more barriers in the way of the black
> performer in those days than there are now, because with
> the exception of Negro minstrels, the black entertainer
> was little known through the Northern and Western states.
> The opposition on account of racial and color prejudice
> and white comedians who "blacked up" stood in the way of
> natural black performers.
>   How to get before the public and prove that ability we
> might possess was a hard problem for us to solve. We
> thought that as there seemed to be a great demand for
> blackfaces on the stage, we would do all we could to get
> what we felt belonged to us by the laws of nature. We
> finally decided that as white men with black faces were
> billing themselves "coons," Williams and Walker would do
> well to bill themselves as "The Two Real Coons," and so
> we did. Our bills attracted the attention of managers,
> and gradually we made our way in.

Many black performers opted not to work in blackface or do
low comedy. Beginning with the Fisk and Hampton "Jubilee Singers"
in the 1870's and 1880's and continuing with the Pekin and Lafayette
Players and other dramatic stock companies, there was a strong
tradition of blacks to perform on the stage with a high level of
dignity and self respect. But always there was the financial pres-
sure to "blacken-up" as explained by Laura Bowman in the April 16,
1927, issue of the Baltimore Afro American:

> The whites offer you long time booking if you darken your
> face and sing "Old Black Joe" and for the Race. The
> Lafayette Players were recently offered $1500 to bring a
> musical comedy to a local theatre and only $800 for a
> week's engagement of comic or serious drama.

In order to secure booking in vaudeville many lightskinned
blacks, who chose not to "darken up," frequently passed for white
or concealed their racial identity by billing themselves as "Two
Creole Maids" or the "Filipino Beauties," etc. This was especially
true for black women performing without male partners who were
sometimes encouraged by theatre managers to "cut out" their racial
identity. These same managers, however, would book blackface
acts in which white women used cork and curled their hair.

The popularity of Negro blackface comedians such as Tim
Moore, Eddie Green and Miller and Lyles and others continued well
into the 1930's. In an article which appeared in the Baltimore Afro
American in 1930, George Santa offered an analysis of the popularity of the American blackface performer during this period.

> The fancies of audiences are much more demanding than
> one would even think. In the blackface artist, the theatre

audiences receive an effect that has never yet been dupli-
cated and it reaches the "funny bone" or their sympathies
as no other artifice known to the American stage.

The whole condition is one which would lend itself un-
doubtedly to the analysis of psychological experts. It has
no counterpart either here or abroad.

The tragic condition of the American Negro in the popularity of the blackface artist paradoxically gives rise to
a much more hilariously funny type of entertainment than
any situation in the United States. Nor does the accepta-
bility show any signs of abating.

That during a period when blacks, suffering from widespread
racial discrimination and from the psychological effects of the propaganda of inferiority, were being imitated to achieve fame and fortune by many performers on the stage who made generous use of
distorted "negroid" characteristics, is a curious anomaly of early
American theatre.

BIOGRAPHIES

ALBERT ANDERSON

Al Anderson, of the famous vaudeville team of Anderson and
Goines, was born in Keokuk, Iowa, August 25, 1869. He went on
the stage at the age of 15 with McFadden's "Uncle Tom's Cabin."
He had two brothers, Morris and York, with whom he teamed sep-
arately, but York Anderson was first to become famous as a quartet man and was with Ben Payne and George Moore. The two
brothers formed the Euclid Quartet which became popular in the
East. Next, they joined Martell's "South Before the War." When
Al began to shine as a comedian, Sam T. Jack signed him with his
Creole Company which was booked in all the top burlesque houses.
It was in this company that he met Mamie Riley whom he later married. He then proceeded to train his wife for vaudeville and after
they had opened on the Keith Circuit as the team of Al and Mamie
Anderson, they immediately became famous. Anderson's former
travels with minstrel shows led him to dress in clean tailor-made
expensive, floppy clothes and he wore a little cap on his head,
which made his handsomeness and smile all the more captivating.
He originated the comedy act in vaudeville which consisted of chas-
ing his shadow around the stage with a spotlight. This act was
later to be used many times in later years by many of the famous
comedians.

In the early 1900's, when musical comedy became popular,
the Andersons starred in the production "Lady Africa." By then,
Al Anderson had become so popular in Boston, Massachusetts that
he had a standing contract for a summer run of minstrelsy at the

Crescent Gardens, then an elite summer resort at Winthrop.   He
would surname his show "Lady Africa's Minstrel" which had an
afterpiece "On Broadway in Dahomey" which was beautifully set.
This was in 1904, and members of the company were Happy Billy
Briggs, J. Hamilton Goines and Mr. Hazard, "Christian," the foot
cyclist and roller skater, Bobby Kemp and his Wang Doodle Four
which included Johnny Green, Will Cook and a chorus.   Soon after
Anderson's wife retired from the stage, Anderson and Billy Briggs
formed a partnership for a brief period.   He next teamed with
Hamilton Goines, a fine singer, and toured the country for over
twenty years.   Al Anderson died in Keokuk, Iowa in 1926 at the
age of 57.

EDDIE ANDERSON

Born in Oakland, California on September 18, 1905, Eddie
Anderson attended grammar schools in Oakland and in San Francisco.
He completed his formal education with two years of high school in
San Mateo.   He entered show business at the age of 13 when he
ferried across the bay with a dime he'd found, and won an amateur
contest in a San Francisco vaudeville house.   During this period,
he also had a brief fling at being a jockey, but quit after he became too heavy.   In the next few years, he established himself as
a comedian with a versatile dancing act, and soon began to get hoof-
ing booking at the better vaudeville houses.   In 1923, he was engaged to perform in the black musical comedy "Struttin' Along"
which featured Mamie Smith.   Anderson was a chorus boy and general utility performer.   Later, with his older brother Cornie, he
appeared in a Los Angeles vaudeville act.

In 1924, Anderson appeared in the Los Angeles production of
"Steppin' High" as a member of the dance team, the "Three Black
Aces," which included Cornie and "Flying" Ford.   After this show
the Aces played fourteen weeks at the Plantation Club, and then
went on tour with "Steppin' High" and the California Collegians dance
band.   Anderson received his first big break when the company
broke up in Omaha, Nebraska.   Eddie got a temporary spot as a
song and dance man at the World Theatre, and his reception there
gained for him a Pantages Circuit contract for the rest of the season.

Returning to Los Angeles in 1926, Anderson did a tour of
the Coast and then signed as a regular on the Keith Orpheum Circuit, which lasted 35 weeks.   It was at this time that he began to
inject comedy routines into his song and dance act.

After a brief appearance at the Apex nightclub on Central
Avenue in Los Angeles, Anderson went into Sebastian's Cotton Club,
where he appeared for two and a half years.

It was during his vaudeville days in the East that Eddie
first met Jack Benny.   They first did little more than shake hands,

but Jack remembered Eddie's name, and this encounter paved the
way to Anderson's eventual selection for the role of "Rochester" on
the Jack Benny radio show.

Anderson's start in motion pictures came when he did a
dance number in Mervyn Leroy's first feature, "No Place to Go, "
which starred Lloyd Hughes and Mary Astor. His first film speaking part was as a valet in "What Price Hollywood. " After a series
of film comedy roles, Anderson next attracted attention as "Noah"
in the film "Green Pastures" and was hailed by critics everywhere
for his whimsical characterization.

A year later, Jack Benny was looking for a black to play a
porter on his radio program. When he issued his audition call,
Jack made sure that Eddie, whose work he remembered, was invited to try out. The following Sunday, "Rochester" was born and
Eddie won a permanent place as a regular member of the cast.

After his radio debut, Anderson was more and more in demand for picture parts. He is best remembered for his roles in
"Cabin in the Sky, " his scene-stealing performance in "Jezebel"
and as Donald in "You Can't Take It With You. " Anderson died in
Los Angeles in 1977.

IDA ANDERSON

Ida Anderson was born Ida Gwathmey in King William County,
Virginia, the 11th of 13 children. At an early age she went to New
York City and took up dancing. She had always wanted to be an
actress, so when she asked Anita Bush in 1915 to give her a chance
in a dramatic play, Miss Bush (a former chorine in the famous
Williams and Walker company and then the director of the Anita
Bush Players) responded by giving Miss Anderson a small part.
Miss Anderson made her debut in a play entitled "Barbara Fritchie. "

In 1916 Miss Anderson joined the Lafayette Players Stock
Company at the Lafayette Theatre in New York City. At that time
the salary of the featured players averaged from $153 to $150 per
week. The Company was so successful in Harlem that additional
companies were organized and sent on the road to play Philadelphia,
Washington, D. C. , Baltimore and Chicago.

After a season with the Players, Miss Anderson left the
company and during the next two years took out a dramatic company
of her own playing the major cities of the East. After that she returned to New York and again joined the Lafayette company which
by that time had come under the ownership of E. C. Brown. After
the parent company temporarily disbanded, Miss Anderson organized
her own company of Lafayette Players and for the next eighteen
months toured the East and Midwest playing such cities as Richmond, Raleigh, Durham, Norfolk, Cleveland, Chicago, Detroit,
Indianapolis, St. Louis, Kansas City, and Memphis. Then her

health broke under the strain and she retired from the stage con-
valescing in Chicago and California.

In 1925, Miss Anderson returned to New York from California to see if drama couldn't be revived in Harlem. However, because of the growing popularity of musical comedies, the theatre
managers were hard to convince that drama would pay. After
months of trying she got on at the Lincoln Theatre and for ten successive weeks she presented such plays as "The Scrubwoman," "The
Branding Iron," "Gypsy Harlot," "Kick In," "Why Wives Go Wrong,"
"The Getaway," "The Unborn," "Within the Law," "The Murder of
Eddie Griggs," and "The Love of Su Shong." The featured players
in Miss Anderson's company included Monte Hawley, Billy Andrews,
Hilda Oftley, Inez Clough, Arthur Ray, Charles Olden, Babe Townsend, Clarence Walker, Ricardo Londez, Alfred "Slick" Chester,
and Lawrence Chenault.

"MA" BAILEY

"Ma" Bailey, who performed with her own company as a
blackface comedienne in 1926, started her stage career in 1888.
She was born in New York City and lived on 42nd and on 73rd
streets after the death of her parents. When Helen Morrell, a
white singer, was at the top of her popularity in the 1880's, she
thought of the idea of having two little black girls sing and dance
with her on stage. In that day they were called pickaninnies.
Eager for the new experience, the young Miss Bailey made a tour
of the East and West with Miss Morrell. They later toured Hawaii
and the Orient and went to Spain where they first had an opportunity
to entertain royalty. The two young black girls were considered a
novelty and the act was a sensation in Europe.

After returning to New York City, Miss Bailey attended
school again, although she continued to appear on the stage at inter-
vals. In 1899 the lure of the stage reached her again and she sailed
with Ernest Hogan's Show to Australia. Later she made another
trip abroad with Hogan. In the late 1920's, "Ma" Bailey headed
her own show on the T. O. B. A.

JAMES (JIMMY) BASKETTE

Jimmy Baskette, who appeared in at least five black films
between 1932 and 1940, and is probably best remembered for his
portrayals of Uncle Remus in Walt Disney's "Song of the South,"
and Gabby Gibson, the fast talking lawyer on the Amos and Andy
radio series, was born in 1904 in Indianapolis, Indiana. In his
youth he aspired to be a pharmacist, but became interested in show
business as a career when, as a teen, he was asked to take a small
part in a show to relieve a member of the cast who had taken ill.

When a young man, he went to New York and joined the

Lafayette Players and soon became one of the best known black actors of the period.   In the 1920's and early 1930's, Baskette attracted attention on the musical comedy stage starring in such black
shows as "Go Get 'Em" (1926), "Fancy Trimmings" (1928), "The
Toy Boat" (1930), "Goin' to 'Town'" (1934), and "Lucky Me" (1935).
He also gained prominence in the New York stage production of
"Green Pastures," portraying the role of "De Lord."   During the
1930's, Baskette turned film actor gaining his first film acting experience in such all-black cast films as "Policy Man," "Comes
Midnight," "Gone Harlem," "Harlem is Heaven" and "Straight to
Heaven."   Baskette won an Academy Award for his portrayal of
Uncle Remus in Disney's "Song of the South" in which he introduced
the song, "Zip-A-Dee-Doo-Dah."

        Baskette died at his home, 3443 South Arlington Ave., in
Los Angeles in 1948, at the age of 44.

PEG LEG BATES

        Peg Leg Bates was one of America's greatest dancers and
his spectacular success was due to his amazing courage early in
his life.   He lost his leg in 1918 in an auto accident in his hometown of Greenville, South Carolina.   He was twelve years old and
his playmates thoughtlessly taunted him when he hobbled around on
his crutches, and the 12-year-old boy cried bitter tears.   To show
them, he threw down his crutches in defiance and hopped up and
down gallantly on his one leg and fell down.   With his face buried
in the earth of a baseball diamond, he heard the cruel jeers from
his peers.

        That night, sleeping in the attic of his home, he made up
his mind he would make good in a two-legged world.   His uncle
built him a crude peg leg and for three years he walked two miles
to school.   That strengthened his good leg and he was ready to
start his dancing career.

        His first Broadway appearance was in Lew Leslie's "Black-
birds," and the courageous youngster figuratively tore down the
house.   That was in 1928.   During the next five years he was the
number one dancer in the country.

BERRY BROTHERS

        The Berry Brothers dance team gained fame around the
world for their strut number done to the tune "Papa De Da Da."
As topflight artists, the Berry Brothers, Ananias, Warren and
James, always fought for their full rights as American citizens and
racked up many victories over Jim Crow in the entertainment world
of years past.   They were the first black act to be booked into the
new Copacabana Club in New York City in 1929, and a year later
achieved similar prominence by appearing on the bill which opened

the Radio City Music Hall.   Their fight against discrimination continued throughout their professional careers.   They were in the first interracial show in the state of Florida in Allen Gale's Celebrity Club, and this was followed by being the first black act to appear in the major nightclubs in Tampa.

Ananias, the older brother, and James, two years his junior, got their start doing elocution on the Chicago church circuit.   Later, they moved to Denver with their parents where the youngest of the Berry Brothers, Warren, was born in 1922.   Attending an amateur contest one night, Ananias persuaded his father to permit him to enter a contest.   He floored the audience and took his father by surprise by doing a dance act.   Being a religious man, the father had forbidden dancing in the family.   Ananias had carefully memorized the steps he had seen in other contests and later improved upon them himself.

That was the beginning of the Berry Brothers act.   The theatre manager, responding to the prolonged applause for Ananias' act, offered a week's contract at $75.   This was a lot of money in 1922, when many of the good acts were playing for $25.   Since both James and Ananias had been working as a team reciting poems by Paul Laurence Dunbar, their father demanded they be hired as a team.

By the time Ananias and James were 11 and 9, respectively, they were veterans of the stage and screen.   Hal Roach had signed James and Ananias for a contract calling for about $125 a week to work in some of Roach's "Our Gang" comedies.   Although they both appeared in several of these films, it was not steady work, so the brothers kept busy by entertaining in the homes of such Hollywood stars as Mary Pickford and Douglas Fairbanks.

When their contract with Roach expired, the Berry Brothers act went out on the T. O. B. A. circuit and worked with such stars as Bessie Smith and Joe King Oliver.

The Berry Brothers opened at the famed Club Alabam in New York City in 1925, and worked alongside such stars as Ethel Waters, Josephine Baker, Edith Wilson, Johnny Hudgins and Adelaide Hall.   Then they moved to the Cotton Club a year later, where they remained as headliners for more than four years.   At the time, a young pianist named Duke Ellington played with the Cotton Club's Plantation Orchestra and a young lady named Lena Horne was one of the club's chorines.

In 1927, the Berry Brothers went abroad with "Blackbirds" in which Florence Mills starred, and other featured performers included the great dancer "Snakehips" Tucker and Adelaide Hall.

After eight months overseas, they returned to open the Radio City Music Hall and went on to make appearances in top night spots and theatres across the country; a few years later the three brothers

returned to Hollywood where they played featured parts in "Panama
Hattie, " "Lady Be Good, " and "You Are My Everything. "

Then, at the peak of their careers in the mid-1940's, they
toured Latin America, where they were especially successful in
Havana and Rio de Janeiro. Ananias remained in Rio for five years,
and James and Warren returned to the States to carry on until
Ananias again joined them in 1948.

After Ananias passed away unexpectedly while taking a shower
in October 1951, Warren and James retired from the stage, but
James continued to be active in other fields. He became co-partner
with Mrs. Mura Dehn, a pioneer in the concert jazz field, in 1954.
Together they produced a documentary film on dance, and did concert work and educational work in the jazz field. James Berry
helped produce the films "The Spirit Moves" and "A History of
Afro-American Dance from Rag to Bop. " He also wrote and produced a film short "The Dancing James Berry" which summed up
all the forms of jazz dances and presented a portrait of the jazz
musician. The film received rave notices from critics when it was
shown in cinematiques, museums, and universities in France, England, Holland, Switzerland, Belgium and Canada.

In collaboration with Mrs. Dehn, James Berry organized the
Jazz Dance Theatre Company which included such outstanding artists
as Avon Long, Johnny Hudgins, George Peach (the gospel singer),
Cook Brown, Albert Gibson, Buster Brown and Mabel Lee.

James Berry also appeared in a number of jazz dance concerts from Carnegie Hall to Cooper Union, creating a new repertory
for each performance. He gave lecture demonstrations at the New
School for Social Research and conducted a course on the history of
jazz dancing at the Philadelphia Academy of Dance and Music.

Mr. Berry was the founding spirit and inspiration of the
Afro-American Folk Dance Theatre which was invited to Washington
for a concert sponsored by the Rebekah Harkness Foundation, and
the Smithsonian Institution. Subsequently, the company was invited
as the first black American folk dance organization to appear at the
Olympic Festival held in Mexico City. A year later, James Berry
died in New York at age 54.

EUBIE BLAKE

Without a doubt, Eubie Blake is the dean of ragtime piano
players and has done more than any other performer during his
seventy years in show business to keep this musical form before
the public. Not only a gifted performer, Blake's composing genius
has produced many of America's greatest song hits.

James Hubert Blake was born on February 7, 1883, in East
Baltimore, Maryland, the son of John Sumner and Emily Johnson

Blake who were former slaves.   From his deeply religious mother he learned humility and through his father he acquired an independence that has carried him through his long life.

As a child prodigy on the pump organ and piano he exhibited a measure of musical genius.   While still wearing knickers the young Eubie was acclaimed by his associates and admiring public as the "best piano player" across town.   At fifteen he was playing piano for $3 a week at Agnes Shelton's sporting house.   By the time he was sixteen, he had composed the "Charleston Rag," a very intricate ragtime piece, very difficult to play.

In 1907, he was engaged by Joe Gans, onetime lightweight boxing champion, to play piano at the fabulous Goldfield Hotel which was built by Gans.   Eubie worked with a quartet which, in addition to himself, included J. Madison Reed, Miss Mary Stafford, a singer, and Joe McIntosh, a sensational drummer.   The group was a big success and stayed together at the Goldfield until the death of Gans in 1910.

On the week of May 20th, 1912, William H. Daly, a Baltimore man, engaged the team of Reid and Blake to perform at Daly's Theatre which was later changed to the Lincoln.   The engagement was an experiment to find out if the pair could make good in a large theatre as they had in the hotels and cabarets.   They were paid $35 per week for the two.   Their big hit song during that engagement was the "Memphis Blues."

Theirs was the feature act and standing room was at a premium during the entire week.   Coleman Minor and his wife, the Meyers Mules and Christian along with Lottie Gee and her partner Effie King were on the same bill.   Eubie and all the other performers were paid the unheard of salary of $40 per week.

Blake's debut as an orchestra conductor was at Albaugh's Theatre, then located on North Charles Street in Baltimore.   The occasion was a minstrel show staged by the Monumental Lodge of the Elks.   About the same time, he began to study harmony with Llewellyn Wilson.

It was an engagement at Riverview Park in 1915 under the direction of Bob Young that Blake first met the brilliant young lyricist Noble Sissle.   They formed a song writing team with Eubie composing the music and Sissle taking care of the lyrics.   Their first piece "It's All Your Fault" was bought by the great Sophie Tucker and became one of her early hits.   Earlier, Noble Sissle had written a comedy sketch called "A Dangerous Girl."

Eubie's publishing career began in 1915 when Luckeyth Roberts introduced him to the Joseph Stern Company which later published two of his rags, "Chevy Chase" and "Fizz Water."

In 1916, Noble Sissle persuaded Blake to join him in New

York to begin writing an all black Broadway show under the direction of James Reese Europe, a brilliant arranger and orchestra conductor.   But the project was shelved at the start of World War I
when Sissle and Europe enlisted and later formed an all black regi-
mental band that was considered to be the best on the continent.
Eubie, too old for the army, remained in New York and took care
of business.

        In 1919, after the Armistice was signed, Sissle and Europe
again returned to New York and again plans were made to resume
production of the show, but the project was again terminated at the
untimely death of Europe who was stabbed by one of the drummers
in his band.   Sissle and Blake then went into vaudeville on Keith
Orpheum Circuit, this time billing themselves as the "Dixie Duo."

        The "Duo" toured the country and soon became one of the
most successful acts in vaudeville.   In 1920 they found themselves
on the same bill with Miller and Lyles at a benefit for the NAACP
in Philadelphia.   They met and made plans to combine the comic
genius of Miller and Lyles with the music of Sissle and Blake to
produce a musical comedy, "Shuffle Along."

        "Shuffle Along," written, staged and directed by Miller,
Lyles, Sissle and Blake, opened at the Sixty-third Street Theatre
in New York City in 1921.   The show created a sensation and was
largely responsible for bringing black shows back to the Broadway
stage in the fashion of Williams and Walker and Cole and Johnson
some fifteen years previous.

        After "Shuffle Along," the teams Miller and Lyles and Sissle
and Blake went their separate ways.   In 1923 Sissle and Blake made
one of the earliest sound films, "Snappy Tunes," which was produced by Lee DeForrest using the Phonofilm system which he invented.   The film in which Sissle and Blake sang some of their
vaudeville favorites was first shown at the Rivoli Theatre in New
York City.

        In 1924, Sissle and Blake came out with their second big
show, "In Bamville."   The show opened on the road and the title
was changed to "Chocolate Dandies" for its New York City opening.
The show ran for a year and was unique in its staging in that it
included a simulated racetrack with real horses.   After the show
closed in 1926, Sissle and Blake toured Europe with their song act.
After leaving Sissle in Europe, Blake returned to America and
brought out a road show, "Shuffle Along, Jr.," which had only
moderate success.

        In 1930, Blake collaborated with the famous lyricist Andy
Razaf to write the music of "Blackbirds of 1930."   In 1932, Sissle,
Blake and Miller joined up again to produce "Shuffle Along of 1933."
After this show, Blake retired from the musical comedy field.   In
1932, Eubie and his orchestra performed in the classic black musi-
cal short, "Pie Pie Blackbirds" with Nina Mae McKinney and the

young Nicholas Brothers. After ragtime fell out of popularity, he
retired from show business in 1942. Soon after, he completed a
course in the Shillinger System of music and later composed "Dicty's
on Seventh Avenue."

Around 1943, Eubie came out of retirement and toured the
U. S. with a USO show. Edith Wilson was the featured singer and
Eubie played the piano and conducted the orchestra.

Eubie again retired from show business in 1951, but was
persuaded by friends to begin playing and recording the old rags
again. The 1970's found Blake writing rags and traveling across
the country appearing on almost all of the major television talk
shows. In 1976, he was honored by being inducted into the Black
Filmmakers Hall of Fame in Oakland, California.

Sometimes collaborating with Andy Razaf and Noble Sissle,
Mr. Blake's song hits include: "Shuffle Along, Jr.," "I'm Just
Wild About Harry," "Love Will Find a Way," "You Were Meant for
Me," "Shuffle Along," "Bandana Days," "Crying Blues," "Goodnight
Angeline," "Slave of Love," "Lowdown Blues," "Memories of You,"
"You're Lucky to Me," "Lindy Hop," "Lovin' You the Way I Do,"
"Green Pastures," and "My Handy Man."

JAMES BLAND

James Bland was one of America's greatest composers, having written such well-known songs as "Carry Me Back to Old Virginny," "Oh, Dem Golden Slippers," "In the Evening by the Moonlight," and "In the Morning by the Bright Light." He was also a
performer having appeared as a member of Sprague's Georgia Minstrels, Hyer Sisters Company, The Original Georgia Minstrels,
Callender's Minstrels, and Harvey's International Minstrels.

Bland was born in Flushing, Long Island, New York on October 22, 1854. His father, Allan M. Bland, moved his family
from Flushing to Washington, D. C. after he was appointed as Ex-
aminer in the United States Patent Office.

While a student at Howard University in Washington, D. C.,
where he studied music, Bland had an opportunity to listen to songs
and stories from many black people around Washington who had been
slaves. He soon started putting some of the tunes on paper. During his career, Bland composed over 600 songs.

Bland died on May 5, 1911. Years later, the Virginia Con-
servation Commission recommended that "Carry Me Back to Old
Virginny" be adopted as the official state anthem. Many of the
commission were astounded to later learn that the song was not
written by Stephen Foster, but by James Bland. The song was of-
ficially adopted on January 1940, 66 years after its composition.

Vaudeville Act of Laura Bowman and Sidney Kirkpatrick

LAURA BOWMAN

Laura Bowman, an accomplished dramatic actress as well as a vaudeville star, was born in 1889 in Quincy, Illinois. She attended the public schools in Quincy and showed a strong interest in the theatre. With a remarkable singing voice and an unusual ability to project her acting talents into various characterizations, it was not long before she decided to go to New York City to begin an acting career.

After several years of concert appearances, Miss Bowman organized her own group called the Dark Town Entertainers. It was composed of three men and herself. She later married one of its members, Sidney Kirkpatrick. The Dark Town Entertainers under the management of Miss Bowman, who also proved to be equally talented in business matters, soon found themselves in demand. After many successful tours in the States, they went to Europe where they played before Royalty in several countries.

The repertoire of the Dark Town Entertainers was something unique in theatrical circles. They sang, danced and Miss Bowman

highlighted the evening with varied characterizations in costume.
One of her favorites was "Salome" from the opera of the same
name.

Upon the return of the company to the United States, Miss
Bowman dissolved the group and soon after separated from her husband and went out in vaudeville as a single.   Later she became associated with the Lafayette Players Stock Company in New York
City.   For several seasons she appeared in almost every performance of this celebrated company.

In the late 1920's, Miss Bowman came to Los Angeles with
the Lafayette Company which did a schedule of performances at the
Lincoln and Belasco Theatres.   When the Players disbanded in the
early 1930's, Miss Bowman continued her theatrical activities by
giving recitals and plays at social and church functions.

She made her film debut in an all-black film, "Louisiana,"
which was adapted from a play of the same name authored by J.
Agustus Smith.   Later she appeared in Oscar Micheaux's "Lem
Hawkin's Confession" (1935) and "God's Stepchildren" (1938).   She
also appeared in the first all-black horror film, "Son of Ingagi"
(1940).   Miss Bowman retired from the stage in the late 1940's
and died in her home in Los Angeles in 1957.

PERRY BRADFORD

Perry Bradford along with Shelton Brooks were two American
composers who originated songs that included instructions in the lyrics on how to perform a dance.   Bradford was born in about 1890
in Atlanta, Georgia.   He began his theatrical career by touring the
South and North with a song and dance act billed as Bradford and
Jeanette between 1908 and 1911.   Perry acquired his nickname
"Mule" from his vocal specialty in vaudeville, "Whoa, Mule!"   His
first song "Crazy Blues" was made popular by Mamie Smith's recording of it in the early 1920's.

In 1921, Bradford achieved success when Ethel Waters sang
his song "Messin' Around" on the T. O. B. A.   In 1917, Bradford
published "Scratchin' the Gravel" and in 1922 he published "The
Original Blackbottom Dance" which became popular nationally after
being introduced on Broadway in Irvin C. Miller's "Dinah" in 1923.

Perry Bradford is given credit for introducing the Blackbottom dance to New York City.   In the April 1927 edition of
McClure's Magazine, Bradford gave the following account of how he
discovered the dance:

> Down home, my folks live in a little Negro settlement
> called "Darktown" just on the outskirts of Atlanta.   Dark-
> town is probably the dancing capital of the American Ne-
> gro.   The people dance in the open, and indoors, at pic-

Perry and Jeanette Bradford, circa 1915

nics and house parties, and in the churches, most of all.
Every prayer meeting of the African Methodist Church
ends in a sort of Black Bottom circle dance, with the
dancers clapping their hands and crooning, and the preacher calling the steps.   Well, visiting my mother and dad
down there in 1922, I saw a girl and man dancing a step
that looked pretty good to me.   And they were waving their
hands and singing over and over:
 Hop down front and then
 doddle back,
 Mooch to the left and then you Mooch to the right--
 Your hands on your hips and do
 a mess around
 Break a lot until you're under the ground.

I asked them what it was and wrote down the Black
Bottom. I wrote down the Black Bottom words and the
melody, and when I came back to New York, I trained
Ethel Ridley, a Negro dancer, to do the steps. She
danced the first Black Bottom in New York in a Harlem
musical show called "Dinah," produced in 1923. Broadway producers on a sight-seeing trip in Harlem noticed
the dance and imported it to Broadway. Within a few
weeks every stage dancer was clamoring for instruction
in the dance and society belles were paying Harlem Negroes hundreds of dollars a night to attend debutante
parties and demonstrate the "step."

BESSIE BRADY

Bessie Brady was born in Frankfort, Kentucky in 1882. She
first gained recognition as an actress with the William and Walker
Abyssinia Company in 1906. She remained with this company for
several seasons appearing in "Bandanna Land" and later with Bert
Williams' company in "Mr. Lode of Koal." When the Williams
company disbanded, she entered vaudeville in Chicago, and her first
appearance at the Pekin Theatre met with success. Later she
joined hands with Leona Mitchell and the two performers successfully toured the vaudeville circuits with repeated engagements at the
Grand and Monogram Theatres in Chicago where they reached the
heights of popularity.

Miss Brady, who was beautiful in form and features, ranked
next to Aida Overton Walker in Spanish dancing. Her last professional appearance before her death in 1912 was at the Crescent
Theatre in New York City.

MARION BROOKS

Marion Brooks was born in Dallas, Texas in 1874. He first
gained notice with the Dumas Dramatic Club and his greatest ambition was to become a noted dramatic actor. He made his first professional debut in "Damon and Pythias" in New Orleans, Louisiana,
with Charles Hunter, his partner. Brooks and Hunter first became
well known at the Elysium Theatre and later in Panama. Later,
J. Ed. Green engaged Brooks as assistant producer at Bob Motts'
Pekin Theatre in Chicago, Illinois. He and Flournoy E. Miller
were the founders of the Bijou Stock Company at the Columbia
Theatre in Montgomery, Alabama. Later, when J. Ed. Green
formed a circle of theatres including the Grand, Chester and Monogram in Chicago and three in Cincinnati, Ohio, Brooks was the
manager with an office in Chicago. He also went to Jacksonville,
Florida where he was engaged as manager and producer for Frank
Crowd at the Globe Theatre. While there, he organized the Brooks
Stock Company and met with much success. The most pretentious
effort of his career was as the manager of the New Lincoln Theatre

in Cincinnati, Ohio. His last stage appearance was in Chicago in a
play entitled "On the Border" at the Monogram Theatre. Brooks
died in 1914.

SHELTON BROOKS

Shelton Brooks, an internationally famous composer, was
born in Amestberg, Canada on May 4, 1896, and first came to the
United States in 1901. Brooks began his professional career playing "gut-bucket" piano in Cleveland. In 1911, Brooks composed the
hit song "Some of These Days" which became world famous as
Sophie Tucker's theme. In the same year, he appeared in his first
musical comedy, "Dr. Herb's Prescription, or It Happened in a
Dream," which was produced by Jesse Shipp. Brooks later went
out in vaudeville doing a single turn and for several months traveled with Danny Small's "Hot Harlem Band" as a trap drummer.

In the 1920's, Brooks appeared in a number of black shows
including "Miss Nobody from Starland" (1920) and "K of P" (1923).
He became prominent as a song and dance man with the cast of
"Dixie to Broadway" which starred Florence Mills. In 1928 he pro-
duced and performed in the revue "Nifties of 1928." In the early
1930's, he appeared in "Chocolate Scandals" with Mantan Moreland,
"Lazy Rhythm," and "Harlem Express" which was put out by Irvin
C. Miller. Brooks went to Europe with Lew Leslie's "Blackbirds
of 1932" and appeared in a command performance before English
Royalty.

Brooks wrote songs for some of America's best known performers including Nora Bayes, Al Jolson, and Sophie Tucker. He
also appeared in Ken Murray's "Blackouts" for two years. Brooks'
hit songs include: "Some of These Days," "The Darktown Strutter's
Ball," "All Night Long," "Jean," "Walkin' the Dog," "You Ain't
Talking to Me," "Honey Gal," and "If I Were a Bee and You Were
a Red, Red Rose."

TOM BROWN

Although Tom Brown never reached the heights of stardom
in the theatrical world, he was one of the most respected pioneer
black actors. He possessed a technical knowledge of the theatre
which was surpassed by few of his peers.

Brown was born in Indianapolis, Indiana on June 14, 1868,
and when twenty years old was already making a name for himself
in show business. He was first seen as an end man with the
McCabe and Young Minstrels and could play every part in the show.

At the time of the Chicago World's Fair, Mr. Brown was a
member of the Richard and Pringle's Minstrels, then the largest
black minstrel troupe on the road. He was one of the big features,

Tom Brown, circa 1907

and one of his specialties was that of doing a Chinaman under cork. When Jesse A. Shipp first saw him in Chicago in the Chinese role, Shipp bought him a complete Chinese costume, the first Tom Brown had ever owned.

In about 1895, Tom Brown went into vaudeville and did a single turn in the Keith houses, appearing in his Chinese act.

In 1897, Brown helped Bob Cole and Billy Johnson to organize the A Trip to Coontown Company which included Jesse A. Shipp, the Freeman Sisters and other well-known performers. After severing his connection with this company, Brown returned to vaudeville and later took on Siren Nevarro as a partner. At first, however, Brown had trouble convincing vaudeville managers to accept a black woman doing a Chinese part. For several months Miss Nevarro accompanied Brown as they toured the theatres, Brown paying all the expenses although she was not getting paid. Brown finally won over the managers and Nevarro joined the act as a paid performer.

Brown and Nevarro were given the best booking in vaudeville and made several trips to Europe appearing with much success in London, Paris and at the Winter Garden in Berlin. On one of their trips to Europe they remained for over two years.

In 1906, the team returned to the United States and joined Cole and Johnson's "Shoo Fly Regiment." They did not remain any length of time with this show and during the middle of 1906-7 joined Ernest Hogan's Rufus Rastus Company. The last big musical comedy show in which Brown and Nevarro appeared in was Bert Williams' "Mr. Lode of Koal."

Returning to vaudeville, Brown and Nevarro met with success until Tom Brown had a disagreement at Hammerstein's Victoria Theatre over going on first. After this controversy, Brown experienced much difficulty in getting work on the big time circuits, and the team went to Europe.

While in Europe, Tom Brown and J. Rosamond Johnson formed a vaudeville act, and in the early part of 1914 came back to the United States. The act made only a few appearances before it was disbanded, Tom Brown going to Chicago, where he became associated with Billy Johnson.

Shortly after the Lafayette Players were organized, Tom Brown went back to New York City and became one of the Players' most respected members. He played a prominent part in many of the dramatic successes presented at the famous Lafayette Theatre. Tom Brown died in Chicago in June 1919.

IVAN HAROLD BROWNING

Ivan Harold Browning, who was a member of the famous Four Harmony Kings quartet, was born in Brenham, Texas in 1891. His first professional job came in 1915 when he joined the Exposition Four as a tenor. The quartet was a big hit at the World's Fair in San Francisco the same year. Later, they went into vaudeville, playing West Coast theatres on the Pantages circuit.

Browning later joined the Four Harmony Kings and toured with the quartet over the Keith circuit before they were engaged to appear in "Shuffle Along" in 1921. Browning played the romantic lead opposite Lottie Gee and together they sang one of the hits of the show, "Love Will Find a Way." Eubie Blake recalls that this was the first time a love song between a man and woman alone on the stage was attempted in a black show. Common practice among white show producers of this period was not to allow on the stage the open show of romantic affection between black men and women.

The year 1924 found Browning as the leading man in the next big Sissle and Blake show, "Chocolate Dandies." After the close of the show, Browning with the Harmony Kings made a successful tour of Europe for several years. Still in Europe, Browning left the quartet in 1933 and joined up with Henry Star, singer, pianist and composer. They toured all of Europe with much success. During this period, they were featured in the "Baltabarin Revue" in Paris. This show was similar to the famous "Follies Bergere." They wrote two numbers especially for this show, one of which was "Jungle Nights in Gay Montmartre."

At the beginning of World War II, Browning returned to the States and settled in California where he began a film career in Hollywood portraying black stereotypes in numerous films. He had a featured role in the film "Sunrise at Campobello." He also made several appearances on the Amos and Andy television show in the early 1950's.   During the 1970's, Browning was still active in show business appearing in concerts at colleges and churches all over California.

OLLIE BURGOYNE

Ollie Burgoyne was born in Chicago, Illinois in 1885.   She began her stage career in 1901 when she was six, with a group of singing and dancing girls that toured Europe for nine years, returning to the United States in 1910.   Between 1910 and 1928 she toured Europe at least fifteen times with various shows.   Miss Burgoyne's specialty was dancing and her forte was the Brazilian dance, the Snake dance and the famous Spanish dance.   Her arms, hand motions, and the swing of her graceful body in doing these dances caused the theatrical critics to rate her the peer of any dancer in the world.

Miss Burgoyne lived in Russia for several years where she operated a lingerie shop in which she employed 27 people, and also sang and danced before the notables of that country.   She also had the privilege of performing in various other countries including Germany, Denmark, Sweden, Hungary, France, Switzerland, Egypt and Turkey where she mastered the oriental dances.   At one time, in the 1920's, she was billed as an "Algerian Girl" when she performed on the various vaudeville circuits.   In 1923, she was a featured performer of the show "Follow Me."

ALSTON BURLEIGH

Alston Burleigh was the son of Harry T. Burleigh, baritone soloist at St. George Church in New York City and the composer of "Deep River" and other spirituals.   From his mother, who in her youth toured with Williams and Walker company, he inherited his talent for the stage.   Born in New York City and educated in England and at Howard University, Washington, D. C., Burleigh's first stage experience was through the Howard Dramatic Club, which supported Charles Gilpin in a single performance of O'Neil's "The Emperor Jones."   Later he toured with Gilpin in this play.   After serving with Abbie Mitchell's company of Lafayette Players, he played in Paul Green's "In Abraham's Bosom," a Pulitzer Prize play, at the Provincetown Playhouse, and later had a leading role in "Harlem."   Later he supervised the music in "Rope" and performed in "Blackbirds," in Ziegfeld's "Show Girl" and in "Hot Chocolates."   Between 1931 and 1933 he was the head of the music and dramatic department of Virginia State College at Petersburg, Virginia.

SANDY BURNS

Sandy Burns' career in show business spanned three decades

Sandy and Gretchen Burns, circa 1915

in which he became one of the best known comedians and show producers of his time.   He was born in Oklahoma City, Oklahoma in
1884 and moved with his parents to Huntsville, Texas where he
lived until he was fifteen years of age.   By this time, young Burns
had already acquired a love for the theatre and it was around this
time that he acquired a job with an opera company that came through
his home town.   After traveling with this company for some time,
he drifted among black performers and found his first real engagement on the stage with the Stafford Brothers and he remained with
this company for two years.   His next engagement was with the
Parker Concert Company and then he joined the Sells-Flotow Circus
Band where for the next year and a half he beat his way about the
country on a bass drum.

        In 1909, he went into vaudeville with Al Boyd as a partner.
This partnership lasted for five years and then he teamed with
Glenn (later of the team of Glenn and Jenkins).   The act was billed
as "Glenn and Burns, Street Sweepers."   This partnership lasted
for nearly three years and then Burns, who by this time had married Miss Gretchen Roberts, began to produce his own shows.   His
wife died shortly after this venture and he then joined Irvin C.

Miller's Company. He toured with this organization for a while,
and then joined Bob Russell's Company with which he remained for
a year.

 After leaving Russell, Burns signed a five-year contract
with John T. Gibson, then owner-manager of the Standard Theatre
in Philadelphia. The contract called for Burns to produce shows
in partnership with Sam Russell who worked opposite him on the
stage. During their run at the Standard, the Burns Russell Company became one of the most celebrated of the period. A young
George Wiltshire, who went on to become a well-known straight
man and who worked with virtually every well-known black comedian on the stage for the next thirty years, got much of his early
stage experience with the Sandy Burns Company. Marcus Slayter
who became a well-known show producer in partnership with Quintard Miller also got his start with Burns.

HARVEY BURRIS

 Harvey Burris, at the early age of ten, entered show business in New York City. He was one of the first members of the
original "Georgia Minstrels," the company being one of the first
black shows on the road. He did songs, dances and monologues
and was associated with such comics as Billy Kersands, Billy
Green, Billy Banks, Sam Lucas and Charley White. Kersands was
leading man of the show and made millions laugh with the little
donkey that was his inseparable pal.

 When the "Georgia Minstrels" were in their hey-day, there
were only two well-known black theatres in the United States and
they were the Adelphia and Walnut Street Theatres in Philadelphia.
The majority of minstrel audiences were white and the company
usually played under a tent or in the largest white theatres. After
several tours of the United States, the company went abroad and it
was there that they made their biggest pay days.

 It was the custom when in England and Germany to put on
performances in big beer gardens. These performances, in the
nature of extra acts, would be solely for the benefit of the individual minstrel members, and many were the times that two or three
of the men would pass hats around and return with them loaded to
the brim with coins and paper money.

 After eight or ten years with Callender's "Georgia Minstrels,"
Burris joined a show that had been organized by Kersands and remained with him about two years. After that he enlisted in the
Army serving a number of years, and was discharged for disabil-
ities in 1885.

 At one time, Burris was employed as a correspondent for
the Chicago Mascot, a white paper. He was then living in Pennsylvania, and wrote so many exposes of scandal and corruption that he

was forcibly invited to leave town. He also worked on the Cleveland Gazette, one of the oldest black newspapers in America. Burris also composed a number of songs including "Angel Gabriel, "
"Great Camp Meeting in the Promised Land, " "Who Broke the Lock
on the Hen House Door" and "Creep on the Hen House Door. "

BUTTERBEANS AND SUSIE
(JODIE AND SUSIE EDWARDS)

Without a doubt one of the most famous husband and wife
teams in show business was that of Butterbeans and Susie. Butterbeans was born Jodie Edwards in Marietta, Georgia and started in
show business in 1910 with the Moss Brothers Carnival doing what
at the time was called a "pickaninny bit. " He was just a youngster
then, but by his singing and dancing worked himself up the show
business ladder.

On May 15, 1917, Butterbeans and Susie were married on a
stage in a little theatre in Greenville, South Carolina as part of a
publicity stunt, and for which they were paid $50. Jodie and Susie
were both fifteen years of age and, with thoughts of the marital ob-
ligations, they became so scared that it took many hours of pleading by members of the troupe to convince them that everything
would turn out all right.

A few weeks later, Charles H. Dudley was short of an act
at the old Douglass Theatre in Macon, Georgia. Jodie and Susie had
so much talent that members of Alex Talbert's company encouraged
them to form a team and try for the job at the Douglass. Rosetta
Brown, then a well-known singer, taught the kids a few songs and a
couple of gags, and later the team opened at the Douglass and
scored a big hit at the first performance. This event marked the
beginning of over thirty years of trouping for Jodie Edwards and
Susie Hawthorne.

In the early 1920's, there was a famous comedian by the
name of Butler "Stringbeans" May who wore tightfitting pants as
part of his comedy regalia. He always got a big laugh when he
came on. When he died in 1929, Charles Turpin, then a well-
known theatre owner and booking agent, attempted to provide a suc-
cessor to May. He then tagged Jodie Edwards "Butterbeans"--a
monicker that stuck all through the years.

Butterbeans and Susie were one of the first teams to build
their act around the comic situations arising from conflict between
man and wife. In their act they sang duets between which Susie
sang the blues and cakewalked while Butterbeans performed eccentric dances. He was famous for his Heebie Jeebies, a dance routine known in the trade as "the itch" in which he scratched in

Opposite: The Comedy Team of Butterbeans and Susie, circa 1925

syncopated rhythm. Butterbeans' trademark was his tight pants and
when he kept his hands in his pockets he looked like he was "itch-
ing to death. "

        The team was an overnight success and so great was their
commercial value, a record company contracted them to do their
songs on records. Their records sold like hotcakes and are now
collector's items.

        In the mid-1920's, Jimmy Cooper, a white producer, put out
black and white revues on the Columbia Burlesque Circuit. These
shows consisted of two parts; the first part in which Butterbeans
and Susie were the stars was performed by about 20 black performers while about the same number of whites put on the second part
of the show. These shows were very popular in the South and Midwest and in many cities were performed before segregated audiences
with the Blacks occupying balcony seats in white theatres.

        For more than a decade the marquee billing of Butterbeans
and Susie was an integral part of the Consolidated Booking Office
and every year they played the circuit--Louisville, Cincinnati,
Indianapolis, Columbus, St. Louis, Kansas City, Detroit, Chicago,
Tulsa, Oklahoma City, Cleveland, and Toledo.

        During World War II they played a part in the entertainment
of service men by visiting hospitals and training camps time and
time again for the USO camp shows.

        Susie Edwards died in 1963 shortly before a group of friends
and admirers in the entertainment and business fields were preparing to fete her and Jodie with a huge theatrical testimonial on
February 9 at the Trionon Ballroom in Chicago.

        After the death of his wife, Edwards teamed up with his
adopted daughter, Miss Dixie Gibson. Six weeks before his death,
he was married to Eva Wheatley. In November 1967, Jodie Edwards at age 70 succumbed to a fatal heart attack just after walking
off the stage at the Dorchester Inn located in a Chicago suburb.

LAWRENCE E. CHENAULT

        Lawrence Chenault was born in Mount Sterling, Kentucky in
1877. At an early age Lawrence moved with his family to Cincinnati, Ohio, where he attended the public and high schools. For
years he was a soloist at Allen Temple Church in Cincinnati. He
made his debut in the theatrical profession in 1895 when he joined
Al G. Field's Negro Minstrels. So successful were his efforts
with this company the first season that he was engaged for a second season. In 1897, Mr. Chenault joined A. G. Field's Darkest
America company. With this show he was featured tenor and his
impression of the character "Golden Hair Neil" kept the audiences
in an uproar with laughter. And in the opera scene, portraying the

Lawrence Chenault, circa 1897

role of "Furride" from Cavalier Rusticanni, his brilliant voice and acting was seen to great advantage. His rendition of the "drinking song" from the same opera was one of the sparkling gems of the show.

After six or seven seasons with Fields, he became a member of the Black Patti's Troubadours, one of the greatest shows of the time. He then became a member of the M. B. Curtis Minstrels, which had as "star comedian" Ernest Hogan. He toured America with the show and later toured Australia, New Zealand and Tasmania, returning by way of the Hawaiian Islands and making a long appearance in Honolulu. After returning stateside to

San Francisco, Lawrence decided to remain on the coast for a time, and for two years sang in all the principal places of amusement in San Francisco.   He then rejoined Hogan, who was starring in the original "Smart Set" and remained with the show after Hogan's death. He was a member of the Williams and Walker Company doing a part in "Abyssinia, " and was also with the Pekin Stock Company of Chicago for three years.   He then rejoined Dudley, whose "His Honor the Barber" was recognized at the time as a great success. Later Chenault appeared in vaudeville and doubled as a member of the teams of Allen and Chenault and Martin and Chenault.   About this time, Anita Bush organized the first dramatic company in the East, and Lawrence joined her.   Later he went to the company of the Griffin Sisters.   Through the aid of Charles Gilpin, the cele- brated actor, Chenault was made the first leading man with the then newly formed Lafayette Players Stock Company.   He remained with the players a number of years and appeared in several black films.

INEZ CLOUGH

        Inez Clough was one of the original members of the Lafayette Players.   She was born in Worcester, Massachusetts and was edu- cated in that town and in Boston specializing in vocal and piano. She was also coached in the former in London, England and Austria during her ten-year stay abroad.   Her first experience in show business was gained with Isham's Oriental America Company in 1896.   After a season playing the principal cities in America, the troupe toured England where Miss Clough remained.   She lived in London and performed as a single in all the principal halls of the British Isles.   For five years she worked in the English Panto- mimes, three as a "principal boy" and two as fairy queen in the musicals "Red Riding Hood, " "Dick Whittington, " and "Robinson Crusoe. "

        After her return to America she toured with Cole and John- son's "Shoo Fly Regiment, " leaving it to join the Williams and Walker Company, with which she remained for five years until the death of George Walker.   She then toured vaudeville until she joined the Lincoln Stock Company at the Lincoln Theatre in New York City. After this company disbanded, she joined the famous Lafayette Players.   Miss Clough retired from the stage in the late 1920's.

LULU COATES

        One of the most successful performers in the 1920's was Lulu Coates whose company "Lulu Coates and Her Crackerjacks" were box office smashes wherever they appeared.   Miss Coates was born in Chicago, Illinois.   As a young girl she was something of a "child prodigy" and consequently was engaged to dance at lawn fetes of the ultra-wealthy families in Chicago.   During that time she appeared at the Field's mansion, and later she was the feature of a fete held at the home of a prominent theatrical manager who

recognized the potential of her talent. As a result, she was engaged to play the part of the dancing flower girl in the big pageant
"Parsifal." Her work was so impressive that she was engaged to
play a big musical show and during this time she married Sherman
Coates, who at the time was a member of the then celebrated
"Golden Gate Quartette." A short time later, the Coates and
Grundy Watermelon Trust was organized. The act was a riot in
vaudeville and it was later booked as a headline attraction with the
best burlesque shows.

A few months after Mr. Coates died, Lulu Coates formed
her "Crackerjacks" company. Every big circuit in vaudeville
played "Lulu Coates and her Crackerjacks." During World War I,
Miss Coates took an active part in the sale of Liberty Bonds and
was credited with making a record of over $500,000 worth of sales.
For this service she received a letter honoring her from the United
States Government. In 1918, she accepted a six-year contract from
Hurtig and Seamon to act as a featured attraction along with her
Crackerjacks with burlesque shows on the "big wheel."

CHARLES "HONI" COLES

Charles "Honi" Coles, one of America's greatest tap dancers,
was born and raised in Philadelphia. He learned how to dance as
a youngster on the streets of Philadelphia and in amateur contests
around the city. His first professional experience came when he
joined the Three Millers and went with the group to New York in
1931 when they opened at the Lafayette Theatre. After the act
broke up, Coles returned to Philadelphia and later returned to New
York in 1932 where he joined the Hoofers Club which assisted him
in finding jobs. Later he performed with the Lucky Seven Trio, a
comedy act, and later with Cab Calloway between 1940 and 1943.
Around that time, he met Holly Atkins and with Atkins and Atkins'
wife formed a song and dance act with assistance from Calloway.
The act broke up after Coles and Atkins joined the Army in 1943.

After World War II, Honi Coles and Atkins formed a team
and their first engagement was at the Apollo Theatre in Harlem.
Between 1945 and 1949 they danced with a number of bands including Cab Calloway, Louis Armstrong, Charlie Barnett, Lionel Hampton, Billy Eckstine and Count Basie. In 1948 they toured England
with great success.

In 1949, Coles and Atkins joined "Gentlemen Prefer Blondes"
on Broadway which starred Carol Channing. They stayed with the
show for two years and after the show closed in 1951, the team
played summer stock for a while and appeared in the musical "Kiss
Me Kate."

After a few years' separation, Coles and Atkins went back
together in 1958 joining Tony Martin's act in Las Vegas. In 1965,
Coles and Atkins appeared in CBS Television's "Camera 3" and in

1966 Coles appeared in the opening of a series entitled, "U. S. A. Dance" on National Educational Television. Later, Coles was elected president of the Negro Actors' Guild and in 1976 he appeared in the black musical, "Bubbling Brown Sugar."

EDGAR CONNORS

Edgar Connors broke into the entertainment world in 1906 when he was brought from Jacksonville, Florida to New York City by J. Rosamond Johnson to play a juvenile role in Cole and Johnson's "Shoo Fly Regiment." He made a hit in the show singing a number about "Sambo" and later was given a part in a skit having the same name in the next Cole and Johnson musical comedy "Red Moon."

After the death of Bob Cole in 1911, Connors appeared in vaudeville on the big time with his Sambo Girls. He headed "Shuffle Along" company no. 2 which toured the South. Later in his career, he worked in several motion pictures with some success playing opposite Al Jolson in "Hallelujah I'm a Bum" and had parts in "Rufus Jones for President" with Ethel Waters and Sammy Davis, Sr. in 1933, and in "Black and Tan Fantasy" with Duke Ellington and Fredie Washington.

Edgar Connors died in New York City in 1934.

WILL MARION COOK

One of the great American composers, and the musical genius behind the Williams and Walker shows, Will Marion Cook, was born in Washington, D. C. in 1865. His father, John Cook, was professor of law at Howard University. As a child Cook developed a love for music and demonstrated such talent that his parents sent him to study music at Oberlin when he was 13 years old. While there he excelled in his studies to such a degree that he won a scholarship to study violin in Berlin, Germany under Josef Joachim, then one of the celebrated authorities in music. Cook studied in Berlin for five years after which he returned to the United States, in 1895, and studied briefly under the famous Anton Dvorak at the National Conservatory of Music.

In 1898, Cook and the celebrated poet, Paul Laurance Dunbar, collaborated to write and produce the operetta "Clorindy, or the Origin of the Cakewalk." This show which opened at the Casino Roof Garden in New York City introduced a new kind of music to the American stage. The hour long show had a cast of about forty singers and dancers and was based on a Southern plantation love story. It featured the comedian Ernest Hogan whose hit songs were "Jump Back, Honey," "Who Dat Say Chicken in Dis Crowd," "Hottest Coon in Dixie" and "Darktown Is Out Tonight." The show ended with a 20-minute cakewalk. These songs and "On Emancipa-

Will Marion Cook

tion Day" immediately gained fame for the young Cook and brought him to the attention of all the big music publishers.

After a successful New York run, Ernest Hogan left the show to join Black Patti Troubadours and "Clorindy" was incorporated into Williams and Walker's "Senegambian Carnival" as an afterpiece. With a cast of 60 performers, this show was booked into theatres in Boston, Philadelphia, Cincinnati and Washington. The show, however, did not draw well and was subsequently disbanded.

During the next ten years, Cook became nationally known for his music compositions for the Williams and Walker shows: "In

Dahomey," "Abyssinia," "Bandanna Land" and also for "Darkydom" which starred Flournoy E. Miller and Aubrey Lyles.

Cook's great songs included: "Mandy Lou," "Happy Jim," and "Red, Red Rose." He also produced such remarkable choral pieces as "Swing Along," "Exhortation," and the "Rain Song." He also wrote the opera "St. Louis Woman."

In 1919, Cook took his New York Syncopated Orchestra to Europe and was largely instrumental in creating the vogue for black musicians in England and all over Europe.

At one time, Cook was married to Abbie Mitchell, a talented and well-known singer and actress. They separated after the birth of their second child.

Will Marion Cook died on July 20, 1944 in New York City.

HENRY CREAMER

Henry Creamer of the vaudeville team of Creamer and Layton was born in Richmond, Virginia. Creamer became interested in the stage as a very young man and during a 15-year period he worked as an usher, stage manager, manager, director and writer of songs, some of which came to the attention of the great Williams and Walker team. He gained rapid success because of the fresh and original nature of his syncopated melodies and before long he was associated with Alex Rogers as coproducer of a musical show, "The Old Man's Boy," in 1913.

In 1916, Creamer met Turner Layton who had studied music until age sixteen when he gave it up for a medical career, having obtained a degree from the University of Pennsylvania. Creamer met Layton through a mutual friend, Lt. Jim Europe, in Paris, France where Layton was studying music. The two seemed to have a musical affinity for each other, a kind of complementary understanding that made them work together as one man.

First they tried a number of simple melodies, more in fun than in earnest, and later, finding that the melodies were not half bad, they developed them into what were successes and before long the music publishers were anxious to publish their work. They composed the music for several well-known black shows including "Strut, Miss Lizzie" and wrote many song hits including "Sweet Emalina," "My Gal," "Strut, Miss Lizzie," "Mandy," "Breaking a Leg," "Dear Old Southland," and "New Orleans." In addition, they wrote special songs for many well-known white performers including Nora Bayes, Fannie Brice, Al Jolson, Eddie Cantor, and others. Also, their songs appeared in several editions of the Ziegfeld Follies.

With the aid of J. C. Robinson, Creamer wrote the popular

song "If I Could Be With You One Hour Tonight. " This song did
not make much of a hit at the time, although it was plugged heavily
by George Randol and Andy Razaf in one edition of Irvin C. Miller's
"Brownskin Models. " The song, however, became one of America's
favorites. Creamer retired from show business in the late 1920's
and died in New York City in 1930.

SAM CROKER, JR.

Sam Croker, Jr. was born in 1876 in Charleston, South Carolina.
Going to New York City in about 1895, Croker showed a fondness
for theatricals and he had not been there long before he secured a
position at the old Daly's Theatre as usher. He first attracted attention in 1897 as business manager for Bob Cole's "A Trip to
Coontown" company. It was Sam Croker with Bob Cole, Billy Johnson, Jesse Shipp, Tom Brown and Bob Kelly who struggled to keep
the first black musical comedy on the road using their personal
funds. Remaining with this aggregation until it disbanded, Croker
next associated himself with Cole and J. Rosamond Johnson in
vaudeville, taking care of their business matters.

In 1904, Croker joined Norman J. Norman's Dahomey Company No. 2 with Avery and Hart as principals. This company was
taken to England where it played the provinces with great success.
In 1906, when Cole and Johnson starred in "The Shoo Fly Regiment, "
Croker joined the company as business manager. With the closing
of Cole and Johnson's company, Croker was next seen as manager
of the Pekin Theatre in Chicago, returning to New York City shortly after the closing of the pioneer black show house.

In 1913, Croker secured several well-known black performers for the "Lime Kiln Club" series of motion pictures which were
to be produced by Klaw and Erlanger with Bert Williams as the
star. This venture fell through, however. At the time of his
death in 1914, Mr. Croker was actively engaged in promoting a
spectacular entitled "The Autumn Exposition" which was held at the
Manhattan Casino in September of that year.

SAMMY DAVIS, JR. and WILL MASTIN TRIO

Sammy Davis, Jr. celebrated his first birthday in the dressing room at the old Hippodrome Theatre in New York City. The
52 intervening years have seen him develop into one of the most
electric and popular entertainers in America and abroad. He and
the Will Mastin Trio commanded kings ransoms for nightclub appearances and his records have sold in the millions. Will Mastin
and Sammy's father, Sam Davis, Sr. , were well established in
vaudeville for years before Sammy came along. In 1921, Will
Mastin organized the Holliday in Dixie Company which enlisted the
services of fifteen well-known performers including Virginia Richards,
Sam Davis, Sr. , and Ida Forsyne. Their act consisted of songs,

Will Mastin Trio: Sammy Davis, Sr. [left], Sammy Davis, Jr. [center], and Will Mastin

sketches and comedy, in addition to a dance novelty that was sweeping the nation, the "Texas Tommy." During this period, Mastin put out "Struttin' Hannah from Savannah" and "Miss Creole."

Sammy was born in 1926 and by the time he was two, the toddler kept busy mimicking the various members of the "Miss Creole" company as the delighted piano player fed him cues. With the coming of the depression era of the 1930's, Mastin was forced to cut his act to five men; Sammy, all of four, was one of the "men." A few more seasons of depression and the act was whittled down to a trio, where it remained until Sammy went out on his own in the late 1950's. During the early years, Sammy never appeared

in any other setting, with the exception of two movie appearances
in "Rufus Jones for President" with Ethel Waters in 1932 and "Seasons Greetings." It was during the depression years that Sammy
developed into the incredible versatile entertainer that he is today.
The Trio played in vaudeville, in burlesque, in big cities and tank
towns. Sometimes they were broke, sometimes stranded, sometimes stranded and broke, but they always managed somehow to get
to the next date. And always, Sammy was learning, learning.
Once at a theatre in Michigan, the late, great Bill Robinson caught
the act, and was vastly impressed with its youngest member and
asked Will Mastin to bring the youngster to him for some extra
tutelage.

In 1943, Sammy went into the Army and combined the usual
chores of a soldier with producing camp shows, many of which he
wrote and directed himself. Discharged in 1945, he immediately
rejoined his father and uncle in Seattle. The Trio was back in
business again and this time it skyrocketed. In April 1946, the Trio
opened at Slapsie Maxie's, a then popular Hollywood nightclub. Ben
Blue was the headliner, while the Trio, unknown and unheralded,
merely opened the show. So deafening was the reception for Sammy
and his family that they were signed for a return engagement as
headliners. From then on, the Trio worked the best nightclubs in
America including Ciro's in Hollywood, the Copacabana in New York
City, and all the hotels on the Strip in Las Vegas. Television appearances on such shows as Ed Sullivan's "Toast of the Town" and
the Milton Berle Show further enhanced their popularity.

In November 1954, Sammy suffered a blow that might well
have ruined a less determined man for life; while driving from Las
Vegas to Hollywood for a recording session, he was involved in an
automobile accident that completely wrecked his car and cost him
his left eye. Eleven weeks after the accident, Sammy was back
with the Trio at Ciro's. The result: a ten-minute standing ovation,
and the breaking of every box-office record in the club's history.

In 1956, Sammy, his father, and his uncle made their Broadway debut in the hit musical comedy, "Mr. Wonderful" which starred
Sammy, Jack Carter, Olga James and Pat Marshall. Sammy's next
starring role on Broadway was in "Golden Boy," which was adapted
from a play by Clifford Odets. Sammy's records have sold in the
millions and he is considered by many to be America's most versatile entertainer. Will Mastin died in Los Angeles in 1978.

GALLIE DE GASTON

Gallie DeGaston, whose real name was Melton, was born in
Huntsville, Alabama in 1890. The comedian appeared on the stage
for over thirty years. He was the star on the T. O. B. A. circuit
with his partner Lilly "Pontop" Yuen. He also appeared with several
editions of "Brownskin Models." His last important engagement was
with Lew Leslie's "Blackbirds" in London. After the close of that

production, he remained in Europe for several more weeks, returning to the United States in October 1937 when he resumed his partnership with George Williams, with whom he had worked on and off
for seven years between 1930 and 1937.

Gallie DeGaston died in 1937 shortly after completing the
first day's performance of a week's engagement at the Howard
Theatre in Washington, D. C. with his partner, George Williams.

SIDNEY EASTON

Sidney Easton was born in Savannah, Georgia in 1891. As a
young lad he worked in various capacities at the Savannah Theatre
from call boy to stage manager. In 1907, at the age of sixteen,
Easton started on the road and during his long career he played on
the Mutual, Columbia, T. O. B. A. and various other circuits. He
composed several songs and lyrics and is credited with two of the
hit songs of Ethel Waters. In the mid-1920's, Easton toured with
the Easton Trio which included Bert Howard and Martha Copeland.
Easton was also featured in several black-cast films in the 1930's
and 1940's including: "Murder on Lenox Avenue," "Fight That
Ghost," "Sunday Sinners" and "Paradise in Harlem."

JODIE AND SUSIE EDWARDS   see   BUTTERBEANS AND SUSIE

JAMES REESE EUROPE

James Reese Europe, one of America's great band and orchestra leaders, was born in Mobile, Alabama in 1879. When quite
young, he moved with his family to Washington, D. C., where he attended public school and first began to study music. He was from
a musical family; his sister, Mary Europe, and a brother, John
Europe, were excellent musicians.

In 1904, Europe first went to New York City and secured
jobs as a piano player. During the season of 1906-7 he went out
as musical director for "Jolly" John Larkin's Company, and the next
season was employed in a similar capacity with Cole and Johnson's
"Shoo Fly Regiment." Europe wrote one of the musical hits of the
show "Gay Laneta" which was sung by Theodore Pankey. Europe's
next engagement as musical director was with the Smart Set Company followed by a similar position with Bert Williams' Mr. Lode
of Koal Company.

It was in 1910 that Europe conceived an idea for dignifying
and uplifting black musicians in New York City. He organized the
Clef Club which was a booking house for black musicians which en-
abled them to get steady work at higher salaries.

A few years later, Europe withdrew from the Clef Club and

organized the Tempo Club. About this time, dancing was becoming
a popular form of entertainment and black musicians were in great
demand. Through the efforts of James Reese Europe hundreds of
musicians were booked to play engagements for the Four Hundred
and the wealthy black and white people in and out of New York City
at top salaries. On some occasions entertainers were sent as far
as Chicago.

When Col. William Hayward organized the 15th Regiment,
Europe was one of the first black men to secure a commission.
Later Col. Hayward authorized Lt. Europe to organize a crack band,
and in order to do this, Europe went as far as Puerto Rico to secure some of his musicians.

The 15th later became the 369th and was sent overseas after
America's entry into the First World War. Europe went with the
Regiment as First Lieutenant in charge of the band which was later
named the "Hell Fighters." This aggregation later played before
royalty and won the commendation of General Pershing. They made
the biggest hit in France of any band in the American Expeditionary
Forces.

When the 369th returned from France in 1919, well-known
theatrical promoters, quickly recognizing the prestige Lt. Europe
and his band were enjoying, made arrangements to send Europe's
"Hell Fighters" on a nationwide tour. Their first performance was
given at the Manhattan Casino and was a smashing success. It
was during a subsequent engagement of the band in Boston in May
1919 that Europe and Herbert Wright, a drummer in the band, had
a dispute which developed into a fight which resulted in Europe's
death.

BILLY EWING

Billy Ewing was born in Chattanooga, Tennessee, his parents
moving to Cleveland, Ohio when he was six years old. Billy's father was a Methodist minister and was affiliated with the Parham
Lodge of the Masons. Billy developed an interest in magic at a
very young age and while in school spent many hours reading all of
the books on magic that the local library afforded. Ewing centered
his interest on card and coin manipulation until he had become pro-
ficient in both of these somewhat difficult skills which required much
ability and dexterity to mystify audiences without being detected.
His mother and other relatives were horrified at the thought of their
son with a deck of "devil" cards and predicted that Billy was on his
way to ruin.

During one vacation period, Billy secured a shoe-shining job
in a washroom of the Kennard House, a Cleveland hotel. Soon
after he began to work on the new job, he began to amaze his fellow employees between shines with his card tricks. It so happened
that Thurston, then a famous magician, checked in at the same hotel

while playing a date in the city.   Some admirer of Billy's (as a
man of magic) informed the great Thurston that there was a young
black man who knew a thing or two about the secrets of producing
aces from the air and making them disappear.

Eventually Thurston sat in on one of these impromptu exhibitions in the hotel basement and was pleased to the extent of praising the skill of Ewing and offered him a position at $25 per night
as one of his assistants.   Ewing accepted and traveled many months
appearing twice daily in the garb and makeup of a Hindu assistant
in Thurston's famous "Basket Trick" in which a sword was passed
through a basket in which a person was concealed.

While in Chicago, Ewing left the services of Thurston and
formed a partnership with Joe Byrd in a vaudeville act.   During the
1920's, Byrd and Ewing travelled extensively, playing both vaudeville and musical comedies.

IDA FORSYNE

Ida Forsyne, who was famous in vaudeville for her unique
style of Russian dancing, was born in Chicago, Illinois in 1883.
She started dancing at the age of 10 in front of a candy store near
her home for pennies.   She also learned dance steps from Willie
Mason who played a piano in the saloon over which Ida and her
mother lived and by watching such shows as "South Before the War"
and the "Coontown 400" rehearse at the Alhambra Theatre.

While still a young girl, Ida ran away from home with a tab
show "The Black Bostonian" when she was fourteen.   She sang "My
Hannah Lady" and did buck dances.   Later she worked with "Black
Patti's Troubadours" from 1898 to 1902 for a salary of $5 per week.
In 1899, when she was sixteen, she accompanied the Black Patti
troupe to San Francisco which was the start of an extensive West
Coast tour.

After returning to New York, Ida got jobs in Atlantic City
and Coney Island.   In 1903 she joined the original "Smart Set" company which at the time was owned by Gus Hill, a white producer.
The show starred Ernest Hogan, Billy McClain, and the Henry
Brothers.   Ida sang and did a solo dance.   In 1904, Ida danced a
solo with Will Marion Cook's "The Southerners" at the Roof Garden
in New York City.   This was a mixed show and one of the few at
that time where black and white performers worked on the stage at
the same time.

The following year, Ida went abroad with the "Tennessee
Students," a troupe of seventeen performers, most of whom played
string instruments and sang.   Included in the troupe were Abbie
Mitchell, Ernest Hogan, and Henry Williams.   Billed as "Abbie
Mitchell and Her Coloured Students" the show opened at the Palace
Theatre in London in 1906, where it was a smash hit.   Ida was
billed as "Topsey, the Famous Negro Dancer."

Ida Forsyne, Russian Dancer

Ida did not return home with the troupe. She remained in
Europe for the next five years playing Moulin Rouge in Paris and
was booked throughout England. She first learned Russian-style
dancing during a year's stay in St. Petersburg, Russia and later
appeared for a triumphant engagement in Moscow.

In 1914, Ida returned to America where she had trouble
finding a job. Later, she tried T. O. B. A. first with partner Billy
Sells and then as a single. Later, she appeared with Billy King
and with Will Mastin's "Over the Top" company. Finding jobs hard
to get, Ida worked as a maid, on stage and off, for Sophie Tucker
for two years between 1920 and 1922. She was paid $5 per week.
Sophie sang and Ida danced at the end of the act to whip up applause.
In 1924, she was back on T. O. B. A. as one of six dancing girls
with Mamie Smith's act which included a comedian and the pit band.
In 1926, she toured the South with the Smart Set Company, headed
by Salem Tutt Whitney and J. Homer Tutt. After returning to New
York, Ida tried to get jobs at the big nightclubs such as Small's
Paradise, Cotton Club, Connie's Inn and the Nest, but she was re-
fused because they featured light-skinned chorus girls.

In 1927, Ida again toured the T. O. B. A., this time with
Bessie Smith's show which paid $35 per week. The show included
Hooton and Hooton, a husband and wife comedy team. Ida worked
in the chorus and did a Russian dance specialty. In 1930, Ida had
a bit part in "Lily White" and in 1932 she played the part of Mrs.
Noah in "Green Pastures. " In the same year, she appeared with
Rex Ingram in "Emperor Jones. " In 1935 she appeared in Oscar
Micheaux's film "The Underworld" which was one of her last jobs
in show business.

LOTTIE GEE

Lottie Gee, who rose from chorus girl to star, began her
stage career as a chorus girl with the Cole and Johnson's "Red
Moon" company and remained with them until it closed. She then
entered the chorus with the Smart Set company and for two years
toured with S. H. Dudley as the star. Later Mrs. Aida Overton
Walker (wife of George Walker of Williams and Walker) hired her
as one of her dancing girls. After Mrs. Walker's retirement from
the stage, Miss Gee returned to the chorus line. Later she decided to try it as a single and was given her first engagement at
Ford Dabney's Theatre where she at once became very popular. It
was during this engagement that she formed a trio with Effie King
and Lillian Gillam. After the trio disbanded, she formed a sister
act of King and Gee which was considered to be one of the best in
the business. They toured the various vaudeville circuits for a
number of years and finding all the roads to the top barred against
them because of their color, they gave up temporarily. Miss Gee's
first big opportunities came when she was offered a position with
the Southern Syncopated Orchestra. After a short tour of the U. S.
the company went abroad with Miss Gee as the featured soloist.

Lottie Gee [left] and Effie King As They Appeared in Vaudeville

She toured Europe with the company winning praise in England,
France, Italy and Asia. Her first big hit show was when she
played the daughter of the proprietor of the Jim Town Hotel in
Miller, Lyles, Sissle and Blake's show "Shuffle Along" in 1921.
Later, she was one of the featured performers in Sissle and
Blake's "Chocolate Dandies."

CHARLES S. GILPIN

Born November 20, 1878 in Richmond, Virginia, Charles
Gilpin's parents died when he was a young boy and he was raised
by an uncle, Joseph Gilpin.   Educated at St. Francis School, he
did not complete high school because of his ambition to go on the
stage.   His first work was with the Canadian Jubilee singers in 1903.
He appeared with Williams and Walker's "Abyssinia" company and
Gus Hill's "Smart Set" company in 1905, and was a member of the
Pekin Stock Company in Chicago between 1907 and 1908.   He was
with the Pan-American Octette between 1911 and 1913, and he
toured with the "Old Man's Boy" show between 1913 and 1914 before
entering vaudeville in 1914.

In 1915, Anita Bush introduced Negro drama in New York
City by organizing the Colored Dramatic Stock Company which she
later renamed the Anita Bush Dramatic Stock Company.   For her
first play, "The Girl at the Fort," she secured Billie Burke as her
director and Gilpin for the male lead, and Mrs. Charlotta Freeman
for the female lead.

In 1916, the Quality Amusement Company produced its first
play, "Abraham Lincoln," in which Gilpin played the black character, William Curtis.

In 1920, the Provincetown Players staged "Emperor Jones"
in which Gilpin played the leading role.   His performance created
a sensation and later Gilpin was honored by the Drama League of
New York as one of the persons who had contributed most during
the year to the art of the theatre.

In September 1921, "Emperor Jones" ran for several weeks
to capacity audiences at the Playhouse on 410 South Michigan Avenue
in Chicago.   Never in the history of Chicago theatre had any artist
received the glowing notices that were accorded Gilpin.

On tour with the Provincetown Players, Gilpin had the distinction of being received in the White House by President Warren
Harding.

In 1921, Major Joel Spingarn, in behalf of the NAACP, presented Gilpin the Spingarn Medal, which for eight years had been
presented to the black who, during the year, had made the greatest
contribution to art or science.

In 1926, Gilpin appeared in his first and only all-black film, "Ten Nights in a Barroom," produced by the Colored Players Film Corporation of Philadelphia, Pennsylvania. Charles Gilpin died in 1930.

SAM GRAY

Sam Gray, along with Johnny Hudgins, James Riley and Eddie Green, started his theatrical career around the Daley Theatre, then located on Pennsylvania Avenue in Baltimore, Maryland, and soon became a vaudeville headliner and tab favorite with Rachel King. During the 1920's, Gray appeared in such big time attractions as "Scarlet Sister Mary," "Rhapsody in Black," and his own production, "Wrap It in Black." He left the "Rhapsody" cast in Chicago early in 1932 and went south to produce for Silas Green, then a well-known traveling tent show. Gray died in Greenville, North Carolina in 1932 shortly after completing a performance of the Silas Green Show.

AURORA GREELEY

Aurora Greeley was born in Jacksonville, Florida in 1905 and as a young girl moved with her parents to New York City where she first gained success as a musical comedy actress. Her first stage role was as a chorus girl in Irvin C. Miller's "Liza." At the time, she was a student at Wadleigh High School in New York City. She was in the chorus for six months and when Margaret Sims became ill, she took the latter's role as one of the principals. She portrayed it so successfully that Miller gave her a similar role in "Broadway Rastus" and later she was featured in Flournoy E. Miller and Aubrey Lyles' show "Runnin' Wild." In 1926 she joined "4-11-44" and worked with the company until it closed in 1927.

It was with this show that she first met Leroy Broomfield. At the time, Broomfield was a first rate dancer in his own right and he objected very rigorously to being teamed with a girl who had relatively little experience. However, by the end of the first rehearsal he accepted her and their dancing was one of the high points of the show "4-11-44." Soon after, they decided to team together and played for a while in Chicago before going to Los Angeles where they performed from 1928 to 1931 in Frank Sebastian's Cotton Club. Miss Greeley, besides leading the chorus of thirty chorines, did a specialty number each night with Leroy Broomfield. At the time, the Cotton Club orchestra was considered to be one of the best in the country and for a while it broadcast nightly over KFVD with Leroy Broomfield announcing.

CORA GREEN

Cora Green, a native of Baltimore, Maryland, began her

stage career at the age of fourteen.   Although she never received
any formal voice training, she was born with a rich contralto voice
which she developed early in her life by singing in school productions.   Her first professional appearances were in musical tabloid
shows with an act of Green and Pugh.   Later she went to Chicago
and became a member of the Panama Trio, with the other two members being Florence Mills and Ada "Bricktop" Smith.   This act was
a vaudeville headliner for three years and each member was a star
in her own right.   Later, she performed with Creamer and
Dayton's "Strut, Miss Lizzie."   She also teamed with Hamtree Harrington and for five years was the sensation of
Broadway and Europe.   She was featured in "Put and Take"
in 1921 which was produced by Irvin C. Miller with music
by Spencer Williams, and "Dixie to Broadway" in 1924.   In
1929, she was the star of "Ebony Showboat."   Miss Green also
performed in several all black films including Oscar Micheaux's
"Swing."

EDDIE GREEN

        Eddie Green, actor and founder of the Sepia Art Picture
Company, was born in Baltimore in 1901, and was the son of a
ship's carpenter.   His only job outside of show business was for
a menswear manufacturing company.

        His first stage experience was at the age of twelve when he
originated a magic show by reading do-it-yourself magic books.   At
about age sixteen, he began hiring assistants and renting halls and
put on magic shows for any audience that would come in.   After
completing high school, he made a few changes in the act and took
it into vaudeville, sometimes working in blackface.

        After several years in vaudeville, he began to double between
his regular act (now without magic) and burlesque.   He worked for
four years in the latter on the Columbia circuit.   In the 1930's,
Eddie began a musical comedy career that won him top roles in
"Hot Chocolates" and "The Hot Mikado."   In 1932, he was
featured performer in "Blackbirds," which he helped write.

        His first network radio assignment was on the Rudy Vallee
Show where he did historical sketches.   Later he worked on the
show "Duffy's Tavern" playing the role of "Eddie the waiter."   He
also produced and managed "All in Fun" for Barney Girard.

        In 1938, Eddie organized the Sepia Art Picture Company and
made several film shorts.   In 1948, Eddie moved the company to
Los Angeles and opened an office at 2640-1/2 Jefferson Avenue.
His last production was "Mr. Atom's Bomb" in 1949.   Eddie Green
wrote many hit songs, among them, "A Good Man Is Hard to Find."

GREENLEE AND DRAYTON

Rufus Greenlee and Thaddeus Drayton were born in the South around 1895. They both came to New York with their families, where they decided to become dancers after viewing shows produced by Sherman Coats and J. Grundy. They met for the first time at Hattie Anderson's dancing school on 53rd Street in New York, where they learned both the waltz and the two step. Drayton progressed from choir boy to professional dancer at the age of twelve. Wearing a wig and dressed as a girl, Drayton later worked as a pick with a long series of white acts including Gertie LeClair.

Rufus Greenlee started at the age of seventeen when he worked with Moor's "New Orleans Minstrels" at the Fourteenth Street Theatre in New York City. Later he went on tour with "The Georgia Campers" company.

In about 1909, Greenlee and Drayton teamed up and went on a tour of Europe with the famed act "Johnson and Dean" (Charles and Dora) which lasted over a year. After Johnson and Dean broke up in 1914, Greenlee and Drayton stayed in Paris. Later they went to St. Petersburg in Russia where they stayed for a while with Ida Forsyne, an American performer.

After returning to New York, they were booked at the Rivera Theatre on 97th Street and scored a hit before a white audience. Later they played the Winter Garden and then went on the Loew Vaudeville Circuit. They also played the Palace in New York during World War I when they and Bert Williams were the only black performers allowed to appear there.

The act was at its peak during the 1920's. Two of their big successes came when they performed in "Liza" in 1922 and "Lovin' Sam from Alabam'. " In 1926 they toured Russia with Sam Wooding's band where they sang and danced for Stalin. When the depression set in during the 1930's, Greenlee and Drayton broke up. Greenlee continued to work with his wife for six more years and then retired to New Haven, Connecticut, where he opened the Monterey Cafe on Dixwell Avenue. Greenlee died in New Haven, Connecticut in 1963.

GRESHAM AND GRESHAM

Leroy Gresham was the male member of the team of Gresham and Gresham, one of the foremost sketch teams playing in vaudeville and musical comedy shows in the 1920's and 1930's. Leroy Gresham was a native of Baltimore where, as a young lad, he attended Girard Avenue School. He was the son of a Baptist clergyman and also attended Hampton Institute in Virginia. He made his theatrical debut at the old Queen Theatre on Lexington Street in Baltimore as a singer of illustrated songs and for this he

received the sum of $2 a week.   During this engagement the young
actor, realizing his talent for mimicry, tried out a "Hebrew" character.   So successful was he that he was known throughout his professional career as "Kike" Gresham.   Season after season the young
man added new impersonations to his repertoire which included
blackface, Italian, western characters, and a female impersonation
that was a classic.   He also excelled in the art of makeup and
could fashion an appropriate costume seemingly out of nothing.

During the appearance of the great Bert Williams at the
Maryland Theatre in Baltimore, Gresham was filling a cabaret engagement at a local hotel.   Mr. Williams "caught" the act after
work that night and invited the young man, the writer Kennard Williams, and a few others to a little impromptu party.   The fatherly
advice was considered invaluable by the young Gresham.   The great
Bert Williams and the young man swapped Jewish dialect stories.
Gresham stories caused Mr. Williams to guffaw as loudly as had
the rest of the party at his own tales told in his inimitable style.
Gresham recalled that Williams' parting word was "Leroy, keep
on. "

Later, during World War I, Gresham served as a sergeant
in the 305th Field Artillery.

Mrs. Gresham was the daughter of Mr. Edward Eason, then
a prominent contractor who constructed the Masonic Temple in
Birmingham, Alabama.   She specialized in music at Miles College
in Birmingham.   Gresham and Gresham were box office hits on all
the big vaudeville circuits in the 1920's and 1930's.

JAMES GRUNDY

James Grundy, who was born in Little Rock, Arkansas in
about 1861, first went on the stage at the age of six with his brother, Will, in the "Little Nugget" company and later with Dr. Fitz-
gibbon's Medicine Show.   They were next seen in Whalen and Martell's "South Before the War" company where James met and married his wife, Susie Grundy, who was also a performer in this
famous show.   Next he and his wife joined Sam T. Jack's Creoles
and later Sheriden and Flynn's "Big Sensation. "   During James
Grundy's second season with this show, he joined hands with Sherman Coats, and formed the famous act known as "The Watermelon
Trust" in about 1899.   During this long stage career Grundy appeared in many successful shows including "Dainty Paree, " Katherine Rober in repertoire, Sam Seribner's New York City Stars.
His last appearance on the stage was at St. Joseph, Missouri
shortly before his death in November 1914.

LEONARD HARPER

Leonard Harper, whose genius as a producer of classy revues

was demonstrated by many hit nightclub and theatre shows during
the 1920's and 1930's, was born in Birmingham, Alabama in 1899.
He first went to New York City in 1913 where he worked at Connie's
Inn for George Immerman, who produced George White's "Scandals"
and the spectacular Winter Garden shows.   In 1923 he married
Osceola Banks, later to become his dancing partner in vaudeville.
The pair was the first black team featured abroad in the shows of
the Schuberts.   In 1926, he was a featured performer in "Blackbirds" with Florence Mills.

        In later years, Harper became best known for the jobs he
did as main producer of the revues of the famed Apollo Theatre on
125th Street in Harlem.   The Harperettes girls under his direction
and the various scenery designs and stage settings which were a
tribute to his genius helped establish the Apollo as one of the top-
notch show houses of the country.

        One of his most talked of shows was "Hot Chocolates."
Leonard Harper died in 1943, shortly after suffering a heart attack
during the rehearsal of a show at Murrains' Nightclub in New York
City.

CHARLES "CHARLIE" HART

        Charles Hart, who made his biggest reputation in the theatri-
cal world as a member of the team of Avery and Hart, was born
in San Jose, California in 1873.   When he was about eight years
old, he was taken to Cleveland, Ohio by his parents.   At one time,
he attended Wilberforce University.

        Hart first came to New York City in the spring of 1900.
His first appearance on the stage was in "Uncle Eph's Christmas,"
which was put on in Washington by Ernest Hogan in the fall of that
year.

        In the spring of 1901, Clarence Logan put Hart in Williams
and Walker's play, "The Sons of Ham," the comedian having been
selected because of his strong resemblance to Bert Williams.   The
piece was put on at the old Hertig and Seamon's Music Hall on
125th Street in New York City.

        Hart then teamed with Dan Avery and they did well in vaude-
ville.   Dan Avery was born in Texas in 1872.   His first partner
was Sam Loak.   Later he married Lizzie Harding and toured with
her as his partner in vaudeville and minstrelsy.   In the Georgia
Minstrels Avery was a shining star.   Next he succeeded Williams
and Walker in Hyde's Comedians.   Avery first met Hart when the
latter was doing an imitation of Bert Williams in vaudeville and the
two comedians decided to form a partnership.   For the next few
seasons they starred successfully in Williams and Walker's castoff
plays, "Sons of Ham" and "In Dahomey."

In 1904, Avery and Hart went to England with the "In
Dahomey" company, playing the provinces. Williams and Walker
had previously played the piece in London and the larger English
cities.

Returning to America in 1905, Avery and Hart again went
into vaudeville and were a big success. At the time of Dan Avery's
death, the act was drawing $350 a week.

In 1913, J. Rosamond Johnson and Charles Hart formed an
act which they later took to England. While in England, they performed in several big English musical comedy productions. After
Johnson returned to America, Hart stayed in England to perform in
several other musical shows.

In 1914, shortly after the start of World War I, Hart returned to America for a brief period before returning to England in
1915 to perform in a new show. At the time of his death in 1917,
he was starring in an English pantomime.

BILLY HIGGINS

Billy Higgins, whose real name was William Weldon, was
one of the most popular comedians on the stage in the 1920's. He
was born in Columbia, South Carolina in 1888 and began his acting
career in his hometown as a ballad singer at private concerts in
1912. Before his advent into the concert field he had been a machinist. After about a year in the concert business, he attracted
the attention of Billy King, then a famous show producer and comedian. Higgins remained with the Billy King Company until 1917,
when he entered the U. S. Army and was assigned to the 805th Pioneer Infantry and later rose in the ranks to become color sergeant.
He did not see service at the front and was mustered out after the
signing of the Armistice in 1918.

After leaving the Army, Higgins went into vaudeville playing
the Loew Circuit for a time and then joining Quintard Miller's Company. His next engagement was with the Coleman Brothers' Creole
Follies Company. It was while playing the Lafayette Theatre in
New York as a member of this company that Marcus Levey saw
him one night and the next day asked him to play the lead comedy
role in "Gold Dust," a show which then was in rehearsal. Billy
was offered a contract which called for a 25-week engagement which
he subsequently signed. His next big show was "Follow Me" in
which he played the principal comedy role with Clifford Ross as his
assistant. At one time, he was married to Valaida Snow, well-
known actress and singer. Higgins usually worked in blackface
(under cork) and played major roles in musical shows. Billy Higgins also wrote the popular song "There'll Be Some Changes Made."

Ernest Hogan, circa 1906

ERNEST HOGAN

Ernest Hogan, whose real name was Ernest Reuben Crowders, was born in Bowling Green, Kentucky in about 1859, and became one of the most well-known entertainers of his time, having performed from coast to coast in America and in Canada, Australia, Europe and Hawaii.

Hogan's early life was spent in minstrelsy and he later branched out as a quartet singer. His first professional recognition came when he toured with Richard and Pringle's Georgia

Minstrels. With the financial aid of his first wife, a white woman,
he wrote and published the song "All Coons Look Alike But Me."
Hogan did not consider this song to be an insult to his race, but
rather conceived it as a popular ragtime music. It was during the
first season of this song's popularity that he managed to attract the
attention of R. Voelckel, manager of Black Patti's Troubadours,
who later featured him as the "Unbleached American" on almost
equal billing as the star, Black Patti. After a few seasons with
the Black Patti Company, a difference arose between Hogan and a
Southern manager at New Orleans and caused Hogan to suddenly close
and leave for New York City where he opened as a headliner at
Hammerstein's Victoria at an enormous salary.

In the season 1899-1900, Hogan traveled to Australia with
Curtis' Afro-American Minstrels. On their return they stopped by
Honolulu where they presented a comedy, "My Friend from Georgia."
The Pacific Commercial Advertiser of Honolulu had this to say about
their performance:

> Hogan's capabilities are well-known but in Billy McClain,
> a former partner, he has support which is the best he has
> ever received. McClain is an actor. He is not only a
> dancer, the best Negro minstrel, that has been seen here
> in years but in fact he has made some strides along the
> way and his poise, his quiet demeanor and his command
> of a situation show real dramatic instinct. Wise, as a
> blackface Hebrew, was fairly good there being a strain-
> ing at some points, but with all the careful representation
> of the anxious real estate man. Mrs. McClain was seen
> to advantage and the return of Laura Moss, the "bronze
> Patti," with the quartette, gave a real lift to the quality
> of the choruses. The best song of the evening was "My
> Sweet Moano" written by Wise and the music by Hogan,
> sung by Miss Mamie Harris. The most striking specialty
> was the burlesque hula "Tommy" in which Kitty Milton,
> Wise and Hogan (who wrote it) sung and danced, the first
> made the whole go so well that the trio ran out of verses
> and had to stop. Altogether there was just enough of
> specialty to take the performance out of the pure dramatic
> and a sufficient story to keep up the interest.

While in Honolulu, Hogan and McClain got their heads together on an idea of constructing a new play embodying some of the
entrancing features of Hawaii. Their dream was realized on their
return to the States when Gus Hill agreed to finance the new show.
The new production which became the Original Smart Set Company
featured McClain and Hogan as the stars. The principle character
"George Washington Bullion" which Hogan created was based on a
person he had met during his boyhood in Bowling Green, his hometown. It was the work in this particular organization that convinced
all managers and critics that Hogan was a comedian of exceptional
ability. During the first tour with the Smart Set, Hogan fell in love
and married Miss Mattie Wilkes, then a famous singer and soubrette.

However, after a summer in vaudeville doing a one-act play entitled "The Military Man," they parted.

It had been Hogan's dream to have manager Hill take the Smart Set Company to Europe. It was Hill's refusal to carry the Company abroad that caused Hogan to leave the Smart Set after two seasons.

In the season of 1903, Hogan starred in the vaudeville production "Uncle Eph's Christmas." Paul L. Dunbar was the author of the play and the music was composed by Will Marion Cook. The roster of this talented company included Ernest Hogan, Will Marion Cook, Kid Frazier, Charles Hart, Aaron Tyler, Louis Salsberry, Judson Hicks, Walter Gaston, Theo. Pankey, Fletcher Cole, Albert Young, Allie Gilliam, Clarence Logan, Frank Williams, Abbie Mitchell, Mattie Evans, Gene Moore, Ollie Burgoyne, Leventa Ellis, Estella Pugsley, and Muriel Ringgold. Shortly after this show closed, Hogan produced and starred in a one-act farce in vaudeville entitled "Missionary Man."

Later, managers Hertig and Seamon secured Mr. Hogan for a new comedy, "Rufus Rastus." They engaged J. Ed. Green to produce and stage the show. During this first season as the star of this production, Hogan's popularity reached its zenith. He also performed the greatest song hit of the show, "Oh, Say! Wouldn't That Be a Dream."

In 1907 Hogan started rehearsing for what he hoped would be his greatest production, "The Oyster Man." Hogan wrote the book assisted by F. E. Miller and A. Lyles, two young playwrights then associated with the Pekin Stock Company in Chicago. After several weeks of rehearsal in New York City, the company traveled to Lima, Ohio where they opened on December 24, 1907. Hogan was quite ill and required the services of a physician. By January 1908, Hogan's illness had grown worse and he was forced to temporarily leave the show. Overwork was probably a contributing factor. Besides assisting in composing the music and writing the book, Hogan staged the show. After a few days rest, Hogan felt well enough to return to the show, but after a performance at the Globe Theatre, Boston, Hogan collapsed from physical exertion. Hertig and Seamon, managers of the company, decided to send their star to the mountains for a few weeks rest, where he died in 1909.

JAMES A. JACKSON

James A. Jackson was a leading newspaper man and had a major influence in promoting black theatricals in the early 1920's. Not only did he compile statistical data on all aspects of black participation in show business, but he brought the achievement of black performers and the merits of black shows to national attention through his page which appeared every week in Billboard, one of America's oldest and most respected theatrical publications.

Jackson was born in Belefonte, Pennsylvania in 1879, and received his first training in newspaper work at the age of 15 on the Daily News, a hometown newspaper. Passing successively from managing the business end of a theatrical company, a bank clerk with the Jennings Trust Company of Chicago, he joined Today, an afternoon daily in Detroit. After one year with this newspaper, Jackson branched out into railroad work, minstrel interlocutor, assistant musical comedy manager, traveling investigator and railroad policeman. He stayed with this last occupation for the next sixteen years, and during World War I he was attached to the United States Military Intelligence Service, general staff.

During this period, Jackson never lost his proclivity to write. Perhaps his best two serial works, both published by the New York Globe, were "The Negro at Large" in 1912 and "The Underlying Cause of Race Riots" in 1919. Both of these articles were syndicated by the Globe and quoted extensively by other publications throughout the country. Several of his feature stories were published during 1921 by the New York Sun and the New York Herald in the magazine section of their Sunday editions. Between 1921 and 1923, Jackson wrote a page of black theatrical news which appeared in Billboard. After leaving Billboard, Jackson joined the Washington Tribune as executive and theatrical editor.

In addition to his own work, Jackson collaborated with several well-known authors in national magazines and foreign papers. Jackson, who was essentially an observer, investigator, and analyst, was one of the best known and respected black dramatic reviewers of the period.

SEYMOUR JAMES

Seymour James was born in Wrightsville, Georgia in 1899. He started out in show business as a juvenile dancer at the age of 12, and soon after toured with the Original Florida Blossoms company, Richard and Pringle's Minstrels, the Georgia Minstrels, and later was featured with the Auto Girls company on the Mutual Circuit. Later he teamed with Wallace Stovall, a straight man. So successful was the team that they formed a company under the name of Stovall and James, and toured several years on the T. O. B. A. until Stovall's illness and death.

When Jeanette Taylor severed partnership with Perry Bradford, the song writer of the team of Bradford and Taylor, she saw the merits of talent in Seymour James and took him on as a partner and later married him. They had considerable success in straight vaudeville, but gained their first real success as one of the featured teams of O'Neil and Greenwald's celebrated "Plantation Days" which toured from coast to coast.

Mrs. James was unique and original in crazy-eyed expression, and in eccentric dancing. After Jeanette and Stovall left

"Plantation Days" they toured with their own orchestra until Seymour James' sudden death in 1926 at the age of 27.

JOHN WESLEY JENKINS

John Jenkins was born in Winchester, Virginia in 1859. He went to school in Pittsburgh until he was about 14 years old, then went to work to help his mother and the older children. He worked as a bootblack in the barber shop at a hotel until he was promoted to bellboy. He was quite a singer even as a young boy and at the age of twelve he organized a quartet of boys then known as the "Stars." They sang together around Pittsburgh until Wesley was about 15 years old; then he and the quartet joined the Gottholt and Ryles "Uncle Tom's Cabin" company. After one season with the Gottholt and Ryles company, he joined his brother, Robert, in the New Orleans Jubilee Singers.

Later, Jenkins formed the Oriole Quartet with Charles Preston, Charles Mahoney and John Hill as members. The quartet played successfully throughout the country. After that, Jenkins joined Whalen and Martell's "South Before the War" company. It was during this time he met his wife whom he married on March 17, 1898, at Bloomington, Indiana.

Jenkins and his wife and Sam Lucas created the well-known "Bode of Education" for Cole and Johnson's "Shoo Fly Regiment" and with the same writers performed in "Red Moon" where Jenkins was one of the famous "Four Bills" in the 1908-9 season.

In Bert Williams' picture "A Natural Born Gambler," Jenkins was Williams' principal support as "Brother Gardner." After that, Jenkins was with Eddie Leonard in one of Leonard's big vaudeville acts. Between 1911 and 1930, Jenkins played principal character parts in numerous pictures for Vitograph, Cosmopolitan, Distinctive, Inspiration, Kermar, Famous Players, Lasky, Thomas Ince, Selznick, Metro, Fox, Biograph, World Films, Universal, Delsarte, Goldwyn and J. E. Williamson.

John Jenkins died at the age of 71 in 1930 in Brooklyn, New York.

BILLY JOHNSON

Billy Johnson, who gained national fame as Bob Cole's first partner and the co-producer of "A Trip to Coontown," was born in Charleston, South Carolina in 1858. His first prominent appearance on the stage was with J. W. Hyatt's Colored Minstrels during the season of 1881 when he introduced the song "The Trumpet in the Cornfield Blows" which he wrote himself and used in an "old man" specialty in the stock dance which he originated. In 1886 he toured with Lew Johnson's "Black Baby Boy Minstrels," and later with

Hicks and Sawyer's Minstrels in 1888.   Next he joined W. S. Cleveland's "Big Double Minstrels."   He was next with Sam T. Jack's
Creoles, but soon left to join John W. Isham's Original Octoroons
in the seasons of 1895-1896.   It was in this company that he first
began to gain attention as a song writer.   "The Sporty Coon" and
"Oh, Henrietta," "Honolulu Song," and "Rehearsal for the Cake
Walk" were some of his songs which he and Frank Mallory staged.

He also appeared in descriptive songs with the talented Fred
J. Piper in an olio.   When Isham put out his second company "Oriental America," Voelckel and Nolan signed Madam Sissieretta Jones
to contract with plans to put out a show to compete with Isham.
The company was called Black Patti's Troubadours, and Voelckel
engaged Billy Johnson and Bob Cole to write songs and stage the
show.   It was in this company that Bob Cole and Billy Johnson became the talk of the country.   They wrote and produced a musical
sketch entitled "At Jolly Coney Island" which eclipsed all efforts of
other black producers.   Billy Johnson's "The Black 400 Ball" was
introduced and "At Jolly Coney Isle," "Song of the Bathers," "Red
Hots," and "Play 4-11-44" were also big hits.   After a dispute with
Voelckel, Johnson and Cole left the show and conceived the idea of
producing a musical comedy of their own.   Their project, with the
help of Tom Brown, Jesse Shipp, and Bob A. Kelly, was launched
in the season of 1898 and was the first complete original black musical comedy on the American stage and was entitled "A Trip to
Coontown" in three acts.   Although the opening performance of the
production was a hit at the Catskills in New York State, the company soon hit a snag.

Their funds had been exhausted in staging the presentation.
In the meantime Ernest Hogan had succeeded them as the strong
featured star in Black Patti's Troubadours and many white theatre
managers made it hard for them to get bookings in the better theatres.   In the meantime, Cole and Johnson discovered Sam Croker,
a bright young man from the South who had theatrical inspirations
and was industrious and had managed to save a considerable sum of
money.   They took in young Croker whose money was put in the
show.   Although they were all broke, the play was beginning to attract attention.   It was later that a man by the name of Cook took
over the management and the company met with big success just in
time to meet the distinct competition of the Williams and Walker
company which had just been launched by the two comedians and
which was beginning to make a hit at Koster and Bial's Music Hall
in New York City.

Among the songs Bob Cole and Billy Johnson wrote together
and made famous in "A Trip to Coontown" were "There's a Warm
Spot in My Heart for You," "You'll Have to Choose Another Baby
Now," "Wedding of the Chinese and the Coon," "The Luckiest Coon
in Town," "In Dahomey," "The Way to Kiss a Girl," "Sweet Savannah," "Ma Chicken," "I Hope These Few Lines Will Find You Well,"
and "For All Eternity."   Bob Cole who played the tramp and Billy
Johnson who played the bunco man were the distinct stars.   After

the first real successful season Jesse Shipp and Bob A. Kelly retired from the company. Jesse Shipp had left to write and stage plays for Williams and Walker. Cole and Johnson immediately hired Sam Lucas to replace him. It was perhaps the third season of the successful tour that Bob Cole became very ill and had to retire from the company for many weeks. Billy Johnson continued on the road with the show. When Cole recovered and returned to the show he accused his partner of financial disloyalty and the two comedians separated. Cole soon entered vaudeville with J. Rosamond Johnson.

Billy Johnson opened in vaudeville in New England but his pride and reputation were crushed as a result of the dispute with Cole. He later married and moved to Chicago where he temporarily retired from the stage to write songs and stage productions. In the meantime, he tried his hand at politics running for County Commissioner in Chicago in 1908, but he was defeated. He then returned to vaudeville with a big act including girls, which he did in addition to song writing and staging shows.

When Tom Brown returned from Europe because of the First World War, he and Billy Johnson joined hands to produce one act plays and on Monday, November 6, 1914 they opened at the Grand Theatre in Chicago in "Twenty Miles from Home," a musical comedy with Mattie Wilkes in the leading female role. The comedy was a hit and Billy Johnson did his old graceful stick dance. This play was followed by the Pierot Minstrels in which Billy Johnson made his last stage appearance. At the time of his death in 1916, Johnson had been working on the music and lyrics for a burlesque show for Mr. Friedenwald, the white manager of the Honolulu Girls, which took to the road on the day of Johnson's death. Johnson died as a result of a fall from the balcony of the Pioneer Club then located at 3512 State Street in Chicago.

CHARLES AND DORA DEAN JOHNSON

Charles Johnson and his beautiful partner and wife, Dora Dean, were one of the best-known vaudeville dance teams in the gay '90's and early 1900's. They were not only very talented, but also were considered to be the best dressed dance team on the American stage. They were the first black dance team to play Broadway in 1897, and the first dance team, white or black, to wear evening clothes on the stage. That was at Hammerstein's Roof Garden in 1901.

Mr. Johnson made his first appearance on the stage at Brown's Theatre in Minneapolis in an amateur show in 1889. Later he joined up with Sam T. Jack's "Creole" show in St. Louis at a salary of $7 a week and room and board. Dancing in the chorus of the "Creole" show was shapely Dora Dean Babbige whose brother had been the first black judge in her home state of Kentucky during Reconstruction following the Civil War. Johnson fell madly in love

with Dora Dean and made her his partner after he got the idea of
forming a dance team.

After the couple had learned their routines, they left the
"Creole" show for vaudeville bookings and were an almost immediate success; in 1893 they were married.

As their fame grew in the United States and abroad, so did
their reputation for fine clothes. On April 8, 1901, the New York
Telegraph called them the "best dressed team in vaudeville" and
the next year the Boston Globe marvelled at one of Dora's gowns:
"It must have bankrupted a thousand dollar bill." At the peak of
their success, many of Dora's gowns cost more than $1000 each
and they were copied by Lillian Russell, Sarah Bernhardt and other
big names on Broadway.

Overseas it was the same. In Germany, artist Ernest von
Heilmann bought Dora Dean's theatrical contract so she could pose
for him. The picture was exhibited throughout America after it
was first unveiled at the coronation of King Edward in London in
1902.

The team's bookings in Europe included two months a year
for five years in Berlin's Wintergarten, three summer months for
three years in Budapest, and two months for three years in London's Palace Theatre. They also played six weeks at the old Madison Square Roof Garden and three months every summer for three
years at Hammerstein's Roof Garden in New York City.

Harry Bradford, a writer with the Indianapolis Freeman,
wrote the following about the performance of Johnson and Dean
presented at the American Theatre, New York City, October 10,
1909:

> In the first part Johnson and Dean enter with a pretty
> little song, "I Wouldn't Leave My Little Wooden Hut for
> You." Mr. Johnson wore a black fall dress suit of the
> latest pattern, while Miss Dean wore a pretty evening
> coat of costly appearance, with a beautiful pair of dia-
> mond earrings in her ears, and presented a fine appear-
> ance. They finished the first part of their present of-
> fering with soft-shoe dancing a la Charles Johnson, to
> good applause. Second part: Mr. Johnson enters in a
> salmon-colored broad cloth suit, and Miss Dean enters
> in a long train dress. They sing "Billy, I Love You,"
> while Johnson does some wing dancing that brought down
> the house. Third part: Mr. Johnson enters in a suit
> of an English soldier. I think the uniform of a private
> solider--I am not positive, but I've seen the Canadian
> soldiers wear similar suits. Miss Dean enters in white
> tights, and they sing and dance, the song being "I'm an
> English Coon." Mr. Johnson did some clever and origi-
> nal dancing at the finish of his act that won the team a
> great many encores.

While at the top of their fame, the team and the marriage split up. This was in 1910, after Dora decided that she wanted her own show and Charles wanted his. They both went out with acts consisting of four men and four women. During the next few years, Johnson appeared on the same bills with name performers such as Bert Williams, Bessie Smith and Florence Mills.

In 1934, Dora Dean went to Hollywood to do an all-black film, "Georgia Rose," and while there she decided to contact Charles Johnson about going back to him. She did, and they revived their old act and played Connie's Inn in New York City, and subsequently toured the country.

The revival was shortlived, however, because by that time vaudeville was giving way to motion pictures and the impeccably-dressed couple returned to Minneapolis where they lived quietly until Dora Dean's death on December 13, 1949.

HALL JOHNSON

Hall Johnson, who was the founder of the famous Hall Johnson Choir, was born in Athens, Georgia in 1888 and was the son of a minister who later became president of Allen University, Columbia, South Carolina. Johnson was educated in the South, the University of Pennsylvania, and at the Institute of Musical Arts in New York. He organized the Hall Johnson Choir in December 1925, and it made it's first public debut outside of Harlem over two years later and immediately achieved a reputation which spread across the country. Serving as director of the spirituals in the original production of "The Green Pastures," Johnson was determined to work out in dramatic form the community background in which black spirituals were born. The result of this effort was his first play "Run Little Chillun" in 1933. Johnson was the author, composer and arranger of the play's incidental music, but did not appear in the cast. The play was also successfully produced in Los Angeles in 1938. Hall Johnson and his Choir provided the music for a number of Hollywood films including "Green Pastures," "Lost Horizon," "Way Down South," and "Cabin in the Sky." Hall Johnson died in 1971.

SISSIERETTA JONES
(BLACK PATTI)

Madam Sissieretta Jones, who was best known by her stage name, Black Patti, was born Matilda Joyner in Portsmouth, Virginia on January 5, 1870. Her father, J. M. Joyner, was pastor of the Afro-American Methodist Church of that city and was also the choir director. In this latter duty, he was assisted by his wife who at the time was a soprano of exceptional ability. In 1876, Mr. Joyner received a call to come to Providence, Rhode Island, where the family later moved.

Hall Johnson

As a small child, Sissieretta Jones developed a voice of
such remarkable power and quality that she was soon in great demand to give concerts in the churches of Providence.   By 1888,
Mme. Matilda Jones was gaining attention as a result of her brilliant concert appearances in the East.   In April she made her first
New York appearance at the Bergen Star Concert performed at
Steinway Hall.   A month later, she created a great impression at
a concert at the Academy of Music in Philadelphia.   In August of
the same year, Mme. Jones and a company of black singers sailed
for Jamaica, arriving in Kingston on the 10th.   They opened at the
Royal Theatre to an overflow house which included J. C. Johnson
the Governor.   They gave sixty performances in Jamaica and then

Sissieretta Jones (Black Patti), circa 1905

traveled through the neighboring islands, playing to packed houses. After that they crossed the Isthmus of Panama, stopping at Aspinwall, where they played a week at the celebrated Sarah Bernhardt Theatre.   Then they played Panama for two weeks and Mme. Jones was a tremendous success.   Nightly the stage was covered with floral tributes presented by the ladies; she also received seven solid gold medals during the tour.

After playing Panama, they went to Colon, Trinidad and to Barbados.   From there to Dutch Guiana, they played a week to an audience who did not speak or understand English.   The last stop was at St. Kitt where the chorus made a hit singing jubilee selections.   They were abroad for about six weeks.

Upon her return to the United States, she was selected to appear as the stellar attraction of the Grand Negro Jubilee at Madison Square Garden in April 26-28, 1892. Her performance at this concert was so sensational that the New York Clipper, then one of the leading theatrical newspapers in the country, gave her the name by which she later became world famous, "Black Patti." For her one week's engagement at the Pittsburgh Exposition, Major Pond demanded and received $2000, which was at the time the highest salary ever paid a black artist. Other performers appearing on the same bill included Campanini, Materna, and the famous Pat Gilmore.

As her fame spread along the East Coast, she received an invitation from then President Harrison to appear at a private concert in the Blue Room of the White House on February 25, 1892. The selections presented were "Cavatina" by Meyerbeer, "Suwanee River," "Waltz," and "Home Sweet Home." Professor Charles Dunger accompanied her on the piano. Mrs. Harrison, the President's wife, was so delighted that she personally presented Mme. Jones with a bouquet of White House orchids. The White House concert was followed by numerous invitations to appear at the houses of other Washington notables.

Morris Reno, then President of the Carnegie Music Hall Association of New York City, next engaged Sissieretta Jones for a concert tour of the United States and Europe under the management of R. Voelckel, who at the time was Reno's associate. She made her first European appearance at Berlin, Germany, and the Berliner Zeitung, in commenting upon her debut, said: "No sooner had the real Adeline Patti departed than a most worthy substitute appeared in the person of Madama Sissieretta Jones, 'The Black Patti.'"

The European engagement lasted about 18 months, and no singer was ever received with greater enthusiasm and applause. London, Paris, Berlin, Cologne, Munich, Milan, and St. Petersburg seemed to vie with each other in their approval, and the Continental newspapers fairly showered the most favorable praise on her voice and art. While in London, Mme. Jones received a royal command to appear before King Edward, then the Prince of Wales, who expressed the most delight with her performance.

When Mme. Jones returned from Europe, her managers, Voelckel and Nolan, decided to put her out in al all-black show. They engaged Bob Cole to write it and the show went on the road in 1896 billed as "Black Patti's Troubadours." At first the show followed the minstrel pattern with the first part being a sketchy farce interspersed with song and chorus ending with a buck-wing dance contest. Then followed an olio. The finale was entitled, "The Operatic Kaleidoscope" and it was in this part that Black Patti appeared singing operative selections with the chorus. She took no other part in the show.

The following review of "Black Patti's Troubadours" appeared in the December 12, 1896, edition of the Indianapolis Freeman:

Vaudeville, comedy, burlesque, and opera interpreted by
fifty of the best artists ever organized for this style of
entertainment will be the stage offering of "Black Patti's
Troubadours" on the occasion of their performance in this
city.   The company is practically a double one with
"Black Patti" as the star of the operatic and singing forces
and Tom McIntosh, the greatest of all ebony comedians as
the leader of funmakers.   The first part of the entertainment is devoted to the comedy forces which include Henry
Wise, Bob Cole, and Stella Wiley, delsartean dancers,
Billy Johnson, descriptive vocalists, Goggin and Davis,
knock-about acrobats, Kingsbury and Cousins, instrumentalists, May Bobee, the Creole nightingale and a chorus of
thirty pretty girls with well trained voices.   "At Jolly
Coney Island" is the title of the opening skit which introduces the company on the "Bowery" of this famous resort,
a scene which has been faithfully reproduced on canvass
by Harley Merry and sons, and which was painted from
sketches taken on the spot.   Here is where the fun begins
and where the audience is led to view all the humorous
characteristics of this resort by the sea.   The skit, to
use a theatrical term, is full of "hot stuff, " song, story
and dance in which the entire company took part.   This
travesty is followed by a great vaudeville olio and selections from the various standard grand and comic operas.
In the operatic olio Black Patti has great opportunities to
display her wonderful voice.   She sustains the principal
roles of "The Grand Duchess, " "Carmen, " "Bohemian
Girl, " "Trovatore, " "Lucia, " "Maritana, " "Tar and Tar-
tar, " and "The Daughter of the Regiment. "   The rendition
which she and the entire company give of this repertorical
opera selections is said to be incomparably grand.   Not
only is the solo singing of the highest order, but the
choruses are rendered with a spirit and musical finish
which never fail to excite genuine enthusiasm.   The work
of Black Patti and the company has received the highest
marks of public approval, and the forthcoming performances
here will doubtless be highly appreciated.

Later the shows took on more of a conventional musical
comedy format with a story and the billing of the company was
changed to "Black Patti Musical Comedy Company. "   About this
time, Mme. Jones was given small speaking parts, but she remained the featured singer.

In the season of 1905, the Black Patti Troubadours made
their second tour of California.   The Los Angeles Daily Times had
the following to say about one of their performances:

A Colored aggregation of genuine fun-makers is shimmer-
ing across the footlights of the Grand this week.   A year
ago they were here, and made hundreds laugh.   They have
come back, and apparently the luster of humor is undimin-
ished.

Chief among the celebrants is John Rucker, a Negro so homely that a single look at his black countenance is enough to make one laugh. Rucker had great vivacity and inexhaustible stock of facial contortions, and jokes which-- if not new--are told in a humor creating way.

Sissieretta Jones--"Black Patti"--is a handsome colored woman possessed with a melodious soprano voice, beautifully trained and entirely unworn. She sings with artistic discretion, confining her efforts almost entirely to simple genre melodies. Whether she is "Black Patti" first, second or third, makes little difference--she can sing.

The remainder of the company deport themselves in musical comedy fashion, extracting an average amount of uproariousness from their time and situations.

For more than twenty years the famous Troubadours with Black Patti as the star toured every season and established their popularity in the principal cities of the United States and Canada.

Mme. Jones retired from the stage around 1920 and lived quietly in her home in Providence, Rhode Island until her death in 1933.

BOBBY KEMP

Bobby Kemp was born in Galveston, Texas in 1867, and showed a decided preference for the stage while still a young lad, much to the chagrin of his father.

Kemp first began to attract attention as a performer while a member of the team of Moore and Kemp. Later, his work with McCabe and Young's Minstrels demonstrated his exceptional talent. He was next seen with the Black Patti Troubadours and other road companies.

For a number of years, Kemp enjoyed success over the big time vaudeville circuits, appearing with Mae Kemp in an act billed as The Kemps. At one time he filled a short engagement in vaudeville with Aida Overton Walker, actress and wife of the famous George Walker.

In the fall of 1919, the Kemps left New York City to work in vaudeville theatres in the West and Midwest. While playing in Kansas City, Missouri in January 1920, Bobby Kemp suddenly lost his voice and became too ill to continue the performance. He was taken to Chicago where he recuperated until September 1920, when the Kemps once more returned to the stage. Soon after, however, Bobby Kemp became seriously ill and later died in June 1921.

BILLY KERSANDS

Billy Kersands, America's greatest minstrel performer, was

Billy Kersands--Foremost Comedian of the Minstrel Era, circa 1899

born in Baton Rouge, Lousiana in 1842 and went to New York City
at an early age. His first engagement was with Callender's Georgia
Minstrels. Later the Callender show was sold to J. H. Haverly
and, with Kersands as principal comedian, made a tour of Europe,
under the management of Charles Frohman, where the show appeared
before the crowned heads of numerous countries. Upon his return
to America, Kersands organized the Hicks and Kersands Minstrels,
touring the United States for five successful seasons before the
partnership broke up. Kersands then joined the Richard and Pringles
show with which he remained for many years as principal comedian.

After the death of Richard and Pringles, the company was
taken over by Rosco and Holland, who retained Kersands as star,
traveling the country for several seasons. After the dissolution of

this firm, the Kersands Minstrels were launched and ran for four successful seasons.

During his long career Kersands circled the globe several times. His last tour abroad was with the Hugo Brothers Minstrels. Starting at Honolulu, the show covered the entire Orient.

At the time of his death, Mr. Kersands was under the management of Nigro and Stevenson of the Dixie Minstrels and was running his own show. Death came suddenly, Kersands appearing to be in perfect health. Kersands was appearing with his company and doing the biggest business of the season and he had been working with more vim and vigor than he had been for weeks. After his last performance, he returned to his private railroad car, as usual, and had just seated himself for a short chat before retiring when he fell over dead. This was on June 29, 1915.

Sam Lucas wrote the following article about his friend Kersands in the August 15, 1915 edition of the New York Age:

> Forty-one years ago Callender's Georgia Minstrels was a body of strong and healthy men numbering twenty-one, but Father Time has mowed them down until there is only one stalk left standing in the field. Of the members of that splendid company, I am the sole survivor. It is mine to take up the melancholy task of writing a word of remembrance and farewell to my friend and associate of former years. As I have said, the death of Billy Kersands leaves me the sole survivor of Callender's original Georgia Minstrels. We were together in 1872, 1873 and part of 1874, during which period we toured the principal towns and cities throughout the United States. At that time the stars of the organization were Bob Hight, Billy Kersands, Pete Deavenear, Dick Little, and Sam Lucas. In our band parade before the show Billy would be on one side and I on the other, leading the procession. Being young, we were both natural mashers and at that time the minstrels were the people of the land.
> Billy was unfortunate in the matter of an early education. He could neither read nor write. I took great delight in teaching him his songs for the stage. Among them were "Angel Gabriel," "Old Aunt Jemima," and "Mary, Gone with a Coon." As he sang them in his unique way it was beyond the power of imitation. Nature had done much for him in natural talents and originality. Billy's big mouth and skill with which he handled it and his pretty teeth were a great asset. It was the songs he sang and the smile he wore that made the sun shine everywhere.
> I often sit and think of the funny stories he used to tell me of himself and the old folks at home when he was a boy. Among them, one of his duties was to fill and light his grandmother's pipe, which task had to be performed many times a day. Billy, by way of diversion and occa-

sion, placed a little charge of gunpowder in the bowl of
the pipe, piled the tobacco upon it, lighted it and passed
it to his grandmother. The mild explosion which ensued
gave her a great shock and him amusement.

His main specialty was his dance, "The Essence of
Old Virginia." In that dance he would lie flat on his
stomach and beat first his head and then his toes against
the stage to keep time with the orchestra. He would look
at his feet to see how they were keeping time, and then
looking out at the audience he would say, "Ain't this nice?
I get seventy-five dollars a week for doing this!"

Billy Kersands' reputation was surpassed by none. In
the South, after Callender's and Haverley's shows were
gone he was excelled by none as a single star. The reputation he made in Europe was equally great. Billy was
born in Baton Rouge, Louisiana seventy-three years ago.
He died a few weeks ago of heart disease at Artesia, New
Mexico.

The minstrel was the first door of entrance opened to
Negroes on the American stage, just as now men and
women of the race possessing unusual talent for serious
roles of legitimate drama are compelled to confine themselves to comedy.

But it will not be many years before the new public will
applaud the rise of the curtain upon the Negro actors and
musicians who will shine as stars of the first magnitude
both as composers and performers of the highest forms of
amusement and entertainment that have ever given interest
to the stage.

By some strange fate I stand alone, the last of that
merry company which was the first of our race to amuse
the fun-loving public. On Billy Kersands the curtain has
now gone down for the last time.

FORD WASHINGTON LEE   see   JOHN WILLIAM SUBLETT

SAM LUCAS

Sam Lucas, who was considered the dean of black theatricals
in the early 1900's, was born in Washington, Fayette County, Virginia on August 7, 1848, of poor parents who were formerly slaves
belonging to Samuel Lucas of Rommey, Virginia after whom Lucas
was named. During Lucas' childhood he attended public school for
five years, and was then put to work as a farmhand, which was his
occupation until he was nineteen years old.

He then went to Cincinnati, Ohio and became a barber. It
was during this period that his initial taste for music developed.
He first attracted attention while connected with Hamilton's celebrated Colored Quadrille Band as guitarist and caller. In 1869,
Lucas went to New Orleans and taught school for a few months,

Sam Lucas, circa 1905

but it was not long before he went to St. Louis where he made his initial appearance as a minstrel performer with Lew Johnson's Plantation Minstrels as middle man and balladist. After about three weeks, the minstrel company disbanded and he was left stranded. However, it was not long before he again returned to the stage joining Jake Hamilton's minstrel company as general performer where he made a hit in the original role of "Hungry Jake."

In 1871, Lucas returned to St. Louis and again joined Lew Johnson's company. This time the company remained on the road a year, after which Lucas returned once more to teaching school.

On July 4, 1873, Lucas became a member of the Original Georgia Minstrels as a ballad singer and general manager. His first act to gain prominence was "The Vegetable Peddler" which made a hit. The enormous success enjoyed by the Georgia Minstrels throughout the West and South was such that similar minstrel companies were formed. The Georgia Minstrels were first brought to New York City in 1874 where it did a big business.

Later in 1874, Lucas joined the Hyer Sisters in the musical comedy "Out of Bondage" which was one of the first musical shows to be produced by a black theatrical organization. The show was in two acts and had six characters. It was in the role of "Mischievous Henry" that Lucas made his first big hit.

After leaving the Hyer Sisters, Lucas joined the ranks of the variety (vaudeville) artists and had the distinction of being the first black man to appear in what later became legitimate vaudeville. His work consisted of comic and motto songs, monologues and dancing. At Ben Trumble's Variety Theatre, Lucas played one week as the principal drawing card to record-breaking business. Subsequently, Lucas starred in a blood-and-thunder play entitled "The Black Diamonds of Molly McGuires" but the show lasted only four weeks. His appearance in the show surrounded by a white cast marked the first time a black starred in a melodrama.

Later Lucas was selected to play the part of Uncle Tom in the C. H. Smith Double "Uncle Tom's Cabin" company, being the first black man to fill the role. The author of the book, Harriet Beecher Stowe, witnessed a production of the piece and afterward wrote Lucas a letter stating that his conception of the character of Uncle Tom was better than any she had seen. Lucas remained with the company until 1879.

Later, Lucas went to Boston where he remained until 1899 working as a single in vaudeville. He was finally engaged by the Bergen Concert Company. It was with this organization that he met Miss Carrie Melville of Providence, Rhode Island, whom he married after a brief courtship. Soon after, they formed a musical act and played all the principal variety halls. During this time, he conceived the idea of producing a Creole Show and sought to interest several black men with money in the project, but was not

successful in interesting anyone of them to back the show. It was
at the Olympic Theatre, Denver, Colorado where the Lucas act
played for nine months that Mr. Lucas met and talked with Sam T.
Jack, a white man, and told him of the idea he had for a black
show. Jack thought the proposition was a good idea and organized
a company headed by Mr. and Mrs. Lucas which was known as Sam
T. Jack's Creole Company. Lucas and his wife remained with the
show for three years and then went abroad, appearing in vaudeville,
and opening at the Oxford Theatre, London, England. They were an
instant success and played for three months. They remained in
England for six years and enjoyed success everywhere.

Upon their return to America, they were starred in A. G.
Fields' Darkest American Company, but they became dissatisfied
within a few months and left the aggregation.

Sam Lucas' next big engagement was with Cole and Johnson
in "A Trip to Coontown" where he played the part of "Silas Green."
Later, Lucas played "Brother Doolittle--On the Board of Education"
in Cole and Johnson's "Shoo Fly Regiment" and later appeared as
"Bill Webster" in Cole and Johnson's "The Red Moon."

After Cole and Johnson's Company was disbanded, Lucas was
a big feature on the Loew vaudeville circuit doing a monologue.
Later he was engaged to play the part of Uncle Tom in the movie
version of "Uncle Tom's Cabin." In one of the scenes in this picture, Uncle Tom had to jump into a partially frozen river to save
little Eva. As a result of this action, Lucas caught pneumonia and
did not recover; he died in New York City on January 15, 1916.

TONY LUCAS

In 1859, when John Brown made his memorable attack on the
slave holders at Harper's Ferry, West Virginia, Tony Lucas was a
youngster of nine in France. He was born in Indiana in 1850 and
went to France with his parents as an infant and did not return to
America until he was a lad of fourteen. He attended the public
schools of Columbus, Ohio immediately following the Civil War and
was constantly ridiculed by his classmates because he spoke with a
French accent.

After leaving the public schools, he worked at various odd
jobs before returning to France, where he continued his education.
He later returned to America and completed his education at Wilberforce University in 1897.

Lucas began acrobatic tumbling while a youngster in France
and performed professionally as an acrobatic dancer in vaudeville.
During his long career on the stage, he saw the black theatre rise
from a few blackface comics to large musical comedy companies
and hundreds of vaudeville acts. Lucas retired from show business
in 1928 at the ripe old age of 78.

CECIL MACK

Cecil Mack, who was the first black music publisher in New York City, was born in Norfolk, Virginia. His real name was Cecil McPherson. He attended Lincoln University in Pennsylvania, class of 1902, but left in his junior year because of a shortage of funds. He then went to New York City where he found a job and earned enough money to enter the University of Pennsylvania Medical School, but stayed only one semester.

He returned to New York in about 1905 and met George Walker who encouraged him to enter show business. In the latter part of the 1920's he organized the Cecil Mack Choir which made its debut in Lew Leslie's "Blackbirds." Mr. Mack also wrote many songs including the hit of Aida Overton Walker, "I'm Miss Hanna from Savannah" and "That's Why They Call Me Shine." He also wrote music for Bert Williams and the score for Miller and Lyles' "Runnin' Wild" in collaboration with James P. Johnson.

DEWEY "PIGMEAT" MARKHAM

Dewey "Pigmeat" Markham was born in Durham, North Carolina on April 18, 1906, where he attended West Durham High School. He wrote and acted in school plays and after graduation he traveled with carnivals for five years before joining Ganzel White's Minstrel Show in which Count Basie was a pianist.

During 1925-1927, he toured with A. D. Price's "Sugar Cane" revue. Price later became one of the leading undertakers in Richmond, Virginia.

Markham acquired the nickname "Pigmeat" during his minstrel days with White because he featured a song entitled "Sweet Papa Pigmeat."

Markham's first New York appearance was a year and a half stay at the Alhambra Theatre. He later appeared at the Standard Theatre in Philadelphia, and then went back to Broadway where he appeared in "Hot Rhythm" in 1930 and "Cocktails of 1932." He played Harlem's Apollo Theatre for three years between 1935 and 1938. He was a featured performer in Lew Leslie's "Blackbirds of 1939," "Sugar Cane" and "Extatic Ebony" produced in 1939 by Ralph Cooper.

In 1938 Markham went to Hollywood and was featured in several black-cast films including "Mr. Smith Goes Ghost," "The Big Mistake," and "Am I Guilty?" opposite Ralph Cooper. He also played the role of a butler in the RKO production "That's My Baby," and appeared in "Moonlight and Cactus" with the Andrews Sisters.

In 1940 Markham went back to the Apollo for a short run

then back to the coast for a two-year run at the Lincoln Theatre in
Los Angeles.   At about the same time, he played the role of "Ala-
mo, " chief cook in the Andrews Sisters radio show "Eight to the
Bar" for 16 weeks and later for a short engagement at New York's
Paramount Theatre in their stage production.

After the show closed, he appeared at the Regal Theatre in
Chicago and then returned to the Apollo where he played 15 weeks
and teamed with John Bunn, Jr., a native of Birmingham.   He later
added Sybil Lewis to the act.   Before joining Markham, Bunn had
appeared in musical comedies, films and radio.   Markham's first
partner was Johnny Lee Long who died suddenly after a performance
at the old Minsky Burlesque House in New York in 1934.

In 1947 Markham returned to Hollywood and was featured in
"House Rent Party" produced by Toddy Pictures.   Markham also has
made numerous comedy phonograph albums during his long career
in show business.

JOHN MASON

In 1940 John (Spider Bruce) Mason was one of the last of a
then vanishing breed of blackface comedians.   He was born in
Spartanburg, South Carolina and was reared in Gaffney, South Caroline.   He made his stage debut in 1910 when he joined the Joeney
Pierce's Carnival which opened in Winston-Salem, North Carolina
and played for three weeks.   When the show closed, Mason found
himself stranded, but a friend, Carter Lockhart, paid Mason's fare
to Charlotte, North Carolina where Mason worked in a vaudeville
house for several weeks with Walter Long.

Later, Mason and Long joined a state fair which was held at
Spartanburg, South Carolina where they worked twenty-two shows a
day.   Mason then joined a show in Augusta, Georgia where he slept
as well as acted in a tent.

After that, Mason joined the Honolulu Minstrel where he met
a friend, Hambone Jones, who was the star of the show.   After a
successful run, Mason joined the Johnnie J. Jones Carnival and
stayed with the show for three years.

During Mason's long stage career, he worked with almost all
of the leading black entertainers and appeared in many hit shows including "Brown Buddies" with Bill Robinson and several editions of
"Blackbirds. "

WILL MASTIN TRIO see SAMMY DAVIS, JR.

LIVINGSTON MAYS

Livingston Mays, who managed the first black carnival

company in America, was born in Nashville, Tennessee. His first
venture in show business began when he was about 12; he paid a
magician to teach him a few tricks. Soon, he began to invent some
tricks of his own. In 1903 he opened a movie and vaudeville theatre in Columbia, Tennessee which he named "Livingston" after himself. Because at the time the T. O. B. A. and other vaudeville booking agencies had not yet been formed, presenting worthwhile attractions was not only costly, but almost impossible and the theatre
failed.

Mays' next undertaking was the organizing of the Jubilee
Minstrels which consisted of 30 performers and traveled under can-
vas throughout Tennessee, Georgia, and other parts of the South.
This show discontinued after two seasons and Mays, not being discouraged, put together a few magic tricks and illusions and traveled
throughout Louisiana, Indiana, Georgia and Tennessee giving performances in schoolhouses, churches and halls. Mays then worked
in minstrel shows in connection with several circuses.

Mays was one of the first to join Dao Michael when the latter formed the first all black carnival company to play black state
fairs in the south. Later, the entire troupe left Michael and persuaded Hill, then owner of a New York City taxi company, to take
over the management of the show. Because of Mays' years of experience and wide knowledge of the carnival game, Mays was made
general manager. The carnival carried four shows consisting of a
minstrel, illusion show, and Hawaiian show. There were also a
number of rides and about 30 regular concessions which were augmented by a number of game operations. The route of the show
included Manassas, Suffolk, Virginia, Greensboro, North Carolina
and other states in the South. In the winter the company played
indoor engagements for various fraternal orders.

BILLY McCLAIN

Billy (or Billie) McClain was one of the most talented and
versatile performers on the American stage. He was one of the
first actors to write and star in his own plays including "Down on
the Suwanee River," "Before and After the War," "From the Jungles
to the Senate," and "The Black Politician." He was also the author
of the following popular songs: "Pretty May," "Don't Forget Mother
at Home," "Hand Down the Robe," "Dar's Gwine to be a Great
Resurrection," "Phonograph De News," and "The Old School House."
At one time he was the amusement director and stage manager of
"Black America," amusement director and stage manager of "South
Before the War" and he was one of the feature performers in Pain's
"Storming of Vicksberg."

McClain was born on Elm Street in Indianapolis, Indiana on
October 12, 1866. As a boy he played cornet in Bell's Band and
made his first public appearance at Crone's Garden in 1881. His
first professional appearance came with Lew Johnson's Minstrels in
1883. Soon after this engagement he joined Heck and Sawyer's

"BILLIE" M'CLAIN.

William McClain, circa 1894

Minstrels and later went with Blythe's Georgia Minstrels. In 1886
McClain joined Sells Brothers Circus which toured the Hawaiian Islands. In 1887 he took out the Gigantic Comedy Company which was
forced to disband in Texarkana, Texas. Next he joined Cleveland's
Minstrels in 1890 and toured the United States and Canada in 1891.
He also had successive engagements with Lewis Turner's Company,
the Nashville Students, Hyer Sisters, Whalen's "South Before the
War," Callender's Minstrels, and Jas. Pane and Sons. In June
1894, McClain went west with Davis and Kehoe's "On the Mississippi," a comedy drama company consisting of 50 people, two car loads
of scenery, one huge alligator and two horses.

     Sometime in the early 1890's, McClain married Cordellia
Scott who was a very talented actress in her own right. Miss Scott
made her professional debut in 1889 with the Nashville Students
where she remained for two seasons before leaving to join the
Hyer Sisters' Company. Next John Whalen convinced her to join
the "South Before the War" company where she remained three seasons. During the season of 1898, William Hawarth, who wrote "On
the Mississippi," was looking for the best talent for Messrs. Davis
and Kehoe's first production of this play and happened to see a performance of "South Before the War" at the old Niblo's Garden, New
York City. After giving the performers careful study he approached
Mrs. McClain and engaged her for the new show. She soon became
one of the leading actresses of the company. Later, Edward J.
Nugent selected her to join Billy McClain in the "Suwanee River"
which was her first starring role in the big production. In the seasons of 1897 and 1898, he was prima donna in Vogel's "Darkest
America."

     In the season 1899-1900, McClain, his wife, and Ernest
Hogan joined Curtis' Afro-American Minstrel Company for a tour of
Australia. The July 12, 1899 edition of The Referee, Sidney, had
the following comments about the show:

> Mr. Curtis' Afro-American Minstrel Company entered
> upon its second week on Saturday night, when there was a
> splendid house and most of the items on the very lengthy
> programme were new. The dual scene, which concluded
> the first part, between Mr. "Billy" McClain and Mr.
> Ernest Hogan, aroused great merriment. The same cou-
> ple of artists also kept the house in splendid humor by
> their antics in the "Rag Time Opera," while the former
> who is practically the life and soul of the show contributed
> several coon songs and gags in his own inimitable fashion.
> Miss Madah A. Hyer, "The Bronze Patti," was heard to
> great advantage in a couple of operatic selections; The
> Kentucky Four did some exceedingly clever buck and wing
> dancing and Siren, the lilliputian creole contortion
> danseuse, twisted and twirled in a risque and an alarming
> fashion. The performance concluded with the laughable
> Cake Walk in which the competition between the various
> couples was very keen.

After returning from Australia, McClain and Hogan organized the Original Smart Set Company under the management of Gus Hill. After Hogan left the show the featured role was played by Tom McIntosh. After McIntosh's death, S. H. Dudley moved into the starring role.

In 1906, McClain and his wife went to Paris where they remained for many years playing the French Music Halls and Clubs.

In the April 2, 1910, edition of the Indianapolis Freeman was published the following letter written by Billy McClain in Paris:

Looking back to former as well as present triumphs, it has been my fate to be the first of my race to accomplish everything that I have done that is worthy of note, whether good, bad, or indifferent. To begin with, I was the first boy to sell the Indianapolis World and the first colored page in the Indiana Senate Chambers before the present Court House was built. I was the first to write the Freeman on theatrical news, the first boy cornet player in the old Indianapolis Capitol City Band under George Bell. Dan Palmer and I were the first acrobats and trapeze performers out of Indianapolis. Later, with Cleveland's Minstrels, Tom Brown and I were the first to do a sketch of a Chinaman, and a "Coon" in Kansas City in 1887 at the Gaiety Theatre, where colored performers' reputation extended from Walnut Street to Independence Avenue, an area of ten blocks. The stars were Tom Brown, Dave Jackson, Johnny Coats, Walter Smart, George Williams, Harry Goodman, Al Ackman, Ambrose Lewis, Dan Palmer, Palmer Carroll, Burt Grant, Coley Grant, Frank Kennedy and about every four dark faces you saw was a quarter, including yours truly.

I was the first to put on a cake walk on the stage, with the Hyer Sisters. Harry Stafford was with the show and I introduced him to Anna Hyer. Then I called it a "walk around." After that I produced it with the "South Before the War" and called it the "cake walk." It has become famous all over the world. I produced and starred in "Suwanee River" and the first to write and to do the same. I produced the "Black America," with 365 colored people, including Victor Herbert and band all under my direction. I wrote and starred in the Smart Set. I was the first colored man to open a music hall and picture show in St. Louis.

I am the first Negro to produce, play, sing, dance, and talk in French. It seems so strange that it always falls to my lot to break the ice, but there is one thing that I am sure of not being first in, and that is the finish.

After returning from France in 1913, Billy McClain settled in Tulsa, Oklahoma where he secured half ownership of the Tulsa Star, then one of the leading black newspapers in the West.

After retiring from show business, McClain and his wife moved to Los Angeles where he died in 1949.

TOM McINTOSH

Tom McIntosh, pioneer black actor who reached the height of his popularity during the era just before and after 1900, was born in Kentucky. He joined a minstrel show as a teenager and later enjoyed his first success with Callender's Georgia Minstrels on tour in America and in England. When the Company returned to New York from Europe and opened at the Fourteenth Street Theatre, the press was lavish in its praise of his performances.

After Callender's Minstrels had disbanded and after a short season with Hicks and Sawyer's Minstrels, W. C. Cleveland engaged him as principle comedian of his all black minstrels at a salary of $100 per week. James Bland, the famous black composer, was with the company at the time. After W. C. Cleveland's Minstrels closed, McIntosh joined hands with Willie Ganze, a female impersonator of great renown. As a team, McIntosh and Ganze played over all the leading vaudeville circuits and theatres of the country. Finally, the "Great Ganze," as Willie was billed, was engaged and featured with Rusco and Holland's Georgia Minstrels. McIntosh's next team venture was with his wife, Hattie, whom he married soon after he and Ganze had parted. He had a hard time breaking her into being an actress, but her sweet contralto voice and beauty carried her to success. When their maiden vaudeville tour was over, they joined Harry S. Eaton's Afro-American Vaudeville Company as leading features, but for a short season only.

When John W. Isham's Octoroons were organized with Mme. Flower and Fred J. Piper as the stars, Tom and Hattie McIntosh were engaged as special features and remained with the company for several seasons.

McIntosh, who was of light complexion and always blacked up his face, gave up burnt cork for a while and put on a new act--that of a red-nosed drunkard--and scored a lasting hit. This act, with the assistance of his wife, proved to be a masterpiece. His next venture was a starring tour in a farce comedy entitled "A Hot Old Time in Dixie." This company remained on the road for one season and finally had to close. It was said at the time that in this venture Tom McIntosh lost a great deal of money.

After this tour was over, Tom and his wife worked separately. Hattie McIntosh joined the last Isham Octoroon Company (after John W. Isham had retired) under the management of Will Isham. The company featured Billy Kersands in a vaudeville comedy entitled "King Rastus" with the Mallory Brothers and Smart and Williams as stars and with scenery owned by a Miss Belle Davis, who later foreclosed on the company because of nonpayment on the scenery.

Tom McIntosh returned to minstrelsy and worked with the
Mahary Company and other shows.   Later, he worked as a monologue specialist in Graham's Southern Specialty Company.   Next,
he entered vaudeville alone, but was soon engaged by Gus Hill to
replace Ernest Hogan in the Smart Set Company to play the principal part in "Southern Enchantment. "   He was employed in this
capacity at the time of his death in 1904.   His wife, Hattie, was
on tour with the Williams and Walker Company in London at the
time of his death, which occurred on a train en route from Indianapolis, Indiana to Columbus on March 2.   He was 64 years of age.

FLORENCE MILLS

The following poem was dedicated to the late Florence Mills,
who died November 1, 1927.

<u>All the World is Lonely</u>
<u>(For Our Little Blackbird)</u>

All the World is Lonely
    For a Little Blackbird
For our one and only
    Little Florence, so dear
We Thought so much of her,
    Angels up above her,
Wonder if they love her
    Much as we love her here.
Poor little Blackbird,
    You've never been so blue,
Your little Blackbird
    Can sing no more for you.
Heaven had the power,
    Took a precious flower,
Sadness rules the hour
    Left us only in tears.
                    --Andy Razaf

Florence Mills was unquestionably one of the greatest American entertainers of the twentieth century.   During her brief career
on the stage, she captivated audiences all over America and abroad.

Florence Mills' first big show engagement came at the age
of eight at the Bijou Theatre in Washington, D. C. , when she appeared in a production of the "Sons of Ham. "   She was billed as
"Baby Florence Mills, an Extra Added Attraction" and she sang
"Miss Hannah from Savannah. "   This song was taught to her by
Aida Overton Walker, pioneer show performer and wife of the
famous George Walker.   She was a big hit and was encored for
her dancing.   During the early stages of her career, she did quite
a bit of entertaining, often appearing before "The most exclusive
set in Washington" and she had captured cakewalking and buck dancing championships by the time she was six.   Soon after her initial

stage debut, she joined the Bonita Company and later travelled for several years as one of the "picks" with Lew Hern.   After leaving the latter company, she and her two sisters, Olivia and Maude, formed the Mills Sisters team.   The trio eventually dwindled to Maude and Florence and then, after Maude left the act, Florence teamed with Kinky Clark to form "Mills and Clark."   Next, she joined the Panama Trio consisting of Cora Green, Ada Smith and Florence.   The trio played the Pantages Circuit from coast to coast for three years.

Following the Panama Trio, Florence Mills joined the "Tennessee Ten," remaining with this show for four seasons.   It was during this engagement that Miss Mills met and married U. S. Thompson, then one of the leading comedians and dancers of the company and formerly of the team of Thompson and Covan (Willie).

After the Tennessee Ten closed, Florence Mills and U. S. Thompson decided to team up in vaudeville.   Soon after, Florence was called to take the female lead in "Shuffle Along" in 1921, replacing Gertrude Saunders.   She scored so heavily that she came into immediate demand by several white Broadway producers. Florence later left the "Shuffle Along" company and joined Lew Leslie who placed her at the lead of "Plantation Revue," which included Paul Robeson.   Leslie later took the troupe to London where they were well received by the British.

In 1925 she got her first break on Broadway in "From Dixie to Broadway."   The cast of this show included Shelton Brooks, Hamtree Harrington, and others.   Her next hit show was "Blackbirds," produced by Lew Leslie.   Following a successful New York season, Miss Mills led the show to Paris, France where it was the acclaim of the populace.   Lew Leslie, who had Miss Mills under contract, later took the company to London where it opened at the Pavilion on May 14, 1926.   The company played for a solid year without missing one of 300 performances.   While there, it was heralded as the smartest revue that had come from America.   The Prince of Wales visited the show numerous times.   Miss Mills' popularity was so great that dolls were named for her and the shops designated light brown goods as the Florence Mills shade.

"Blackbirds" left the Pavilion on June 1, and began a tour of the provinces after a short run at the Strand Theatre.   Miss Mills left the company to take a much needed rest and vacation in the States.   Her place in the revue was taken by Mabelle Mercer, a black English performer.   During her stay with the company, Miss Mills caused a wave of "Blackbird" songs which later earned thousands for publishers.   On her return passage to the United States in the latter part of September, accompanied by her husband, U. S. Thompson, Miss Mills was honored by the passengers which included Jimmy Walker, then the Mayor of New York City.

After her return, a bid was made for her services by Leonard Harper, then a leading Harlem nightclub producer.   Club

Ebony and other smart clubs around New York were also vying for
her appearance, when she was stricken with a fatal illness.

While in London, Miss Mills was interviewed by the Sun-
Chronicle regarding her career in show business.   The following is
the concluding part of that interview:

> But it was a hard struggle.   I know for I have been through
> it.   For years before I became a success and the white
> people smiled on me, I struggled against adversity and
> prejudice.
> When I was born, I was just a poor pickaninny, with
> no prospects but a whole legacy of sorrow.   My parents
> were far too poor to afford me a good education, and it
> was obvious that I would have to fend for myself.
> One day, when I was playing in the street with a num-
> ber of other children, a white comedian who was appear-
> ing close to my house saw me and took a fancy to my
> face.   From him I learned my first song "Don't Cry My
> Little Pickaninny. "
> That was the beginning.   At the age of four, I ap-
> peared with him on the stage with the proud intention of
> singing my little song.   Half-way through I saw a black-
> faced comedian standing in the wings waiting to go on.
> His make-up was so startling that I broke off in terror
> and had to be led off the stage weeping bitterly.
> From the age of eight when I appeared in a production
> called the "Sons of Ham" it has just been one long fight
> for success.   Always there was the bogy of my color bar-
> ring the way.   That I was able to win through it all was
> due to sheer determination to rise superior to prejudice.

Florence Mills died in New York in 1927.

ABBIE MITCHELL

Abbie Mitchell was one of the most accomplished actresses
on the American stage.   Born in 1884, she studied voice as a
youngster under Harry T. Burleigh who later placed her under Mme.
E. Serrano with whom she studied for four years.   At the tender
age of fourteen, she left a Baltimore convent to audition for Will
Marion Cook's "Clorindy. "   She eventually took over the leading
role and later married the composer of the piece.

Abbie Mitchell was a member of the original "Nashville
Students" which starred Ernest Hogan.   When the show toured
Europe, the name was changed to "Tennessee Students. "   Abbie
Mitchell was not only a prima donna, but a clever soubrette as
well.   She had a beautiful voice and proved to be a singing sensa-
tion during the show's European tour.   After the show closed, Miss
Mitchell remained in Europe for a concert tour which lasted be-
tween 1905 and 1908.

After returning to the U.S., she did a short concert tour and later joined the second edition of the "Students"--the "Memphis Students"--in which she starred with Tom Fletcher. During the same period she was the prima donna of Cole and Johnson's "Red Moon" company and later she played vaudeville dates and concerts.

Later, Miss Mitchell retired from musical comedy to study music theory and harmony under Metville Charlton. Later she went to Paris where she studied for two years.

After returning to America, Miss Mitchell turned to the stage and soon after became one of the leading performers with the famous Lafayette Players Stock Company in New York City. One of her early successes with the company was "Madam X" and "Help Wanted." In 1926 she had a leading role in the Pulitzer Prize play "In Abraham's Bosom."

Miss Mitchell also spent several summers at the Hodgeman Theatre in Philadelphia under the direction of Jasper Deeter. Later she joined the "Little Foxes" company and also appeared in "Coquette" which starred Helen Hayes. This play had a long and successful run on Broadway.

For three years Abbie Mitchell taught at Tuskegee Institute in Alabama where she also assisted with dramatics. During the American Negro Exposition in Chicago, she was the technical advisor for the production "Cavalcade of the Negro Theatre" in which she also played the role of Abbie Mitchell.

Abbie Mitchell died in 1960 at age 76.

CHARLES L. MOORE

Charles L. Moore, an original member of the Lafayette Players Stock Company, was born in North Carolina in 1870. When he was quite young he was brought to Brooklyn where he was reared and received his schooling. He joined Williams and Walker's company as a baritone singer and later was engaged as the personal representative of the two famous comedians, looking after their financial interests at the box office of the theatres where the show played. Moore severed his connection with Williams and Walker in about 1905. From 1915 until his death in 1919, Charles Moore was a featured player with the famous Lafayette Players Stock Company at the Lafayette Theatre in New York City.

TIM MOORE

Tim Moore, who is best known for his role of "Kingfish" on the Amos and Andy television show, also was in the famous "Chicago Follies" company. Moore was born in Rock Island, Illinois, where in early life he decided that he wanted a life of show business.

He was first inspired by the original Nashville Students, a black-cast musical extravaganza which played in his home town many times.   He was seven years old when he saw this show and the very next day staged a show in his father's barn.

At twelve he ran off and joined Dr. Mick's medicine show. Dr. Mick was at the time well-known throughout the Middle West. His medicine could cure, as it was then said, anything from hard-ening of jello to the landlord's heart, and Tim Moore would sing and dance on a platform in the lot to attract those who sought en-tertainment for nothing.   Moore saw so much medicine sold that he was glad to get away from the good doctor and join up with Cora Miskel and her Pickaninnies.   He and Romeo Washburn were the original "gold dust twins" in this act and they won special acclaim both in America and in Europe.

About the same time, horse racing began to appeal to the youthful Moore and he quit the stage to become a jockey.   For a time this life appealed to him, but when he saw his first prize-fight, he thought the ring offered more adventure and excitement and he donned the boxing gloves.   He began as a featherweight un-der the name of Kid Noble and finished his boxing career in the middleweight division.   His best fights were in the lightweight divi-sion against Young Klondike, whom he defeated in twelve rounds, and against Jimmy Shannon, to whom he lost in 27 rounds at Muscatine, Iowa in 1908.

In 1908 Tim Moore returned to the stage and created a sensation doing a one-man edition of "Uncle Tom's Cabin."   With one-half of his face in white chalk and the other half in burnt cork, Moore turned the white side of his face to the audience when he spoke the lines of Simon Legree, and turned the other side when he spoke as Uncle Tom.

Again the lights of the stage lured Moore and soon he was in vaudeville with his first wife, Hester Moore.   The two proved so successful that they toured Japan, Australia, China, New Zea-land, Hawaii and the Fiji Islands.   Then followed some more vaude-ville dates with his second wife, Gertie Moore, until he produced Tim Moore's Chicago Follies, a black musical which played the T. O. B. A. circuit from 1921 to 1925.   Ed Daly, then a well-known show promoter, saw him in his own show and signed him as the star of "Rarin' to Go."   He also was featured comedian in "South-land Revue" in 1927.

Lew Leslie, in seeking a black comedian for "Blackbirds," thought Tim Moore was the best in his field.   So in 1928, for the first time in his life, Tim Moore appeared on Broadway.   In 1932 he was featured with Mantan Moreland in "Harlem Scandals" and "Blackberries."   Later in his career he continued to play night-clubs in a comedy act and in the early 1950's he starred in the Amos and Andy television show.   Tim Moore died at age 71 in Los Angeles, California.

MANTAN MORELAND

Mantan Moreland, who is best remembered for his more than 300 film appearances, received much of his early stage experience in the all-black musical comedies and revues in the late 1920's and early 1930's. He was born in 1901 in Monroe, Louisiana and when he was fourteen years old, ran away from home to join a circus followed by a short stay with Huntington's Minstrels. Moreland's comic genius began to surface when he played second comedian to Tim Moore and Flournoy E. Miller in such shows as "Connie's Inn Frolics of 1927," the 1928, 1930 and 1932 editions of "Blackbirds," "Chocolate Scandals," "Cotton Club Parade" which starred Lena Horne, "Shuffle Along of 1933" and "Singing the Blues."

Mantan came to Hollywood in 1935 with Flournoy E. Miller. Joe Louis (former heavyweight boxing champion of the world) got him a role in "The Spirit of St. Louis," an all-black film. Mantan wrote and appeared in the first all-Negro "horse opera," "Harlem on the Prairie," with Herb Jeffries as the singing cowboy. He also appeared in a number of films produced by Toddy Pictures and Dixie National Pictures.

Mantan made a total of 310 screen appearances, most with the major motion picture companies. One of Mantan's special routines which he became famous for in the Charlie Chan picture series was what he called his "indefinite" routine, which he performed with Benny Carter. One would begin a sentence, the other would interrupt, and the exchanges would lead into mental brick walls. Nothing made sense to the viewer, but it did to them.

One of Mantan's trademarks was his pop-eyed expression and his line, "Feets, do your stuff."

Mantan worked Harlem's Apollo Theatre in the 1940's and 1950's with Redd Foxx. He was the featured comedian in the black-cast show "Rhapsody in Rhythm" in 1945. In 1957 he appeared on stage in New York in a black production of Samuel Beckett's "Waiting for Godot." He played Estragon (Gogo). Reviewing the production for the New York _Times,_ Brooks Atkinson praised the veteran comic's performance for bringing to the role "a suspicious joyousness of manner, a crack-voiced laugh, a teetry walk, a general feeling that he is the one who is going to be slapped."

Mantan also appeared in such television shows as "Love American Style," "Adam 12," and "The Bill Cosby Show." In 1953 Mantan Moreland hosted a short-lived variety show series on TV. The programs were seen on WOR-TV in New York City. The series was called "Club Mantan" and featured some of the most popular black performers of the time.

In 1959, Mantan, in an article for a Cleveland newspaper, stated that he would "never play another stereotype, regardless of what Hollywood offers." In Mantan's view, "The Negro, as a race,

has come too far in the last few years for me to dash his hopes,
dreams, and accomplishments against a celluloid wall, by making
pictures that show him to be a slow-thinking, stupid dolt. " Mantan
also said, "Millions of people may have thought that my acting was
comical, but I know now that it wasn't always so funny to my own
people. " "I'll work in Movies anytime they want me to play a role
that shows me to be as intelligent as all the other characters. " In
the same article Moreland contended that up to that time he and
Stepin Fetchit were the only Negro actors who held longtime Hollywood contracts. Other Negroes had picture contracts, but this did
not guarantee weekly checks when work was slow.

Mantan Moreland died in Los Angeles on September 28, 1973.

MOSS AND FRYE

Arthur G. Moss and Edward Frye were one of the best
vaudeville comedy teams in show business. They were not only
talented performers, but also produced several shows including
"Dumb Luck. " Moss came from a family of actors and singers
and he was the first black to graduate from high school in Fairfield,
Iowa. He continued his education at Parson Presbyterian College
and, after graduation, Moss joined the Georgia Minstrels and was
one of the featured performers.

Frye, who was the older partner, was born in Lawrence,
Kansas and was a veteran of the Spanish American War. He met
Moss in 1912 and they decided to form an act and try vaudeville.
In the 1920's, they were one of the best known comedy teams play-
ing the Keith circuit. Following the success of Sissle and Blake,
Miller and Lyles' "Shuffle Along, " Moss and Frye starred in "Dumb
Luck" in 1922, and later appeared in a black film short of the same
title. The stage production was presented by Louis Rosen, a theatrical costumer, who formed the Louis Rosen Producing Company
with A. G. Moss as the manager. The show carried a cast of 90
including such well-known performers as Revella Hughes, Ethel
Waters, Rubie Mason, Inez Clough, Cleo Desmond, Justa (toe
dancer), Ethel Williams, Lottie Tyler (niece of Bert Williams),
A. B. Comathiere, J. Lawrence Criner, Jesse A. Shipp, and a
ten-piece orchestra directed by Robert W. Ricketts. The show
opened on the road at Stamford, Connecticut on September 11, but
it was a failure and closed for good on September 23 at Worcester,
Massachusetts, stranding the entire cast without sufficient funds to
return to New York City.

It happened that the "Shuffle Along" company was playing in
Boston, and when the producers, Messrs. Miller, Lyles, Sissle and
Blake, were informed of the financial difficulties of the "Dumb
Luck" company, they, after working their own show, jumped in
their car and traveled to Worcester. There, they contacted Moss
and offered financial assistance towards getting the people of the
company back to New York. However, Moss and his attorney,
M. B. Marshall, refused the offer.

The following Saturday, the situation for the "Dumb Luck" company became desperate and William C. Elkins, who was with the company as director of the chorus, phoned Noble Sissle long distance and informed him of the situation.

The "Shuffle Along" producers forgot all about the contemptuous reception given their voluntary offer of aid, and Mrs. Sissle went to Worcester bringing with her $400 which she gave to Mr. Elkins. This money enabled 50 of the "Dumb Luck" cast to return to New York City. Shortly afterwards, an additional $300 was sent and the remaining members of the "Dumb Luck" company were able to return to New York.

Arthur Moss died in 1932 at his home at 150 West 118th Street in New York City and was survived by his partner.

CLARENCE MUSE

Clarence Muse was born October 7, 1889, in Baltimore, Maryland, the son of Alexander and Mary Muse. He studied at Dickinson College at Carlisle, Pennsylvania where he graduated in 1911 with a degree in International Law. After leaving school, he put aside his lawbooks for a career in music. His start in show business was in 1912 when he performed as a singing entertainer on the Hudson River boats and in Palm Beach cafes. After closing out the season in Palm Beach, Muse was introduced to the owners of the Airdome Theatre (theatre without a roof) in Jacksonville, Florida. As the owners were in debt, Muse bought into the show using a large sum of money he had won playing cards. It was there that he first met Tim Moore who was doing a one-man edition of "Uncle Tom's Cabin" and who later became the "Kingfish" of Amos and Andy TV series.

Clarence Muse first gained notice on the stage as a member of the Freeman-Harper-Muse stock company at Frank Crowd's Globe Theatre in Jacksonville, Florida, in 1912. The company's big hit play of this season was entitled "Stranded in Africa." The play was written by Frank Crowd and Clarence Muse portrayed "King Gazu," a role in which he demonstrated his creative make-up artistry. The roster of the company for this engagement included: J. D. Taylor, tenor and character man; William Burrell, character and straight; Otis Hall, tenor and comedian; Oscar Hagamin, pianist and female impersonator; Leonard Harper, straight and female impersonator; Essie Whidby, leading lady; Lulu Whidby, chorus; Lucile Nelson, soubrette; Annie Morgan, chorus; Gussie Freeman, character lady; Clarence E. Muse, character, secretary and business manager; George Freeman, comedian, stage manager, producer.

The season of 1910 found Clarence Muse and his wife, Ophelia, in vaudeville billed as the Two Muses and playing the black theatres on the East Coast. It was during this period that the Muses teamed with Lillard Pugh and formed the Muse and Pugh Stock Company at the Franklin Theatre in New York City. After a

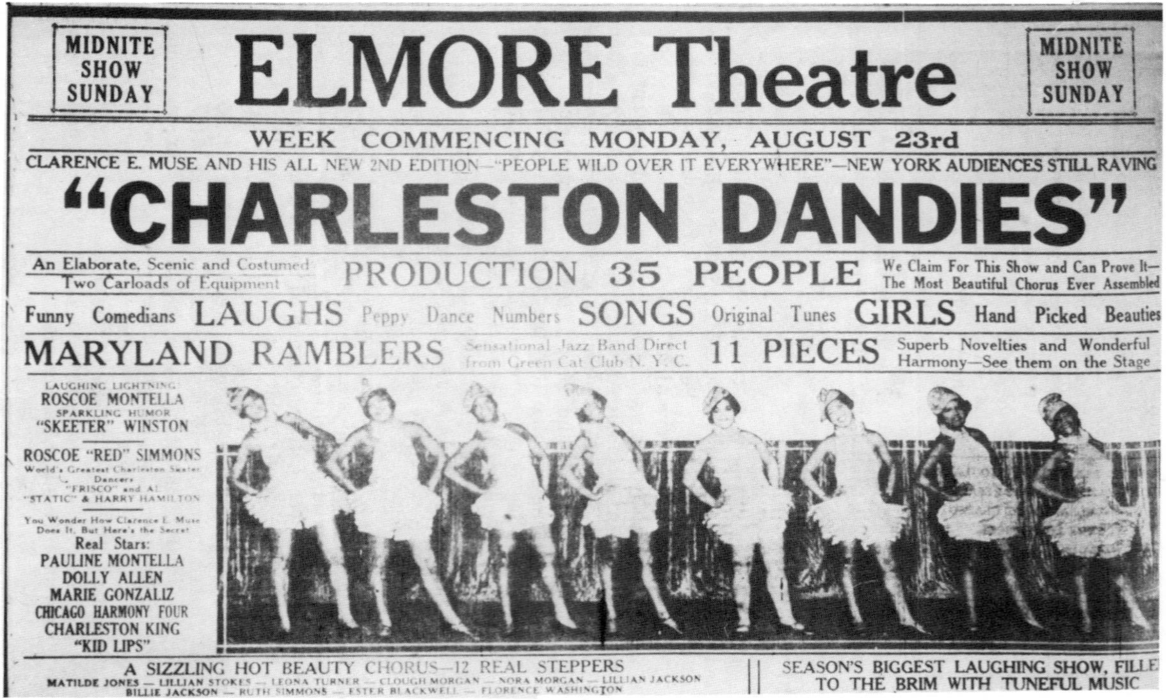

Ad for Clarence Muse's "Charleston Dandies," circa 1926

successful engagement of several weeks, the Muses moved to the
Crescent Theatre in New York City where they organized the Crescent Players.   Their first production was entitled "Another Man's
Wife. "   Their plays drew large crowds and significantly improved
the financial situation of the theatre.   In addition to the stock company, the Muses act also included two vaudeville artists, a singer,
Edmona Adison, and the team of Hodge and Lauchmere.   The stock
company's production of "Another Man's Wife" had Mrs. Muse playing an orphan girl and Clarence in the role of the comedian and
masher.

Shortly after Anita Bush moved her company of dramatic
players to the Lafayette Theatre in February 1916, Billy Burke organized the New Lincoln Stock Company which included Clarence and
Ophelia Muse, Walker Thompson, Charles F. Olden, Margaret Scott
and Cecil Jones.   For the next several months the Lincoln and Lafayette stock companies staged a new dramatic production every
week and vied with each other for the patronage of the black upper
class in Harlem.   During this period the most successful production of the Lincoln players included "Golden Heart, " "The Man Who
Came Back, " "Lena Rivers, " "The Savage, " "Paying the Price" and
"Parson Bill. "

Muse joined the Lafayette Players in October 1916 in a play
entitled "Fine Feathers" and because of his brilliant performance
his place among the famous players was secure.   In the 1916-1917
season, Muse received high critical acclaim for his performances
in "The Master Mind" and "The Escape. "   Other members of this
talented company included Charles Gilpin, J. Francis Mores, George
Demerest, Helen Morris, Andrew Bishop, Mrs. Charles Anderson,
Cleo Desmond, C. Creighton Thompson, and Bob Slater.

Muse became the first black of the American stage to make
up as a white man, using wigs and a facial preparation of his own
devising.   He remained with the Lafayette Players for several years
and his notable characterizations included the dual title role in "Dr.
Jekyll and Mr. Hyde. "   He repeated his Jekyll-Hyde interpretation
for Los Angeles audiences years later after he came to Hollywood
to perform in pictures.

Muse appeared in a long succession of dramatic roles, including the priest in the opera "Thais" which was presented in
Chicago and St. Louis.   He directed and supervised the production
of "Thais" with a cast of 190 black actors.

In 1921 Muse became one of the directors of the Del Sarte
Film Company.   In the same year Muse and other actors and directors of the company went to Vicksburg, Mississippi where they made
the all-black film "The Custard Nine. "

Muse later settled in Chicago and put on shows for the Royal
Gardens owned by Virgil Williams, a black businessman who organized the Royal Gardens Motion Picture Company and who later

brought Louis Armstrong and others from New Orleans to introduce
the Chicago patrons to the new Jazz craze.   One of his big shows
was the "Chicago Plantation Revue" in 1921.   In 1922 Muse directed
and produced the black show "Hoola Boola, " and "Ramblin' Round"
in 1923.   His next big show was the "Charleston Dandies" in 1926,
which toured the country playing T. O. B. A. time.

Muse's first motion picture experience came in 1929, when
he was invited by William Fox of Fox Studios of Hollywood to appear in the role of "Nappus" in the second all-talkie movie "Hearts
in Dixie. "

After completing a 12-week contract with the studio, Muse
remained in Hollywood where later he gained new acclaim when he
sang the title role in the DuBose Heyward play "Porgy. "   Muse was
also the first director for the Federal Theatre Project and produced
"Run Little Chillun" which was written by Hall Johnson.   The play
had a two-year run in Los Angeles and a later revival on Broadway.

Muse has composed a number of songs and is a member of
the American Society of Composers, Authors and Publishers.   His
best known song is "When It's Sleepy Time Down South, " a peren-
nial favorite.   He also wrote "Muse a While, " taking the title from
the name of his 160-acre dude ranch which is located between Per-
ris and Lake Elsinore in Southern California.

In 1938 he collaborated with Elliott Carpenter on the lyrics
and music for the film "Spirit of Youth. "   In this film he played
Joe Louis' manager and coached Louis on his dialogue and acting.

In 1940 he was featured in the black film "Broken Strings, "
and he also coauthored the screenplay.   In 1921 he wrote the screenplay for "The Sport of Gods, " a black film based on a story by Paul
Laurance Dunbar.

During World War II he served as an executive member of
the Hollywood Victory Committee, which arranged for the appearances of screen stars before overseas troops and in camps and
hospitals.   He also was a member of the Hollywood Writers Mobili-
zation, preparing material for propaganda and entertainment uses.
He made a series of hospital tours, entertaining soldiers throughout
the war.

In 1933, Clarence originated an annual memorial radio program for the late Evelyn Preer.   Muse prepared and directed the
program which was broadcast over KRKD in Los Angeles, California.

In 1972 the Honorary Degree of Doctor of Humanities was
conferred on Muse by Bishop College, Dallas, Texas for his contribution to the arts and humanities.   In June 1978, he was awarded
the Honorary Degree of Doctor of Laws by his alma mater, the
Dickenson School of Law.

At age 88 Muse was still active in films, and his Muse-A-While Ranch was a mecca for young writers and actors seeking to "sit at the feet" of one of the pioneers of the American stage and screen. He died in November 1979 at age 90.

NICHOLAS BROTHERS

Harold and Fayard Nicholas are considered one of the most talented and best known dance teams in the history of American entertainment. Growing up in Philadelphia, the Nicholas Brothers were sons of musicians who had their own band and frequently played John Gibson's Standard Theatre. It was there that the older brother, Fayard, used to set in the front row every night so that by the time he was ten he had seen almost all of the famous black entertainers and shows. He taught himself to dance by imitating famous dancers like Bill Robinson and performing acrobatics and clowning for the kids in the neighborhood. Harold, six years younger, first learned to dance by imitating his older brother, but it wasn't long before he had developed a style of his own.

The young Nicholas Brothers were dancing prodigies and their unique dancing style was so popular that they soon gained prominence in Philadelphia that led to their first professional engagements at the Standard, Pearl and other local theatres. It was during this time that the manager of the Lafayette Theatre saw them and immediately signed them to play the famous New York City Playhouse.

The fourteen-year-old Fayard and eight-year-old Harold created a sensation at the Lafayette. Immaculately attired in top hat and tails, the brothers sang and danced with such brilliance that they captivated the hearts of their Harlem audiences.

Leaving the Lafayette, the Nicholas Brothers opened at the Cotton Club where they were first seen by whites who also were thrilled by their dazzling dance routines which included spins, flips and tap dancing to the jazz tempo of "Bugle Call Rag." During their successful two-year stay at the Cotton Club, they performed with many of the country's top orchestras including Duke Ellington, Cab Calloway, Lucky Millinder and Jimmy Lunceford.

During their first year at the Cotton Club in 1932, they made their film debut in a black-cast film short, "Pie Pie Blackbirds," with Eubie Blake and his Orchestra and the beautiful Nina Mae McKinney. Two years later, they went to Hollywood to appear in Sam Goldwyn's "Kid Millions" with Eddie Cantor. After returning to the Cotton Club for a short engagement, they went back to Hollywood where they were cast as Dot and Dash in the film "The Big Broadcast of 1936." During this time they made three more all-black cast musical shorts: "Black Network" with Nina Mae McKinney and Amanda Randolph, "All Colored Vaudeville Show" with Adelaide Hall, and "Dixieland Jamboree" with Cab Calloway and Adelaide Hall.

The Nicholas Brothers made their spectacular debut on Broadway in "The Ziegfeld Follies of 1936" which included such stars as Fannie Brice, Bob Hope, Eve Arden, and Josephine Baker.   Their act stopped the show so frequently that Fannie Brice, who followed in a skit with Judy Canova, was always forced to fall back regularly on a line at her first opportunity: "Do you think we can talk now?, " and this made the audience laugh and then quiet down.

The year 1937 found the Nicholas Brothers touring England with a production of "Blackbirds" and after returning to the United States they appeared in the Rodgers and Hart musical "Babes in Arms" during the 1937 Broadway season.

Back to the Cotton Club in 1938, the Nicholas Brothers came into competition with the Berry Brothers, another famous black dance team.   In a legendary confrontation, the two teams engaged in a "dance-off" which is now part of show business history.

During the next few years, in addition to their nightclub appearances, they appeared in several Hollywood films including "Down Argentine Way" (1940), "The Great American Broadcast" (1941), "Sun Valley Serenade" (1941), "Orchestra Wives" (1942), and "Stormy Weather" (1943) in which they performed their amazing, leapfrog staircase number.

Next, they returned to nightclubs and later toured South America and Europe before performing in the Broadway musical "St. Louis Woman" in 1946.

From 1958 to 1964, the Nicholas Brothers did not perform together.   Harold lived in Paris while Fayard toured the United States and Mexico doing a single.   Back together again in 1964, the brothers performed in Las Vegas and made many television appearances.   In 1965 they performed for the U. S. troops overseas.

In 1976 they were inducted into the Black Filmmakers Hall of Fame at the third Oscar Micheaux Awards Ceremony held in February at the Paramount Theatre in Oakland, California.

MURIEL RAHN

Muriel Rahn was a graduate of Tuskegee and the music school of the University of Nebraska.   She made her professional debut about 1929 as a singer with Eva Jessye's "Dixie Jubilee Singers. "   A few months later, she was engaged to perform in "Blackbirds of 1929" as an understudy for the female leads and as a foil to the comedians in some of their sketches.   In 1930, Miss Rahn was cast in "Connie's Hot Chocolates" with many other headliners such as Cab Calloway, Edith Wilson, Roland Holden, Five Crackerjacks, and Billy Higgins.   She sang Fats Waller's hit song "Ain't Misbehavin' " with Cab Calloway.   In 1933, Miss Rahn made appearances at the "Chez La DuBarry" in Paris, where she was the

acclaim of the Parisian critics.   Shortly after her return, she appeared in the Broadway play "Come of Age" with Judith Anderson
and several editions of "Hot Chocolates" at Connie's Inn.

AMANDA RANDOLPH

Amanda Randolph, who started out in show business at an
early age, was born in Louisville, Kentucky.   She began her career
at age fourteen in Cleveland.   She was a musician as well as an
actress and appeared in nightclubs and musical comedies.   Between
1926 and 1932, she also appeared in many hit shows including "Joy
Cruise," "In the Alley," "Chili Peppers," "Dusty Lane" with Clinton "Dusty" Fletcher, "Fall Frolics," "Radiowaves," and she toured
Europe in 1930 with the Scott and Whaley show.   In 1932, Amanda
and Catherine Handy (daughter of composer W. C. Handy) were
billed as the Dixie Nightingales and sang in several shows including
Glenn and Jenkins' Review.

She succeeded her sister, Lillian Randolph, in the role of
the housekeeper on "The Great Gildersleeve" radio show, and she
played the maid "Louise" for eleven years on the Danny Thomas
television show.   She also played the role of the "mother-in-law"
on the Amos and Andy radio show.   Her motion picture credits include "No Way Out" and "She's Working Her Way Through College"
as well as "Lying Lips," "Swing" and "Comes Midnight."   She died
in 1967.

EDDIE RECTOR

Eddie Rector, one of America's greatest soft shoe and tap
dancers, was a major influence on many dance teams of the 1920's.
He was born in Orange, New Jersey on December 12 in the late
1890's.   His first professional job in show business was as a pickaninny with Mayme Remington at the age of fifteen.   In 1914, he
played the role of "Red Cap Sam" in J. Leubrie Hill's "My Friend
from Kentucky," replacing Eddie Stafford.   Later he formed a
partnership with Toots Davis and went on tour on the T. O. B. A.
circuit.   After this, Rector teamed with his wife, Grace, and still
later with Ralph Cooper.   Rector's next big show appearance was
in "Dixie to Broadway" where he introduced his "Bambousa" dance
routine.   In 1928, Rector took Bill Robinson's place in Lew Leslie's
"Blackbirds" on a tour abroad.

On his return to the United States, Rector worked with Duke
Ellington at the Cotton Club in New York City where he originated
the routine of tapping on a big drum.   This routine was later made
famous by Bill Robinson in the film "Stormy Weather."   Later in
1930, he performed at Sebastian's Cotton Club in Los Angeles where
he played the trumpet and led the house band.   Later, back in New
York City, Rector appeared in the shows "Hot Rhythm" in 1930 and
"Yeah, Man" in 1931.   In the late 1940's and early 1950's he again

Eddie Rector

teamed with Ralph Cooper.   Eddie Rector died in 1962.   Like King
Rastus and Jack Ginger Wiggins, Rector was never given full recognition as one of the major influences on American dance.   As Ethel
Waters said in her book "His Eye Is On the Sparrow":   "White people never saw them, but that's the white folks' loss. "

C. LUCKEYTH ROBERTS

C. Luckeyth Roberts, whose song hit "Moonlight Cocktail"
was the number one American song hit of World War II and sold
over one million recordings by Bing Crosby and Glenn Miller, was
born in Philadelphia, Pennsylvania on August 7, 1893, the son of
William and Elizabeth Roberts.   By the tender age of five, Roberts
had learned to sing, dance and play the piano and later was engaged
by Gus Sulky for theatres.   One night his father saw him perform
for the first time dressed only in a raffia shirt.   Enraged, Roberts,
Sr. , stopped the show.   The packed house roared, thinking the scene
was part of the show.

Later, relenting, his father took him to hear Lonnie Hicks,
then the leading pianist of the day, and the youngster was entranced.
Mr. Hicks advised him to keep up his playing and study hard.
Roberts gave Hicks credit for starting him on his career of music
and helping him often in the early days.

Next season, young Roberts joined the Mamye Remington
company as a "Pickaninny. "   He went to Europe three times with
her and Gus Sulky.   The latter paid him $1.25 weekly plus room
and board and tutoring, and sent his father five dollars weekly for
five years.

On December 28, 1911, Roberts married Miss Lena Stanford
of New York City when both were in their teens and traveling with
J. Leubrie Hill's My Friend from Dixie Company.   Later, Mrs.
Roberts appeared with Roberts' band as a soloist.

In 1912, the seventeen-year-old Roberts wrote a syncopated
tune he called "Ripple of the Nile, " but it did not catch on.   Thirty
years later, the tune, now "Moonlight Cocktail, " was the number
one hit of the nation.   From the night when Glenn Miller and his
Orchestra introduced the number over New York's Station WABC,
the song was among the first ten tunes on the Hit Parade.   In
March 1942, it was weekly No. 9, No. 7, and No. 8; in April,
No. 6, No. 5, and No. 4; in May it swung between No. 4 and
No. 7.   Variety hailed it as "No. 1 all over the nation. "   Bill-
board gave it a leading position for several weeks.   The New York
Enquirer listed it as No. 1 in sheet music sales of the Eastern
States and the West Coast, and No. 2 in the Middle West.

On April 11, Glenn Miller thanked the men of the armed
forces for sending in letters and cards which voted "Moonlight
Cocktail" the Glenn Miller No. 1 Hit of America.   On April 18,

Mary Martin sang it over the radio for Hollywood to the armed forces of the nation.   Horace Heidt, Tommy Tucker, Reichman and His Orchestra, Dolly Dawn and her Dawn Patrol, and several other popular bands soon followed Glenn Miller and Bing Crosby in recording it.   In short, "Moonlight Cocktail" was the song of wartime America.

In 1913, as a result of the efforts of Lester Walton, Roberts began his successful partnership with Alex Rogers which lasted until September 1930, when Rogers died.   During that period, they were among the leading song writing teams of the nation, with Rogers writing the lyrics and Roberts composing the music.   They wrote successful numbers for such famous show folk as Molly Williams, Nora Bayes, Bert Williams, Al Jolson, Sophie Tucker, and Marrie Cahill.   Among their great shows were "Baby Blues," "This and That," "Follies of the Stroll," and "Magnolia."   They were the leading song writing team for the Quality Amusement Company and wrote John Cort's successful musical "Go! Go!" which thrived on Broadway nine months before taking to the road and was known as the fastest white show on record.   Roberts did the finale of Florenz Ziegfeld's Follies called "Midnight Frolic Glide" which clicked on the New Amsterdam Roof for two continuous seasons, 1916-1917.

Rogers and Roberts wrote all the material for the radio show "Two Black Crows," featuring Moran and Mack, which was broadcast every Sunday night at 9 p.m. over Station WABC for several months.   Both Rogers and Roberts worked in the sketch, with Roberts playing piano solos and Rogers playing a character in the skit.

Some of the song hits that made the name of Roberts and Rogers internationally famous were "Shy and Sly," "Helter Skelter," "Bon Bon Buddy," "Bon Ton," "Why Adam Sinned," "Railroad Blues," and the "Elder Eatmore Sermons," immortalized by the great Bert Williams.

Every winter between 1924 and 1930, Roberts and his entertainers were in Palm Beach, Florida.   He was the first black to be regularly mentioned in the leading papers there, except in connection with a lynching.   At the time, he was getting paid about $1700 for a single engagement and his musicians were among the highest paid in the profession.

Roberts performed his first Carnegie Hall concert on August 30, 1939 and received excellent reviews from his critics.   Among his patrons was Mrs. Franklin D. Roosevelt.   A second concert was held at Town Hall on May 28, 1941.   This concert almost failed to come off, for on July 1, 1940, Roberts was involved in a serious automobile accident in which his jaw, his right hand and both feet were broken.

Roberts retired from show business in the late 1940's and

opened a club in Harlem which he managed for several years before
his death in 1948.

BILL "BOJANGLES" ROBINSON

    Bill Robinson was born in Richmond, Virginia on May 25,
1878.   His mother and father died when he was very young and he
lived with his grandmother.   Robinson attended the public schools
of Richmond until he was eight years old when he and his grandmother moved to Washington, D. C. , where Bill got a job in a racing stable.   After working hours he earned a bit of change tapping
out syncopated rhythms on beer garden floors.

    His professional career was launched in 1908 when he be-
came a vaudeville performer and teamed up with George Cooper.
A booking agent, Marty Porkins, saw their act and signed them.
The Cooper-Robinson combination broke up and Bill became a "single. "   The nickname of "Bojangles" was given to him by a pal in
1914.

    Not long after he won the name "Bojangles, " he was a vaude-
ville headliner and star of black musicals.   His salary hit $2000
per week and he became known as the greatest of all tap dancers.
Although he was not accepted, Bill tried to enlist for the Spanish-
American War.   Bill traveled along with a company anyway, and he
got as far as Battleboro, North Carolina before he got a bullet in
the knee.   A second lieutenant was cleaning his rifle and shot him
accidentally.

    On his 62nd birthday, Bill danced up Broadway for 52 blocks
to show his amazing vitality.   In the 1920's, Bill scored on Broadway in such shows as "Brown Buddies" and "Blackbirds of 1927. "

    Bill, who earned and spent approximately $3,000,000 during
his 66 years in show business, died almost broke.   Friends planned
to stage a nightclub benefit for him on December 5, 1949 to help
him take care of his medical expenses.   He died in November 1949.

    Bill appeared in a number of Hollywood pictures and also
one independent all-black film, "Harlem is Heaven" in 1932.   As a
dancer he contributed remarkable stepping routines.   Allegedly he
was also the father of a word which now appears in many diction-
aries, "copacetic, " and is now in general use.   Bill claimed he
made up the word when he was a kid and that it means "very okay. "

    A Few Pertinent Facts about the World's Greatest Tap
Dancer--As Told by Mrs. Bill Robinson, to Annabelle
Darden*

    That he made his terrestrial debut at Richmond,

*Reference: Baltimore Afro American, December 23, 1930.

Bill Robinson

Virginia, on May 25, fifty-five years ago.

That he doesn't remember his parents, as they died while he was very young.

That he started dancing when he was barely able to walk.

That his childhood ambition was to be a dancer.

That he never had a dancing lesson in his life.

That new steps just come to him.

That his first stage appearance took place in the "South Before the War."

That he and Eddie Leonard worked side by side years ago.

That he and Al Jolson, the Jewish mammy singer, came up from Washington together.

That he has been on the RKO Circuit for thirty-five years.

That he appeared in the flicker "Dixiana," with Bebe Daniels, was the star of the film, "Harlem Is Heaven," and he has also made a few movie shorts.

That he has many proteges, including the Nicholas youngsters appearing at the Cotton Club.

That he first came to New York when he was a young man around twenty or twenty-two years old.

That before he became a box office attraction, his jobs included: work in the tobacco factories in Richmond, Virginia; work in the public markets; shelling peas at two cents a quart; stage work; and work in the stockyards in Chicago.

That he went to the Spanish-American War.

That the nickname, "Bojangles" was picked up at the race tracks.

That he has originated countless tap dancing steps.

That his education began and ended in the public schools of Richmond.

That being orphaned during infancy, he found it necessary to shift for himself at an early age.

That he "coined" the word "copacetic," which means: Everything is all right; is always using words of his own invention.

That he is very athletic.

That he can run backward as fast as he can run forward.

That among his souvenirs is a gold revolver which was presented to him by New York's "finest."

ALEX ROGERS

Alexander Claude Rogers, who wrote many of the hit songs for Bert Williams and George Walker, was born in Nashville, Tennessee. Later Rogers went to Philadelphia before finally winding up in New York City in about 1900. During the next twenty-five years he wrote the book and lyrics for a half dozen black musical comedies that were performed on Broadway.

Collaborating with Jesse Shipp, Rogers wrote one of the pioneer black musical comedies "Abyssinia" which starred Bert Williams and George Walker. Other of his works include: "In Dahomey," "The Sons of Ham," "Bandanna Land," "Mr. Lode of Koal," "Go, Go, My Magnolia," and "Sheriee." In 1907 he was one of the actors in the Williams and Walker Company, giving a performance before the King and Queen of England at Buckingham Palace. About eight years later in New York, he and Henry Creamer produced "The Old Man's Boy" which premiered at the Empire Theatre in Brooklyn.

Rogers was the author of the words of nearly 2,000 songs, many of which he wrote for Bert Williams. Some of the best were written in collaboration with the celebrated Williams and include such songs as: "Bon Bon Buddy," "Swing Along," "Elder Eatmore's Sermon," one of Bert Williams' most famous records containing material used by Moran and Mack in their radio broadcasts, and Bert Williams' theme song, "Nobody."

Alex Rogers died in New York City in 1930.

MARSHALL ROGERS

Marshall (Garbage) Rogers, famous stage comedian, nightclub entertainer, got his start with the Billy King Stock Company at the old Grand Theatre in Chicago a few years before World War I. Rogers at one time was Billy King's chauffeur before King gave the young Rogers a few parts in his productions. Rogers soon became one of the principal performers playing the straight man to King. "Moonshine," a skit written by Billy King, was Rogers' first starring play. Marshall made his first New York appearance in "Miss Calico" which starred Ethel Waters and Billy King, and in 1924 he played the part of a saloon keeper in Oscar Micheaux's film "Body and Soul" which starred Paul Robeson.

In 1928 Rogers opened at the Regal Theatre in Chicago and enjoyed the longest run at that house of any performer up to that time. He married Gladys Mike, then a well-known girl, in the same year, taking her with him to play certain parts on the stage.

After leaving the Regal, Marshall went to the Golden Lily Cafe where he acted for several seasons as master of ceremonies and comedian. Following this, he went East, where he was a star in nightclubs and theatres. His first starring role in the East was with Noble Sissle and others in "Harlem on Parade." Marshall Rogers died in Philadelphia in December 1934.

CLIFFORD ROSS

Clifford Ross was born in Cincinnati, Ohio in 1879 and began his career as a concert singer at the age of 14. He followed this line of entertainment as a young man and appeared in concerts as a baritone singer and dramatic reader with such artists as Madam Hackley, Joe Douglass and Clarence Cameron White, a noted violinist.

Later, Ross went into vaudeville and when the Pekin Stock Company, the first black dramatic company organized in America, was established in Chicago, he became a member along with other well-known players who at the time were gradually climbing the ladder of success. Chief among these was Charles H. Gilpin. After the Pekin Company folded, Ross drifted back into vaudeville and for a time toured with the Russell and Owens Stock Company where he gained a reputation as a funmaker and singer. One of the high points of his career was when he appeared in "Follow Me" as assistant comedian to Billy Higgins.

JOHN RUCKER

John Rucker, who was billed for most of his professional life as the "Original Alabama Blossom," was born in Murphysboro, Tennessee in 1866, and reared in Huntsville, Alabama. He served apprenticeship and received his first schooling as a comedian under the famous minstrel man, Al G. Fields of Columbus, Ohio. Rucker remained with Fields' White Minstrels before he joined Fields' World Famous Negro Minstrels in 1894. He remained with this organization for two seasons as principal end man. He next starred in the great black musical drama "Darkest America," where he remained as a featured performer for four seasons playing the part of "Uncle Amos Jackson." After two seasons Fields sold the show to John W. Vogel.

In 1899, Rucker joined Rusco and Holland's Georgia Minstrels as principal end man and one of the stars. He remained with this company for two years before joining Black Patti's Troubadours in 1902. He stayed with the Troubadours for four seasons and held the position as one of the leading comedians.

Rucker's next engagement was with the Dixie Minstrels in 1906. As in the case of Black Patti's Troubadours, this show was under the management of Voelckel and Nolan. His stay with the Dandy Dixie Company was short, for after half a season with this company he closed at New Orleans and returned to New York City.

Rucker next joined Ernest Hogan's "Oyster Man" company playing the opposite comedy co-star part with the great Ernest Hogan. Critics said that Rucker and Hogan were two of the funniest men ever seen on the stage together, especially in the "collection box" and the "raft" scenes. After Hogan's retirement from "Oyster Man" because of illness, John Rucker played the leading role in several large cities including New York, Boston, and Providence, Rhode Island before the show closed.

John Rucker, circa 1899

        Rucker's next important starring venture was with his own
company billed as "John Rucker's Own Minstrels." This show opened
in 1907 at the 125th Street Theatre in New York. After this show
closed, Rucker returned to vaudeville where he remained for most
of the remaining part of his professional career.

SYLVESTER RUSSELL

        Sylvester Russell, theatrical critic, and performer, was born
in East Orange, New Jersey and started his career as a valet for

Sylvester Russell, Pioneer Theatrical Critic, circa 1902

the wealthy Colby boys, serving them at Brown University.   Later
he was a tenor singer with Al Field's famous minstrel "Forty Whites
and Thirty Blacks. "   After his minstrel days, Russell toured the
country on the concert stage.   His first newspaper job came when
he joined the staff of the Indianapolis <u>Freeman</u>, then a leading black
weekly.   He worked as dramatic critic and Chicago correspondent.

     A few years before the start of World War I, State Street
between 31st and 35th Streets was the center of black business ac-
tivity in Chicago.   It was Sylvester Russell who nicknamed that
stretch of thoroughfare "The Stroll. "   For a number of years he
published a tabloid newspaper on activities on the "Stroll. "

     After the <u>Freeman</u> suspended publication, Russell became a freelance writer for a number of newspapers. He also edited and published several weekly pamphlets in Chicago including one he issued under a sealed cover which dealt with fair-skinned black actors and actresses who were "passing" for white.

Sylvester Russell died in Chicago in 1930.

GERTRUDE SAUNDERS

Gertrude Saunders, who was born in Asheville, South Carolina, was a feature singer in many musical comedies for over fifteen years. She was a student at Benedict College in Columbia, South Carolina before she left school for a career on the stage at the age of seventeen. She was in her senior year at the college when her fellow students, sensing her superior talent for comedy and song, urged her to take up a professional career on the stage. Her first engagement was with the Billy King Company where she remained for several years. During this period, her talent as a singing comedienne was recognized whenever she was given special song numbers and she soon had the leading booking agents praising her work.

Her success was eventually noted by Messrs. Blake and Sissle, Miller and Lyles, and they engaged her for the original "Shuffle Along" in 1921 preceding Florence Mills as the feminine star of the show. She was lured away from the "Shuffle" show by Hertig and Seamon with fabulous offers to join a burlesque company. This venture soon blew cold and she took to vaudeville doing a singing specialty on the Keith, Loew and other circuits until 1924, when she performed in Irvin C. Miller's "Liza" show. One of her last stage appearances was in the Los Angeles production "Run Little Chillun" in 1938.

JESSE A. SHIPP

Jesse Shipp, playwright and producer, whose creative genius produced books for the great Williams and Walker shows, got his start in show business as a performer in the 1870's with a partner named Dave Simms. The team was not successful and later Shipp went to Cincinnati where he got a job driving for a laundry. While working for the laundry, he became part of a quartet which also included Joe Hagerman who later was the first black to be appointed to the Cincinnati police force, Gilbert Fredericks and Ed Monroe. Known as the Beethoven Quartet, the group played beer gardens on Saturday nights until they were picked up by a man named Snyder who booked them in variety halls for seven years.

Shipp then toured with Draper's "Uncle Tom's Cabin" company until the Eureka Minstrels were organized. The later company included Shipp, Grill Wilson, Billy Allen, Billy Windom, Billy Cook, Ed Monroe, Jim Tyler, and a white band of seven Englishmen.

Later Shipp joined the Primrose and West "Forty Whites and Thirty Blacks," remaining until he went with the "Octoroons" and then to the Oriental America Company. He was also a member of the original company of Cole and Johnson's "A Trip to Coontown," and he also wrote the book for the show. Later he turned exclusively to playwriting.

Soon after, he wrote "The Sons of Ham" and joined the Williams and Walker company and remained with the famous team until the end of their producing career. During this period he wrote the book for "In Dahomey," "In Abyssinia," and "Bandanna Land." Jesse Shipp died in Jamaica, British West Indies in 1934.

JOE SIMMS

Joe Simms was born in Vicksburg, Mississippi where his father was pastor of King David Baptist Church. In 1901, the young Simms accepted the opportunity to go to LaGrange, Illinois with his grandmother. He attended high school in LaGrange and later drifted to Chicago and began to make professional use of the amateur stagecraft that he had gained in church functions in Vicksburg. His first professional work came in a State Street saloon which went under the name of Beer Garden. A performer was allowed to come in, blacken his face, deliver a line of chatter and some buck and wing dancing, and collect a dollar every night if he were satisfactory. Simms was satisfactory and found himself with an engagement, three years later, at the Old Pekin Theatre, near 27th Street in Chicago. Among his partners during this period were Walker Thompson, who was a member of the Lafayette Players, Wilber Sweetman, and Crickett Smith, then leader of a famous jazz band.

Simms replaced Aubrey Lyles in the original cast of "Shuffle Along" in 1923 and played with the show for 23 weeks. Later, after making a tour on the Keith Circuit, he and Sidney Easton produced the show "Sons of Rest" in 1927.

NOBLE SISSLE

Noble Sissle was born in Indianapolis, Indiana on July 10, 1889. He organized a Glee Club in high school and later attended Butler University to study the ministry. He quit school, however, before graduating in order to support his family after his father died. After taking up music, he toured for two years with the Thomas Jubilee Singers and later became the protege of bandmaster Jim Europe and entertained at various nightclubs in New York City. In 1915 Sissle first met Eubie Blake and they formed a song writing team.

When America entered World War I, Sissle enlisted as a private in the 369th Regiment and later earned a commission as second lieutenant. He became drum major for Jim Europe's Army

Noble Sissle [left] and Eubie Blake, circa 1930

Band and succeeded as leader after the war. In 1921 Sissle and
Blake again teamed up and produced and wrote "Shuffle Along" in
collaboration with Miller and Lyles.   They followed this very successful show with "The Chocolate Dandies."

Later, Sissle organized an orchestra and toured Europe,
taking in London, Paris, Monte Carlo and subsequently throughout
the United States.   His hit songs, many in collaboration with Eubie
Blake, include: "I'm Just Wild About Harry," "Love Will Find a
Way," "Bandana Days," "Gypsy Blues," "Hello, Sweetheart" and
"Boogie Boogie Beguine."

Noble Sissle and his Band appeared in several black-cast
movies in the late 1930's and early 1940's including "Murder with
Music." He also appeared with Eubie Blake in "Snappy Tunes"
which was an early sound film.   The film was produced in 1923 by
Lee DeForrest using the Phonofilm system which he invented in
1920.   The film was first shown at the Rivoli Theatre in New York
City.

Sissle was the founder of the Negro Actor's Guild and was
once known as the unofficial mayor of Harlem.   He was also a mem-
ber of the American Society of Composers, Authors and Publishers.
During his long career he wrote the lyrics to many songs including
"Love Will Find a Way" and "You Were Meant for Me."   Noble
Sissle died at age 86 in December 1975, in Tampa, Florida.

ROBERT SLATER

Robert Samuel Slater was born in New Orleans, Louisiana, June 22, 1869, and entered the theatrical profession at a young age, traveling for several years with the Dr. Hi Cooper's Medicine Show which was then famous. A short time later, he went East, where he formed a partnership with Bert Murphy, the team making their first appearance at a benefit performance at Madison Square Garden, given for Gussie L. Davis, a black song writer. While there, they were seen by Bob Cole and engaged by him for the musical comedy "Trip to Coontown." After a successful season with the company, they went into vaudeville, then called variety, and soon became one of the leading black acts of the day, playing the Orpheum Circuit and the Keith Proctor Circuit. Later, Mr. Slater was a partner with Henry Williams and still later with Fred Rogers.

After leaving vaudeville, Slater established the first licensed vaudeville booking agency by and for black performers. He also was the organizer of the Colored Vaudeville Benevolent Association.

For a time, he also managed the Ruby Theatre in Louisville, Kentucky and formed the first black American musical comedy company to play Cuba.

Bob Slater died in New York City on June 20, 1930.

J. AGUSTUS SMITH

J. Agustus Smith was born in Gainsville, Florida in 1891. He made his stage debut in 1905 at the age of 14 with the Rabbit's Foot Minstrels. Smith's entry into show business was largely a matter of accident (a friend of the family owned a minstrel show, so it was best for the young lad to get a job but once he'd chosen it as a profession, he was determined to learn everything about it that he could). Consequently, he toured with vaudeville acts, and minstrel shows, did a stint for a while in a wild west show, and even did a few motion pictures. In 1907 Smith appeared in the first film version of "Uncle Tom's Cabin," a two-reeler which was shot on location on the Delaware River near Philadelphia.

Smith's first Broadway appearance was in 1933 in the production "Louisiana" which he also authored and staged. Unfortunately, "Louisiana" opened just before every bank in the country closed (the Bank Holiday) and that doomed the production before it could get off the ground.

For many years Smith served as the Director of the Negro Section of the Federal Theatre. He was responsible for staging and producing such shows as "Androcles and the Lion," "Walk Together, Children," "Haiti," "The Case of Philip Lawrence," "Conjure Man Dies" and a number of others. It was during this time that he met Canada Lee with whom he performed in "On Whitman Avenue" in 1946.

MAMIE SMITH

Mamie Smith had already received nationwide fame as a recording artist before she appeared in black-cast films. She was
born in Cincinnati, Ohio and went out at the age of 10 with a white
act, the "Four Dancing Mitchels." She later joined the then celebrated Salem Tutt Whitney show, "The Smart Set," doing her regular turn in the chorus at the age of 15. She came to Harlem in
1913 at a time when the population was centered around 134th and
Fifth Avenue; at a time when Lenox Avenue was known as the Negro's "International Boulevard." She wanted to stay in New York
so she quit the Whitney outfit and began singing and entertaining
around such Harlem spots as Baron Wilkin's, Leroy's, Edmunds',
Connie's Inn, Percy Brown's and Banks' Place.

Later she appeared in the musical production, "Maid in Har-
lem," with such stars of the time as Brown of Brown and Gulfport,
Phillip Giles, Daisey Vervalian, Jeanette of Mule Bradford and
Jeanette, and Leigh Whipper.

Mamie Smith's first big song hit was "Harlem Blues" which
was written for her by Perry Bradford. In 1920, the song was recorded by Okeh Recording Company and the title was changed to
"Crazy Blues." The recording was a smash and theatres begged
dates from the heavy-hipped, deep-voiced blues shouter who had
created a name for herself. Other big records for Mamie during
this period were "The Thing Called Love," and "You Can't Keep a
Good Man Down," both written by Perry Bradford.

Some time later, Mamie went into the movies and did several
shorts at the old RCA Company. The most outstanding of them was
the "Jail House Blues" with Porter Grainger, J. Homer Tutt,
and Billy Mills, then a well-known comedian.

In the late 1920's and 1930's, she toured the country with
her orchestra the Jazz Hounds. The group changed frequently during the several years it was popular. Some of the more well-known
members of the group were Buster Bailey, Ernest Elliot, Willie
(the Lion) Smith, Dope Andrews, Sam Walker, Johnny Dunn and
Coleman Hawkins who joined the group when he was 18 years old.

After the Jazz Hounds disbanded, Mamie continued to record
and appeared in black-cast movies such as "Murder on Lenox Avenue" and "Sunday Sinners."

VALAIDA SNOW

Born in 1903, Valaida Snow was a headline attraction during
the 1920's and 1930's. She was recognized as a great jazz musician and could play every instrument in the band, although she was
better known for her artistry on the trumpet. She toured Europe
six times, starting when she was just 12 years old. By the time

she was 15, she was starring abroad and playing command performances. Later, she was one of the singing and acting stars of Lew
Leslie's European "Blackbirds."

Miss Snow made her last trip to Europe in 1939 and in
Copenhagen, Denmark she was arrested and spent 20 months in a
Nazi concentration camp. After her release, she returned to the
United States, in 1943, a 68-pound shadow of her former self.

Late in her career Miss Snow made several recordings as a
singer and for a time produced shows at the Cotton Club in Culver
City, California. She was also the creative talent behind many of
the shows at the Old Grand Terrace in Chicago. Miss Snow died
in New York City in 1957.

JUANITA STINNETTE

Juanita Stinnette of the celebrated dancing team of Chappelle
and Stinnette was born in Baltimore, Maryland in 1899, where as a
youngster she attended Carey Street School. She began her career
on the stage in 1917 as a member of the chorus of Whitney and
Tutt's "Smart Set" Company. It was while singing and dancing in
the chorus of the company that Thomas Chappelle saw her and at
once singled her out as a potential dancing partner in his vaudeville
act which up to that time he had been performing as a single. He
found her willing to make the change and, after several days of rehearsal, they "went on" and were an instant success.

It was not long after the formation of their partnership that
they were married. They played all the black and white vaudeville
circuits. In addition to her work, Stinnette made a number of recordings and she and her husband formed a company of 30 people
and produced several musical comedy shows. Miss Stinnette died
in 1932. Her last Broadway show was "Sugar Hill."

FORD WASHINGTON LEE AND JOHN WILLIAM SUBLETT
(BUCK AND BUBBLES)

Ford Washington Lee (Buck) and John William Sublett (Bubbles) were born in Louisville, Kentucky. When a young lad, Buck
was with a small carnival touring Indiana when he first met Bubbles. They became friends and worked together riding horses at
Churchill Downs Race Track in Louisville and later they worked as
janitors at the old Mary Anderson Theatre in Louisville. Later,
they worked in a carnival, dancing and jigging for the "Midnight
Madness" side show. At the start of World War I, the carnival
business went bad and the boys got a job as bat boys for the Louisville Colonels baseball team, then managed by Joe McCarthy who
later achieved fame as manager of the New York Yankees.

After the baseball season ended in the fall, Buck and Bubbles

Buck [left] and Bubbles, circa 1943

joined up with a black troupe touring the South and finally ended up
in New Orleans washing dishes in a little nightclub.   They usually
came to work early and practiced dancing and singing with Buck
playing the piano.   One night the manager of the club gave them a
chance to perform and when they finished they divided twelve dollars which had been thrown to them by the enthusiastic patrons.
With this money the lads returned to Louisville and their old jobs
at the Mary Anderson Theatre.   Each night, after completing their
work, the boys would practice, Buck at the piano and Bubbles doing
the dancing.   The stagehands and other theatre employees found the
two-man show very enjoyable, but the night watchman complained of
the noise.   The manager of the theatre stayed late one night to see
what it was all about and was amazed at what he saw.   Later in
the season, when an act fell out of the show, the manager gave
Buck and Bubbles a chance to perform.   They were an instant success.

       In 1921, they went to New York City and applied for a job at
a music publishing house.   The manager of the house gave them an
audition and by chance Nat Nazarro, then a well-known vaudeville
star, happened to be present and liked their act so much that he
asked the youngsters to perform at a Sunday night concert at the
old Columbia Theatre on Broadway.   Nazarro brought them out as
an encore to his own act and the boys went over so well that
Nazarro signed them to a five-year contract, and Buck and Bubbles
appeared as a part of Nazarro's act in all the big-time theatres.

       When the contract with Nazarro expired, Buck and Bubbles
tried to go it alone, but in a few weeks, after being cancelled at
several theatres, they wired Nazarro for railroad fare to New York.
After returning, they again signed with Nazarro and soon became a
big-time vaudeville act and were the first black team to be held
over for two weeks at the then famous Keith's Palace Theatre in
New York.   This engagement led them to play the Paramount Public Circuit and then to an extensive engagement as featured performers with Lew Leslie's "Blackbirds."   Later they went to Hollywood to do a series of Pathe comedies that were adapted from Hugh
Wiley's short stories dealing with various aspects of Negro life
which were published in the Saturday Evening Post.

       In 1931, Buck and Bubbles went to Europe and enjoyed great
success when they played for two weeks at the famous Palladium
Theatre in London.   After returning to America, they enjoyed perhaps their greatest success when they performed in the Ziegfeld
Follies at the old Ziegfeld Theatre in New York.

ULYSSES "SLOW KID" THOMPSON

       Ulysses "Slow Kid" Thompson, comedian, innovator of the
slow motion dance, and husband of Florence Mills, was born in
Prescott, Arizona in 1888.   He ran away from home at the age of
fourteen and his first job in show business was with a medicine

show which toured Louisiana.   Later he worked for a while with
several carnivals including the Patterson Carnival in Texas, Parker's
Mighty Show in Kansas, and George J. Loose's Carnival in Florida.
Thompson's tap dancing and acrobatic skills were spectacular and he
soon made it to the Keith vaudeville circuit in 1920.   In 1917 Jesse
Shipp organized the Tennessee Ten for the Keith Orpheum vaudeville
circuit.   The act included Florence Mills and Thompson, who conducted the jazz band and danced.   Thompson left the act when he
was drafted in World War I.

Thompson's first musical comedy success was in "Shuffle
Along" in 1921 in which he played the porter in the Mayor's (Flournoy A. Miller) office.   He also did an eccentric soft shoe and lego-
mainia dance.   Thompson and his wife, Florence Mills, later left
the "Shuffle Along" show to appear in Lew Leslie's "Plantation Revue" in 1922.   The revue opened at the Forty-eighth Street Theatre
in 1922 with Will Vodery's Band, Shelton Brooks as master of ceremonies, and Lew Leslie as producer.   Later, Thompson appeared
in "Dixie to Broadway" in which Florence Mills was the star.

ANDREW TRIBBLE

Andrew Tribble, who gained fame on the musical comedy
stage as a female impersonator, was a product of the old Pekin
Stock Company which also produced such noted actors as Lawrence
Chenault, Lottie Gee, Lottie Grady, Charles Gilpin and Miller and
Lyles.   Tribble, who stood about 5 feet 4 inches tall, was born in
1879 and attended school in Richmond, Kentucky.   Tribble's first
job in show business came when he joined a pickaninny band and
traveled with "In Old Kentucky."   When he grew too large to be a
"pick, " Tribble quit the road and stayed off the stage until 1904; in
the meantime, he got married.

Returning to show business in Chicago, Tribble sang and
danced on a music hall stage on State Street.   It was there that
Robert Motts saw him and later booked him into the Pekin Theatre
where Tribble soon found himself playing any and every kind of
part.

One night in an afterpiece, Tribble slipped on a dress and
the audience screamed at his performance.   Tribble found his dress-
wearing characterizations so effective that he frequently worked in
drag for the remainder of his career.   It was at the Pekin that he
was first seen by Cole and Johnson who later brought him to New
York City to play in their second production, "Shoo Fly Regiment. "

When Cole and Johnson formed the "Shoo Fly Regiment" in
1906, Tribble created the role of "Ophelia Snow. "   This highly successful character was that of a single minded woman, careless,
kindly, tough, and above all desirous for an affair of the heart just
the same as her sisters blessed with more beauty.   In the third
Cole and Johnson production "Red Moon, " Tribble portrayed "Lilly

Andrew Tribble, circa 1907

White" to the delight of all those who saw this clever and faithful
delineation of a type unique on the stage.   During his long career
on the stage Tribble was a featured performer with many companies including The Smart Set, Eddie Hunter Company, J. Leubrie
Hill Company, the Miller (Quintard) and Slater Company and many
others.   Among his show credits are "Shuffle Along," "Rarin' to
Go," "Smart Set," "In Old Kentucky," "Jazz Regiment," and "Brown
Buddies."   Andrew Tribble died in 1935.

ELOISE UGGAMS

        Eloise Uggams, who first gained recognition in the hit show
"Rhapsody in Black," was born in Gainesville, Florida.   Her parents
were Rev. Coyden H. and Mamie Hughes Uggams.   Her dad was a
Presbyterian minister and both of her parents were school teachers.
Miss Uggams was educated in a parochial school in Charleston,
South Carolina, where most of her early childhood was spent.   Lat-
er, she attended Avery Normal Institute, Haines Institute and finally
Fisk University in Nashville, Tennessee.   She was a brilliant stu-
dent with a special aptitude for languages, mathematics and music.

        She made her debut in church concerts along with her elder
sister at the age of three.   The Uggams girls, Eloise and Louise,
won a host of admirers because of their unique talents in singing,
both being able to alternate alto and soprano in their duet appearances.   She was encouraged by her home town friends to attend
Fisk University.   After the first quarter's study at Fisk, she won
a scholarship and made her debut as offertory soloist after seven
weeks of study.   For several years she was soloist of the Mozart
Society at Fisk which was composed of 75 picked voices.

        She represented Fisk in solo and quartette work in the vicin-
ity of Nashville, and finally went on tour with the Fisk Quartette,
traveling for a year and six months all over the United States and
Canada.   After that, she returned to Fisk where she completed her
courses.

        Miss Uggams was at one time the soloist at Nazarene Con-
gregational Church in Brooklyn and served in the same capacity at
St. James Presbyterian Church, New York City, for over three
years, which served to introduce her to the musical elements of
New York.

        At one time, Miss Uggams was a member of the Hall John-
son and the William Elkins Chorus.   She was with the Dixie Jubilee
Singers, directed by Eva Jessye in 1927, and with this aggregation
appeared at the Central Theatre, Capital Theatre in New York, and
other leading theatres in the East including an engagement at the
Fox Theatre in Philadelphia in support of Jules Bledsoe.

        In 1928, Miss Uggams joined Cecil Mack's Choir with Lew
Leslie's "Blackbirds," going abroad with the company in 1928.

Later she worked with Eva Jessye in the radio series "Aunt Mandy's Children" which was broadcast over WOR in New York. Later, she returned to Leslie in 1930, performing as a featured soloist in "Rhapsody in Black" in 1932.

Miss Uggams' voice had a range of three octaves, but it was usually adjudged lyric soprano. During her stay with "Rhapsody in Black," she had on various occasions substituted for Aida Ward and Geneva Washington whose voices and selections were directly opposite. After leaving "Rhapsody in Black," she went back to the Eva Jessye Choir where she remained for several years before retiring from show business.

WILL H. VODERY

Will Henry Bennett Vodery was born in Philadelphia, Pennsylvania in 1885. He attended Central High School in Philadelphia, and his excellent academic record won him a scholarship to the University of Pennsylvania in 1902. While at the University, he organized an orchestra which became well known in Philadelphia and he also studied piano and violin under Hugh A. Clark, then a well known teacher of music.

Mr. Vodery credited Bert Williams for his entry into the field of professional music. Whenever Williams played in Philadelphia, he stopped at Vodery's house. One day, after hearing Vodery play, Williams told him that he had exceptional talent and took him to New York in 1904, where he wrote the music for his first show, "A Trip to Africa," put on by Black Patti's Troubadours company. He went on tour with the show and later was stranded in Chicago after the show closed following a short run in that city. He then obtained a position with Charles K. Harris and was engaged to become custodian of the Theodore Thomas Orchestra. During this period, he wrote the music for "The Isle of Bang-Bang" for Mort Singer and also for "South Africa" and "Time, Place and Girl."

In 1906, Bert Williams sent for Vodery to come to New York to compose the music for their new show "Abyssinia." The following season he helped write the music for Ernest Hogan's show "The Oyster Man," and composed one of his most famous works "After the Ball Is Over." Next, Vodery arranged the music for Williams and Walker's "Bandanna Land" and traveled with this show in the United States and Europe as musical director. Between 1909 and 1910 he composed "Two Much Isaacs," "Girls From Happy Land," "Saucy Maid" and "Me, Hen and I."

When Bert Williams went with the "Follies," he commissioned Vodery to write his songs, which included "Can't Get Away from It," "Dark Town Poker Club," and "My Land Lady." In this capacity Vodery attracted the attention of Flo Ziegfeld who engaged Vodery to write the score and musical arrangements for the "Follies." Vodery worked as arranger for Ziegfeld into the late 1920's.

Between 1911 and 1913 Vodery had charge of Aida Overton Walker's vaudeville show and later wrote the music for "Porto Rico Girls" and "Happy Girls" in 1914.

During World War I, Vodery organized bands for the U. S. Army. He was at Camp Dix for nine months before he "went across" with the 807th, a black regiment. Later, the 807th band was selected by Lt. General Liggett as the best band in the A. E. F. The General then sent Vodery to Chanmont, then the general head-quarters of the A. E. F. and also the location of the bandmasters school. Vodery attended the school and graduated with high honors and also won a scholarship to the Paris Conservatory.

After his return to America, he wrote the music for Bert Williams' show "The Pink Slip," which was produced by A. H. Woods. In 1922, Vodery was engaged to organize his own orchestra for the Plantation, then one of the very smartest cabarets in New York City. In 1925, he was a member of the "Dixie to Broadway" company which featured Florence Mills. He also arranged the score for "Keep Shufflin'," several editions of "Blackbirds," "Show Boat," and for more than 50 other musical comedies. Mr. Vodery died on November 18, 1951 in New York City.

AIDA OVERTON WALKER

Aida Overton Walker, who was a pioneer black actress and one of the most popular performers on the stage during her career, was born in Richmond, Virginia in 1870, and later went with her mother to New York City to live. In 1886, at the age of 16, she began to attract attention as a soubrette with the Black Patti Compa-ny and later with the Oriental America Company in 1888. In 1898, she became a member of the famous Williams and Walker company and it was with this well-known organization that she won her great-est stage laurels.

Of all the songs sung by Aida Overton Walker while associ-ated with the Williams and Walker Company, none gave her a better opportunity to demonstrate her powers as an entertainer than "Hanna from Savannah" which was regarded by many at the time as the song hit of "Sons of Ham." This number was instrumental in making her one of the important figures in the Williams and Walker Company.

When the Williams and Walker Company was playing England in "In Dahomey," Aida Overton Walker was eagerly sought after by titled persons to teach them the cakewalk (dance).

Aida Overton Walker not only dignified the cakewalk, but also other dances originated by blacks.

She was married to George Walker on June 22, 1899. After the closing of the Williams and Walker Company following the death of George Walker, Mrs. Walker joined Cole and Johnson Company

Ad for "His Honor the Barber" with Aida Overton Walker, circa 1910

during the season of 1908-1909 and in the next season, 1909-1910, she was a member of the "Smart Set" Company. After that, she appeared in vaudeville with success during the season of 1911-1912 appearing in the East and West. For the next two years, Mrs. Walker devoted more of her time to producing acts than to appearing on the stage and was financially interested in the Porto Rico Girls and the Happy Girls. The last entertainment under her management was given at the Manhattan Casino on August 16, 1914. She died shortly afterwards on October 11, 1914.

BILLY WALKER

Billy Walker was born in 1891 and reared in Pittsburgh. He started in show business at an early age as one of the clever set of "pickaninny" dancers that performed in his home town. It was with the Billy King Stock Company that he showed first promise as a comedian. Later, he formed a partnership with Edgar Martin and headed several shows that played on the T. O. B. A. circuit. Walker's cleverness as a comedian soon won his larger salaries on all the large vaudeville circuits. Later, he married Babe Brown and after he broke with Martin he and his wife formed the Walker and Brown Company with George Crawford as assistant comedian. The company toured for several seasons on the T. O. B. A.

Billy Walker was not only a great dancer, but he was one of the few comedians who could really put a song over and hold his audience in its delivery with a gifted voice of high tenor. His greatest song success was "Toodle Toodle" and no other performer could dance like him. Billy Walker died in 1927.

THOMAS "FATS" WALLER

Thomas "Fats" Waller, famous composer, pianist and organist, was born in New York City in 1905. He learned to play the piano at age five but never took music lessons until he was 10; by that time, he could play any tune he heard whistled or hummed. Mrs. Edna Perrin, black, was his first teacher. He later took organ lessons from Professor Carl Bohn of the Guilmont Conservatory, and as the theatre organist "Fats" soon became one of the best in the country. "Fats" quit Wadleigh High School in New York in his junior year to take a cabaret job. Later he went to Chicago where he became Bessie Smith's first accompanist.

In 1921, Waller first started composing music for publication; among his early successes were "Senorita Mine," "Squeeze Me," "I've Got a Feeling I'm Falling," and "I Can't Give You Anything But Love." The latter was introduced in one edition of Lew Leslie's "Blackbirds." Waller, in need of cash, sold this song to Jimmy McHugh, white, for $500 and since then the song has brought many thousands of dollars.

> "Say, boy, you goin' to that dance tonight?"
> "Ain't Misbehavin', podner, ain't misbehavin'."

The scene was in Gary, Indiana during the summer of 1928, and the characters were two of the local folks. Waller was spending a few days in the city when he first heard the above refrain. As he toured the city, he heard the same bit repeated again and again. "Some day," said Fats, to himself, "I'm going to write a piece around that bit of slang." For a while he forgot that he had even heard it.

"Fats" Waller

Back in New York, however, the memory of the phrase seemed to haunt him, so much so that four days before Christmas in 1928 he sat down and composed a rough draft of the song. Later he called in Andy Razaf, then a noted young lyric writer, and in four days the pair had completed the song "Ain't Misbehavin'" which later became one of America's all-time song hits. But they kept it "on the shelf" until February 1929. One day, when Connie Immerman, then owner of Connie's Inn, was planning the show "Hot Chocolates," Waller, who was working at the Inn, took the song to Connie and played it for him. However, Connie didn't like the song and threw up his hands in desperation saying, "Take it away, I can't use it." But Waller was not so easily discouraged. He called in Andy Razaf and the two insisted that Connie hear the number again. After much persuasion the producer decided to give it a try and it later became one of the hits of "Hot Chocolates" in 1929.

During the 1930's, Waller became nationally known through his record sales ... and a long series of radio broadcasts over WLW in Cincinnati. Later, he made a brief trip to France in 1932 and after his return to America he started working with a small bank in New York City. In May 1934, he began a famous series of Victor record sessions with six-piece groups, usually featuring his own satirical renditions of current pop tunes which was to become his trademark. Waller was also the first musician to play jazz successfully on the Hammond organ and the pipe organ. He appeared in several movies and probably is best remembered for his role as the cabaret piano player in "Stormy Weather" in 1943. Waller, one of America's most creative musicians, died in 1943.

LESTER A. WALTON

Lester A. Walton, a brilliant and nationally known journalist and drama critic, started his career in St. Louis as a freelance writer for the St. Louis Globe-Democrat. For a long time the City Editor didn't know the racial identity of the young writer. Finally, Walton was asked to come to St. Louis and, although the Editor was shocked to learn that Walton was a black man, he was given an assignment to cover court news. He soon worked up through different departments and became an expert golf reporter. Later, he left the Globe-Democrat and secured a position with the St. Louis Star and later from the Star to the Post-Dispatch. While there, he met Herbert Bayard Swopes who later became editor of the New York World.

While working on the St. Louis newspapers, Walton learned to be a dramatic critic and in 1907 he was induced to come to New York by Ernest Hogan to write the lyrics for the musical comedy "Rufus Rastus." This started his theatrical career which carried for several seasons on the road as personal representative and business manager of the company.

In 1908, he joined the New York Age as dramatic editor, but

before long was promoted to managing editor. At the close of
World War I he made a tour of France with Dr. R. R. Morton.
In 1920, he took over the management of the Lafayette Theatre in
New York City and remained in the theatrical business until he
joined the New York World in 1922.

During his long journalistic career, Mr. Walton also contributed articles to many of the leading national magazines of the
period including The Outlook and Literary Digest.

FREDIE WASHINGTON

Fredie Washington was born in Savannah, Georgia and was
educated at St. Elizabeth's Convent, Philadelphia. Her first experience on the stage was in "Shuffle Along" in 1921. After a long
engagement at the Club Alabam, where Lee Shubert saw her, she
was recommended by Shubert to Horace Liveright for the leading
role opposite Paul Robeson in "Black Boy" which she played under
the stage name of Edith Warren. At the end of this run, with no
other serious black productions in view, she reverted to dancing at
Roger Wolfe Kahr's Parakeet. Later she toured Europe as a dancer
and after her return she appeared in Vincent Youman's "Great Day,"
"Sweet Chariot," "Singing the Blues" and Hall Johnson's "Run Little
Chillun" in 1933.

Fredie Washington also appeared in a number of films including "Emperor Jones," "Black and Tan Fantasy," "Imitation of
Life," Drums in the Night," and "One Mile from Heaven." Her
other stage credits include "Mamba's Daughters" and "A Long Way
from Home."

Miss Washington was one of the founders of the Negro Actors
Guild of America, Inc., serving as its executive secretary for one
year. She also worked for several years as drama editor and col-
umnist with the People's Voice, a New York weekly published by
Adam Clayton Powell, Jr.

ETHEL WATERS

One of the great women of the American stage, Ethel Waters
was born into a large family in Chester, Pennsylvania in 1886. Her
first employment of record was in a second class Philadelphia hotel,
doing menial work for $3.50 a week, with $1.25 added for extra
laundry chores. For a time, she also worked as a maid at Swarth-
more College.

Her debut on the stage came in an amateur contest in Philadelphia at the age of 14. Three years later, she began her professional career in vaudeville as a protege of the Hill Sisters,
Maggie and Jo, on the Carnival or "Kerosene Circuit." They were
billed as "The Hill Sisters, Featuring Sweet Mama Stringbeans

Ethel Waters As She Appeared in "While Thousands Cheer."

singing 'St. Louis Blues'." Miss Waters worked in blackface in Frank Montgomery's show "Hello, 1919," and in 1921 she made her first record for the Cardinal Company, "The New York Glide" and "At the New Jump Steady Ball." About the same time she made her film debut, playing a bit part in Oscar Micheaux's film "The Gunsaulus Mystery" in 1921.

The early 1920's found Miss Waters gaining attention as a singer in the clubs of New York City. It was during this period that Harry Pace signed her to record for his Black Swan records. Her first record was "Down Home Blues" on one side and "Oh, Daddy" on the other. In 1922 her recording of "Sweet Georgia Brown" on the Black Swan label set a new high for record sales. Later she toured the East and Midwest with a group billed as "The Black Swan Troubadours" which was sponsored by Harry Pace and which was essentially a promotional tour for his company. The band was led by Fletcher Henderson and included such great musicians as Joe Smith, Gus Aiken, Lorenzo Brashear and Raymond Green. Pace hired Lester A. Walton, then with the New York World, as advance man.

One of Ethel Waters' Earliest Recordings; Released in May 1921

Although Miss Waters was the star of the troubadours, she frequently had to share top honors with Ethel Williams, another member of the company. Miss Williams, who had worked in the chorus with J. Leubrie Hill's Darktown Follies Company, was an exceptional dancer who specialized in the shimmy.

Later, Miss Waters recorded with much success for Brunswick and Mary Howard labels.

Miss Waters' first musical comedy appearances as a name performer were in "Oh, Joy" and "Jump Steady" in 1922, written, produced and staged by Whitney and Tutt. Her next appearance in a black show was in "Get Set" in 1923 which was produced by the Harlem Producing Company. After several more years of singing in Harlem nightclubs, she went downtown to star in the black revue "Africana" at Daley's Sixty-Third Street Theatre in 1927.

Later, Miss Waters starred in Lew Leslie's "Blackbirds of 1931" and in 1932 she created an equal sensation in Leslie's "Rhapsody in Black."

After hearing her sing "Stormy Weather" at the famous Cotton Club, Irving Berlin engaged her to appear in her first white Broadway show, "While Thousands Cheer." Soon after, she was seen in "At Home Abroad" in which she shared star billing with the great Beatrice Lillie. When the show went on tour without Bea, Ethel Waters starred alone.

Having reached the pinnacle of musical comedy achievement, Miss Waters turned to movies, to the radio, and to the concert stage at Carnegie Hall. In 1932, she appeared with the then seven-year-old Sammy Davis, Jr. in the black film musical short "Rufus Jones for President" in which she sang "Am I Blue" and "Underneath a Harlem Moon." Soon after, she played the role of Hager in "Mamba's Daughters" which Dorothy and DuBose Heyward had dramatized for her. This show catapulted Ethel Waters to the top ranks of the acting profession. The Broadway run of this play was followed by an extended tour.

Her next bit of stage success came in "Cabin in the Sky" in 1941 in which she played the role of Petunia. Later, she starred in the film version.

In 1949, Miss Waters received an Academy Award nomination as best supporting actress in the film "Pinky." In the same year, she performed briefly in the title role of the "Beulah" television show broadcast over the ABC network.

One of her last stage appearances was in "The Member of the Wedding" in 1950 in which she sang the popular hit "His Eye on the Sparrow."

In the last 15 years of her life, Miss Waters toured the

United States and the world singing with Billy Graham's Crusades.
Ethel Waters died in Los Angeles on September 1, 1977.

DEWEY WEINGLASS

Dewey Weinglass, who was the foremost male exponent of
Russian style dancing in the early 1920's, was born in Georgetown,
South Carolina in 1900. He moved to New York City with his family when he was six years old. In his early youth he was a champion broad jumper for two years in the Public School Athletic League
in New York City. He began his theatrical career at the age of
fifteen with a black act billed as "Mattie Phillips and her Jungle
Kids" with which she earned $12.50 per week while the act played
the "gas light circuit." In 1915, Weinglass toured Cuba for six
months with an act called "Gengette Hamilton and Her Picks" at
$18 per week. In 1916, he joined Mayme Remington and they
opened at the Bushmack Theatre in Brooklyn on the same bill as
the Marx Brothers. Weinglass did his Russian dance for the finale
and was the hit of the show.

Deciding to form his own act, Weinglass took on Dave Strat-
ton, Nina Hunter, and Charlotte Settle and called the act the "Dancing Demons." They opened at the Alhambra Theatre in Brooklyn.
However, the other acts, all white, were paid, but the Demons were
not; because of that the act broke up temporarily.

Later, the Demons got back together and toured the T. O. B. A.
playing southern theatres. It was a new experience for Weinglass,
who had never been South. The act soon became headliners and
after a few years returned to New York on the Keith Circuit. In
1921, the group appeared at the Victoria Theatre in London where
they were a hit and Weinglass earned $500 per week for this en-
gagement.

After returning to the U. S., Weinglass worked in "Liza" and
"Dixie to Broadway," and he and the Dancing Demons were featured
in "Harlem Rounders" in 1925. Later, he produced "Who's Doing
It?" in 1927. After another short stint in vaudeville, he managed
the Pearl Theatre in Philadelphia. Weinglass retired from show
business in the late 1930's to become the manager of a bar and
grill in Harlem.

AL WELLS

Al Wells, who was a pioneer black American aerialist,
was among a score of blacks trouping with circuses in the 1920's.
Almost all of them, because of the existing racial discrimination,
called themselves Arabs, Bedouins, or by any other name than
what they racially were. Al Wells was born in West Virginia
and was taught the art of walking the tight wire by members of a
circus troupe, who became interested in him. The young Wells

was an apt pupil and soon received a regular job. His first appearances were with "Connie Cal's" and "Sutton and Jackson's 10 and 20 Cent Wagon Circus" that trouped the Ohio Valley, covering the states of Ohio and Pennsylvania. No longer an amateur, he performed nightly on the horizontal bar and trapeze like a veteran. Later he joined the Rich Brothers, white, with which he performed a clown act. About this time, he decided to take on a partner who later became his wife.

While working in a hotel in New York City, Mr. Wells taught his wife acrobatics at the St. Cyprian's Gymnasium during his off duty hours. For about a year and a half, she was put through an intense course of training. At the end of this time, she was ready and the couple began performing together. On January 11, 1910, the act received an engagement in Madison Square Garden, New York, and made history by being the first black aerial act to work in New York City. Mrs. Laura Wells was at the time the first black woman to do a "flying break-away" with a 25-foot drop without a net. Other pioneer black circus performers of this period included the Gaines Brothers (Charles and Albert), acrobats, Harper Puggeley, Watts Brothers, "Jolly" Saunders and the Reese Brothers. Wells and Wells were also a featured vaudeville act in the 1920's.

MATTIE WILKES

Mattie Wilkes, whose career began back in the early 1890's, was one of the best known character actresses. She came to prominence with Isham's Octoroons and later with Isham's Oriental America, appearing as a member of a famous quartet composed of Bell Davis, Dora Dean, Ollie Burgoyne, and Mattie Wilkes. Mrs. Wilkes toured abroad several times and performed in all of the European capitals. In the latter part of her career, she played the heavy parts in various productions staged by the famous Lafayette Players and later was one of the featured performers in the play "Lula Bell." Mrs. Wilkes died in New York City, July 1927.

SPENCER WILLIAMS

Spencer Williams, actor, film technician, and film producer, is probably best remembered for his characterization of "Andy Brown" on the Amos and Andy TV show. The versatile and multitalented Williams was born on July 14, 1893 in Vidalia, Louisiana, a quaint little city across the Mississippi River from Natchez, Mississippi. As a young man he drifted to New York City where he secured a position as call boy for Oscar Hammerstein and gained his first stage experience. While in New York, he became acquainted with Bert Williams and studied the art of comedy at the feet of the great master. He later served in the U. S. Army during World War I.

In the wake of the sound picture craze, he came to Hollywood not to be an actor but to be a technician, a job he finally obtained at the old Christy Studios in Hollywood and where he helped to install the first sound equipment. He worked at this job for some time until Octavious Roy Cohn, a writer from Birmingham, Alabama, came to the studio to write a series of all-black comedies. Williams, because of his knowledge of Negro dialect, was engaged to help write the scripts and later became one of the first black scenario writers in Hollywood. Williams was later featured in several Christy comedies.

He appeared in a number of all-black films including "Georgia Rose, " "The Bronze Buckaroo, " "Harlem Rides the Range, " "Harlem on the Prairie, " and "Juke Joint. " He also appeared in "The Virginia Judge" which was released by Paramount. He also wrote and directed several black films including "Blood of Jesus, " "Go Down Death, " and "Tenderfeet. " Williams appeared in and wrote the story for the first all-black horror film, "Son of Ingagi, " in 1940.

At the time he was summoned to Hollywood for a principal role in the Amos and Andy TV show, Williams was in Tulsa, Oklahoma where he had gone to live in 1946 and to form a partnership with Masonic fraternal leader Amos T. Hall in the organization of the American Business and Industrial College, a GI school.   A professional photographer himself, Williams instituted a six-vocation curriculum which included photography and radio.

Unknown to him, he was being sought by Flournoy E. Miller who had been enlisted in a national search for an actor to fill the role of Andy as well as that of the Kingfish.   The search ended when Williams learned that Tulsa's radio station KTUL had been broadcasting for him to come and try out for the role.   With Tim Moore portraying Kingfish, Williams gained nationwide attention in the TV show which was filmed at the old Hal Roach Studio in Culver City, California between 1951 and 1954.   Following the TV series, Williams went into semi-retirement and later died in Los Angeles in 1969.

ARTHUR "DOOLEY" WILSON

Arthur Wilson, pioneer actor, singer and pianist, was born in 1885 in Tyler, Texas, the youngest son of a poor family.   His father died when he was seven, so he went out and got a job singing for five dollars a week "and cakes" in carnivals and tent shows. By the time he was eight, he had played a full year of one night stands and his salary had increased to eighteen dollars a week "and cakes. "   He sang popular ballads of the day such as "The Bird in the Gilded Cage. "

During the next few years, the young Wilson worked in min-

"Dooley" Wilson

strel shows and whatever else he could find, all over the Midwest
before winding up in Chicago where he became associated with the
famous Pekin Stock Company founded by Bob Motts.   Charles Gilpin
was one of the stars of the company during this time.   During this
period, Wilson displayed an incredibly wide versatility, specializing
in Irish roles which he did with a brogue and in "white face."   Wilson, Clarence Muse and Tim Moore were three of the relatively few
black actors who worked in white face on the stage.

One of Wilson's most popular Irish characterizations was his
song called "Mr. Dooley."   The name stuck and from then on he
was never billed as anything but Dooley Wilson.

After the Pekin, Wilson played the drum in small bands and
he was beating it out at the Sontag Cabaret on Lenox Avenue in
Harlem when Irving Berlin, then a young song writer, would come
in and slip Wilson five or ten to plug a tune called "Alexander's
Ragtime Band."

Later, Wilson went to Europe where he was joined by his
old band, the Red Devils.   He remained in Europe until the late
1920's when he returned to the United States and took up a variety
of jobs which ranged from playing stock with Bette Davis in New
Hampstead to beating the skins in the Nest Club in Harlem.

During the next few years, he appeared in "The Strangler
Fig," "Of Mice and Men," and created the role of Little Joe opposite Ethel Waters in "Cabin in the Sky."

Wilson then went to Hollywood to work in pictures, but could
only get small parts as a porter or butler.   However, he later
gained national fame in his role of Sam the piano player in the film
"Casablanca."   His rendition of the song "As Time Goes By" is a
film classic.

Later in his career, he appeared on the "Beulah" radio show
with Ethel Waters.   Dooley Wilson died in 1953 at the age of 67.

EDITH WILSON

Edith Wilson was one of the most popular and talented entertainers in the 1920's and 1930's.   She got her first chance to perform before a large audience at the age of 13, when she sang for
several nights during a Centennial celebration in her hometown of
Louisville, Kentucky.   The youngster had to keep her appearance a
secret until she could convince her parents that she was serious
about going into show business as a career.

Edith first went to New York City in 1921 where she met the
famous song writer Perry Bradford, who arranged her first recording date.   In 1922, she was cast in her first bit show "Put and
Take" produced by Irvin C. Miller.

Her first professional break came in 1924 when she was hired by Lew Leslie to co-star with Florence Mills in the Plantation Revue. The show was a smashing success and the English producer C. B. Cochran was so impressed that he later took the entire cast to England and combined it with an English cast to create "Dover Street to Dixie." During this period, she rose to become an established star and was much in demand at home and abroad.

During her long career Miss Wilson starred in many hit shows including "Rhapsody in Black," Dixie to Broadway," "Hot Chocolates," and "Memphis Bound" with Bill Robinson. She also made several appearances with Duke Ellington at the Cotton Club in Harlem. In "Hot Chocolates" Miss Wilson, Fats Waller and Louis Armstrong were billed as "1000 pounds of harmony." "Black and Blue," one of her numbers in that show, was written especially for her by Fats Waller and Henry Brooks with the lyrics by the great Andy Razaf.

Miss Wilson was also a very successful recording artist. Between 1921 and 1930 she made about 35 records, most of which were issued. She also worked with Eubie Blake in the 1932 edition of "Shuffle Along." Later, during World War II, they appeared together touring the country with a USO show.

After the war, she moved from New York City to California where she was active in the theatre, radio and television. She played the Kingfish's mother-in-law on the Amos and Andy show and appeared as Aunt Jemima as part of an advertising promotion for Quaker Oats pancake mix. She was also very active in touring the country raising funds for various youth programs. At one time, she also had the honor of being elected to the position of Vice President of the Negro Actors Guild. Her many TV appearances included the Bill Cullen and Gary Moore shows.

FRANK WILSON

Frank Wilson, nationally known playwright and performer, was born in New York City. He first gained recognition when he organized the Carolina Comedy Four in 1908 and played in vaudeville until 1911 when he temporarily quit show business, and took a job as a mail carrier.

While carrying the mail around Harlem, he came across what he regarded as excellent material for black plays. His first dramatic was produced at the Lincoln Theatre on West 135th Street near Lenox Avenue. For three years he wrote an average of one playlet every six or eight weeks for the theatre.

Wilson's debut as a legitimate actor was in about 1917 as a member of the Lafayette Players Stock Company in a play titled "Deep Purple" at the Lafayette Theatre, Seventh Avenue and 131st Street. Towards the end of World War I, when Franklin P. Sargent of the American Academy of Dramatic Arts organized a dramatic class which met at Carnegie Hall, Wilson was one of the students. Later, when Anno Wolter undertook to carry on the work started by Sargent, Wilson became a pupil and took lessons for three and a half years.

In 1921, a theatrical manager turned to Mr. Wilson for a playlet dealing with black life for a company of the Lafayette Players. Wilson's "Confidence" was successfully produced in New York City, Philadelphia, Washington, D. C. and other cities.

In the 1920's, Wilson appeared in supporting roles in almost all of the dramatic productions in New York. He appeared with Charles S. Gilpin in "The Emperor Jones," he was with Paul Robeson in the stage and film productions of "The Emperor Jones" and in "All God's Chillun' Got Wings." In 1925, when Robeson was at the 52nd Street Theatre, Wilson had the principle part as "Dreamy Kid" the curtain raiser.

It was during this engagement that marked the turning point in his career. In 1926, he appeared in the prizewinning play "In Abraham's Bosom." In the 1930's, Wilson produced and performed in many shows and plays and he also appeared in several all-black films including "Paradise in Harlem."

"RASTUS" WINFIELD

"Rastus" Winfield was born in Greenville, South Carolina and his mother was a concert associate of the famous Anita Patti Brown and his father was manager of a musical comedy company. In 1909, the young Winfield divided his time between the public schools and playing juvenile parts in the productions of his parents.

His first opportunity to strike out on his own came with an offer from A. L. Walcott of the "Rabbit's Foot Minstrels" in 1916. His success was almost immediate. From there he went from fair and celebration engagements to a position with "Billy" Watson on the Columbia Burlesque Circuit. After leaving Watson in 1913, Winfield and his wife Marie played in a dance act over the T. O. B. A.

Their offering was a pronounced success and was given a berth on the Keith and Lowe circuits for three years. The Tap, Charleston, Eccentric, Waltz Clog and other then popular dances were included in Winfield's dance repertoire. In 1927, Winfield headed his own "Dancing Dan from Louisian' Company" with a cast of fifteen people.

HENRY WINFRED

Henry Winfred, of the team of Winfred and Mills (Billy), was born in Windsor, Canada, and raised in Louisville, Kentucky.

As a boy he did chores around the Buckingham Theatre, which created his desire to be a performer.   Later he joined the original Whalen and Martell's "South Before the War" company where he performed with such success that he soon branched out into other shows such as Sam T. Jack's "Creole" company, Isham's famous "Octoroons" and the "Oriental Americans" during the season of 1896-1897.

Winfred later formed the original Golden Gate Quartet which was a featured act in one of the best known shows of the time, "Darkest American."   Leaving this, he played with the Williams and Walker company until he went into vaudeville where he remained until 1901 at which time the quartet joined Miacos City Club burlesque company.

In about 1908, the Golden Gate Quartet, then consisting of Winfred, Frank Sutton, Jim Burris and Paul C. Floyd, dissolved. Winfred then formed a trio with his wife and Martin, calling it the Golden Gate Trio.   After the termination of the trio, Winfred formed an act with John Rucker, and later he worked with Billy Brown.   After spending some time in warm California in an effort to improve his health, Winfred worked for a while with Slim Thompson.   He then formed an act with Billy Mills, billing it Winfred and Mills "In China" and it opened at the Plantation Club in New York City.

APPENDIX A

TYPICAL T. O. B. A. SHOW CONTRACT
OF THE LATE 1920's*

It is agreed between the said Artist and said Manager that there will be great damage to the business of the Manager if said Artists fails to perform his act on the stage of said Theatre aforesaid, and that said Artist and said Manager agree that such damages are not easily ascertainable, and that the said Artist agrees to pay the said manager for such failure to perform his act the sum of Fifteen Hundred Dollars ($1500) as liquidation damages.

It is agreed between the said Artist and said Manager that there will be great damage to the business of the Manager if the said Artist appears and performs his act upon the stage of any other theatre or place of amusement in the city aforesaid at any time after the date of the making of this contract and prior to the times said contract is to be performed by said Artist at said theatre of said Manager aforesaid, and the said Artist and said Manager agree that such damages for the said Artist appearing and performing his act upon the stage of such other theatre or place of amusement in said city mentioned aforesaid are not easily ascertainable, and said Artist agrees to pay said Manager for appearing and performing his said act at said other theatre or place of amusement in said city after the date of the making of this contract the sum of Fifteen Hundred Dollars ($1500) as liquidated damages.

This contract being entered into through the instrumentality of the T. O. B. A. and in consideration of the service rendered to the parties hereto in procuring this contract said parties hereby agree to and do hereby save the said T. O. B. A. harmless from any and all claims of every character whatsoever, which the parties hereto or either of them may sustain because of the failure on the part of either party to faithfully carry out the terms of this contract. The said Artist agrees that the sum of $50 of the amount received by the said Artist on this contract shall be deducted by the said Theatre Owners and Booking Association, in full consideration of the services rendered to said Artist in securing this engagement.

*From an article by Clarence Muse, Pittsburgh Courier, Jan. 8, 1928.

455

Party of the second part agrees not to appear at any theatre
in above mentioned city ninety days before or sixty days after this
engagement, violation of this clause subject to liquidated damages
contained in this contract.

The Manager or Artist reserve the right to cancel this contract by giving at least six days notice in writing.   Also Manager
reserves the right to cancel act after the first performance.

In witness whereof, said parties have hereunto set their
hands and seals the day and year first above written.

This contract signed and executed in triplicate.

BANDANA AMUSEMENT CO.,
INC.
per Clarence Muse
CHARLESTON DANDIES CO.

APPENDIX B

A PARTIAL LIST OF BLACK MUSICAL SHOWS, 1900-1940*

1900-1910

"Black Patti Troubadours," 1908. Producer: Sissieretta Jones, Black Patti Musical Comedy Co. Principal Cast: Sissieretta Jones (Black Patti), Slim Henderson, Salem Tutt Whitney.

"Black Politician," 1908. Producer: S. H. Dudley. Principal Cast: Smart Set Company.

"A Blackville Corporation," 1910. Producer: J. Leubrie Hill. Principal Cast: J. Leubrie Hill, Brown and Shelton (Richard), Louie Mitchell, Leona Marshall.

"De Cider Man," 1909. Producer: Edward Denton. Principal Cast: No data.

"George Washington B," 1910. Producer: Salem Tutt Whitney. Principal Cast: The Smart Set Company.

"His Honor the Barber," 1909. Producer: S. H. Dudley. Book: Edwin Hanford. Music, Lyrics: Brown, Smith, Burris. Principal Cast: S. H. Dudley, Chris Smith, Jennie Pearl, James Burris, Alene Caspel, Irving Allen, Matt Johnson, Andrew Tribble.

"The Music Man," 1910. Producer: No data. Principal Cast: Tom Lockhart, Lena Lockhart, Mitchell Sisters, Billy Scott (The Drool Comedian).

"A Night in New York's Chinatown," 1910 (Pekin Theatre, Chicago). Producer: Sam Croker, Jr. Book: Jesse A. Shipp. Principal Cast: Esmeralda Straham, Fannie Wise, Broadway Girls (Misses Davis, Jones, and Brown), Jesse A. Shipp, Tom Brown, Charles Gilpin, Jerry Mills, Sidney Perrin, Goldie Crosby, Gibson and Amose.

"No Place Like Home," 1910 (Pekin Theatre, Chicago). Producer:

---

*Shows included in Chapter 5 are not listed here.

Jesse A. Shipp, Jesse A. Shipp's Stock Company. Principal
Cast: Tom Brown (Italian Man), Sidney I. Perrin (Willie
Brown), Jesse A. Shipp (Rod Staff), Goldie Crosby (Lucy White),
Fanny Wise (Anna Bell), Hattie McIntosh (Mrs. White), Jerry
Mills (Mr. White).

"Our Friend from Dixie," 1910. Producer: J. Leubrie Hill.
Principal Cast: William Simmon, J. Leubrie Hill, George
Williams, Lois A. Mitchell, Maggie Miller, Mayme Butler,
Abe Lewis, Alonzo Govern, Leona Marshall, Kate Krew, Evon
Robinson, Quetta Watts.

"The Whitman Sisters Review," 1910. Producer: Whitman Sisters.
Principal Cast: Whitman Sisters, Little Thomas (Thomas Hawkins), Baby Alice.

1911-1915

"Bombay Girls," 1915. Producers: Drake and Walker, The Great
Eastern Stock Company. Principal Cast: Drake and Walker.

"Broadway Rastus," 1915. Producer: Irvin C. Miller. Principal
Cast: Irvin C. Miller, Henry Jines, Leigh Whipper, Russell
Lee, Billy Young, Eloise Johnson, Marie Hendricks, Lulu
Whidby, Juanita Hicks, Esther Bigeou, Tillie Cotterman,
Carrie Purnell.

"The Cabaret," 1913. Producer: Flournoy E. Miller, Aubrey
Lyles. Principal Cast: Flournoy E. Miller, Aubrey Lyles,
Lizzie Wallace, Cook and Bernard, Pekin Trio, Lottie Grady,
Davis and Walker, Clarence M. Jones, Jordan and Jones, Jerry
Mills, Kid Brown, Johnny Woods.

"Captain Bogus of the Jim Crow Regiment," 1913. Producer: No
data. Principal Cast: Star (Theatre, Savannah, Ga.) Stock
Co.; Williams and Rajou, Bradford and Bradford, The Williams
Sisters, Papa String Beans, Mabel Johnson.

"Carnation," 1914. Producer: Billy King. Principal Cast: Billy
King Stock Company.

"The Darktown Politician," 1913. Producer: Salem Tutt Whitney.
Music: T. L. Corwell, Salem Tutt Whitney, J. Homer Tutt,
Watterson. Principal Cast: Salem Tutt Whitney (title role),
J. Homer Tutt, Blanche Thompson, 25 songs.

"Dr. Herbs' Prescription, or It Happened in a Dream," 1911 (Pekin
Theatre, Chicago). Producer: Jesse A. Shipp. Principal
Cast: Jesse A. Shipp, Allie Gilliam, Shelton Brooks, Hattie
McIntosh, Fanny Wise, Ada Banks, Lottie Grady, Billy John-
son, Charles Gilpin, Will C. Elkins, Jerry Mills, Clarence
Tinsdale, W. D. Coleman, Kattie Jones, Daisy Brown, Ethel
Marlowe, Gertie Brown.

"The Epic of the Negro," 1913. Producer: No data. Principal
Cast: The Dixie Chorus.

"The Frog Follies," 1913. Producer: Will Marion Cook, J. Rosa-
mond Johnson, James Reese Europe. Principal Cast: Bert A.
Williams, Julius Glenn, Henry Troy, James Reese Europe's
Band, Harper and Gilliam, Alex Rogers, Sam Lucas, Lloyd
Gibbs, Jesse A. Shipp, Charles Gilpin, Barber and William,
S. H. Dudley, Kelly and Catlin (all members of the famous
Frog Club).

"The Ham Tree," 1911 (3 acts). Producer: William M. Benbow,
"Alabama Chocolate Drop Company." Principal Cast: W. Benbow, Edna Benbow, Mose Graham, Rebecca Kinzy.

"His Excellency the President," 1914. Producer: Salem Tutt
Whitney, J. Homer Tutt. Principal Cast: Salem Tutt Whitney,
J. Homer Tutt, Blanche Thompson.

"Hottest Coon in Dixie," 1911, 1912. Producer: No data. Principal Cast: Harry Morgan, Bud Halliday, Alan Richardson,
Viola Harris, Otis Benson, Alex Wheeler's Rag Time Band.

"The Lime Kiln Club," 1911 (Pekin Theatre, Chicago). Producer:
Sam Croker, Jr. Book: Jesse A. Shipp. Music: Bob Bailey.
Principal Cast: Allie Gilliam, Charles Gilpin, Billy Harper,
Jimmy Brown, Hattie McIntosh, Fanny Wise, Clarence Tisdale,
Lottie Grady, Will C. Elkins, The Dahomian Trio.

"Lucky Sam from Alabam'," 1914. Producer: Sissieretta Jones,
Black Patti Musical Comedy Company. Principal Cast:
Sissieretta Jones (Black Patti), Harrison Stewart, Viola
Stewart, W. A. Cook, Jeanette Murphy, Tillie Sequin, C.
Payne.

"Mr. John Green in the Tropics of Mexico," 1915. Producers:
Drake and Walker. Principal Cast: Drake and Walker Players.

"Out in the Street," 1914. Producer: Billy King. Principal Cast:
Billy King Stock Company.

"Professor Ebenezzer," 1915. Producer: Harrison Stewart.
Principal Cast: Harrison Stewart, Sam Gains, Viola Stewart,
Zerobia Allen, Beulah Brown, Lawrence Chenault, George Hall,
Rena Blunt, Beulah Bishop, Ethel Jacobs, Loretta Jacobs,
Maude Gaines, Sallie Walker, Gertrude Jones, Hattie Wallace,
Charles Cantry, Marrie Gibson, Pete Jones, Will Sulzer, J. C.
Liverpool, Lottie Bryant.

"Royal Sam," 1911. Producer: Morrow and Mindlin. Principal
Cast: "Jolly" John Larkins, Jennie Pearl, Irving (Boots) Allen,
J. Francis Mores, Irene Tasker, William Wilkins, James A.
Lillard, Luke A. Scott, Ethel Johnson, Anna Tyler, George

George McClain, Ethelyn Green, Ora Dunlop, Arthur C. Simmons, T. J. Sadler, Richard Webb.

"Runaway Slaves," 1911.   Producer: No data.   Principal Cast: Edwards and Edwards, Lee and Lee, Edna Campbell.   Songs: "That Was Me," "If Dreams Are True," "Stop, Stop, Stop," "There Is No Place Like the Old Folks After All."

"The Runaway's Return," 1914.   Producer: Billy King.   Principal Cast: Billy King Stock Company

"Spoony Sam," 1911 (1 act).   Producer: William M. Benbow, Alabama Chocolate Drop Company.   Principal Cast: W. Benbow (Spoony Sam), Mose Graham, Rebecca Kinzy (the Black Swan), Edna Benbow.   Songs: "Tell Her No, That's All," "All That I Ask is Love," "In the Land Harmony."

"Tallaboo," 1913.   Producer: No data.   Book: N. R. Harper. Principal Cast: Jenie Lacey, Nellie Lane, Fannie Hall, Clara Hutchinson, Aida Cunningham, George Hutchinson, A. C. Simms, George Gamway, Slim Walls.

"Ten Dark Nights," 1911.   Producers: Rolf and Smith.   Principal Cast: Jane Smith, Jimmie Brown, Henderson Smith, Alexander Wood, Wright Mobley, Haley Trio, Martha Russell, The Erie Quartet.

"Tom Boys--Easy Breezy Girls," 1914.   Producer: Billy Johnson. Principal Cast: Tom Brown, Billy Johnson.

"A Tragedy on the Town," 1913.   Producer: Porter and McDaniel. Principal Cast: Porter and McDaniel Stock Company.

"The Traitor," 1914 (2 acts).   Producer: The Famous Colored Players.   Principal Cast: Billy Harper, Charles H. Gilpin, Alice Gorgas, Grayce LeCook, Ruth Cherry, Andrew Bishop, Cassie Norwood, Invincible Quartette (Jordan, Derry, Reevs, Crawford).

"Two Bills from Alaska," 1913.   Producer: Billy King.   Principal Cast: Billy King, Hattie McIntosh, Cordelia McClain, Howard Kelly, Georgia Kelly, the Jolly Hendersons (Billy and Beulah), Ursell Burnette, Walter Watkins.

"Two Story," 1911 (1 act).   Producer: William M. Benbow, Alabama Chocolate Drop Company.   Principal Cast: Mose Graham ("Porter"), Edna Benbow, William Benbow, Rebecca Kinzy. Songs: "China Town Rag," "Miss Malinda."

"When Luck Bill Came to Town," 1914.   Producer: No data. Principal Cast: McDaniel and White, Nina Stovall, Robinson and Robinson, Billy Cross.

"The Whitewash Man," 1915. Producer: Harrison Stewart. Principal Cast: Harrison Stewart and Company.

"Who's to Win," 1913. Producers: Bragg and Mahone. Principal Cast: Madame Endora Lockett.

"The Wrong Cook and Waiter," 1915. Producers: Drake and Walker, The Great Eastern Stock Company. Principal Cast: Drake and Walker.

"The Wrong Mr. President," 1913. Producers: Salem Tutt Whitney, J. Homer Tutt. Principal Cast: The Smart Set Company.

"The Wrong Mr. Right," 1913 (Pekin Theatre, Savannah, Georgia). Producer: No data. Principal Cast: Pekin Stock Company.

1916

"The Black Coachman," 1916. Producers: The Whitman Sisters. Principal Cast: The Whitman Sisters.

"Chicago Follies," 1916. Producer: Tim Moore. Principal Cast: Tim Moore Company.

"45 Minutes from Broadway," 1916. Producer: No data. Principal Cast: Abbie Mitchell, "Babe" Townsend, Susie Sutton, Laura Bowman, Walker Thompson, Tom Brown, Alice Gorgas, Susie Smith.

"From Speedville to Broadway," 1916. Producer: Frank Montgomery. Sponsor: Quality Amusement Co., Robert Levey. Principal Cast: Frank Montgomery, Fanny Wise, Mae Brown, Blanche Harris, Josephine Lazzo, Marion Whitfield, Howard and Mason, Dave Struffin, Gertrude Struffin, Hattie James, Alice Saunders, George Stamper, Earl West, Lillian Williams, Florence McClain, Clarice Wright, Dewey Weinglass.

"Good Time Tonight," 1916. Producers: Drake and Walker. Principal Cast: Drake and Walker, Madeline Cooper, William Bally, Jack "Ginger" Wiggins.

"Holiday in Dixie," 1916. Producer: Will Mastin. Principal Cast: Will Mastin, Vergie Richards, C. Owen, Cora Hunter, Alice Owen, Essie Wallace, Burt Smith, Sam Bailey, Arthur Malone, Miles Williams.

"In the Old Home Town," 1916. Producer: Frank Montgomery. Sponsor: Quality Amusement Company, Robert Levey. Principal Cast: No data.

"Lizzie and Pete of the Cabaret Show," 1916. Producer: No data. Principal Cast: Mable Decard.

"On the Way to Boston, " 1916.   Producer: Frank Montgomery.
Sponsor: Quality Amusement Company, Robert Levey.   Prin-
cipal Cast: Frank Montgomery, Fanny Wise, Mae Brown,
Blanche Harris, Josephine Lazzo, Marion Whitfield, Howard
and Mason, Dave Struffin, Gertrude Struffin, Hattie James,
Alice Saunders, George Stamper, Earl West, Lillian Williams,
Florence McClain, Clarice Wright, Dewey Weinglass.

"The Return of Sam Langford, " 1916.   Producer: Billy Watts,
Watts Big Stock Company.   Principal Cast: Madam Patti Willis,
Billy Watts.

"The Rivals, " 1916 (Grand Theatre, Chicago).   Producer: Billy
King.   Principal Cast: Billy King Company.

"The Three Twins, " 1916.   Producer: Quality Amusement Compa-
ny, Robert Levey.   Principal Cast: Francis Mores, Abbie
Mitchell, Laura Bowman, "Babe" Townsend, Mildred Smallwood,
Susie Sutton, Tom Brown.

"The Undertaker's Daughter, " 1916 (Grand Theatre, Chicago).
Producer: Billy King.   Principal Cast: Billy King, Billy
Walker, Greensbery Holmes, John Boone, Gertrude Saunders,
Stella Harris, W. B. Overstreet, Howard Kelly.

1917

"Bombay Girls, " 1917.   Producers: Drake and Walker.   Principal
Cast: Drake and Walker, Russell Lee, Ethel Walker, Willie
Hampton.

"The Bon Ton Minstrels, " 1917.   Producer: Frank Montgomery.
Sponsor: Quality Amusement Company, Robert Levey.   Prin-
cipal Cast: Frank Montgomery, Fanny Wise, Mae Brown,
Blanche Harris, Josephine Lazzo, Marion Whitfield, Howard
and Mason, Dave Struffin, Gertrude Struffin, Hattie James,
Alice Saunders, George Stamper, Earl West, Lillian Williams,
Florence McClain, Clarice Wright, Dewey Weinglass.

"Exploits in Africa, " 1917 (Grand Theatre, Chicago).   Producer:
Billy King.   Principal Cast: Billy King, Howard Kelly.

"The Face at the Window, " 1917 (Grand Theatre, Chicago).   Pro-
ducer: Billy King.   Principal Cast: Billy King, Gertrude
Saunders, Weber and Wilson, Blaskston Quartette, Howard
Kelly.

"The Final Rehearsal, " 1917 (Grand Theatre, Chicago).   Producer:
Billy King.   Principal Cast: The Billy King Company.

"The Heart Breakers, " 1917 (Grand Theatre, Chicago).   Producer:
Billy King.   Principal Cast: Billy King Company.

"Hotel Nobody, " 1917 (Grand Theatre, Chicago). Producer: Billy
    King. Principal Cast: Marguerita Jackson, Leon Brooks,
    Billy King, Mary Young, Georgia Kelly, Howard Kelly.

"The Kidnapper, " 1917 (Grand Theatre, Chicago). Producer: Billy
    King. Principal Cast: Billy King and Company.

"A Lady for a Day, " 1917 (Grand Theatre, Chicago). Producer:
    Billy King. Principal Cast: Billy King Company.

"The Lonesome Mile, " 1917 (Grand Theatre, Chicago). Producer:
    Billy King. Principal Cast: Billy King Company.

"Lucky Sam from Alabam', " 1917. Producer: Irvin C. Miller.
    Principal Cast: Irvin C. Miller, Sandy Burns, Helen Bumbry.

"A Mother-in-Law's Disposition, " 1917 (Grand Theatre, Chicago).
    Producer: Billy King. Principal Cast: Billy King and Com-
    pany.

"My People, " 1917. Producers: Salem Tutt Whitney, J. Homer
    Tutt. Lyrics: Tutt and Whitney. Music: C. Luckeyth Rob-
    erts. Principal Cast: Salem Tutt Whitney, J. Homer Tutt,
    T. L. Corwell, B. Hillman, Luck Scott, Sam Gray, Al Watts,
    Nat Cash, William Fountain, Julian Costello, Wesley Mitchell,
    Charles Lawrence, Alex White, Edward Marshall, Buster Wil-
    liams, Emma Jackson, Lena Roberts, Daisy Martin, Carrie
    King, Estelle Cash, Ora Dunlop, Virginia Wheeler, Gladys
    Dennis, Ferrell White, Julia Moody, Marion Artie, Theresa
    West, Mattie Brooks, Ethel Pope.

"Neighbors, " 1917 (Grand Theatre, Chicago). Producer: Billy
    King. Principal Cast: Billy King Company.

"Raiding a Cabaret, " 1917 (Grand Theatre, Chicago). Producer:
    Billy King. Principal Cast: Billy King, Gates and Davis,
    Gertrude Saunders, Everett Butler, India Allen, Ernest Whit-
    man, Georgia Kelly, Howard Kelly.

"Sambo Jones in New York, " 1917. Producers: James and Stovall.
    Principal Cast: James and Stovall.

"The Senator, " 1917 (Grand Theatre, Chicago). Producer: Billy
    King. Principal Cast: Billy King, Theresa Brooks, Gertrude
    Saunders, Vera Carmen Trio, Wright and Davis, Bergoulst
    Brothers.

"Sergeant Ham of the 13th District, " 1917. Producers: Perry
    Bradford and Jeanett. Principal Cast: Bradford and Jeanett,
    Hatch and Hatch, Mason and Brown, Billy McLauren, Mamie
    Smith, Elsie Perry.

"Sultan for a Night, " 1917. Producer: Irvin C. Miller. Princi-
    pal Cast: Irvin C. Miller, Dink Stewart.

"The Two Detectives," 1917.   Producer: Frank Montgomery.
Principal Cast: Frank Montgomery, Florence McClain, Sam
Gaines, Garland Howard, Hattie James.

"Wolves and Lambs," 1917.   Producers: James and Stovall.
Principal Cast: James and Stovall.

1918

"At the Beach," 1918 (Grand Theatre, Chicago).   Producer: Billy
King. Principal Cast: Billy King, Howard Kelly, Bessie
Brown, Gertrude Saunders, Ernest Whitman.

"Catching the Burglar," 1918 (Grand Theatre, Chicago).   Producer:
Billy King. Principal Cast: Billy King, Howard Kelly.

"The Charming Widow," 1918.   Producers: Bob Russell, Bob
Russell Stock Company. Principal Cast: Blanche Thompson,
Cora Green, Carolyn Williams, Florence Mills.

"Chief Outlanchette," 1918 (Grand Theatre, Chicago).   Producer:
Billy King. Principal Cast: Billy King, Jerry Mills, Jim
Reed, Leon Brooks, Howard Kelly, Bessie Brown.

"The Con Man," 1918 (Grand Theatre, Chicago).   Producer: Billy
King. Principal Cast: Billy King, Howard Kelly, James Reed,
Bessie Whitman, Ernest Whitman.

"The Final Rehearsal," 1918 (Grand Theatre, Chicago).   Producer:
Billy King. Principal Cast: Billy King, Howard Kelly, Gertrude Saunders, Genevieve Stern, Blaine and Brown.

"The Flat Below," 1918.   Producers: Flournoy E. Miller, Aubrey
Lyles. Stage Director: Clarence Muse. Principal Cast:
Flournoy E. Miller, Aubrey Lyles, Leon Diggs, Myrtle Porter
Lyles, Bessie Oliva Miller, William D. Rivers, Charles H.
Bruce, Cassie E. Slaughter, Roger Jones, Aaron Twigg, Bessie
Tribble, Ethyl Patton, Minnie Brown, Solomon Bruce, Clarence
Muse.

"Goodby Everybody," 1918 (Grand Theatre, Chicago).   Producer:
Billy King. Principal Cast: Billy King, Ernest Whitman,
Anita Wilkins, Bessie Brown, Leon Brooks, Blanche Thompson,
Howard Kelly.

"The Heart Breakers," 1918 (Grand Theatre, Chicago).   Producer:
Billy King. Principal Cast: Billy King, Howard Kelly, James
Thomas, Gertrude Saunders, Bessie Brown.

"His Honor the Mayor," 1918.   Producer: No data. Principal
Cast: Walker Thompson, Thressa Bluford, Marjorie Shipp,
Sidney Kirkpatrick, Laura Bowman.

"In the Draft," 1918 (Grand Theatre, Chicago). Producer: Billy
    King. Principal Cast: Billy King, Howard Kelly, James Reed,
    Gertrude Saunders.

"Mr. Jazz from Dixie," 1918 (Grand Theatre, Chicago). Producer:
    Billy King. Principal Cast: Billy King Company.

"My People," 1918. Producers: Salem Tutt Whitney, J. Homer
    Tutt. Principal Cast: Salem Tutt Whitney, J. Homer Tutt,
    Luke Scott, Alonzo Fenderson, Sam Gray, Nat Cash, Wesley
    Mitchell, Charles Lawrence, Al Watts, Larry Williams, Jim
    Lee, William Fountain.

"My Wife's Sweetheart," 1918. Producer: Dunell Bright Company.
    Principal Cast: Esther Bigeou Miller, Irvin C. Miller.

"The Night Raid," 1918 (Grand Theatre, Chicago). Producer:
    Billy King. Principal Cast: Billy King, Georgia Kelly, Babe
    Brown.

"Now I'm a Mason," 1918 (Grand Theatre, Chicago). Producer:
    Billy King. Principal Cast: Billy King Company featuring
    Bessie Brown and Howard Kelly.

"The Rich Uncle," 1918 (Grand Theatre, Chicago). Producer:
    Billy King. Principal Cast: Howard Kelly and Billy King.

"Trouble in a Chinese Laundry," 1918. Producer: Big Six Musi-
    cal Comedy Company. Principal Cast: Jules McGarr, Billy
    McLaurin, Hardtack Jackson, Maude McGarr, Kitty Brown.

"20 Minutes in Hell," 1918. Producer: Benbow's Merry Makers.
    Principal Cast: William Benbow, Bob Davis, Baby Benbow,
    Williams and Taylor.

<u>1919</u>

"Bowman's Cotton Blossoms," 1919. Producer: Henri Bowman.
    Principal Cast: W. Henri Bowman (straight), Leroy White
    (comedian), Sam P. Gardner (character man), Johnnie Sawyer
    (principal), James Phoenix (dancer), S. H. Dudley (agent),
    Bonnie Bell Drew (leading lady), Chorus: Alice McDonald,
    Jackie Mabley, Sweetie May, Ethel Gardner, Ruth Wilson.

"Broadway Rastus," 1919 (edition). Producer: Irvin C. Miller.
    Principal Cast: Flo Brown, Irvin C. Miller, Cecil Rivers,
    Blanche Thompson, John Henderson, Lilly Yuen, Lloyd Mitchell.

"Darktown After Dark," 1919. Producer: Perry Bradford. Prin-
    cipal Cast: No data.

"Darktown Follies," 1919. Producer: Sherman H. Dudley. Prin-

cipal Cast: Sherman H. Dudley and his mule "Patrick," George
Glasco, Emma Fredericks, Rena Mitchell, Helen Bumbraye,
Wilton Crawley, West & Fredericks.

"Hello 1919," 1919-20. Producers: Frank Montgomery and Florence
McClain. Principal Cast: Frank Montgomery, Gus Butler,
Dike Thomas, Daisy Martin, Florence McClain.

"The Hunter Horse," 1919. Producer: Sandy Burns. Principal
Cast: Sandy Burns Stock Company.

"Over the Top," 1919 (Grand Theatre, Chicago). Producer: Billy
King. Principal Cast: Billy Higgins, Gertrude Saunders,
Theresa Brooks, Margaret Scott, James E. Stevens, Ernest
Whitman, Marcus F. Slayter, Ollie Burgoyane, Ida Forsyne,
Berlena Blanks, Laura Hall, Dean Gloves, Elvira Johnson.

"Rock and Rosey Lee," 1919. Producer: Sandy Burns. Principal
Cast: Sándy Burns Stock Company.

"Seeing Chinatown," 1919. Producer: Quality Amusement Company,
E. C. Brown. Staging: Jesse Shipp. Principal Cast: No
data.

"Sergeant Ham," 1919. Producer: Perry "Mule" Bradford. Prin-
cipal Cast: Perry Bradford, Ruth Coleman, Jerome Johnson,
Gladys Thompson, Marion Bradford, Charley Young, Larabell
Wise, Anita Spencer, The Dixie Four.

"This and That," 1919 (2 acts, 11 scenes). Producers: Alex
Rogers, C. Luckeyth Roberts. Book, Lyrics: Alex Rogers.
Music: C. Luckeyth Roberts. Dances: Hazel Thompson Davis.
Stage Director: Alex Rogers. Principal Cast: Dink Stewart,
Edna Brown, Charley Woody, Lottie Harris, Ellis Stevens,
Eddy the Curry, Charles H. Williams, Lelia Mitchell, Jesse
Paschall, Terry Williams, Macie Walters, Willa Dotson, Rose
Delta, Lena S. Roberts, A. F. Watts, Mattie Lewis, Arthur
Mason, Anna Crowder, P. Colston, Wolsie Simmons, Frank
O'Cause, Laymable Dover, Lucille Stone, Jessie Edmondson,
Jennie Smith, Violet Cash, Charles Young, Lydie Webb, E. E.
Coldwell, Gladys Boyd, Richard Courtney, Irene Summers,
Margaret Trimble, Irma Waters, Nora Brown, Edna White,
Ethel Wells.

"A Trip to South Africa," 1919. Producer: Sandy Burns. Principal Cast: Sandy Burns Stock Company.

"Up Stairs and Down Below," 1919. Producer: Flournoy E. Miller,
Aubrey Lyles. Principal Cast: Miller and Lyles.

"A Wedding in Jazz," 1919. Producer: Stovall & Macks' Merry-
Makers. Principal Cast: Joe Sheftell and his Eight Black Dots,
Tim and Gertie Moore, Walker and Brown, Thomas and Martin.

1920

"Beale Street to Broadway," 1920. Producer: Aaron Gates. Principal Cast: Gulfport and Brown, Gertrude Saunders, Anna
Freeman, Alice Ramsey, Leonard Scott, James Thomas, Ida
Forsyne, Mary Hubbard, Clara Lewis, India Allen.

"Bringing Up Husband," 1920. Producer: Hambone Jones. Principal Cast: Hambone Jones, Sam H. Gray, Virginia Liston.

"Broadway Gossips," 1920 (10 scenes). Producer: Quintard Miller.
Principal Cast: Quintard Miller, B. B. Joyner, Ethel Marshall,
Doe Doe Green, Cleo Mitchell, Aaron Gates, Joe Carmouche,
Lulu Whidby, Tressie Mitchell, Minnie Cos, Theresa Burroughs
Brooks.

"Broadway Rastus of 1920," 1920 (edition). Producer: Irvin C.
Miller. Principal Cast: Irvin C. Miller, The McCarvers,
Blanche Thompson, Leggett Sisters, William Fountain, Candy
Purnell, Emmett Anthony, Anita Wilkins, Quintard Miller,
Ernest Whitman, Earl Evans, Leon the Magician, Charlie
Williams Jazz Band.

"China Town," 1920 (2 acts). Producer: Billy King, Darktown
Follies Company. Principal Cast: Billy King, George Catlin
(Chinese impressionist), Lottie Gee, Will Cook, Leon Diggs,
Dink Stewart, Jesse Paschall, Helen Baxter, Lottie Harris,
May Crowder, Evon Robinson, Percy Colston.

"The Cotton Brokers," 1920. Producer: Hambone Jones Company.
Principal Cast: Hambone Jones, Virginia Liston, Sam H. Gray.

"Follies and Fancies of 1920," 1920. Producers: Frank Montgomery and Florence McClain. Principal Cast: Laura Brown and
others.

"45 Minutes from Nowhere," 1920. Producer: Hardtack Jackson.
Principal Cast: Hardtack Jackson, Effie Moore, Annie Mae
Ryan, Laura Badge, Carrie Huff.

"Fun in a Music Shop," 1920. Producer: Gains Brothers Variety
Players Comapny. Principal Cast: No data.

"Hello Dixieland," 1920 (Grand Theatre, Chicago). Producer:
Billy King. Principal Cast: Billy King, Arthur Bruce, Lelia
Mitchell, Berlena Blanks, Ollie Hickman, Clarence Beasley.

"Lime Kiln Club," 1920. Producer: Billy King, Darktown Follies
Company. Principal Cast: Billy King, Andrew Tribble, Dink
Stewart, W. A. Cook, E. R. Fraction, Mattie Wilkins.

"My Friend from Kentucky," 1920 (edition). Producer: Evon
Robinson. Music: E. Dowell, Jim Vaughn. Principal Cast:
Dink Stewart, Andrew Tribble.

"Show Folks," 1920.   Producer: Sidney Perrin's High Flyers
    Company.   Principal Cast: Iris Hall, Inez Dennis, George
    Wiltshire, Willie Richardson, Jimmie Stewart.

"Sultan Sam," 1920.   Producer: Irvin C. Miller.   Principal Cast:
    Emmett Anthony, Blanche Thompson, Anita Wilkins, Ernest
    Whitman, Leggett Sisters, Ralph Brown.

"The Time, The Place, The Horse," 1920.   Producer: Stovall &
    Macks' Stock Company.   Principal Cast: No data.

"Tunes and Funnies of 1920," 1920.   Producers: Flournoy E. Mil-
    ler, Aubrey Lyles.   Principal Cast: Leon Diggs, Flournoy E.
    Miller, Aubrey Lyles, Lem Ross, A. J. Twiggs, Edna Hicks,
    Rosa Grodon, Bessie Tribble, Julia Rector, Trixie Butler,
    Ethel Patton, Mary Carpenter, Cordelle Richardson, Alma
    Jones.

1921

"Darktown Frolics," 1921.   Producer: W. D. Henderson.   Princi-
    pal Cast: Carrie Hall, Beatrice Howe, "Rare Back" (billed as
    S. H. Dudley's mule), Madame Brannin, Tucker and Gresham.

"Darktown Scandals of 1921," 1921.   Producer: Quintard Miller.
    Principal Cast: B. B. Joyner, Lulu Whidby, Tom Cross,
    Margaret Jackson, James Howell, Grace Johnson, Clarence
    Jackson, Clarence Foster, George Lynch, Theresa Burroughs
    Brooks, Earl Evans, Billy Higgins, Margaret Lee.

"Dixie Girls," 1921.   Producer: Pal Williams.   Principal Cast:
    Billy Mack, Floyd Young, Mrs. Mack, Madame Williams,
    Olivia Zalatte.

"Folly Town," 1921.   Producer: Quintard Miller.   Principal Cast:
    B. B. Joyner, Lulu Whidby, Margaret Lee, Teressa Brooks.

"Fun at the Picnic Grounds," 1921.   Producer: Hardtack Jackson.
    Principal Cast: No data.

"Hello 1921," 1921.   Producer: Frank Montgomery.   Lyrics and
    Music: Frank Montgomery and Marie Lucas.   Additional Lyrics
    and Music: Florence McClain and Jim Vaughn.   Musical Ar-
    rangements: Marie Lucas.   Dance Arrangements: Frank
    Montgomery.   Principal Cast: Frank Montgomery, Blondie
    Robinson, Chinese Walker, Toots Hoy, Pat Ford, Wells and
    Wells, Royal Sutton, James Jasper, Josie Graham Austin,
    Johnnie Virgel, Alexander Peel, Eleanor Wilson, Montgomery
    Beauty Chorus, Florence McClain.

"Hello Sue," 1921.   Producer: Sandy Burns.   Principal Cast:
    Sandy Burns and Company.

"High Flyers," 1921. Producer: Sid Perrin. Principal Cast: Iris Hall, George Wiltshire, "One String" Willie, Brooks and Jackson, Allen and Stokes, Margreto Rice, Ike Thompson's 10-piece orchestra.

"Holiday in Dixie," 1921 (edition). Producer: Will Mastin. Principal Cast: Virginia Richards, George McClennon, Jack Thornton, Will Mastin, Norman Willes, Mathew White, George Taylor, George Allen, Mabel Johnson, Ida Forsyne, Gladys Thompson.

"In Mexico," 1921. Producer: Doe Doe Green. Music Director: Lovey (Percy) Saunders. Principal Cast: Doe Doe Green, Arthur Williams, Helen Butler, Mary Jackson, Bobby Wilson, Rosa Lee Saunders, Louise Wilson, Coleman Titus, Ed Pickett, Kid Bruce.

"The Insane Asylum," 1921. Producer: Eddie Hunter, The Standard Stock Company (John Gibson, manager). Principal Cast: Jim Burris, Evon Robinson, Lottie Harris, Nina Hunter, Theodore Robinson, Elizabeth Moulton, Bee Palmer, Marie Warren, Mae Lambert, Madeline Belt, Maggie Crosh, Alfred Curtis, Marcus Slayter, Charles Lawrence, Fred Hollins.

"Joyland Girls," 1921. Producer: Edgar Martin. Principal Cast: Pearl Ray, Peggie Barnette, Edgar Martin (in blackface), Helen Thomas, Isabelle Foster, Bobby Bramlet.

"Mexico," 1921. Producer: Doe Doe Green. Principal Cast: Charles Smith, Geradine Cardwell, Lena Wiggins, Lovie Taylor, Georgie White, Gene Collins, May Crowder, Henrietta Loveless, Doe Doe Green.

"Midnight in Chinatown," 1921. Producer: Luke Scott. Principal Cast: Luke Scott, Irene Elmo Scott (Mrs. Scott). Songs: "Sweet Adaline" by Scott and Scott, "Rusty."

"Miss Nobody's Hotel," 1921. Producer: Hardtack Jackson. Principal Cast: Hardtack Jackson, E. E. Pugh, Louise Jackson.

"New Americans," 1921 (Grand Theatre, Chicago). Producer: Billy King. Principal Cast: Billy King, Marshall Rogers, Maud Russell, James Thomas, "Kid" Bumsky, Edna Hicks, Viola Young, Margaret Scott, Beatrice Bruce, Sons of Ham Quartet (Messers Vaughn, Burton, Smith and Gunn), Berlena Blanks, Dink Thomas, James E. Stevens.

"Noyes and Watts Musical Comedy Company," 1921. Producer: No data. Principal Cast: Hazel Gray, Juanita Jones, Evelin Winfield, Sam Rhodes, Rastus Winfield, William Floyd.

"Put and Take," 1921. Producer: Irvin C. Miller. Music: Spencer Williams. Principal Cast: Perry Bradford, Tim Brymm, Hamtree Harrington, Earl Dancer, Andrew Tribble,

Cora Green, Mildred Smallwood, Irvin C. Miller, Emmett Anthony, Fred LaJoy, Florence Parham, Lillian Goodner, Mae Crowder and Maxie.

"Small Town Doings, " 1921.   Producers: Salem Tutt Whitney, J. Homer Tutt.   Principal Cast: Smart Set Company.

"Some Baby, " 1921.   Producer: Quintard Miller.   Principal Cast: Quintard Miller, B. B. Joyner, Lulu Whidby, Marquette Lee, Jimmy Howell, Ruth Cherry, Theresa Burroughs Brooks.

"Trip Around the World, " 1921 (Grand Theatre, Chicago).   Producer: Billy King.   Principal Cast: Billy King (Kid Bumpsky), Marshall Rodgers, Jason Stevens, Arthur Bruce, Fred Vaughn, Leonard Burton, Mrs. Bryant, Lelia Mitchell, Allegrate Anderson, Maude Russell, Ollie Hickman, "Gator" and the "Bull. "

"Tunes and Topics, " 1921.   Producer: Quintard Miller.   Principal Cast: B. B. Joyner (Long Gone), Johnny Hudgins (Fashion Plate of Musical Comedy), James Howell, Mildred Martlene, Lulu Whidby, Theressa Brooks.

"Two Neighbors, " 1921.   Producer: Hardtack Jackson.   Principal Cast: No data.

"Two Nuts from Brazil, " 1921.   Producer: Hardtack Jackson. Principal Cast: No data.

"Why Worry?" 1921. Producer: Quintard Miller.   Principal Cast: B. B. Joyner, Lulu Whidby, Margaret Lee, James Howell, Theresa Burroughs Brooks, Billy Higgins.

1922

"Abraham the Barber, " 1922.   Producer: Eddie Hunter.   Principal Cast: Eddie Hunter, Evon Robinson, Madeline Belt, Nina Hunter, Alec Lovejoy, "Babe" Townsend, Andrew Tribble, Al Curtis, Dick Conway, May LaVern, Stella Atkins, Florence Sussen, Nona Butler.

"Anita Bush Company, " 1922.   Producer: No data.   Principal Cast: Anita Bush, Billy Mitchell, Baby Hazel Wallace (6-year old girl), Raymond Wallace, Doris Wallace, Seba Banks, Corinne Sneed, Kitty Stevens, Marie Harris.

"Beulah Benbow's Dancing Fools, " 1922.   Producer: Beulah Benbow.   Principal Cast: Beulah Benbow, Floyd Young.

"Billy Mack's Merry Makers, " 1922.   Producer: Billy Mack. Principal Cast: Billy Mack, Leroy Johnson (comedian), Jack Ryers (straight), Mary Mack (Mrs. Mack), Chorus: May Evans, Thelma Paris, Bobby Powell, Belle Waters, May Dixon,

Viola Belle; Billy Mack's Jazz Band: William Paris, director and trombonist, Walter Harry, cornetist, Westley Wilson, pianist, Harold Wallace, drummer.

"Black Swan Troubadours," 1922. Producer: Harry Pace. Principal Cast: Ethel Waters, Ethel Williams (eccentric dancer), Black Swan Jazz Masters, directed by Fletcher H. Henderson at the piano, Gus Smith, Maude DeForrest, Virginia Smith, "Little Different Trio," Raymond Green (xylophonist), Anderson and Gray.

"Breezy Times," 1922. Producer: No data. Book, Lyrics: Herbert Byron. Stage Director: Clarence Muse. Orchestra Director: Herbert Byron. Principal Cast: Laura Hall, Leon Diggs, Bud Harris, Susie Sutton, Orphelia Muse, Babe Brown, Elizabeth Williams, Billy Walker (comedian), Slim and Johnnie Woods, Billy Young, Clarence Muse.

"Chappelle and Stinnette Revue," 1922. Producer: Chappelle and Stinnette. Principal Cast: Chappelle and Stinnette, Jazz Hounds (Bobby Lee, pianist; Percy Glasco, clarinet; Seymour Errick, cornet; M. Fleming, trombone; Faulkner, banjo).

"Chuckles," 1922. Producer: No data. Book: William Pierson. Music: Johnnie Anderson and his Orchestra. Principal Cast: Williams Pierson, Richard Count, Catherine Reese, Fern Calswell, T. A. Perkins, George Bronson, Lottie Bolds, James Moore, Janet Cooper, Lena Boyd, Alyena Cauldwell, Clittle Adams, Nell Pierson, Bessie Ricketts, Joy Morris, Gene Rushing, Edna Douglass, Victoria Powell, Mae Provost, Alice Walker, Epsie Lee, Helen Boyd, Charlotte Strange, Lelia Johnson, Milton Douglass, Herman Higgs.

"Clorifena's Wedding Day," 1922. Producers: Joe Simms, Robert Warfield. Principal Cast: Lovie Taylor, Billy Starksy, James Edwards, Edward Williams, Robert Warfield, Joe Simms, Eloise Johnson, Ethel James, Edna Hicks, Lizzie Taylor, Virginia Hartley, Heatrice Valentine.

"The Coal Heavers," 1922. Producer: James Crescent Players. Principal Cast: Freddie James (13 year-old), Willie Glover, Crawford Jackson, Tillie James, Frank Delyon, Weegie Payne, Roxie Caldwell, Lena Jackson, Ida Carry, Evelyn Handcock.

"Creole Bells," 1922. Producer: Edward Lee. Principal Cast: Josephine Thomas, Albert Allen, Landow Crosby, Pace and Pace, Edith Williams, Jessie Brooks, Lavinta Moore, Bessie Stones, Eddie Bonner and his band.

"Creole Follies Revue," 1922. Producer: No data. Principal Cast: Billy Higgins, Emmett Anthony, Blanche Thompson, Johnny Hudgins, Mildred Martine, Lulu Whidby, W. C. Richardson, Freeman and McGinty.

"Creole Jazz Babies," 1922.   Producer: Slim Henderson.   Principal Cast: Slim Henderson (comedian), Royal Sutton (comedian), Frank King (straight), Rosa Henderson (singer), Marietta Foster (dancer), Isabel Dabner (singer, dancer), Chorus: Louise Sutton, Marion Summers, Julia Taylor, Irene Poindexter.

"Daffy Dill Girls," 1922.   Producers: Mills and Frisby.   Principal Cast: Mills and Frisby, Doris Hudson (in blackface), Zarelda Larue (blues singer), John Larue (straight).   Songs: "High Yellow and Seal-Skin Brown" (Mills, Maude Frisby, Zarelda Larue, Doris Hudson, Rastus Brown), "Tuck Me to Sleep" (Terry Williams), "Chick" (Green and Jene Fradley).

"Darktown Jubilee," 1922 (Grand Theatre, Chicago).   Producer: Billy King.   Principal Cast: Susie Brown (attorney), Billy King (judge), Dink Thomas (dope fiend), Anna Belle (plaintiff), Ida Cox (defendant, accused of kidnapping the plaintiff), Doc Straine (officer of the court).

"The Devil," 1922.   Producer: Quintard Miller.   Principal Cast: Quintard Miller, Henrietta Lovelass, Purcelle Cuff, Estelle Cash, "Monkey" Jim, Marion Ablaunche, Helen Chapelle, Eugene Shields, Ruby Jones, Catherine Peace.

"Dixie Flyer Girls," 1922.   Producer: Jimmy Cox.   Principal Cast: Jimmy Cox, Baby Ernestine Jones (8 years old), Henry Thomas, Ana Mae Cox, Roy Lee, Bobby Sullivan, Louise Howard, Gladys Williams, Margaret Lyon, Buster Lee, Pearl Jones.

"The Eddie Hunter Company," 1922 (1 act, 2 scenes).   Producer: Eddie Hunter.   Book: Eddie Hunter.   Music: William Fountain.   Principal Cast: Eddie Hunter, Evon Robinson, William Fountain, James Burris, Alec Lovejoy, Al Curtis.

"Go Get It," 1922.   Producer: Sherman H. Dudley.   Principal Cast: Sherman H. Dudley, Slim Henderson, John Mason, Sam H. Gray, Aaron Gates, C. J. Davis, D. D. Petty, Virginia Liston, C. Huff, Stella White, Eva Metcalf, Millie Lovelass, Rose Henderson, Perry Wood, Oscar Bray, Herman Rodgers, Wizard Quartette, Grace Smith, Marion Sumter, Irene Poindexter, Irene Saunders, Solade Banks, Kittie Stevens, Chaterine Petty, Tressa Beatty, Bobby Lee, Millie Lee, George Cayaire, James E. Carroll, Lloyd Hollis, Gray and Gray, Oliver Blackwell's Jazz Orchestra.

"Hardtack Jackson's Company," 1922.   Producer: Hardtack Jackson.   Principal Cast: Joseph Jones, Hardtack Jackson, Baby Benbow, Eugene Jones, Peggy Richards, Jack Richards, Ida Wilson, Marie Biddings, Little Alton Choristers.

"Hearts of Men," 1922.   Producer: Quintard Miller.   Principal Cast: No data.

"Hello Sue," 1922 (Grand Theatre, Chicago). Producer: Billy King.
   Book: Billy King. Music: William Overstreet. Principal
   Cast: Billy King, Billy Gunn, Rastus Lee, "Hoss" Crawford,
   Leonard Barton, Marshall Rogers, Charles H. Berry, Edward
   Taylor, Dean Glover, Margueritte Scott, Anita Wilkins, Gene-
   vieve Stearn, Madelene Deakler, Iola Young, Rebecca (Dink)
   Thomas, Ethel Jackson, The Russell Sisters.

"Henri Bowman's Cotton Blossoms," 1922. Producer: Henri Bowman. Principal Cast: Leroy White (comedian), Henri Bowman
   (straight), Bonnie Bell Drew (leading lady), James Phoenix,
   Jessie Wilson, Belle Johnson.

"High Life Scandals," 1922. Producers: Benbow and Cohen. Principal Cast: Margie Cohen, Harry Brock, George Green, Henrietta Lovelass, Macklin White, John Dunsey, Belle Waters,
   Mattie Miles, May Smith, Dorothy Waters.

"Hits and Bits," 1922 (edition) (Grand Theatre, Chicago). Producer:
   Billy King. Principal Cast: Billy King, Cox-Thomas-Moore,
   Rastus Lee, Billy Cornell, Margaret Scott, Sarah Martin, Eight
   Folly Girls, Marshall Rodgers, Scott-Thomas-Ray, Billy Gunn,
   Rastus Brown, Genevieve Stearn, Edmonia Henderson, Six
   Dancing Masters.

"Hoola-Boola," 1922. Producer: Clarence Muse. Principal Cast:
   "Babe" Townsend, Gladys Jordan, Elsie Fisher, Dorothy
   Sweetny, Evelyn Riley, Ella Thomas, Carrie Hutt, Lena Wil-
   son, Lillian Gilliam, E. C. Caldwell.

"Hot Dogs," 1922 (2 acts, 12 scenes). Producer: Irvin C. Miller.
   Principal Cast: Irvin C. Miller, Wilber Blanks, Joe Peterson,
   Madeline Belt, Evon Robinson, Troy Brown, B. B. Joyner, Doe
   Doe Green, Clarence Foster, Jimmy Ewell, May Barnes.

"In Honolulu," 1922. Producer: Mae Kemp, Ragtime Steppers
   Company. Principal Cast: Mae Kemp, Lyons Daniels, "Skunk"
   Tom Bower, Zachariah White, Billy Nichols, Elmer Lloyd
   (straight), Estelle Carrol, Hector Patterson, Louise Patterson,
   Hazel Wallace, Eloise Howard, Viola Dorsey.

"In Slam," 1922. Producers: Byrd and Byrd. Principal Cast:
   No data.

"Keep It Up," 1922. Producer: I. M. Weingarden. Principal
   Cast: Billy Higgins, Ernest Whitman, Clifford Ross, Alice
   Gorgas, Susie Sutton, Lena Leggett, Henrietta Leggett, Edna
   Hicks, Ollie Burgoyne, Bob (Monk) Brawlet, Al Curtis, Iola
   Young.

"Me and You," 1922. Producer: No data. Principal Cast: Andrew
   Tribble, Alec Lovejoy, Eddie Gray, James P. Johnson, Bradford and White, Parker Anderson, Dink Stewart.

"Moonshine," 1922 (Grand Theatre, Chicago). Producer: Billy
    King. Principal Cast: Billy King, Marshall Rodgers, Margaret
    Scott, Ethel, Genevieve Stern, Rastus Lee, Billy Cornell, Wil-
    liam Gunn, Edmonia Henderson, Dink Thomas, Sally Gates,
    Irene Cornell, Christine Russell, Lillie Jackson, Stell Brown,
    Willie Thrill, Doc Straine.

"Radio Girls," 1922. Producer: Roscoe and Mitchell. Principal
    Cast: Roscoe and Mitchell, Edmonia Henderson, Emma John-
    son, Pauline Montella, Mamie Jefferson, Bobby Powell, Baby
    Badge, Annie McReynolds, Bessie Williams.

"Shades of Hades," 1922. Producer: J. Samuel Stanfield. Book:
    Tim E. Dudley. Music, Lyrics: Dave Payton. Stage Director:
    Julia Rector. Principal Cast: Sidney Kirkpatrick, Laura Bow-
    man, B. B. Joyner, Walter Richardson, Charles Moore, Allie
    Smith, Hester Kenton, Mary Bradford, Earl Simms, Charles
    Grundy, Isadora Mitchell.

"That Gets It," 1922. Producer: Chicago Producing Company
    (Tennan Jones and Dave Payton). Principal Cast: Tim Owsley,
    Sylvia Mitchell, Sidney Kirkpatrick, Laura Bowman, Charles
    Richardson, Ellanora Wilson, Berlena Blanks, Robert Warfield,
    Ferdo Robinson, Jodie Edwards, Susie Edwards, Mabel Gant,
    Alberta Perkins.

"This One Night," 1922. Producer: Sandy Burns. Principal Cast:
    Sandy Burns Stock Company.

"This Way Out," 1922. Producer: Quintard Miller. Principal
    Cast: Quintard Miller, Henrietta Lovelass, Purcell Cuff,
    Eugene Shields.

"Tim Moore's Follies," 1922. Producer: Tim Moore. Principal
    Cast: Tim Moore, Gertie Moore, Eddie Stafford, Ethel Watts,
    Eva Smith, Kid Brown, Eugene Thomas, Jessie Conway,
    Florence Seales.

"Title Not Known," 1922. Producers: Sandy Burns, Sam Russell,
    Burns and Russell Stock Company. Principal Cast: Sandy
    Burns, Sam Russell, Marcus Slayter, George Wiltshire, Alex-
    ander Peel, Fred Hart, Edna Burns, Helen Dolly, Inez Wilt-
    shire, Anita Spencer, Tiny Gray, Mary Deever, Lillian Carroll.

"Vamping Liza Jane," 1922. Producer: Billy Ewing. Principal
    Cast: Goldie Ewing, Jenkins and Johnson, Billy Ewing.

"We Got It," 1922. Producer: No data. Principal Cast: E.
    E. Pugh, Cleo Mitchell, Joe Carmouche.

"Wesley Varnell's Revue," 1922. Producer: Wesley Varnell.
    Principal Cast: Brown and Hudson, Coleman and Johnson,
    Henry (Gang) Jines, Houston and Houston.

"Whirl of Joy," 1922 (Grand Theatre, Chicago). Producer: Billy King. Principal Cast: Billy King Stock Company.

"Why Spoil It?," 1922. Producer: Frank Montgomery. Principal Cast: Frank Montgomery, Florence McClain, Dink Thomas.

1923

"Bombay Girls," 1923. Producers: Drake and Walker. Principal Cast: Drake and Walker, Ethel Walker, James Rutherford, Helen Battle, Edwards and Edwards.

"Broadway Rastus of 1923," 1923. Producer: Irvin C. Miller. Book: Irvin C. Miller. Lyrics: Pousseau Simmons. Music: W. Aston Morgan. Stage Director: Quintard Miller. Principal Cast: Irvin C. Miller, Quintard Miller, Jimmie Parker, Trixie Smith, Ruby Mason, Henry Saparo.

"Burgleton Green vs. Spark Plug," 1923 (Grand Theatre, Chicago). Producer: Billy King. Principal Cast: Billy King, Chick Beamon, Esther Bigeou, Frank Kirk, Alice Ramsey, Clarence Muse, Beauty Chorus.

"The Chocolate Scandals," 1923. Producer: No data. Principal Cast: Sam Russell, Sarah Martin, Doc Straine, Curtis Mosby's Dixieland Blue Blowers, Ali Brothers and Jackson.

"Chocolate Town," 1923. Producer: Raymond Day. Stage Director: Coy Herndon. Principal Cast: Coy Herndon, Leon Diggs, Billy Arnett, Jazz Warren, Bessie Brown, "Pork Chops" Gibson, Cecelia Coleman, Elaine Horn, Louise Washington, Josephine Jones, Ernest Montague's 18-piece jazz band, W. Kelly's 18-piece orchestra, Flapper Chorus.

"The Frolics," 1923. Producer: Leonard Harper. Music Director: Allie Ross. Principal Cast: Mason and Henderson, Eva Metcalf, Bryon Brothers, The Three Eddies, Billy Mitchell and Moore, Ada "Bricktop" Smith, Harper and Blanks, Johnnie Virgel, Fred Davis, Roy White, Rosa Henderson, Aida Ward. 20 songs, four specialties, 12 dance numbers.

"The Girl with the Beauty Spot," 1923. Producer: No data. Principal Cast: Medell Thomas, Edward Williams, Will Jeedman, Josephine Legget, Sylvia Mitchell, India B. Edwards.

"Hot Chops," 1923. Producer: Nat Nazarro. Book and Music: Joe Trent. Stage Director: Frank Montgomery. Principal Cast: Buck and Bubbles, George McGlennon, Sam Russell, Tony Green, Willie Spencer, B. Wiggins, Jean Starr, Gene Kane, E. McKinney. Songs: "Hot Chops" (Buck and Bubbles), "Moanin' and Groanin'" (George McGlennon on clarinet).

"The Jazz Express," 1923. Producers: Salem Tutt Whitney and J. Homer Tutt. Principal Cast: Salem Tutt Whitney, J. Homer Tutt, Julian Costello, Maude DeForest, Alma Daniels. Hit Song: "Betwixt and Between" (composed by Donald Heywood).

"Jones Syncopated Syncopators," 1923. Producer: Joseph Jones (Jewish impersonator). Principal Cast: Speedy Wilson (in black face), Joseph Jones, George Gould, Raymond Jefferson, Violetta Howell, Eva Mason, Lilly Yuen, Marie Bidding, Minnie Lee, Bobby Vinson.

"Just for Fun," 1923. Producer: Irvin C. Miller. Principal Cast: Billy Mills, Will Marion Cook, Irvin C. Miller, Ida Andrews.

"K of P," 1923. Producer: Collington Hayes. Principal Cast: Collington Hayes, Helen Hayes, Bessie White, Newell Morse, Olivette West, Malachia Smith.

"Let 'Em Have It," 1923. Producers: Byrd and Ewing. Principal Cast: Byrd (chief comedian), Billy Ewing (chief straight), Louis Talley (assistant, blackface comedian), Madam Cherrie Blossom, Elsie Fisher, Libby Robinson, Alma Henderson, Gladys Foster, Gladys Jordan, Beulah Getting, Beatrice Moody.

"Man from Bam," 1923. Producer: No data. Principal Cast: Emmett Anthony, B. B. Joyner, Clarence Foster, Alberta Perkins, Valaida Snow.

"The Mayor of Jimtown," 1923. Producer: Miller and Slater Company. Principal Cast: Emmett Anthony, Blanche Thompson, Glenn of the team of Glenn and Jenkins.

"Mr. Sambo from Gaston, South Carolina," 1923. Producer: Delaney and Delaney Stock Revue Company. Principal Cast: Tom Delaney, Eugene Thomas, Pearl Delaney, Catherine Stanley, Gladys Dorsey.

"North Ain't South," 1923. Producers: Salem Tutt Whitney, J. Homer Tutt. Book: Jesse Shipp. Dances: Frank Montgomery. Principal Cast: J. Homer Tutt, Salem Tutt Whitney, George McGlennon, Paul Bass, Walter Richardson, Jesse Shipp, Harold Demond, Joe Purnell, Marion Harrison, Mae Kemp, Edna Gibbs, Frank Shipp, Loraine Sampson.

"Oh Yes," 1923. Producer: No data. Principal Cast: Hezekiah Jenkins, S. H. Gray, Virginia Liston, Hermon Brown and Dorothy Jenkins, Bert Houze and Carrie Houze.

"Plantation Days," 1923. Producer: No data. Principal Cast: Chappelle and Stinnette, Austin and Delaney, Pepper Choir, Five Cracker Jacks, Allen and Lee, Seymore and Jeannette,

James P. Johnson, Harper and Blanks, Eddie Green.

"Plantation Revue," 1923. Producer: Earl Dancer. Principal Cast:
Lawrence Deas, Gulfport and Brown, Jean Starr, Dan Small,
Eight Kangaroo Steppers.

"Raisin' Cain," 1923. Producer: Nat Nazarro. Book and Music:
Frank Montgomery. Music Director: Jules Laster. Principal
Cast: Emery Hutchins, Sam Russell, Buck and Bubbles, Demos
Jones, Josephine Gray, Percy Wiggins.

"Ramblin' Round," 1923. Producer: Clarence Muse. Principal
Cast: Emmett Anthony, Blanche Calloway, Ollie Powers,
Valaida Snow, Esther Bigeou, Clarence Muse.

"Rosie's Weddin' Day," 1923. Producer: Tim Moore. Principal Cast:
Tim Moore (principal comedian), Willie Singleton, Pete Gentry,
Fred Moore (dancer), Fred Durrel (juvenile straight), Edna
Brown, Early Smith, Rachel King, Eva Simmons.

"Runnin' Wild," 1923. Producers: Miller and Lyles. Music:
Will Marion Cook, James P. Johnson at the piano. Principal
Cast: Flournoy E. Miller, Aubrey Lyles, Revella Hughes,
George Stephens, Georgette Harvey, Ina Dungan, Adelaide Hall,
Arthur D. Porter, Elizabeth Welch, Clarence Robinson, Ralph
Bryson, George Stamper, Lionel Monagas, Charles Olden,
"Onion" Jeffrey, Florence Covan.

"7-11," 1923. Producer: No data. Principal Cast: Elenora Wilson,
Josephine Gray, Eddie Gray, Dink Thomas, Evon Robinson,
Mae Brown, Garland Howard, Speedy Smith, Sam Cook, Bar-
rington Carter, Will Grundy.

"Shake Your Feet," 1923 (2 acts, 9 scenes). Producer: Will
Mastin. Principal Cast: E. E. Pugh (featured comedian),
Will Mastin, Vergie Richards, Joe Carmouche, Cleo Mitchell,
Harris and Holly (offered comedy sketch "Push 'Em and Pull
'Em").

"Sheik of Harlem," 1923. Producer: Irvin C. Miller. Principal
Cast: Irvin C. Miller, Billy Mills, Quintard Miller, Paul
Bass, Edith Spencer, Hattie Revas, Bessie Arthur, Ida Ander-
son, Alonzo Fenderson, Will A. Cook.

"Step-Children," 1923. Producers: Boatner and Clark. Principal
Cast: Clark, Clem Mills (straight), Eulalia Smith, Mary Hicks,
Vergie Williams, Mary Green, Katie Smith.

"Step Lucky Girls," 1923. Producers: Bailey and Harris. Principal Cast: Laura Bailey, Johnny Bird, O. Robinson, Stella
Harris.

"Struttin' Along, " 1923. Producer: Jack Joy. Principal Cast:
Mamie Smith and her Jazz Hounds, John Rucker, Sid Perrin,
Richard Courtney, William Pierson, Frisco Nick, Zoe Rames,
Carolyne Snowden, Sussie Harris, William Mitchell, Lawrence
Ford, Earl West, Norman Stewart, Eddie Anderson (Rochester
of the Jack Benny Radio Show), Billy Moore, C. Anderson,
Mlle. Augusta Petit.

"Swanee River Home, " 1923 (2 acts, 12 scdnes). Producer: Sandy
Burns. Book: Sandy Burns. Music: Benton Overstreet.
Stage Director: Inez Dennis. Principal Cast: Sandy Burns,
Sam Russell, Helen Dolly, Inez Davis, Grace Smith, Millie
Holmes, Alec Lovejoy, Fred Hart, George Wiltshire, Dinah
Scott, Brownie Campbell, Al Curtis, Leroy and Rastus, The
Swanee Four.

"Tunes and Topics, " 1923. Producers: Quintard Miller and Marcus
Slayter. Principal Cast: Bessie Smith, Andrew Tribble, George
Cooper, Carrie Yates, Greenlee and Drayton, Emmett Anthony,
Quintard Miller.

"Unloved Wife, " 1923. Producer: No data. Principal Cast:
Evelyn Ellis, Bessie Allison.

"Watermelon Girls, " 1923. Producer: Charles Taylor. Principal
Cast: Charles Taylor, Reggie Taylor, Emma Nash, George
Tuggett, George Nash, Hattie Storey, Lucile Rankin, Cecile
McKay, Hattie Owen.

"Whirl with Pleasure, " 1923. Producer: Billy King. Principal
Cast: Billy King Stock Company.

"Who Struck John?" 1923. Producer: Salem Tutt Whitney and J.
Homer Tutt. Principal Cast: The Smart Set Company.

1924

"Annie Oakley, " 1924. Producers: Quintard Miller and Marcus
Slayter. Principal Cast: Marcus Slayter, Quintard Miller,
Amon Davis, Eddie Lemons, Carrie Yates, Rosa Henderson,
Bill Causby.

"Broadway Rastus of 1924, " 1924. Producer: Irvin C. Miller.
Principal Cast: Emmett Anthony, Cecil Rivers, Aurora Greeley,
Blanche Thompson, Ida Brown, Lloyd Mitchell, John Henderson.

"The Broadway Vamps, " 1924. Producer, owner: Thomas Mason.
Principal Cast: William "Babe" Townsend, Kid Townsend,
Flossie Townsend, "Buzzie Boozie. "

"Brown Beauties, " 1924. Producer: Mary Milson. Principal Cast:
Charlie "Fat" Hayden.

"Brown Skin Vamps," 1924. Producer: Billy McLaurin. Principal Cast: Buster Lee, Joe Clark, Miss "Boy" Lee (soubrette), Catherine Jackson, "Little Bits" Hall, Margaret Warren, Viola Williams (leading lady), Guy Jackson.

"Cotton Land," 1924. Producer: No data. Music: James P. Johnson. Principal Cast: Billy Higgins, Gertrude Saunders, James P. Johnson, Dickie Wells, Billy Mitchell, Jimmy Mordecai, The Three Browns, Cotton Land Chorus.

"Creole Bells," 1924. Owner, Manager: Ed Lee. Stage Manager: Joe Brown. Musical Director: A. C. Davis. Principal Cast: Joe Stephens and Lockhart (principal comedians), William Pace (singer, straight), Prince and Princess Alimona (magicians), Chorus: Aileen Breeden, Goldberta Hudson, Hattie Watkins, Etta May Cade, Mattie Alice Pace.

"Creole Revue of 1924," 1924. Producers: J. Berry, Earl Hailstock. Stage Manager: Roger Bell. Principal Cast: Roger Bell (comedian), Marie Bell (leading lady), Eleanor Hamilton (chorus), Catherine Ross (soubrette, blues singer), Louie Kepplinger (chorus), Charles Duffis (straight, chorus), James Berry (orchestra director), Earl Hailstock (straight).

"The Darktown Bazaar," 1924. Producers: Allen and Stokes. Stage Manager: Al Wells. Principal Cast: Raymond Jefferson (straight), Harry Brooks and Arthur Allen (comedians), Tylas Bailey, Helen Stokes, Luella Wells, Bertha LaJoy, Anna Brock, Jennie Finch, Amelia Smith.

"The Devine," 1924. Producer: No data. Principal Cast: Sarah Martin, Davenport Trio, Julian Costello, White and Moore.

"Ethiopia Shall Win," 1924. Producer: Joe Bright. Principal Cast: Joe Bright, "Bobby" Tolliver Bright, Theresa Burroughs Brooks.

"The Flat Above," 1924. Producers: Quintard Miller, Marcus Slayter. Principal Cast: No data.

"Follow Me," 1924 (edition). Producer: I. M. Weingarden. Principal Cast: Ernest Whitman, Alice Gorgas, Clifford Ross, Eddie Mathews, Susie Sutton, Edna Hicks, Follow Me Four.

"From Baltimore to Turkey," 1924. Producer: Joe Bright. Principal Cast: Joe Bright, Dink Stewart, Andrew Tribble, Theresa Burroughs Brooks.

"Georgia Red Hots," 1924. Producer: Jimmy Cox. Principal Cast: Jimmy Cox (principal comedian), Baby Ernestine Jones (singer), Leroy Johnson (comedian), Master Henry Thomas (dancer), Anna Mae Cox (female lead), Billy Wright (straight), Mabel Granger, Parlee Cox, Madam Pearl Jones at piano.

"The Girl from Philly," 1924. Producers: Drake and Walker.
Principal Cast: Henry Drake, Ethel Walker (Mrs. Drake),
Alta Oats, Willie Drake (straight), George Crawford, "Sambo"
Reid.

"Happy Days," 1924. Producer: No data. Principal Cast: Dancing Demons, Bill H. Ward, Frank R. Murphy.

"Happy Go Lucky," 1924. Producer: No data. Principal Cast:
Kelso Brothers, Chester Nelson, Juggling Delisle, Arlove Johnson, Thomas A. Brooks, Madeline Ashton, Johnny Brown.

"Hide and Seek," 1924. Producer: Salem Tutt Whitney and J.
Homer Tutt. Principal Cast: The Smart Set Company.

"Hit and Run," 1924 (2 acts, 8 scenes). Producer: No data.
Owners: Smith and Carter. Principal Cast: Andrew Tribble,
Speedy Smith, Al Young, Sam Cook, Marion Davis, Estelle
Floyd, Sterling Grant, Johnny Nit, Charles Prime, Barrington
Carter, Garland Howard, George Myrick, Charles Young,
Mamie Lewis, Howard Cook; 24 songs, 4 dance specialties.

"Hits and Bits," 1924 (edition). Producer: Billy King. Principal
Cast: "Buzzin' Sparrow" Harris, Alberta Harris, Verlar Lee
Woodward.

"Honey," 1924 (2 acts, 7 scenes). Producers: Flournoy E. Miller
and Aubrey Lyles. Book: Miller and Lyles. Music and Lyrics:
Porter Grainger, Bob Ricketts, Joe Trent. Orchestra Director:
J. Rosamond Johnson. Choral Director: Bob Ricketts. Prin-
cipal Cast: Flournoy E. Miller, Doe Doe Green, Eddie Rector,
Julia Rector, Elizabeth Williams, Alma Daniels, Edgar Conners,
Alonzo Fenderson, May Dent, George Stamper, Dorothy Rhodes,
Juanita Boyd, Zenaide Anderson, A. W. Jason.

"Hot Feet," 1924. Producer: Jimmy Cooper. Principal Cast:
Emmett Anthony, Bessie DeSota, Reuben Brown, Joe Peterson,
Hilaria Friend, Bob Thompson, Jazzlips Richardson, Octavia
Slayter, Ida Roley, Sam Cross, Gertie Miller, Four Dancing
Fools.

"Jolly Time Follies," 1924. Producer: No data. Principal Cast:
Louis Deppe, Vance Dixon, Earl Hines, Bo Diddley.

"Let's Go," 1924. Producer: Fred Clark. Principal Cast: Sonny
Thompson's Colored Jazz Band, Mabel Kemp, Manny King,
Kitty Madison, Burton Sash.

"Mamie Smith Revue," 1924. Producer: Ocey Wilson. Principal
Cast: Mamie Smith, Mitchell and Harris, Ethel Harris,
Frederic Johnson, Billy Gulfport, Dewey Weinglass and his
Dancing Demons, George Cooper, Jr., Bobby Shields, Ruby
Mason.

"Milinda's Wedding Day," 1924. Producer: Joe Bright. Principal
Cast: Joe Bright, Dink Stewart, Andrew Tribble, Theresa
Burroughs Brooks, "Bobby" Tolliver Bright.

"Negro Nuances," 1924. Book: Abbie Mitchell. Lyrics and Music:
Will Marion Cook, James P. Johnson. Principal Cast: Abbie
Mitchell, Lucille Handy (daughter of W. C. Handy), Louis
Douglass.

"New Orleans Vampires," 1924. Producer: Jim Green. Principal
Cast: Roberta Green, Elenora Moore, Lucille Smith, Julies
Shedrick, Catherine Simmons, Emma Thomas, Jim Green, Kid
Thomas, Blanche Nelson, Spencer Anthony Orchestra; James
Sykes, William Turner, Clarence Simmons, Bob Johnson,
Charles Mason.

"Nut Brown Lady," 1924. Producer: H. D. Collins. Principal
Cast: Salem Tutt Whitney and J. Homer Tutt; Smart Set
Company.

"Oh Honey," 1924. Producer: Agustus Smith. Music, band and
orchestra direction: Genee Jones (Mrs. J. Agustus Smith).
Principal Cast: J. Agustus Smith, Leo Boatner, Sherman
Dirkson, Herbert Latham, A. C. Flower, Roseta Swan, Bertha
LaJoie, Anna Whitfield, Viola Walker, Ora Carpenter, Marrie
Williams, George Bascom (manager of the company).

"Oriental Serenaders," 1924. Producer: No data. Principal Cast:
Buster Lee and "Boy" (Mrs. Lee), Elmira Washington, "The
Cut-Out Kid," Little Jeff, Margarett Warren, Dorothy Dunbar,
"Little Bits" Hall, Mary Lou Berlin, Musicians: Guy Jackson,
John Ricketts, James Hall.

"Ragtime Sailors," 1924. Producer: Bob Russell. Principal Cast:
Josephine Russell, Fred Lajoy, E. E. Pugh, "Kid" Williams,
John Mason, Baby Mack, Freeman and McGinty, Petrona Lazzo,
Creole Mays, Leonora Morgan, Ivy Black, Ethel Watts, Mabel
Brown, Elenora Wilson, Carrie Huff.

"Rastus Brown in Bad Company," 1924. Producer: No data.
Principal Cast: Billy English (Kansas City Brown), Miss "Lindy,"
"Rastus" Brown, Herbert Skinner, Sleepy Harris, Albert Celes-
ton, Billy Henderson, Stella Johnson, Beulah Gittings, Mary
Williams, Virginia Barker.

"Record Breakers," 1924. Producer: Joe Reed. Principal Cast:
Billy Cumby (The Black Spear), Kewpie Doll Chorus.

"Rompin' Through," 1924. Producer: Mabel Whitman. Principal
Cast: Whitman Sisters.

"Sailors' Jazz," 1924. Producer: Bob Russell. Principal Cast:
Elinor Wilson, Freeman McGinty, Howard Mason.

"The Sheik of Harlem, " 1924.   Producer: Irvin C. Miller, Liza
    Company.   Principal Cast: Irvin C. Miller, Ethel Ridley.

"Southland Follies, " 1924.   Producer: Joe Sheftell.   Principal
    Cast: Nina Cato, "Ukulele" Bob Williams (comedian), Russell
    Brown (dancer), Joe Peterson (dancer), Reuben Brown, Joe
    Sheftell (singer).

"Steppin' High, " 1924.   Producer: William (Billy) Pierson.   Prin-
    cipal Cast: Hazel Myers, Dike Thomas, Strawberry Russell,
    Mary Richards, Dusky Beauty Chorus, Glennie Cheesman,
    Three Black Aces (Eddie Anderson, Lawrence Ford, Connie
    Anderson), Thomas and Russell, Ernestine Porter.

"Steppin' Time, " 1924.   Producers: Alex Rogers and Luckeyth
    Roberts.   Principal Cast: Alex Rogers, Luckeyth Roberts,
    Billy Higgins, Eddie Hunter.

"Steppin' Up, " 1924.   Producer: No data.   Book: Jessie Gines.
    Music Director: "Doc" Perkins.   Principal Cast: Happy
    Holmes, Jessie Gines, Alice Perkins, Byrd and Byrd, "Kid"
    Bruce, and May Allen.

"Struttin' Along Liza, " 1924.   Producers: Flournoy E. Miller,
    Aubrey Lyles.   Principal Cast: Eddie Lemons, Marcus Slayter,
    Birch Williams, Lulu Whidby, Wrightson and Williamson, Lemons
    and Williams.

"Struttin' Time, " 1924.   Producer: No data.   Book: Eddie Hunter.
    Principal Cast: Eddie Hunter, Alex Rogers, Dink Stewart,
    Andrew Tribble, Ada Brown, Katherine Yarborough, Nina
    Hunter, Lena Roberts, Alberta Hunter.   Song: "Magnolia" by
    Paul Bass and Norman Astwood, Katherine Yarborough and
    Chorus.

"Take It Easy, " 1924.   Producers: Quintard Miller, Marcus
    Slayter.   Principal Cast: No data.

"Talk of the Town, " 1924.   Producer: No data.   Principal Cast:
    James "Slim" Parker, Little Jeff.

"Their Gang, " 1924.   Producers: Whitman Sisters (Mabel, Essie,
    Alberta [Bert], Alice).   Principal Cast: Whitman Sisters,
    Maxie Jr. , Bernice Ellis.

"Trip to Cannibal Isle, " 1924.   Producer: Drake and Walker.
    Principal Cast: No data.

"We Got It, " 1924.   Producer: Joe Carmouche.   Principal Cast:
    Joe Carmouche, Willie Ognesby, Cleo Mitchell, Susie Wrotan,
    S. H. Dudley, Jr. , Troy "Bear" Brown, Queenie Price,
    Georgine Holm, Mary Covinton.

"When Malinda Sings, " 1924. Producers: Salem Tutt Whitney, J. Homer Tutt. Principal Cast: Smart Set Company.

"A Wife Wanted, " 1924. Producer: Drake and Walker. Principal Cast: No data.

"Who Struck John?" 1924. Producer: Salem Tutt Whitney, J. Homer Tutt. Principal Cast: Smart Set Company.

"Yaller Gal, " 1924. Producer: Chappelle and Stinnette. Principal Cast: Chappelle and Stinnette, John Mason, Baby Cox.

1925

"Backbiters, " 1925. Producer: Flournoy E. Miller. Principal Cast: Henrietta Lovelass, Mildred Smallwood, Hilda Mannigault, Percy Verwayne, Oswell Lyles (son of Aubrey Lyles).

"Brown Babies, " 1925. Producer: Irvin C. Miller. Principal Cast: No data.

"Brown Skin Quinan Revue, " 1925. Producer: Lew Leslie. Principal Cast: Florence Mills, Johnny Nit, U. S. Thompson (husband of Florence Mills), Will Vodery's Orchestra, Edith Wilson, Leon Simmons, Dorothy Belk, Leonard Harper, Hinton Jones, Claude Lawson, Archie Cross, Henry Winfred, Billy Mills, Alma Smith.

"Chocolate Box Revue, " 1925. Producer: John Gibson (then owner of Standard and Dunbar Theatres in Philadelphia). Principal Cast: Roy B. Arthur (That Grasshopper Comedian), Johnnie Stevens, Berthel Gibson, Gladys Kirkland, Rastus Brown, Marie Kitchen, Will Sibley, Happy Bolden, Fats Johnson, The Gibson Trio.

"Darktown Puzzles, " 1925. Producer: "Strawberry" Russell. Principal Cast: "Strawberry" Russell, Billy Maxie, DeLoach and Corbin, Gold and Goldie, "Ragtime" Billy Tucker, Margaret Scott.

"Darktown Strutters, " 1925. Producer: Ollie Burgoyne. Principal Cast: Ollie Burgoyne (classic dancer), Harrison Blackburn (one-man circus), The Harmony Four, Ida Forsyne (Russian Dancer), Katherine Jacks (soubrette).

"Dusty Miller Revue, " 1925. Producer: Dusty Miller. Principal Cast: Belle Johnson Murray, Tillie Marshall, Bruce Johnson, James Phoenix (straight), Henry Mitchell, Daisy Randolph; Chorus: Bebe Johnson, Eula Dolly, Margaret Brown, Annie Hathaway, Pearl Young, Ella May.

"Ebony Vampires, " 1925. Producer: Billy Watts. Principal Cast:

Billy Watts, Madame Pattie Williams, Bertha Hill, Mary Hicks, Alondo Johnson, Bennie Johnson.

"Fan Fan Follies," 1925. Producer: Earl B. Westfield. Principal Cast: Lean Kinbrough.

"Get Happy," 1925. Producer: William Benbow. Principal Cast: Deatta Robinson, Margie Cohen, Odell Irvins, "Rastus" Winfield, Shorty Edwards, Elnora Mantley.

"Get-It-Fixed," 1925. Producer: Joe Bright. Principal Cast: Joe Bright, Dink Stewart, Andrew Tribble, Eddie Lemons, Maybella Brown, Millie Holmes.

"Go Getter Revue," 1925. Producer: John Mason. Principal Cast: "Bobby" Covington (female singer), Blanch McLancom (straight), Eva Metcalf, Willie DeLoach, Perry and Perry, Mary Wood Mason, John Mason.

"Going Some," 1925. Producer: Mabel Whitman. Principal Cast: Whitman Sisters, Creole Mike, Sambo Jenkins.

"Happy Days in Dixie," 1925. Producers: Joe Carmouche and Cleo Mitchell. Principal Cast: Zachariah White, "Buckwheat" Stringer, S. H. Dudley, Jr., George Green, Nathanial Lane, James Cash, "Sugarfoot" Mitchell, Cleo Mitchell, Joe Carmouche.

"Hello Dixie," 1925. Producer: Andrew Downey. Principal Cast: Gus Smith, Buck Price, Genee Jones (Mrs. Gus Smith), Carrie Crutchfield, Cecilia Coleman, George Williams (comedy dancer), Broadway Eddie.

"How've You Been," 1925. Producer: Pollock Productions. Dances: George Stamper. Music: Donald Heywood. Principal Cast: Sidney Easton (the happy bootblack), Lottie Brown.

"Melody Lane Girls," 1925. Producer: No data. Principal Cast: James Isom, Emma J. Mitchels, Ernest "Baby" Seals, Willie Gunn and his beauty chorus.

"Miss Georgia Brown," 1925. Producer: Irvin C. Miller. Principal Cast: Irvin C. Miller, Aurora Greeley, Gallie DeGaston, Lilly Yuen.

"Mooching Along," 1925. Producer: Billy Mitchell, Broadway Revue Company. Stage Manager: Dick Conway. Book: Jesse Shipp, Cecil Mack, Jimmie Johnson. Principal Cast: Thelma Jordan (dancer), J. Hartwell Cook (dancer), 75 people.

"New Orleans Vampire," 1925. Producer: Jim Green. Principal Cast: No data.

"A Night in Turkey," 1925. Producer: Carmouche and Mitchell.
Principal Cast: Joe Carmouche and Cleo Mitchell.

"Non-Sense," 1925. Producer: Salem Tutt Whitney, J. Homer
Tutt. Principal Cast: Salem Tutt Whitney, J. Homer Tutt,
Joseph Purnell, Charles H. Hawkins, Baynard Whitney, Mabel
Ridley, Frances Watts, Arlyne Brooks; Chorus: Bobby Lee
Frederick, Janet White, Julia Wilber, Tony Ridley, Ruby
Williams, Minnie Gertles, Helen Jackson.

"Ollie Burgoyne and Her Darktown Strutters," 1925. Producer:
Ollie Burgoyne. Principal Cast: Ollie Burgoyne (classic danc-
er), Harrison Blackburn (one-man circus), The Harmony Four,
Ida Forsyne (Russian dancer), Katherine Jacks (soubrette).

"Plantation Days," 1925. Producer: Lew Leslie. Principal Cast:
Florence Mills, Five Crackerjacks, Madeline Belt, Farrell and
Chadwick, Jones and Jones, The Three Eddies (Scott, Allen,
and Lee), Blanche Calloway.

"Plantation Revue," 1925. Producers: Ethel Waters, Earl Dancer.
Principal Cast: Ethel Waters, Earl Dancer, Bessie Allison,
Eddie Rector, Ralph Cooper, Eight "Plantation Vamps."

"Radio Girls," 1925. Producer: Roscoe Montella. Principal Cast:
Roscoe Montella (comedian), Kid Lips (The Charleston King).

"Ragtime Steppers," 1925. Producer: Jules McGarr. Principal
Cast: Melvin Hunter, Mabel Dilworth, Howell and Ogburn,
Fred Clarkston, Eugene Landrum, Chicago Jazz Five.

"Rarin' to Go," 1925. Producer: Edward E. Daley. Principal
Cast: Tim Moore, Jimmie Ferguson, Dancing Dane, Lena
Wilson, Lovey Taylor, Alex Kent, Gertie Moore, Gladys Smith.

"Sands of Honolulu," 1925. Producer: Sandy Burns. Principal
Cast: Sam Russell, Bonnie B. Drew, Lee and White.

"Shake Your Feet," 1925. Producer: No data. Principal Cast:
Zacariah White (principal comedian), Joe Carmouche (second
comedian), Billy McOwens (third comic), "Baby" Ernestine
(child singer), Willie Oglesby (dancer), Susie Wroten (toe
dancer), Robert Wright (dancer).

"Shu-Shin-Shi," 1925. Producer: Johnny Lee Long. Principal
Cast: Johnny Lee Long, creole chorus.

"Steppin' High," 1925 (edition). Producers: Thomas and Russell.
Principal Cast: Hazel Myers, Dike Thomas, "Strawberry"
Russell, Three Black Aces, Leonidas Simmons, Richard Courtney,
Glennie Chessnut, Bill Pierson, Webb King.

"T. O. B. A. Revue," 1925. Producer: Albert Gibson. Principal

Cast: Gibson Trio (Little Albert, Baby Corine, Gibson), "Grasshopper" (comedian), Wilton Crawley (the "human worm").

"What's Up?" 1925.   Producer: Roscoe Montella.   Principal Cast:
Radio Girls.

"When Malinda Sings," 1925.   Producers: Salem Tutt Whitney, J.
Homer Tutt.   Principal Cast: Salem Tutt Whitney, J. Homer
Tutt, Joe Purnell, Mabel Ridley, Charles Hawkins, Wilber
White, Duncan Sisters, Lula Duncan, Edna Bass, Ida Brown,
Chorus: Hazel Terry, Jeannette White, Bobbie Frederico,
Irene Lauda.

"Whim Wham Wharblers," 1925.   Producers: Martin and Walker.
Principal Cast: Edgar Martin, Billie Walker, Babe Brown,
Sylvia Mitchell, Lawrence Nash, Singing Slim Howard.

1926

"Atlantic City Revue," 1926.   Producer: Billy Mitchell.   Principal
Cast: Billy Mitchell, Luther Toy (singer), Johnson and Taylor
(two black dots), Reed C. Moore (a name comedian), Delois
Mitchell (soubrette), Chorus: Margaret Jones, Evelyn Ray,
Christine Cooper, Deloris Pettus, Hazel Stokes, Edna Carroll.

"Bamville Dandies," 1926.   Producer: S. H. Dudley.   Principal
Cast: No data (company appeared on same bill as the black
film "Easy Money" which starred S. H. Dudley).

"Bessie Smith Revue," 1926.   Producer: No data.   Principal Cast:
Bessie Smith, Mason and Henderson (in blackface), Mrs. Mason,
Mrs. Henderson, Taskiana Quartet, Dick and Dick, George
Wiltshire (character actor), Lloyd Hollis (straight), Chorus:
Gladys Gregory, Jessie Lawson, Eleanora Jones, Bessie Wil-
liams, Helen Green, Anna Williams.

"Blue Moon," 1926 (1 act).   Producer: Irvin C. Miller.   Book,
Lyrics: Irvin C. Miller, Donald Heywood.   Principal Cast:
Princess Mysteria, Lorenzo McLane, Stewart Hampton, "Babe"
Townsend, Henrietta Lovelass, Edna Barr, Belle Hampton,
George Nixon, Buster Newman, Reginald York, Lucy Smith,
Sarah Mckey, May Welch, Sadie Williams, Mary Ellisby,
Louise Jeter, Thelma Thomas, Bob James, Billy Chase, Art
Johnson, Rinal (with Princess Mysteria).

"Bon Ton Revue," 1926.   Producer: Susie Sutton.   Principal Cast:
Susie Sutton, Eunice Washington, Billy Gunn, Harold Brown,
The Novelty Quartet, Colmen Titus and Richard Huff (dancers
and impersonations).

"Broadway Brevities," 1926.   Producers: Quintard Miller, Marcus
Slayter.   Principal Cast: Quintard Miller, Marcus Slayter,

Amon Davis, Montrose Brooks, John Freeman, Inez Dennis, Helen Dolly, Emma Hawkins, Lucille Henderson.

"Brown Beauties," 1926. Producer: Jessie Cobb, Mae Wilson. Principal Cast: Mae Wilson, Joe LaRose (straight), "Sleepy" Harris (comic), R. E. Foster (singer), Clentonia Babb (soubrette), W. Benton Overstreet (pianologue), Antonio Grant (chorus boy), Geraldine Jones, Corinne Jones, Eva Overstreet, Leona Perrilliat, Edna Duplessie, Alice Thomas, Olivet West, Willie Mae Veals.

"Brownskin Models of 1927," 1926. Producer: Irvin C. Miller. Principal Cast: Irvin C. Miller, George Randol, George Williams, Sammy Vanderhurst, Minstrel Morris, Shelton Brooks (special appearance for Baltimore production), Blanche Crompton, Lilly Yuen, Eva Metcalf, Rose Johnson, Lavenia Mack, St. Clair Dodson.

"Brownskin Vamps," 1926. Producer: Lew Payton. Principal Cast: Josephine Oliver (soubrette), Paul C. Floyd (straight), Freda Griffin (muscle dancer), Artie McGinity (of Freeman and McGinity), Dick Webb, Grace Conoway, Myrtle Dillard, Chorus: Minnie Harris, Lillian Watts, Ethel George, Marion Ford, Margaret Dorsey, Ailene Lewis, Dee Simmons.

"Charleston Dandies," 1926. Producer: Clarence Muse. Principal Cast: Clarence Muse, Eloise Bennett, John Churchill, Teddy Peters, Norman Astwood, Andrew Tribble, Hardtack Jackson (in blackface), Crawford Jackson, George Jenkins, Hope Black; Chorus: Catherine Jarvis, Happy Jones, Francis Walton, Lena Crawford, Lillian Stokes, Sadie Tappan.

"Charleston Fricassee," 1926. Producers: Quintard Miller and Marcus Slayter. Principal Cast: Amon Davis, Enez Davis, Montrose Brooks, Emma Hawkins, Bessie Wright, George Wiltshire, Robert Rice, Tondelayo, Quintard Miller, Marcus Slayter.

"The Charleston Steppers," 1926. Producer: No data. Principal Cast: Vivian Brown, Helen Dolly, Rose Young, Floyd Young, Mose Williams.

"Charleston Syncopaters," 1926. Producers: Bruce and Skinner. Principal Cast: Madam Bruce, Herbert Skinner, Troy Brown, Odel Irvin, Josie Austin.

"Chicago Pacemakers," 1926. Producer: No data. Principal Cast: Ragtime David Wiles, Humming Bird Beauty Chorus.

"Chocolate Box Revue," 1926. Producer: John Gibson. Principal Cast: Baby Corrine, Little Albert.

"Club Alabam Revue," 1926. Producers: Doc Straine, Bessie

Brown. Music Director: Aaron Thompson. Principal Cast: Helen Stokes, Clifton and Batis, Henry Myres, Robert Wade, C. J. Davis, Doc Straine, Bessie Brown, Jackie Young, Helen Stokes, Claude Collins; Chorus: Dolly Conway, R. Young, Bessie Williams, Philis Martin, Babie Wilson, Jean Gillespie, Nettie Adams, Mildred Williams.

"Connie's Inn Frolics," 1926. Producer: No data. Principal Cast: Emmett Anthony, George Cooper, Archie Crown, George Taylor, John Dancy, Jennie Dancy, Alta Oates, Billy Young, "Baby" Johnson, Octovia Sumter; Sketch: "Twenty Minutes to Hell," Emmett Anthony and Sam Cross.

"Creole Bells," 1926. Producer: Jimmie Cooper. Principal Cast: Doc Straine, Billy Cumby, Bessie Brown, Grace Smith, Barrington Carter, Jimmie Marshall, Wesley Hill, The Dancing Browns, Famous Runnin' Wild Quartette.

"Desires of 1927," 1926. Producer: Irvin C. Miller. Lyrics and Music: Andy Razaf and J. C. Johnson. Book and Stage Direction: Irvin C. Miller. Principal Cast: Adelaide Hall, J. Homer Tutt, Henry (Gang) Jines, Arthur Porter, Frankie Watts, Bee Freeman, Jaquelene White, Stewart Hampton, Mabel Ridley, Arlyne Brooks, Clarence Nance, William McKelvey.

"Dixiana," 1926. Producer: Johnny Lee Long. Principal Cast: Johnny Lee Long, Catherine Patterson.

"Dixie Brevities," 1926. Producer: Quintard Miller, Marcus Slayter. Music: Marcus, Slayter, Inez Dennis. Book: Quintard Miller. Principal Cast: Covan and Florence, George Wiltshire, Montrose Brooks, Ruth Lambard, Emma Hawkins, Andrew Fairchild, Inez Dennis.

"Dixie Strutters," 1926. Producer: No data. Principal Cast: "String Beans" Price, Inez Saunders, Johnson and Rector, Joe Slater.

"Dots and Dashes," 1926. Producer: Ocey Wilson. Principal Cast: Arty Bell, Gladys Smith, Edward DeGaston, Irene and May, Williams and Williams, Scott and Evans.

"Ebony Vampires," 1926. Producers: Watts and Wills. Principal Cast: Watts and Wills, Mme. Patti Wills (primadonna), Charles Shaw, Alonzo Johnson, Rosetta Branum, Mildred Crimes, Rosa Tucker.

"Everybody's Talking," 1926. Producer: Salem Tutt Whitney. Principal Cast: Clarence Nance, Joe Purnell, Mabel Ridley, Frankie Watts, Arlyne Brooks, Ida Foster, Charlie Hawkins, Marion Davis, Selma Sayles, Julia Thomas, Rosa Knight, Mae Austin, Emma Marshall.

"4-11-44," 1926. Producer: No data. Principal Cast: Eddie
Hunter (principal comedian), Andrew Tribble, Nina Hunter,
Grayce Rector, Alberta Perkins, Norman Astwood, Aurora
Greeley, Emma Jackson, George Cooper, Billy Mitchell, Claude
Lawson.

"Fun Festival," 1926. Producer: Lonnie Fisher. Principal Cast:
Lonnie Fisher, "Stompy" Watson, "Lollipop," Mrs. Fisher.

"Georgia Red Hots," 1926. Producer: No data. Principal Cast:
Baby Cox, Betty Snow, Clarkston "The Strong Man," Lee and
Eckart.

"Get Happy," 1926. Producer: William Benbow. Principal Cast:
William Benbow, Ozie Stennis, Henrietta Leggett, Mabel Jones,
"Shorty" Edwards, Zue Robinson and his Jazz Band.

"Get Set," 1926. Producer: Harlem Producing Company (Joe
Bright, Mann, Luigi). Principal Cast: John Mason, Alex
Fairchild, Joe Russell, Boots Marshall, Ethel Williams,
Walter Richardson, Rose Brown, Ethel Waters, Lawrence
Chenault, Henry Rector, Rennie Clark, Hilda Thompson, Jennie
Lawson, Ruby Mason, Mabel Johnson, Rose Brown, Ida Ander-
son, Tootsie Delk, Ella Deas, Louise Dunbar, Mattie Harris,
Edwin Scotron, Lloyd Gibbs, Joe Bright.

"Go Get 'Em," 1926 (edition). Producers: Henry Drake and Ethel
Walker. Principal Cast: Ethel Walker, Henry Drake, Baby
Mack (singing and dancing soubrette), Claude Collins (singer and
leading man), Sambo Reid, Robert Wade, Clifton Drake, Jim-
mie Baskette, Eddie Johnson, William Mitchell Dancers; Chorus:
Marion Jones, Wilhelmena Baker, Maria DeCosta, Arlina Sisco,
Gene Calloway, Christina Daniel, D. Williams, Pearl Jackson.

"Goin' Some," 1926. Producer: Mabel Whitman. Principal Cast:
Whitman Sisters.

"Golden Brown Reasons of 1926," 1926. Producer: No data.
Principal Cast: Sarah Martin, John Henderson, Willis Rogers,
Alvin Beman, Happy Cole, Rogers and Rogers, Annie White,
Josephine Byrd, Herby Leonard, Pete Nugent; Chorus: Billy
Henderson, Rosa Barbis, Rosa Bell Anderson, Florence Blake,
Hortense Lightfoot, Ethel Blake, "Little Bits" Smith, Bob
Knight, Mattie Sutton, Jewel Thomas.

"Harlem Butterflies," 1926. Producers: Quintard Miller, Marcus
Slater. Principal Cast: Quintard Miller, Marcus Slater, Inez
Dennis, Amon Davis, Helen Dolly, Emma Hawkins.

"The Harlem Scandals," 1926. Producer: Billy Crumby. Principal
Cast: Billy Cumby, Jimmy Marshall, Cooper and Thomas, Bee
Freeman, Edith Young, May Dewit, Eleanor Wilson, Jerry
Wiley, Irene Louder.

"Hello Sambo," 1926.   Producer: Jules McGarr.   Principal Cast:
    Jules McGarr, "Kid Lips," Dorothy Scott, Jimmy Howell,
    Ethel Ogburn, Mabel Dilworth, "Buckwheat" Stringer, Melvin
    Hunter, Beulah Benson.

"Hottentot Revue," 1926.   Producers: Petway and Rector (Eddie).
    Principal Cast: Eddie Rector, "Onions" Jeffrey, Anconia
    Turner, Shirley Abby, Ed. Peat (talking, singing, dancing),
    Aaron Thompson, Ten Dixie Dandies Band.

"Kentucky Sue," 1926.   Producers: Chappelle and Stinnette.   Prin-
    cipal Cast: Chappelle and Stinnette, Doe Doe Green, Billy
    Maxey, Dink Thomas, James Thomas, George Cooper, Arthur
    Johnson, "Babe" Townsend, Loveless and McLane, Larry Sey-
    mour, Grace Smith; Chorus: Irene Davis, Thelma Thomas,
    Miamie Ellis, Minnie Webster, Edna Fletcher, Leronia Parham,
    Marion Jeffreys, Audrey Purnell, Gladys Osoris, Mildred
    Pritchard, Lillian Pollard, Marion Cheeks, Pauline DeCosta,
    Edith Carrington, Carmen Lopez.

"Louisiana Mess-Around," 1926.   Producer: No data.   Principal
    Cast: Daybreak Nelson, Madge Young, William McConnicoe,
    Marie Daniels, Travil Tucker, Stella Young, Odelina Johnson,
    Mary Daniels, Agnes Levi, Susie Taylor, Margaret Wilkens.

"Lucky Sambo," 1926.   Producer: No data.   Principal Cast: Billy
    Higgins (husband of Valaida Snow), Joe Byrd, Julia Moody,
    Ernest Whitman, Jim Vaughn and his Jazz Hounds, Arthur
    Porter, James Watts, Nina Hunter, Three Dixie Songbirds
    (Hilda Perleno, Berlena Blanks, Amanda Randolph), Billy
    Ewing, Al Watts, George Phillips.

"Ma' Rainey and Her Georgia Jazz Hounds," 1926.   Producer: Ma'
    Rainey.   Principal Cast: Ma' Rainey, Geneva Washington,
    Queen Dora (dancer), "Jolly" Saunders (juggler), John "Jiggs"
    Briedy (whistler, dancer, singer); Chorus: Madeline Carter,
    Margaret McDonald, Grace McDaniels.

"Mamie Smith Revue," 1926.   Producer: Mamie Smith.   Principal
    Cast: Mamie Smith, Ethel Williams Dotson (soubrette), "Ace,
    King and Jack" (Herbert Taylor, Eugene Taylor, Daniel Win-
    stead, dancers), Clinton "Dusty" Fletcher and Mose Gaston
    (comics); Chorus: Sadie Montgomery, Lillian Stokes, Billie
    Henderson, Phoebe Helms, Lucille Basey, Bessie Williams.

"Miss Dinah of 1926," 1926.   Producers: Quintard Miller, Marcus
    Slayter.   Principal Cast: Inez Dennis (dancer), Rosa Hender-
    son (blues singer), Annie White (singer), Quintard Miller, Mar-
    cus Slayter (straight), George Wiltshire (character), Brownie
    Cambell, Dick Webb, Montrose Brooks; Chorus: Bessie
    Wrightson, Irene Poindexter, Emma Hawkins, Catherine Watts,
    Edith Randolph, Jennie Hill, Lillian Denning, Hattie Carpenter.

"Miss New York, " 1926. Producer: Mabel Whitman. Principal
Cast: Whitman Sisters, Bobbie Kyle, Zelma Straighter, Alberta
Whitman, Alice Whitman, Willie Brandon, Pops and Billie,
Walter Johnson, Tony Grant, Charlie Jones, Willie Braudon,
Josephine Oliver, James Rogers. Chorus: Ethel Frye,
Christine Haines, Harriet Calloway.

"My Magnolia, " 1926. Producer: Lew Leslie. Principal Cast:
Eddie Hunter, Alex Rogers, C. Luckeyth Roberts, Dink Stewart,
Barrington Carter, Percy Colston, George Randol, Lionel Mona-
gas, Charles Davis, Lena Sanford Roberts, Alberta Perkins,
Mabel Gant, Catherine Parker, Estell Floyd, Charlie Lawson.

"A Night in the Cabaret, " 1926. Producers: Joe Clark, Joy
Makers Company. Principal Cast: No data.

"Nobody's Girl, " 1926. Producer: No data. Principal Cast: Hamtree Harrington, Cora Green.

"Race Horse Charlie's Last Chance, " 1926. Producer: Dad James.
Principal Cast: Marion Ford, Melvin Butler, Gertrude Demond,
Hortence Lewis, Annie Mason.

"Ragtime Sailors, " 1926. Producer: Bob Russell. Principal Cast:
Sam Robinson, Eleanor Wilson, Arthur Boykin, Fred LaJoy,
Rogers Duo, Baby Mack.

"Rainbow Chasers, " 1926. Producers: Salem Tutt Whitney and J.
Homer Tutt. Principal Cast: Salem Tutt Whitney, J. Homer
Tutt, L. Baynard Whitney (tenor), Clarence Nance (comedy),
Charles Hawkins (character), Ida Forsyne (Russian dancer),
Nona Marshall (Queen of the Charleston), Joseph Purnell (light
comedy), Melody Maids Trio, Mabel Ridley (mezzo soprano),
Miss Frankie Watts (contralto, blues singer); Chorus: Marion
Davis, Selma Sayles, Jewel Thomas, Arlyne Brooks, Rosa
Night, Mae Anderson.

"Rarin' to Go, " 1926. Producer: No data. Principal Cast: The
show consisted of two parts, each performed separately by black
and white performers. The black cast included: Tim Moore,
Lovey Taylor, Florence McClain.

"Red Hot Mama, " 1926. Producer: Irvin C. Miller. Principal
Cast: Gertrude Saunders, Gallie DeGaston, Snow Fisher, Alice
Gorgas, Alonzo Fenderson, Albert Jackson, Percy Colston,
Westly Hill, Archie Cross, Marion Bradford, Billy Andrews.

"Red Hots, " 1926. Producer: No data. Principal Cast: Baby
Cox, Leo Edwards, Fred Clarkson, Hattie V. Snow (sister of
Valaida Snow), Lillian Barbrey.

"Roll-On, " 1926. Producer: Brown (Lillian) and DuMont. Princi-

pal Cast: "Slim" Jones, Allen and Allen, Clifton and Batle,
Brown and DuMont, Wells and Wells, Freddie Tunsdall.

"Rompin' Through," 1926. Producer: Mabel Whitman. Principal
Cast: Alberta (Bert) Whitman, Alice Whitman, Essie Whitman,
Ernest Michaels, Alberta La Bastiste.

"Round the Globe," 1926. Producer: Mary Mack, Merry Makers
Company. Principal Cast: No data.

"Shuffle Along," 1926 (Kansas City Production). Producers:
Quintard Miller and Marcus Slayter. Principal Cast: Quintard
Miller, Marcus Slayter, Amon Davis, Inez Davis, George Wilt-
shire, Bessie Wrightson, Robert Rice, Emma Hawkins, Theo.
McDonals, Josephine Leggett.

"Shufflin' Sam from Alabam," 1926. Producers: Gardner and
Horton. Band Conductor: Jeff Smith. Principal Cast: Nay
Brothers (Harr, Hurl, Lawrence), S. H. Dudley, Jr., Bee
Haines, Earl Brown, Elmer Moore, Victor Scott, Hoyt Jenkins,
Virginia Liston, Frank Kirk, Sidney Rink and Gunpowder (his
trick mule); Chorus: Lily Turner, Jessie Scott, Bee Haines,
Kitty Ratin, Roberta Rountree, Thelma Sales, Laura Nichols,
Hattie Williams, Mildred Pettibone, Belish Nay, Gladys Robin-
son, Mamie Smith, Lily Davies, Hattie Roberts, May Simmons,
Gertie Perkins, Billie Warren.

"So Different Revue," 1926. Producer: No data. Principal Cast:
Melvin Hunter, Jimmie Howell, J. Revis, Floyd Young, Beulah
Benbow, Ethel Oydbraum.

"Steppin' Along," 1926. Producer: Standard Amusement Company.
Principal Cast: Margurite Johnson, Rose Henderson (Little
Miss Jazz).

"Steppin' Babies," 1926. Producer: Eddie Lemons. Principal Cast:
Eddie Lemons, Olive Lopez Lemons, Yanks Bronson, "String
Beans" Price, Lulu Whidby, Albert McClelland, Charles A.
Berry.

"Tan Town Topics," 1926. Producer: Eddie Rector and Ralph
Cooper. Principal Cast: Eddie Rector (dancer), Ralph Cooper
(dancer), Maude Mills (sister of Florence Mills), Phillip Giles
(comic), Adelaide Hall, Leondies Simmons, Gulfport and Brown
(in a skit "Leave My Wife Alone"), Arthur Gaines (singer),
Walter Brown (whistler), Fats Waller and his band; Chorus:
Goldie Cisco, Alma Sutton, Mildred Brown, Thelma McLoughlin,
Tina Curly, Hazel Valentine, Evelyn Keyes, Babe McClendon,
Sadie Maxie, Donald Heywood and his Orchestra.

"That's My Baby," 1926. Producer: Irvin C. Miller. Principal
Cast: Irvin C. Miller, Albert Jackson (son of J. A. "Bill-
board" Jackson), Gallie DeGaston, John Henderson, Alice
Gorgas, Aurora Greeley, Happy Simpson, George McArthur.

"Vanities," 1926. Producer: Earl Dancer. Principal Cast: Ethel
Waters, Earl Dancer, Billy King, Marshall Rogers, Nuggle
Johnson.

"Vanities of 1926," 1926. Producer: Edward Langford. Principal
Cast: Gonzell White, Rogers and Rogers, Doris Rhinebottom,
Kitty Aublanche, "Crackshot" and Hunter, George Aiken, George
Ray, Dandy Brown, Bill Baisey's Band.

"Watermelon Morn," 1926. Producer: Mabel Whitman. Principal
Cast: Alberta Whitman, Essie Whitman, Mattie Dorsey (singer),
Hamilton and Hamilton (Mr. and Mrs.), Miss Calloway, W. B.
Johnson, Charley Jones, Princess Wee Wee, Albert Palmer,
Shine Bones, Katie Franklin.

"Who's Dat," 1926. Producer: Eddie Lemons. Principal Cast:
Eddie Lemons, Rose Henderson, Eva Mason, Theresa Brooks,
Elizabeth Scott, Olive Lopez (Mrs. Eddie Lemons), Petway and
Rector.

"Yellow Gal," 1926. Producer: John Mason. Principal Cast:
Dixie Beach Girls Company.

"Yes Sir," 1926. Producers: Martin and Walker (Edgar and Billy).
Principal Cast: Babe Brown, Lawrence Nash, Myrtle Quarrels,
Edgar Martin, Billy Walker (in blackface), Ray Moore, Chorus:
Baby Green, Jessie Taylor, Marion Hall, Doris Saunders,
Erlaine Lane, Gene Forster.

1927

"Ace High Revue," 1927. Producer: Mae Wilson. Principal Cast:
Mae Wilson, Ernest Whitman, Joe Byrd, Henry Crackshot,
Suzanne Brown, Rena Curry.

"All-Nation's Revue," 1927. Producer: Irvin C. Miller. Principal Cast: Margaret Simms.

"Aunt Jemima's Revue," 1927. Producer: No data. Principal
Cast: Ella Ringgold (Aunt Jemima), "Dollar" Jones (Old Black
Joe), Sammie Lewin, George Craft, Johnny Williams (in black-
face), Baby Lewis (soubrette), Chorus: Ruth Williams, Madeline
Belt, Leona Miller, Ethel Burley, Tiny Odum, Norma Burke,
Helen Green.

"Bad Habits of 1928," 1927. Producer: Irvin C. Miller. Principal Cast: Gallie DeGaston (comedian), Margaret Simms (singer),
Elizabeth Smith (girl with the ukulele), Archie Cross (harmon-
ica), Albert Jackson (funster), Percy Colston, Marion Bradford,
George Randol, Bass Lawson, Four Miller Dancers.

"Bare Facts," 1927. Producer: Quintard Miller. Principal Cast:

Quintard Miller, Margaret Simms, Joe Russell, Edgar "Sambo" Conner's Trio, Troy Brown, Gladys Ferguson.

"Black Bottom Revue," 1927. Producer: Jack Goldberg. Principal Cast: Clare Smith, Clarence Paison, Nuggie Johnson, Williams and Ferguson, Happy Holmes, Quinton Redd, Green and Green, Ana White, "Washboard" Johnson, Ruth Trent.

"Black Pepper Revue," 1927. Producer: No data. Principal Cast: Flo Brown, Cecil Rivers, Bill "Bojangles" Robinson (in Harlem production only), Monte Hawley, Edgar Conners.

"Blackbirds of 1927," 1927. Producer: Lew Leslie. Principal Cast: Florence Mills, Edith Wilson, Johnny Nit, Winfred and Mills, Joynes and Foster, Leonard Harper, Three Eddies.

"Blue Baby," 1927. Producer: Irvin C. Miller. Principal Cast: Elizabeth Smith, Billy Young, Lovie Austin, Edgar Martin, Nona Marshall, Teddye Frazier, Albert Jackson, Louise Williams, Alfred "Slick" Chester, Blue Baby Dancing Girls.

"Broadway Flappers," 1927. Producer: Rosa Johnson. Principal Cast: Rosa Johnson, May Smith, James Miller, Bennie Robinson, Marie Hampton, Willie Townsend, Lola Belle Wells, "Slick" Porter and "Kid Country" (blackface comedy).

"Bubbling Over Revue," 1927. Producers: Mitchell and Rector (Lelia, Julia). Principal Cast: Lelia Mitchell, Julia Rector, Dewey Weinglass, Bertha Roe, Tommy Woods, Lawrence Lomax.

"Chicago Plantation Revue," 1927. Producer: Clarence Muse. Principal Cast: Rossoe (Red) Simmons, Dolly Allen, Rosco Montella, Chicago Four, Pauline Montella, Marie Gonzales, "Skeeter" Winston, Johnnie Jones, Valley Inn Orchestra.

"The Chocolate Scandals," 1927. Producer: No data. Principal Cast: Sam Russell, Sarah Martin, Doc Straine, Halen Stokes, Gill and Warner (Two Ebony Nights).

"Club Kentucky Revue," 1927. Producer: Lenard Harper. Principal Cast: Lenard Harper, Radcliffe and Radcliffe, Hunter and Ledman, Blanche Thompson, Doris Rhuebottom, "Jazz Lips" Jr., Cambell and Powell, Henry Crackshot.

"Connie's Inn Frolics of 1927," 1927. Producer: George Immerman. Principal Cast: Emmett Anthony, Mantan Moreland, Sam Cross, Johnny Lee, James Jackson, John Dancy, Alto Oates, Jennie Dancy, Baby Lee, Ruth Payne.

"Dancing Fools," 1927. Producer: Whitman Sisters. Principal Cast: Mabel, Essie, Alice and Alberta (Bert) Whitman, Little Jazzlips (juvenile), Little "Pops" Albert, Mike Bow and Willie "Toosweet" (blackface comedy).

"Dashing Dinah," 1927. Producer: Eddie Lemons. Principal Cast: Eddie Lemons, Homer Hubbard, Rogers and Rogers, Leroy Phillips, Charles Barry, Isadore Price, Willie Taylor, Jack "Ginger" Wiggins, Christina Gray, String Beans Price.

"Dixie Brevities," 1927. Producer: Quintard Miller. Principal Cast: Marcus Slayter, Quintard Miller, Covan and Florence, Andrew Fairchilds, Inez Dennis.

"Fanticies of 1927," 1927. Producer: No data. Principal Cast: Margaret Johnson, "Baby" Juanita Johnson, Earl Howard, Strand Serenaders.

"Gay Harlem," 1927. Producer: Irvin C. Miller. Principal Cast: Billy Cumby, Tom Cassidy, Elizabeth Smith, Ruby Mason, Ethel Dudley, Charles Alexander, Ike Paul, Louise Williams, Lorraine Harris, Claude Winifrey.

"Great Temptations," 1927. Producers: Donald Heywood, Jimmy Marshall. Principal Cast: Dink Stewart, Viola Colston, Percy Verwayne, Lottie Brown, Four Melody Maids, Monroe and Daley, Edna Barr, Geraldine Gooding, Adelle Hargrave, Mildred Mitchell.

"The Harlem Follies," 1927. Producer: Jack Gee. Principal Cast: Bessie Smith, Clarence Smith, Dina Scott, Red Hot Chorus, Gert, Darlin, and Phillips (dancers), "Long" Johnnie Madlock, James Collins, Tucker and Tucker, Clarence Smith, Louise Alexander, Chorus: Rae Tucker, Annie Mae Cole, Helen Hill, Catherine Brown, Edna Payne, Hazel Echels, Elsie Freby, T. Powell, Lena Madlock, Maude Smith, Hilda Reed, Lorenzo Tucker.

"The Harlem Strutters," 1927. Producer: Clinton "Dusty" Fletcher. Principal Cast: Dusty Fletcher, Billie McKensey, Willie Mae, Marie Miller, "Dollar Bill," Hard Back "King of the Uke," "Won't Don't" Orchestra.

"Heebee Jeebies," 1927. Producer: Jimmy Cooper. Principal Cast: Butterbeans and Susie, Five Crackerjacks (Florence Parham, Harry Jones, Clifford Carter, Irish Hammet, Raymond Carter), Gulfport and Brown, Brown and Marguerite, Octavia Sumler, Florence Parham, Eddie Heywood and his orchestra.

"Hey Hey," 1927. Producer: Amy Ashwood Garvey (Mrs. Marcus Garvey). Principal Cast: Sam Manning, Sam Davis, Cotton-belt Four, Evelyn Ray, Charlotte Ringgold, Dorothy McClemont, Catherine Beas.

"His Honery, the Judge," 1927. Producer: No data. Principal Cast: Our Gang Revue Company.

"Jigfield Follies," 1927. Producer: No data. Principal Cast: Henry Drew, Billy Mitchell, Billy Bradford, Calloway Sisters

(Jenne and Harriett), Frank Keith (female impersonator), Tommie Davis (toe dancer), Billy Hayes, W. Davis, Bootsie Wilson, Betty Lockwood, Lillian White.

"Keep Movin'," 1927. Producer: E. E. Daley. Principal Cast: "Skeeter" Winston, Pauline Montella, Billy Young, Onnie Jones, Williams and Scott, Roscoe Montella, Nona Marshall, Troy Brown, Edgar Haynes.

"Look Who's Here," 1927. Producer: Drake and Walker. Principal Cast: Henry Drake, Ethel Walker (Mrs. Drake), Baby Mack, Estella Edwards, Jackie Mabley (in blackface), Jimmie Baskette, Louis Dandridge, Clifton and Williams, Drake Black Bottom Dancers, William Mitchell and Herman Carbin (dance specialty).

"Lulu Belle," 1927. Producer: J. W. Jackson. Principal Cast: Ollie Burgoyne, Louis Decail, Elvire Johnson, Alberta Pope, Edna Davis, Lionel Monagas, Percy Wade.

"Mannequins of 1927," 1927. Producer: Johnny Lee Long. Principal Cast: Catherine Patterson, "Baby Kid," Johnny Bodidly, Teddy Smith, Howard Dorsey, Chorus: Elsie Frebee, Dorothy Lee, Dorothy Wiggins, Chestine Wooten, Ethel McCoy, Anna May Coles.

"Midnight Steppers," 1927. Producer: Leonard Harper. Principal Cast: Billy Higgins, Paulis and Jimmie Johnson, Nina May, Joe Byrd, Dewey Brown, Three Dixie Song Birds (Hilda Perleno, Berlena Blanks, Amanda Randolph), Alabama Four (dancers), "Midnight Steppers" (Joe Wilson, Sam Burnham, Edward Chenault), George Phillips (acrobatic dancer), Linda Garnette (contortionist), Gomes Monsanto, Helario Friend, Shirley Abbey, Goldie Cisco, Julia Noisette, Peggy Morris, "Baby" Fisher.

"Miss Bandana," 1927. Producer: Clarence Muse. Principal Cast: Mabel Ridley, Alice Gorgas, Angeline Mitchell, Ollie Burgoyne, Geraldine Gooding, Beatrice Brown, Salem Tutt Whitney, Walter Crumby, Ike Paul, "Onion" Jeffries, George Booker (juvenile lead), L. J. Randall, J. W. Mobley, Gordon Wilson, Cecil Graham, John Henderson, Sheldon Hoskins, R. M. Cooper.

"Modern Cocktail," 1927. Producer: Norman Thomas. Musical Director: Grant Williams. Principal Cast: Susie Sutton (character), Wells and Wells (aerialists), Lloyd Hollis and Coleman Titus (straight and character), Robert Perry and Willie Richardson (comedians), Viola Richardson; Chorus: L. E. Butler, Bertha Perry, Louise Owsley, Helen Little, Baby Jones, Christine Russell, Florida Hall.

"Neath the Southern Moon," 1927. Producer: Bill "Bodidley" Pierson. Principal Cast: Lovey Austin, Hazel Myers, Dink Stewart, Mann and Cole, Walter Smith.

"Peppy Steppers," 1927. Producer: Carter Lockhart. Principal Cast: Carter Lockhart, Rose Brown, Sol Speights and Myrtle, Lockhart and Bozo (blackface comedians).

"Rock Dinah," 1927. Producer: Grant and Wilson. Principal Cast: Coot Grant, Kid Wilson, Baby Hines (leading lady, singer), Johnny Bragg (leading man, straight), "Big Boy" Anderson and Shorty Ford (comedians), Raymond Shackelford (parts and light comedy), Jeanette Jackson (soubrette); Chorus: Georgette Walker, Francis Tyler, Billy Clay, Elizabeth Chandler, Mamie Ford, Louise Shackelford.

"Royal Flush Revue," 1927. Producer: No data. Principal Cast: Garland Howard, Mae Brown, Bernice Robinson, Sterling Grant, Julia Moody, Campbell and Farrell, Pauline Montella (singer), Sketter Winston (comedian), Roscoe Montella, Billy Mitchell.

"Runnin' Wild," 1927 (edition). Producer: Irvin C. Miller. Principal Cast: Gallie DeGaston, Albert Jackson, Alonzo Fenderson, Archie Cross, Alice Gorgas, Hazel Randolph, Percy Colston, Derby Wilson, Irvin Beamon.

"Slim Slivers," 1927. Producer: J. W. Jackson. Principal Cast: Ollie Burgoyne, Louis Deckail, Elvira Johnson, Alberta Pope, Edna Davis, Lionel Monagas, Frank Badham, Percy Wade.

"Shake, Rattle and Roll," 1927. Producer: No data. Principal Cast: Jones and Jones, Viola McCoy, Wesley Hill, Bobby Perry, George Huges, George Stafford, "Honey" Brown (toe dancer), Hatch and Hatch.

"Southland Follies," 1927. Producer: Joe Sheftell. Principal Cast: Johnnie Woods, Little Henry, White Brothers, Mamie Moon, Esther Bigeou, Charles Moore, Dude Kelly.

"Southland Revue," 1927. Producer: Tim Moore. Principal Cast: Tim Moore, Freddie Johnson, Berry Brothers, Campbell and Farrow, Clinton "Dusty" Fletcher, Ethel Williams, Viola Speedy.

"Stoppin' the Traffic," 1927. Producer: Dewey Weinglass. Principal Cast: Dewey Weinglass (Russian dancer), Billy McLaurin and Slim Thomas, Cecil Rivers, Flo Brown, Bertha Roe, Lomax and Blue, Bloudina Stern, Marion More, "Birdie" Baker, Tommy Woods, Lee Allen, "Song Birds."

"Syncopation," 1927. Producer: No data. Principal Cast: Inez Dennis, Billy McLaurin, Monette Moore.

"That's My Baby," 1927. Producer: Irvin C. Miller. Principal Cast: Elizabeth Smith, Bee Freeman, Hampton and Hunter, Lois Williams, Charles Hawkins, John Alexander, Harriet Calloway.

"Three Thieves Musical Comedy," 1927. Producer: No data.

Principal Cast: K. Pierson, Tim Owsley, Hazel Myers, Rags Cole, Silvertone Toye.

"A Trip to Araby," 1927. Producer: Mat Housley. Principal Cast: "Dike" Thomas and Slim Austin ("Sheiks of Araby"), Angeline Mitchell, Baby DeLeon, Josephine Dean, Moxie Jackson, Baby "Kid" Hall.

"Watermelon," 1927. Producer: Jack Goldberg. Principal Cast: Andrew Tribble, Guy and Jacqueline Jines, Bob Bramlet, Elverta Brown, Harrie Carter.

"You've Got to Step Lively," 1927. Producer: Bailey and Wiggins. Principal Cast: Laura Bailey (in blackface), Jack (Ginger) Wiggins, the Three Inkspots (dancers), Anna Thomas, Slim Russell, Jesse Gordon, James Lancaster, "Dollar Bill" Jones, Chorus: Anna Thomas, Bernice Williams, May Thompson, Coley Williams, Eleanor Jones, Myrtle Speights, Camile Chase.

1928

"A La Carte," 1928. Producer: Walter Douglass. Principal Cast: Ralph Cooper, Eddie Rector, Billy Higgins, Alec Lovejoy, Margaret Beckitt, Theresa Mason, Eloise Bennett and Baby DeLeon, Roscoe Simmons, Eddie Taylor, Earl Taylor.

"Ace of Clubs," 1928. Producer: Harry Thomas, William Parvus. Principal Cast: Harry Smith, Patterson and Patterson, "Dollar Bill" Jones, Frederick Mitchell, Billy Petway, Purnell Murray, Ike Perkins, Henry Mitchell, Odella Johnson, Lillian Jackson, Violet Field, Charlotte Goodman, Daisy Brown, Mary Johnson.

"Bandanna Days," 1928 (edition). Producer: Majestic Theatrical Circuit (Jack Goldberg). Principal Cast: Hooten and Hooten, Julia Moody, Larry Seymour, Bee Middleton, Willie Williams, Ruth Trent, Billy McLaurin, Ralph DeMont.

"Benbow's New York Colored Follies," 1928 (staged in Trinidad). Producer: William Benbow. Principal Cast: Margie Cohen, Elnora Wilson, Jay Goins, Leon Diggs, Henrietta Leggett, Elmo and Bobbie Moore, Willa May Veal, Willie Thompson, Harvey Meyer, Maude Maxwell, Tiny Ridley, Geraldine Robinson, Hope Renepez, Estelle Cook, Violet Brown, Nina Cozac, Bessie Dean, Ada Lewis, Mrs. Edna Givens, Don Dawleigh's Nine Jazz Kings, F. W. Benbow and Master Richard Benbow, Jr.

"Black Diamond Express," 1928. Producer: Mamie Smith. Principal Cast: Mamie Smith, Apus Brooks, Joe Russell, Amon Davis, Sonny Lee, Henry Williams, Clarence Peterson, Lon Claxton, Whirley Wiggins, Lorenzo Tucker; Chorus: Helen Battles, Emm Hawkins, May Evans, Helen Little, Rae Tucker, Fay Polard, Emmon Hawkins, Eva Allen, Lena Williams.

"Blackbirds of 1928," 1928 (London, England Production). Producer: Lew Leslie. Principal Cast: Eddie Hunter, Eva Sherman, Anita Ward, Anita Edwards, Norman Astwood, Johnny Nit.

"Blue Baby," 1928. Producer: Irvin C. Miller. Principal Cast: Elizabeth Smith, Billie and Mona, Edgar Martin, Louise Williams, Teddy Frazier, Albert Jackson, Billy Young.

"Broadway Rastus," 1928 (edition). Producer: Irvin C. Miller. Principal Cast: Emmett (Gang) Anthony, Ida Brown, S. H. Dudley, Jr., Brown and Jones; Chorus: Eddy Herd, Llewellyn Crawford, Ernest Morman, Taft Price, Cleo Johnson, Beatrice Stewart, Mildred Pritchard, Dolores Minor, Billy Hayes, Wealthy Davis, Claudina Heyward, Fredrica Seymour.

"Brownskin Models," 1928 (edition). Producer: Irvin C. Miller. Music Director: Cuney Conners. Principal Cast: Maidina Brown, Teddy Johnson, Eva Metcalf, Helen Stewart, George Crawford, Harrison Blackburn, Willie Jackson, Charlie Salter, Wells and Wells, Blanche Thompson, Salter and Boatner, Joe Russell.

"Brownskin Models of 1929," 1928. Producer: Irvin C. Miller. Principal Cast: Maudina Brown, Teddy Johnson, Ancomia Turner, Eva Metcalf, Helen Stewart, George Crawford, Harrison Blackburn, John Henderson, Marcellus Sherwood, Charlie Salter, Willie Brown.

"Bubblin' Over," 1928. Producer: No data. Principal Cast: Willie Richardson (blackface comedian), "Boll Weevil" (blackface comedian), Ola Mae Waters (soubrette), Johnny Williams (straight), Tillie Johnson (character); Chorus: Vernon Hogan, Valetta Ridgel, Jessie Tanner, Mary Bell.

"Butterbeans and Susie Revue," 1928. Producer: Butterbeans and Susie. Principal Cast: Butterbeans and Susie, Baby Cox, Billy Mitchell, Russell Lee, Daisy Wright, Johnson, Wells, and Blue Trio, Chorus: "Dimples" Williams, Fannie Cotton, May Goodwin, Ollie Shoomaker, Helen Penn, Alice Brown, Otis Stigrave, Billy Fisher.

"Carolina Nights," 1928. Producer: No data. Book: Doe Doe Green. Principal Cast: Gladys Thompson, Arlyne Brooks, Frankie Watts, Doe Doe Green, Arthur Porter, Paul Floyd, Alonzo McLane, Evelyn Preer, Edward Thompson, Chorus: Elizabeth McManus, Rose Mitchell, Joyse Richardson, Bessie Mitchell, Alberta Atkins, Sally Simms, Billy Wilson, Jessie Oxendine.

"Chicago Follies," 1928. Producer: No data. Principal Cast: Raymond Shackelford, Johnson and Rector, Julia Davis.

"Circus Day Revue," 1928. Producer: No data. Principal Cast: Slim Thompson, Hilda Rogers, King Knappie and Dewey Miles.

"Dancing Days, " 1928. Producer: Joe Simms. Principal Cast:
    Joe Simms, Laura Bailey, Reginald York, William Simpson,
    Catherine Brown (in blackface), Kitty Goodwin, James Sheffey,
    Clarence Jones Orchestra.

"Deep Harlem, " 1928. Book: Salem Tutt Whitney and J. Homer
    Tutt. Principal Cast: Salem Tutt Whitney, J. Homer Tutt,
    Mabel Ridley, Grant and Sterling, Doe Doe Green, Four
    Northern Bros. , Pearl McCormack, Louis Cole, Harry Mays,
    Charlie Willis, Alice Gorgas, Howard Elmore.

"Dixie Brevities of 1928, " 1928. Producers: Quintard Miller and
    Marcus Slayter. Principal Cast: Lottie Gee, Edith Spencer,
    Doris Rhenbottom, Inez Dennis, Gallie DeGaston, Montrose
    Brooks, George Wiltshire (sings "No Foolin' "), Quintard Miller,
    Marcus Slayter, Dinah Scott, Robert ("snow") Rice (dancer in
    blackface), Chorus: Mary Denvers, Otis Sitgraves, Marion
    Sumler, Elizabeth Scott, Lillian Stokes, Jennie Hill, Sybil
    Gentry, Mae Diggs, Eva Bradley, Benie Wrightson.

"The Dixie Vagabond, " 1928. Book: No data. Principal Cast:
    Roscoe Montella, Lillian Westmoreland, Ernest Whitman, Lilly
    Yuen, Pauline Montella, Hazel Lee, Marion Moore, Chorus:
    Mildred Pritchard, Hazel Miller, Minnie Harris, Edith Oliver,
    Bernice Cameron, Evelyn Plunkett.

"Dusky Follies, " 1928. Producer: Majestic Theatrical Circuit
    (Jack Goldberg). Principal Cast: Skeeter Winston, Lena Cury,
    Lovey Austin, Jan Jeanet.

"Ebony Follies, " 1928. Producer: S. H. Dudley. Stage Director:
    S. H. Dudley, Jr. Principal Cast: S. H. Dudley, Madam
    Tolliver, S. H. Dudley, Jr. , Lonnie Fisher, Ozie McPherson,
    Cash and Smith, Cyclonic Jazz Band, Georgia Brownskin Peaches
    Chorus.

"Fancy Trimmings, " 1928. Producer: Addison Carey. Principal
    Cast: Billy Higgins, Ernest Whitman, Johnny Lee Long, Putney
    Dandridge, George Green, Mrs. Johnny Lee Long.

"Gettin' Hot, " 1928. Producer: Speedy Smith. Principal Cast:
    Speedy Smith, Zudora DeGaston, Pete Peters, Teddy Smith,
    George Lynche, Billie Wilson, Sadie Crawford, Jessie Love.

"Happy Go Lucky, " 1928. Producer: No data. Principal Cast:
    William and Brown, George Williams, Charles Taylor, Johnson
    and Lee, Henry Williams.

"Here We Are, " 1928. Producer: Ed. E. Daley. Principal Cast:
    Brown and Jones, Buster Newman, Grace Rector, Spencer
    Barnes, Kitty Abblanche.

"Jazz Town Capers, " 1928. Producer: Marshall Rogers. Principal

Cast: Marshall Rogers, Fess Williams, Margie Lorraine,
Joyce Robinson, Rookie Davis (in blackface), Walter Richardson,
Jimmie Bartrand, Aggie and White.

"Levee Days, " 1928.   Producer: Al Rogers.   Director of Music:
Clarence Austin.   Principal Cast: Chappelle and Stinnette,
Ollie Burgoyne, Marion Moore, Frank Badham, Willie Porter,
Charlie Doyle, George Morton, Lillian Westmoreland.

"Mandy Green from New Orleans, " 1928.   Producer: Majestic
Theatrical Circuit (Jack Goldberg).   Principal Cast: "Babe"
Brown, Johnny Stevens, John LaRue.

"Miss Broadway, " 1928.   Producer: "Boots" Hope.   Principal Cast:
"Boots" Hope, Pete Gentry, Minnie, John "Rastus" Murray, Kid
Hawks, Joe Watts, Ruth Carter, Lillian Hayes, Rose Morris,
Georgia Celletta, Helen Bush, Lorraine Lockhart.

"Mississippi Steppers, " 1928.   Producer: Hezekiah Jenkins.   Principal Cast: Hezekiah Jenkins, Bertha Idaho, Herman Higgs,
Walter Smith, Billie Dedway, Hattie Snow, Jessie Winston.

"My Friend from Kentucky, " 1928 (edition).   Producer: Evon Rob-
inson (Mrs. J. Leubrie Hill).   Principal Cast: Dink Stewart,
Jim Towel, LeRoy Morton, Rudolph Fraction, Billie Henderson
(in blackface), Margaret Anderson, Isadora Kenney, James
Smith, Fred Gordon, India Allen, Blondie LaMarr, Coleen
Morton, Viola, Constance Anderson, Evon Robinson, Josephine
Winn, Margaret Klendon, Hilda Nelson, Frank DeCarlos.

"The Nifties of 1928, " 1928.   Producer: Shelton Brooks.   Principal Cast: Shelton Brooks, King Hunter, Popo Warfield, St.
Clair Dotson, Ivette, Lena Wilson, Anna White, Wilbur White.

"Ophilia Snow from Baltimo', " 1928 (edition).   Producer: No data.
Principal Cast: Andrew Tribble, Billy Mitchell, Harold De-
mund, Buddy Green, Elveta Brown, Kitty Arlanie, Carl Robin-
son, Gertrude Smith, Dot Campbell, Chorus: Mildred Coleman,
Stella Johnson, Lottie Byrd, Virncee Mack, Jewel Thomas, Mae
Berkley, Hope Allen, Evelyn Plunkett.

"Plantation Days, " 1928.   Producer: No data.   Principal Cast:
Billy Cornell, Johnny Gardner, Wilber "Toosweet" (straight),
Bee Bee Allen and A. McSwan (dancers), Edna Lewis (soubrette),
Beatrice Banks, J. Homer Hubbard, Billy Lewis (dancer),
Sammy Louis.

"Playmates, " 1928.   Producer: Buster Lee.   Principal Cast:
Buster Lee, Geneva Pichon, Edna Brisco, Laura Smith, Hattie
Jones, Lucille Harris, William Charleston, Fred LaJoie, James
Langston.

"Raisin' Cain, " 1928.   Producer: Majestic Theatrical Circuit (Jack

Goldberg). Principal Cast: Ida Cox, Eddie Mathews, David
Wills, Willie Mae, Gussie Gould, Charlie Anderson, Billy
McKenzie, Mae Williams, Stewart York.

"Rolling On," 1928. Producer: Dewey Weinglass. Principal Cast:
Dewey Weinglass, Gertrude Saunders, Jackie Young, Billy
Mitchell.

"Roseland Revue," 1928. Producer: No data. Principal Cast:
Pan American Four, Gaines Brothers (acrobats), Dusty Fletcher,
Andrew Tribble.

"Shuffle Along, Jr.," 1928. Producers: Eubie Blake, "Broadway"
Jones (Henry Jones). Principal Cast: Broadway Jones, Panama
Pansies, Eubie Blake.

"Shufflin' Sam from Alabam'," 1928 (edition). Producer: George L.
Barton. Principal Cast: Babe Brown, John (Ashcan) LaRue,
Shrimp Brock, Johnny Woods, Coleman Titus, "Snuffy" Stevens,
Alvira Margaret Watkins, Darling Sisters.

"Steamboat Bill from Louisville," 1928. Producer: George L.
Barton. Principal Cast: Billy Ewing and Sam Robinson
(comedians), "Bozo" Nickerson and J. C. Davis (tenor and piano
artists), The Dixie Quartet, Jackson and Jackson (delux dancers),
Hattie Noel (comedienne), Brown Skin Radio Beauty Chorus,
Tommy Woods (eccentric dancer).

"Steamboat Days," 1928. Producer: No data. Principal Cast:
Bessie Smith, Ethel Williams, Nat Cash, Lloyd Hollis, Sam
Davis, Bootsey Swan, Hackback and Willie Holmes.

"Sugar Cane," 1928. Producer: Coleridge Davis (for Majestic
Theatrical Circuit). Principal Cast: Coleridge Davis, Jessie
Cryor, D. Martin, John Davis (sock), Geneva Washington,
Harry James, Marie Williamson, Florine Jenkins, Alma Bell,
Willie Greek, Pigmeat.

"Sugar Cane," 1928. Producer: Homer Hubbard. Principal Cast:
Maybelle Brown, Homer Hubbard, Kate Price, Sox Jenkins,
Marie Williams, Harvey James, Macon Scott, Florence Jenkins,
Peg and Peg.

"The Surprise Company," 1928. Producer: Rosa Hostler. Princi-
pal Cast: Rastus Murray, Sam Theard, Louise Redder, Baby
Doris Wallace, Chorus: Susie Turner, Jessie Mae Turner,
Bobbie White, Margaret Johnson, Tiny Marshall, Frances Clark.

"Swannee Club Revue," 1928. Producer: Leonard Harper. Principal Cast: Willie Jackson, Doris Rheubottom, Wells and Mordecia.

"Tabasco Queens," 1928. Producer: No data. Principal Cast:

Hooten and Hooten, Billy Higgins, Leonia Williams, Joe Byrd, Vivian Brown, Walter Thomas.

"That's It, " 1928.   Producer: Majestic Theatrical Circuit (Jack Goldberg).   Principal Cast: Edgar Martin, Hazel Vanverlah, Elizabeth Smith.

"Tokio, " 1928.   Producer: Irvin C. Miller.   Principal Cast: Irvin C. Miller, Emmett "Gang" Anthony, Jota (dancer), Edna Ban, Gladys Robinson, Queenie Price, John Churchill.

"20 Dark Spots of Joy, " 1928.   Producer: No data.   Principal Cast: "Ornie" (Lollypop) Jones, Grace Rector, Johnny Snow (comedian), Lottie Harris, Anna Mae Fritz (character), Jazz Lips, Jr. (9 years old), William Brown, Wiley and Silvers (dancers), Chorus: Bettie Bee, Violet Gray, Peggy Whitefield, Blanche Jones, Vance Logan, Jessie McMorty, Ada Chaplan, Irene Bateaste, Oilly Barns, Blanche Robinson.

"Why Girls Go Wrong, " 1928.   Producer: Joe Bright (Record Breakers Company).   Principal Cast: Bobbie Toliver Bright, Alonzo Jackson (character), Baby Kid, Laura Miller, Katie Jones (comedienne), Willie Toosweet (juvenile), Betty Evans, "Cutout" and Leonard (blackface comedy), Billy "Scarecrow" McOwens (blackface comic), Chorus: Hazel Wallace, Mary Jackson, Stella Goodloe.

1929

"Abraham from Alabam', " 1929.   Producer: Henri Bowman. Principal Cast: Henri Bowman, Leroy White, "Dinah" Scott, Mae Williams.

"Birth of the Blues, " 1929.   Producers: Ringgold and Watts. Principal Cast: Watts and Ringgold, Anita Walkins, Hodge and Hodge, Felton and Felton, Babe Manley, Dan Dawley's Tornado Band.

"Brown Gal, " 1929.   Producer: John Henderson.   Principal Cast: John Henderson, Queenie Price (dancer featured in "Diga Diga Do" and "Shy Violets" numbers), Hokum Kids (two banjoes and saxophone), "Simp" and Marion, George Crawford (comic impersonations of several stage and screen celebrities), Inez Drew (singer).

"Brownskin Models of 1929, " 1929.   Producer: Irvin C. Miller. Principal Cast: Blanche Thompson, Eva Metcalf, Mildred Smallwood, George Byen, Antone Grant, Troy Brown, Ornie "Lollypop" Jones, Blain and Allen; Models: Coleen Morton, "Boots" Bryant, Margaret Nelson, Myrtle Dascane.   Chorus: Mae King, Rosabelle Anderson, Bertha McElroy, Jessie Mae Janner, Jules Hasson, Marie Wilson, Katheryn Brown, Adelaide Marshall.

"Devil's Frolics," 1929.   Producer: No data.   Principal Cast:
    John Mason, Doris Rheubottom, Gallie DeGaston, Jackie Mabley,
    Red Rudolph, "Jelly Beans" Smith, Addison Carey's Band, Put-
    ney Dandridge.

"Fashion Shoe Revue," 1929.   Producer: No data.   Principal Cast:
    Amanda Randolph.

"Gee Whiz," 1929.   Producer: No data.   Principal Cast: Alice
    Ramsey (blues singer), Evon Robinson (song and dance), Leroy
    Morton, Greechie Haywood, Boyton Webb, "Cut Out" Ellis
    (dance), George Green (Juvenile straight).

"George Stamper's Revue," 1929.   Producer: George Stamper.
    Principal Cast: George Stamper, Audry Thomas, Mabel
    Richards, PeeWee and Eddie, Wilber DeParis Orchestra.

"Georgia Peaches," 1929.   Producers: Jenkins and Idaho.   Prin-
    cipal Cast: Hezekiah Jenkins, Idaho Jordan, Willie Mitchell,
    Willie Holmes, Jessie Wilson, Herman Higgs.

"Harlem Darlings," 1929.   Producer: Charlie Davis.   Principal
    Cast: Eva Metcalf, Joe Bryd, Emmett Anthony, Cooper and
    Hunter, Sammy Payne, Roscoe (Red) Simmons.

"Hello Dixieland," 1929.   Producer: Mabel Whitman.   Principal
    Cast: Whitman Sisters, Princess WeeWee, Sambo Reed (comic),
    Bernice Ellis, Willie "Toosweet," Little Albert "pops," Charles
    Anderson.

"Hot Ella," 1929.   Producer: Ella B. Moore.   Principal Cast:
    Brown and Brown, Jones and Johnson, Lorine Winn, Boyd and
    Boyd, Martin and Martin.

"Hottentots of 1930," 1929.   Producer: No data.   Principal Cast:
    Marion Moore, Lilly Yuen, Beulah Benbow, Rastus Airship,
    Midget George Brown.

"It's a Plenty," 1929.   Producer: No data.   Principal Cast: Eva
    Metcalf, Roscoe (Red) Simmons, Al Watts, Mary Clemons,
    Swan and Lee, S. H. Dudley, Jr., Amanda Randolph, Alhambra
    Girls.

"Jail Birds," 1929.   Producers: Henry Drake and Ethel Walker.
    Principal Cast: Henry Drake, Ethel Walker, George Williams,
    Flora Wilson, "String Beans" Price (comedian), Coristine
    Daniels (soubrette), Elenor Wilson (female lead), Jay Goines
    (character impersonator); Dancing Boys: Alen Noble, Cleon
    Johnson, Robert Wade, "Rastus" Hill; Female Dancers: Maelon
    Davis, Marion Jones, Grace Robinson, Lydia Wilson, Doris C.
    Scott, Ethel Welch, Dorothy Blackmore, Sadie Mitchell, Peggy
    Cisco, Dorothy Moppins.

"Jazz Regiment," 1929. Producer: No data. Principal Cast: Sam
  Corman, Gertrude Saunders.

"Jumble Jazzbo Jamboree," 1929. Producer: No data. Principal
  Cast: Billy Watts, Mary Hicks, Maryland Harmony Four, Watts
  and Wills, Oliver Price's Jazz Wizards Orchestra.

"Leonard Harper's Revue," 1929. Producer: Leonard Harper.
  Principal Cast: Midnight Steppers, Palmer Brothers, Jazzlips
  Richardson, Baby Cox, Louise Cook, Madeline Belt, Billy
  Maxey, Leona Williams, Two Black Dots, Dudley Dixon, Pearl
  McCormack, Louis Anthony's Orchestra.

"Loose Feet Follies," 1929. Producer: Joe Carmouche. Principal
  Cast: No data.

"Make Me Know It," 1929. Producer: No data. Principal Cast:
  Vivian Barber, A. B. DeComathiere, Barrington Guy, Ethel
  Moses, Enid Raphel, Lucia Moses, Brevard Burnett, Lee
  Bailey, Edna Ellington, Janes Dunsmore, Lorenzo Tucker,
  Allen Gilliard, Louis Schooler, Frances Carter, Napoleon
  Whitney, James McAtec, Marion Fleming, Charles Hawkins,
  Pearl Ford, Walter Dike, Florence Lee, Ollie Burgoyne, Elmer
  Snoden's Band.

"Messin' Around," 1929. Producer: Louis Isquith. Music: James
  P. Johnson. Lyrics: Perry Bradford. Principal Cast: Cora
  LaRedd, Sterling Grant, Monett Moore, Hilda Perlena, Billy
  McLaurin, James (Slim) Thompson, Walter Brogdale, Arthur
  Porter, William McKelvy, Olive Ball, Audrey Thomas, "Bam-
  boo" McCarver, Paul Floyd, Susie Worten, Emma Maitland,
  Aurelin Wheldin, Joe Willis.

"Midnight Frolic," 1929. Producer: No data. Principal Cast:
  Frisco Bowman, Mae Bonds, Virginia Meck, Mabel Hite.

"Midnight Steppers," 1929. Producer: No data. Principal Cast:
  Bessie Smith, Lonnie Johnson, Hattie Noel, Black and Tan
  Trio, Lee Randall, H. Jenkins, Lorenzo Tucker.

"Miss Creola," 1929. Producer: Will Mastin. Principal Cast:
  Will Mastin, Eddie Williams, Rastus Murray, Jessie Cryor,
  Sam Davis, Al Parker, Chick McIntosh, Kathleen Bart, Obie
  Smith, Nora Collins.

"Miss Inez," 1929. Producer: No data. Principal Cast: Charlie
  Smith, Sol Speights, Myrtle Speights, Beulah Benbow, Gladys
  Dorsey, Waneta Gonzales, Allen and Allen, Randolph Johnson,
  Anna Rose Turner.

"My Gal," 1929. Producer: Garland Howard. Principal Cast:
  Garland Howard, Mae Brown, Clarence Parson, Nettie Hays,

Coley Grant, Hattie Neels, Joe Boyd, Bob Davis, Al Young, Maxey and Al, Joe Lumes, William Elkins' Jubilee Choir.

"Naughty But Nice," 1929.   Producer: Milton Fruckman.   Principal Cast: Doorkey Singleton, Ruth Trent, Hack Back, Katherine Brown.

"Pancy," 1929.   Music, Lyrics: Maceo Pinkard.   Dances: Nat Cash.   Principal Cast: Nat Cash.

"Pickings from Dixie," 1929.   Producer: No data.   Principal Cast: No data.

"Radio Sam the Melody Man," 1929.   Producer: George L. Barton. Principal Cast: No data.

"Shake Your Feet," 1929 (edition).   Producers: Joe Carmouche, Cleo Mitchell.   Principal Cast: Joe Carmouche, Cleo Mitchell, Van Epps and Beatie (singing, talking, dancing), Grant Ross (tap dancer), Mattie Brown (singer), Billie Gunn and Henry Williams, Sue Parker (singer), Edna Young (toe dancer), Mattie Hedgeman (dancer).

"Sizzling Oriental Sunflower Revue," 1929.   Producer: No data. Principal Cast: Lovey Austin, Peat and Leroy White, Chippy Hill, Christine Russell and Jessie Taylor, Atta Blake, Dave Brown, Lawrence Nash.

"Sonny Boy Sam," 1929.   Producer: No data.   Principal Cast: Sam Robinson (Sonny Boy Sam), Zablo Jenkins, Hunter and Warfield, C. D. Davis, James "Kid" Austin, O'Brien and McKenny, Paul Foster, Blake Morril, Gertie Davis.

"Spirit of 1930," 1929.   Producer: Mabel Whitman.   Principal Cast: Whitman Sisters, Princess WeeWee, Pops and Dotty.

"Summertime," 1929 (2 acts, 12 scenes).   Producer: Carleton "Ritz" Moss.   Dances: Ruth Krygar.   Lyrics, Music: Dick Handel.   Principal Cast: Thelma Hall, Russell White, Walker L. Smith.

"Sun Flower Revue," 1929.   Producer: Lovey Austin.   Principal Cast: Clara and Della, Chippy Hill, Lida Lee, Dant and Roy, Rastus Jones, Roy Blanks.

"Syncopated Sue," 1929.   Producer: No data.   Principal Cast: Alice Stewart (Syncopated Sue), Inez Saunders (soubrette), Francis Wallace (female lead), Alex Craig, Ted Smith, Willie Smith, Raymond Jefferson, William Jones and William Green (dancers), Ralph Franklin (straight), Zepeck Craig.

"We've Got It," 1929.   Producer: Sam Robinson.   Principal Cast: Sam Robinson, Jay Goins, Wallace Curtis, Paul Foster, Bessie McKinney, C. S. Davis, Jimmy Simmons, Ma Bailey.

1930

"Blackbirds of 1930," 1930. Producer: Lew Leslie. Principal Cast: Ethel Waters, Flournoy E. Miller, Mantan Moreland, "Broadway" Jones (Henry Jones), Marion Harrison, Blue McAllister, Minto Cato, Neeka Shaw, Berry Brothers, Buck and Bubbles, Jimmy Baskette, Estelle Bernier, Mametta Newton, Louise Uggams, Eubie Blake and his Blackbird Orchestra.

"Brownskin Models of 1930," 1930. Producer: Irvin C. Miller. Principal Cast: Blanche Thompson, Troy Brown, Lollypop Jones, Eva Metcalf, Blair and Allen, Tony Grant, Chorus: Margaret Helson, Marie Wilson, Colleen Morton, Bert McElroy, Rosabelle Anderson, Boots Bryant, Jessie Mae Turner.

"Dixie on Parade," 1930. Producer: Noble Sissle. Principal Cast: Noble Sissle and his Paris Ambassadeurs, Joyce Robinson, George Crawford, Marshall Rogers, Harold Reed, Dewey Weinglass, Oscar Newman, Alice Harris, Izzy Ringgold, Ace Graham, Wilton Crawley; The Four Bob Bobs, Lucky Seven Trio, Miller Brothers, Mills and Tiddler, The Chocolate Steppers.

"Gingersnaps," 1930. Producer: No data. Book: Salem Tutt Whitney, J. Homer Tutt, George Morris. Dances: George Stamper. Costumes: Hilda Barum. Music: Donald Heywood. Principal Cast: Swan and Lee, Barrington Guy, "Baby" DeLeon, Vivian Barber, Roscoe "Red" Simmons, Maude DeForrest, Southland Choir, Ginger Snaps and Snapperettes, Donald Heywood's Band.

"Harlem Girl," 1930. Producer: Irvin C. Miller. Principal Cast: Shelton Brooks, Hamtree Harrington.

"Hello Everybody," 1930. Producers: Henry Drake and Ethel Walker. Principal Cast: Henry Drake, Ethel Walker, Sam "Bilo" Russell, Baby and Billy English, The Harmony Four.

"Hollywood Revue," 1930. Producer: Lincoln Perry (Stepin Fetchit). Principal Cast: Stepin Fetchit.

"Hot Heels," 1930. Producer: Louis Azorsky. Principal Cast: Buddy Green, George Cooper, Jr., Buster Lee, Snake Hips, Jr., Marie Moore, Billy Griffin, Two Dancing Demons.

"The Joy Boat," 1930. Producer: No data. Principal Cast: Johnny Hudgins, Clinton "Dusty" Fletcher, Izzy Ringgold, Marion Bradford, Jimmie Baskette, George Brown, George Crawford, Three Aces, Jackie Mabley (in blackface), Alma Travis, Billie Wyler, James Lancaster.

"Look Who's Here," 1930. Producers: Drake and Walker. Principal Cast: Henry Drake, Ethel Walker, Moore and Moore.

"Maytime Revue," 1930. Producer: No data. Principal Cast:
    Grant and Wilson, Fat Head, Johnny Lee Long.

"Midnight Steppers," 1930. Producers: Gertrude Saunders, John
    Dancy. Principal Cast: Gertrude Saunders, Harold Randolph,
    Bruce Johnson, Teddy Bunn and "Chick" Smith, the Washboard
    Serenaders, George Williams, Melvin Hunter, William Charles-
    ton, Otins Blake, James Allen, Norman Wright, The Three
    Black Sams (dancers), "Peaches" Wilson (soubrette), Chorus:
    Thelma Simmsons, Ira Fredericks, Bernie Henderson, "Toots"
    Daniels, Mildred Johnson, Dorothy Stevens, Edith Jones,
    Thelma Erickson, Alberta Jones, Steve Stevens.

"Miss Broadway," 1930. Producer: Billy Pierson. Principal
    Cast: Billy "Bodidley" Pierson, Irene Butler, "Soap" and
    "Towel," Simmons and Jenkins, Theophile Sisters, Helen
    Jackie Morrison, Lenora Jones, Dot Johnson, Ishamel Watkins,
    Joe Ivory, Earl Palmer.

"Moaning Low," 1930. Producer: No data. Principal Cast:
    Bessie Smith, Ethel Williams, Hope Blank.

"My Wife," 1930. Producer: Drake and Walker. Principal Cast:
    Henry Drake, Ethel Walker, Sam "Bilo" Russell, Billy English,
    Lucy Strayhorne, The Harmony Four.

"Pickings from Dixie," 1930. Producer: Billy and Mary Mack.
    Principal Cast: Billy Mack, Mary Mack (leading lady), Charles
    Taylor (straight), D. Bubiskit (singer), Mack and Leonard
    Rogers (comedians), "4 Periods," (Charles Taylor, Leonard
    Rogers, Ed Braxos, Bill Thomas), J. J. Mims (tap dancer),
    Irene Cooper (singer), Chorus: Alma Fuller, Lucile Grass,
    Hazel Baskett, Willie Lee Martin, Willie Mae Neil, Elizabeth
    Richardson.

"Red Pastures," 1930. Producer: Irvin C. Miller. Principal
    Cast: Albert Jackson, Jackie Mabley, Billie Young, Mary
    Wheeler, Hayes Prior, Edgar Martin.

"Runnin' De Town," 1930. Producer: Aubrey Lyles. Lyrics,
    Music: J. C. Johnson. Book: Leigh Whipper. Principal Cast:
    Leigh Whipper, Aubrey Lyles, Paul Ford, Sam Cross, Henry
    Davis, Angeline Lawson, Susie Brown.

"Sandy Burns and Bilo," 1930. Producers: Sandy Burns, Sam "Bilo"
    Russell. Principal Cast: Sandy Burns, "Bilo," George Wilt-
    shire.

"Sepia Vagabonds," 1930. Producer: No data. Principal Cast:
    Mamie Smith, Eloise Bennett, Alec Lovejoy, Virginia Four
    (male quartet), Buddy Green, Bernice Bennett, Kay Mason.

"Sidewalks of Harlem," 1930. Producers: Addison Carey, Charles

Davis. Principal Cast: John (Rareback) Mason, Gaines Brothers, Doris Rheubottom, Johnnie Virgel, Struggles and Red, "Washer Board," Jackie Mabley.

"Tight Like That," 1930. Producer: No data. Principal Cast: Rivers and Brown, Simms and Bowie, Barnes and Jackson, George Crawford, Earl Edwards.

"Velvet Brown Babies," 1930. Producer: Eddie Lemons. Principal Cast: Eddie Lemons, Joe Sheftell, Fred Lajoie, Elizabeth Welch, Sadie McKinney, Mike and Ike.

"Wake Up Chillun'," 1930. Producer: Mabel Whitman. Principal Cast: Whitman Sisters.

"Whoopee Girls," 1930. Producer: No data. Principal Cast: Gertrude Saunders, "Crackshot" Hackley, Gladys Bentley, John LaRue.

"Zonky," 1930. Producer: Addison Carey. Principal Cast: John Mason, Gallie DeGaston, Struggle and Red.

1931-1932

"Blackberries," 1932 (edition). Producer: Max Radnick. Book: Eddie Green. Lyrics, Music: Donald Heywood, Tom Peluso. Dances: Sidney Sprague, Lew Crawford. Costumes: Gladys Douglas. Settings: Meyer Kavin. Stage: Ben Benard. Orchestra: Sam Wooding's Chocolate Kiddies. Principal Cast: Jackie Mabley (comedy, singing, impersonation), Gertrude Saunders, Eddie Green, Georgette Harvey's Bon Bons, Tim Moore, Mantan Moreland, Dewey "Pigmeat" Markham, Johnny Lee Long, Sam Paige, Midnight Steppers, The Three Yorkers, The Three Bubbles, Charles Ray, Alice Harris, Robert Haines, Billy Shepard, Monte Hawley, Baby Goins, Susie Brown, Helen Powell.

"Blackbirds," 1932. Producer: Lew Leslie. Music: Rube Bloom. Lyrics: Dorothy Sachs, et al. Dialogue: Nat N. Dorfman, Fred F. Finklehofte. Principal Cast: Lena Horne, Hamtree Harrington, Dewey "Pigmeat" Markham, Tim Moore, Bobby Evans, Joe Byrd, Laurene Hines, Kate Hall, Ralph Broen, Norman and Blake, Rosetta Crawford.

"Brownskin Models," 1932. Producer: Irvin C. Miller. Principal Cast: Irvin C. Miller, Lester Williams, George Bias, "Rags" Cole, Blanche Thompson, Cutout Ellis, Alto Oates, Teddye and Estelle, Miller Dancing Girls.

"Careless Love," 1931 (Radio Sketches). Author: Carleton Moss. Performers: Frank Wilson, Edna Lewis Thomas, Clarence Williams, Eva Taylor, "The Southernaires" Quartette (30-

minute weekly programs broadcast over station WAEF in
Baltimore, Maryland).

"Chocolate Scandals," 1931.   Producer: Al Davis.   Principal Cast:
Mantan Moreland, Shelton Brooks, Percy Verwayne, Lottie
Brown, Kitty Aublanche, Hanna Sylvester, Smart Brothers.

"Club Hollywood Revue," 1931.   Producer: Irvin C. Miller.
Principal Cast: Aaron Palmer, Brown and Jones, Leroy
Maton, Evon Robinson, Gertrude Saunders.

"Deep Central," 1932.   Producer: No data.   Book: John Larkins,
Alec Lovejoy.   Principal Cast: Alec Lovejoy, John Larkins,
Mae Johnson.

"Do Your Stuff," 1932.   Producer: Ralph Thomas.   Dances:
Sammy Dyer.   Principal Cast: Blanche Walton Choir, Eva
Waters, Sammy Dyer, Three Rhythm Ramblers (dancers),
Ruby Mason (singer), Three Brown Brothers, Four Cotton
Pickers Quartette, Wiona Short, Patti Patterson (banjo wizard),
"Tiny" Parham and his Grandes Life Orchestra.

"Ebony Scandals," 1932.   Producer: No data.   Principal Cast:
Bowie and Simms, Leviana Mack, Julia Noisette, Sarah Smith,
Freddie Seymour, Albert W. Jackson, May Barnes, Cecil
Rivers, Flo Brown.

"Echoes of a Plantation," 1931.   Producer: Earl Dancer.   Staged
by the Fred Whittaker Legion Post No. 372 for the benefit of
black Boy Scouts of Los Angeles.   Principal Cast: Eddie Anderson, Clarence Muse, Hattie McDaniels, Stepin' Fetchit, Butler's
Old Time Southern Singers.

"Harlem on Parade," 1931.   Producer: No data.   Principal Cast:
Bud Harris.

"Hot Chocolates of 1932," 1932.   Producer: Connie Immerman.
Principal Cast: Louis Armstrong, Baby Cox, Frey and Harrington, Billy Maxey, Pearl McCormack, Three Brown Buddies, Sally Gooding, The Cyclones, Madeline Belt, Chick
Webb's Band.

"Hot from Harlem," 1931.   Producer: No data.   Principal Cast:
Bill "Bojangles" Robinson, John Mason, Neeka Shaw, Jelli
Smith, Mary Prevall, Putney Dandridge.

"Hot Rhythm," 1932.   Producer: Dewey Weinglass.   Principal
Cast: Dewey Weinglass, Sandy Burns, Billy Higgins, George
Wiltshire.

"Jail Birds," 1930.   Producers: Drake and Walker.   Principal
Cast: Henry Drake, Ethel Walker, Sam "Bilo" Russell, Helen
Stokes, Baby and Billie English, The Kennetts, Lucy Stray-
horne, The Harmony Four.

"January Jubilee," 1931. Producer: Mabel Whitman. Principal Cast: Whitman Sisters, Princess Wee Wee, Four Cotton Pickers.

"Lazy Rhythm," 1931. Producer: Miller and Lyles. Principal Cast: Flournoy E. Miller, Aubrey Lyles, Shelton Brooks, Eddie Rector, Louise Cook.

"Lucky to Me," 1931. Producer: No data. Principal Cast: Ethel Waters, Jimmy Baskette, "Dusty" Fletcher, Blue McAllister, Gallie DeGaston, Melody Monarchs.

"Old Kentucky," 1932. Producer: No data. Principal Cast: George Dewey Washington, Hamtree Harrington, Marjorie Sterner, Murial Rahn, Clara Smith.

"Step Lively Girls," 1931. Producer: Mabel Whitman. Principal Cast: Whitman Sisters.

"Vanities of 1932," 1932. Producer: No data. Principal Cast: Butterbeans and Susie, Jimmy Ferguson.

"Wrap It in Black," 1931. Producer: Sam H. Gray. Principal Cast: Sam H. Gray, Tim Robinson, Irene Robinson, Trixie Smith, Irene Castle, Billy Mitchell, Prof. Toby (the wonder horse), Sammy Paige, Jean Calloway, Paul Floyd, Doe Doe Green, George ("Bugle Blues") Williams, Emmett Anthony.

1933

"Plantation Follies," 1933. Producer: James P. Johnson. Principal Cast: Carrie Marerro, Joe Byrd, Billy Higgins, Rogers and Rogers, Three Little Words, "Snake Hips" Tucker, Bearnice and Scott, Maitland and Wheeler, Cecilia Williams, Twelve Sepia Dancers, James P. Johnson's Black Diamond Aces.

"Ragtime," 1933. Producer: Earl B. Westfield. Principal Cast: "Babe" Townsend, A. B. DeComathiere, Frank Wilson, Brown and Brown.

"Runnin' Sam," 1933. Producer: No data. Principal Cast: Gertrude "Baby" Cox, Speedy Smith, Lionel Monagas, Lorenzo Tucker, Madeline Belt, Edith Wilson.

"Shuffle Along of 1933," 1933. Producers: Noble Sissle, Eubie Blake, Flournoy E. Miller. Principal Cast: Flournoy E. Miller, Noble Sissle, Eubie Blake, Mantan Moreland, Edith Wilson.

"So This Is Africa," 1933. Producer: No data. Principal Cast: Wheeler and Woosey.

"Sugar Cane, " 1933 (edition).   Producer: No data.   Principal Cast:
    Harriet Calloway, Dewey "Pigmeat" Markham, Charles Ray,
    Lavanda Snow, Rudolph Craig, Willie and "Smoak. "

"Tan-Town Topic Revue, " 1933.   Producer: No data.   Principal
    Cast: Smith's Entertainers: Jessie Belle Hicks, Pamala Moore,
    Dorothy Mayes, Helen Morrison, Dorothy Perry, Alice Duran,
    Ralph Wills, Ruby Williams.

1934

"Brownskin Models, " 1934.   Producer: Irvin C. Miller.   Principal
    Cast: No data.

"Dixie Follies, " 1934.   Producer: No data.   Principal Cast:
    Wilton Crawley, Joyner and Foster, William Brown, The Two
    Tan Tippers, Three Brown Buddies.

"Flying Down to Harlem, " 1934.   Producer: "Rubber Leg" Wil-
    liams, Three Cyclones, "Uke" Bob.

"Get Lucky, " 1934.   Producer: Quintard Miller.   Book: Quintard
    Miller and Flournoy E. Miller.   Principal Cast: Quintard
    Miller, George McClennon, Billy Mitchell, Margaret Cosby,
    Oliver Childs, Joseph Stubbs, Hattie Knowles, Cook and Brown,
    Margaret Watkins, Sammy Ayer.

"Goin' to Town, " 1934.   Producer: No data.   Principal Cast:
    Jazz Lips Richardson (eccentric and acrobatic dancer), Ada
    Brown (blues singer), Jimmie Baskette (singer), Russell
    Wooding's Choir, "Brown Buddies" Chorus, Bill Baily, Harry
    Swangegen.

"Harlem Scandals, " 1934.   Producer: Irvin C. Miller.   Principal
    Cast: Alta Oates, Edgar Martin, Ernest "Baby" Seals, Jesse
    James (one-legged crutch dancer), Teddy and Estelle, Fred
    Jennings.

1935

"Get Lucky, " 1935.   Producers: Quintard Miller and Marcus
    Slayter.   Principal Cast: Butterbeans and Susie, Quintard
    Miller, Marcus Slayter, Irene Wiley, Woods Sisters, Billie
    Hunter, Joe Paige, Three Red Hots, Hot Dixie Club Orchestra.

"Harlem Express, " 1935.   Producer: Irvin C. Miller.   Principal
    Cast: Shelton Brooks, Three Hot Flashes, Billie Young,
    Margaret Simms, Quintard Miller, Marion Davis, Boots Bryant,
    Madeline Carter.

"Harlem on Parade, " 1935.   Producer: No data.   Principal Cast:

Buck and Bubbles, Ada Brown, Earl Handy's Cotton Club Orchestra, Harry Swanagan, The Three Sams (dancers), Susaye Brown (soubrette), "Jigsaw" Jackson (contortion dancer), Edna Taylor (singer, dancer), Twelve Sepia Strutters (dancers from "Blackbirds of 1934").

"Honeymoon Cruise," 1935. Producer: Earl Partello. Principal Cast: Bea Moore, Monzella Lewis, Ernestine McLain, Marie Wade.

"120° in the Shade," 1935. Producers: Earl Dancer, Eddie Joseph, Nat Perrin. Music, Lyrics: Otis and Leon Rene. Principal Cast: Jeni LeGon, Etta Moten. Other Shows Produced by Dancer Include: "Lucky Day," "Miss Calico," "Deep Harlem," "Ebony Brevities," "Plantation Revue," "Cafe De Paree."

"Rhythm Hotel," 1935. Producer: Leonard Reed. Book: Leonard Reed. Principal Cast: George Dewey Washington, Ida Brown, Rubie Blakley, Three Lightning Flashes, Show Boy and Ann.

1935-1949

"Atlantic City Follies of 1946," 1945. Producer: Joe "Ziggy" Johnson. Dances: Hortense Allen. Principal Cast: Marva Louis, Peg Leg Bates, Coleridge Davis and his Orchestra.

"Bronze Manikins," 1941. Producer: Don Kay. Principal Cast: "Flip" Murdock, Vivian Henderson and the Royal Bermudian Orchestra, Baby Seals.

"Brownskin Models of 1937," 1937. Producer: Irvin C. Miller. Principal Cast: Barney Johnson and his Swingsters, "Funny" Bowe Ferebee, Margaret Simms (billed as Aarzanya, Queen of the Jungle Dances), Leroy Watts, Chocolate Jones, Ada Cotton, Lee Twins, Hot Dancing Chorus.

"Brownskin Models," 1938. Producer: Irvin C. Miller. Principal Cast: Jesse James, Charlie Banks, Fay Canty, "Florida Nightingale," Alta Oats, Three Cyclones, Sylvester Brisco, George Bias, Baby Seals, Al Stewart's Swing Band.

"Brownskin Models of 1941," 1941. Producer: Irvin C. Miller. Principal Cast: Irvin C. Miller, Wahuetta Sam, Emily Santos, Margaret Simms, Clarence Metcalf, Philips and Philips, Robert Freebee, Pearl McCormack, Jean and Helen, Claude Jones, Wahgi (Queen of Shake).

"Brownskin Models, 1949 edition," 1949. Producer: Irvin C. Miller. Principal Cast: William Earl, Willie Jones, Bertha Hays, Evelyn Whorton, Clay Tyson, Earl Jackson, Alex and Gracie Shavers, Three Melody Tones, Barney Johnson Orchestra.

"Cotton Club Parade," 1935.   Producer: Ted Koehler.   Book,
   Lyrics: Ted Koehler.   Music: Rube Bloome.   Dances: Elida
   Webb, Leonard Harper.   Orchestration: Will Vodery, Claude
   Hopkins, Alex Hill.   Principal Cast: Nina Mae McKinney,
   Flournoy E. Miller, Mantan Moreland, Butterbeans and Susie,
   Cora LaRedd, Juano Hernandez, B. Matthews, Cook and Brown,
   Lena Horne, "Babe" Wallace, Three Rhythm Queens, Jessie
   Crynor, Rhythm Rascals, Connie Smith, Claude Hopkins Or-
   chestra, Orlando Robeson.

"Darktown Scandals," 1936.   Producer: No data.   Principal Cast:
   Ida Cox, Bell and Bell, "Peg Leg" Jefferson, Cotton Pickers
   Swing Band.

"Dixie Goes High Hat," 1938.   Producer: Flournoy E. Miller.
   Principal Cast: Flournoy E. Miller, Mantan Moreland, Mae
   Turner, Spencer Williams, Marcus Slayter, Quintard Miller,
   Dorothy Dandridge.

"Ecstatic Ebony," 1939.   Producer: Ralph Cooper.   Principal Cast:
   Ralph Cooper, Dewey "Pigmeat" Markham, Edith Wilson, Reg-
   inald Fenderson, Shirley Howard, Myrtle Quinlan, Williams and
   Grant, Ernestine and Pal, Leroy White's Band.

"Harlem Broadcast," 1936.   Producer: Irvin C. Miller.   Principal
   Cast: Margaret Simms, Marcus Slayter, S. H. Dudley, Estelle
   Blackman, Dolores Smith.

"Harlem Is Heaven," 1937.   Producer: No data.   Principal Cast:
   Cristola Williams.

"Harlem on Parade," 1936.   Producers: Quintard Miller, Marcus
   Slayter.   Principal Cast: Troy Brown, Baby Cox, Lew Crawford, Viola Ford.

"Here 'Tis," 1941.   Book: Jesse James.   Music, Lyrics: Eddie
   Hunter, J. C. Johnson.   Principal Cast: Peg Leg Bates, Crip
   Heard, Jesse James, Eddie Hunter, Joe Jordan and his Orches-
   tra, Charlie Davis, Marion Worthy, Deanie Larey (daughter of
   Larence Deas).

"Hollywood Revue," 1939.   Producer: Flournoy E. Miller.   Principal Cast: Flournoy E. Miller, Mantan Moreland, Edith Wilson.

"Hot Chocolates," 1935 (edition).   Producer: Connie Immerman.
   Lyrics: Andy Razaf.   Music: Paul Denniker.   Principal Cast:
   Gertrude "Baby" Cox, Alberta Hunter, Pete Peaches, Edna
   Mae Harris, Muriel Rahn, Tim and Freddie.

"Rhapsody in Rhythm," 1945.   Producer: Paul Small.   Principal
   Cast: Ethel Waters, Mantan Moreland, Timmie Rogers,
   "Dusty" Fletcher, Four Step Brothers, Savage Dancers.

"Royal American Show," 1939. Producer: Leon Claxton. Princi-
pal Cast: Gwendolyn Bates, Hilda Smith (snake dancer),
Sparkey and Spencer (rhythm tap dancers), "Too Sweet" (comic),
Dorris Williams (rumba dancer).

"Sing for Your Supper," 1936. WPA Federal Theatre Project.
Principal Cast: Rose Poindexter, Dorothy Turner, Dorothy Gee.

"Swing It," 1937. Sponsored by the WPA. Book: Cecil Mack.
Principal Cast: Edward Frye (of the old team of Moss and
Frye), Walter Crumbley, Joe Loomes, James Green, Henry
Jines, Al Young, Lee Bailey, John Fortune, Sonny Thompson,
Frank Jackson, Sherman Dirkson, James Mordecai, George
Booker, Anita Bush, Lawrence Lomax, Cliff Parker, Billy
Young, Herbie Brown, Edna Deas, Flash Riley, Levee Har-
monizers, Northern Brothers, Joe and Ralph, J. B. McRiley.

"The Swing Mikado," 1939. Presented by the Federal Theatre of
Chicago. Principal Cast: Bill "Bojangles" Robinson, Gladys
Boueree, Herman Green.

"Swing Revue," 1936. Producer: Whitman Sisters. Principal Cast:
Whitman Sisters, Pops and Louie, Alice Whitman.

"Tropicana," 1941. Producer: Donald Heywood. Principal Cast:
Edna Mae Harris, George Wiltshire, Alec Lovejoy, Freddie
Robinson, Sister Roseta Thorpe, Conway and Parks, Mary
Bruce Orchestra.

"Tropics After Dark," 1940 (presented at American Negro Exposi-
tion at the Chicago Coliseum in July 1940). Producer: Teddy
Blackman. Principal Cast: Pork Chops Patterson, Dick
Montgomery, Pop and Lourie, Dick Landry, Jeanette Girder,
"Sweetie Pie" DeHart, Mitzie Mitchell, Rubie Blakley, Katherine
Day.

"Ubangi Club Follies," 1935. Producer: Leonard Harper. Music,
Lyrics: Andy Razaf. Dances: Lou Crawford. Costumes:
Hilda Furnam. Principal Cast: Velma Middleton, Billy
Daniels, "Dusty" Fletcher, Pearl Baines, Edna Mae Harris,
Gladys Bently, Mae Johnson, Lee Simmons, Three Speed
Demons, Brown and Brown, Helen Smith, Bobby Evans, "Bunny"
and Don, Erskine Hawkins and his Bama State Collegians Or-
chestra.

APPENDIX C

PARTIAL LIST OF U.S. BLACK NEWSPAPERS, 1900-1940

Alabama

Advocate (Mobile)
The Emancipator (Montgomery)
Forum (Mobile)
Reporter (Birmingham)
Student (Tuskegee)
Voice of the People (Birmingham)
Weekly Press (Mobile)

Arkansas

Banner (Little Rock)
Inter-State Reporter (Helena)
Weekly Herald (Pine Bluff)
Western Review (Little Rock)

Arizona

Spokesman (Tucson)
Statesman (Denver)

California

*Eagle (Los Angeles)
Independent (Oakland)
New Age (Los Angeles)
*Sentinel (Los Angeles)
*Sunshine (Oakland)
Times (Oakland)
*Western American (Oakland)
*Western Out Look (San Francisco)

Delaware

Outlook (Wilmington)

District of Columbia

*Bee (Washington)
*Colored American (Washington)
Eagle (Washington)
Odd Fellows Journal (Washington)
Tribune (Washington)

Florida

Bulletin (Tampa)
The Colored Citizen (Pensacola)
Sentinel (Jacksonville)

Georgia

*Age (Atlanta)
Chronicle (Columbus)
*Daily World (Atlanta)
Gazette Land Bulletin (Waycross, Brunswick)
*Independent (Atlanta)
Inquirer (Atlanta)
Journal (Savannah)
Sentinel (Macon)
News (Augusta)
Post (Atlanta)
*Tribune (Savannah)
Union (Augusta)
Voice (Atlanta)

*Used as source material for this book.

Appendix C

Illinois

Broad Ax (Chicago)
*Defender (Chicago)
Enterprise (Chicago)
Plaindealer (Chicago)
Star (Chicago)
*Whip (Chicago)
World (Chicago)

Indiana

*Freeman (Indianapolis)
Ledger (Indianapolis)
Recorder (Indianapolis)
World (Indianapolis)

Iowa

Bystander (Des Moines)

Kansas

Daily American (Kansas City)
Founder (Quindard)
Herald (Topeka)
The Hutchinson Blade (Hutchinson)
Parsons Weekly Blade (Kansas City)
Plaindealer (Topeka)

Kentucky

Columbia Herald (Louisville)
Leader (Louisville)
The New Age (Hopkinsville)
News (Louisville)
Reporter (Louisville)
Standard (Lexington)
Weekly News (Lexington)

Louisiana

Advocate Messenger (Alexandria)
Republican Courier (New Orleans)
Southern Republican (New Orleans)
Southwestern Christian Advocate (New Orleans)
Tribune (New Orleans)

Maryland

*Afro-American (Baltimore)
The Commonwealth (Baltimore)
Negro Appeal (Baltimore)
Weekly Herald (Baltimore)

Massachusetts

Advocate (Boston)
*Guardian (Boston)
Journal (Boston)

Michigan

Chronicle (Detroit)
The Contender (Detroit)
Leader (Detroit)
State News (Grand Rapids)

Minnesota

National Advocate (Minneapolis)
The Appeal (St. Paul)
Twin City Star (Minneapolis)

Mississippi

Advocate (Jackson)
Enterprise (Jackson)
Free State (Brandon)
Golden Rule (Vicksburg)
Guardian (Holly Springs)
The Light (Vicksburg)
National News (Mound Bayou)

Missouri

*The Argus (St. Louis)
*Call (Kansas City)
The Independent Clarion (St. Louis)
Independent News (St. Louis)
Kansas City Sun (Kansas City)
Missouri Messenger (Kansas City)
Protest (St. Joseph)
Rising Sun (Kansas City)
Searchlight (Sedalia)
The Voice of Missouri (Kansas City)

Western Messenger (Jefferson City)

Nebraska

Enterprise (Omaha)
Monitor (Omaha)

New Jersey

Advocate (Atlantic City)

New Mexico

Southwest Review (Albuquerque)

New York

*Age (New York City)
American (Buffalo)
*Amsterdam News (New York City)
Colored American (New York City)
Dispatch (New York City)
National Negro Tailors Journal (New York City)
*Negro World (New York City)
News (New York City)
Rochester Weekly (Rochester)

North Carolina

Gate City Argus (Greensboro)
Gazette (Raleigh)
Independent (Raleigh)
Negro American Presbyterian (Charlotte)
Presbyterian (Charlotte)
The Voice (Rocky Mount)

Ohio

Advocate (Cleveland)
*Afro-American (Cleveland)
*Call and Post (Cleveland)
Colored Teacher (Wilberforce)
Fall Express (Cleveland)
Forum (Dayton)
Fraternal Monitor (Cincinnati)
*Gazette (Cleveland)
Journal (Cincinnati)

Standard and Observer (Wilberforce)
Union (Cincinnati)

Oklahoma

American (Wagoner)
Baptist Informer (Muskogee)
Black Dispatch (Oklahoma City)
The Guide (Oklahoma City)
Langston City Herald (Langston)
Safeguard (Guthrie)
Scimeter (Muskogee)
The Sun (Tulsa)
Watchman-Lantern (Muskogee)

Oregon

Advocate (Portland)

Pennsylvania

*Afro-American (Philadelphia)
American (Philadelphia)
American (Pittsburgh)
Baptist Defender (Philadelphia)
Christian Banner (Philadelphia)
Christian Recorder (Philadelphia)
*Courier (Pittsburgh)
Defender (Philadelphia)
Odd Fellow's Journal (Philadelphia)
Politician (Pittsburgh)

South Carolina

Afro-American Citizen (Charleston)
New Era (Charleston)
Peoples' Recorder (Orangeburg)
Messenger (Rock Hill)
Southern Indicator (Columbia)

Tennessee

Buff City News (Memphis)
Defender (Chattanooga)
East Tennessee News (Knoxville)
Fisk University News (Knoxville)
Globe (Nashville)

Headlight (Jackson)
Southern Christian Recorder
   (Nashville)

Texas

The City Times (Galveston)
The Colored American (Galves-
   ton)
Express (Dallas)
Forward Times (Houston)
Freeman (Texas City)
The Gate City Bulletin (Denison)
The Herald (Austin)
Hornet (Fort Worth)
The Independent (Houston)
Informer (Dallas)
*Informer (Houston)
Informer (Texarkana)
Inquirer (San Antonio)
The Item (Dallas)
The New Idea (Galveston)
Observer (Houston)
Oil City Afro-American
   (Corsicana)
Paul Quinn Weekly (Waco)
The Pioneer (Waco)
The Sentinel (San Antonio)
Western Star (Houston)

Virginia

*Journal and Guide (Norfolk)
Messenger (Charlottesville)
National Pilot (Petersburg)
Planet (Richmond)
Reformer (Richmond)
Southern Workman (Hampton)
Weekly Review (Petersburg)

Washington

Republican (Seattle)
World (Seattle)

West Virginia

Observer (Charleston)
Pioneer Press (Martinsburg)
Times-American (Huntington)

Wisconsin

Defender (Milwaukee)

A LA CARTE 498
ABRAHAM FROM ALABAM'
503
ABRAHAM THE BARBER 470
ABYSSINIA 9, 25, 81, 136, 138,
343, 354, 368, 422, 427,
437
ACE HIGH REVUE 493
ACE OF CLUBS 498
ACES AND QUEENS 139
Ackers, Hattie 208, 257, 326,
327
AN AFRICAN PRINCE 140
AFRICANA (1927) 141, 446
AFRICANA (1934) 143
AFRO-AMERICAN VAUDEVILLE
CO. 401
ALABAMA BOUND 143
Alabama Chocolate Drop Compa-
ny see Benbow, William
ALABAMA CHOCOLATE
DROPS 144
ALL GOD'S CHILLUN' GOT
WINGS 120
ALL-NATION'S REVUE 493
All Star Stock Co. 68
Allen, Bunny 233
Allen, G. W. 317, 318
Allen, Hortense "The Body"
513
Allen, India 197, 313, 463,
467, 501
Allen, Irvin 148, 149, 457
Allen, Irving "Boots" 223,
255, 459
Amos and Andy 114, 328, 333,
343, 405, 406, 415, 448,
449, 452
Anderson, Albert 330, 331
Anderson, Eddie "Rochester"
331, 332, 478, 482, 485,
510

Anderson, Ida 32, 123, 209,
332, 333, 477, 489
Anderson, Ivy 242, 244
Andrews, Billy 139, 140, 158,
491
Andrews Sisters 396
ANITA BUSH COMPANY (1922)
470
Anita Bush Stock Company see
Bush, Anita
ANNIE OAKLEY 478
Anthony, Emmett "Gang" 100,
143, 144, 156, 161, 162,
250, 251, 256, 273, 467,
468, 470, 471, 476, 477,
478, 480, 488, 494, 499,
503, 504, 511
Arden, Eve 414
Arlen, Harold 299
Armstrong, Henry 74
Armstrong, Louis 225, 355,
412, 452, 510
Arnett, Billy 475
AS THOUSANDS CHEER 445,
446
Astwood, Norman 231, 482,
487, 489, 499
AT THE BEACH 464
Atkins, Holly 355
ATLANTIC CITY FOLLIES 513
ATLANTIC CITY REVUE 486
Attucks Theatre (Norfolk, Vir-
ginia) 29, 48, 128
Auditorium Theatre (Atlanta,
Georgia) 28, 45, 128
AUNT JEMIMA'S REVUE 493
Avenue Theatre (Chicago) 37,
122, 126, 127
Avery, Dan 373, 374